Tony Sintes

SAMS
Teach Yourself
Object Oriented Programming

in 21 Days

SECOND EDITION

SAMS

West 103rd St., Indianapolis, Indiana, 46290 USA

Sams Teach Yourself Object Oriented Programming in 21 Days

Copyright © 2002 by Sams Publishing

International Standard Book Number: 0-672-32109-2

Library of Congress Catalog Card Number: 2001089626

Printed in the United States of America

First Printing: September 2001

04   03   02   01   4   3   2   1

Trademarks

Warning and Disclaimer

EXECUTIVE EDITOR
Michael Stephens

ACQUISITIONS EDITOR
Carol Ackerman

DEVELOPMENT EDITOR
Tiffany Taylor

MANAGING EDITOR
Matt Purcell

PROJECT EDITOR
George E. Nedeff

COPY EDITOR
Susan Hobbs

INDEXER
Tom Dinse

PROOFREADER
Harvey Stanbrough

TECHNICAL EDITOR
Mark Cashman

TEAM COORDINATOR
Lynne Williams
Pamalee Nelson

INTERIOR DESIGNER
Gary Adair

COVER DESIGNER
Aren Howell

Contents at a Glance

Introduction   1

WEEK 1 Defining OO   **3**

Day 1   Introduction to Object Oriented Programming   7

Day 2   Encapsulation: Learn to Keep the Details to Yourself   25

Day 3   Encapsulation: Time to Write Some Code   53

Day 4   Inheritance: Getting Something for Nothing   75

Day 5   Inheritance: Time to Write Some Code   103

Day 6   Polymorphism: Learning to Predict the Future   125

Day 7   Polymorphism: Time to Write Some Code   151

WEEK 2 Learning to Apply OO   **181**

Day 8   Introduction to the UML   185

Day 9   Introduction to Object Oriented Analysis (OOA)   203

Day 10   Introduction to Object Oriented Design (OOD)   229

Day 11   Reusing Designs Through Design Patterns   249

Day 12   Advanced Design Patterns   277

Day 13   OO and User Interface Programming   305

Day 14   Building Reliable Software Through Testing   329

WEEK 3 Putting It All Together: A Complete OO Project   **359**

Day 15   Learning to Combine Theory and Process   363

Day 16   Blackjack Iteration 2: Adding Rules   399

Day 17   Blackjack Iteration 3: Adding Betting   429

Day 18   Blackjack Iteration 4: Adding a GUI   447

Day 19   Applying an Alternative to MVC   469

Day 20   Having Some Fun with Blackjack   485

Day 21   The Final Mile   497

Appendices

Appendices **511**

XA Answers   513

XB Java Primer   569

XC UML Reference   595

XD Selected Bibliography   603

XE Blackjack Code Listings   607

Index   681

Contents

Introduction   **1**

About the Examples 2

What You Need to Know to Use This Book................................2

Week 1 Defining OO   **3**

Week 1 At a Glance   **5**

Day 1 Introduction to Object Oriented Programming   **7**

Object Oriented Programming in a Historical Context 8

    Precursors to OOP...9

    Object Oriented Programming 10

    How Object Oriented Programming Builds Upon the Past 18

Benefits and Goals of OO..19

    Natural 19

    Reliable 19

    Reusable...20

    Maintainable 20

    Extendable 20

    Timely 21

Pitfalls 21

    Pitfall 1: Thinking of OOP as Simply a Language 21

    Pitfall 2: Fearing Reuse...21

    Pitfall 3: Thinking of OO as a Cure-All 22

    Pitfall 4: Selfish Programming 22

The Week Ahead..22

Summary..23

Q&A 23

Workshop 24

    Quiz 24

    Exercises 24

Day 2 Encapsulation: Learn to Keep the Details to Yourself   **25**

The Three Pillars of Object Oriented Programming 26

Encapsulation: The First Pillar 26

    An Example of Interface and Implementation 28

    Public, Private, and Protected 29

    Why Should You Encapsulate? 30

Abstraction: Learning to Think and Program Abstractly 30
What Is Abstraction? 31
Two Examples of Abstraction 31
Effective Abstraction 33
Keeping Your Secrets Through Implementation Hiding 34
Protecting Your Object Through the Abstract Data Type (ADT) 34
Protecting Others from Your Secrets Through Implementation Hiding 39
A Real-World Example of Implementation Hiding 40
Division of Responsibility: Minding Your Own Business 42
Encapsulation Tips and Pitfalls..46
Abstraction Tips and Pitfalls 46
ADT Tips and Pitfalls 47
Implementation Hiding Tips 48
How Encapsulation Fulfills the Goals of OO Programming 48
Caveats 49
Summary 50
Q&A 50
Workshop 51
Quiz 51
Exercises 52

Day 3 Encapsulation: Time to Write Some Code   53

Lab 1: Setting Up the Java Environment 54
Problem Statement..54
Lab 2: Class Basics..54
Problem Statement..57
Solutions and Discussion...59
Lab 3: Encapsulation Roundup...60
Problem Statement..61
Solutions and Discussion...61
Lab 4: Case Study—The Java Primitive Wrappers (Optional) 66
Problem Statement..70
Solutions and Discussion...70
Q&A 71
Workshop 72
Quiz...72
Exercises 73

Day 4 Inheritance: Getting Something for Nothing   75

What Is Inheritance?...76
Why Inheritance? 78
"Is-A" Versus "Has-A": Learning When to Use Inheritance 79

Learning to Navigate Inheritance's Tangled Web..81
  Inheritance Mechanics...83
Types of Inheritance 89
Inheritance for Implementation 89
  Implementation Inheritance Problems...89
  Inheritance for Difference 90
  Inheritance for Type Substitution 94
Tips to Effective Inheritance...97
Summary 98
How Inheritance Fulfills the Goals of OO 99
Q&A 100
Workshop 101
  Quiz 101
  Exercises 102

Day 5 Inheritance: Time to Write Some Code   **103**

Lab 1: Simple Inheritance...103
  Problem Statement...104
  Solutions and Discussion...105
Lab 2: Using Abstract Classes for Planned Inheritance 106
  Problem Statement...109
  Solutions and Discussion...109
Lab 3: Bank Account—Practicing Simple Inheritance 110
  A Generic Account 111
  The Savings Account..111
  The Timed Maturity Account 111
  Checking Account 111
  Overdraft Account 112
  Problem Statement...112
  Extended Problem Statement 114
  Solutions and Discussion...115
Lab 4: Case Study—"Is-A," "Has-A," and the java.util.Stack...........................120
  Problem Statement...121
  Solutions and Discussion...121
Summary 123
Q&A 123
Workshop 123
  Quiz 124
  Exercises 124

Day 6 Polymorphism: Learning to Predict the Future   **125**

Polymorphism...126
Inclusion Polymorphism..130

Parametric Polymorphism..135
    Parametric Methods..135
    Parametric types 137
Overriding...138
Overloading...139
    Coercion..141
Effective Polymorphism 141
Polymorphic Pitfalls 144
    Pitfall 1: Moving Behaviors Up the Hierarchy 144
    Pitfall 2: Performance Overhead 144
    Pitfall 3: Blinders..145
Caveats 146
How Polymorphism Fulfills the Goals of OO 146
Summary 147
Q&A 148
Workshop 149
    Quiz 149
    Exercises 149

Day 7 Polymorphism: Time to Write Some Code   151

Lab 1: Applying Polymorphism 151
    Problem Statement...158
    Solutions and Discussion...159
Lab 2: Bank Account—Applying Polymorphism to a Familiar Example 160
    Problem Statement...160
    Solutions and Discussion...163
Lab 3: Bank Account—Using Polymorphism to Write Future-Proof Code 164
    Problem Statement...166
    Solutions and Discussion...167
Lab 4: Case Study—The Java Switch and Polymorphism...................169
    Fixing a Conditional 171
    Problem Statement...173
    Solutions and Discussion...174
Summary 176
Q&A 176
Workshop 177
    Quiz 177
    Exercises 177

Week 1 In Review   179

Week 2 Learning to Apply OO   181

Week 2 At a Glance   5

Day 8 Introduction to the UML   185

Introduction to the Unified Modeling Language 186
Modeling Your Classes 187
   Basic Class Notation 188
   Advanced Class Notation 189
   Modeling Your Classes to Suit Your Purposes 190
Modeling a Class Relationship..191
   Dependency 191
   Association 193
   Generalization 197
Putting It All Together 198
Summary..199
Q&A 200
Workshop 200
   Quiz 200
   Exercises 201

Day 9 Introduction to Object Oriented Analysis (OOA)   203

The Software Development Process..204
   The Iterative Process 205
   A High-Level Methodology 208
Object Oriented Analysis (OOA) 208
   Using Use Cases To Discover System Use 209
   Building the Domain Model 223
So Now What? 225
Summary..226
Q&A 226
Workshop 227
   Quiz 227
   Exercises 228

Day 10 Introduction to Object Oriented Design (OOD)   229

Object Oriented Design (OOD) 230
How Do You Apply OOD?..231
   Step 1: Generate an Initial List of Objects 232
   Step 2: Refine Your Objects' Responsibilities..234
   Step 3: Develop the Points of Interaction 241
   Step 4: Detail the Relationships Between Objects 243
   Step 5: Build Your Model 243

Summary 245
Q&A 245
Workshop 246
    Quiz 246
    Exercises 247

Day 11 Reusing Designs Through Design Patterns   **249**

Design Reuse 250
Design Patterns 250
    The Pattern Name 251
    The Problem 251
    The Solution 251
    The Consequences 252
Pattern Realities 252
Patterns by Example 253
    The Adapter Pattern 253
    The Proxy Pattern 257
    The Iterator Pattern 260
Making a Pattern Yours 267
Summary 268
Q&A 268
Workshop 268
    Quiz 269
    Exercises 269
Answers to Quiz 272
Answers to Exercises 273

Day 12 Advanced Design Patterns   **277**

More Patterns by Example 278
    The Abstract Factory Pattern 278
    The Singleton Pattern 283
    The Typesafe Enum Pattern 289
Pattern Pitfalls 295
Summary 296
Q&A 296
Workshop 297
    Quiz 297
    Exercises 297
Answers to Quiz 299
Answers to Exercises 300

Day 13 OO and User Interface Programming   **305**

OOP and the User Interface 306
The Importance of Decoupled UIs 306

How to Decouple the UI Using the Model View Controller Pattern 310
    The Model 310
    The View 313
    The Controller 317
Problems with the Model View Controller...319
    An Emphasis on Data 320
    Tight Coupling..321
    Inefficiency 321
Summary..321
Q&A 322
Workshop 322
    Quiz 323
    Exercises 323

Day 14 Building Reliable Software Through Testing   **329**

Testing OO Software 330
Testing and the Iterative Software Development Process 330
Forms of Testing 333
    Unit Testing 333
    Integration Testing 334
    System Testing..334
    Regression Testing..335
A Guide to Writing Reliable Code 335
    Combining Development and Testing...335
    Writing Exceptional Code 350
    Writing Effective Documentation 352
Summary..354
Q&A 355
Workshop 356
    Quiz 356
    Exercises 356

Week 2 In Review   **357**

Week 3 Putting It All Together: A Complete OO Project   **359**

Week 3 At a Glance   **361**

Day 15 Learning to Combine Theory and Process   **363**

Blackjack...364
    Why Blackjack?...364
    Vision Statement 365
    Overriding Requirements 365

Initial Blackjack Analysis 365
    The Blackjack Rules 366
    Identifying the Actors 368
    Creating a Preliminary List of Use Cases 369
Planning the Iterations 369
    Iteration 1: Basic Game Play 370
    Iteration 2: Rules 370
    Iteration 3: Betting...371
    Iteration 4: User Interface 371
Iteration 1: Basic Game Play 372
    Blackjack Analysis 372
    Blackjack Design...376
    The Implementation...381
    Testing 395
Summary 396
Q&A 396
Workshop 396
    Quiz 397
    Exercises 397

Day 16 Blackjack Iteration 2: Adding Rules   399

Blackjack Rules 399
    Rules Analysis 400
    Rules Design 404
    Rules Implementation 412
    Testing 425
Summary..425
Q&A 426
Workshop 426
    Quiz 426
    Exercises 427

Day 17 Blackjack Iteration 3: Adding Betting   429

Blackjack Betting 430
    Betting Analysis..430
    Betting Design...433
    Betting Implementation 436
    A Little Testing: A Mock Object..444
Summary..445
Q&A 445
Workshop 446
    Quiz 446
    Exercises 446

Day 18 Blackjack Iteration 4: Adding a GUI   **447**

Blackjack Presentation 447

Command Line Tweaks 448

Blackjack GUI Analysis 449

    GUI Use Cases 450

    GUI Visual Mock Ups 452

    Blackjack GUI Design..453

    GUI CRC Cards..454

    GUI Structure 455

    Refactoring 456

    GUI Class Diagram 456

    Blackjack GUI Implementation..457

    Implementing the VCard, VDeck, and CardView..457

    Implementing the PlayerView 460

    Implementing the OptionView and the OptionViewController 461

    Implementing the GUIPlayer 461

    Putting It All Together with the BlackjackGUI..464

Summary..465

Q&A 466

Workshop 466

    Quiz 466

    Exercises 466

Day 19 Applying an Alternative to MVC   **469**

An Alternative Blackjack GUI 469

    The PAC Layers..470

    The PAC Philosophy 470

    When to Use the PAC Design Pattern..471

Analyzing the PAC Blackjack GUI 471

Designing the PAC Blackjack GUI 471

    Identifying the Presentation Layer Components..472

    Designing the Abstraction Layer Components 473

    Designing the Control 474

    Using the Factory Pattern to Avoid Common Errors 474

Implementing the PAC Blackjack GUI 476

    Implementing the VCard and VHand 476

    Implementing the VBettingPlayer..478

    Implementing the VBlackjackDealer 480

    Implementing the GUIPlayer 481

    Putting It All Together with the Control 481

Summary..483

Q&A 484

Workshop 484

    Quiz 484

    Exercises 484

Day 20 Having Some Fun with Blackjack **485**

Having Fun with Polymorphism...485

    Creating a Player 486

    The Safe Player 486

    Adding the SafePlayer to the GUI 486

    Polish 487

OOP and Simulations 488

    The Blackjack Players 488

Summary 493

Q&A 493

Workshop 494

    Quiz 494

    Exercises 494

Day 21 The Final Mile **497**

Tying Up the Loose Ends 497

    Refactoring the Blackjack Design for Reuse in Other Systems 498

    Identifying the Benefits the OOP Brought to the Blackjack System 504

    Industry Realities and OOP..505

Summary 506

Q&A 506

Workshop 506

    Quiz 506

    Exercises 507

Week 3 In Review **509**

Appendices **511**

Appendix A Answers **513**

Day 1 Quiz Answers 513

    Answers to Quiz 513

Day 2 Quiz and Exercise Answers 515

    Answers to Quiz 515

    Answers to Exercises...517

Day 3 Quiz and Exercise Answers 517

    Answers to Quiz 517

    Answers to Exercises...518

Day 4 Quiz and Exercise Answers 521
    Answers to Quiz 521
    Answers to Exercises..523
Day 5 Quiz Answers...523
    Answers to Quiz 523
Day 6 Quiz and Exercise Answers 524
    Answers to Quiz 524
    Answers to Exercises..525
Day 7 Quiz Answers...526
    Answers to Quiz 526
Day 8 Quiz and Exercise Answers 527
    Answers to Quiz 527
    Answers to Exercises..528
Day 9 Quiz and Exercise Answers 530
    Answers to Quiz 530
    Answers to Exercises..532
Day 10 Quiz and Exercise Answers 533
    Answers to Quiz 533
    Answers to Exercises..535
Day 11 Quiz and Exercise Answers 535
    Answers to Quiz 535
    Answers to Exercises..536
Day 12 Quiz and Exercise Answers 538
    Answers to Quiz 538
    Answers to Exercises..539
Day 13 Quiz and Exercise Answers 542
    Answers to Quiz 542
    Answers to Exercises..543
Day 14 Quiz and Exercise Answers 545
    Answers to Quiz 545
    Answers to Exercises..547
Day 15 Quiz and Exercise Answers 547
    Answers to Quiz 547
    Answers to Exercises..548
Day 16 Quiz and Exercise Answers 548
    Answers to Quiz 548
    Answers to Exercises..549
Day 17 Quiz and Exercise Answers 550
    Answers to Quiz 550
    Answers to Exercises..551
Day 18 Quiz and Exercise Answers 554
    Answers to Quiz 554
    Answers to Exercises..554

Day 19 Quiz and Exercise Answers 558
    Answers to Quiz 558
    Answers to Exercises..559
Day 20 Quiz and Exercise Answers 562
    Answers to Quiz 562
    Answers to Exercises..562
Day 21 Quiz and Exercise Answers 567
    Answers to Quiz 567
    Answers to Exercises..567

Appendix B Java Primer   **569**

Java Developer's Kit: J2SE 1.3 SDK 569
    Development Environment Configuration 570
SDK Tools Overview 571
    Java Compiler: javac 571
    Java Interpreter: java 572
    Java Archive Utility: jar..572
    Java Documentation and the Documentation Generator: javadoc 573
Java Playpen: Your First Java Program...574
    Compiling and Running 575
    Creating a .jar File..576
    Generating javadoc 577
Java Language Mechanics 578
    Simple Java Class 578
    Data Types 580
    Variables 581
    Constants 582
    Operators 583
    Conditional Statements 584
    Loops 585
Classes and Interfaces—Building Blocks of Java 586
    Using Existing Classes 586
    Creating Your Own Classes..587
    Interfaces 590
    Inner Classes and Anonymous Inner Classes 591
Summary..593

Appendix C UML Reference   **595**

UML Reference 595
Classes..595
    Object...596
    Visibility 596
    Abstract Classes and Methods...596

Notes 597
Stereotypes 597
Relationships..598
    Dependency 598
    Association 598
    Aggregation 599
    Composition 600
    Generalization 600
Interaction Diagrams..600
    Collaboration Diagrams..600
    Sequence Diagrams 601

Appendix D Selected Bibliography   **603**

Analysis, Design, and Methodologies 603
C++ Programming 604
Design Patterns 604
General OO Principals and Theory 604
"Hard Core" Theory (But Don't Let That Scare You!) 605
Java Programming 605
Miscellaneous 605
Smalltalk 605
Testing..606

Appendix E Blackjack Code Listings   **607**

blackjack.core 608
blackjack.core.threaded..633
blackjack.exe 635
blackjack.players..641
blackjack.ui 649
blackjack.ui.mvc 650
blackjack.ui.pac...663

Index   **681**

About the Author

TONY SINTES has worked with object-oriented technologies for 7 years. In that time, Tony has been part of many large-scale object-oriented development efforts. Currently, Tony works for First Class Consulting, a company that he founded in order to help large enterprises integrate their various systems under a unified framework. Before starting First Class Consulting Tony worked at BroadVision as a Senior Principal Consultant, where he has helped build some of the world's largest Web sites. Today, Tony's main responsibilities are as architect, technical lead, and as team mentor, helping build the skills of less-experienced developers.

Tony is a widely published technical author whose works have appeared in *JavaWorld*, *Dr. Dobb's Journal*, *LinuxWorld*, *JavaOne Today*, and *Silicon Prairie*, where he co-authored a highly-regarded monthly column on object-oriented programming. Tony currently writes *JavaWorld*'s monthly Q&A column. You can contact Tony at `styoop@firstclassconsulting.net`.

Dedication

For Amy

Acknowledgments

Writing a book is a process like none other. The number of people who contribute to a book, the number of people that it takes to produce the final copy that you are reading right now, is simply amazing. I would like to extend my gratitude to the entire Sams publishing team. Without their hard work this book simply would not exist.

By name, I would like to thank Michael Stephens, Carol Ackerman, Tiffany Taylor, and George Nedeff. Carol's guidance and gentle prods are truly what kept this book moving towards completion. Tiffany's ability to structure and word technical material clearly and concisely is simply amazing. Not only did Tiffany's editing make this book more understandable, but I feel that her editing taught me some valuable lessons about technical writing. I would also like to thank William Brown. William contacted me about the STY OOP project in early August of 2000. Trusting such a project to a relatively unknown author was risky and I thank William for giving me the chance to write this book.

Special thanks go out to the technical editors, Mark Cashman and Richard Baldwin, who made sure that the material presented was technically sound. Thank you for your technical input.

To my colleagues, thank you. I'd like to extend special thanks to David Kim and Michael Han. I began this book while at BroadVision and I would like to thank David Kim for allowing me those panic vacations when deadlines began to loom. I would also like to thank Michael Han for his technical insight and for writing the Java appendix for this book.

Last but not least I'm privileged to thank my wonderful wife, Amy, for her unyielding support, proofreading, and patience. Thanks are also due to my family and friends who offered their support and listened to my complaining.

Tell Us What You Think!

As the reader of this book, *you* are our most important critic and commentator. We value your opinion and want to know what we're doing right, what we could do better, what areas you'd like to see us publish in, and any other words of wisdom you're willing to pass our way.

As an executive editor for Sams Publishing, I welcome your comments. You can fax, email, or write me directly to let me know what you did or didn't like about this book—as well as what we can do to make our books stronger.

Please note that I cannot help you with technical problems related to the topic of this book, and that due to the high volume of mail I receive, I might not be able to reply to every message.

When you write, please be sure to include this book's title and author as well as your name and phone or fax number. I will carefully review your comments and share them with the author and editors who worked on the book.

Fax: 317-581-4770
Email: feedback@samspublishing.com
Mail: Michael Stephens
         Executive Editor
         Sams Publishing
         201 West 103rd Street
         Indianapolis, IN 46290 USA

Introduction

Sams Teach Yourself Object Oriented Programming in 21 Days takes a practical approach to teaching object-oriented programming (OOP). Rather than teaching OOP at an academic level, this book presents accessible, user-friendly lessons and examples designed to let you begin applying OOP right away. Instead of trying to teach every agonizing, theoretical detail, this book highlights those topics that you need to know to be able to apply OOP to your daily projects—and not waste your time fighting some theoretical debate.

The goal of this book is to provide you with a solid foundation in object-oriented programming. After 21 days you should have a good footing in the basic concepts of OOP. Using this foundation you can begin to apply OOP concepts to your daily projects as well as continue to build your OO knowledge through additional study. You will not learn all there is to know about OOP in 21 days—that's simply not possible. It is possible, however, to build a solid foundation and get off on the right foot. This book helps you do just that.

I've divided this book into three parts. Week 1 presents the three tenets of OOP (also known as the three pillars of OOP). These three tenets form the basis of object-oriented theory. Understanding of these three tenants is absolutely critical to understanding OOP. The week's lessons are split between presenting the theory and giving you hands on experience through labs.

Week 2 presents the OO software development process. While the lessons of Chapter 1, "Introduction to Object Oriented Programming," are important, sending you out to program without any other guidance is like giving you lumber, a saw, a hammer, and some nails, and telling you to go build a house. Week 2 shows you how to apply the tools presented in the lessons of Week 1.

Week 3 steps you through a full case study of an OO card game. This study will allow you to go through an entire OO development cycle from beginning to completion, as well as to get your hands dirty with some code. It is my hope that this case study will help bring the OO theory down from the clouds and into something concrete.

There are also a number of appendices at the end of the book. Of special important is the Java primer in Appendix B and the selected bibliography in Appendix D. Appendix B serves as an excellent primer to the Java programming language. The bibliography points you to the resources that you'll want to consult as you continue your study of OOP. These resources were certainly invaluable while writing this book.

About the Examples

All source code examples are written in Java. Some Java experience will help; however, Appendix B should help bring you up to speed if you're rusty or have never seen the language before. Great pains were taken to make the examples as accessible as possible, as long as you have some programming knowledge. Special Java features and tricks were especially avoided in the examples.

What You Need to Know to Use This Book

This book does assume some previous programming experience, and it does not attempt to teach basic programming. This book takes the knowledge that you already have and shows you how you can use it to write object-oriented software. or write better object-oriented software. This isn't to say that you need to be a programming guru to read and understand this book—an introductory programming course or simply reading through one of Sams' *Teach Yourself* programming books is all the background that you should need.

To be able to take full advantage of the examples and exercises, you will also need a computer with Internet access. The choice of operating environment and editor is completely up to your personal taste. The only requirement is that you can download, install, and run Java. Appendix B walks you through the process of obtaining a Java SDK.

Finally, you need determination, dedication, and an open mind. Object-oriented programming is not easy, and it will take longer than 21 days to master, but you can get a good, solid start here.

The wonderful world of OOP awaits....

WEEK 1

Defining OO

1 Introduction to Object Oriented Programming

2 Encapsulation: Learn to Keep the Details to Yourself

3 Encapsulation: Time to Write Some Code

4 Inheritance: Getting Something for Nothing

5 Inheritance: Time to Write Some Code

6 Polymorphism: Learning to Predict the Future

7 Polymorphism: Time to Write Some Code

1

2

3

4

5

6

7

WEEK 1

At a Glance

The next seven days provide you with a solid foundation in object-oriented programming. Day 1 describes the basics of OO. You learn about object oriented from a historical perspective and see how OO evolved from existing programming languages. You also learn basic terminology as well as benefits and pitfalls of object-oriented programming.

Days 2, 4, and 6 introduce you to the three pillars of object-oriented programming: encapsulation, inheritance, and polymorphism. These chapters not only explain the basics of object-oriented programming, but how and when to use them as well as mistakes to avoid.

Days 3, 5, and 7 provide labs corresponding to each of the three pillars. Each lab chapter provides hands on experience that allows you to get familiar with the pillars introduced on Days 2, 4, and 6.

After finishing the first week, you should have a thorough understanding of what constitutes an object-oriented program. You should be able to identify the three pillars of OO, and be able to apply them to your code.

Quizzes and exercises follow each day's lesson to help further your understanding of the topics covered. The answers to each quiz question and exercise appear in Appendix A.

WEEK 1

DAY 1

Introduction to Object Oriented Programming

Although object-oriented languages have been around since the 1960s, the past 10 years have seen unparalleled growth in the use and acceptance of object technologies throughout the software industry. Although it began as an underdog, recent successes such as Java, CORBA, and C++ have propelled object-oriented (OO) techniques to new levels of acceptance. That's no accident. After years of being stuck in academia and having to fight an uphill battle against entrenched practices, object-oriented programming (OOP) has matured to a point where people are finally able to realize the promises that the technique holds. In the past, you would have had to convince your boss to let you use an object-oriented language. Today, many companies mandate its use. It is safe to say that people are finally listening.

If you're reading this book you've finally come around. You're probably someone with an intermediate level of programming experience. Whether your background is in C, Visual Basic, or FORTRAN, you've been around the block but you've decided that you have to give object-oriented programming a serious look and make it part of your skill set.

Even if you do have some experience with an object-oriented language, this book can help you solidify your understanding of OO. But don't panic if you are not familiar with an OO language. Although this book uses Java to teach OO concepts, pre-existing Java knowledge isn't necessary. If you ever do feel confused or need a syntax refresher, simply consult Appendix B, "Java Primer."

Whether you need OO to keep yourself marketable, get yourself through your newest project, or satisfy your own curiosity, you've come to the right place. Although no book can possibly teach you everything there is to know about OO, this book promises to give you a solid OO foundation. With this foundation, you can start practicing OOP. More importantly, the foundation will give you the lasting basis that you need in order to continue to learn and eventually master this programming paradigm.

Today you will learn

- Object-oriented programming in a historical context
- The basics of object-oriented programming
- The benefits and goals of object-oriented programming
- The common fallacies and pitfalls associated with object-oriented programming

Object Oriented Programming in a Historical Context

In order to understand the current state of OOP, you must know a little about the history of programming. No one conceived of OOP overnight. Instead, OOP is just another stage in the natural evolution of software development. Over time, it becomes easier to pick out the practices that work and those that prove themselves to fail. OOP combines proven, time-tested practices as efficiently as possible.

NEW TERM   *OO* is shorthand for object-oriented. OO is an umbrella term that includes any development style that is based on the concept of an "object"—an entity that exhibits characteristics and behavior. You can apply an object oriented approach to programming as well as to analysis and design.

You can also say that OO is a state of mind, a way of looking at the world and seeing everything terms of objects.

Simply, OO contains everything that can be prefixed as object-oriented. You'll see the term OO a lot in this book.

Precursors to OOP

Today, whenever you use a computer you benefit from 50 years of refinement. Early programming was ingenious: Programmers entered programs directly into the computer's main memory through banks of switches. Programmers wrote their programs in the machine's binary languages. Such machine language programming was extremely error prone, and the lack of overriding structure made code maintenance nearly impossible. In addition, machine language code was not very accessible.

As computers became more common, higher-level, procedural languages began to appear; the first was FORTRAN. However, later procedural languages such as ALGOL had more influence on OO. Procedural languages allow the programmer to boil a program down to a number of fine-grained procedures for processing data. These fine-grained procedures define the program's overall structure. Sequential calls to these procedures drive a procedural program's execution. The program terminates once it is done calling its list of procedures.

This paradigm presented a number of improvements over machine language, including the addition of an overriding structure: the procedure. Smaller functions are not only easier to understand, they are easier to debug. On the other hand, procedural programming limits code reuse. And, too often, programmers produced spaghetti code—code whose execution path resembled a bowl of spaghetti. Finally, procedural programming's data-centric nature caused some problems of its own. Because data and procedure are separate, there is no encapsulation of data. This requires each procedure to know how to properly manipulate the data. Unfortunately, a misbehaving function could introduce errors if it didn't manipulate the data just right. Since each procedure needed to duplicate the knowledge of how to access the data, a change to the data representation would require changes in each place that accesses the data. So, even a small change can lead to a cascade of changes throughout the program—in other words, a maintenance nightmare.

Modular programming, with a language such as Modula2, attempts to improve on some of the deficiencies found in procedural programming. Modular programming breaks programs down into a number of constituent components or modules. Unlike procedural programming, which separates data and procedures, modules combine the two. A module consists of data and the procedures for manipulating that data. When other parts of the program need to use a module, they simply exercise the module's interface. Because modules hide all of the internal data from the rest of the program, it is easy to introduce the idea of state: A module holds onto state information that might change over time.

NEW TERM   An object's *state* is the combined meaning of an object's internal variables.

NEW TERM   An *internal variable* is a value held within an object.

But modular programming suffers from major shortcomings of its own. Modules are not extendable, meaning that you cannot make incremental changes to a module without breaking open the code and making changes directly. You also cannot base one module on another other than through delegation. And, although a module might define a type, one module cannot share another module's type.

In modular and procedural languages, structured and unstructured data has a "type." The type is most easily thought of as the in-memory format of the data. Strongly-typed languages require that every object has a specific and defined type. However, types cannot be extended to create another type except through a style called "aggregation." For instance, in C, we might have two related data types:

```
typedef struct
{
    int a;
    int b;
} aBaseType;

typedef struct
{
    aBaseType    Base;
    int c;
} aDerivedType;
```

In this example, `aDerivedType` is based on `aBaseType`, but a structure of `aDerivedType` cannot be treated directly as an structure of `aBaseType`. One can only reference the Base member of an `aDerivedType` structure. Unfortunately, this arrangement leads to code that relies heavily on case and if/else blocks because the application must know how to manipulate each module that it encounters.

Finally, modular programming is also a procedural hybrid that still breaks a program into a number of procedures. Now instead of acting upon raw data, these procedures manipulate modules.

Object Oriented Programming

OOP takes the next logical step after modular programming by adding inheritance and polymorphism to the module. OOP structures a program by dividing it into a number of high-level objects. Each object models some aspect of the problem that you are trying to solve. Writing a sequential lists of procedure calls to direct program flow is no longer the focus of programming under OO. Instead, the objects interact with one another in order to drive the overall program flow. In a way, an OOP program becomes a living simulation of the problem that you are trying to solve.

An OOP Approach to Software Using Objects

Imagine that you had to develop an OOP program to implement an online shopping cart or a point-of-sales terminal. An OOP program will contain item, shopping cart, coupon, and cashier objects. Each of these objects will interact with one another in order to drive the program. For example, when the cashier totals an order, it will check each item for its price.

Defining a program in terms of objects is a profound way of viewing software. Objects force you to see everything at the conceptual level of what an object does: its behaviors. Viewing an object from the conceptual level is a departure from looking at how something is done: the implementation. This mindset forces you to think of your programs in natural, real-world terms. Instead of modeling your program as a set of separate procedures and data (terms of the computer world), you model your program in objects. Objects allow you to model your programs in the nouns, verbs, and adjectives of your problem domain.

NEW TERM   *Implementation* defines how something is done. In programming terms, *implementation* is the code.

NEW TERM   The *domain* is the space where a problem lives. The domain is the set of concepts that represent the important aspects of the problem you are trying to solve.

When you step back and think in the terms of the problem you are solving, you avoid getting bogged down in implementation details. Sure, some of your high-level objects will need to interact with the computer in some low-level, computer-oriented ways. However, the object will isolate those interactions from the rest of the system. (Day 2, "Encapsulation: Learn to Keep the Details to Yourself," explores these benefits further.)

Note

> In terms of the shopping cart, *implementation hiding* means that the cashier doesn't look at raw data when totaling an order. The cashier doesn't know to check a certain array of memory location for item numbers and another variable for a coupon. Instead, the cashier interacts with item objects. It knows to ask the item how much it costs.

At this point you can formally define *object*:

NEW TERM   An *object* is a software construct that encapsulates state and behavior. Objects allow you to model your software in real-world terms and abstractions.

Strictly speaking, an object is an instance of a class. The next section will introduce the OOP concept of *class*.

Just as the real world is made up of objects, so too is object-oriented software. In a pure OO programming language, everything is an object, from the most basic types such as integers and Booleans to the most complex class instances; not all object oriented languages go so far. In some (such as Java), simple primitives such as int and float are not treated as objects.

What Is a Class?

Just like objects in the real world, the OOP world groups objects by their common behaviors and attributes.

Biology classifies all dogs, cats, elephants, and humans as mammals. Shared characteristics give these separate creatures commonality. In the software world, classes group related objects in the same way.

A class defines all of those characteristics common to a type of object. Specifically, the class defines all of those attributes and behaviors exposed by the object. The class defines specifically what messages its objects respond to. When one object wants to exercise another object's behavior it does not do so directly but asks the other object to change itself, usually based on some additional information. Often this is referred to as "sending a message."

NEW TERM   A *class* defines the common attributes and behaviors shared by a type of object. Objects of a certain type or classification share the same behaviors and attributes. Classes act very much like a template or cookie cutter in that you use a class to create or *instantiate* object instances.

NEW TERM   *Attributes* are the outwardly visible characteristics of a class. Eye color and hair color are example of attributes.

An object can expose an attribute by providing a direct link to some internal variable or by returning the value through a method.

NEW TERM   A *behavior* is an action taken by an object when passed a message or in response to a state change: It's something that an object does.

One object can exercise another object's *behavior* by performing an operation on that object. You might see the terms *method call*, *function call*, or *pass a message* used in place of performing an *operation*. What is important is that each of these actions elicits an object's behavior.

Note

Message passing, *operation*, *method call*, and *function call*; which you use often depends upon your background.

Thinking in terms of *message passing* is a very object oriented way of thinking. *Message passing* is dynamic. It conceptually separates the *message* from the object. Such a mindset can help when thinking about your objects' interactions.

Languages such as C++ and Java come from procedural heritages where function calls are static. As a result, these languages often refer to one object performing a *method call* upon another. A *method call* is tightly coupled to the object.

This book will normally use *method call* because of its close Java ties. However, there may be times when *message* is used interchangeably.

Putting It All Together: Classes and Objects

Take an item object for example. An item has a description, id, unit price, quantity, and an optional discount. An item will know how to calculate its discounted price.

In the OOP world you would say that all item objects are instances of the Item class. An Item class might look something like this:

```java
public class Item {

    private double unit_price;
    private double discount;     // a percentage discount to apply to the price
    private int    quantity;
    private String description;
    private String id;

    public Item( String id, String description, int quantity, double price ) {
        this.id = id;
        this.description = description;

        if( quantity >= 0 ) {
            this.quantity = quantity;
        }
        else {
            this.quantity = 0;
        }

        this.unit_price = price;
    }

    public double getAdjustedTotal() {
```

```
        double total = unit_price * quantity;
        double total_discount = total * discount;
        double adjusted_total = total - total_discount;

        return adjusted_total;
    }

    // applies a percentage discount to the price
    public void setDiscount( double discount ) {
        if( discount <= 1.00 ) {
            this.discount = discount;
        }
        else {
            this.discount = 0.0;
        }
    }

    public double getDiscount() {
        return discount;
    }

    public int getQuantity() {
        return quantity;
    }

    public void setQuantity( int quantity ) {
        if( quantity >= 0 ) {
            this.quantity = quantity;
        }
    }

    public String getProductID() {
        return id;
    }

    public String getDescription() {
        return description;
    }
}
```

Methods such as

```
public Item( String id, String description, int quantity, double price )
```

are called *constructors*. Constructors initialize an object during its creation.

NEW TERM *Constructors* are methods used to initialize objects during their instantiation. You call object creation *instantiation* because it creates an object instance of the class.

Note

In the constructor and throughout the `Item` example you might notice the use of `this`. `this` is a reference that points to the object instance. Each object has its own reference to itself. The instance uses that reference to access its own variables and methods.

1

Methods such as `setDiscount()`, `getDescription()`, and `getAdjustedTotal()` are all behaviors of the `Item` class that return or set attributes. When a cashier wants to total the cart, the cashier simply takes each item and sends the object the `getAdjustedTotal()` message.

`unit_price`, `discount`, `quantity`, `description`, and `id` are all internal variables of the `Item` class. These values comprise the object's *state*. An object's state may vary over time. For example, while shopping a shopper may apply a coupon to the item. Applying a coupon to the item will change the item's state since it will change the value of `discount`.

Behaviors such as `getAdjustedTotal()` and `getDiscount()` are called *accessors* since they allow you to access an object's internal data. The access may be direct as in the `getDiscount()` case. On the other hand, the object may perform processing before returning a value, such as in the `getAdjustedTotal()` case.

NEW TERM *Accessors* give you access to an object's internal data. However, *accessors* hide whether the data is in a variable, a combination of variables, or is calculated. *Accessors* allow you to change or retrieve the value and to have "side-effects" on the internal state.

Behaviors such as `setDiscount()` are called *mutators* since they allow you to alter the object's internal state. A mutator may process its input as it sees fit before altering the object's internal state. Take `setDiscount()` for example. `setDiscount()` makes sure that the discount is not greater than 100% before applying the discount.

NEW TERM *Mutators* allow you to alter an object's internal state.

When running, your programs use classes such as `Item` to create, or instantiate, the objects that make up the application. Each new instance is a duplicate of the last. However, once instantiated the instance carries out behaviors and keeps track of its state. So what begins its life as a clone might behave very differently over its lifetime.

For example, if you create two item objects from the same `Item` class, one item object may have a 10% discount while the second may not have a discount. Some items are also a bit pricier than others. One item might cost $1,000, while another might only cost

$1.98. So while the state of an item might vary over time, the instance is still an `Item`. Think back to the biology example; a gray colored mammal is just as much of a mammal as a brown colored mammal.

Putting Objects to Work

Consider the following `main()` method:

```
public static void main( String [] args ) {
        // create the items
        Item milk   = new Item( "dairy-011", "1 Gallon Milk", 2, 2.50 );
        Item yogurt = new Item( "dairy-032", "Peach Yogurt", 4, 0.68 );
        Item bread  = new Item( "bakery-023", "Sliced Bread", 1, 2.55 );
        Item soap   = new Item( "household-21", "6 Pack Soap", 1, 4.51 );

        // apply coupons
        milk.setDiscount( 0.15 );

        // get adjusted prices
        double milk_price   = milk.getAdjustedTotal();
        double yogurt_price = yogurt.getAdjustedTotal();
        double bread_price  = bread.getAdjustedTotal();
        double soap_price   = soap.getAdjustedTotal();

        // print receipt
        System.out.println( "Thank You For Your Purchase." );
        System.out.println( "Please Come Again!" );
        System.out.println( milk.getDescription()   + "\t $" + milk_price   );
        System.out.println( yogurt.getDescription() + "\t $" + yogurt_price );
        System.out.println( bread.getDescription()  + "\t $" + bread_price  );
        System.out.println( soap.getDescription()   + "\t $" + soap_price   );

        // calculate and print total
        double total = milk_price + yogurt_price + bread_price + soap_price;
        System.out.println( "Total Price\t $" + total );
    }
```

This method shows you what a small program that uses `Item`s might look like. First, the program instantiates four `Item` objects. In a real program, the program might create these items as a user browses an online catalog or as a cashier scans groceries.

This program creates a number of items, applies discounts, and then prints out a receipt. The program performs all object interaction by sending various messages to the items. For example, the program applies a 15% discount to the milk by sending the `setDiscount()` message to the item. The program totals the items by first sending each item the `getAdjustedTotal()` message.

Finally, this program sends a receipt to the screen. Figure 1.1 illustrates the sample output.

FIGURE 1.1

Printing a receipt.

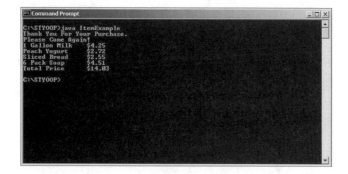

It is important to realize that all the programming was done in terms of Items and the behaviors exposed by the Item's methods —the nouns and verbs of the shopping cart domain.

Object Relationships

How objects relate is a very important component of OOP. Objects can relate in two important ways.

First, objects can exist independently of one another. Two Item objects can appear in the shopping cart at the same time. If these two separate objects ever do need to interact, they will interact by passing each other messages.

 Objects communicate with one another through *messages*. Messages cause an object to do something.

"Passing a message" is the same as calling on a method to change the state of the object or to exercise a behavior.

Second, one object might contain other objects. Just as objects make up an OOP program, objects can make up other objects through aggregation. From the Item example you might notice that the item object contains many other objects. For example, the item object also contains a description and id. Description and id are both String objects. Each of these objects has an interface that offers methods and attributes. Remember, in OOP everything is an object, even those pieces that make up an object!

Communication works the same way between an object and those objects that it contains. When the objects need to interact, they will do so by sending each other messages.

Messages are an important OO concept. Messages allow objects to remain independent. When one object sends a message to another object, it does not generally care how the object chooses to carry out the requested behavior. The requesting object just cares that the behavior happens.

You'll learn more about how objects interrelate next week.

Caution

> The definition of object is open to debate. Some people do not define an object as an instance of a class. Instead, they define everything in terms of being an object: From this point of view, a class is an object that creates other objects. Treating a class as an object is important for concepts such as the meta-class.
>
> Whenever this book encounters a disagreement in terminology, we will pick one definition and stick to it. The choice will very often be a pragmatic one. Here, we have chosen to use the definition of object as instance. This is the Unified Modeling Language (UML) definition and the one most encountered in industry. (You'll learn more about UML later.) Unfortunately, the other definition is a purer object-oriented definition. However, you will not run into it very often, and the concept of a meta-class is beyond the scope of this book.

How Object Oriented Programming Builds Upon the Past

Just as the other paradigms attempt to leverage the strengths and correct the faults of the preceding paradigms, OOP builds upon procedural and modular programming.

Modular programming structures a program into a number of modules. Likewise, OOP breaks a program into a number of interacting objects. Just as modules hide data representations behind procedures, objects encapsulate their state behind their interface. OOP borrows this concept of encapsulation directly from modular programming. Encapsulation differs greatly from procedural programming. Procedural programming does not encapsulate data. Instead, data is opened for all procedures to access. Unlike procedural programming, object-oriented programming tightly couples data and behavior together in the object. You'll learn more about encapsulation on Day 2 and Day 3, "Encapsulation: Time to Write Some Code."

Although objects are similar in concept to modules, they differ in a number of important ways. First, modules do not readily support extension. Object-oriented programming introduces the concept of inheritance to clean up this deficiency. Inheritance allows you to easily extend and enhance your classes. Inheritance also allows you to classify your classes. You'll learn more about inheritance on Day 4, "Inheritance: Getting Something for Nothing" and Day 5, "Inheritance: Time to Write Some Code."

OOP also leverages the concept of polymorphism, which helps build flexible programs that do not resist change. Polymorphism adds this flexibility by cleaning up the module's limited typing system. You'll learn more about polymorphism on Day 6, "Polymorphism: Learning to Predict the Future" and Day 7, Polymorphism: Time to Write Some Code."

1

OOP certainly did not invent encapsulation and polymorphism. Instead, OOP combines these concepts in one place. Throw in OOP's notion of objects, and you bring these technologies together in a way never done before.

Benefits and Goals of OO

Object-oriented programming sets six overriding goals for software development. OOP strives to produce software that has the following characteristics:

1. Natural

2. Reliable

3. Reusable

4. Maintainable

5. Extendable

6. Timely

Let's look at how it works to meet each of these goals.

Natural

OOP produces natural software. Natural programs are more understandable. Instead of programming in terms of an array or region of memory, you can program using the terminology of your particular problem. You don't have to get bogged down in the details of the computer while designing your program. Instead of force-fitting your programs into the language of the computer world, OO frees you to express your program in the terms of your problem.

Object-oriented programming allows you to model a problem at a functional level, not at the implementation level. You do not need to know how some piece of software works in order to use it: You simply concentrate on what it does.

Reliable

In order to create useful software, you need to create software that is as reliable as other products, such as refrigerators and television sets. When was the last time that your microwave crashed?

Well-designed, carefully written, object-oriented programs are reliable. The modular nature of objects allows you to make changes to one part of your program without affecting other parts. Objects isolate knowledge and responsibility where they belong.

One way to increase reliability is through thorough testing. OO enhances testing by allowing you to isolate knowledge and responsibility in one place. Such isolation allows you to test and validate each component independently. Once you validate a component, you can reuse it with confidence.

Reusable

Does a builder invent a new type of brick each time he builds a house? Does an electrical engineer invent a new type of resistor each time she designs a circuit? Then, why do programmers keep "re-inventing the wheel?" Once a problem is solved, you should reuse the solution.

You can readily reuse well-crafted object-oriented classes. As with modules, you can reuse objects in many different programs. Unlike modules, OOP introduces inheritance to allow you to extend existing objects and polymorphism to allow you to write generic code.

OO does not guarantee generic code. Creating well-crafted classes is a difficult skill that requires focus and attention to abstraction. Programmers do not always find that easy.

Through OOP you can model general ideas and use those general ideas to solve specific problems. Although you will build objects to solve a specific problem, you will often build these specific objects using generic pieces.

Maintainable

A program's life cycle does not end when you ship it out the door. Instead, you must maintain your code base. In fact, between 60% and 80% of the time spent working on a program is maintenance. Development is only 20% of the equation!

Well-designed object-oriented code is maintainable. In order to fix a bug, you simply correct the problem in one place. Since a change to the implementation is transparent, all other objects will automatically benefit from the enhancement. The natural language of the code should enable other developers to understand it as well.

Extendable

Just as you must maintain a program, your users will call upon you to add new functionality to your system. As you build a library of objects, you'll also want to extend your own objects' functionality.

OOP addresses these realities. Software is not static. Software must grow and change over time in order to remain useful. OOP presents the programmer with a number of features in order to extend code. These features include inheritance, polymorphism, overriding, delegation, and a variety of design patterns.

Timely

The life cycle of the modern software project is often measured in weeks. OOP aids these quick development cycles. OOP trims time off of the development cycle by providing reliable, reusable, and easily extendable software.

Natural software simplifies the design of complex systems. While you cannot ignore careful design, natural software can streamline design cycles because you can concentrate on the problem that you are trying to solve.

When you break down a program into a number of objects, the development of each piece can go on in parallel. Multiple developers can work on classes independently. Such parallel development leads to quicker development times.

Pitfalls

When you first learn OO, there are four pitfalls that you need to avoid falling into.

Pitfall 1: Thinking of OOP as Simply a Language

Often people equate object-oriented languages with OOP. The mistake arises in assuming that you are programming in an object-oriented way simply because you use an object-oriented language. Nothing could be further from the truth.

OOP is much more than simply using an object-oriented language or knowing a certain set of definitions. You can write horribly non–object-oriented code in an object-oriented language. True OOP is a mindset that challenges you to see your problems as a group of objects and to use encapsulation, inheritance, and polymorphism correctly.

Unfortunately, many companies and programmers assume that if they simply use an object-oriented language they will enjoy all of the benefits that OOP offers. When they fail, they tend to blame the technology, not the fact that they didn't train their employees properly or that they latched onto a popular programming concept without truly understanding what it meant.

Pitfall 2: Fearing Reuse

You must learn to reuse code. Learning to reuse without guilt is often one of the hardest lessons to learn when you first pick up OOP. Three problems lead to this difficulty.

First, programmers like to create. If you look at reuse the wrong way, it will seem to take some of the joys of creation away. However, you need to remember that you are reusing pieces in order to create something larger than the piece that you reuse. It may not seem exciting to reuse a component, but it will enable you to build something even better.

Second, many programmers suffer from the sentiment of "not written here"—meaning that they don't trust software they didn't write. If a piece of software is well tested and it fulfills your need, you should reuse it. Do not dismiss a component out of hand because you did not write it. Remember that reusing a component will free you to write other wonderful software.

Pitfall 3: Thinking of OO as a Cure-All

Although OOP offers many benefits, it is not the cure-all of the programming world. There are times when you should not use OO. You still need to use judgment in picking the right tool for the job at hand. Most importantly, OOP does not guarantee success of your project. Your project will not automatically succeed just because you use an OO language. Success only comes with careful planning, design, and coding.

Pitfall 4: Selfish Programming

Don't be selfish when you program. Just as you must learn to reuse, you must learn to share the code that you create. Sharing means that you will encourage other developers to use your classes. However, sharing also means that you will make it easy for others to reuse those classes.

Keep other developers in mind when you program. Craft clean, understandable interfaces. Most importantly, write documentation. Document assumptions, document method parameters, document as much as you can. People will not reuse what they cannot find or understand.

The Week Ahead

In the week ahead, you will continue your introduction to OOP by learning about the three pillars that form the basis of OOP theory: encapsulation, inheritance, and polymorphism.

Each pillar will be broken over two lessons. The first lesson will introduce the pillar and the theory behind it. The second lesson will give you hands-on experience with the concepts introduced the day before. This approach mirrors the lecture/lab approach used successfully by many universities and colleges.

You will complete all of these labs using Sun Microsystem's Java programming language. You can obtain all of the tools used within this book free of charge over the World Wide Web. Day 3 as well as Appendix B, "Java Primer," at the end of the book will step you through obtaining and setting up your development environment.

> **Note**
>
> **Why Java?**
>
> There are two reasons to use Java as a teaching tool. First, Java nicely abstracts you away from machine and operating system details. Instead of having to worry about memory allocation and de-allocation, you can simply concentrate on learning about objects. Finally, learning good object-oriented practices in Java is practical. You can take the knowledge and get a job. Some languages are more object-oriented than Java. However, it's easy to find Java work.

Summary

Today you took a tour of object-oriented programming. You began by taking a look at the evolution of the major programming paradigms, and you learned some of the basics of OOP. By now you should understand the conceptual ideas behind OO, such as what a class is and how objects communicate.

Definitions are important, but we must never lose track of what we are trying to accomplish by using OO by getting stuck in the "hows" of what we are doing. The six benefits and goals summarize what object-oriented programming hopes to accomplish:

1. Natural
2. Reliable
3. Reusable
4. Maintainable
5. Extendable
6. Timely

You must never lose sight of these goals.

Q&A

Q What can I do to master OOP?

A Books such as this are a good way to get started on your road to OO mastery. It's important to build a solid foundation; one that you can build upon.

Once you have a foundation, you need to start actively practicing OO. True mastery only comes through experience. Start as a developer on an OO project. Learn the ropes. As you become more familiar with OO, begin to involve yourself in the analysis and design of your projects.

It also helps to find a mentor. Find someone who is willing to take the time to impart wisdom. Learning from others is the best and fastest way to learn OOP.

Finally, continue your personal study. Read books, read articles, attend conferences. You can never absorb enough information.

Workshop

The quiz questions and answers are provided for your further understanding. See Appendix A, "Answers," for the answers.

Quiz

1. What is procedural programming?
2. What benefit does procedural programming have over unstructured programming?
3. What is modular programming?
4. What benefits does modular programming have over procedural programming?
5. List a shortcoming of procedural and modular programming.
6. What is object-oriented programming?
7. What are the six benefits and goals of object-oriented programming?
8. Explain one of the goals of object-oriented programming.
9. Define the following terms:

   Class

   Object

   Behavior
10. How do objects communicate with one another?
11. What is a constructor?
12. What is an accessor?
13. What is a mutator?
14. What is this?

Exercises

Rejoice! For today, you have no written exercises. Instead, go for a walk.

DAY 2

Encapsulation: Learn to Keep the Details to Yourself

Hopefully, Day 1, "Introduction to Object Oriented Programming," piqued your interest, and you probably have many questions. As you can guess, there is a lot more to object-oriented programming than a few simple definitions. When taking an OO approach to software development, you can't simply plod and hack your way along. Instead, you must have careful planning and a sound grounding in the important theories behind OOP. Unfortunately, there is no practical way to become an OOP expert in a few years, let alone in 21 days! Instead, you need to step back and ask, "What am I trying to accomplish?" Are you trying to become a theoretical expert or a practical practitioner? You see, you need to be a bit more practical if you ever want to learn enough OO to do your job. Fortunately, you don't need a Ph.D. to understand and apply OO to your software projects effectively. What you do need is an open mind and the willingness to learn—or unlearn in many cases.

Today and for the rest of the week, you will take a practical look at the theories behind OOP: the tools of OO. These theories should give you enough background to begin experimenting with OOP. Mastery will not come quickly, however. Like any other skill, your OOP skills will improve and grow only with study and practice.

Today you will learn

- About the three pillars of object-oriented programming
- How to apply encapsulation effectively
- How to program abstractly
- How the Abstract Data Type forms the basis of encapsulation
- The difference between interface and implementation
- About the importance of responsibility
- How encapsulation fulfills the goals of OO

The Three Pillars of Object Oriented Programming

In order to build your understanding and mastery of OO, you must first lay down a solid foundation upon which you can expand your understanding. First, you'll need to identify, define, and explore the basic concepts of OO. Only when you are fully grounded in the basic theories of OO can you properly apply OO to the software that you write. Such a discussion naturally brings you to the three concepts that must be present for a language to be considered truly object oriented. These three concepts are often referred to as the *three pillars* of object-oriented programming.

 The *three pillars* of object-oriented programming are *encapsulation*, *inheritance*, and *polymorphism*.

Because OOP builds upon them, the three pillars are a lot like a tower of blocks: Remove the bottom block and everything else will come crashing down. Encapsulation, which you will cover today, is an extremely important piece of the puzzle because it forms the basis for inheritance and polymorphism.

Encapsulation: The First Pillar

Instead of looking at a program as one large monolithic entity, encapsulation allows you to break down a program into a number of smaller, independent pieces. Each piece is self-contained and does its job independently of the other pieces. Encapsulation maintains this independence by hiding each piece's internal details, or implementation, through an external interface.

 Encapsulation is the OO characteristic of self-containment. Encapsulation allows you to build self-contained pieces of software by taking some piece of functionality and hiding its implementation details from the outside world.

Note

If you are not familiar with the term *encapsulation*, you might recognize the terms *module, component,* or *bean.* You can use these terms in place of "encapsulated piece of software."

Once encapsulated, you can view a software entity as a black box. You know what the black box does since you know the box's external interface. As Figure 2.1 illustrates, you simply send the black box messages. You don't really care what happens inside of the box; you just care that it happens.

FIGURE 2.1

A black box.

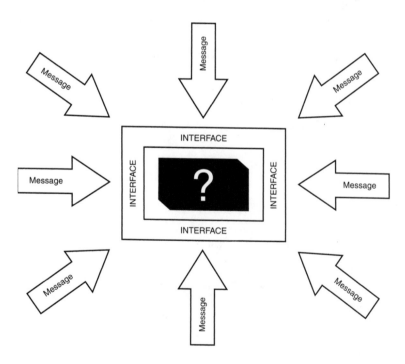

NEW TERM An *interface* lists the services provided by a component. The interface is a contract with the outside world that defines exactly what an outside entity can do to the object. An interface is the control panel for the object.

Note
An interface is important because it tells what you can do to the component. Of more interest is what an interface does *not* tell you: how the component will do its job. Instead, the interface hides the actual implementation from the outside world. This frees the component to change its implementation at any time. Changes to the implementation don't require changes to code that uses the class, so long as the interface remains unchanged. Changes to the interface will necessitate changes in the code that exercises that interface.

Note
You might be familiar with the programming term application program interface (API). An *interface* is akin to the API for an object. The interface lists all of those methods and arguments that it understands.

NEW TERM The implementation defines how a component actually provides a service. The implementation defines the internal details of the component.

An Example of Interface and Implementation

Consider the following Log class:

```java
public class Log {

        public void debug( String message ) {
                print( "DEBUG", message );
        }

        public void info( String message ) {
                print( "INFO", message );
        }

        public void warning( String message ) {
                print( "WARNING", message );
        }

        public void error( String message ) {
                print( "ERROR", message );
        }

        public void fatal( String message ) {
                print( "FATAL", message );
                System.exit( 0 );
        }

        private void print( String message, String severity ) {
```

```
         System.out.println( severity + ": " + message );
    }
}
```

The Log class provides your objects with a way to report debugging, informational, warning, and error messages during runtime. Log's interface is made up of all the behaviors available to the outside world. The behaviors available to the outside world are known as the public interface. Log's public interface includes the following methods:

```
public void debug( String message )
public void info( String message )
public void warning( String message )
public void error( String message )
public void fatal( String message )
```

Everything else in the class definition besides these five method declarations is implementation. Remember, implementation defines how something is done. Here the how is the fact that Log prints to the screen. However, the interface completely hides the how. Instead, the interface defines a contract with the outside world. For example, public void debug(String message) is a way of telling the outside world that if you pass it a String it will report a debug message.

What is important to note is what the interface does not say. debug() does not say that it will print to the screen. Instead, what it does with the message is left up to the implementation. The actual implementation might write to the screen, dump to a file, write to a database, or send a message to a network-monitoring client.

Public, Private, and Protected

You might have noticed that the public interface does not include

```
private void print( String message, String severity )
```

Instead, the Log object restricts access to print() to itself.

What does and does not appear in the public interface is governed by a number of keywords. Each OO language defines its own set of keywords, but fundamentally these keywords end up having similar effects.

Most OO languages support three levels of access:

- Public—Grants access to all objects
- Protected—Grants access to the instance and to any subclasses (more about subclasses on Day 4, "Inheritance: Getting Something for Nothing")
- Private—Grants access to the instance only

What access level you choose is very important to your design. Any behavior that you want to make visible to the world needs to have public access. Anything that you wish to keep from the outside world needs to have either protected or private access.

Why Should You Encapsulate?

When used carefully, encapsulation turns your objects into pluggable components. For another object to use your component, it only needs to understand how to use the component's public interface. Such independence has three valuable benefits:

- Independence means that you can reuse the object anywhere. When you properly encapsulate your objects, they will not be tied to any particular program. Instead, you can use them wherever their use makes sense. In order to use the object elsewhere, you simply exercise its interface.

- Encapsulation allows you to make transparent changes to your object. As long as you don't alter your interface, all of the changes will remain transparent to those that are using the object. Encapsulation allows you to upgrade your component, provide a more efficient implementation, or fix bugs—all without having to touch the other objects in your program. The users of your object automatically benefit from any changes that you make.

- Using an encapsulated object won't cause unexpected side effects between the object and the rest of the program. Since the object is self-contained, it won't have any other interaction with the rest of the program beyond its interface.

You are now at a point where we can make a few generalities about encapsulation. You have seen that encapsulation enables you to write self-contained software components. The three characteristics of effective encapsulation are

- Abstraction
- Implementation hiding
- Division of responsibility

Let's look closely at each characteristic in order to learn how to best achieve encapsulation.

Abstraction: Learning to Think and Program Abstractly

While OO languages encourage encapsulation, they do not guarantee it. It is easy to build dependent, fragile code. Effective encapsulation comes only with careful design, abstraction, and experience. One of the first steps to effective encapsulation is to learn how to abstract software and the concepts behind it effectively.

What Is Abstraction?

Abstraction is the process of simplifying a difficult problem. When you set out to solve a problem, you don't overwhelm yourself with every detail. Instead, you simplify it by addressing only those details germane to a solution.

Imagine that you have to write a traffic flow simulator. It is conceivable that you would model classes for streetlights, vehicles, road conditions, highways, two-way streets, one-way streets, weather conditions, and so on. Each of these elements would affect the flow of traffic. However, you wouldn't model insects and birds into the system even though they might appear on an actual road. Furthermore, you would leave out specific types of cars. You simplify the real world and include only those pieces that actually affect the simulation. A car is very important to the simulation, but a Cadillac or having the car track its gas level is superfluous to the traffic simulation.

Abstraction has two benefits. First, it allows you to solve a problem easily. More importantly, abstraction helps you achieve reuse. Software components are often overly specialized. This specialization, combined with unnecessary interdependency between the components, makes it difficult to reuse an existing piece of code elsewhere. When possible, you should strive to create objects that can solve an entire domain of problems. Abstraction allows you to solve a problem once and then use that solution throughout that problem domain.

Note

Although it is desirable to write abstract code and avoid over specialization, writing abstract code is hard to do, especially when you first start practicing OOP.

There is a very fine line between too much and too little specialization. The line can be discerned only with experience. However, you need to be aware of this powerful concept.

Two Examples of Abstraction

Consider two examples.

First, imagine people in line at a bank waiting for a teller. As soon as a teller becomes available, the first person in line advances to the open window. People always leave the line in a first-in, first-out (FIFO) order: This order is always maintained.

FIGURE 2.2

A line at a bank.

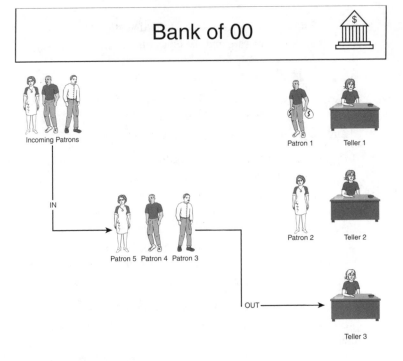

Second, consider a fast food burger establishment. As a new burger comes off the line, it is placed behind the last burger in the steamer; see Figure 2.3. That way, the first burger pulled out is also the oldest burger. FIFO is the restaurant's motto.

FIGURE 2.3

Burgers coming off the line.

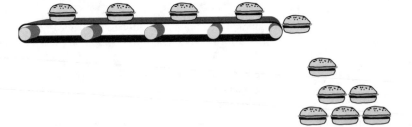

Although each of these examples is specific, you can come up with a generic description that will work in each situation. In other words, you can arrive at an abstraction.

Each domain is an example of a first-in, first-out queue. It doesn't really matter what kind of elements appear in the queue. What does matter is that elements enter at the back of the queue and leave the queue from the front, as illustrated in Figure 2.4.

FIGURE 2.4

An abstraction of both domains.

By abstracting the domains, you can create a queue once and reuse it in any problem that models a domain where there is a FIFO ordering of elements.

Effective Abstraction

At this point you can formulate a few rules for effective abstraction:

- Address the general case, not the specific case.
- When confronting a number of different problems, search for commonality. Try to see a concept, not a specific case.
- Don't forget that you have a problem to solve. Abstraction is valuable, but don't neglect the problem in hopes of writing abstract code.
- Abstraction might not be readily apparent. Abstraction might not jump out at you the first, second, or third time you solve a problem that is subject to being abstracted.
- Prepare for failure. It is almost impossible to write an abstraction that will work in every situation. You'll see why later in this day.

Caution

Do not fall into abstraction paralysis. Solve the problems that you face first. Look at abstraction as a bonus, not the end goal. Otherwise you face the possibility of missed deadlines and incorrect abstraction. There are times to abstract and times when abstraction is not appropriate.

A good rule of thumb is to abstract something you've implemented three times similarly. As you gain experience you will learn to pick out abstraction sooner.

Note

You might not always recognize opportunities for abstraction. You might have to solve a problem several times before an abstraction becomes apparent. Sometimes, different situations help to bring out an effective abstraction and, even then, the abstraction might need some coercion. Abstraction might take time to mature.

Abstraction can make an encapsulated component more reusable because it is tailored to a domain of problems, not one specific use. However, there is more to encapsulation than simple component reuse. It is also important to hide the internal details. The Abstract Data Type is a good place to look next in the search for effective encapsulation.

Keeping Your Secrets Through Implementation Hiding

Abstraction is only one characteristic of effective encapsulation. You can write abstract code that isn't encapsulated at all. Instead, you also need to hide your objects' internal implementations.

Implementation hiding has two benefits:

- It protects your object from its users.
- It protects the users of your object from the object itself.

Let's explore the first benefit—object protection.

Protecting Your Object Through the Abstract Data Type (ADT)

The Abstract Data Type is not a new concept. ADTs, along with OO itself, grew from the Simula programming language introduced in 1966. In fact, ADTs are decidedly non-OO; instead, they are a subset of OO. However, ADTs present two interesting characteristics: abstraction and type. It is this idea of type that is important, because without it, you cannot have true encapsulation.

 Note

> *True encapsulation* is enforced at the language level through built-in language constructs. Any other form of encapsulation is simply a gentlemen's agreement that is easily circumvented. Programmers will work around it because they can!

NEW TERM An *ADT* is a set of data and a set of operations on that data. ADTs allow you to define new language types by hiding internal data and state behind a well-defined interface. This interface presents the ADT as a single atomic unit.

ADTs are an excellent way to introduce encapsulation because they free you to consider encapsulation without the extra baggage of inheritance and polymorphism: You can focus on encapsulation. ADTs also allow you to explore the idea of type. Once type is understood, it is easy to see that OO offers a natural way of extending a language by defining custom user types.

What Is a Type?

When you program you will create a number of variables and assign values to them. Types define the different kinds of values that are available to your programs. You use types to build your program. Examples of some common types include integers, longs, and floats. These type definitions tell you exactly what kinds of types are available, what the types do, and what you can do to them.

We will use the following definition of type:

 Types define the different kinds of values that you can use in your programs. A type defines the domain from which valid values of the type can be drawn. For positive integers, this is numbers with no fractional parts, and which are greater than or equal to 0. For structured types the definition is more complex. In addition to the domain, the type definition includes which operations are valid on the type and what their results are.

> **Note** The formal treatment of *type* is well beyond the scope of an entry-level book on OOP.

Types are atomic units of computation. This means that a type is a single self-contained unit. Take the integer, for example. When you add two integers, you don't think about adding individual bits; you just think about adding two numbers. Even though bits represent the integer, the programming language presents the integer as just one number to the programmer.

Take the `Item` example from the Day 1. Creating the `Item` class adds a new type to your programming vocabulary. Instead of thinking about a product id, a product description, and a price as separate entities, probably disconnected regions of memory or variables, you simply think in terms of `Item`. Thus, types allow you to represent complex structures at a simpler, more conceptual level. They protect you from the unnecessary details. This frees you to work at the problem level instead of the implementation level.

While it is true that a type protects the programmer from underlying details, types offer you an even more important advantage. The definition of a type protects the type from the programmer. A type definition guarantees that any object that interacts with the type will interact in a correct, consistent, safe manner. The constraints imposed by a type prevent objects from inconsistent, possibly destructive interaction. The type declaration prevents the type from unintended and arbitrary use. A type declaration guarantees proper use.

Without a clear definition of the allowed operations, one type could interact with another type in any way that it wanted to. Often such undefined interaction can be destructive.

Think about the Item from Day 1 again. Imagine that we altered the Item definition a bit:

```
public class UnencapsulatedItem {

    // ...

    public double unit_price;
    public double discount;     // a percentage discount to apply to the price
    public int    quantity;
    public String description;
    public String id;
}
```

You'll notice that all of the internal variables are now publicly available. What if someone wrote the following program using the new UnencapsulatedItem:

```
public static void main( String [] args ) {
        UnencapsulatedItem monitor =
            new UnencapsulatedItem( "electronics-012",
                                    "17\" SVGA Monitor",
                                    1,
                                    299.00 );

        monitor.discount = 1.25; // invalid, discount must be less than 100%!

        double price = monitor.getAdjustedTotal();

        System.out.println( "Incorrect Total: $" + price );

        monitor.setDiscount( 1.25 ); // invalid
                                     // however the setter will catch the error

        price = monitor.getAdjustedTotal();

        System.out.println( "Correct Total: $" + price );
    }
```

Figure 2.5 shows what happens when you execute the main() method.

FIGURE 2.5

An invalid total.

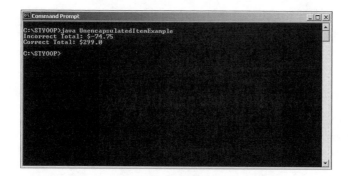

2

By opening the UnencapsulatedItem type to unfettered access, others can come along and leave an UnencapsulatedItem instance in an invalid state. In this case, main() creates an UnencapsulatedItem and then directly applies an invalid discount. The result is a negative adjusted price!

ADTs are valuable tools of encapsulation because they enable you to define new language types that are safe to use. Just as new words are added to the English language each year, an ADT enables you to create new programming words whenever you need to express a new idea.

Once it is defined, you can use a new type as any other type. Just as you may pass an integer to a method, you can pass an ADT to a method as well. This is known as being a first class object. You can pass first class objects around as parameters.

NEW TERM A *first-class object* is one that can be used exactly the same way as a built-in type.

NEW TERM A *second-class object* is a type of object that you can define but not necessarily use as you would a built in type.

An Example ADT

Let's consider the example of the abstract queue presented earlier. When implementing a queue, you have a number of implementation choices. You can implement the queue as a linked list, a doubly linked list, or as an array. However, the underlying implementation does not change a queue's defined behavior. Regardless of implementation, items still enter and exit in a FIFO manner.

The queue is a prime candidate for an ADT. You've already seen that you do not need to know the underlying implementation in order to use the queue. In fact, you don't want to have to worry about the implementation. If you don't turn the queue into an ADT, each object that needs a queue will need to reimplement the data structure. Each object that wants to manipulate the data on the queue will need to understand the implementation and understand how to interact with it correctly. You've already seen the dangers of unintended use!

Instead, you should construct the queue as an ADT. A well-encapsulated queue ADT guarantees consistent, safe access to the data.

When sitting down to design an ADT, you need to ask yourself what the ADT does. In this case, what can you do to a queue? You can

- Place elements into the queue: enqueue
- Remove elements from the queue: dequeue
- Query the state of the queue
- Look at the front element without removing it: peek

Each of the bullets will translate to an entry in Queue's public interface.

You also need to name the ADT. In this case, the ADT's name is Queue. The ADT is defined as follows:

```
public interface Queue {
    public void enqueue( Object obj );
    public Object dequeue();
    public boolean isEmpty();
    public Object peek();
}
```

Notice that the queue interface doesn't say anything about how the queue holds its internal data. Also note that the interface does not provide unfettered access to any of the internal data. All of those details are hidden.

Instead, you now have a new type, a queue. You can now use this type in any of your programs.

Since it is a first-class object, you can use the queue as a parameter. You can treat the abstraction as one unit because all the pieces are self-contained. This is powerful; it allows the programmer to be more expressive. Instead of thinking in terms of pointers and lists, the programmer can think at a much higher level: in terms of the problem to be solved. When the programmer says queue, the word includes all the details of a list and pointer but also allows the programmer to ignore those details and think of a high-level FIFO data structure.

Note

As you'll see as you continue, a type might be composed of other types through containment. Although this hides details, it also furthers your expressability. Types that contain other types can encompass many concepts.

For example, when you program and say int, the meaning is very simple; you have simply declared a single integer. However, when you say Queue your statement is much more expressive. There is much more going on inside of Queue than inside of int.

2

Let's consider the interface a bit more. Note that this interface is very generic. Instead of saying that this is a queue of ints or hamburgers, the interface simply queues and enqueues Objects. In Java, you can treat all objects as Object. However, each language provides its own similar mechanism. By declaring the parameters in this way, you can queue any object that you want on the queue. Thus, this definition makes the Queue type useable in many different situations.

Caution

Generic interfaces have dangers of their own. A Queue of Integers is very exact. You know that each element on the Queue is an Integer. A Queue of Objects however, is weakly-types. When you pull off an element, you might not know what type it is.

For truly effective encapsulation, there are a few more characteristics that you'll need to address. We've touched on one aspect of implementation hiding. But what about the other side of the coin—protecting the users of your objects?

Protecting Others from Your Secrets Through Implementation Hiding

So far, you've seen that an interface can hide an object's underlying implementation. When you hide the implementation behind an interface you protect your object from unintended or destructive use. Protecting your object from unintended use is one benefit of implementation hiding. However, there is another side to the story: the users of your object.

Implementation hiding leads to a more flexible design because it prevents the users of your object from becoming tightly coupled to the object's underlying implementation. So, not only does implementation hiding protect your object, it also protects those that use your object by encouraging loosely coupled code.

NEW TERM *Loosely coupled code* is independent of the implementation of other components.

NEW TERM *Tightly coupled code* is tightly bound on the implementation of other components.

You might wonder, "What good is loosely coupled code?"

Once a feature appears in an object's public interface, anyone who uses the feature becomes dependent upon the feature being there. If the feature suddenly goes away you'll need to change the code that had grown dependent on that behavior or attribute.

NEW TERM *Dependent code* is dependent on the existence of a given type. Dependent code is unavoidable. However, there are degrees to acceptable dependence and over dependence.

There are degrees to dependence. You cannot eliminate dependence totally. However, you should strive to minimize inter-object dependence. Normally, you limit such dependence by programming to a well-defined interface. Users can only become dependent upon what you decide to place in the interface. However, if some of the object's implementation becomes part of the interface, the users of the object might become dependent upon that implementation. Such tightly coupled code removes your freedom to change the implementation of your object as you see fit. A small change to your object's implementation might necessitate a cascade of changes throughout all of the users of the object.

> **Caution** Encapsulation and implementation hiding are not magic. If you need to change an interface, you will need to update the code that is dependent upon the old interface. By hiding the details and writing software to an interface, you create software that is loosely coupled.

Tightly coupled code defeats the point of encapsulation: creating independent, reusable objects.

A Real-World Example of Implementation Hiding

A concrete example of implementation hiding will drive this lesson home. Consider the following class definition:

```
public class Customer {
    // ... various customer methods ...
    public Item [] items; // this array holds any selected items
}
```

A `Customer` holds onto selected items. Here, `Customer` makes the `Item` array part of its external interface:

```
public static void main( String [] args ) {
        Customer customer = new Customer();

        // ... select some items ...

        // price the items
        double total = 0.0;
        for( int i = 0; i < customer.items.length; i++ ) {
                Item item = customer.items[i];
                total = total + item.getAdjustedTotal();
        }
}
```

This `main()` takes a customer, adds some items, and totals the order. Everything works, but what happens if you want to change the way a `Customer` holds onto items? Suppose that you would like to introduce a `Basket` class. If you change the implementation you'll need to update all of the code that accesses the `Item` array directly.

Without implementation hiding you lose your freedom to enhance your objects. In the `Customer` example you should make the `Item` array private. Provide access to the items through accessors.

> **Note**
>
> Implementation hiding does have its downsides. There are times that you might need to know a bit more than what the interface can tell you.
>
> In the programming world, you will want a black box that works within a certain tolerance or uses the right amount of precision. You might know that you need 64-bit integers because you are dealing with very large numbers. When defining your interface, it is important not only to provide an interface but to document these types of specifics about the implementation as well. However, like any other part of the public interface, once you declare a behavior, you cannot change it.

Implementation hiding allows you to write code that is independent and loosely coupled with other components. Loosely coupled code is less fragile and more flexible to change. Flexible code facilitates reuse and enhancement since changes to one part of a system will not affect other unrelated parts.

Tip

How do you achieve effective implementation hiding and loosely coupled code?

Here are a few tips:

- Only allow access to your ADT through a method based interface. Such an interface ensures that you do not expose information about the implementation.
- Do not give inadvertent access to inner data structures by accidentally returning pointers or references. After someone gets a reference, he can do anything to it.
- Never make assumptions about the other types that you use. Unless a behavior appears in the interface or in the documentation, do not rely on it.
- Be careful while writing two closely related types. Do not accidentally program in assumptions and dependencies.

Division of Responsibility: Minding Your Own Business

Implementation hiding naturally evolves into a discussion of the division of responsibility. In the previous section, you saw how you could uncouple code by hiding implementation details. Implementation hiding is only one step toward writing loosely coupled code.

In order to have truly loosely coupled code, you must also have a proper division of responsibility. Proper division of responsibility means that each object must perform one function—its responsibility—and do it well. Proper division of responsibility also means that the object is cohesive. In other words, there is no point in encapsulating a random bunch of functions and variables. They need to have a tight conceptual bond to each other. The functions must all work toward a common responsibility.

Note

Implementation hiding and responsibility go hand in hand. Without implementation hiding, responsibility can seep out of an object. It is the object's responsibility to know how to do its job. If you leave the implementation open to the outside world, a user might begin to act on the implementation directly—thus duplicating responsibility.

> As soon as two objects begin doing the same task, you know that you do not have a proper division of responsibility. Whenever you notice redundant logic, you'll need to rework your code. But don't feel bad; rework is an expected part of the OO development cycle. As your designs mature, you'll find many opportunities to improve it.

Let's consider a real-life example of the division of responsibilities: the relationship between manager and programmer.

Imagine that your manager comes to you, gives you the specs of your piece of a project, and then leaves you to your work. He knows that you have a job to do and that you know how to do your job best.

Now imagine that your boss isn't so clever. He explains the project and what you'll be responsible for. He assures you that he's there to facilitate your work. But when you begin, he pulls up a chair! For the rest of the day, your boss sits over your shoulder and gives you step-by-step instruction as you code.

While the example is a bit extreme, programmers program this way in their code all the time. Encapsulation is like the efficient manager. As in the real world, knowledge and responsibility need to be delegated to those who know how to do the job best. Many programmers structure their code like an overbearing boss treats his workers. This example is easily translated to programming terms. Let's consider such an example:

```java
public class BadItem {

    private double unit_price;
    private double adjusted_price;
    private double discount;    // a percentage discount to apply to the price
    private int    quantity;
    private String description;
    private String id;

    public BadItem( String id, String description,
                    int quantity, double price ) {
        this.id = id;
        this.description = description;

        if( quantity >= 0 ) {
            this.quantity = quantity;
        }
        else {
            this.quantity = 0;
        }
```

```
        this.unit_price = price;
    }

    public double getUnitPrice() {
      return unit_price;
    }

    // applies a percentage discount to the price
    public void setDiscount( double discount ) {
        if( discount <= 1.00 ) {
            this.discount = discount;
        }
    }

    public double getDiscount() {
        return discount;
    }

    public int getQuantity() {
        return quantity;
    }

    public void setQuantity( int quantity ) {
        this.quantity = quantity;
    }

    public String getProductID() {
        return id;
    }

    public String getDescription() {
        return description;
    }

    public double getAdjustedPrice() {
      return adjusted_price;
    }

    public void setAdjustedPrice( double price) {
      adjusted_price = price;
    }
}
```

BadItem no longer contains the responsibility of calculating adjusted price. So how do you generate an adjusted price? Consider the following main():

```
    public static void main( String [] args ) {
        // create the items
        BadItem milk   = new BadItem( "dairy-011", "1 Gallon Milk", 2, 2.50 );

        // apply coupons
```

```
        milk.setDiscount( 0.15 );

        // get adjusted prices
        double milk_price    = milk.getQuantity() * milk.getUnitPrice();
        double milk_discount = milk.getDiscount() * milk_price;
        milk.setAdjustedPrice( milk_price - milk_discount );

        System.out.println( "Your milk costs:\t $" + milk.getAdjustedPrice() );
    }
```

Now instead of simply asking the Item for its adjusted price you have to behave like the inefficient manager. You need to tell the item object what to do step by step.

Having to call multiple functions to calculate the adjusted total moves the responsibility out of the item and places it in the hands of the user. Moving responsibility around in this way is just as bad as exposing internal implementations. You end up with responsibility duplicated throughout your code. Each object that wishes to calculate the adjusted total will need to repeat the logic found in the main().

When writing your interfaces, you have to be sure that you are not simply presenting the implementation through a different set of names. Think back to the queue—you don't want methods named addObjectToList(), updateEndListPointer(), and so on. These types of behaviors are implementation specific. Instead, you hide the implementation through the higher level enqueue() and dequeue() behaviors (even though internally you might update pointers and add the object to a list). In terms of BadItem, you wouldn't want to have to call a calculateAdjustedPrice() method before you could retrieve the adjusted price through the getAdjustedPrice() method. Instead, getAdjustedPrice() should know to do the calculation.

When you have objects that do not properly divide responsibility you end up with procedural, datacentric code. The main for calculating the adjusted price is very procedural. A main that would instruct a Queue in each step of its enqueue() process is procedural. If you simply send a message to an object and trust it to do its job, it is true object-oriented development.

Encapsulation is all about hiding details. Responsibility places knowledge of certain details where it belongs. It is important for objects to have only one or a small number of responsibilities. If an object has too many responsibilities, its implementation becomes very confusing and difficult to maintain and extend. In order to alter one responsibility, you'll run the risk of inadvertently altering another behavior if an object contains many behaviors. It also centralizes a lot of knowledge that would be better spread out. As an object gets too large, it almost becomes a program in its own right and falls into procedural traps. As a result, you face all the problems that you would face in a program that doesn't use encapsulation at all.

When you find that an object performs more than one responsibility, you need to move that responsibility into its own object.

 Caution Implementation hiding is only one step to efficient encapsulation. Without proper divisions of responsibility, you simply end up with a list of procedures.

At this point, you can enhance the definition of encapsulation.

NEW TERM *Effective encapsulation* is abstraction plus implementation hiding plus responsibility.

Take away abstraction, and you have code that is not reusable. Take away implementation hiding, and you are left with fragile, tightly coupled code. Take away responsibility, and you are left with datacentric, procedural, tightly coupled, decentralized code.

Without all three pieces, you cannot have effective encapsulation, but a lack of responsibility leaves you with the biggest mess of all: procedural programming in an object-oriented environment.

Encapsulation Tips and Pitfalls

When applying encapsulation there are a number of tips to follow and traps to avoid.

Abstraction Tips and Pitfalls

When writing a class, you might get yourself into trouble if you try to work too abstractly. It is impossible to write a class that will satisfy all users and each situation. Imagine that you had to write a person object for an enterprise payroll system. That person object is going to be a lot different than a person object in the traffic flow simulator that we discussed earlier.

 Caution Abstraction can be dangerous. Even if you have abstracted some element, it might not work in every case. It is very difficult to write a class that will satisfy every user's needs. Don't fall into abstraction fixation—solve your problems first!

It all comes back to doing enough to solve the problem at hand. To include all the details necessary for the person object to work in both contexts would be very expensive. It opens you up to all the problems that you saw today because of muddled responsibility. Although you can plug your person into two situations, it is no longer an abstract person. You lose all of the simplification that abstraction offers.

Caution

Don't put more into a class than is necessary to solve the problem. Don't set out to solve all problems, solve the problem at hand. Only then should you look for ways to abstract what you have done.

2

Of course, there are times where a problem is complex, such as a difficult calculation or an intricate simulation. I'm talking about complexity from a responsibility point of view. The more responsibilities an object takes on, the more complex it is and the harder it will be to maintain.

Tip

Remember that adding a new class to your system is the same as creating a new type. Keeping this idea in mind helps focus on what you are actually doing. When talking about your problem, you will find that you talk in terms of the objects and interactions, not data and methods.

Finally, true abstraction can only come with time.

True abstraction normally is born from real-life uses, not a programmer sitting down and deciding to create a reusable object. As the saying goes, invention is born of necessity. Objects work the same way. You cannot normally sit down and write a truly abstract reusable object the first time. Instead, reusable objects are normally derived from mature code that has been put through its paces and faced many changes.

True abstraction also comes with experience. It is a goal to strive for in your mastery of OOP.

ADT Tips and Pitfalls

Transforming an ADT into a class is language specific. However, there are a few language-independent points that you can make about classes.

Most OO languages provide keywords that help you define encapsulated classes. First, there is the class definition itself. The class is kind of like the ADT but with some important features that you will see in the coming days.

Within a class, you normally have methods and internal variables—the data. Access to these variables and methods is provided by access functions. Everything in the ADT interface should appear as part of the object's public interface.

Caution ADTs are not directly analogous to the OO class. ADTs lack inheritance and polymorphic capabilities. The importance of these capabilities will become evident as you study Day 4 and Day 6, "Polymorphism: Learning to Predict the Future."

Implementation Hiding Tips

What to expose and what to hide in your interface is not always easy to decide. However, we can make a few language-independent points on access. Only methods that you intend others to use should be in the public interface. Methods that only the type will use should be hidden. In the queue example, dequeue() and enqueue() should be in the public interface. However, you should hide helper methods such as updateFrontPointer() and addToList().

You should always hide internal variables unless they are constants. I maintain that they should not only be hidden but accessible only by the class itself. You'll explore this concept more closely on Day 4. Opening internal variables to outside access exposes your implementation.

 Note You can open internal variables to outside use only if your language treats these values the same as methods. Both Delphi and Borland C++ treat internal variables this way.

If outside users can access methods and values without knowing they are touching a value, it is okay to open it up. In such a language, an exposed internal variable would look the same as a method that takes no parameters. Unfortunately, not many OO languages treat values and methods the same way.

Finally, do not create interfaces that just present the internal representation with a different name. The interface should present high-level behaviors.

How Encapsulation Fulfills the Goals of OO Programming

Day 1 states that the goal of OO programming is to produce software that is

1. Natural
2. Reliable

3. Reusable

4. Maintainable

5. Extendable

6. Timely

Encapsulation fulfills each of these goals:

- Natural: Encapsulation allows you to divide responsibility in a way that is natural to the way people think. Through abstraction, you are free to model the problem in terms of the problem, not in terms of some specific implementation. Abstraction allows you to think and program in the general.

- Reliable: By isolating responsibility and hiding the implementation, you can validate each individual component. Once the piece is validated, you can use it with confidence. This allows for thorough unit testing. You still need to perform integration testing to make sure that the software that you construct works properly.

- Reusable: Abstraction gives you code that is flexible and usable in more than one situation.

- Maintainable: Encapsulated code is easier to maintain. You can make any change that you like to the implementation of a class without breaking dependent code. These changes can include changes to the implementation as well as adding new methods to the interface. Only changes that violate the semantics of the interface will require changes to dependent code.

- Extendable: You can change implementations without breaking code. As a result you can make performance enhancements and change functionality without breaking the existing code. Furthermore, since the implementation is hidden, the code that uses the component will automatically be upgraded to take advantage of any new features that you introduce. If you do make such changes, be sure to run your unit tests again! Breaking an object can have a domino effect throughout all of the code that uses the object.

- Timely: By breaking your software into self-contained pieces, you can split the task of creating the pieces between multiple developers, thereby speeding development.

Once these components are constructed and validated, they will not need to be rebuilt. Thus, the programmer is free to reuse functionality without having to re-create it.

Caveats

You might be thinking, "But I don't need OO to abstract and encapsulate my code." You know what? You're right—you do not need OO to have encapsulated code. ADTs themselves are not OO. It is very possible to have encapsulation in just about any language.

However, there is a problem. In other types of languages, you often need to create your own mechanisms for encapsulation. Since there is nothing in the language that forces you to respect your standards, you need to be vigilant. You have to force yourself to follow your guidelines. You'll also have to re-create your guidelines and mechanism for each program that you write.

That's fine for one developer. What about two developers? Ten? An entire enterprise? As more developers are added, the harder it is to get everyone on the same page.

A true OO language provides a mechanism for encapsulation. It enforces the mechanism so that you do not have to. The language encapsulates the details of the encapsulation mechanism from the user. An OO language provides some keywords. The programmer simply uses the keywords, and the language takes care of all the details.

When working with the features provided by the language, the language presents all programmers with the same consistent mechanism.

Summary

Now that you understand encapsulation, you can begin programming with objects. By using encapsulation you can leverage the benefits of abstraction, implementation hiding, and responsibility in your day-to-day code.

With abstraction, you can write objects that are usable in a number of situations. If you properly hide your object's implementation, you are free to make any enhancements to your code that you want—at any time. Finally, if you properly divide responsibility among your objects, you'll avoid duplicate logic and procedural code.

If you put this book down now and never came back to it, you've learned enough new OO skills to write self-contained components. However, the OO story does not end with encapsulation. Stick around and you'll learn how to take advantage of all the features offered by OOP.

Q&A

Q How do you know what methods to include in an interface?

A It's simple to know what methods to include. You need to include only those methods that make the object useful; the methods that you need in order for another object to get its job done.

When you set out to write an interface you'll want to produce the smallest interface that still satisfies your needs. Make your interface as simple as possible. Don't include methods that you "might" need. You can add those when you truly need them.

Beware of certain types of convenience methods. If you're object holds onto other objects, you'll normally want to avoid creating methods that simply forward a method call onto one of the contained objects.

For example, say that you have a shopping cart object that holds onto items. You shouldn't add a convenience method on the cart that will query an item for its rice and return it. Instead, you should have a method that allows you to obtain the item. Once you have the item you can request the price yourself.

Q You mentioned the public, protected, and private keywords. Are there any other access modifiers?

A Each language defines its access modifiers in its own way. However, most OO languages define those three levels. Java also has a default package access modifier. You specify this level by leaving a modifier off. This level restricts access to only those classes in the same package. For more information about packages check out Appendix B, "Java Primer."

Q Do the access modifiers double as a security mechanism?

A No. The access modifiers only restrict how other objects may interact with a given object. Modifiers have nothing to do with computer security.

Workshop

The quiz questions and answers are provided for your further understanding. See Appendix A, "Answers," for the answers.

Quiz

1. How does encapsulation fulfill the goals of object-oriented programming?
2. Define abstraction and give an example demonstrating abstraction.
3. Define implementation.
4. Define interface.
5. Describe the difference between interface and implementation.
6. Why is the clear division of responsibility important to effective encapsulation?
7. Define type.
8. Define ADT.

9. How do you achieve effective implementation hiding and loosely coupled code?

10. What are some dangers inherent in abstraction?

Exercises

1. Consider the classical stack data structure. A stack is a "Last In First Out" (LIFO) structure. Unlike a LIFO queue, you can only add and remove elements from the same end of a stack. Like a queue, a stack allows you to check to see if it is empty and to peek at the first element that you can remove.

   Define an ADT for the stack class.

2. Take the stack ADT from Exercise 1 and sketch out an implementation. When done, define a second implementation.

3. Look back at Exercises 1 and 2. Was the interface that you designed in Exercise 1 adequate for both implementations that you formulated in Exercise 2? If so, what benefits did the interface provide? If not, what was lacking in the original interface?

DAY 3

Encapsulation: Time to Write Some Code

Yesterday, you learned all about encapsulation. As you begin today's lessons, you should have a good idea of what encapsulation is, how to apply it effectively, and what common mistakes to keep an eye out for. What you don't have at this point is hands-on experience with the technique. Sure, you know the theory, but nothing beats getting down and dirty with code. For the rest of the day, you'll complete a number of labs that should cement the lessons of Day 2.

Today you will learn

- How to set up the Java environment
- About class basics
- How to implement encapsulation
- About the Java primitive wrappers

Lab 1: Setting Up the Java Environment

You will use the Java programming language to complete all of the labs this week as well as the final project. In order to program in Java, you need to obtain a version of the Java 2 Platform, Standard Edition. To complete these labs, you need to have at least version 1.2 of the SDK.

If you don't already have one, you'll have to download and install a development kit now. There are many different development kits available. However, you can easily obtain the newest version from `http://www.javasoft.com/j2se/`.

Sun supports three main platforms: Solaris, Linux, and Windows. At the time of this writing, Sun's newest version is Java 2 SDK, Standard Edition, v 1.3.

IBM also offers a number of development kits at `http://www.ibm.com/java/jdk/index.html`.

In addition to the platforms supported by Sun, IBM also provides support for a number of platforms, such as OS/2, AS/400, and AIX.

Each development kit comes with adequate installation instructions. Please follow these instructions in order to install the kit on your development machine. You can also refer to Appendix B, "Java Primer," for more help.

You can also choose to use a popular Java IDE such as Forte, JBuilder, or Visual Age for Java. These examples and labs will work in these environments as well.

This book assumes a basic familiarity with programming, but you do not need a deep understanding of Java to complete these labs. If you do need some help getting up to speed on Java basics, please see Appendix B.

Problem Statement

Indeed, you need the horse before you get the cart. Before you can program you need to obtain and set up a Java development environment. If you have not already done so, obtain a Java development kit and follow the steps outlined in Appendix B in order to install it. Once installed, the appendix will step you through setting your classpath as well as compiling and running your first Java program. Once you complete this lab you'll know that your Java installation works. You'll also know all that you need to know in order to compile and run your Java programs.

Lab 2: Class Basics

It is very important that you keep the lessons of Days 1 and 2 in mind as you write your first classes.

In Day 1 you learned some basics about classes and objects. Day 2 showed you how you can leverage encapsulation to produce well-defined objects.

The Java class library contains a rich set of classical data structures such as lists and hashtables. Consider the DoubleKey class of Listing 3.1.

LISTING 3.1   DoubleKey.java

```java
public class DoubleKey {

    private String key1, key2;

    // a no args constructor
    public DoubleKey() {
        key1 = "key1";
        key2 = "key2";
    }

    // a constructor with arguments
    public DoubleKey( String key1, String key2 ) {
        this.key1 = key1;
        this.key2 = key2;
    }

    // accessor
    public String getKey1() {
        return key1;
    }

    // mutator
    public void setKey1( String key1 ) {
        this.key1 = key1;
    }

    // accessor
    public String getKey2() {
        return key2;
    }

    // mutator
    public void setKey2( String key2 ) {
        this.key2 = key2;
    }

    // equals and hashcode omitted for brevity
}
```

When you place an object into any implementation of java.util.Map you can specify any object as a key to that object. When you need to retrieve an object you simply use the key to retrieve the value. DoubleKey allows you to hash on two String keys instead of one.

You'll notice that `DoubleKey` has two constructors:

```
public DoubleKey() {
    key1 = "key1";
    key2 = "key2";
}

public DoubleKey( String key1, String key2 ) {
    this.key1 = key1;
    this.key2 = key2;
}
```

Constructors come in two forms: those without arguments (*noargs* constructors) and those with arguments.

NEW TERM *Noarg constructors* are constructors that do not take any arguments.

> **Note** *Noarg constructor* is a Java term. The C++ equivalent is *default constructor*.

No argument constructors instantiate an object with default values, whereas those that accept arguments use the arguments to initialize the objects internal state.

`public DoubleKey()` is an example of a noargs constructor, whereas `public DoubleKey( String key1, String key2 )` accepts arguments.

As Day 1 taught you, methods such as `public String getKey1()` and `public String getKey2()` are known as accessors because they allow you to access the internal values of the object.

> **Note** The Java world recognizes two types of accessors: setters and getters. *Setters* allow you to set an instance variable, whereas *getters* allow you to read an instance variable.
>
> Sun Microsystems has developed an entire naming convention around setters and getters known as JavaBean Design Patterns. JavaBeans is a standard way of writing your components. If your components conform to this standard, you can plug them into any JavaBean compatible IDE. Such an IDE could allow you to construct your programs visually using the beans.
>
> The Java naming conventions are simple. The JavaBean convention for naming getters and setters is
>
> ```
> public void set<VariableName>( <type> value )
> public <type> get<VariableName>()
> ```

> where *<type>* is the type of the instance variable and *<VariableName>* is the
> name of the instance variable.
>
> Take a *Person* object as an example. A *Person* has a name. The name getter
> and setter might take the following format:
>
> ```
> public void setName( String name )
> public String getName()
> ```

Finally, you call methods such as `public void setKey1( String key1 )` and `public void setKey2( String key2 )` mutators because they allow you to alter the internal state of the object.

`DoubleKey` demonstrates the proper use of encapsulation. By employing a well-defined interface, `DoubleKey` hides its implementation from the outside world. `DoubleKey` is also fairly abstract. You can reuse `DoubleKey` anywhere you need to hash by two String keys. Finally, `DoubleKey` properly divides responsibility by only providing those methods necessary to act as a map key.

Problem Statement

On Day 2 you saw the Bank of OO. At the Bank of OO, customers enter a queue while waiting for a teller. But don't worry, you won't be writing a `Queue` class. Java has plenty of built-in support for classical data structures. Instead, you'll program an account class—Java still leaves the programmer with a few jobs to do.

Whether it is a brokerage account, a checking account, or a money market account, all accounts have a few shared characteristics. All accounts have a balance. An account will also allow you to deposit funds, withdraw funds, and query the balance.

Today you will write an account class. Lab 2 comes complete with a `Teller` class. The `Teller` class has a `main()` that you will use to test your account implementation.

The `Teller` expects a specific public interface. Here are the rules:

- You must name the account class `Account`.
- The class must have the following two constructors:
  ```
  public Account()
  public Account( double initial_deposit )
  ```
  The noargs constructor will set the initial balance to 0.00. The second constructor will set the initial balance to `initial_deposit`.
- The class must have the following three methods. The first method credits the account with the value of `funds`:
  ```
  public void depositFunds( double funds )
  ```

The next method debits the account by the value of `funds`:

```
public double withdrawFunds( double funds )
```

However, `withdrawFunds()` should not allow an overdraft. Instead, if `funds` is greater than the balance, only debit the remainder of the balance. `withdrawFunds()` should return the actual amount withdrawn from the account.

The third method retrieves the account's current balance:

```
public double getBalance()
```

Beyond these few rules you can add any other methods that you might think helpful. However, be sure to implement each of the methods exactly as listed above. Otherwise, the teller cannot do its job!

Once you are done writing the `Account` class be sure to compile both the `Account` and `Teller` classes. Once you do that, execute the main in `Teller` by typing **java Teller**.

If you've done your work correctly you should see the output shown in Figure 3.1.

FIGURE 3.1

The proper output from
`Teller`.

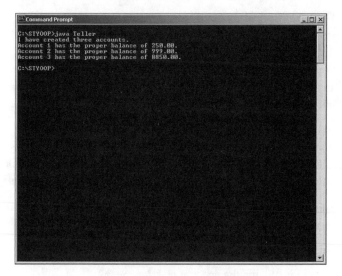

 Caution | The next section discusses the solutions to Lab 2. Do not proceed until you complete Lab 2!

Solutions and Discussion

Listing 3.2 presents one possible implementation of Account.

LISTING 3.2   Account.java

```java
public class Account {

    // private data
    private double balance;

    // constructor
    public Account( double init_deposit ) {
        balance = init_deposit;
    }

    public Account() {
        // no need to do anything, _balance will default to 0
    }

    // deposit monies into account
    public void depositFunds( double amount ) {
        balance = balance + amount;
    }

    // query the balance
    public double getBalance() {
        return balance;
    }

    // withdraw funds from the account
    public double withdrawFunds( double amount ) {

        if( amount > balance ) {  // adjust the amount
            amount = balance;
        }

        balance = balance - amount;
        return amount;
    }
}
```

The Account class illustrates the important concepts behind encapsulation. Account is fairly abstract. It will work as the basis for many different types of accounts. The Account hides its implementation behind a well-defined interface. Finally, the Account shows a proper division of responsibility since it contains all of the knowledge of how to debit and credit the account balance. Knowledge of how to accomplish these tasks does not "leak" outside of the object.

However, `Account` is not perfect; there is still some room for improvement. For the sake of brevity, this `Account` class solution skips argument validation beyond simple overdraft checking. For use in the real world you would need to include code to validate all method parameters.

Lab 3: Encapsulation Roundup

Day 2 covered three characteristics of effective encapsulation:

- Abstraction
- Implementation hiding
- Division of responsibility

Each characteristic is an important skill to master while designing and writing your classes. You need to apply all three characteristics in order to have well encapsulated objects.

Let's apply these three characteristics to a game of cards.

First, let's apply abstraction. Remember not to overdo abstraction. You still have a problem to solve and you can't solve all problems. So you should first try to solve the problems that you know about!

What can you say generically about card games played with a standard poker deck?

A good place to start is the deck of cards itself. A standard deck contains 52 cards. You can shuffle a deck as well as pick a card out of the deck from any position. Likewise, you can return a card to any position in the deck. Any other draw is just a specialization on picking a card from any part of the deck.

What can you say about the cards themselves?

All cards share a common structure. Each card has a suit: diamonds, hearts, spades, or clubs. Each card also has a value: 2–10, Jack, Queen, King, or Ace. The only difference from one card to the next is the value of these two attributes.

Taken to an extreme you could try to describe every type of card deck whether they are baseball cards or tarot cards. Again, when you start abstracting you need to be sure not to over abstract.

How about implementation hiding?

Unless you cheat while playing cards you never get to see inside of the deck until you are dealt a card. You also do not get to insert cards that are not part of the deck.

Finally, what about responsibility?

In the real world, cards themselves do not do too much. A card simply displays its suit and value. A card does have a state: face-up or face-down. Likewise, a deck does not do too much in the real world. Instead, the dealer is the one who does all of the shuffling and dealing. The deck simply contains the playing cards.

In the computer world, a card will hold onto its suit, value, and state. In a simple program, a card will also know how to display itself. A deck will create and hold onto the cards. Finally, the dealer will know how to shuffle the cards and deal a card.

> **Note** Later you will learn the importance of separating display from your model/data. However, for your purposes here you can mix the two.

3

Problem Statement

Use the poker card description design classes to represent the cards, the deck of cards, and the dealer. You should then write a small `main()` that instantiates the dealer and your deck of cards, shuffles the cards, and then prints out the deck.

This lab leaves you with a great deal of leeway while designing your cards, deck, and dealer. When thinking about the classes that you will create, be sure to consider implementation hiding and division of responsibility. Only place responsibility where it belongs and once you do place it, make sure it does not "leak" out.

> **Note** Please see `java.lang.Math.random()` for generating random numbers. `random()` will come in handy for shuffling the deck. You can obtain full documentation of the Java APIs from `http://www.javasoft.com/`.
>
> For example, `(int)(Math.random() * 52)` will give you a number between 0 and 51.

> **Caution** The next section discusses the solutions to Lab 3. Do not proceed until you complete Lab 3!

Solutions and Discussion

Listing 3.3 presents one possible `Card` class.

LISTING 3.3 Card.java

```java
public class Card {

    private int rank;
    private int suit;
    private boolean face_up;

    // constants used to instantiate
    // suits
    public static final int DIAMONDS = 4;
    public static final int HEARTS   = 3;
    public static final int SPADES   = 6;
    public static final int CLUBS    = 5;
    // values
    public static final int TWO   = 2;
    public static final int THREE = 3;
    public static final int FOUR  = 4;
    public static final int FIVE  = 5;
    public static final int SIX   = 6;
    public static final int SEVEN = 7;
    public static final int EIGHT = 8;
    public static final int NINE  = 9;
    public static final int TEN   = 10;
    public static final int JACK  = 74;
    public static final int QUEEN = 81;
    public static final int KING  = 75;
    public static final int ACE   = 65;

    // creates a new card - only use the constants to initialize
    public Card( int suit, int rank ) {
        // In a real program you would need to do validation on the arguments.

        this.suit = suit;
        this.rank  = rank;
    }

    public int getSuit() {
        return suit;
    }

    public int getRank() {
        return rank;
    }

    public void faceUp() {
        face_up = true;
    }

    public void faceDown() {
```

LISTING 3.3   continued

```
        face_up = false;
    }

    public boolean isFaceUp() {
        return face_up;
    }

    public String display() {
        String display;

        if( rank > 10 ) {
            display = String.valueOf( (char) rank );
        } else {
            display = String.valueOf( rank );
        }

        switch ( suit ) {
            case DIAMONDS:
                return display + String.valueOf( (char) DIAMONDS );
            case HEARTS:
                return display + String.valueOf( (char) HEARTS );
            case SPADES:
                return display + String.valueOf( (char) SPADES );
            default:
                return display + String.valueOf( (char) CLUBS );
        }
    }
}
```

The Card class definition starts by defining a number of constants. These constants enumerate the valid card values and suits.

You'll notice that once instantiated you cannot change the value of the card. Card instances are immutable. By making the card immutable, someone cannot come along and wrongly change a card's value.

NEW TERM   An *immutable* object is an object whose state does not change once constructed.

The Card class is responsible for holding onto its suit as well as value. The card also knows how to return a String representation of itself.

Listing 3.4 presents one possible Deck implementation.

LISTING 3.4   Deck.java

```java
public class Deck {

    private java.util.LinkedList deck;

    public Deck() {
        buildCards();
    }

    public Card get( int index ) {
        if( index < deck.size() ) {
            return (Card) deck.get( index );
        }
        return null;
    }

    public void replace( int index, Card card ) {
        deck.set( index, card );
    }

    public int size() {
        return deck.size();
    }

    public Card removeFromFront() {
        if( deck.size() > 0 ) {
            Card card = (Card) deck.removeFirst();
            return card;
        }
        return null;
    }

    public void returnToBack( Card card ) {
        deck.add( card );
    }

    private void buildCards() {

        deck = new java.util.LinkedList();

        deck.add( new Card( Card.CLUBS, Card.TWO   ) );
        deck.add( new Card( Card.CLUBS, Card.THREE ) );
        deck.add( new Card( Card.CLUBS, Card.FOUR  ) );
        deck.add( new Card( Card.CLUBS, Card.FIVE  ) );
        // full definition clipped for brevity
        // see source for full listing
    }

}
```

The Deck class is responsible for instantiating the cards and then providing access to the cards. The Deck provides methods for retrieving and returning the cards.

Listing 3.5 presents the Dealer implementation.

LISTING 3.5   Dealer.java

```java
public class Dealer {

    private Deck deck;

    public Dealer( Deck d ) {
        deck = d;
    }

    public void shuffle() {
        // randomize the card array
        int num_cards = deck.size();
        for( int i = 0; i < num_cards; i ++ ) {
            int index = (int) ( Math.random() * num_cards );
            Card card_i = ( Card ) deck.get( i );
            Card card_index = ( Card ) deck.get( index );
            deck.replace( i, card_index );
            deck.replace( index, card_i );
        }
    }

    public Card dealCard() {
        if( deck.size() > 0 ) {
            return deck.removeFromFront();
        }
        return null;
    }

}
```

The Dealer is responsible for shuffling the deck and dealing cards. This Dealer implementation is honest. Another Dealer implementation might deal from the back of the deck!

All three classes have a clear division of responsibility. The Card represents poker cards, the Deck holds onto cards, and the Dealer deals the Cards out. All three classes also hide their implementation. Nothing suggests that the Deck actually has a LinkedList of cards.

Although Card may define a number of constants, this does not compromise its implementation integrity since the Card is free to use the constants however it likes. It is also free to change the values of the constants at any time.

The Deck's buildCards() method does highlight a shortcoming of implementation hiding. You could instantiate cards with rank 2–10 in a for loop. If you look at the constants you will see that TWO through TEN count from 2 to 10 sequentially. Such a loop is much simpler than instantiating each card individually.

However, such an assumption ties you to the current values of the constants. You should not allow your program to become dependent on a certain value behind the constant. Instead, you should blindly use the constant by calling Card.TWO, Card.THREE, and so on. You should not make any kinds of assumptions about the value. Card could redefine the constant values at anytime. In the case of buildCards() it is easy to become tempted and use the constant values directly.

Here, the contract between Card and the user of the Card constants is the constant names, not their underlying value. Day 12, "Advanced Design Patterns," will present a solution that is a bit more elegant than this use of constants.

Lab 4: Case Study—The Java Primitive Wrappers (Optional)

 Note

Lab 4 is an optional lab. Although completing the lab will offer you additional insights into object-oriented programming, its completion is not necessary in order for you to succeed in the coming days.

Each object-oriented language has its own rules for determining what is and what is not an object. Some object-oriented languages are more "pure" than others. A purely object-oriented language, such as Smalltalk, considers everything an object, even operators and primitives.

NEW TERM   A *pure* object-oriented language supports the notion that everything is an object.

In a purely object-oriented language everything—classes, primitives, operators, even blocks of code—is considered an object.

Java has its own rules for determining what is and is not an object. In Java not everything is an object. For example, the Java language declares a number of primitive values. The primitives are not considered objects in Java. These primitives include boolean, char, byte, short, int, long, float, and double.

NEW TERM An *object-enabled* language does not consider everything an object.

Primitives do provide some benefits over objects. In order to use a primitive you do not need to instantiate a new instance using new. As a result, using a primitive is much more efficient than using an object because it does not suffer from the overhead associated with objects.

On the other hand, you'll find using primitives limiting at times. You cannot treat primitives as objects. This means that you cannot use them in places that require an object. Consider java.util.Vector from the generic collection classes. In order to place a value in the vector, you need to call the vector's add() method:

```
public boolean add( Object o );
```

In order to store a value on the vector, the value must be an object. Put plainly, if you want to place a primitive on a vector you're out of luck.

In order to get around these shortcomings, Java has a number of primitive wrappers including Boolean, Character, Byte, Double, Float, Integer, Long, and Short. These classes are called wrappers because they contain, or wrap, a primitive value.

NEW TERM A *wrapper* is an object whose sole purpose is to contain another object or primitive. A wrapper will provide any number of methods for obtaining and manipulating the wrapped value.

Let's consider the Boolean's public interface, which is outlined in Listing 3.6.

LISTING 3.6 java.lang.Boolean

```
public final class Boolean implements Serializable {
    public Boolean( boolean value );
    public Boolean( String s );

    public static final Boolean FALSE;
    public static final Boolean TRUE;
    public static final CLASS    TYPE;

    public static boolean getBoolean( String name );
    public static Boolean valueOf( String s );

    public boolean booleanValue();
    public boolean equals( Object obj );
    public int hashCode();
    public String toString();
}
```

> *Final* refers to the concept of preventing descendant classes from changing this element when inherited. Inheritance is discussed in Day 4, "Inheritance: Getting Something for Nothing."
>
> *Implements* has to do with the special "interface" construct of Java, discussed in Appendix B, "Java Primer."

Internally, the `Boolean` wrapper will contain a `boolean` primitive. So in order to pass a `boolean` to a vector you would need to first instantiate a `Boolean` wrapper, wrap the `boolean` primitive, and pass that wrapper to the vector.

The `Boolean` interface introduces another feature of object-oriented languages: class methods and class variables.

Up until now all of the methods and variables that you have seen are instance methods and instance variables. That is, each variable and each method is tied to some object instance. In order to call the method or access the variable you must have an instance of the object.

The fact that you need an instance is often logical. Consider `Boolean`'s `booleanValue()` method. The `booleanValue()` method is an instance method. The value that the method returns will depend upon the internal state of the individual `Boolean` instances. One instance may wrap `true`, another may wrap `false`. The value returned will depend on which value the instance holds internally.

Now consider `Boolean`'s `getBoolean()` method. This is a class method. If you study the definition of `getBoolean()` you will notice the keyword `static`. In Java, the keyword `static` declares that the method or variable is a class method or variable.

Unlike instance variables and methods, class methods and variables are not tied to any one instance. Instead, you access class methods through the class itself. So to call `getBoolean()` you do not need an instance (though you could still call the method as if it were an instance method). Instead, you can simply call `Boolean.getBoolean()`. The response to `getBoolean()` is not dependent upon the state of any one instance. For that reason it can get away with being declared as a class method.

NEW TERM *Class variables* are variables that belong to the class, not a specific instance. Class variables are shared among all instances of the class.

NEW TERM *Class methods* are methods that belong to the class, not a specific instance. The operation performed by the method is not dependent upon the state of any instance.

Class variables work the same way. You do not need an instance to access them. However, they have another use as well. Because the variable is kept at the class level, all instances share the same variable (and if it is public, every object can share it). Class variables cut down on memory requirements. Consider `public static final Boolean FALSE`. This is a constant that wraps false. Because it is static, all instances share this same constant. Each instance does not need its own copy.

Consider the following class, CountedObject:

```java
public class CountedObject {

    private static int instances;

    /** Creates new CountedObject */
    public CountedObject() {
        instances++;
    }

    public static int getNumberInstances() {
        return instances;
    }

    public static void main( String [] args ) {
        CountedObject obj = null;
        for( int i = 0; i < 10; i++ ) {
            obj = new CountedObject();
        }
        System.out.println( "Instances created: " +
                                obj.getNumberInstances() );
        // note that this will work too
        System.out.println( "Instances created: " +
                                CountedObject.getNumberInstances() );
    }
}
```

CountedObject declares a class variable named instances. It also declares a class method for retrieving the value, getNumberInstances(). Within the constructor, the value is incremented each time an instance is created. Because all instances share the variable, the instances variable acts as a counter. As each object is created it increments the counter.

The main() creates 10 instances. You'll note that you can either use an instance to make the call to getNumberInstances() or the class itself.

Whether or not to declare a method or variable static is a design decision. If the method or variable is independent of the state of any instance, it is probably a good idea to make it a class method or variable. However, you may not declare variables and methods that are instance dependent as static, such as Boolean's booleanValue().

You might have made a few observations regarding Boolean. If you study the interface you will notice that there is no way to change the wrapped boolean value once you've instantiated the Boolean instance! Because you cannot change its value, instances of Boolean are said to be immutable.

There are times when using an immutable object is valuable. If you are familiar with threading, an immutable object is inherently thread-safe since its state can never change.

However, there are times when immutable objects cause more harm than good. In the case of the primitive wrappers, the overhead of instantiating a wrapper for each primitive can become expensive.

Problem Statement

For Lab 4 you need to create a mutable `Boolean` primitive wrapper. At a minimum, this wrapper should allow you to get and set the wrapped value. The wrapper should also provide two constructors: a noargs constructor and a constructor that takes the wrapper's initial value.

Feel free to add any other methods that you would find convenient. However, do not forget to follow the rules of effective encapsulation.

You may find it helpful to review Appendix B's discussion of the keyword `static` if you decide to provide all of the methods provided by the `Boolean` primitive wrapper.

 Caution | The next section discusses the solutions to Lab 4. Do not proceed until you complete Lab 4!

Solutions and Discussion

Listing 3.7 presents one possible solution for Lab 4.

LISTING 3.7   MyBoolean.java

```
public class MyBoolean  {

    // some constants for convenience
    public static final Class TYPE = Boolean.TYPE;

    private boolean value;

    // no arg constructor - default to false
    public MyBoolean() {
        value = false;
    }

    // set the initial wrapped value to value
    public MyBoolean( boolean value ) {
        this.value = value;
```

LISTING 3.7   continued

```
    }

    public boolean booleanValue() {
        return value;
    }

    public void setBooleanValue( boolean value ) {
        this.value = value;
    }

    // for getBoolean and valueOf we can simply delegate to Boolean
    // you'll learn more about delegation in chapter 4
    public static boolean getBoolean( String name ) {
        return Boolean.getBoolean( name );
    }

    public static MyBoolean valueOf( String s ) {
        return new MyBoolean( Boolean.getBoolean( s ) );
    }

    // definitions of hashCode, equals, and toString omitted for brevity
}
```

MyBoolean maintains the public interface found in Boolean with three exceptions:

- MyBoolean adds a mutator: public void setBooleanValue(boolean value). This mutator allows you to change the wrappers value.

- MyBoolean redefines valueOf() so that it returns an instance of MyBoolean instead of Boolean.

- MyBoolean removes the constants TRUE and FALSE. Now that MyBoolean is mutable, those values do not make adequate constants since their values may be changed by anyone at any time.

The solution to Lab 4 also gives you some sneak peaks into Day 4, "Inheritance: Getting Something for Nothing." Methods such as valueOf() demonstrate delegation. The full source solution to Lab 4 also gives you some early exposure to inheritance and overriding through the toString(), hashCode(), and equals() methods.

Q&A

Q In lab 3 you wrote, "This **Dealer** implementation is honest. Another **Dealer** implementation might deal from the back of the deck!" What do you mean by another implementation?

A You can say that the `shuffle()` and `dealCard()` methods make up the `Dealer`'s public interface. The `Dealer` presented is honest. He deals from the front of the deck. You could write another dealer named `DishonestDealer` that has the same public interface. However, this dealer might deal from the bottom of the deck.

You call this dealer another implementation because it reimplements the same interface as the one found in `Dealer`. However, this class implements the functionality behind the method slightly differently.

Q Can encapsulation be harmful?

A Indeed, encapsulation can be harmful. Imagine that you have a component that performs mathematical calculations. Suppose that you need to keep a certain precision as you complete your calculation. Unfortunately, the component may completely encapsulate the amount of precision that it keeps. You might end up with an incorrect value if the implementation uses a different precision than the one that you need. You can end up with strange bugs if someone comes along and alters the component.

So encapsulation can be harmful if you need precise control over the ways that an object handles your requests.

The only defense is good documentation. You should document any important implementation details and assumptions. Once documented, you can not easily make changes to any documented details or assumptions. Like the mathematical component, if you make a change, you risk breaking all of the users of that object.

Workshop

The quiz questions and answers are provided for your further understanding. See Appendix A, "Answers," for the answers.

Quiz

1. Look back at the `Account` class from Lab 2. Which method(s) is a mutator? Which method(s) is an accessor?

2. What are the two types of constructors? From the lab solutions, find an example of each type of constructor.

3. (Optional) `Boolean` as discussed in Lab 4 declares three public variables. In this case the use of public variables is acceptable. Can you explain why public is okay in this case?

4. (Optional) How can you make the solution to Lab 3 more efficient?

5. Why do you think that the solution to Lab 3 didn't create a separate Card class for each suit?

6. In Lab 3 you explored division of responsibility. What benefits did dividing up responsibility give to the Card, Deck, and Dealer classes?

Exercises

1. (Optional) Take Lab 2 and abstract DoubleKey further. Redesign DoubleKey so that it can accept any sort of object as a key—not just a String.

   In order for your new DoubleKey to work, you'll need to alter the definition of the equals() and hashCode() methods. These methods were left out for brevity in the printed solutions. However, the methods are available in the full source to the solutions.

2. (Optional) In Lab 3, Card instances know how to display themselves. However, the Deck does not know how to display itself. Redesign Deck so that Deck instances know how to display themselves.

3

DAY **4**

Inheritance: Getting Something for Nothing

For the past three days, you've concentrated on learning about the first pillar of object-oriented programming: encapsulation. Although encapsulation is a fundamental concept in OOP, there is more to the story than supporting simple ADTs and modules. In fact, OOP would offer very little over older-style programming if all it did was offer simple encapsulation. Of course, OOP offers much more.

OOP goes further by adding two other features: inheritance and polymorphism. You will spend the next two days considering inheritance, the second pillar of OOP.

Today you will learn

- What inheritance is
- The different types of inheritance
- Some of the pitfalls of inheritance

- Tips to effective inheritance
- How inheritance fulfills the goals of OO

What Is Inheritance?

Yesterday, you saw how encapsulation allows you to write well-defined, self-contained objects. Encapsulation allows one object to *use* another object through messages. *Use* is only one way that objects may relate in OOP. OOP also provides a second way for objects to interrelate: inheritance.

Inheritance allows you to base a new class's definition upon a pre-existing class. When you base a class on another, the new class's definition automatically inherits all of the attributes, behavior, and implementations present in the pre-existing class.

NEW TERM   *Inheritance* is a mechanism that allows you to base a new class upon the definition of a pre-existing class. By using inheritance, your new class inherits all of the attributes and behaviors present in the pre-existing class. When one class inherits from another, all the methods and attributes that appear in the pre-existing class's interface will automatically appear in the new class's interface.

Consider the following class:

```
public class Employee {

    private String first_name;
    private String last_name;
    private double wage;

    public Employee( String first_name, String last_name, double wage ) {
        this.first_name = first_name;
        this.last_name  = last_name;
        this.wage = wage;
    }

    public double getWage() {
        return wage;
    }

    public String getFirstName() {
        return first_name;
    }

    public String getLastName() {
        return last_name;
    }
}
```

Instances of a class such as `Employee` may appear in a payroll database application. Now suppose that you needed to model a commissioned employee. A commissioned employee has a base salary plus a small commission per sale. Other than this simple requirement, the `CommissionedEmployee` is exactly the same as `Employee`. A `CommissionedEmployee` is an `Employee`, after all.

Using straight encapsulation, there are two ways that you can write the new `CommissionedEmployee` class. You could simply repeat the code found in `Employee` and add the code necessary to track commissions and calculate pay. However, if you do that you'll have to maintain two separate but similar code bases. If you need to fix a bug, you'll have to do it in each place.

So simply copying and pasting the code is not really an option. You'll need to try something else. You could have an employee variable inside the `CommissionedEmployee` class and delegate all messages such as `getWage()` and `getFirstName()` to the `Employee` instance.

NEW TERM   *Delegation* is the process of one object passing a message to another object in order to fulfill some request.

However, delegation still forces you to redefine all of the methods found in `Employee`'s interface in order to pass on all messages. So neither of these two options seems satisfactory.

Let's see how inheritance can fix this problem:

```
public class CommissionedEmployee extends Employee {

      private double commission; // the $ per unit
      private int    units;      // keep track of the # of units sold

      public CommissionedEmployee( String first_name, String last_name,
                               double wage, double commission ) {
            super( first_name, last_name, wage ); // call the original
                                                  // constructor in order to
                                                  // properly initialize
            this.commission   = commission;
      }

      public double calculatePay() {
            return getWage() + ( commission * units );
      }

      public void addSales( int units ) {
            this.units = this.units + units;
      }
```

4

```
        public void resetSales() {
            units = 0;
        }
}
```

Here `CommissionedEmployee` bases its definition on the existing `Employee` class. Because `CommissionedEmployee` inherits from `Employee`, `getFirstName()`, `getLastName()`, `getWage()`, `first_name`, `last_name`, and `wage` all become part of its definition.

Because `Employee`'s public interface becomes part of `CommissionedEmployee`'s interface, you can send any message to `CommissionedEmployee` that you could send to `Employee`. Consider the following `main()`, which does just that:

```
public static void main( String [] args ) {
    CommissionedEmployee c =
        new CommissionedEmployee("Mr.","Sales",5.50,1.00);
    c.addSales(5);
    System.out.println( "First Name: " + c.getFirstName() );
    System.out.println( "Last Name: "  + c.getLastName()  );
    System.out.println( "Base Pay: $" + c.getWage() );
    System.out.println( "Total Pay: $" + c.calculatePay() );
}
```

Figure 4.1 illustrates what you will see upon execution of this code.

FIGURE 4.1

Output generated
from the
`CommissionedEmployee`.

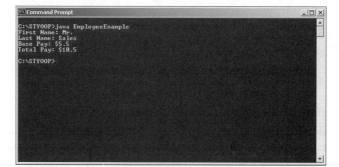

Why Inheritance?

As you saw in the last example, sometimes encapsulation's simple *use* relationship isn't enough. However, there's more to inheritance than simply inheriting a public interface and implementation.

As you will see later today, inheritance allows the inheriting class to redefine any behavior that it does not like. Such a useful feature allows you to adapt your software as your requirements change. If you need to make a change, you simply write a new class that inherits the old functionality. Then, override the functionality that needs to change or add the functionality that is missing and you're done. Overriding is valuable because it allows you to change the way an object works without touching the original class definition! You can leave your well-tested, validated code base intact. Overriding even works if you don't have the original source to a class.

Inheritance has another very important use. On Day 1, "Introduction to Object Oriented Programming," you saw how a class groups related objects. Inheritance allows you to group related classes. OOP always strives to produce natural software. Like the real world, OOP allows you to group and classify your classes.

"Is-A" Versus "Has-A": Learning When to Use Inheritance

In order to introduce you to the mechanisms of inheritance, the first section covered what is known as *implementation inheritance*. As you saw, implementation inheritance allows your classes to inherit the implementation of other classes. However, just because one class can inherit from another doesn't mean that it should!

So how do you know when you should use inheritance? Luckily, there is a rule of thumb to follow in order to avoid incorrect inheritance.

Whenever you are considering inheritance for reuse or any other reason, you have to first ask yourself if the inheriting class is the same type as the class being inherited. Thinking in terms of type while inheriting is often referred to as the "Is-a" test.

NEW TERM   *Is-a* describes the relationship in which one class is considered the same type as another.

To use "Is-a" you say to yourself, "A `CommissionedEmployee` 'Is-an' `Employee`." This statement is true and you would know right away that inheritance is valid in this situation. Now stop and consider the Java `Iterator`:

```java
public interface Iterator {
    public boolean hasNext();
    public Object next();
    public void remove();
}
```

Say that you would like to write a class that implements this interface. If you think back to Day 2 you might realize that a `Queue` implementation might be useful in constructing your `Iterator`. You could use all of the pre-existing `Queue` implementation to hold onto the elements in the `Iterator`. When you need to check `hasNext()` or `remove()`, you can simply call the proper `Queue` method and return the result.

4

Inheritance in this case will provide a quick way to implement an `Iterator`. However, before you begin coding, don't forget the "Is-a" test.

"An `Iterator` 'Is-a' `Queue`." Clearly this statement is false. Forget about inheriting from `Queue`!

> **Note**   A `Queue` may "have an" `Iterator` that knows how to traverse over the elements.

There will be many situations where the "Is-a" test fails when you want to reuse some implementation. Luckily, there are other ways to reuse implementation. You can always use composition and delegation (see the following sidebar). The "Has-a" test saves the day.

 Has-a describes the relationship in which one class contains an instance of another class.

 Composition means that a class is implemented using internal variables (called member variables) that hold onto instances of other classes.

Composition is a form of reuse that you have seen before. If you can't inherit, nothing prevents you from using instances of the other class inside of the new class. Whenever you want to use the features of another class, you simply use an instance of that class as one of your constituent pieces. Of course, you do suffer the limitations presented earlier.

Consider the `Queue`/`Iterator` example again. Instead of inheriting from `Queue`, the `Iterator` can simply create an instance of `Queue` and store it in an instance variable. Whenever the `Iterator` needs to retrieve an element or check whether it is empty, it can simply delegate the work to the `Queue` instance as demonstrated in Figure 4.2.

FIGURE 4.2

An `Iterator`
delegating method
calls to the `Queue`.

Iterator Instance

HasNext()   IsEmpty()   Queue
Instance

When you use composition, you get to pick and choose what you use. Through delegation, you may expose some or all features of your constituent objects. Figure 4.2 illustrates how the `Iterator` routes the `hasNext()` method to the `Queue`'s `isEmpty()` method.

It is important to point out that delegation differs from inheritance in two important ways:

1. With inheritance you only have one object instance. There is only one indivisible object because what is inherited becomes an intrinsic part of the new class.
2. Delegation generally only supplies the user with what is in the public interface. Regular inheritance gives you more access to the internals of the inherited class. We'll talk about such access in detail toward the end of today's lesson.

Learning to Navigate Inheritance's Tangled Web

The concepts of "Is-a" and composition change the nature of the discussion of inheritance from one of greedy implementation reuse to one of class inter-relationships. A class that inherits from another must relate to that class in some way so that the resulting relationships, or inheritance hierarchies, make sense.

NEW TERM An *inheritance hierarchy* is a treelike mapping of relationships that form between classes as a result of inheritance. Figure 4.3 illustrates a real-life hierarchy taken from Java.

FIGURE 4.3

A sample hierarchy from `java.text`.

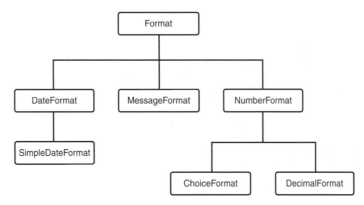

Inheritance defines the new class, the *child*, in terms of an old class, the *parent*. This child parent relationship is the simplest inheritance relationship. In fact, all inheritance hierarchies begin with a parent and child.

NEW TERM The *child class* is the class doing the inheriting; also known as the subclass.

NEW TERM The *parent class* is the class that the child directly inherits from; it's also known as the superclass.

Figure 4.4 illustrates a parent/child relationship. `NumberFormat` is the parent of the two children `ChoiceFormat` and `DecimalFormat`.

FIGURE 4.4

A parent with multiple children.

```
                    ┌──────────────────┐
                    │   NumberFormat   │
                    └──────────────────┘
                             │
              ┌──────────────┴──────────────┐
    ┌──────────────────┐          ┌──────────────────┐
    │   ChoiceFormat   │          │  DecimalFormat   │
    └──────────────────┘          └──────────────────┘
```

Now that you've seen a few more definitions, you can refine the definition of inheritance.

NEW TERM *Inheritance* is a mechanism that allows you to establish "Is-a" relationships between classes. This relationship also allows a subclass to inherit its super-class's attributes and behaviors.

Note

When a child inherits from a parent, the child will get any attributes and behaviors that the parent might have inherited from another class.

As you have seen, in order for the inheritance hierarchy to make sense, you must be able to do everything to the child that you can do to its parent. That is what the "Is-a" test really tests. A child is only allowed to augment functionality and add functionality. A child is never allowed to remove functionality.

Caution

If you do find that a child needs to remove functionality, this is an indication that the child should appear before the parent in the inheritance hierarchy!

Like real-life parents and children, class children and class parents will resemble one another. Instead of sharing genes, classes share type information.

> **Note**
>
> Unlike real life children, a class may have only one physical parent. It all depends on how the language implements inheritance.
>
> Some languages allow a class to have more than one parent. That is known as *multiple inheritance*.
>
> Some languages constrain the child to one parent.
>
> Other languages, such as Java, allow only one parent for implementation, but provide a mechanism to inherit multiple interfaces (but no implementation, just the method signatures).

Like flesh-and-blood children, child classes may add new behaviors and attributes to themselves. For example, a flesh-and-blood child may learn to play the piano even though the parent never did. Likewise, a child may redefine an inherited behavior. For example, the parent may have been a poor math student. A child can study extra hard and become a good math student. When you want to add new behavior to a class, you can do so by adding a new method to the class or by redefining an old one.

Inheritance Mechanics

When one class inherits from another, it inherits implementation, behaviors, and attributes. This means that all the methods and attributes available in the parent's interface will appear in the child's interface. A class constructed through inheritance can have three important kinds of methods and attributes:

- Overridden: the new class inherits the method or attribute from the parent but provides a new definition
- New: the new class adds a completely new method or attribute
- Recursive: the new class simply inherits a method or attribute from the parent

> **Caution**
>
> Most OO languages do not allow you to override an attribute. However, the overridden attribute is included here in order to be thorough.

First, let's consider an example. Then we'll explore each type of method and attribute.

```
public class TwoDimensionalPoint {

    private double x_coord;
    private double y_coord;

    public TwoDimensionalPoint( double x, double y ) {
        setXCoordinate( x );
```

```
            setYCoordinate( y );
        }

        public double getXCoordinate() {
            return x_coord;
        }

        public void setXCoordinate( double x ) {
            x_coord = x;
        }

        public double getYCoordinate() {
            return y_coord;
        }

        public void setYCoordinate( double y ) {
            y_coord = y;
        }

        public String toString() {
            return "I am a 2 dimensional point.\n" +
                    "My x coordinate is: " + getXCoordinate() + "\n" +
                    "My y coordinate is: " + getYCoordinate();
        }
    }

    public class ThreeDimensionalPoint extends TwoDimensionalPoint {

        private double z_coord;

        public ThreeDimensionalPoint( double x, double y, double z ) {
            super( x, y ); // initialize the inherited attributes
                            // by calling the parent constructor
            setZCoordinate( z );
        }

        public double getZCoordinate() {
            return z_coord;
        }

        public void setZCoordinate( double z ) {
            z_coord = z;
        }

        public String toString() {
            return "I am a 3 dimensional point.\n" +
                    "My x coordinate is: " + getXCoordinate() + "\n" +
                    "My y coordinate is: " + getYCoordinate() + "\n" +
                    "My z coordinate is: " + getZCoordinate();
        }

    }
```

Here you have two point classes that represent geometric points. You might use points in a graphing tool, a visual modeler, or a flight planner. Points have many practical uses.

Here, TwoDimensionalPoint holds onto an x and y coordinate. The class defines methods for getting and setting the points as well as creating a String representation of the point instance.

ThreeDimensionalPoint inherits from TwoDimensionalPoint. ThreeDimensionalPoint adds a z coordinate as well as a method for retrieving the value and setting the value. The class also provides a method to obtain a String representation of the instance. Because ThreeDimensionalPoint inherits from TwoDimensionalPoint, it also has the methods contained within TwoDimensionalPoint.

This example demonstrates each type of method.

Overridden Methods and Attributes

Inheritance allows you to take a pre-existing method or attribute and redefine it. Redefining a method allows you to change the object's behavior for that method.

An overridden method or attribute will appear in both the parent and the child. For example, ThreeDimensionalPoint redefines the toString() method that appears in TwoDimensionalPoint:

```
// from TwoDimensionalPoint
    public String toString() {
            return "I am a 2 dimensional point.\n" +
                    "My x coordinate is: " + getXCoordinate() + "\n" +
                    "My y coordinate is: " + getYCoordinate();
    }
```

TwoDimensionalPoint defines a toString() method that identifies the instance as a 2-dimensional point and prints out its 2-piece coordinate.

ThreeDimensionalPoint redefines the toString() method to identify the instance as a 3-dimensional point and print out its 3-piece coordinate:

```
// from ThreeDimensionalPoint
    public String toString() {
            return "I am a 3 dimensional point.\n" +
                    "My x coordinate is: " + getXCoordinate() + "\n" +
                    "My y coordinate is: " + getYCoordinate() + "\n" +
                    "My z coordinate is: " + getZCoordinate();
    }
```

Consider the following main():

```
    public static void main( String [] args ) {
            TwoDimensionalPoint two = new TwoDimensionalPoint(1,2);
```

```
                ThreeDimensionalPoint three = new ThreeDimensionalPoint(1,2,3);

                System.out.println(two.toString());
                System.out.println(three.toString());
        }
```

Figure 4.5 illustrates what you will see after executing the main().

FIGURE 4.5

Testing the overridden
toString() *method.*

As you can see in Figure 4.5, ThreeDimensionalPoint returns its overridden String representation.

Overriding a method is also known as *redefining* a method. By redefining a method, the child provides its own tailored implementation of the method. This new implementation will provide new behavior for the method. Here the ThreeDimensionalPoint redefines the behavior of the toString() method so that it is properly translated into a String.

NEW TERM   *Overriding* is the process of a child taking a method that appears in the parent and rewriting it in order to change the method's behavior. Overriding a method is also known as *redefining* a method.

So how does the object know which definition to use?

The answer depends on the underlying OO plumbing. Most OO systems will first look for the definition in the object that is passed the message. If a definition is not found there, the runtime will travel up the hierarchy until a definition is found. It is important to realize that this is how a message is handled and that's why overriding works. The child's definition will be the one called because that is the first one found. The mechanism is the same for recursive methods and attributes, which you will cover later.

Figure 4.6 illustrates the method propagation among the point objects for a call to getXCoordinate(). A method call to getXCoordinate() will go up the hierarchy until it finds a definition for the method.

FIGURE 4.6

Message propagation among the point objects.

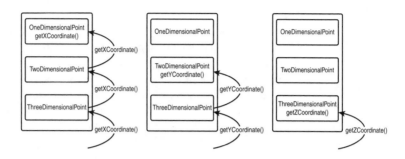

When considering overriding a method or attribute, it is important to realize that not all methods and attributes are available for your child to override, let alone use. Most object-oriented languages have some idea of access control. Access control keywords define just who is allowed to see and access methods and attributes. Generically, these access levels fall into three categories, as discussed briefly on Day 2:

- Private: An access level that restricts access only to the class.
- Protected: An access level that restricts access to the class and to children.
- Public: An access level that allows access to everyone and anyone.

Protected methods and attributes are those methods or attributes to which you only want subclasses to have access. Do not leave such methods public. Only those with extensive knowledge of the class should use protected methods and attributes.

You should make all non-constant attributes and any method meant solely for the class itself private. Private prevents any other object from calling the method except for the object itself. Don't make private methods protected just in case some subclass might want access to them someday. Only use protected for those methods that you *know* a subclass wants to use. Otherwise, use private or public. Such a rigid practice will mean that you might have to go back into your code at a later time and change a method's access level. However, this leads to a tighter design than one that opens everything up to a subclass.

Note

Going back and changing access levels may seem like a bad practice. However, inheritance hierarchies should never happen by accident. Instead, hierarchies should develop naturally as you program. There is no shame in refactoring your hierarchies over time. Real-life OOP is an iterative process.

Remember though, making everything private is a rule of thumb. There are cases in which this advice will not work to your advantage. It really all depends on what you are programming. For example, if you sell generic

> class libraries without supplying source code you should probably default to protected so that your customers can use inheritance to extend your classes.
>
> In fact, there are times when you will want to design a subclass with inheritance in mind. In such a case it makes sense to establish an inheritance protocol. An inheritance protocol is an abstract structure only visible through the protected elements of the class. The parent class will call these methods, and the child class can override these methods to augment behavior. You'll see such an example tomorrow.

Using these definitions and rules, it is easy to see that protected and public methods/attributes are the most important to inheritance.

New Methods and Attributes

A new method or attribute is a method or attribute that appears in the child but does not appear in the parent. The child adds the new method or attribute to its interface. You saw new methods in the `ThreeDimensionalPoint` example. `ThreeDimensionalPoint` adds new `getZCoordinate()` and `setZCoordinate()` methods. You can add new functionality to your child's interface by adding new methods and attributes.

Recursive Methods and Attributes

A recursive method or attribute is defined in the parent or some other ancestor but not in the child. When you access the method or attribute, the message is sent up the hierarchy until a definition of the method is found. The mechanism is the same as the mechanism introduced in the section about overridden methods and attributes.

You saw recursive methods in the source for `TwoDimensionalPoint` and `ThreeDimensionalPoint`. `getXCoordinate()` is an example of a recursive method because it is defined by `TwoDimensionalPoint`, not by `ThreeDimensionalPoint`.

Overridden methods may also behave recursively. While an overridden method will appear in the child, most object-oriented languages provide a mechanism that allows an overridden method to call the parent's (or some ancestor's) version of the method. This ability allows you to leverage the superclass's version while defining new behavior in the subclass. In Java, the keyword `super` gives you access to a parent's implementation. You'll get a chance to use `super` in the labs on Day 5, "Inheritance: Time to Write Some Code."

 Note

Not all languages provide a `super` keyword. For those languages you will need to be careful to properly initialize any inherited code.

Not properly referencing the inherited classes can be a subtle source of bugs.

Types of Inheritance

In all, there are three main ways to use inheritance:

1. For implementation reuse

2. For difference

3. For type substitution

Be forewarned, some types of reuse are more desirable than others! Let's explore each use in detail.

Inheritance for Implementation

You've already seen that inheritance allows a new class to reuse implementation from another class. Instead of cutting and pasting code or instantiating and using a component through composition, inheritance makes the code automatically available as part of the new class. Like magic, your new class is born with functionality.

Both the Employee hierarchy and the misguided Queue/Iterator demonstrate implementation reuse. In both cases, the child reused a number of behaviors found in the parent.

4

Tip

Remember that when you program with implementation inheritance, you are stuck with whatever implementation you inherit. Choose the classes that you inherit from carefully. You'll need to weigh the benefits of the reuse against any negatives in actually reusing some implementations.

However, a class that is properly defined for inheritance will make heavy use of fine-grained protected methods. An inheriting class can override these protected methods in order to alter the implementation. Overriding can lessen the impact of inheriting a poor or inappropriate implementation.

Implementation Inheritance Problems

So far, implementation inheritance seems great. Beware, though—what seems like a useful technique on the surface proves to be a dangerous practice in use. In fact, implementation inheritance is the weakest form of inheritance and you should normally avoid it. The reuse may be easy, but as you will see, it comes at a high price.

To understand the shortcomings, you have to consider types. When one class inherits another, it automatically takes on the type of the inherited class. Proper type inheritance should always take precedence when designing class hierarchies. You'll see why later, but for now take it as truth.

Take a look at the Queue/Iterator example again. When Iterator inherits from Queue it becomes a Queue. This means that you can treat the Iterator as if it were of type Queue. Since the Iterator is also a Queue, the Iterator has all of the functionality that was present in the Queue. That means that methods such as enqueue() and dequeue() are also part of the Iterator's public interface.

On the surface this does not seem like a problem, but take a closer look at the definition of Iterator. An Iterator simply defines two methods, one for retrieving an element and another to test whether the iterator has any elements left. By definition, you cannot add items to an iterator; however, Queue defines the enqueue() method for just such a case. Instead, you may only remove elements. You cannot take an element and at the same time leave it inside the Iterator. Again, the Queue defines the peek() method for just such a case. It is simple to see that using Queue as an inherited base for Iterator isn't a good choice; it gives you behaviors that just do not belong in an Iterator.

> **Note**
>
> Some languages allow a class to simply inherit implementation without inheriting the typing information. If your language allows such inheritance then the Queue/Iterator example isn't that much of a problem. However, most languages do not allow the separation of interface and implementation while inheriting. Of the languages that do make the separation some do it automatically. Yet others, such as C++, will allow the separation, but require the programmer to explicitly request it. Such a language requires the programmer to design and request the separation explicitly while coding the class. Obviously, it can be fairly easy to overlook the fact that you'll need to separate the implementation and type if you are not careful.

> **Note**
>
> This book uses a simple definition of inheritance. The discussion of inheritance assumes that inheritance includes both implementation and interface when one class inherits from another.

Poor inheritance is the Frankenstein's monster of programming. When you use inheritance solely for implementation reuse without any other considerations, you may often end up with a monster constructed from parts that do not belong together.

Inheritance for Difference

You saw inheritance for difference in the TwoDimensionalPoint and ThreeDimensionalPoint example. You also saw it in the Employee example.

Programming by difference allows you to program by only specifying how a child class differs from its parent class.

 Programming by difference means inheriting a class and only adding code that makes the new class different from the inherited class.

In the case of the ThreeDimensionalPoint, you see that it differs from its parent class by adding a Z coordinate. In order to support the Z coordinate, ThreeDimensionalPoint adds two new methods for setting and retrieving the attribute. You also see that ThreeDimensionalPoint redefines the toString() method.

Programming by difference is a powerful concept. It allows you to only add enough code necessary to describe the difference between the parent and the child class. This allows you to program incrementally.

Smaller, more manageable code causes your designs to be simpler. And since you program fewer lines of code you should, theoretically, introduce fewer bugs. So when you program by difference, you write more correct code in a shorter amount of time. Like implementation inheritance, you can make these incremental changes without altering existing code.

Through inheritance, there are two ways to program by difference: adding new behaviors and attributes and redefining old behaviors and attributes. Either case is known as specialization. Let's take a closer look at specialization.

Specialization

 Specialization is the process of a child class defining itself in terms of how it is different from its parent. When all is said and done, the child's class definition includes only those elements that make it different from its parent.

A child class specializes upon its parent by adding new attributes and methods to its interface as well as redefining pre-existing attributes and methods. Adding new methods or redefining existing ones allow the child to express behaviors that are different from its parent.

Don't become confused over the term specialization. Specialization only allows you to add to or redefine the behaviors and attributes that the child inherits from its parent. Specialization, contrary to what the name might suggest, does not allow you to remove inherited behaviors and attributes from the child. A class does not get selective inheritance.

What specialization does is restrict what can and cannot be a three-dimensional point. A ThreeDimensionalPoint can *always* be a TwoDimensionalPoint. However, it is incorrect to say that a TwoDimensionalPoint can always be a ThreeDimensionalPoint.

Instead, a `ThreeDimensionalPoint` is a specialization of a `TwoDimensionalPoint` and a `TwoDimensionalPoint` is a generalization of a `ThreeDimensionalPoint`.

Figure 4.7 illustrates the difference between generalization and specialization. As you travel down a hierarchy, you specialize. As you travel up the hierarchy, you generalize. As you generalize, more classes can fall under that grouping. As you specialize, fewer classes can meet all criteria to be categorized at that level.

FIGURE 4.7

As you travel up a hierarchy, you generalize. As you travel down a hierarchy, you specialize.

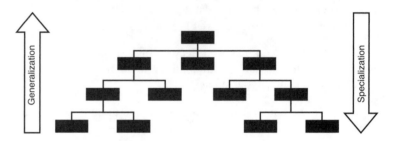

So you see, specialization does not mean restricting functionality, it means restricting type categorization.

The specialization does not have to end with `ThreeDimensionalPoint`. In fact, it does not necessarily even need to begin with `TwoDimensionalPoint`. Inheritance can go as deeply as you want it to. You can use inheritance to form complex class hierarchy structures. The idea of hierarchy that was introduced earlier leads to two more new terms: ancestor and descendant.

> **Caution**
>
> Just because you can have complicated hierarchies does not mean that you should. You should strive to have shallow hierarchies as opposed to overly deep hierarchies. As a hierarchy deepens, it becomes more difficult to maintain.

 Given some child, an *ancestor* is a class that appears in the class hierarchy before the parent. As Figure 4.8 illustrates, `Format` is an ancestor of `DecimalFormat`.

 Given a class, any class appearing after it in the class hierarchy is a *descendant* of the given class. As Figure 4.8 illustrates, `DecimalFormat` is a descendant of `Format`.

FIGURE 4.8

DecimalFormat *is a descendant of* Format.

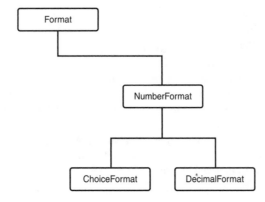

Say we have the class inheritance hierarchy shown in Figure 4.9. We say that OneDimensionalPoint is the parent of TwoDimensionalPoint and an ancestor of ThreeDimensionalPoint and FourDimensionalPoint. We can also say that TwoDimensionalPoint, ThreeDimensionalPoint, and FourDimensionalPoint are all descendants of OneDimensionalPoint. All descendants share their ancestors' methods and attributes.

FIGURE 4.9

The point hierarchy.

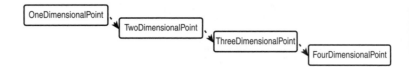

We can make a few more interesting statements about the class hierarchy. OneDimensionalPoint is the root and FourDimensionalPoint is a leaf.

NEW TERM The *root class* (also commonly referred to as a base class) is the topmost class in the inheritance hierarchy. Figure 4.9 shows that OneDimensionalPoint is a root class.

NEW TERM A *leaf class* is a class with no children. In Figure 4.8, DecimalFormat is a leaf class.

It is important to note that descendants will reflect changes made to the ancestors. Say that you find a bug in TwoDimensionalPoint. If you fix TwoDimensionalPoint, all of the classes from ThreeDimensionalPoint down to FourDimensionalPoint will benefit from the change. So whether you fix a bug or make an implementation more efficient, all descendant classes in the hierarchy will benefit.

Multiple Inheritance

Throughout the examples you've seen single inheritance. Some implementations of inheritance allow a single object to directly inherit from more than one other class. Such an implementation of inheritance is known as *multiple inheritance*. Multiple inheritance is a controversial aspect of OOP. Some claim it only makes software harder to understand, design, and maintain. Others swear by it and claim that a language is not complete without it.

Either way, multiple inheritance can be valuable if used carefully and correctly. There are a number of problems introduced by multiple inheritance. However, a full discussion of the dos and don'ts of multiple inheritance is beyond the scope of this day.

Inheritance for Type Substitution

The final type of inheritance is inheritance for type substitution. Type substitution allows you to describe substitutability relationships. What is a substitutability relationship?

Consider the Line class:

```java
public class Line {

    private TwoDimensionalPoint p1;
    private TwoDimensionalPoint p2;

    public Line( TwoDimensionalPoint p1, TwoDimensionalPoint p2 ) {
        this.p1 = p1;
        this.p2 = p2;
    }

    public TwoDimensionalPoint getEndpoint1() {
        return p1;
    }

    public TwoDimensionalPoint getEndpoint2() {
        return p2;
    }

    public double getDistance() {
        double x =
            Math.pow( (p2.getXCoordinate() - p1.getXCoordinate()), 2 );
        double y =
            Math.pow( (p2.getYCoordinate() - p1.getYCoordinate()), 2 );
        double distance = Math.sqrt( x + y );

        return distance;
    }

    public TwoDimensionalPoint getMidpoint() {
        double new_x = ( p1.getXCoordinate() + p2.getXCoordinate() ) / 2;
```

```
        double new_y = ( p1.getYCoordinate() + p2.getYCoordinate() ) / 2;
        return new TwoDimensionalPoint( new_x, new_y );
    }
}
```

Line takes two TwoDimensionalPoints as arguments and provides some methods for retrieving the values, a method for calculating the distance between the points, and a method for calculating the midpoint.

A substitutability relationship means that you can pass *any* object to Line's constructor that inherits from a TwoDimensionalPoint.

Remember that when a child inherits from its parent you say that the child "Is-a" parent. So because a ThreeDimensionalPoint "is-a" TwoDimensionalPoint you can pass a ThreeDimensionalPoint to the constructor.

Consider the following main():

```
public static void main( String [] args ) {
        ThreeDimensionalPoint p1 = new ThreeDimensionalPoint( 12, 12, 2 );
        TwoDimensionalPoint p2   = new TwoDimensionalPoint( 16, 16 );

        Line l = new Line( p1, p2 );

        TwoDimensionalPoint mid = l.getMidpoint();

        System.out.println( "Midpoint: (" +
                            mid.getXCoordinate() +
                            "," +
                            mid.getYCoordinate() +
                            ")" );
        System.out.println( "Distance: " + l.getDistance() );
    }
```

You'll notice that the main passes both a TwoDimensionalPoint and a ThreeDimensionalPoint to the line's constructor. Figure 4.10 illustrates what you will see if you execute the main().

FIGURE 4.10

Testing substitutability relationships.

Note

> Try to imagine the possibilities that substitutability relationships give you. In the example of the line it might allow for a quick way to switch from a 3D view to a 2D view in a GUI.

Pluggability is a powerful concept. Since you can send a child any message that you could send its parent, you can treat it as if it were substitutable for the parent. This is the reason that you should not *remove* behaviors when creating a child. If you do pluggability will break.

Using pluggability, you can add new subtypes to your program at any time. If your program is programmed to use an ancestor it will know how to use the new objects. The program will not need to worry about the exact type of the object. So long as it has a substitutability relationship with the type that it expects it can use it.

Caution

> Be warned that substitutability relationships can only go so far up the inheritance hierarchy. If you program your object to accept a certain type of object, you cannot pass it the parent of the expected object. However, you can pass it any descendant.
>
> Take the `Line` constructor as an example:
>
> `public Line( TwoDimensionalPoint p1, TwoDimensionalPoint p2 )`
>
> You can pass the constructor a `TwoDemensionalPoint` or any decendant of the `TwoDimensionalPoint`. However, you can't pass the constructor a `OneDimensionalPoint`, because that class appears in the hierarchy before `TwoDimensionalPoint`.

NEW TERM A *subtype* is a type that extends another type through inheritance.

Pluggability increases your opportunity for reuse. Say that you've written a container for holding `TwoDimensionalPoints`. Because of pluggability, you can use the container for any descendant of `TwoDimensionalPoint` as well.

Pluggability is important because it allows you to write generic code. Instead of having a number of case statements or if/else tests to see what kind of point the program was currently using, you simply program your objects to deal with objects of type `TwoDimensionalPoint`.

Tips to Effective Inheritance

Inheritance comes with its own set of design issues. While powerful, inheritance truly gives you a rope to hang yourself when used improperly. The following tips will help you use inheritance effectively:

- In general, use inheritance for interface reuse and for defining substitution relationships. You can also use inheritance to extend an implementation, but only if the resulting class passes the "Is-A" test.

- In general, prefer composition over inheritance for simple implementation reuse. Only use inheritance if you can apply the "Is-A" test to the resulting hierarchy. Don't use inheritance for greedy implementation reuse.

- Always use the "Is-A" rule.

Proper inheritance hierarchies don't happen by themselves. Often you will discover hierarchies as you go along. When that happens, rework your code. Other times, you will need to deliberately design your hierarchies. In either case, there are some design principles to follow:

- As a rule of thumb, keep your class hierarchies relatively shallow.

- Carefully design inheritance hierarchies and move commonalities out to abstract base classes. Abstract base classes allow you to define a method without providing an implementation. Because the base class does not specify an implementation you cannot instantiate it. However, the abstract mechanism forces an inheriting class to provide an implementation. Abstract classes are valuable for planned inheritance. It helps the developer to see what they need to implement.

Note

If your language does not provide an abstract mechanism, create empty methods and document the fact that subclasses should fully implement those methods.

- Classes often share common code. There's no sense in having multiple copies of code. You should remove common code and isolate it into a single parent class. However, don't move it too far up. Only move it up to the first level before it is needed.

- You simply cannot always plan your hierarchies completely. Commonality won't jump out at you until you write the same code a few times. When you see commonality, don't be afraid to rework your classes. Such rework is often referred to as *refactoring*.

Encapsulation is just as important between parent and child as it is between unrelated classes. Don't get lax with encapsulation when you are inheriting. The practice of using a well-defined interface is just as valid between parent and child as it is between completely unrelated classes. Here are some tips that will help you guard against breaking encapsulation when you inherit:

- Use well-defined interfaces between the parent and child just as you would use them between classes.
- If you add methods specifically for use by subclasses, be sure to make them protected so that only the subclass can see them. Protected methods allow you to offer your subclasses a little more control without opening that control to every class.
- In general, avoid opening your object's internal implementation to subclasses. A subclass can become dependent upon the implementation if you do. Such coupling has all of the problems outlined on Day 2.

Here are some final keys to effective inheritance:

- Never lose sight that substitution is the number one goal. Even if an object should "intuitively" appear in a hierarchy that does not mean that it should. Just because you can or your intuition screams to do so doesn't mean that you should.
- Program by difference in order to keep code manageable.
- Always prefer composition to inheritance for implementation reuse. It is generally easier to change the classes involved in composition.

Summary

There are two types of relationships provided by OOP: a *use* relationship between objects and an inheritance relationship between classes. Each relationship provides a form of reuse. However, each comes with its own benefits and problems.

Simple instantiation and use often limits the flexibility of a class. Through simple reuse, there is no way to reuse or extend a class. Instead, you are left with simple instantiation or cut and paste. Inheritance overcomes these shortcomings by proving a built-in mechanism for the safe and efficient reuse of code.

Implementation reuse gives you a quick and dirty way of using pre-existing code in your new classes. Unlike simple cut and paste, there is only one copy of the code to maintain. However, simply inheriting for reuse is shortsighted and limits your designs.

Implementation for difference allows you to program your new classes in terms of how they are different from the original class. You only program those attributes that differentiate the child from the parent.

Finally, inheritance for substitution allows you to program generically. With substitution you can swap in subclasses for the parent at any time without breaking your code. This allows your program to be flexible to future requirements.

How Inheritance Fulfills the Goals of OO

Inheritance fulfills each of the goals of OOP. Inheritance helps produce software that is

1. Natural
2. Reliable
3. Reusable
4. Maintainable
5. Extendable
6. Timely

It accomplishes these goals as follows:

- Natural: Inheritance allows you to more naturally model the world. Through inheritance you can form complex relationship hierarchies between your classes. As humans, it is our natural tendency to want to categorize and group the objects around us. Inheritance allows you to bring those tendencies to programming.

  Inheritance also embraces the programmer's wish to avoid repetitive work. There's no sense in doing redundant work.

- Reliable: Inheritance results in reliable code.

  Inheritance simplifies your code. When you program by difference, you only add the code that describes the difference between the parent and child. As a result, each class can have a smaller footprint. Each class can be highly specialized to what it does. Less code means fewer bugs.

  Inheritance allows you to reuse well-tested, time-proven code as the basis for your new classes. Reuse of proven code is always more desirable than writing new code.

  Finally, the inheritance mechanism itself is reliable. The mechanism is built in to the language so you don't need to construct your own inheritance mechanism and make sure that everyone follows your rules.

  However, inheritance isn't perfect. When subclassing, you must be vigilant against introducing subtle bugs by inadvertently destroying unexposed dependencies. Tread carefully while inheriting.

- Reusable: Inheritance aids reuse. The very nature of inheritance allows you to use old classes in the construction of new classes.

4

Inheritance also allows you to reuse classes in ways never imagined by the person who wrote the class. By overriding and programming by difference you can change the behavior of existing classes and use them in new ways.

- Maintainable: Inheritance aids maintainability. Reuse of tested code means that you will have fewer bugs in your new code. And when you do find a bug in a class, all subclasses will benefit from the fix.

  Instead of diving into the code and adding features directly, inheritance allows you to take pre-existing code and treat it as the basis for the construction of a new class. All methods, attributes, and type information become a part of your new class. Unlike cutting and pasting, there is only one copy of the original code to maintain. This aids maintenance by decreasing the amount of code that you have to maintain.

  If you were to make changes directly to the existing code you could damage the base class and affect portions of the system that use that class.

- Extendable: Inheritance makes class extension, or specialization, possible. You can take an old class and add new functionality at any time. Both programming by difference and inheritance for pluggability encourage the extension of classes.

- Timely: Inheritance helps you write timely code. You've already seen how simple reuse can cut down development time. Programming by difference means that there is less code to write, thus you should finish faster. Pluggability means that you can add new features without having to change much of the pre-existing code.

  Inheritance can also make testing easier since you will only need to test new functionality and any interaction with the old functionality.

Q&A

Q Today, you list three separate reasons for using inheritance. Do these reasons need to be mutually exclusive or can I combine them? For example, when I inherit for difference it seems that I could also be inheriting for implementation.

A No, the reasons behind inheritance do not need to be mutually exclusive. You could use inheritance and end up satisfying each of the reasons.

Q Inheriting for implementation reuse seems to have a negative connotation. Isn't reuse one of the main reason for using object oriented programming.

A Reuse is just one of the goals of OOP. OOP is an approach to programming that allows you to model the solutions to your problems in a more natural way: through objects. While reuse is important, you should not simply pursue reuse while ignoring the other goals of OO. Think back to the Iterator/Queue example. Is that a natural model of an Iterator? Of course not!

Besides, inheritance for implementation reuse is only one way to achieve reuse. Delegation is often the best way to achieve simple implementation reuse. Inheritance is just not the right tool if your goal is to just reuse an implementation. Inheritance is the right tool when you want to program by difference or establish type substitutability.

Workshop

The quiz questions and answers are provided for your further understanding. See Appendix A, "Answers," for the answers.

Quiz

1. What are some of the limitations of simple reuse?
2. What is inheritance?
3. What are the three forms of inheritance?
4. Why is implementation inheritance dangerous?
5. What is programming by difference?
6. When inheriting a class can have three types of methods and attributes. What are those three types of attributes and methods?
7. What benefits does programming by difference offer?
8. Consider the hierarchy in Figure 4.11, taken from Java security.

FIGURE 4.11

The Permission *hierarchy.*

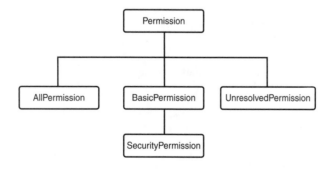

If you focus your attention on the Permission class, which classes are its children? Which are descendants?

Considering the entire hierarchy which class is the root class? Which classes are leaf classes?

Finally, is Permission an ancestor of SecurityPermission?

9. What is inheritance for type substitution?

10. How can inheritance destroy encapsulation? How can you enforce encapsulation when using inheritance?

Exercises

1. Given the following class definition, what problems might occur if it is inherited?

```java
public class Point {
    public Point( int x, int y) {
        this.x = x;
        this.y = y;
    }
    public Point getLocation() {
        return new Point( x, y );
    }
    public void move( int x, int y ) {
        this.x = x;
        this.y = y;
    }
    public void setLocation( int x, int y ) {
        this.x = x;
        this.y = y;
    }
    public void setLocation( Point p ) {
        this.x = p.x;
        this.y = p.y;
    }
    public int x;
    public int y;
}
```

2. How would you prevent these problems?

DAY 5

Inheritance: Time to Write Some Code

Inheritance is a powerful tool. Today you will explore the use of this new tool through a number of hands-on lab exercises. By the end of today's lesson, you should feel a bit more comfortable with the theory presented on Day 4.

Today you will learn

- How to use inheritance while programming
- How abstract classes help you plan inheritance
- About the importance of the "Is-A" and "Has-A"
- How Java may have violated the "Is-A" and "Has-A" relationship

Lab 1: Simple Inheritance

Listing 5.1 presents the personified MoodyObject baseclass.

LISTING 5.1 MoodyObject.java

```java
public class MoodyObject {

    // return the mood
    protected String getMood() {
        return "moody";
    }

    // ask the object how it feels
    public void queryMood() {
        System.out.println("I feel " + getMood() + " today!");
    }

}
```

MoodyObject defines one public method: queryMood(). queryMood() prints the object's mood to the command line. MoodyObject also declares one protected method, getMood(). queryMood() uses getMood() internally to get the mood that it places in its response. Subclasses can simply override getMood() in order to specialize their mood.

If a subclass would like to change the message written to the command line it will need to override queryMood().

Problem Statement

In this lab you will create two subclasses: SadObject and HappyObject. Both subclasses should override getMood() in order to supply their own specially tailored mood.

SadObject and HappyObject should also add some methods of their own. SadObject should add a method: public void cry(). Likewise, HappyObject should add a method: public void laugh(). laugh() should write "hahaha" to the command line. Likewise, cry() should write "boo hoo" to the command line.

Listing 5.2 sets up a test driver that you should compile and run once you have completed writing HappyObject and SadObject.

LISTING 5.2 MoodyDriver.java

```java
public class MoodyDriver {
    public final static void main( String [] args ) {
        MoodyObject moodyObject = new MoodyObject();
        SadObject   sadObject = new SadObject();
        HappyObject happyObject = new HappyObject();

        System.out.println( "How does the moody object feel today?" );
```

LISTING 5.2   continued

```
            moodyObject.queryMood();
            System.out.println( "" );
            System.out.println( "How does the sad object feel today?" );
            sadObject.queryMood(); // notice that overriding changes the mood
            sadObject.cry();
            System.out.println( "" );
            System.out.println( "How does the happy object feel today?" );
            happyObject.queryMood(); // notice that overriding changes the mood
            happyObject.laugh();
            System.out.println( "" );
        }
    }
```

Caution

The next section discusses the solutions to Lab 1. Do not proceed until you complete Lab 1.

Solutions and Discussion

Listings 5.3 and 5.4 present one solution to the lab.

LISTING 5.3   HappyObject.java

```
public class HappyObject extends MoodyObject {

    // redefine class's mood
    protected String getMood() {
        return "happy";
    }

    // specialization
    public void laugh() {
        System.out.println("hehehe... hahaha... HAHAHAHAHAHA!!!!!");
    }
}
```

LISTING 5.4   SadObject.java

```
public class SadObject extends MoodyObject {

    // redefine class's mood
    protected String getMood() {
        return "sad";
```

5

LISTING 5.4 continued

```
    }

    // specialization
    public void cry() {
        System.out.println("'wah' 'boo hoo' 'weep' 'sob' 'weep'");
    }
}
```

When you run the test driver you should see output similar to Figure 5.1.

FIGURE 5.1

The proper output of
MoodyDriver.

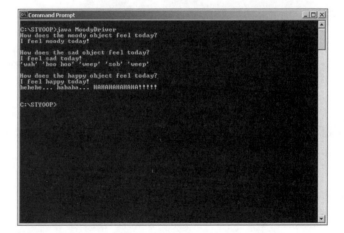

Of interest is the call to queryMood(). When you call queryMood() on SadObject, "I feel sad today!" prints out to the screen. Likewise, HappyObject prints, "I feel happy today!" Such behavior may seem surprising since neither class redefines queryMood().

You need to look closely at queryMood(). Internally queryMood() calls getMood() to obtain the mood. Since the subclasses do redefine getMood(), queryMood() will call the child's version of getMood(). This behavior is an example of the process illustrated in Figure 4.6 on Day 4.

Lab 2: Using Abstract Classes for Planned Inheritance

There are times when you will want to develop a class specifically so that others can inherit from it. As you develop a few related classes you may find code that is common to all of your classes. Good practice dictates that when you see common code you move it out into a base class. When you wrote that base class you planned for other classes to inherit from it.

However, once you are done moving the code around you may notice that it makes no sense to ever instantiate the base class directly. While the base class holds common code that is very valuable to subclasses, it may not offer any value for direct instantiation and use. Instead, it only makes sense to use the subclasses. The subclasses specialize upon the base class and provide what is missing.

Consider the Employee class:

```
public class Employee {

    private String first_name;
    private String last_name;
    private double wage;

    public Employee( String first_name, String last_name, double wage ) {
        this.first_name = first_name;
        this.last_name  = last_name;
        this.wage = wage;
    }

    public double getWage() {
        return wage;
    }

    public String getFirstName() {
        return first_name;
    }

    public String getLastName() {
        return last_name;
    }

    public double calculatePay() {
        // I don't know how to do this!
        return 0;
    }
    public String printPaycheck() {
        String full_name = last_name + ", " + first_name;
        return ( "Pay: " + full_name + " $" + calculatePay() );
    }
}
```

You may use the Employee as a base class for CommissionedEmployees, HourlyEmployees, and SalariedEmployees. Each subclass knows how to calculate its pay. However, the algorithm used to calculate pay will vary depending on the employee's type. When I created this hierarchy, I envisioned that each subclass would need to define its own calculatePay() method.

There is a small problem: `Employee` doesn't have any rules for calculating its pay. It doesn't make any sense to say `calculatePay()` for an `Employee`. There is no algorithm to calculate pay for a generic employee.

One solution is to not define `calculatePay()` in the base class. However, not defining the method in the base class would be an unfortunate decision. It does not model an employee very well. Each employee will know how to calculate its pay. All that differs is the actual implementation of the `calculatePay()` method. So the method really does belong in the base class.

If you do not define `calculatePay()` in the base class, you cannot treat the employees generically. You'll lose subtype pluggability for the `calculatePay()` method. Another solution is to simply hard-code a canned return. The method could simply return `wage`.

A hard-coded return is not a very clean solution. There is no guarantee that another developer will remember to override the method when developing a new subclass. Plus, it doesn't make a whole lot of sense to even instantiate an `Employee`. Luckily, OOP offers a special type of class meant specifically for planned inheritance: the abstract class.

An abstract class looks a lot like any other class definition. The class definition may define behaviors and attributes just like a normal class. However, you cannot directly instantiate an abstract class since an abstract class can leave some methods undefined.

New Term   A declared but unimplemented method is called an *abstract method*. Only abstract classes can have abstract methods.

Instead, you may only instantiate the descendants of the abstract class that actually implement the abstract methods.

Let's take a look at an abstract `Employee`:

```
public abstract class Employee {
....
    public abstract double calculatePay();
    // the rest of the definition remains the same
}
```

The abstract `Employee` defines a `calculatePay()` method; however, it leaves it undefined. Now it is up to each subclass to actually implement the method. `HourlyEmployee` is one such subclass:

```
public class HourlyEmployee extends Employee {

    private int hours; // keep track of the # of hours worked

    public HourlyEmployee( String first_name, String last_name, double wage ) {
        super( first_name, last_name, wage );
    }
```

```
    public double calculatePay() {
        return getWage() * hours;
    }

    public void addHours( int hours ) {
        this.hours = this.hours + hours;
    }

    public void resetHours() {
        hours = 0;
    }
}
```

By declaring abstract methods, you force your subclasses to specialize upon the base class
by proving an implementation for the abstract methods. By making a base class abstract
and by creating abstract methods you plan in advance what the subclass must redefine.

Problem Statement

In Lab 1 you created a `MoodyObject` class. All of the subclasses redefine `getMood()`. For
Lab 2, change that hierarchy a bit. Make the `getMood()` method abstract. You'll also need
to update the `MoodyDriver` so that it no longer attempts to directly instantiate
`MoodyObject`. You won't have to make any changes to `SadObject` or `HappyObject` since
they already provide an implementation of `getMood()`.

 Caution | The next section discusses the solutions to Lab 2. Do not proceed until you complete Lab 2.

5

Solutions and Discussion

Listings 5.5 and 5.6 present the restructured `MoodyObject` and `MoodyDriver` definitions.

LISTING 5.5   `MoodyObject.java`

```
public abstract class MoodyObject {

    // return the mood
    protected abstract String getMood();

    // ask the object how it feels
    public void queryMood() {
        System.out.println("I feel " + getMood() + " today!");
    }

}
```

LISTING 5.6   MoodyDriver.java

```
public class MoodyDriver {
    public final static void main( String [] args ) {
        //MoodyObject mo = new MoodyObject(); // cannot instantiate MoodyObject
        SadObject    so = new SadObject();
        HappyObject ho = new HappyObject();

        //System.out.println( "How does the moody object feel today?" );
        //mo.queryMood();
        //System.out.println( "" );
        System.out.println( "How does the sad object feel today?" );
        so.queryMood(); // notice that overriding changes the mood
        so.cry();
        System.out.println( "" );
        System.out.println( "How does the happy object feel today?" );
        ho.queryMood(); // notice that overriding changes the mood
        ho.laugh();
        System.out.println( "" );
    }
}
```

The changes are fairly simple. MoodyObject defines an abstract getMood() method and leaves it up to its subclasses to provide the real implementation. When the queryMood() method needs to retrieve the mood it simply makes a call to the abstract method.

Using abstract classes defines the contract that subclasses must fulfill in order to use the base class. As a developer, when you look at an abstract base class, you know exactly what you need to specialize when you inherit it. You can specialize in addition to the abstract methods. However, you know that by defining the abstract methods your new class will fit into the hierarchy properly.

When a base class has many methods, it can be confusing to figure out which ones to override. Abstract classes give you a hint.

Lab 3: Bank Account—Practicing Simple Inheritance

Now it's time to put your inheritance knowledge to the test. Let's go back to the Bank of OO and see what inheritance can do for the bank's accounting system.

The Bank of OO offers its customers a few choices in accounts: a savings account, a checking account, a timed maturity account, and an overdraft account.

A Generic Account

Each account type allows the user to deposit and withdraw funds as well as check the current balance. The generic base account does not allow overdraft.

The Savings Account

The savings account specializes upon the standard bank account by applying interest to the balance when told to do so. For example, if a depositor has a balance of $1,000 and the interest rate is 2%, after an interest payout the balance will read $1020:

```
balance = balance + (balance * interest_rate)
```

The savings account does not allow overdraft.

The Timed Maturity Account

The timed maturity account also applies interest to the balance. However, if the account owner withdraws any of the principal before the account matures, the bank will deduct a percentage from the withdrawal. So, for example, if the depositor withdraws $1,000 before maturity and there is a 5% penalty on the amount withdrawn, the account balance will decrease by $1000. However, the depositor will only receive $950. If the account is mature, the bank will not penalize withdrawals

```
balance = balance - withdraw_amount
```

but

```
amount_given_to_depositor = amount - (amount * penalty_rate)
```

the timed maturity account does not allow overdraft.

Checking Account

Unlike savings and maturity accounts, the checking account does not apply interest to the balance. Instead, the checking account allows the depositor to write checks and make ATM transactions against the account. However, the bank limits the number of transactions per month to some fixed number. If the depositor exceeds this monthly quota the bank will assess a per-transaction fee. So, for example, if the depositor gets five free transactions per month but makes eight transactions at a fee of $1 per transaction, the bank will charge the depositor a $3 fee:

```
fee = (total_transactions - monthly_quota) * per_transaction_fee
```

The checking account does not allow overdraft.

Overdraft Account

Finally, the overdraft account allows the depositor to draw money in excess of the account's balance. However, there is no free lunch. Periodically, the bank will apply an interest charge against any negative balance. So, for example, if the depositor runs a –$1,000 balance at the rate of 20%, he may pay a fee of $200. After the fee, his balance will be –$1200:

```
balance = balance + (balance * interest_rate)
```

Note that the bank only calculates interest on accounts with a negative balance! If not, the bank would end up giving money away. The Bank of OO is not in the business of giving money away. Not even to developers.

Unlike the checking account, the overdraft account does not place a limit on the number of monthly transactions. The bank would like to encourage withdrawals—they might get to charge interest!

Problem Statement

Your task is to formulate an inheritance hierarchy and implement the accounts as defined above. You must create the following account classes:

- BankAccount
- SavingsAccount
- TimeMaturityAccount
- CheckingAccount
- OverdraftAccount

BankAccount is the base class. It contains those tasks common to all accounts. That is the only hierarchical hint that you will get! Part of the lab is for you to experiment with inheritance hierarchies.

There are a number of simplifications that you can make. For fees, timed maturity, and interest calculations, assume that some third party will watch the calendar. Don't program that kind of functionality into your classes. Instead, provide a method for another object to call. For example, the SavingsAccount should have an addInterest() method. An outside object will call that method when it is time to calculate interest. Likewise, the CheckingAccount should expose an accessFees() method. When called this method will calculate any fees and apply them against the balance.

Note   Don't get bogged down in unnecessary details. Remember, you're completing this lab to gain hands-on inheritance experience, not write the most robust account system ever. To that end, don't worry about validating input (unless you really want to). You can assume that all argument values will always be valid.

Day 4 briefly touched on the use of super. super is not a difficult concept. Consider the following selection:

```
public CommissionedEmployee( String first_name, String last_name,
                             double wage, double commission ) {
    super( first_name, last_name, wage ); // call original constructor in
                                          // order to properly initialize
    this.commission   = commission;
}
```

When you call super from within a constructor, it allows you to call the parent's constructor. Of course, you must supply all of the arguments required by the parent's constructor. Most languages, Java included, require that if you call super within the constructor, you do so before doing anything else. In fact, if you don't call super, Java will automatically try to call super() itself.

super allows you to leverage parent's code that you otherwise would have simply overridden. In the case of constructors, super allows the child to call its parent's constructor.

Properly calling the parent's constructor is something that you must not overlook. You need to ensure that the class gets properly initialized.

You can also use super from within a method.

Imagine a VeryHappyObject class:

```
public class VeryHappyObject extends HappyObject {

    // redefine class's mood
    protected String getMood() {
      String old_mood = super.getMood();
      return "very" + old_mood;
    }
}
```

VeryHappyObject overrides getMood(). However, super.getMood() allows a VeryHappyObject to call the parent's version of getMood(). The VeryHappyObject specializes on its parent's getMood() method by doing some extra processing on the value returned by super.getMood().

So even if a child overrides a parent's method, the child can still leverage the existing code that exists in the parent.

Like a constructor, if you use super.<method>() to call a method you must supply any of the arguments that the method may require.

You will find super useful in this lab.

5

Stop now and complete the lab if you feel comfortable. If you need a little more help, read on.

Extended Problem Statement

If you still feel lost, these interfaces should help a bit. These interfaces represent only one way of completing the lab.

BankAccount exposes the following methods:

```
public void depositFunds( double amount )
public double getBalance()
public double withdrawFunds( double amount )
protected void setBalance( double newBalance )
```

SavingsAccount should expose the following methods:

```
public void addInterest()
public void setInterestRate( double interestRate )
public double getInterestRate()
```

TimedMaturityAccount exposes the following methods:

```
public boolean isMature()
public void mature()
public double getFeeRate()
public void setFeeRate( double rate )
```

TimedMaturityAccount will need to redefine withdrawFunds() to check maturity and apply any applicable fees.

CheckingAccount exposes the following methods:

```
public void accessFees()
public double getFee()
public void setFee( double fee )
public int getMonthlyQuota()
public void setMonthlyQuota( int quota )
public int getTransactionCount()
```

CheckingAccount will need to override withdrawFunds() in order to keep track of the number of transactions.

OverdraftAccount exposes the following methods:

```
public void chargeInterest()
public double getCreditRate()
public void setCreditRate( double rate )
```

OverdraftAccount may need to override withdrawFunds() if BankAccount places overdraft checks in the method.

You may also want to start you hierarchy with the Account class that you developed for Lab 2 back on Day 3. The only change that you'll want to make is to the withdrawFunds() method. You should probably put overdraft protection into the withdrawFunds() methods.

Caution   The next section discusses the solutions to Lab 3. Do not proceed until you complete Lab 3.

Solutions and Discussion

Figure 5.2 illustrates the resulting account inheritance hierarchy.

FIGURE 5.2

The bank account hierarchy.

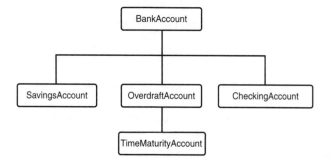

It is important to keep this hierarchy in mind while considering the following solutions.

Listing 5.6 presents one possible BankAccount implementation. This base class keeps track of the balance and handles deposits and withdraws.

LISTING 5.7   BankAccount.java

```
public class BankAccount {

    // private data
    private double balance;

    // constructor
    public BankAccount( double initDeposit ) {
        setBalance( initDeposit );
    }
    // deposit monies into account
    public void depositFunds( double amount ) {
        // the base class applies no policy
```

5

LISTING 5.7 continued

```
        // does not validate input
        setBalance( getBalance() + amount );
    }
    // query the balance
    public double getBalance() {
        return balance;
    }
    // set the balance
    protected void setBalance( double newBalance ) {
        balance = newBalance;
    }
    // withdraw funds from the account
    public double withdrawFunds( double amount ) {
        if( amount >= balance ) {
            amount = balance;
        }
        setBalance( getBalance() - amount );

        return amount;
    }
}
```

SavingsAccount, in Listing 5.8, directly inherits from BankAccount. SavingsAccount specializes upon BankAccount by adding methods to get and set the interest rate as well as a method to apply interest to the account balance.

LISTING 5.8 SavingsAccount.java

```
public class SavingsAccount extends BankAccount {

    // private data
    private double interestRate;

    // Creates new SavingsAccount
    public SavingsAccount( double initBalance, double interestRate ) {
        super( initBalance );
        setInterestRate( interestRate );
    }
    // calculate and add interest to the account
    public void addInterest() {
        double balance  = getBalance();
        double rate     = getInterestRate();
        double interest = balance * rate;

        double new_balance = balance + interest;

        setBalance( new_balance );
```

LISTING 5.8   continued

```
    }
    // set the interest rate
    public void setInterestRate( double interestRate ) {
        this.interestRate = interestRate;
    }
    // query the interest rate
    public double getInterestRate() {
        return interestRate;
    }
}
```

TimeMaturityAccount, in Listing 5.9, inherits from SavingsAccount since interest may apply to its balance. However, it too specializes upon its parent by defining methods to set maturity level and fees. Of interest is the fact that this class redefines the withdrawFunds() method. Through a call to super.withdrawFunds() this method still uses the original functionality, however it adds the checks necessary to see if it needs to access a fee against the transaction. If so, it accesses the fee and returns the withdrawn amount minus the fee.

LISTING 5.9   TimeMaturityAccount.java

```
public class TimedMaturityAccount extends SavingsAccount {

    // private data
    private boolean mature;
    private double  feeRate;

    // Creates new TimedMaturityAccount
    public TimedMaturityAccount( double initBalance,
                                 double interestRate,
                                 double feeRate ) {
        super( initBalance, interestRate );
        setFeeRate( feeRate );
    }
    // override BankAccount's withdrawFunds
    public double withdrawFunds( double amount ) {
        super.withdrawFunds( amount );
        if( !isMature() ) {
            double charge = amount * getFeeRate();
            amount = amount - charge;
        }
        return amount;
    }
    // check maturity
    public boolean isMature() {
        return mature;
```

5

LISTING 5.9   continued

```
        }
        // make mature
        public void mature() {
            mature = true;
        }
        // % fee for early withdraw
        public double getFeeRate() {
            return feeRate;
        }
        // set % fee for early withdraw
        public void setFeeRate( double rate ) {
            feeRate = rate;
        }
    }
```

CheckingAccount, in Listing 5.10, inherits directly from the BankAccount base class.
This class adds the methods necessary to set the per-transaction fee, set the monthly
quota, reset the transaction count, and query the current number of transactions. This
class also overrides the withdrawFunds() method in order to keep track of the number of
transactions. Like the TimedMaturityAccount, CheckingAccount still uses the original
logic by calling super.withdrawFunds().

LISTING 5.10   CheckingAccount.java

```
public class CheckingAccount extends BankAccount {

    // private data
    private int     monthlyQuota;
    private int     transactionCount;
    private double fee;

    // Creates new CheckingAccount
    public CheckingAccount( double initDeposit, int trans, double fee ) {
        super( initDeposit );
        setMonthlyQuota( trans );
        setFee( fee );
    }
    // override BankAccount's withdrawFunds
    public double withdrawFunds( double amount ) {
        transactionCount++;
        return super.withdrawFunds( amount );
    }
    // access fees if went over transaction limit
    public void accessFees() {
        int extra = getTransactionCount() - getMonthlyQuota();
        if( extra > 0 ) {
```

LISTING 5.10 continued

```
            double total_fee = extra * getFee();
            double balance = getBalance() - total_fee;
            setBalance( balance );
        }
        transactionCount = 0;
    }
    // some getters and setters
    public double getFee() {
        return fee;
    }
    public void setFee( double fee ) {
        this.fee = fee;
    }
    public int getMonthlyQuota() {
        return monthlyQuota;
    }
    public void setMonthlyQuota( int quota ) {
        monthlyQuota = quota;
    }
    public int getTransactionCount() {
        return transactionCount;
    }
}
```

Finally OverdraftAccount, in Listing 5.11, inherits directly from BankAccount. However, it also adds methods for setting the overdraft interest rate and for applying any interest charges.

LISTING 5.11 OverdraftAccount.java

```
public class OverdraftAccount extends BankAccount {

    // private data
    private double creditRate;

    // Creates new OverdraftAccount
    public OverdraftAccount( double initDeposit, double rate ) {
        super( initDeposit );
        setCreditRate( rate );
    }
    // charge he interest on any lent monies
    public void chargeInterest() {
        double balance = getBalance();
        if( balance < 0 ) {
            double charge = balance * getCreditRate();
            setBalance( balance + charge );
        }
```

5

LISTING 5.11   continued

```
        }
        // query the credit rate
        public double getCreditRate() {
            return creditRate;
        }
        // set the credit rate
        public void setCreditRate( double rate ) {
            creditRate = rate;
        }

        // withdraw funds from the account
        public double withdrawFunds( double amount ) {
            setBalance( getBalance() - amount );

            return amount;
        }
    }
}
```

Each of these classes specializes upon its parent in one way or another. Some, such as SavingsAccount, simply add new methods. Others, like CheckingAccount, OverdraftAccount, and TimedMaturityAccount override the parent's default behavior to augment the functionality.

This lab exposes you to the mechanics of inheritance as well as inheritance for implementation reuse and programming by difference.

While not shown here, you can also use type pluggability since the common BankAccount class relates all accounts. Anyone who knows how to act on the BankAccount base class can withdraw, deposit, and check on funds from any type of account. You'll explore type pluggability in detail throughout Day 6, "Polymorphism: Learning to Predict the Future" and Day 7, "Polymorphism: Time to Write Some Code."

Lab 4: Case Study—"Is-A," "Has-A," and the `java.util.Stack`

When new to OO it may become tempting to look at Java as an example of perfect object-oriented design. You might say to yourself, "If Java does it, it must be correct." Unfortunately, placing unquestioned trust in any OO implementation is dangerous.

Let's revisit the classical stack data structure. You can push items onto a stack, pop objects off of a stack, and peek at the first element on the stack without removing it. You might also want to check to see whether the stack is empty.

Java has a Stack class. Listing 5.12 illustrates the interface.

LISTING 5.12   `java.util.Stack`

```
public class Stack extends {
    publiv boolean empty();
    public Object peek();
    public Object pop();
    public Object push( Object item );
    public int search( Object o );
}
```

You'll notice that Java tweaks the classical stack definition a bit. Java adds a search() method. The push() method also returns the object that you push.

However, there is a larger problem. The Java Stack also inherits from Vector. From one point of view this is a smart decision. By inheriting Vector, Stack gets all of the implementation held in Vector. To implement Stack all you need to do is wire Stack's methods to internally call the proper inherited Vector methods.

Unfortunately, the Java Stack is an example of poor inheritance. Does Stack pass the "Is-a" test? "A Stack 'Is-a' Vector." No—the test fails. Vector has all kinds of methods for placing elements into the Vector and removing them. A Stack only allows you to place elements onto the top of the Stack. The Vector allows you to insert elements and remove elements anywhere.

Here, inheritance allows you to interact with the Stack in undefined ways that are undefined for a stack.

Problem Statement

Stack passes the "Has-a" test. "A Stack 'Has-a' Vector." For this lab, write a new version of Stack that employs the proper type of implementation reuse.

 Caution   The next section discusses the solutions to Lab 4. Do not proceed until you complete Lab 4.

Solutions and Discussion

Listing 5.13 illustrates one possible implementation of Stack.

LISTING 5.13 A New Stack Implementation

```
public class Stack {

    private java.util.ArrayList list;

    public Stack() {
        list = new java.util.ArrayList();
    }

    public boolean empty() {
        return list.isEmpty();
    }

    public Object peek() {
        if( !empty() ) {
            return list.get( 0 );
        }
        return null;
    }

    public Object pop() {
        if( !empty() ) {
            return list.remove( 0 );
        }
        return null;
    }

    public Object push( Object item ) {
        list.add( 0, item );
        return item;
    }

     public int search( Object o ) {
         int index = list.indexOf( o );
         if( index != -1 ) {
             return index + 1;
         }
         return -1;
     }

}
```

If this lab teaches you anything, it is to not place complete faith on any one OO source. Nothing is perfect.

Summary

Today you completed four labs. Lab 1 allowed you to experiment with simple inheritance. After completing Lab 1 you should understand the basic mechanics inheritance. Lab 2 allowed further exploration of inheritance through the abstract class and planned inheritance. Lab 3 should solidify the lessons of Day 4. Labs 1 and 2 let you see redefined, new, and recursive methods and attributes hands on. You also saw how even if you override a method you could still use the parent's implementation.

Lab 4 illustrates the importance of considering "Is-A" and "Has-A" while forming inheritance hierarchies. Sometimes the best course of action is to not inherit. As Day 4 stresses, composition is often the cleanest form of reuse. Inheritance only makes sense from the relational or "Is-a" point of view. If two objects are not related by type, they should not inherit. Shared implementation is not reason enough to inherit.

Within a system or application you should always plan as much inheritance as possible. However, when you program for a specific application you are limited to that one program. Over time, you will work on many different programs. As you start to notice that you're programming the same things over and over again, opportunities for inheritance will begin to present themselves. You must always be on the lookout for these discovered inheritance hierarchies. You should rework your code whenever you discover these new hierarchies.

Q&A

Q In Lab 4, you point out how even Java makes OO mistakes. When I review the Java APIs or other sources of OO examples, how can I be sure that what I see is "good" OO?

A It is difficult to tell what constitutes "good" OO and "bad" OO, even after gaining a lot of OO experience. The best that you can do is apply what you've learned and never take an example for granted. Approach each example judiciously and if something doesn't seem right discuss it with your peers: Get a second opinion.

Workshop

The quiz questions and answers are provided for your further understanding. See Appendix A, "Answers," for the answers.

Quiz

1. From the lab solutions give an example of a redefined method, a recursive method, and a new method.

2. Why would you declare a class as being abstract?

3. In Lab 4 you explored "Is-A" and "Has-A" relationships. Before you even learned about inheritance you saw "Has-A" relationships. What "Has-A" relationships did you see in the labs from Day 3?

4. How did these labs preserve encapsulation between the base and subclasses?

5. From the solutions, find an example of specialization.

6. How do the solutions to Lab 3 and Lab 4 take a different approach to implementation reuse?

Exercises

There are no exercises today. Do your labs!

DAY 6

Polymorphism: Learning to Predict the Future

So far, you have learned about the first two pillars of object-oriented programming: encapsulation and inheritance. As you know, encapsulation enables you to build self-contained software components and inheritance enables you to reuse and extend those components. However, there is still something missing. Software is always changing. Whether users demand new functionality, bugs appear, or software needs to be integrated into new environments, the only constant is change. The software lifecycle does not end when you ship a product. You need software that can adapt to fit future needs. Wouldn't it be great if you could write "future proof" software?

Future proof software adapts to future requirements without alteration. Future proof software enables you to make changes and add new features easily. Luckily, OOP understands that successful software is not static. To that end, OOP uses the concept of polymorphism to allow you to write that future proof software.

You will spend the next two days considering polymorphism, the third and final pillar of object-oriented programming.

Today you will learn

- What polymorphism is
- What the different types of polymorphism are and what they offer your objects
- Valuable tips for effective polymorphism
- About some common polymorphic pitfalls
- How polymorphism fulfills the goals of OO

Polymorphism

If encapsulation and inheritance are the one-two punch of OOP, polymorphism is the follow up knockout punch. Without those other pillars, you could not have polymorphism, and without polymorphism, OOP would not be effective. Polymorphism is where the object-oriented programming paradigm really shines, and its mastery is absolutely necessary for effective OOP.

Polymorphism means many forms. In programming terms, polymorphism allows a single class name or method name to represent different code selected among by some automatic mechanism. Thus, a name can take many forms and since it can represent different code, the same name can represent many different behaviors.

NEW TERM   *Polymorphism*: the state of one having many forms. In programming terms, many forms mean that a single name can represent different code selected among by some automatic mechanism. Thus polymorphism allows a single name to express many different behaviors.

In its own way, polymorphism is the multiple personalities disorder of the software world because a single name can express many different behaviors.

All this talk of expressing "many different behaviors" may seem a bit abstract. Think about the term *open*. You can open a door, a box, a window, and a bank account. The word *open* can apply to many different objects in the real world. Each object interprets open in its own way. However, in each case, you can simply say open to describe the action.

Not all languages support polymorphism. A language that supports polymorphism is a *polymorphic language*. In contrast, a *monomorphic language* does not support polymorphism and instead constrains everything to one, and only one, static behavior, because each name is statically tied to its code.

Inheritance provides the plumbing needed to make certain types of polymorphism possible. In Day 4, "Inheritence: Getting Something for Nothing," you saw how inheritance allows you to form substitutability relationships. Pluggability is extremely important to polymorphism because it enables you to treat a specific type of object generically.

Consider the following classes:

```
public class PersonalityObject {
    public String speak() {
        return "I am an object.";
    }
}

public class PessimisticObject extends PersonalityObject {
    public String speak() {
        return "The glass is half empty.";
    }
}
public class OptimisticObject extends PersonalityObject {
    public String speak() {
        return "The glass is half full.";
    }
}

public class IntrovertedObject extends PersonalityObject {
    public String speak() {
        return "hi...";
    }
}

public class ExtrovertedObject extends PersonalityObject {
    public String speak() {
        return "Hello, blah blah blah, did you know that blah blah blah.";
    }
}
```

These classes form a fairly straightforward inheritance hierarchy. The base class, PersonalityObject declares one method: speak(). Each subclass redefines speak() and returns its own message based on its personality. The hierarchy forms substitutability relationships between the subtypes and their parent.

6

Consider the following main():

```
public static void main( String [] args ) {
        PersonalityObject personality = new PersonalityObject();
        PessimisticObject pessimistic = new PessimisticObject();
        OptimisticObject  optimistic  = new OptimisticObject();
        IntrovertedObject introverted = new IntrovertedObject();
        ExtrovertedObject extroverted = new ExtrovertedObject();
```

```
// substitutability allows you to do the following
PersonalityObject [] personalities = new PersonalityObject[5];
personalities[0] = personality;
personalities[1] = pessimistic;
personalities[2] = optimistic;
personalities[3] = introverted;
personalities[4] = extroverted;

// polymorphism makes PersonalityObject seem to have
//many different behaviors
// remember - polymorphism is the multiple personalities
//disorder of the OO world
System.out.println( "PersonalityObject[0] speaks: " +
    personalities[0].speak());
System.out.println( "PersonalityObject[1] speaks: " +
    personalities[1].speak());
System.out.println( "PersonalityObject[2] speaks: " +
    personalities[2].speak());
System.out.println( "PersonalityObject[3] speaks: " +
    personalities[3].speak());
System.out.println( "PersonalityObject[4] speaks: " +
    personalities[4].speak());
}
```

The first two thirds of the main() do not present anything new. As you saw in Day 4, substitutability allows you to treat an object generically. However, the following excerpt is where the example becomes interesting:

```
// polymorphism makes PersonalityObject seem to have
//many different behaviors
// remember - polymorphism is the multiple personalities
//disorder of the OO world
System.out.println( "PersonalityObject[0] speaks: " +
    personalities[0].speak());
System.out.println( "PersonalityObject[1] speaks: " +
    personalities[1].speak());
System.out.println( "PersonalityObject[2] speaks: " +
    personalities[2].speak());
System.out.println( "PersonalityObject[3] speaks: " +
    personalities[3].speak());
System.out.println( "PersonalityObject[4] speaks: " +
    personalities[4].speak());
```

Figure 6.1 illustrates the output.

Based on the output it seems that PersonalityObject's speak() method has many different behaviors. Even though PersonalityObject defines speak() to print "I am an object," PersonalityObject is exhibiting more than one behavior. Even though the array supposedly contains PersonalityObject instances, each array member behaves differently when the main calls the speak() method. This is the crux of polymorphic behavior; PersonalityObject, the *name*, seems to have many behaviors.

FIGURE 6.1

Demonstration of polymorphic behavior.

 personalities is an example of a polymorphic variable. A *polymorphic variable* is a variable that may hold onto many different types.

> **Note**
>
> In a typed language, polymorphic variables are constrained to holding values from a specific substitutability relationship. In a dynamically typed language, a polymorphic variable can hold onto any value.

The preceding example explains the mechanism but it might not adequately convey the spirit behind polymorphism. After all, you know exactly what the array contains.

Instead, imagine that you have an object whose method takes a `PersonalityObject` as a parameter:

```
public void makeSpeak( PersonalityObject obj ) {
    System.out.println( obj.speak() );
}
```

Substitutability relationships allow you to pass an instance of the `PersonalityObject` or any descendant of that class into the `makeSpeak()` method as an argument. So, as you create specialized descendants of `PersonalityObject`, such as `ExtrovertedObject`, you do not need to change the logic of the method in order for that method to use instances of the new classes as argument. Instead, you can simply instantiate `ExtrovertedObject` (or any descendant) and pass the instance to the method.

Polymorphism comes into play when the `makeSpeak()` method makes method calls on the object passed in as argument. Polymorphism ensures that the proper method is invoked on the `PersonalityObject` argument by calling the argument's method based on the argument's real class type rather than the class type that the `makeSpeak()` method thinks that it is using. So if you pass in an `ExtrovertedObject`, polymorphism will ensure that `ExtrovertedObject`'s definition of `speak()` gets called, not the one found in

6

the base class. As a result, makeSpeak() will display different messages to the screen depending on the type of argument that it is passed.

You can leverage polymorphism to add new functionality to your system at any time. You can add new classes that have functionality that was not even dreamt of when you first wrote the program—all without having to change your pre-existing code. This is what future proof software is all about.

This example is just the tip of the polymorphic iceberg. In fact, the example only represents one of polymorphism's many forms. That's correct polymorphism is itself polymorphic!

Unfortunately, there is little consensus in the OO community when it comes to polymorphism. Instead of getting caught up in the controversy, this book will present four forms of polymorphism. Understanding these four common forms should give you the foundation that you need to begin to apply polymorphism. Today you will learn about

1. Inclusion Polymorphism
2. Parametric Polymorphism
3. Overriding
4. Overloading

Inclusion Polymorphism

Inclusion polymorphism, sometimes called pure polymorphism, allows you to treat related objects generically. You saw inclusion polymorphism firsthand at the start of the day.

Consider the following methods:

```
public void makeSpeak( PessimisticObject obj ) {
    System.out.println( obj.speak() );
}

public void makeSpeak( OptimisticObject obj ) {
    System.out.println( obj.speak() );
}

public void makeSpeak( IntrovertedObject obj ) {
    System.out.println( obj.speak() );
}

public void makeSpeak( ExtrovertedObject obj ) {
    System.out.println( obj.speak() );
}
```

PessimisticObject, OptimisticObject, IntrovertedObject, and ExtrovertedObject are all related because they are all PersonalityObjects. Substitutability and inclusion

polymorphism allow you to write one method for handling all types of
PersonalityObjects:

```
public void makeSpeak( PersonalityObject obj ) {
    System.out.println( obj.speak() );
}
```

Substitutability allows you to pass any PersonalityObject to the method, and polymorphism ensures that the proper method is called on the instance. Polymorphism will call the method based on the instance's true type (PeronalityObject, OptimisticObject, IntrovertedObject, ExtrovertedObject, or PessimisticObject), not on the instance's apparent type (PersonalityObject).

Inclusion polymorphism is useful because it cuts down on the amount of code that you need to write. Instead of having to write a method for each concrete type of PersonalityObject, you can simply write one method that handles all types. Inclusion polymorphism and substitutability allow makeSpeak() to work on any object that "Is-A" PersonalityObject.

Inclusion polymorphism makes adding new subtypes to your program easier because you won't need to add a method specifically for that new type. You can simply reuse makeSpeak().

Inclusion polymorphism is also interesting because it makes it seem as if PersonalityObject instances exhibit many different behaviors. The message displayed by makeSpeak() will differ based on the input to the method. Through the careful use of inclusion polymorphism, you can change the behavior of your system by introducing new sub classes. The best part is that you can get this new behavior without having to alter any of the pre-existing code.

Polymorphism is the reason that you shouldn't automatically associate inheritance with implementation reuse. Instead, you should use inheritance primarily to enable polymorphic behavior through substitutability relationships. If you properly define substitutability relationships, reuse will follow. Inclusion polymorphism allows you to reuse the base class, any descendant, as well as the methods that use the base class.

By now you probably understand the mechanism, but why would you want to use inclusion polymorphism?

Consider the following logging hierarchy:

```
public abstract class BaseLog {

        // some useful constants, don't worry about the syntax
        private final static String DEBUG   = "DEBUG";
        private final static String INFO    = "INFO";
```

```
private final static String WARNING = "WARNING";
private final static String ERROR   = "ERROR";
private final static String FATAL   = "FATAL";

java.text.DateFormat df = java.text.DateFormat.getDateTimeInstance();

public void debug( String message ) {
      log( message, DEBUG, getDate() );
}
public void info( String message ) {
      log( message, INFO, getDate() );
}
public void warning( String message ) {
      log( message, WARNING, getDate() );
}
public void error( String message ) {
      log( message, ERROR, getDate() );
}
public void fatal( String message ) {
      log( message, FATAL, getDate() );
}

// creates a time stamp
protected String getDate() {
      java.util.Date date = new java.util.Date();
      return df.format( date );
}

// let subclasses define how and where to write log to
protected abstract void log( String message, String level, String time );
}
```

BaseLog is an abstract log that defines a log's public interface as well as some implementation. BaseLog is abstract because each implementer needs to customize how the log is written out. Any BaseLog implementer must define the log() method.

By making the class abstract, you guarantee that any implementer implements the subclasses properly. Such an approach allows you to reuse the log design among many different applications. When a new application comes along, you can simply provide the implementation needed by that application. There is no need to create a new log design. Instead, you can reuse the log design laid out in BaseLog by providing custom implementations.

```
public class FileLog extends BaseLog {

    private java.io.PrintWriter pw;

    public FileLog( String filename ) throws java.io.IOException {
          pw = new java.io.PrintWriter( new java.io.FileWriter( filename ) );
```

```
        }

        protected void log( String message, String level, String time ) {
                pw.println( level + ": " + time + ": " + message );
                pw.flush();
        }

        public void close() {
                pw.close();
        }

public class ScreenLog extends BaseLog {
        protected void log( String message, String level, String time ) {
                System.out.println( level + ": " + time + ": " + message );
        }
}
```

FileLog and ScreenLog both inherit from BaseLog and implement the log() method.
FileLog writes to a file while ScreenLog writes to the screen.

Thinking back to the Employee example from Day 4 it is reasonable to suspect that there
is a class that knows how to retrieve Employees from a database:

```
public class EmployeeDatabaseAccessor {
        private BaseLog error_log;

        public EmployeeDatabaseAccessor( BaseLog log ) throws InitDBException {
                error_log = log;
                try {
                        // initialize the db connection
                } catch( DBException ex ) {
                        error_log.fatal( "cannot access database: " +
                                ex.getMessage() );
throw new InitDBException( ex.getMessage() );
                }
        }

        public Employee retrieveEmployee( String first_name, String last_name )
            throws EmployeeNotFoundException {
                try {
                        // attempt to retrieve the employee
                        return null;
                } catch( EmployeeNotFoundException ex ) {
                        error_log.warning( "cannot locate employee: " + last_name +
                                ", " + first_name );
                        throw new EmployeeNotFoundException( last_name, first_name );
                }

        }
        // and so on, each method uses error_log to log errors
}
```

6

The `EmployeeDatabaseAccessor` takes a `BaseLog` as argument in its constructor. An instance will use that log to record any and all important events. Consider the following `main()`:

```
public static void main( String [] args ) {
        BaseLog log = new ScreenLog();

        EmployeeDatabaseAccessor eda = new EmployeeDatabaseAccessor( log );

        Employee emp = eda.retrieveEmployee( "Employee", "Mr." )
}
```

Conceivably, the `main()` could pass *any* `BaseLog` subclass to the `EmployeeDatabaseAccessor`. An application could do the same. `EmployeeDatabaseAccessor` is future proof—as far as logging goes. Perhaps in the future you need a log file that rolls over every 24 hours or one that creates a filename using the date. Perhaps another log will make logs to an error handler that listens to the network. Who can say for sure? However, with inclusion polymorphism you're ready.

Without inclusion polymorphism, you would need a constructor for each type of log that you would like the accessor to use. However, it doesn't stop there. You would also need switch code inside of the accessor so that it would know which log that it should use. An `EmployeeDatabaseAccessor` that didn't use polymorphism but wanted to support many different logs might look like this:

```
public class EmployeeDatabaseAccessor {
     private FileLog    file_log;
     private ScreenLog screen_log;
     private int        log_type;

     // some 'useful' constants
     private final static int FILE_LOG   = 0;
     private final static int SCREEN_LOG = 1;

     public EmployeeDatabaseAccessor( FileLog log ) throws InitDBException {
          file_log = log;
          log_type = FILE_LOG;
          init();
     }
     public EmployeeDatabaseAccessor( ScreenLog log ) throws InitDBException {
          screen_log = log;
          log_type = SCREEN_LOG;
          init();
     }

     public Employee retrieveEmployee( String first_name, String last_name )
          throws EmployeeNotFoundException {
          try {
               // attempt to retrieve the employee
```

```
            return null;
        } catch( EmployeeNotFoundException ex ) {
            if( log_type == FILE_LOG ) {
                file_log.warning( "cannot locate employee: " +
                    last_name + ", " + first_name );
            } else if ( log_type == SCREEN_LOG ) {
                screen_log.warning( "cannot locate employee: " +
                    last_name + ", " + first_name );
            }
            throw new EmployeeNotFoundException( last_name, first_name );
        }

    }

    private void init() throws InitDBException {
        try {
            // initialize the db connection
        } catch( DBException ex ) {
            if( log_type == FILE_LOG ) {
                file_log.fatal( "cannot access database: " +
                    ex.getMessage() );
            } else if ( log_type == SCREEN_LOG ) {
                screen_log.fatal( "cannot access database: " +
                    ex.getMessage() );
            }
            throw new InitDBException( ex.getMessage() );
        }
    }
    // and so on, each method uses error_log to log errors
}
```

You'll need to update EmployeeDatabaseAccessor each time you would like to add support for a new log. Now, which version would you like to maintain?

Parametric Polymorphism

Parametric polymorphism allows you to create generic methods and generic types. Like inclusion polymorphism, generic methods and types allow you to code something once and have it work with many different kinds of arguments.

Parametric Methods

Although inclusion polymorphism affects how you look at an object, parametric polymorphism affects methods. Parametric polymorphism allows you to program generic methods by deferring parameter type declarations until runtime. Consider the following method:

```
int add(int a, int b)
```

6

add() takes two integers and returns the sum. This method is very explicit; it takes two integers as argument. You cannot pass two real numbers to this method or two matrix objects. If you try you will get a compile time error.

If you want to add two real numbers or two matrices, you must create methods for each type:

```
Matrix add_matrix(matrix a, matrix b)
Real add_real(real a, real b)
```

and so on for every type that you would like to add together.

It would be convenient if you could avoid having to write so many methods. First, having to write so many methods makes your programs larger. You will need a separate method for each type. Second, more code leads to more bugs and more to maintain. You don't want to make maintenance harder than it needs to be. Third, having to write separate methods does not naturally model add(). It is more natural just to think in terms of add(), not add_matrix() and add_real().

Inclusion polymorphism presents one solution to the problem. You could declare a type called addable that has a method that knows how to add itself to another instance of addable.

The type might look like this:

```
public abstract class Addable {
    public Addable add(Addable);
}
```

The new method would look like this:

```
Addable add_addable(Addable a, Addable b)
    Return a.add(b)
```

Note   The previous example is sometimes referred to as *function polymorphism*.

That's all fine and well. You only need to write one method for adding, however the method only works for Addable arguments. You also have to be sure that the Addables that you do pass to the method are of the same type. Such a requirement is error prone and counter to what the interface implies. Either way, you really haven't solved the original problem. You will still need to write methods for each type that you wish to add that are not of type Addable. Not everything that you'll want to add will be an Addable.

Here's where parametric polymorphism comes into play. Parametric polymorphism allows you to write one, and only one, method for adding all types. Parametric polymorphism delays the declaration of the argument types.

Consider the method rewritten to take advantage of parametric polymorphism:

```
add([T] a, [T] b) : [T]
```

[T] is an argument just the same as a and b. The [T] argument specifies the type of argument for a and b. By declaring a method in this way, you defer definition of the arguments' type until runtime. You'll also note that both a and b must have the same [T].

Internally the method may look like this:

```
[T] add([T] a, [T] b)
    return a + b;
```

Polymorphism is not magical. It still expects the argument to have a certain structure. In this case, any argument that you pass in must define + for that type.

Note

> *Certain structure* can be the presence of a certain method or properly defined operator.

Parametric types

Taken to its extreme conclusion, parametric polymorphism can extend its reach to types themselves. Just as methods may have parametric parameters, types can be parametric themselves. Consider the Queue ADT defined in Day 2:

```
Queue [T]
    void enqueue([T])
    [T] dequeue()
    boolean isEmpty()
    [T] peek()
```

The Queue is a parameterized type. Instead of writing a queue class for each type that you would like to queue, you simply specify the types of elements that you would like the queue to hold onto dynamically at runtime. Originally, you could say that the Queue was a Queue of Object. Now the Queue can be a Queue of any type.

So, if you wanted to store Employees you would make the following declaration:

```
Queue[Employee] employee_queue = new Queue[Employee];
```

Now, when you use Queue you may only enqueue() and dequeue() employee instances.

6

If parametric types are not possible, you would need to write a separate queue for integers, another for reals, and yet another for space aliens.

Instead, by using parameterized types, you can write the type once, in this case a queue, and use it to hold onto all possible types.

> **Note**
>
> Parametric polymorphism sounds great on paper, but there is a problem: support.
>
> For those of you familiar with Java, the previous examples may seem strange. As of Java 1.3, Java does not have native support for parameterized types or parametric polymorphism in general. You can fake parameterized types, but the price in efficiency is rather high. There are some Java extensions available for parametric polymorphism support, however none are officially sanctioned by Sun.
>
> The syntax of the previous examples is completely made up. However, it demonstrates the ideas adequately.

Overriding

Overriding is an important type of polymorphism. You saw how each PersonalityObject subclass overrode the speak() method at the beginning of this day. However, you got a sneak peek at an even more interesting example of overriding and polymorphism in Day 5. Specifically, consider the MoodyObject and HappyObject class definitions:

```
public class MoodyObject {

    // return the mood
    protected String getMood() {
        return "moody";
    }

    // ask the object how it feels
    public void queryMood() {
        System.out.println("I feel " + getMood() + " today!");
    }

}

public class HappyObject extends MoodyObject {

    // redefine class's mood
    protected String getMood() {
        return "happy";
```

```
    }

    // specialization
    public void laugh() {
        System.out.println("hehehe... hahaha... HAHAHAHAHAHA!!!!!");
    }
}
```

Here, you see that HappyObject overrides MoodyObject's getMood() method. What's interesting is that MoodyObject's definition of queryMood() internally makes a call to getMood().

You'll notice that HappyObject does not override the queryMood() method. Instead, HappyObject simply inherits the method as a recursive method from MoodyObject. When you call queryMood() on a HappyObject, instance polymorphism makes sure to call HappyObject's overridden version of getMood() behind the scenes.

Here polymorphism takes care of the details of what method to call. This frees you from having to redefine queryMood() yourself so that it calls the correct version of getMood().

Later, you saw how you could make getMood() abstract in the parent:

```
public abstract class MoodyObject {

    // return the mood
    protected abstract String getMood();

    // ask the object how it feels
    public void queryMood() {
        System.out.println("I feel " + getMood() + " today!");
    }

}
```

Abstract methods are often referred to as *deferred methods*, because you defer definition to the descendant classes. However, like any other method, the class that defines the abstract method can make calls to the method. Just like overridden methods, polymorphism will ensure that the proper version of the deferred method is always called in the subclasses.

Overloading

Overloading, also known as *ad-hoc polymorphism*, allows you to use the same method name for many different methods. Each method only differs in the number and type of its parameters.

Consider the following methods defined in java.lang.Math:

6

```
public static int max(int a, int b);
public static long max(long a, long b);
public static float max(float a, float b);
public static double max(double a, double b);
```

The max() methods are all examples of overloading. You'll notice that the max() methods only differ in the type of parameters.

Overloading is useful when a method is not defined by its arguments. Instead, the method is a concept that is independent of its arguments. The method transcends its specific parameters and applies to many different kinds of parameters. Take the max() method. max() is a generic concept that takes two parameters and tells you which is greater. This definition does not change whether you compare integers, floats, doubles, or the pecking order among a flock of birds.

The + operation is another example of an overloaded method. The + concept is independent of its arguments. You can add all sorts of elements.

 Note   You cannot overload or override operators in Java; however, Java does have some built in overloading.

If overloading were not possible you would have to do the following:

```
public static int max_int( int a, int b );
public static long max_long( long a, long b );
public static float max_float( float a, float b );
public static double max_double( double a, double b );
ublic static bird max_bird( bird a, bird b );
```

Without overloading you must give each method a unique name. The max() methods would no longer transcend their parameters. Max would cease to be an abstract concept. Instead, you would have to define the method in terms of its arguments. Having to write the max() method is this way is not a natural way of modeling the concept of max(). It also gives the programmer more to keep straight in his mind.

Of course, naming each method differently is not polymorphic. When all methods share the same name, you get polymorphic behavior because different methods are called behind the scenes dependent of what types of parameters you pass. You can simply call max() and pass your parameters. Polymorphism will take care of calling the proper method behind the scenes.

How polymorphism routes the method call is language dependent. Some languages resolve the method call during compilation while others bind the method call dynamically at runtime.

Coercion

Coercion and overloading often go hand in hand. Coercion can also make a method appear as if it were polymorphic. Coercion occurs when an argument of one type is converted into the expected type behind the scenes.

Consider the following definition:

```
public float add( float a, float b );
```

add() takes two float arguments and adds them together.

The following code segment creates a few integer variables and calls the add() method:

```
int iA = 1;
int iB = 2;

add(iA,iB);
```

However, the add() method calls for two float arguments. This is where coercion comes into play.

When you call add() with int arguments the arguments are converted into floats by the compiler. This means that before the int arguments are passed to add(), they are first converted into floats. Java programmers will recognize this conversion as a cast.

So, coercion causes the add() method to appear polymorphic since the add() method appears to work for floats and ints. As you saw in the last section, you could also have an overloaded add method of the form:

```
public int add( int a, int b);
```

In that case, add(iA,iB) would not result in coercion. Instead, the properly overloaded add() method would get called.

Effective Polymorphism

6

Like any other of the pillars, effective polymorphism does not happen by accident. There are a few steps that you can take to ensure effective polymorphism.

The first step toward effective polymorphism is effective encapsulation and inheritance.

Without encapsulation your code becomes easily dependent on the implementation of your classes. Don't allow encapsulation to break down. If your code becomes dependent upon some aspect of a class's implementation you won't be able to plug in a subclass that reworks that implementation. Good encapsulation is the first step to polymorphism.

Note

It is important to note that *interface* in this context is a bit different than the idea of Java interfaces, though they are similar. Here, *interface* is used to describe the list of messages that you can send to an object. All of those messages comprise an object's public interface.

A Java interface also defines the messages that you can send to a Java object. When a Java class implements an interface, all of the methods in the interface become part of the class's overall public interface.

However, the Java `interface` is not the only way to define the messages that you can send to an object in Java. In Java, any public method defined in the class definition will become part of the object's public interface. This means that if a class implements an interface and defines additional public methods, both sets of methods will become part of its public interface.

Using Java interfaces when you program is a good practice because it separates the definition of the interface from the class implementation of that interface. When you separate the two, many otherwise unrelated classes could implement the same interface. Like inheritance, objects that share a common interface can also take part in substitutability relationships, but without having to be part of the same inheritance hierarchy.

Inheritance is an important factor in inclusion polymorphism. Always try to establish substitutability relationships by programming as close to the base class as possible. This practice will allow more types of objects to participate in your program.

One way to encourage substitutability is through well-thought-out hierarchies. Move commonality into abstract classes and program your objects to use the abstract class, not a specific concrete descendant. That way, you'll be able to introduce any descendant into your program.

Tip

For effective polymorphism, follow these tips:

- Follow the tips to effective encapsulation and inheritance.
- Always program to the interface not the implementation. By programming to an interface, you define specifically what types of objects may participate in your program. Polymorphism will then ensure that those objects participate properly.
- Think and program generically. Let polymorphism worry about the specifics. If you let polymorphism do its job, you won't need to write as much code. It'll take care of the specifics for you!

- Lay the groundwork for polymorphism by establishing and using substitutability relationships. Substitutability and polymorphism will ensure that you can add new subtypes to your program and that the proper code will execute when those subtypes are used.

- If your language provides a way to completely severe interface and implementation, favor that mechanism over inheritance. An example of a mechanism that allows you to define and inherit interface without implementation is the Java Interface. Severing the two allows for more flexible substitutability, thus more opportunity for polymorphism.

- Use abstract classes to separate interface from implementation. All non-leaf classes should be abstract; only program to these abstract classes.

The previous discussion focuses heavily on strongly typed languages such as Java. In a strongly typed language, you must explicitly declare a variable's type. However, some object-oriented languages such as Smalltalk do not have this requirement. Instead, such languages are dynamically typed. Dynamic typing means that you do not need to explicitly state a variable's type when you create the variable. Instead, type is determined dynamically at runtime. So, in essence, every variable is polymorphic.

Polymorphism is a bit simpler in dynamically typed languages. Variables are automatically polymorphic because they can hold any value. As long as the object has the expected method, it can work polymorphically. Of course, everything blows up if you try to call a method that does not exist!

Typed languages are a bit more rigorous. Dynamically typed languages allow you to treat an object polymorphically as long as it has the method in which you are interested. The object does not need to belong to a specific inheritance hierarchy. Strongly typed languages require that the object belong to a specific inheritance hierarchy.

However, the two cases are not really all that different. Behavior is what really defines a type; typed languages just require the presence of all defined behaviors. So, the concepts behind polymorphism in strongly typed and dynamic languages are really the same. It all boils down to an object knowing how to perform some behavior.

The focus on typed languages is deliberate. Focusing directly on strong typing forces you to concentrate on type without glossing over the details. If you can understand polymorphism in a typed language, you can certainly understand it in an untyped language. The converse might not be true!

The choice to focus on type is also a pragmatic one. Most mainstream object-oriented languages are strongly typed.

6

Polymorphic Pitfalls

When using polymorphism there are three main pitfalls to look out for.

Pitfall 1: Moving Behaviors Up the Hierarchy

Too often, inexperienced developers will move behaviors up the hierarchy so as to increase polymorphism. The zeal to treat everything polymorphically can easily blind a developer and result in poorly designed hierarchies.

If you move a behavior too far up a hierarchy not every descendant will be able to support the behavior. Remember, descendants must *never* take functionality away from their ancestors. Do not destroy good inheritance to make your programs more polymorphic.

If you find yourself with the desire to move behaviors up your hierarchy solely to improve polymorphism: *stop*. You are in dangerous territory.

If you find too many limitations in your hierarchy, you may very well want to revisit it. Move common elements into abstract classes; move functionality around. However, do not move methods up a hierarchy past the level where they are first needed. Do not fall into the habit of moving behaviors around at whim simply to add polymorphic support. Be sure that you have another valid reason for the change. You might get lucky a few times, but the practice will catch up with you later and bad programming habits are hard to break.

When developing your hierarchies, it is important to consider the potential evolution of the classes over time. You can break the hierarchy into functional levels. Over time, you can evolve your hierarchy by adding new functional levels as they are needed. However, you should only speculate based on the future requirements that you know. There are an infinite number of undefined "what-ifs." Only plan for the eventualities that you know of.

Pitfall 2: Performance Overhead

Everything comes with a price. True polymorphism will suffer some performance overhead. Polymorphism cannot compete with a method that knows its arguments statically. Instead, with polymorphism, there must be checks at runtime. For inclusion polymorphism, the actual implementation of the object that you send messages to must be determined at runtime. All these checks take time to complete and are slower in comparison to values that statically know their types.

The benefits of maintenance and program flexibility should make up for any performance loss. However, if you're writing a time critical application, you may need to be careful when using polymorphism. However, keep performance in perspective. Create a clean OO implementation, profile the implementation, and carefully tune the performance where profiling reveals problems.

Pitfall 3: Blinders

Inclusion polymorphism has a shortcoming. Although it is true that you can pass a subclass to a method expecting a base class, the method cannot take advantage of any new methods that the subclass might add to its interface. For example, the `FileLog` adds a `close()` method to its interface. The `EmployeeDatabaseAccessor`'s `retrieveEmployee()` will not be able to use it. A method programmed to accept the base class will only know how to manipulate the base class' interface.

Figure 6.2 shows how viewing an instance is relative. Choosing to view a `FileLog` instance as if it were a `BaseLog` instance is like putting on blinders. You only have access to the methods declared in `BaseLog`. Of course, if you treat the `FileLog` instance as a `FileLog` instance, you get all of the functionality defined or inherited by the `FileLog` class as you normally would.

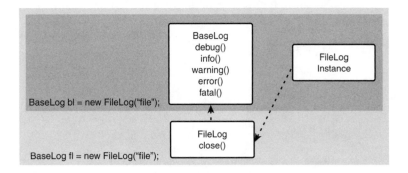

So, when you add new types polymorphically, your old code will be unable to use any new methods. However, new code (or updated code) is free to use anything in the public interface.

This pitfall again points out why a descendant must never remove behaviors from its parent. A method relying on inclusion polymorphism will only know how to exercise the methods defined on the type it is programmed to manipulate. If a behavior is missing, the method will break.

This pitfall also points out that simply swapping a new type into your pre-existing program is often not as easy as it might appear. In the example of the `FileLog` you will need to find a way to call the `close()` method when your program is done with the log.

6

Caveats

There is one major caveat to keep in mind while considering polymorphism. Each language implements polymorphism differently. This discussion has outlined the theoretical definitions behind polymorphism.

Most, if not all languages, support inclusion polymorphism to some degree. On the other hand, few support true parametric polymorphism. Java certainly does not support parametric polymorphism. C++ pretends to implement it.

Most languages do have some form of overloading and coercion. However, the exact implementation will vary from language to language.

So, when you set out to program polymorphically remember the theory but tread carefully. You cannot avoid the limitations of your implementation language.

How Polymorphism Fulfills the Goals of OO

Polymorphism fulfills each of the goals of OOP. Polymorphism produces software that is

1. Natural
2. Reliable
3. Reusable
4. Maintainable
5. Extendable
6. Timely

Polymorphism fulfills these goals in the following ways:

- Natural: Polymorphism enables you to more naturally model the world. Instead of programming for special cases, polymorphism allows you to work at a more generic, conceptual level.

    Overloading and parametric polymorphism enable you to model an object or method at the conceptual level of what that object or method does, not what kinds of parameters it might process. Inclusion polymorphism allows you to manipulate types of objects instead of specific implementations.

    Such generic programming is more natural because it frees you to program at the conceptual level of the problem, not the specific implementations.

- Reliable: Polymorphism results in reliable code.

    First, polymorphism simplifies your code. Instead of having to program special cases for each type of object that you might manipulate, you simply write one case.

If you couldn't program this way, you would have to update your code each time you add a new subclass. Having to update code is error prone.

Second, polymorphism allows you to write less code. The less code that you write, the fewer chances you'll have to introduce bugs.

Polymorphism also allows you to insulate portions of the code from changes to subclasses by ensuring that they only deal with the levels of the inheritance hierarchy that are critical for their function.

- Reusable: Polymorphism aids reuse. For one object to use another, the object only needs to know the second object's interface, not the details of the implementation. As a result, reuse can happen more readily.

- Maintainable: Polymorphism aids maintainability. As you've already seen, polymorphism results in tighter code. So, there is less to maintain. When you do need to maintain code, you're not forced to maintain large case structures.

- Extendable: Polymorphic code is more extendable. Inclusion polymorphism allows you to add new subtypes to your system without having to alter the system to use the new subtype. Overloading allows you to add new methods without having to worry about naming conflicts. Finally, parametric polymorphism allows you to automatically extend your classes to support new types.

- Timely: Polymorphism helps you write timely code. If you can write less code, you can deliver your code sooner. Because polymorphism encourages you to program generically, you can add new types almost instantly to your programs. As a result, maintaining and extending your programs happens at a much quicker pace.

Summary

Polymorphism is the state of one having many forms. Polymorphism is a mechanism that allows a single name to represent different code. Because a single name can represent different code, that name can express many different behaviors. Polymorphism allows you to write moody code: code that exhibits different behaviors.

For the purposes of this book you learned about four different types of polymorphism:

- Inclusion Polymorphism
- Parametric Polymorphism
- Overriding
- Overloading

While there is some disagreement over polymorphism in the OO community, these types describe some of the more common forms of polymorphism. Understanding these types will give you a good foundation in the theory of polymorphism.

6

Inclusion polymorphism allows an object to express many different behaviors at runtime. Likewise, parameteric polymorphism allows an object or method to operate on a number of different parameter types.

Overriding allows you to override a method and know that polymorphism will make sure that the correct method always executes.

Finally, overloading allows you to declare the same method multiple times. Each declaration simply differs in the number and type of arguments. Coercion makes a method appear polymorphic by converting arguments into the type of arguments expected by the method.

Polymorphism allows you to write shorter, more understandable code that is more flexible to future requirements.

Q&A

Q There are three pillars of object-oriented programming. If I don't use all three, is my software somehow not OO?

A At a minimum, you must always use encapsulation. Without encapsulation you really can't have effective inheritance, polymorphism, or OO in general.

As for the other two pillars, you should only use them when it makes sense. Don't use inheritance or polymorphism just so that you can say you used them in your program.

The absence of inheritance and polymorphism doesn't signify that a program is necessarily not OO. However, you need to take a hard look at your program to see if you are squandering an opportunity to properly use the other pillars.

Q Why is there so much disagreement over polymorphism in the OO community?

A There is a great deal of disagreement in the literature that still needs to be worked through. Each author seems to have his own vocabulary. Much of this disagreement stems from the fact that each language implements polymorphism in its own way. All of these different implementations have fragmented the community.

What is important is that you understand the four types presented today. While they may go under different names, these four types are fairly well agreed upon.

Q Will Java ever support parametric polymorphism?

A Only Sun can answer that question. However, there is currently a Java Specification Request (JSR-000014) that has been accepted for development. It adds generic types to the Java programming language. So, it's on the way!

Workshop

The quiz questions and answers are provided for your further understanding. See Appendix A, "Answers," for the answers.

Quiz

1. What are the four types of polymorphism?

2. What does inclusion polymorphism allow you to do?

3. How do overloading and parametric polymorphism more naturally model the real world?

4. When programming, why should you program to an interface rather than an implementation?

5. How do polymorphism and overriding work together?

6. What is another name for overloading?

7. Define overloading.

8. Define parametric polymorphism.

9. What three pitfalls are associated with polymorphism?

10. How do encapsulation and inheritance factor into inclusion polymorphism.

Exercises

1. Give a real-life example of a programming situation where you think you could use inclusion polymorphism. It may help to think of something that you have programmed in the past that could have benefited from polymorphism.

2. Give an example of coercion. Explain why it is coercion.

3. Look through the Java APIs. Find an example of overloading and explain it. Then, find a class hierarchy that you could leverage for inclusion polymorphism. Identify the hierarchy and explain how you can apply inclusion polymorphism to it.

6

DAY 7

Polymorphism: Time to Write Some Code

Yesterday you learned about polymorphism. You should have a good understanding of the four different types of polymorphism. Today you will gain hands-on experience with polymorphism through a number of lab exercises. By the end of today's lesson, you should feel a bit more comfortable with the theory presented in Day 6, "Polymorphism: Learning to Predict the Future."

Today you will learn

- How to apply the different forms of polymorphism
- How to write future proof software
- How polymorphism can help you avoid switch logic

Lab 1: Applying Polymorphism

In Day 5, Lab 2 introduced you to an employee hierarchy. Listing 7.1 presents a slightly altered `Employee` base class.

LISTING 7.1   Employee.java

```java
public abstract class Employee {

    private String first_name;
    private String last_name;
    private double wage;

    public Employee( String first_name, String last_name, double wage ) {
        this.first_name = first_name;
        this.last_name  = last_name;
        this.wage = wage;
    }

    public double getWage() {
        return wage;
    }

    public String getFirstName() {
        return first_name;
    }

    public String getLastName() {
        return last_name;
    }

    public abstract double calculatePay();

    public void printPaycheck() {
        String full_name = last_name + ", " + first_name;
        System.out.println( "Pay: " + full_name + " $" + calculatePay() );
    }
}
```

The new Employee class now has an abstract calculatePay() method. Each subclass must define its own calculatePay() implementation. Listings 7.2 and 7.3 present two possible subclasses.

LISTING 7.2   CommissionedEmployee.java

```java
public class CommissionedEmployee extends Employee {

    private double commission; // the $ per unit
    private int    units;      // keep track of the # of units sold

    public CommissionedEmployee( String first_name, String last_name,
        double wage, double commission ) {
          super( first_name, last_name, wage );
          // call the original constructor in order to properly initialize
```

LISTING 7.2   continued

```
            this.commission   = commission;
        }

        public double calculatePay() {
            return getWage() + ( commission * units );
        }

        public void addSales( int units ) {
            this.units = this.units + units;
        }

        public int getSales() {
          return units;
        }

        public void resetSales() {
            units = 0;
        }

    }
```

LISTING 7.3   HourlyEmployee.java

```
public class HourlyEmployee extends Employee {

    private int hours; // keep track of the # of hours worked

    public HourlyEmployee( String first_name, String last_name,
                           double wage ) {
        super( first_name, last_name, wage );
        // call the original constructor in order to properly initialize
    }

    public double calculatePay() {
        return getWage() * hours;
    }

    public void addHours( int hours ) {
        this.hours = this.hours + hours;
    }

    public int getHours() {
        return hours;
    }

    public void resetHours() {
```

7

LISTING 7.3   continued

```
            hours = 0;
    }

}
```

Each subclass provides its own implementation of calculatePay(). HourlyEmployee simply calculates its pay by multiplying the hours worked by the hourly rate. A CommissionedEmployee is paid a base wage plus a bonus for each unit sold. Each subclass also adds some of its own methods. For example, HourlyEmployee has a method for resetting hours. Likewise, CommissionedEmployee has a method for adding sales.

As you learned in Day 4, "Inheritance: Time to Write Some Code," CommissionedEmployee and HourlyEmployee allow the instances of the two classes to share a substitutability relationship. You can use a CommissionedEmployee instance or an HourlyEmployee instance in place of Employee. However, what does polymorphism allow you to do?

Consider, the Payroll class shown in Listing 7.4.

LISTING 7.4   Payroll.java

```
public class Payroll {

    private int    total_hours;
    private int    total_sales;
    private double total_pay;

    public void payEmployees( Employee [] emps ) {
        for( int i = 0; i < emps.length; i ++ ) {
            Employee emp = emps[i];
            total_pay += emp.calculatePay();
            emp.printPaycheck();
        }
    }

    public void recordEmployeeInfo( CommissionedEmployee emp ) {
        total_sales += emp.getSales();
    }

    public void recordEmployeeInfo( HourlyEmployee emp ) {
        total_hours += emp.getHours();
    }

    public void printReport() {
```

LISTING 7.4 continued

```
        System.out.println( "Payroll Report:" );
        System.out.println( "Total Hours: " + total_hours );
        System.out.println( "Total Sales: " + total_sales );
        System.out.println( "Total Paid: $" + total_pay );
    }

}
```

Caution

Too many get and set methods indicate a bad OO design. In general, you very rarely want to ask an object for its data. Instead, you should ask an object to do something with its data.

In the employee example, it would have been better OO to pass the Employee objects a Report object where they could log their hours, sales, etc. Although this would be better OO, it would have detracted from the example.

"Good OO" is also relative. If you are writing generic objects that will be used in many different situations you may want to add get/set methods so that you can keep the class interface manageable.

Consider the payEmployees(Employee [] emps) method. Substitutability relationships enable you to pass any subclass of Employee to the method. This method treats HourlyEmployees and CommissionedEmployees generally by treating them as simple Employee instances.

Polymorphism is what makes this example interesting. When the payEmployees() methods says

```
total_pay += emp.calculatePay()
```

Polymorphism makes it seem that Employee has many different behaviors. When emp.calculatePay() is called on an object that is really an HourlyEmployee, calculatePay() calculates the pay by multiplying the hourly rate by the number of hours worked. Likewise, when the underlying instance is a CommissionedEmployee, calculatePay() returns the wage plus any sales bonus.

payEmployees() is an example of *inclusion polymorphism*. This method works for any employee. The method doesn't need special code, you won't need to update it each time you add a new subclass to your system—it simply works on all Employees.

7

Methods such as

```
recordEmployeeInfo( CommissionedEmployee emp )
```

and

```
recordEmployeeInfo( HourlyEmployee emp )
```

demonstrate overloading. *Overloading* allows a method to appear polymorphic. For example, it allows the following:

```
Payroll payroll = new Payroll();
CommissionedEmployee emp1 = new CommissionedEmployee( "Mr.", "Sales",
                                                25000.00, 1000.00);
HourlyEmployee emp2 = new HourlyEmployee( "Mr.", "Minimum Wage", 6.50 );

payroll.recordEmployeeInfo( emp2 );
payroll.recordEmployeeInfo( emp1 );
```

`recordEmployeeInfo()` appears polymorphic because it can handle both types of employee.

Overloading is a bit more limited than inclusion polymorphism. With inclusion polymorphism you saw that you only needed one method, `payEmployees()`, to calculate pay for any `Employee`. No matter how many subclasses of `Employee` that you introduce, the method will always work. That's the power of inclusion polymorphism.

Methods that employ overloading are not nearly as robust. Take the `recordEmployeeInfo()` method as an example. Each time that you add a new subclass to the `Employee` hierarchy, you will have to add a new `recordEmployeeInfo()` method for the new type. While a few extra methods may be acceptable for a small hierarchy, you may have to rework your hierarchy so that you can write a generic `recordEmployeeInfo()` as the number of `Employee` subclasses increases.

Listing 7.5 provides a small `main` that exercises the `Payroll` methods.

LISTING 7.5   PayrollDriver.java
_____

```
public class PayrollDriver {
    public static void main( String [] args ) {

        // create the payroll system
        Payroll payroll = new Payroll();

        // create and update some employees
        CommissionedEmployee emp1 = new CommissionedEmployee( "Mr.", "Sales",
                                                25000.00, 1000.00);
```

LISTING 7.5 continued

```
CommissionedEmployee emp2 = new CommissionedEmployee( "Ms.", "Sales",
                                              25000.00, 1000.00);
emp1.addSales( 7 );
emp2.addSales( 5 );

HourlyEmployee emp3 = new HourlyEmployee( "Mr.", "Minimum Wage", 6.50 );
HourlyEmployee emp4 = new HourlyEmployee( "Ms.", "Minimum Wage", 6.50 );
emp3.addHours( 40 );
emp4.addHours( 46 );

// use the overloaded methods
payroll.recordEmployeeInfo( emp2 );
payroll.recordEmployeeInfo( emp1 );
payroll.recordEmployeeInfo( emp3 );
payroll.recordEmployeeInfo( emp4 );

// stick the employees in an array
Employee [] emps = new Employee[4];
emps[0] = emp1; emps[1] = emp2; emps[2] = emp3; emps[3] = emp4;

payroll.payEmployees( emps );
payroll.printReport();
    }
}
```

Figure 7.1 shows the output of the main.

FIGURE 7.1

The proper output of PayrollDriver.

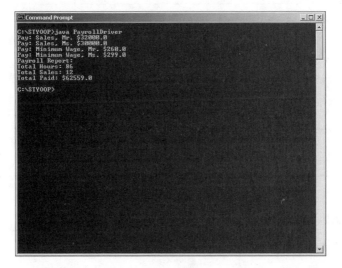

If you step through and manually calculate the pay for each employee you see that
payEmployees() pays out the proper amount. Likewise, all the employee information is
properly recorded.

Problem Statement

Day 5 had you work with MoodyObjects. Listing 7.6 presents a slightly modified
MoodyObject.

LISTING 7.6 MoodyObject.java

```
public abstract class MoodyObject {

    // return the mood
    protected abstract String getMood();

    // ask the object how it feels
    public void queryMood() {
        System.out.println("I feel " + getMood() + " today!");
    }

}
```

Listings 7.7 and 7.8 present two subclasses: HappyObject and SadObject.

LISTING 7.7 HappyObject.java

```
public class HappyObject extends MoodyObject {

    // redefine class's mood
    protected String getMood() {
        return "happy";
    }

    // specialization
    public void laugh() {
        System.out.println("hehehe... hahaha... HAHAHAHAHAHA!!!!!");
    }
}
```

LISTING 7.8 SadObject.java

```
public class SadObject extends MoodyObject {

    // redefine class's mood
```

LISTING 7.8   continued

```
    protected String getMood() {
        return "sad";
    }

    // specialization
    public void cry() {
        System.out.println("'wah' 'boo hoo' 'weep' 'sob' 'weep'");
    }
}
```

Your job is to practice polymorphism. Write a `PsychiatristObject` class.
`PsychiatristObject` should have three methods. `examine()` should take any
`MoodyObject` instance and ask it how it feels. `PsychiatristObject` should also have an
overloaded `observe()` method. `observe()` should call the object's `cry()` or `laugh()`
methods. The `PsychiatristObject` should make a medical comment for each behavior.

Be sure to use the provided `PsychiatristDriver` to test your solution!

 Caution   The next section discusses the solutions to Lab 1. Do not proceed until you
complete Lab 1.

Solutions and Discussion

Listing 7.9 presents one possible `PsychiatristObject`.

LISTING 7.9   `PsychiatristObject.java`

```
public class PsychiatristObject {

    // use inclusion polymorphism to examine all moody objects generically
    public void examine( MoodyObject obj ) {
        System.out.println( "Tell me, object, how do you feel today?" );
        obj.queryMood();
        System.out.println();
    }

    // use overloading to observe objects specifically,
    //but with a generically named method
    public void observe( SadObject obj ) {
        obj.cry();
        System.out.println(
            "Hmm... very, very interesting. Something makes this object sad." );
```

7

LISTING 7.9   continued

```
        System.out.println();
    }
    public void observe( HappyObject obj ) {
        obj.laugh();
        System.out.println(
            "Hmm... very, very interesting. This object seems very happy." );
        System.out.println();
    }
}
```

examine(MoodyObject obj) treats all MoodyObjects generically. The
PsychiatristObject asks the MoodyObject how it feels and calls its queryMood()
method. The PsychiatristObject needs an observe() method for each type of
MoodyObject that it would like to observe.

After completing this lab you should begin to feel comfortable with the basic mechanisms of polymorphism.

Lab 2: Bank Account—Applying Polymorphism to a Familiar Example

In Lab 2 you're going to take what you learned in Lab 1 and apply it to a slightly more
involved problem. This lab centers on the BankAccount hierarchy presented in Day 5.
The hierarchy presented here remains nearly the same as the one presented in Day 5. The
only difference is that BankAccount is now an abstract class. You can no longer directly
instantiate a BankAccount.

Making BankAccount abstract more closely models how bank accounts work. When you
open an account you open a checking account or a money market account. You do not
open a generic bank account. Listing 7.10 lists the only change to the hierarchy.

LISTING 7.10   BankAccount.java

```
public abstract class BankAccount {
    // the rest is the same
}
```

Problem Statement

In this lab you need to write a Bank class. The Bank class has a number of methods.

Bank instances hold onto accounts. However, you need a way to keep track of to whom the accounts belong. addAccount() enables you to specify an owner each time you add a new account:

```
public void addAccount( String name, BankAccount account );
```

You can use the owner name to access the proper account later.

totalHoldings() enables the Bank to report the total amount of money in the bank:

```
public double totalHoldings();
```

totalHoldings() should loop through all the accounts and total the amount held in the bank.

totalAccounts() enables you to query the Bank instance to see how many accounts it currently holds:

```
public int totalAccounts();
```

deposit() allows you to deposit funds into a specific bank account:

```
public void deposit( String name, double amount );
```

deposit() is a convenience method that frees you from having to retrieve a specific account before you can add funds to it. Instead, deposit() allows you to deposit funds directly through the bank.

balance() allows you to retrieve the balance of a specific account:

```
public double balance( String name )
```

Like deposit(), balance() is a convenience method.

---

addAccount() stores an account under a given name. There are a number of ways to implement this functionality. However, some approaches are easier to implement than others.

For this lab you will want to consider java.util.Hashtable. Hashtable allows you to store and retrieve key/value pairs.

Consider this consolidated API:

```
public Object get( Object key );
public Object put ( Object key, Object value );
public int size();
public java.util.Enumeration elements();
```

Here is an example of Hashtable:

```
java.util.Hashtable table = new java.util.Hashtable();
```

7

```
        table.put( "LANGUAGE", "JAVA" );
        String name = table.get( "LANGUAGE" );
```

This example stores the value JAVA under the key LANGUAGE. To retrieve the value later, you simply call get() and pass the proper key.

By studying the API you'll notice that the get() and put() methods return Object. So if you were to store a String, you will get the value back as an Object.

In Java, all objects inherit from Object. The Hashtable was written to deal in Objects so that it will work for all Java objects. However, what if you store a CheckingAccount in the Hashtable and would like to treat it as a CheckingAccount after you retrieve it? How would you do that in Java?

Java provides a way for you to turn an Object reference back to its proper type. The mechanism is known as *casting*. The following statement is illegal in Java:

```
        CheckingAccount account = table.get( "CHECKING_ACCOUNT" );
```

Instead, you will need to perform a cast before you can store an Object reference to a CheckingAccount variable:

```
        CheckingAccount account = (CheckingAccount) table.get( "CHECKING_ACCOUNT"
        );
```

You have to be careful while casting. Casting can be dangerous. For example, the following cast is illegal:

```
        HappyObject o = new HappyObject();
        table.put( "HAPPY", o );
        (CheckingAccount) table.get( "HAPPY" );
```

When you cast, you must be certain that the Object that you are casting is truly the type (CAST_TYPE). So, for this lab, when you retrieve a BankAccount from the Hashtable you'll want to cast to BankAccount. As an example, consider the following cast:

```
        BankAccount b = (BankAccount) table.get( "ACCOUNT1" );
```

If you try to perform an illegal cast in Java, Java will throw a ClassCastException.

Like Lab 1, Lab 2 provides a driver to help you test your solution. Be sure to check out BankDriver.

 Caution   The next section discusses the solutions to Lab 2. Do not proceed until you complete Lab 2.

Solutions and Discussion

Listing 7.11 presents one possible Bank implementation.

LISTING 7.11   Bank.java

```java
public class Bank {

    private java.util.Hashtable accounts = new java.util.Hashtable();

    public void addAccount( String name, BankAccount account ) {
        accounts.put( name, account );
    }

    public double totalHoldings() {
        double total = 0.0;

        java.util.Enumeration enum = accounts.elements();
        while( enum.hasMoreElements() ) {
            BankAccount account = (BankAccount) enum.nextElement();
            total += account.getBalance();
        }
        return total;
    }

    public int totalAccounts() {
        return accounts.size();
    }

    public void deposit( String name, double amount ) {
        BankAccount account = retrieveAccount( name );
        if( account != null ) {
            account.depositFunds( amount );
        }
    }

    public double balance( String name ) {
        BankAccount account = retrieveAccount( name );
        if( account != null ) {
            return account.getBalance();
        }
        return 0.0;
    }

    private BankAccount retrieveAccount( String name ) {
        return (BankAccount) accounts.get( name );
    }
}
```

7

Internally, this solution uses `java.util.Hashtable` to hold onto all the `BankAccounts`. Instead of providing its own mechanism for storage and retrieval, this implementation takes advantage of reuse by using those classes supplied by Java.

`balance()`, `deposit()`, `addAccount()`, and `totalHoldings()` all demonstrate inclusion polymorphism. These methods will work for any subclass of `BankAccount` that you might create.

After completing this lab you should gain further insight into the mechanisms of polymorphism. In Day 5, `BankAccounts` showed you the convenience of inheritance. Inheritance enabled you to quickly create subclasses by just programming what was different between accounts. Polymorphism further simplifies your code by providing a mechanism for generic programming.

Lab 3: Bank Account—Using Polymorphism to Write Future-Proof Code

Throughout the discussion of polymorphism you've heard the term future-proof software. What exactly is future-proof software? Simply, future-proof software is software that easily adapts to changing requirements.

Requirements change all the time. When you first set out to write a program the requirements can change as you learn more about the problem you are solving. Once written, your users will expect and demand new features from your software. If you create future-proof software, you won't have to completely rewrite it each time you get a new requirement.

Let's consider an example of changing requirements. Listing 7.12 presents a new `MoodyObject`: `CarefreeObject`.

LISTING 7.12   `CarefreeObject.java`

```java
public class CarefreeObject extends MoodyObject {

    // redefine class's mood
    protected String getMood() {
        return "carefree";
    }

    // specialization
    public void whistle() {
        System.out.println("whistle, whistle, whistle...");
    }
}
```

Listing 7.13 shows the updated PsychiatristDriver.

LISTING 7.13 PsychiatristDriver.java

```java
public class PsychiatristDriver {

    public static void main( String [] args ) {
        HappyObject happy = new HappyObject();
        SadObject sad = new SadObject();
        CarefreeObject carefree = new CarefreeObject();
        PsychiatristObject psychiatrist = new PsychiatristObject();

        // use inclusion polymorphism
        psychiatrist.examine( happy );
        psychiatrist.examine( sad );
        psychiatrist.examine( carefree );

        // use overloading so that we can observe the objects
        psychiatrist.observe( happy );
        psychiatrist.observe( sad );
    }

}
```

Figure 7.2 shows the output that you will see when executing PsychiatristDriver.

FIGURE 7.2

The proper output of PsychiatristDriver.

Here you see that the PsychiatristObject is future-proof. You can add new MoodyObjects, all with their own customized behavior, at any time. The PsychiatristObject can simply use the new subtypes.

Note
You may notice that this example focuses on the examine() method. Inclusion polymorphism allows for truly future-proof software. However, if the PsychiatristObject wants to observe() a new subtype, you will need to update the PsychiatristObject as well.

MoodyObject is a simple example. However, try to imagine how you could extend this idea to more complex programs!

Problem Statement

Your task is to witness future proof programming first hand. In the last lab you wrote a Bank class. The Bank class can work on any BankAccount subtype. Your task is to create a new BankAccount type: the RewardsAcount.

Like a SavingsAccount, the RewardsAccount applies interest to the balance. However, to increase the number and size of deposits, the bank would like to introduce a rewards system.

The RewardsAccount keeps track of the number of deposits over a certain dollar amount: the reward deposit level. For example, say that the reward deposit level is $500 dollars. Each time the depositor deposits $500 or more, the depositor will earn a reward point.

Note
Keep the RewardsAccount simple. If the reward deposit level is $500 and the depositor deposits $500 the depositor earns one reward point. If the depositor deposits $3,000, the depositor still should only earn one reward point.

Along with the methods defined by BankAccount, RewardsAccount should also provide a mechanism for retrieving and resetting the number of reward points earned. The RewardsAccount also needs a way to set and get the reward deposit level.

For this lab you might want to go back to Day 5 and reread the SavingsAccount and BankAccount descriptions. This lab also includes a RewardsAccountDriver and an updated BankDriver. Be sure to use these to test your solution. You'll also want to look over the BankDriver. The BankDriver demonstrates how you can add a new object type to your program without having to update any of the other objects.

Caution
The next section discusses the solutions to Lab 3. Do not proceed until you complete Lab 3.

Solutions and Discussion

Listing 7.14 presents one possible RewardsAccount solution.

LISTING 7.14   RewardsAccount.java

```java
public class RewardsAccount extends SavingsAccount {
    private double min_reward_balance;
    private int qualifying_deposits;

    public RewardsAccount( double initDeposit, double interest, double min ) {
        super( initDeposit, interest );
        min_reward_balance = min;
    }

    public void depositFunds( double amount ) {
        super.depositFunds( amount );
        if( amount >= min_reward_balance ) {
            qualifying_deposits++;
        }
    }

    public int getRewardsEarned() {
        return qualifying_deposits;
    }

    public void resetRewards() {
        qualifying_deposits = 0;
    }

    public double getMinimumRewardBalance() {
        return min_reward_balance;
    }

    public void setMinimumRewardBalance( double min ) {
        min_reward_balance = min;
    }
}
```

RewardsAccount overrides depositFunds() so that it can check the balance and reward points. The class also adds methods for retrieving the rewards balance, resetting the balance, as well as getting and setting the reward deposit level.

Listing 7.15 presents the updated BankDriver.

7

LISTING 7.15   BankDriver.java

```java
public class BankDriver {

    public static void main( String [] args ) {
        CheckingAccount  ca = new CheckingAccount( 5000.00, 5, 2.50 );
        OverdraftAccount oa = new OverdraftAccount( 10000.00, 0.18 );
        SavingsAccount   sa = new SavingsAccount( 500.00, 0.02 );
        TimedMaturityAccount tma = new TimedMaturityAccount(
                                        10000.00, 0.06, 0.05 );

        Bank bank = new Bank();
        bank.addAccount( "CHECKING", ca );
        bank.addAccount( "OVERDRAFT", oa );
        bank.addAccount( "SAVINGS", sa );
        bank.addAccount( "TMA", tma );

        System.out.println( "Total holdings(should be $25500.0): $" +
                            bank.totalHoldings() );
        System.out.println( "Total accounts(should be 4): " +
                            bank.totalAccounts() );

        RewardsAccount ra = new RewardsAccount( 5000.00, .05, 500.00 );
        bank.addAccount( "REWARDS", ra );

        System.out.println( "Total holdings(should be $30500.0): $" +
                            bank.totalHoldings() );
        System.out.println( "Total accounts(should be 5): " +
                            bank.totalAccounts() );

        bank.deposit( "CHECKING", 250.00 );
        double new_balance = bank.balance( "CHECKING" );
        System.out.println( "CHECKING new balance (should be 5250.0): $" +
                            new_balance );
    }

}
```

To use the new account class there are two steps that you must take.

For the first step you must create your new subtype. After you create your new subtype, you need to alter your program to create new instances of the object.

In the case of RewardsAccount you must update the BankAccount main() to go out and create instances of RewardsAccount. However, you do not have to change anything else!

When you're programming a real program you will go through the same steps to introduce new subtypes to your program. First you'll need to create the new subtype.

Secondly, you'll need to alter your code to get it to create your new subtype. But that's it. You do not need to alter the rest of your program.

Later on you'll see ways to make your programs so flexible that you might not need to alter any of your program's code at all for the program to find and start using new subtypes.

Lab 4: Case Study—The Java Switch and Polymorphism

Java, as well as many other languages, provides a switch mechanism. Consider the following day_of_the_week() method:

```java
public void day_of_the_week( int day ) {
    switch ( day ) {
        case 1:
            System.out.println( "Sunday" );
            break;
        case 2:
            System.out.println( "Monday" );
            break;
        case 3:
            System.out.println( "Tuesday" );
            break;
        case 4:
            System.out.println( "Wednesday" );
            break;
        case 5:
            System.out.println( "Thursday" );
            break;
        case 6:
            System.out.println( "Friday" );
            break;
        case 7:
            System.out.println( "Saturday" );
            break;
        default:
            System.out.println( day + " is not a valid day." );
            break;
    }
}
```

The method takes one parameter: an int representing the day of the week. The method then switches over all of the valid days of the week. If the day argument matches one of the days, the method prints the day's name.

7

Generally speaking you use switches to perform conditional logic. With conditional logic, you check a piece of data for a certain condition. If that condition is met you do something. If another condition is met you do something else entirely. Anyone from a procedural background should be familiar with such an approach to programming.

If you're comfortable with conditionals, it's time for you to do some unlearning. Switch logic is generally considered bad OO practice. It is so bad in fact, that many OO languages do not provide a switch mechanism. Conditional logic does have one benefit; it helps you to detect poor design!

Switches are almost always bad by nature. However, conditionals often sneak up on you, because they come in many forms. Consider a slightly different day_of_the_week() method.

```
public void day_of_the_week( int day ) {
    if ( day == 1 ) {
        System.out.println( "Sunday" );
    } else if ( day == 2 ) {
        System.out.println( "Monday" );
    } else if ( day == 3 ) {
        System.out.println( "Tuesday" );
    } else if ( day == 4 ) {
        System.out.println( "Wednesday" );
    } else if ( day == 5 ) {
        System.out.println( "Thursday" );
    } else if ( day == 6 ) {
        System.out.println( "Friday" );
} else if ( day == 7 ) {
        System.out.println( "Saturday" );
    } else {
        System.out.println( day + " is not a valid day." );
    }
}
```

So what's so wrong with conditionals?

Conditionals are contrary to the concepts of OO. In OO you're not supposed to ask an object for its data and then do something to that data. Instead, you're supposed to ask an object to do something to its data. In the case of the day_of_the_week() method you probably obtain day from some object. You shouldn't be processing raw data. Instead, you should ask the object for a string representation. Conditionals force you to muddle responsibilities. Each place that uses the data will have to apply the same conditional logic.

There are times when conditionals are absolutely necessary. So, how do you detect "bad" conditionals?

There are ways to know when a "good" conditional goes "bad." If you find yourself updating a switch or if/else blocks each time you add a new subtype, chances are the conditional is "bad." Not only is this a bad OO practice it is a maintenance nightmare. You'll have to make sure to update each conditional that switches over the data. It will take a lot of time to guarantee that you didn't forget to update something!

Fixing a Conditional

Consider the following method:

```java
public int calculate( String operation, int operand1, int operand2 ) {
    if ( operation.equals( "+" ) ) {
        return operand1 + operand2;
    } else if ( operation.equals( "*" ) ) {
        return operand1 * operand2;
    } else if ( operation.equals( "/" ) ) {
        return operand1 / operand2;
    } else if ( operation.equals( "-" ) ) {
        return operand1 - operand2;
    } else {
        System.out.println( "invalid operation: " + operation );
        return 0;
    }
}
```

Such a method might appear in a calculator problem. The `calculate()` method takes the operation as well as the two operands as argument. It then performs the requested calculation.

So how might you fix the problem? You can fix the problem with objects, of course!

When you set out to eliminate switch logic, start with the data that you're switching over. Turn the data into an object.

In this case, you should create add, subtract, multiply, and divide objects. All these objects are operations. So they should all inherit from a common base class. As you've seen throughout this day, substitutability and polymorphism will allow you to do some clever things to these objects.

All the objects that you should create are operations, so you know that you need an `Operation` base class. But what does an `Operation` do? An `Operation` calculates some value given two operands. Listing 7.16 presents an `Operation` class.

LISTING 7.16   `Operation.java`

```java
public abstract class Operation {
    public abstract int calculate( int operand1, int operand2 );
}
```

7

Listings 7.17, 7.18, 7.19, and 7.20 present the various operation objects.

LISTING 7.17 Add.java

```
public class Add extends Operation {
    public int calculate( int operand1, int operand2 ) {
        return operand1 + operand2;
    }
}
```

LISTING 7.18 Subtract.java

```
public class Subtract extends Operation {
    public int calculate( int operand1, int operand2 ) {
        return operand1 - operand2;
    }
}
```

LISTING 7.19 Multiply.java

```
public class Multiply extends Operation {
    public int calculate( int operand1, int operand2 ) {
        return operand1 * operand2;
    }
}
```

LISTING 7.20 Divide.java

```
public class Divide extends Operation {
    public int calculate( int operand1, int operand2 ) {
        return operand1 / operand2;
    }
}
```

Each operation implements the calculate() method in its own way. Now that you have
an object for each operation you can rewrite the original calculate() method.

```
public int calculate( Operation operation, int operand1, int operand2 ) {
        return operation.calculate( operand1, operand2 );
}
```

By turning the operation into an object you've gained a good deal of flexibility. In the
past you would have had to update the method each time you wanted to add a new

operation. Now, you can simply create the new operation and pass it to the method. You do not have to alter the method in any way for it to work with the new operation—it simply works.

Problem Statement

Java provides an operator called `instanceof`. `instanceof` allows you to check the underlying type of a reference.

```
String s = "somestring";
Object obj = s;
System.out.println( (obj instanceof String) );
```

This code segment prints true. `obj` holds onto an instance of String. Most OOP languages provide a similar mechanism.

Now, consider the new `Payroll` class in Listing 7.21.

LISTING 7.21   `Payroll.java`

```
public class Payroll {

    private int    total_hours;
    private int    total_sales;
    private double total_pay;

    public void payEmployees( Employee [] emps ) {
        for( int i = 0; i < emps.length; i ++ ) {
            Employee emp = emps[i];
            total_pay += emp.calculatePay();
            emp.printPaycheck();
        }
    }

    public void calculateBonus( Employee [] emps ) {
        for( int i = 0; i < emps.length; i ++ ) {
            Employee emp = emps[i];
            if( emp instanceof HourlyEmployee ) {
                System.out.println("Pay bonus to " + emp.getLastName() +
                                ", " + emp.getFirstName() + " $100.00." );
            } else if ( emp instanceof CommissionedEmployee ) {
                int bonus = ( (CommissionedEmployee) emp ).getSales() * 100;
                System.out.println("Pay bonus to " + emp.getLastName() + ", " +
                                emp.getFirstName() + " $" + bonus );
            } else {
                System.out.println( "unknown employee type" );
            }
        }
    }
}
```

7

LISTING 7.21 continued

```
public void recordEmployeeInfo( CommissionedEmployee emp ) {
    total_sales += emp.getSales();
}

public void recordEmployeeInfo( HourlyEmployee emp ) {
    total_hours += emp.getHours();
}

public void printReport() {
    System.out.println( "Payroll Report:" );
    System.out.println( "Total Hours: " + total_hours );
    System.out.println( "Total Sales: " + total_sales );
    System.out.println( "Total Paid: $" + total_pay );
}

}
```

This `Payroll` class has a `calculateBonus()` method. This method takes an array of `Employees`, figures out what type each is, and calculates a bonus. `HourlyEmployees` receive a flat $100 bonus while `CommissionedEmployees` receive $100 for each sale.

Your job is to eliminate the conditional logic found in `calculateBonus()`. Start by attacking the data the method is switching over. In this case, it's switching over an object. So what's wrong?

Rather than asking the object for the bonus, the method asks the object for some data and then calculates a bonus using that data. Instead, the method should ask the object for the data.

You can download the source to the `Payroll`, `Employee`, `HourlyEmployee`, and `CommissionedEmployee` classes. There is also a `PayrollDriver` provided so that you can easily test your solution.

 Caution | The next section discusses the solutions to Lab 4. Do not proceed until you complete Lab 4.

Solutions and Discussion

To solve this problem you should add a `calculateBonus()` method directly to each `Employee`. This might seem like you're breaking pitfall 1 from Day 6. However, it's okay to move the method into the base class, because all subclasses know how to calculate their bonus. Really, it should have been in the base class all along.

Listings 7.22, 7.23, and 7.24 present the required changes.

LISTING 7.22   Employee.java

```
public abstract class Employee {
    public abstract double calculateBonus();
    // snipped for brevity, the rest stays the same
}
```

LISTING 7.23   HourlyEmployee.java

```
public class HourlyEmployee extends Employee {
    public double calculateBonus() {
        return 100.00;
    }
    // snipped for brevity, the rest stays the same
}
```

LISTING 7.24   CommissionedEmployee.java

```
public class CommissionedEmployee extends Employee {
    public double calculateBonus() {
        return 100.00 * getSales();
    }
    // snipped for brevity, the rest stays the same
}
```

With these changes you can update the Payroll class, as Listing 7.25 demonstrates.

LISTING 7.25   Payroll.java

```
public class Payroll {
    public void calculateBonus( Employee [] emps ) {
        for( int i = 0; i < emps.length; i ++ ) {
            Employee emp = emps[i];
            System.out.println("Pay bonus to " + emp.getLastName() + ", " +
                            emp.getFirstName() + " $" + emp.calculateBonus()
);
        }
    }
    // snipped for brevity, the rest stays the same
}
```

7

Voila! No more nasty conditional logic!

Switch tips:

- Avoid the use of `switch`.
- Look at large `if`/`else` blocks with skepticism.
- Beware of cascading changes. If a change requires many conditional changes, you might have a problem.
- `instanceof` is a very large red flag.
- `if`/`else`, `switch`, and `instanceof` are "guilty until proven innocent."

Tips to switch elimination:

- Objectify the data.
- If the data is already an object, add a method to the object.
- Avoid `instanceof` checks; use polymorphism instead.

Summary

Today you completed four labs. Lab 1 gave you a chance to experiment with some of the basic mechanisms of polymorphism. Lab 2 enabled you to apply what you learned in Lab 1 to a more complicated example. Lab 3 should have finally answered the question, "What exactly is future-proof software." Lab 3 really sums up why you want to use polymorphism. Finally, Lab 4 gave you something to look out for while programming. It also showed how useful polymorphism can be when leveraged correctly.

Together all these labs reinforced the lessons of polymorphism. They give you what you need to know to properly take advantage of the concept. Hopefully, after completing these labs, you will look at your programs from a polymorphism viewpoint. True OO programming requires a different way of thinking about software. The strengths of OO truly come through when you can think polymorphically.

Q&A

Q **It seems that inclusion polymorphism is more convenient that overloading since I only need to write one method and have it work with many different types. Why would I ever use overloading instead?**

A There are times where overloading is a better choice. A method that uses inclusion only works if it's processing related objects. Overloading allows you to reuse a method name among a group of methods whose arguments may not relate at all. You can't do that with inclusion (although you can use a combination of inclusion and overloading).

Workshop

The quiz questions and answers are provided for your further understanding. See Appendix A, "Answers," for the answers.

Quiz

1. From the lab solutions, give an example of an overloaded method.

2. What problem does overriding present?

3. What steps do you need to take in order to alter behavior in a polymorphic hierarchy?

4. From the labs, find an example of inclusion polymorphism.

5. How do you eliminate conditional logic?

6. What is the benefit of inclusion polymorphism over overloading?

7. In OO what is the relationship between objects and data?

8. What's wrong with conditionals?

9. What is a good indication that a conditional is "bad?"

10. In your own words, explain polymorphism.

Exercises

There are no exercises today. Do your labs!

7

WEEK 1

In Review

In week one, you not only learned the basics of object-oriented programming, but how and when to apply them.

You learned that the three pillars of object-oriented programming are encapsulation, inheritance, and polymorphism. Encapsulation allows you to build self-contained pieces of software. Encapsulation is accomplished through abstraction, implementation hiding, and division of responsibility. Inheritance allows you to reuse and extend existing code. You learned that there are three methods of inheritance: for implementation reuse, for difference, and for type substitution. Polymorphism allows a single name to represent different code. Four different types of polymorphism are inclusion polymorphism, parametric polymorphism, overloading, and overriding.

Using the three pillars of object-oriented programming allows you to create code that is

- Natural
- Reliable
- Reusable
- Maintainable
- Extendable
- Timely

While this information is presented in Days 2, 4, and 6, the labs from Day 3, 5, and 7 are what really bring everything together. The hands-on experience in these labs furthered your understanding of how to write object-oriented code that fulfills the above goals.

1

2

3

4

5

6

7

WEEK 2

Learning to Apply OO

8 Introduction to the UML

9 Introduction to Object Oriented Analysis (OOA)

10 Introduction to Object Oriented Design (OOD)

11 Reusing Designs Through Design Patterns

12 Advanced Design Patterns

13 OO and User Interface Programming

14 Building Reliable Software Through Testing

8

9

10

11

12

13

14

WEEK 2

At a Glance

In the first week, you learned the basics of writing object-oriented code. While this is a first step in creating an object-oriented program, there is still much you need to learn before you can start coding.

This week, you move beyond simply coding and cover the entire software development process. The software development process steps that you will cover are analysis, design, implementation, and testing.

Object-oriented analysis (OOA) is the first step in the development process. OOA allows you to understand the problem you are trying to solve. After completing OOA, you should know the requirements for your program as well as any domain specific terminology.

After you have analyzed the problem, you may begin to design your solution. Day 10 describes object-oriented design, the process of taking the domain model and creating the objects model you will use during implementation. Days 11 and 12 present some design short cuts.

The next step is implementation, writing the code. This is where you put to use the information presented in the first week.

Testing is the final stage in the development process. It is important to test throughout the implementation stage as well as at the end to be able to ensure a defect-free system.

These topics will complement the knowledge you gained in the first week, and allow you to take an idea and follow through the development process until you have a fully developed object-oriented program.

DAY **8**

Introduction to the UML

Last week you learned the basic theories of object-oriented programming. However, simply knowing a few techniques and definitions will not adequately prepare you to actually apply them. Do you simply show someone tools, explain their use and purpose, and then send that person to build a home? Of course not! Programming is no different. Successful programming only comes with experience and sound methodology. This week, you will learn how to properly apply the OO tools that you saw last week.

Today you will explore the Unified Modeling Language (UML) as well as some of the finer aspects of object inter-relationship. Today's lessons will give you the common language that you will use while learning how to analyze your problems and design OO solutions.

Today you will learn

- Why you should care about the Unified Modeling Language
- How to model your classes using UML
- How to model the various relationships between classes
- How to put it all together

Introduction to the Unified Modeling Language

When a builder builds a home he doesn't make it up as he goes along. Instead, the builder builds the house according to a set of detailed blueprints. These blueprints explicitly lay out the house's design. Nothing is left to chance.

Now how many times have you, or someone you've known, made it up as you went along while programming? How many times has this practice gotten you into trouble?

The Unified Modeling Language (UML)attempts to bring blueprints to the software world. The UML is an industry-standard modeling language. The language consists of a number of graphical notations that you can use to describe the entire architecture of your software. Programmers, software architects, and analysts use *modeling languages* to graphically describe the design of software.

New Term   A *modeling language* is a graphical notation for describing software design. The language also includes a number of rules to distinguish between correct and incorrect drawings. It is these rules that make UML a modeling language rather than just a bunch of symbols for drawing.

A modeling language is not the same as a process or methodology. A *methodology* tells you how to design software. Instead, a modeling language illustrates the design you will create while following a methodology.

New Term   A *methodology* sets out a procedure for designing software. Modeling languages capture that design graphically.

The UML is not the only modeling language. However, it is a widely accepted standard. When modeling software, it is important to do so in a common language. That way, other developers can quickly and easily understand your design diagrams. In fact, creators of the UML brought together their three competing modeling languages—thus the *U(nified)* in UML. The UML provides a common vocabulary that developers can use to convey their designs.

New Term   The *UML* is an industry standard modeling language. The UML consists of notation for describing each aspect of a software design.

 Note   It is not the purpose of this book to present an exhaustive introduction to the UML. Instead, this book will present those practical pieces that you can use right away to describe your software.

It is important to note that a modeling language doesn't tell you anything about how to arrive at your design. Methodology or processes lay out guidelines for how to analyze and design software.

 A *methodology* or *process* describes how to design software. A methodology often contains a modeling language.

> **Caution**
>
> The UML presents a rich set of modeling tools. As a result there is quite a lot of information that you can put into your models. Beware of trying to use every single notation while modeling. Only use enough notation to convey your design.
>
> Always keep in mind that the purpose of your model is to convey your design. Do what you need to do to convey it and be done with it.

Modeling Your Classes

Last week you saw quite a bit of code. When you get down to it, the code is the lowest level of documentation for your software. If your code works, you are guaranteed to have your design documented.

Although the code is the most complete documentation of your design, it can be extremely difficult for others to get their hands around—especially if they are unfamiliar with the code. The "documentation" is also useless for someone who might not know the implementation language.

Instead, you need a notation that allows you to document your design so that others can understand it at a glance. That way, others can see the high-level class structure and only dive into the details when they need to. In a way, a graphical notation encapsulates you from the details so that you can free yourself to understand the high-level structure of a program.

> **Caution**
>
> Creating documentation separate from the code requires a commitment to keep it in sync with the code.

One way that the UML helps you convey your design is by providing a rich set of notation for describing your classes. By using this notation, others can easily see the main classes that make up your program's design. As you will see, the UML allows you to define the classes, as well as describe the high level relationships between the classes.

Basic Class Notation

The UML provides a rich set of notation for modeling classes. In the UML, a box represents the class. The topmost box always contains the class's name. The center box contains any attributes, and the bottom contains the operations. Graphical notes about your model appear in boxes with folded corners. Figure 8.1 sums up the basic class structure.

FIGURE 8.1

The UML class notation.

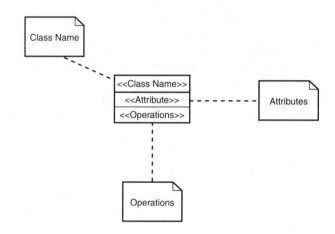

> **Note**
>
> The UML differentiates between operation and methods. In the UML, an operation is a service that you can request from any object of a class while a method is a specific implementation of the operation. Today's lessons will stay true to the UML usage.

Within the model, you can use the characters -, #, and +. These characters convey an attribute's or operation's *visibility*. The hyphen (-) means private, the pound sign (#) means protected, and plus (+) means public (see Figure 8.2).

FIGURE 8.2

The UML's notation to specify visibility.

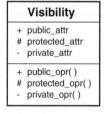

Figure 8.3 illustrates the complete BankAccount class from Days 5 and 7.

FIGURE 8.3

A fully described class.

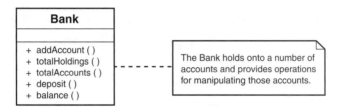

Sometimes a note will help to convey meaning that would otherwise get lost or over-looked, such as the note in Figure 8.4.

FIGURE 8.4

A detailed example of a note.

These notes are modeling analogs of the real-world sticky note.

Advanced Class Notation

The UML also defines a few other, more advanced, notations. The proper use of this notation helps you create more descriptive models.

The UML helps you to be more descriptive by allowing you to extend the vocabulary of the language itself through the use of *stereotypes*.

NEW TERM   A *stereotype* is a UML element that allows you to extend the vocabulary of the UML language itself. A stereotype consists of a word or phrase enclosed in guillemets (<< >>). You place a stereotype above or to the side of an existing element.

For example, Figure 8.1 shows the stereotype <<Attribute>>. This stereotype illustrates where to add attributes to a class rectangle. Figure 8.5 illustrates another stereotype that tells you a bit about the operation.

FIGURE 8.5

A stereotype that qualifies the operation.

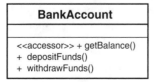

Finally, you may remember that the BankAccount class was originally defined as a concrete class. However, Day 7 redefined the BankAccount as an abstract class. The UML provides a notation to convey that a class is abstract: the abstract class's name is italicized. In the case of BankAccount, the name should be italicized as illustrated in Figure 8.6.

FIGURE 8.6

The abstract BankAccount.

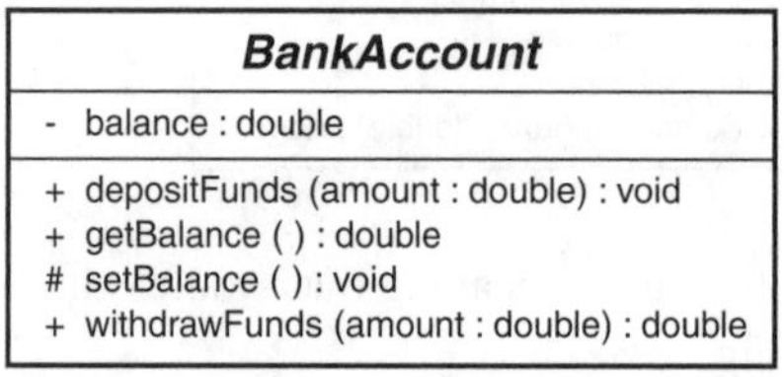

BankAccount
- balance : double
+ depositFunds (amount : double) : void + getBalance ( ) : double # setBalance ( ) : void + withdrawFunds (amount : double) : double

Modeling Your Classes to Suit Your Purposes

The previous two sections presented many different notation choices. Given all these options, how do you know what notations to use?

You always need to go back to the questions, "What am I trying to convey?" and "Who am I trying to convey it to?" The whole purpose of a model is to convey your design as effectively (and as simply) as possible.

Perhaps your purpose is to convey the public interface of a class. Figure 8.7 might suffice. It adequately conveys the public interface of Bank without encumbering you without the details of method arguments or hidden attributes. Such notation will suffice if you would like to simply convey what other objects might do to Bank instances.

FIGURE 8.7

A simple notation for Bank.

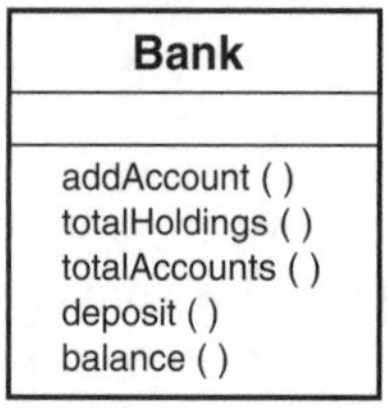

Bank
addAccount ( ) totalHoldings ( ) totalAccounts ( ) deposit ( ) balance ( )

However, take Figure 8.3 as another example. This figure completely documents all attributes and operations (public, protected, and private) for the BankAccount class. You might model a class to this detail if you would like to convey the class's entire definition to another developer. Or maybe as you progress in you OO career you might become an architect. You might give such a model to a developer so that he can go out and create the class.

So the answer to the question "How do I know what notations to use?" is that it depends. When a nontechnical person asks you what you do, you answer in a way that that person will understand. When a peer asks you what you do, you generally give a technical answer. Modeling your design is no different. Use the vocabulary that is appropriate for what you are trying to do.

8

> Tips for effective modeling:
>
> - Always ask yourself the question "What am I trying to convey?" The answer will help you decide exactly what pieces you need to model.
> - Always ask yourself the question "To whom am I trying to convey this information?" The answer will dictate how you model.
> - Always try to produce the simplest model that still succeeds in conveying your design.
> - Don't get caught up in the modeling language. Although you shouldn't be too loose in the semantics you shouldn't let following the notation perfectly stop you from completing your diagrams. The dangers of paralysis while modeling are real—especially when you first start. Don't worry if your model isn't 100% perfect. Only worry if your model doesn't properly convey the design.
> - Finally, remember that the UML (or any modeling language) is simply a tool to help you convey design. It is not a means unto itself. At the end of the day, you still need to produce code.

Modeling a Class Relationship

Classes do not exist in a vacuum. Instead, classes have complex relationships with one another. These relationships describe how classes interact with one another.

 A *relationship* describes how classes interact with one another. In the UML, a relationship is a connection between two or more notational elements.

The UML recognizes three high-level types of object relationships:

- Dependency
- Association
- Generalization

Although the UML may provide notation for each of these relationships, the relationships are not UML specific. Instead, the UML simply provides a mechanism and common vocabulary for describing the relationships. Understanding the relationships independently of the UML is valuable by itself in your study of OO. In fact, if you simply ignore the notation and understand the relationships, you'll be well ahead of the game.

Dependency

Dependency is the simplest interobject relationship. Dependency indicates that one object depends on another object's specification.

> **Note**   *Specification* is a fancy way of saying interface or behavior.

NEW TERM In a *dependency* relationship one object is dependent on another object's specification. If the specification changes you will need to update the dependent object.

Think back to the labs in Day 7. You can say that the PsychiatristObject depends on the MoodyObject for two reasons. First, the PsychiatristObject's examine() method takes a MoodyObject as argument. Secondly, the examine() method calls the MoodyObject's queryMood() method. If the name or argument list of the queryMood() method changes you will need to update how the PsychiatristObject calls the method. Likewise, if the name of the MoodyObject class changes, you'll have to update the examine() method's argument list.

Figure 8.8 illustrates the UML notation of the dependency relationship between PsychiatristObject and MoodyObject.

FIGURE 8.8

A simple dependency relationship.

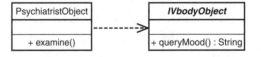

> **Note**   Take note of what Figure 8.8 does not tell you. The PsychiatristObject element does not contain every method found in the PsychiatristObject. The same holds true for MoodyObject. Instead, this dependency model only contains those features necessary to describe the dependency relationship.
>
> Remember, the UML notation is there to convey information. It is not there for you to try to use every modeling trick in the UML book!

Through OOP you always try to minimize dependencies as much as possible. However, it is impossible to remove all dependencies between your objects. Not all dependencies are created equal. Interface dependencies are generally okay, while dependencies to implementation are almost never acceptable.

> **Tip**   When do you model dependencies?
>
> You normally model dependencies when you want to show that one object uses another object. A common place where one object uses another is

through a method argument. For example, the `PsychiatristObject`'s `exam-ine()` method takes a `MoodyObject` as argument. You can say that the `PsychiatristObject` uses `MoodyObject`.

Association

Association relationships run a bit deeper than dependency relationships. Associations are structural relationships. An association indicates that one object contains—or is connected to—another object.

NEW TERM An *association* indicates that one object contains another object. In the UML terms, when in an association relationship one object is connected to another.

Because the objects are connected you can traverse from one object to another. Consider the association between a person and a bank as illustrated in Figure 8.9.

FIGURE 8.9

An association between a person and a bank.

Figure 8.9 shows that a Person *Borrows From* a Bank. In the UML notation every association has a name. In this case the association is named *Borrows From*. The arrow indicates the direction of the association.

NEW TERM The association *name* is a name that describes the relationship.

Each object in an association also has a role as indicated in Figure 8.10.

FIGURE 8.10

The roles in the association.

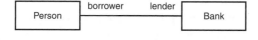

NEW TERM In the association the `Person`'s role is *borrower* and the `Bank`'s role is *lender*.

NEW TERM The association *role* is the part that an object plays in a relationship.

Finally, multiplicity indicates how many objects may take part in an association.

New Term The *multiplicity* indicates how many objects may take part in the instance of an association.

Figure 8.11 illustrates the multiplicity of the association between Person and Bank.

Figure 8.11
Multiplicity.

This notation tells us that a Bank may have 1 or more borrowers and that a Person may bank at 0 or more Banks.

> **Note**
>
> You specify your multiplicities through a single number, a list, or with an asterisk (*).
>
> A single number means that given number of objects—no more and no less—may participate in the association. So, for example, a 6 means that 6 objects and only 6 objects may participate in the association.
>
> * means that any number of objects may participate in the association.
>
> A list defines a range of objects that may participate in the association. For example, 1..4 states that 1 to 4 objects may participate in the association. 3..* indicates that 3 or more objects may participate.

> **Tip**
>
> When do you model associations?
>
> You should model associations when one object contains another object—the *has-a* relationship. You can also model an association when one object uses another. An association allows you to model who does what in a relationship.

The UML also defines two types of association: aggregation and composition. These two subtypes of association help you to further refine your models.

Aggregation

An aggregation is a special kind of association. An aggregation models a *has-a* (or *part-of* in UML speak) relationship among peers. Has-a means that one object contains another. *Peer* means that one object is no more important than the other.

 New Term A *whole/part* relationship describes the interobject relationship where one object contains another object.

NEW TERM An *aggregation* is a special type of association that models has-a of whole/part relationships among peers.

Importance, in the context of an aggregation, means that the objects can exist independently of one another. No one object is more important than the other in the relationship.

Consider the aggregation illustrated by Figure 8.12.

FIGURE 8.12

Aggregation between a Bank and its Customers.

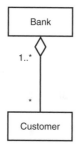

Here you see that a Bank may hold onto any number of Customer objects. The open diamond helps your model indicate which object is the whole and which is the part. Here the diamond tells you that the Bank is the whole. The Bank is the object that has-a in the relationship. The Bank holds onto Customers. In programming terms this might mean that the Bank contains an array of Customer objects.

Note

A clear diamond symbolizes aggregation. The diamond touches the object that is considered the *whole* of the relationship: the class that refers to the other class. The whole is made up of *parts*. In the previous example the Bank is the whole and the Customers are the parts.

Another example of aggregation is a car and its engine. A car has-an engine. In this aggregation the car is the whole and the part is the engine.

Because the Bank and Customer are independent they are peers. You can say that the Bank and the Customer objects are peers because the Customer objects can exist independently of the Bank object. This means that if the bank goes out of business the customers will not disappear with the bank. Instead, the customers can become another bank's customers. Likewise, a customer can withdraw his funds and the bank will carry on.

Aggregation among objects works the same as these real-life examples. One object may contain another independent object. The Queue or Vector is an example of an object that may hold onto other objects through aggregation.

Tip

When do you model aggregation?

You should model an aggregation when the point of your model is to describe the structure of a peer relationship. An aggregation explicitly states the structural whole/part relationship.

However, if you are more interested in modeling who does what in a relationship you are better off using a plain association: one without the diamond.

Composition

Composition is a bit more rigorous than aggregation. Composition is not a relationship among peers. The objects are not independent of one another.

Figure 8.13 illustrates a composition relationship.

FIGURE 8.13

Composition between a Bank and its Branches.

Here you see that a Bank may contain many Branches. The darkened diamond tells you that this is a composition relationship. The diamond also tells you who has-a. In this case, the Bank has-a, or holds onto, Branches.

Note

A blackened diamond symbolizes composition. The diamond touches the object that is considered the whole of the relationship. The whole is made up of parts. In the previous example the Bank is the whole and the Branches are the parts.

Because this is a composition relationship the Branches cannot exist independently of the Bank. Composition tells you that if the bank goes out of business, the branches will close as well. However, the converse is not necessarily true. If a branch closes, the bank may remain in business.

An object may participate in an aggregation and composition relationship at the same time. Figure 8.14 models such a relationship.

FIGURE 8.14

The Bank *in an aggregation and composition relationship at the same time.*

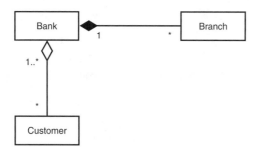

Tip

When do you model composition?

Like aggregation, you should model composition when the point of your model is to describe the structure of a relationship. A composition explicitly states the structural whole/part relationship.

Unlike aggregation, composition does not model peer whole/part relationships. Instead, the part is dependent on the whole. Going back to the Bank example, this means that when the bank goes out of business the branches go out of business.

In programming terms this means that when the Bank is destroyed, the Branches are destroyed as well.

Again, if the point of your model is to capture the roles of the objects in the association, you should use a plain association.

Note

Remember that aggregation and composition are simply refinements or subtypes of association. This means that you can model aggregation and composition relationships as a plain association. It all depends on what you are trying to model in your diagram.

Generalization

A generalization relationship is a relationship between the general and the specific. It is inheritance.

NEW TERM   A *generalization* relationship indicates a relationship between the general and the specific. If you have a generalization relationship you know that you can substitute a child class for the parent class.

Generalization embodies the *is-a* relationship that you first learned about in Day 4. As you learned in Day 4, is-a relationships allow you to define substitutability relationships.

Through substitutability relationships you can use descendants in place of their ancestors, or children in place of their parents.

The UML provides a notation for modeling generalization. Figure 8.15 illustrates how you would model the BankAccount inheritance hierarchy.

FIGURE 8.15

The BankAccount Inheritance Hierarchy.

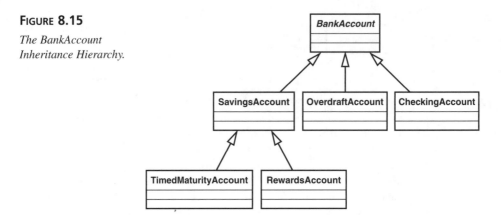

A solid line with a closed hollow arrow indicates a generalization relationship.

Putting It All Together

Now that you've seen basic class modeling and relationships you can begin to craft fairly expressive models. Figure 8.8 presented a simple example of dependency. Taking what you have learned throughout the day, you can make that model a bit more expressive. Figure 8.16 expands on the relationship modeled in Figure 8.8.

FIGURE 8.16

A more expressive dependency model.

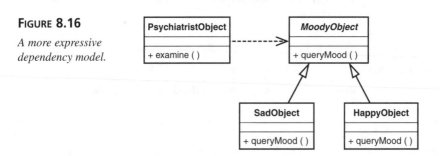

Figure 8.16 adds generalization so that you can see which objects you can substitute for the MoodyObject in this relationship.

Likewise, Figure 8.17 expands on the inheritance hierarchy presented in Figure 8.15.

FIGURE 8.17

A more detailed `BankAccount` *Inheritance Hierarchy.*

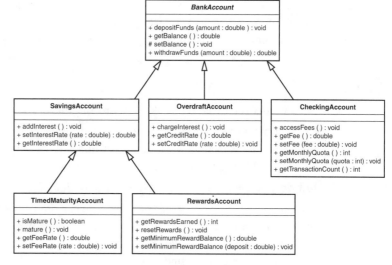

By looking at this model you can see exactly what each class adds to the hierarchy. Such a model could help other developers see what each class offers above and beyond its descendants.

All these models have one common element. Each model contains just enough information, just enough notation, to get the idea across. The point of these models is not to use every available notation.

All these models also combine different elements of the UML. Like a programming language, the UML allows you to combine its various pieces in unique ways. Through combining various elements you can create very expressive models.

Summary

Today you learned the basics of class and relationship modeling. After practicing today's exercises you should be able to begin drawing simple class models using the UML.

The UML provides notations for modeling classes as well as the relationships between objects. The UML provides notations to describe three types of relationships:

- Dependency
- Association
- Generalization

The UML also recognizes two association subtypes: aggregation and composition. By combining all of these elements you can generate expressive class diagrams. Your mastery of UML is important to documenting and conveying your designs to others.

Q&A

Q Can you mix the three types of relationships within the same model?

A Yes. Your model can illustrate any combination of the relationships outlined in this day. The model is there to describe the relationships between your classes. You should model the relationships between your classes.

Q How do you use the UML? Are there specific tools?

A You can use the UML however you want. You can draw your diagrams on a modeling tool, on a white board, or on a paper napkin. It really depends upon the situation. If you are having an interactive discussion about the a design, you'll probably want to use a white board since updating a computer can be distracting.

Computer modeling tools are best used when you want to formally document a design.

Workshop

The quiz questions and answers are provided for your further understanding. See Appendix A, "Answers," for the answers.

Quiz

1. What is the UML?

2. What is the difference between a methodology and a modeling language?

3. What type of relationship exists between Employee and Payroll in Lab 1 of Day 7?

4. Look carefully at the model in Figure 8.15. Using only the model, what can you say about the `MoodyObject`?

5. Look through the labs from Day 7. Find an example of a dependency.

6. In the UML, what do the following symbolize: +, #, -?

7. Day 2 presented the following interface:
```
public interface Queue {
    public void enqueue( Object obj );
    public Object dequeue();
    public boolean isEmpty();
    public Object peek();
}
```

What sort of relationship does a Queue have to the elements that it holds?

8. In Day 3, Lab 3, the Deck class creates a number of cards. What type of has-a relationship does this represent?

9. How do you illustrate that a class or method is abstract?

10. What is the end goal of modeling? What consequences does this goal have?

11. Explain association, aggregation, and composition.

12. Explain when you should use association, aggregation, and composition.

Exercises

1. Model the Queue class defined in question 7.

2. Model a honeybee/hive composition relationship.

3. Model the relationship between Bank and BankAccount from Lab 2, Day 7.

4. Model the association between a shopper and a merchant. Specify the roles, multiplicity, and dependency name.

5. Model the employee hierarchy from Lab 2 of Day 5. Through your model, convey what each class adds above and beyond its descendants.

6. Look back at Day 6. Model the PersonalityObject inheritance hierarchy.

DAY 9

Introduction to Object Oriented Analysis (OOA)

Yesterday you learned how to visualize your class designs through class models. You saw how class models can help other developers better understand your design by highlighting the different kinds of objects and relationships that they will find in your software. Modeling languages such as the UML give you and your fellow developers a common language in which to speak about design.

However, the question still remains; how do you design object oriented software? Models simply capture a snap shot of your design. Models do not help you understand your problems or formulate a solution. Instead, models are simply the end result of software design. How do you get there?

Over the course of the next two days you will learn about Object Oriented Analysis (OOA) and Object Oriented Design (OOD). OOA is an object-oriented approach to understanding a problem. You use OOA to help you get to the meat of the problem you wish to solve. After you understand your problem you can begin to design a solution. That's where OOD comes in. For the rest of today's lesson you will learn about OOA.

Today you will learn:

- About the software development process
- How OOA helps you to understand your software problems
- How to arrive at an understanding of your problem using Use Cases
- How to use the UML to visualize your analysis
- How to build your domain model
- What to do with everything you create during OOA

The Software Development Process

There are as many ways to develop software as there are developers. However, a software development team needs a unified approach to software development. Nothing will get done if each developer is off doing his own thing. Software methodologies define a common way to approach software development. A methodology will often contain a modeling language (such as the UML) and a process.

NEW TERM A *software process* lays out the various stages of software development.

A familiar example of a software process is the waterfall process.

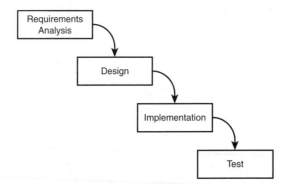

FIGURE 9.1

The waterfall process.

As Figure 9.1 illustrates the waterfall process is a sequential, one-way process. The process is made up of four discrete stages:

1. Requirements Analysis
2. Design
3. Implementation
4. Test

When you follow the waterfall process you go from one stage to the next. However, once you complete a stage there is no going back—just like falling down a waterfall or off a cliff! The waterfall process tries to avoid change by prohibiting change once a stage completes. Such an approach protects developers from constantly changing requirements. However, such a rigid process often results in software that isn't quite what you, or your customer, wants.

As you analyze a problem, design a solution, and begin implementation your understanding of the problem continually deepens. Better understanding of your problem may very well invalidate earlier analysis or design. Requirements may even change while you develop (maybe a competitor has added a new feature to its product). Unfortunately, the waterfall process cannot cope with the reality of modern software development—constantly changing requirements.

Although this book doesn't try to force any specific methodology on you, there is one process that has proven very effective for object-oriented development: the iterative process. This book forces this process on you!

The Iterative Process

The iterative process is the complete opposite of the waterfall process. The iterative process allows change at any point in the development process. The iterative process allows change by taking an iterative and incremental approach to software development.

NEW TERM   An *iterative process* is an *iterative* and *incremental* approach to software development. Another way to think about the process is as an "evolutionary" approach. Each iteration gradually perfects and elaborates a core product into a mature product.

An Iterative Approach

Unlike the waterfall process, the iterative process allows you to continually go back and refine each stage of development. For example, if you discover that the design just does not work while performing implementation, you can go back and perform additional design and even analysis. It is this continual refinement that makes the process iterative. Figure 9.2 illustrates the approach.

An Incremental Approach

When following an iterative process, you don't simply complete one large iteration that builds the entire program. Instead, the iterative process breaks the development effort into a number of small iterations. Figure 9.3 illustrates this incremental approach.

FIGURE **9.2**

An iteration.

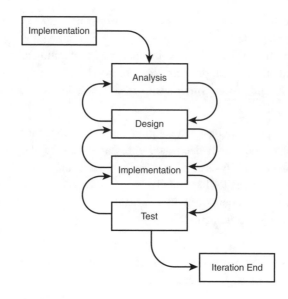

FIGURE **9.3**

The iterative process.

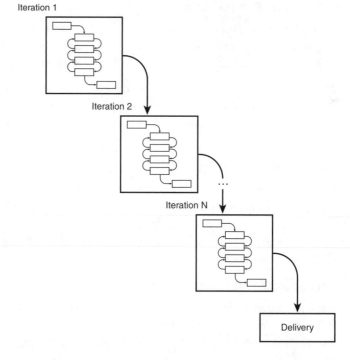

Each iteration of the process introduces a small, incremental, improvement to the program. This improvement might be a new feature or a refinement of an existing feature.

Either way, the iteration has a specific purpose and at the end of the iteration you have a noticeable improvement in functionality.

Imagine that you are creating an MP3 player. During one iteration of the project you might finish the component that plays an MP3 file. To determine that the player works you might hardcode the it to open and play a specific music file. In the next iteration you can add the capability to choose which file to play. At each iteration you have measurable progress. At the end of the first iteration you can hear the component play a song. At the end of the next iteration you have a mechanism that allows you to dynamically choose a song to play.

By following an iterative approach you get to constantly see progress. On the other hand, if you try to do everything at once it can be difficult to see any measurable form of progress. Instead, the project will seem constantly mired in one place—there are never any results. If a project never moves forward morale will slip and it will become difficult to determine what needs to be done next. Low morale and confusion about what to do next will fragment and kill a project.

Caution

> Iterative processes need to be carefully monitored to make sure that they are not simply reduced to "hacking" out a solution. OOA and OOD provide such a sanity check.

Constant progress gives you constant feedback. You can use this feedback as a way to be sure that you are on the right track. If you try to complete the entire project at once, you won't know whether you've created the right solution until you're done. Going back and fixing something that wasn't done right is much more expensive if you have to go back and rewrite the whole program! Iteration, on the other hand, makes going back and fixing something much cheaper. Because you receive constant feedback you are more likely to catch a problem sooner than later. If you catch your problems sooner, it is easier to redo an iteration or two to fix it. It's always more desirable to rewrite an iteration than to rewrite an entire program! If you keep your iterations small, you will not lose too much time if you have to throw a few of them out.

Caution

> If a problem reaches all the way back to the foundation of the original iteration, an iterative approach may not save you. Such a fundamental problem may be too expensive to fix and may damage product quality.

A High-Level Methodology

This book presents an informal object-oriented development methodology. The methodology picks and chooses those techniques that have proven themselves successful from other methodologies. The methodology consists of an iterative process in which an iteration has four stages:

- Analysis
- Design
- Implementation
- Test

 Note

> After the test stage, you may also have release and maintenance stages. These are important stages in the life cycle of a software project. However, for the purposes of today's lesson, these stages are omitted.
>
> Today you will focus on analysis, design, implementation, and test.

"Real" methodologies often enumerate additional stages. However, when you're first learning, these four stages are the ones that matter most. For that reason this book concentrates on these four stages. The remainder of this day covers Object Oriented Analysis.

Object Oriented Analysis (OOA)

Object Oriented Analysis (OOA) is the process that you go through to understand the problem that you are trying to solve. After you complete analysis, you should understand the requirements of the problem as well as the problem domain's vocabulary.

NEW TERM *Object Oriented Analysis* is a process that uses an object-oriented approach to help you understand the problem that you are trying to solve. At the end of analysis you should understand the problem domain and it's requirements in terms of classes and object interactions.

To design a solution to a problem you need to understand how the users will use the system. The answer to this question is the system's requirements. The requirements tell you what the users want to do to the system and what kind of responses they expect back.

NEW TERM *System* is the OOA term for a set of interacting objects. You can say that these objects make up a system or model of the problem.

These objects are instances of classes that are derived from concrete or abstract objects in the problem domain under study.

Analysis also helps you become familiar with the problem domain. By studying the domain you begin to identify the objects that you need to properly model the system.

OOA, as the name suggests, is an object-oriented approach to requirements analysis. OOA takes an OO-based approach by modeling the problem through objects and their interactions. There are two main models. The use case model describes how a user interacts with the system. The Domain model captures the main vocabulary of the system. Using the domain model you begin to identify those objects that belong in your system. A properly constructed domain model can solve many problems in the same domain.

Using Use Cases to Discover System Use

When setting out to analyze a problem you first need to understand how your users will use, or interact, with the system. These uses comprise the system's requirements and dictate the system that you create. By fulfilling your users' requirements you produce a useful system.

NEW TERM The *requirements* are those features that the system must have to solve a given problem.

NEW TERM One way of discovering these uses is through *use case analysis*. Through use case analysis you will define a number of use cases. A use case describes how a user will interact with the system.

NEW TERM *Use case analysis* is the process of discovering *use cases* through the creation of scenarios and stories with the potential or existing users of a system.

NEW TERM A *use case* describes the interaction between the user of the system and the system—how the user will use the system from the user's point of view.

Creating use cases is an iterative process. There are a number of steps that you must take during each iteration to formalize your use cases. To define your use cases you must

1. Identify the actors.
2. Create a preliminary list of use cases.
3. Refine and name the use cases.
4. Define each use case's sequence of events.
5. Model your use cases.

Note

You do not create use cases in a vacuum! While deriving your use cases you must consult those who will use the system—your customers. Customer input is absolutely critical to discovering the use cases (unless you are writing the software for yourself).

Your customers are the domain experts. They know their business space well and know what they need in their software. Always be sure to tap their knowledge and use it to drive your software requirements.

Getting the users to make up stories about their ideal day of interacting with the system can be a good way to break the ice on this activity.

Caution

Before you continue with the day it is important to point out that the examples do not attempt to perform a complete analysis of an online Web site. Instead, the examples teach the steps that you will take while performing an actual analysis. So, many use cases will be left out.

Next week you will work through a complete object-oriented analysis.

Identify the Actors

The first step in defining your use cases is to define the actors that will use the system.

NEW TERM   An *actor* is anything that interacts with the system. It can be a human user, another computer system, or a chimp.

You need to ask your customers to describe the users of the system. Questions might include the following:

- Who will primarily use the system?
- Are there any other systems that will use the system? For example, are there any nonhuman users?
- Will the system communicate with any other system? For example, is there an existing database that you need to integrate?
- Does the system respond to nonuser-generated stimulus? For example, does the system need to do something on a certain calendar day each month? A stimulus can come from sources not normally considered when thinking from a purely user point of view.

Consider an online Web store. An online store allows guest users to browse the product catalog, price items, and request further information. The store also allows registered users to purchase items, as well as track their order and maintain user information.

From this brief description you can identify two actors: guest users and registered users. These two actors each interact with the system.

Figure 9.4 illustrates the UML notation for an actor: a stick figure with a name. You should give each of your actors an unambiguous name.

FIGURE 9.4

The UML actors.

Guest User

Registered User

9

Caution	It is important to avoid confusion while naming your actors. Give each actor a name that uniquely identifies and distinguishes the actor.
	Good naming is critical. Names should be simple and easy to remember.

It is important to note that a given user of the system may take on the role of many different actors. An actor is a role. For example, a user might enter the site as a guest but later on log in as a registered guest so that he can make a purchase.

Note	A user may take on many different *roles* while interacting with a system. An actor describes a *role* that the user may take on while interacting with the system.

Caution	When you first set out to define your use cases, create a preliminary list of actors. Don't get mired while identifying the actors. It will be difficult to find all the actors the first time through.
	Instead, find enough actors to get started and add the others as you discover them.

Actors are the instigators of use cases. Now that you've identified some actors, you can start defining what use cases they perform.

Create a Preliminary List of Use Cases

To define your use cases you need to ask a few questions. Start with your list of known actors. You need to ask what each actor does to the system.

In the case of the online Web store you have registered users and guest users. What does each of these actors do?

Guest users can do the following:

1. Browse the product catalog
2. Search the product catalog
3. Search for a specific item
4. Search the site
5. Add items to a shopping cart and specify the quantity
6. Price the selected items
7. Change the quantity of items in their cart
8. View the popular and new products list
9. Browse other users' wish lists
10. Request further product information

Registered users can do the following:

1. Everything the guest user can do
2. Make a purchase
3. Add items to their wish list
4. View a personalized recommended list
5. Maintain their account
6. Sign up for notifications
7. Take advantage of personalized special offers
8. Track their orders
9. Sign up for various mailing lists
10. Cancel an order

Note

There probably are quite a few more use cases. However, for your purposes here, and for the sake of brevity, this gives you a good start.

Whenever you try to identify use cases you should also ask the question, "How does an actor change its role?"

In the case of the online store, a guest user can become a registered user in these ways:

- The guest user can log into the site.
- The guest user can register with the site.

A registered user becomes a guest user as follows:

- A registered user can log out of the site.

So far, these questions are interaction oriented. You can also take a results-oriented approach to the discovery. For example, you can say that a registered user receives a notification. A second point of view can help you discover use cases that you might have missed if you simply stuck with the first viewpoint.

Finally, consider the various entities that the users manipulate. Here you see products, account information, and various product lists and discounts. How do all these entities get into the system? Who adds new products and edits or deletes old ones?

This system will need a third actor, the administrator. Going through the process that you went through above, you might find that administrators can do the following:

1. Add, edit, and delete products
2. Add, edit, and delete incentives
3. Update account information

Questions may lead to other questions. For example, who updates the popular product list? Who sends out notifications and mailings to the mailing lists? A fourth actor, the system itself, performs all these actions.

Refine and Name the Use Cases

Now that you have a preliminary list of use cases you need to refine the list. In particular, you'll want to look for opportunities to split or combine the use cases.

Splitting Use Cases

Each use case should accomplish one main goal. When you find a use case that's doing too much, you'll want to split it up into two or more use cases. Consider the following use case:

Guest users can add items to a shopping cart and specify the quantity.

You should really split this use case into two use cases:

- Guest users can add items to a shopping cart.
- Guest users can specify an item's quantity.

You can get away with splitting use cases because of the way they can relate to one another. Use cases are a lot like classes. One use case can contain another. So if one use case instance requires another to gets its job done, it can use it.

A use case can also extend the behavior of another use case. As a result, you can place common behavior into one use case and then develop other use cases that specialize on the original. Take "Registered users can make a purchase" as an example. A use case may specialize on order by creating a gift order use case. A gift order might ship without a receipt.

Combining Use Cases

You do not want redundant use cases. One way to avoid redundancy is to keep an eye out for use case variants. When you find them, you should combine the variants into one use case.

NEW TERM   A use case *variant* is a specialized version of another more general, use case.

Consider the following two use cases:

- Guest users can search the product catalog.
- Guest users can search for a specific item.

Here, the second is simply a variant of the more general first use case.

In this case, the use case only differs by the search parameters. It is better to simply have one use case and document the variant in the use case models that you will build later.

A variant is much like an instance of a class. Think back to the `BankAccount` example. A `BankAccount` with a $10,000 balance may have more money that a `BankAccount` with $100. However, both are still `BankAccounts`. All that differentiates one `BankAccount` from another is the value of its attributes. Use cases work much the same way.

The Resulting Use Cases

After you finish refining your use cases you should name each use case. Just as naming actors, you should strive to name your use cases in a way that avoids confusion.

Here are the resulting use cases for guest users and registered users after splitting and combining:

1. Browse the Product Catalog
2. Search the Product Catalog
3. Search the Site
4. Add Item to the Shopping Cart
5. Price the Items
6. Change the Item Quantity
7. View the Highlighted Products List
8. Browse a Wish List
9. Request Product Information
10. Order
11. Maintain Order
12. Add Items to Wish List
13. Update Account
14. Sign Up for Correspondence
15. Apply Incentives
16. Login
17. Logout
18. Register

At this point you have a fairly well-developed list of use cases. Now all you need to do is fully specify each use case.

Define Each Use Case's Sequence of Events

The brief list of use cases only tells part of the story. Internally, a lot more might be going on within a use case. Take Order for example. A user cannot place an order in one step. Instead, the user must take a sequence of steps to successfully complete an order (such as providing a payment method).

The sequence of steps that a user takes to complete a use case is known as a *scenario*. A use case is made up of a number of scenarios.

New Term　　A *scenario* is a sequence or flow of events between the user and system.

As part of your use case analysis you must specify each use cases' scenarios.

Let's develop the Order use case. First, begin by describing the use case in a paragraph:

The registered user proceeds to the checkout to purchase the items in his shopping cart. Once at the checkout page, the user provides shipping information. Once provided, the system totals and displays the order. If everything is correct the customer can choose to continue with the order. Once the user continues with the order the system queries the user for payment information. Once supplied, the system authorizes payment. It then displays a final order conformation page for the user's records and sends a confirmation e-mail.

There are a few interesting aspects to this use case. First, it says nothing about the underlying implementation. Second, you can use it to identify the use case's preconditions and post conditions.

NEW TERM *Preconditions* are those conditions that must be met for a use case to begin. *Post conditions* are the results of a use case.

Note

One of the problems with this type of system is that you are probably not gathering use cases from the users of the system, but from the people who want you to write it. Keep in mind that modern Web applications and other customer-facing apps like kiosks may require you to go out and work with focus groups.

Here the precondition is that the user has already placed items in the cart. The Order use case orders the items in the cart. The post condition is an order. After completing the use case the system will contain an order for the user.

At this point it helps to consider any alternative paths in the order use case. Perhaps payment authorization will fail or the user will decide to cancel the order before completion. You need to capture these alternate paths.

After you feel comfortable with the use case you should write it out formally. One way to write out the use case is to list the steps sequentially. After the steps you should list the preconditions, post conditions, and alternate paths. Consider the Order use case again:

- Order
    1. Registered user proceeds to the checkout
    2. Registered user provides shipping information
    3. System displays the order total

9

4. Registered user provides payment information

5. System authorizes payment

6. System confirms the order

7. System sends a confirmation e-mail

- Preconditions
  - A nonempty shopping cart
- Post Conditions
  - An order in the system
- Alternative: Cancel Order

During Steps 1–4 the user chooses to cancel the order. The user is returned to the homepage.

- Alternative: Authorization Failed

At Step 5 the system fails to authorize the payment information. The user can re-enter the information or cancel the order.

You will need to complete the same process for each use case. Formally defining the scenarios helps you to see the flow of events in the system as well as solidify your understanding of the system.

Tip

When writing out your use cases only include the information that makes sense. Just as in class modeling, your purpose is to convey some kind of information. Only include the information to convey what you are trying to get across.

Only include the preconditions necessary for the use case to begin. Don't include extra, unnecessary information.

Be sure to check out other texts on use cases. There are many ways to write out a use case (there is no standard).

When first writing your use cases consider using an index card with pencil. This way you don't have to be in front of a computer while generating your initial use cases. Depending on who your customers are, it may be difficult to work with them in front of a computer.

Use-Case Diagrams

Just as the UML provides a way to document and convey class design, there are also formal ways to capture your use cases. Of special interest are use case diagrams, interaction diagrams, and activity diagrams. Each helps visualize the various use cases.

Use case diagrams model the relationships between use cases and the relationships between use cases and actors. Although a use case's textual description may help you to understand an isolated use case, a diagram helps you to see how use cases interrelate to one another.

Figure 9.4 shows you how to model actors. Figure 9.5 illustrates the UML notation for a use case: a labeled oval.

FIGURE 9.5

The UML use case.

Put an actor and a use case together in the same diagram and you are left with a use case diagram. Figure 9.6 diagrams the Order use case.

FIGURE 9.6

The Order use case.

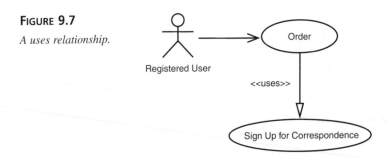

This diagram is fairly simple, however by looking at it you can see that the Registered User performs the Order use case.

Diagrams can be a bit more complicated. The diagram can also show the relationships that exist among use cases themselves. As you've read, one use case may contain and use another. Figure 9.7 illustrates such a relationship.

FIGURE 9.7

A uses relationship.

Here you see that the Register use case uses the Sign Up for Correspondence use case. As part of the registration process the user may elect to receive e-mails and notifications.

Figure 9.8 illustrates the second type of relationship, the *extends* relationship.

FIGURE **9.8**

*An extends
relationship.*

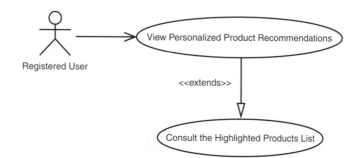

View Personalized Product Recommendations extends the generic View The Highlighted Products List by presenting the registered user with a list of products customized to his shopping preferences. The normal View the Highlighted Products List as seen by a Guest User may simply show the best selling or most requested items. This extension presents the user with products in which his profile suggest he might be interested.

Just like classes it is possible to have an abstract use case. An abstract use case is a use case that other use cases use or extend, but is never directly used by an actor itself. Abstractions are normally discovered after you've done your initial use case analysis. As you study your use cases you may find ways to extract commonality and place them into abstract use cases.

Interaction Diagrams

Use case diagrams help model the relationships between use cases. Interaction diagrams help capture the interactions between the various actors participating in the system.

Let's expand on the use cases that you saw earlier. Let's add a new actor, the Customer Service Representative. Too often, a Registered User may forget his password. The Customer Service Representative is there to help the user regain access to his account. Let's create a new use case, Forgot Password:

> A Registered User calls up the Customer Service Representative and informs the rep that he has lost his password. The Customer Service Representative takes the users full name and pulls up the user's account information. The Customer Service Representative then asks the Registered User a number of questions to establish his identity. After passing a number of challenges, the Customer Service Representative deletes the old password and creates a new one. The user is then e-mailed the new password.

This use case can also be described as follows:

- Forgot Password

    1. Registered user calls the Customer Service Representative

    2. Registered user provides full name

    3. The Customer Service Representative retrieves the customer's information

    4. Registered user answers a number of identifying questions

    5. The Customer Service Representative creates a new password

    6. The user receives the new password by e-mail

- Preconditions

    - The user forgot his password

- Post Conditions

    - A new password is emailed to the user

- Alternative: Identification Failed

    The user may fail to answer the identifying questions in Step 4 correctly. If so, the call terminates.

- Alternative: User Not Found

    At Step 2 the name provided may not be the name of a known user. If so the Customer Service Representative offers to register the caller.

There are two types of interaction diagrams: sequence diagrams and collaboration diagrams. Let's explore each.

Sequence Diagrams

A sequence diagram models the interactions between the Registered User, the Customer Service Representative, and the Web site over time. You should use sequence diagrams when you want to bring attention to the sequence of events of a use case over time. Figure 9.9 presents a sequence diagram for the Forgot Password use case.

As you can see from the illustration, a sequence diagram represents the events between each actor and the system (the Web site). Each participant in the use case is represented at the top of the diagram as either a box or a stick figure (but you can call both a box).

A dashed line known as a *life line* descends from each box. The lifeline represents the box's lifetime during the use case. So if one of the actors goes away during the use case, the line would terminate at the last arrow that either ends or originates from the actor. When an actor leaves a use case you can say that its lifetime has ended.

FIGURE 9.9

The Forgot Password sequence diagram.

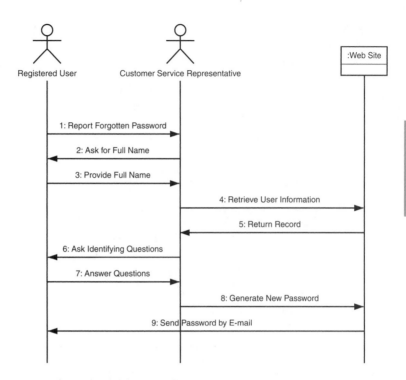

9

A *life line* is a dashed line that descends from a box in a sequence diagram. The life line represents the lifetime of the object represented by the box.

> **NEW TERM**

Arrows originate from the life line to indicate that the actor has sent a message to another actor or to the system. As you move down the life line, you can see the messages as they originate sequentially over time. Time moves from top to bottom in a sequence diagram. So by moving up the life line you can play the sequence of events backward.

Collaboration Diagrams

You should use sequence diagrams if it is your intention to focus attention on the sequence of events over time. If you would rather model the relationships between the actors and the system you should create a collaboration diagram.

Figure 9.10 models the Forgot Password use case as a collaboration diagram.

In a collaboration diagram you model an interaction by connecting the participants with a line. Above the line you label each event that the entities' generate along with the event's direction (who it is directed to). It also helps to number the events so that you know in which order they come.

FIGURE 9.10

*The Forgot Password
collaboration diagram.*

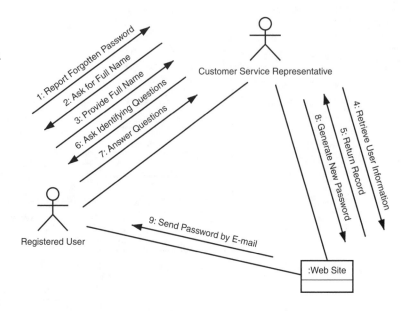

Tip

> Use sequence diagrams to model the sequence of events in a scenario over time.
>
> Use collaboration diagrams to model the relationships between the actors in a scenario.

Activity Diagrams

Interaction diagrams model sequential actions well. However, they cannot model processes that can run in parallel. Activity diagrams help you to model processes that can run in parallel with one another.

Consider another use case Search. Search searches both the Web site and the product catalog at the same time using the Search the Product Catalog use case and the Search the Site use case. There is no reason that these two searches cannot run at the same time. The user would get impatient if he had to wait for the searches to complete sequentially.

Figure 9.11 models these processes through an activity diagram.

An oval represents each state of the process. The thick black bar represents a point where the processes must synchronize—or meet up—before the flow of execution can resume. Here you see that the two searches run in parallel and then meet up before the site can display the results.

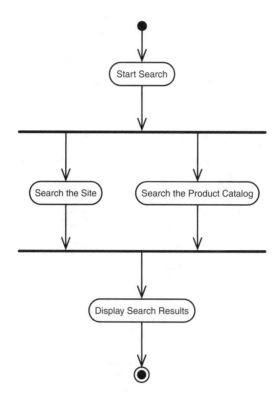

FIGURE 9.11

The Search Activity diagram.

9

We'll take a closer look at interaction diagrams and activity diagrams in the coming days. However, they both prove useful while analyzing a system.

Building the Domain Model

Through use case analysis you capture the system interactions. However, use cases also help you to capture the vocabulary of the system. This vocabulary makes up the problem domain. The domain's vocabulary identifies the main objects in the system.

The domain model lists those objects that you need to properly model the system. Take the online store. Through the use cases you can identify quite a few objects. Figure 9.12 visualizes some of those objects.

At this point you can model the relationships between the domain objects. Figure 9.13 summarizes some of those relationships.

FIGURE 9.12

The domain objects.

FIGURE 9.13

*The domain objects'
relationships.*

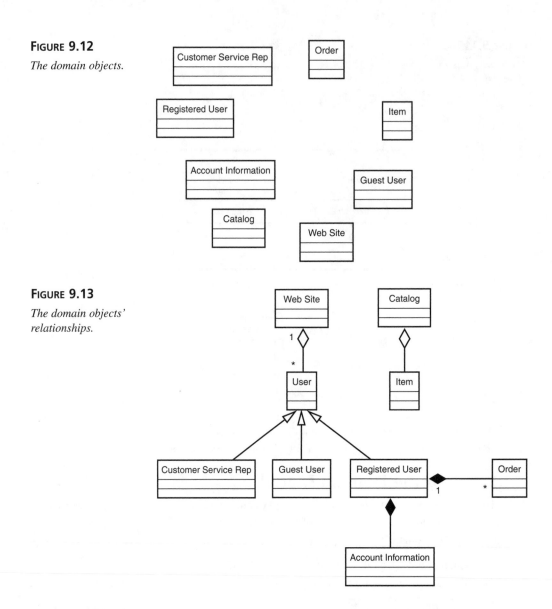

The domain model is important for a number of reasons. First, the domain model models
your problem independently from any implementation concerns. Instead, it models the
system at a conceptual level. This independence gives you the flexibility to use the
domain model that you build to solve many different problems within the domain.

Second, the domain model builds the foundation of the object model that will eventually
become your system. The final implementation may add new classes and remove others.
However, the domain gives you something to start and build your design from—a skeleton.

Finally, a well-defined domain model clearly establishes a common vocabulary for your problem. By finding a common vocabulary everyone involved in the project can approach it from an equal footing and understanding.

So Now What?

You've collected use cases. You've created interaction diagrams. You've even begun a domain model. What's next?

Use cases have three main uses. The first use deals with functionality. The use cases tell you how the system will function. The use cases tell you who will use the system, what those users will do to it, and what the users expect back from the system. Use case analysis helps you learn about the system that you intend to build.

Second, use cases provide a list of "to-do" tasks as you develop the system. You can start by prioritizing each use case and provide an estimate of how long each will take to complete. You can then plan your development timeline around the use cases. Completing a use case can become a milestone. Use cases can also become bargaining chips. Often, time constraints will force you to sacrifice one use case for another.

Finally, use cases help you build your domain model. The domain model will serve as the skeleton of your fledgling system. (And if you've done it right, you might be able to reuse that model elsewhere!)

Once you feel that the domain model and use case analysis is nearly complete you can begin to prototype different parts of the system. However, don't prototype everything. You should only prototype those aspects of the system that seem confusing or risky. Prototyping can deepen knowledge as well as find out if an idea is even possible, thus identifying and reducing risk.

Tip

Tips to effective OOA
- Avoid analysis paralysis. Analysis paralysis sets in whenever you try to perform the perfect analysis. You never move forward because you keep trying to perfectly understand the problem. Sometimes full understanding is not possible without some design and implementation.
- Iterate. Iterate everything. When you first start analysis generate a preliminary list of use cases. Prioritize the use cases and then flesh them out through iterations. Each iteration should encompass a certain amount of analysis, design, and implementation. The amount of implementation will increase as the project moves along: very little in the beginning, much more during later stages.

- Include the domain experts in your analysis—even if the expert is a customer. Unless you are an expert in the domain you will need the input to properly model the system.
- Don't introduce implementation into your analysis. Don't let implementation sneak into your analysis.

Summary

Object-oriented analysis applies objects to the process of problem analysis. OOA helps you uncover the requirements of the system that you intend to build.

Use cases help you identify how the users will interact with the system. The use cases describe the interaction, as well as what the users expect back from the system.

Models such as interaction diagrams and activity diagrams help visualize these interactions. Each type of model views the system from a slightly different vantage point. So you'll need to keep the differences in mind and use each kind when appropriate.

Use cases help you define your domain model. The domain model serves as the skeleton of the system that you eventually build. The domain model has the advantage of being free from any specific implementation or use. As a result, you can apply your domain model to many different problems.

It is important to realize that OOA is truly an object-oriented way of viewing a problem. Use cases are nothing more than objects. A use case can relate to other use cases through use or generalization. Variants of use cases are no different than the difference between class instances. Actors are objects as well.

OOA deconstructs a problem into a number of use cases and domain objects. Once broken down, you can iterate your way to a final solution.

Q&A

Q What happens if you miss a use case?

A If you find that you have missed a use case go back and add it. If you need the use case right away, you should add it right away. If it can wait, make a note and explore it during the next iteration.

Q When elaborating a use case do you always need to do sequence, collaboration, and activity diagrams?

A No. You do not always need to do all three. Do whatever is necessary to help your understanding of the use case.

However, you should probably at least sketch out one of the diagrams. You never know what problems or unknowns that you might discover.

Normally, I always do at least a sequence diagram unless it makes more sense to start with one of the others.

Q How do you know when you have enough use cases?

A Really, you never know if you've found all of the use cases. Knowing when to stop comes with experience. However, you probably have enough use cases when you feel that you have an adequate understanding of the problem and that you feel confident that you can move on.

If you miss a use case you can always go back and add it to your analysis. However, you must be ware of over analyzing a problem. Don't succumb to analysis paralysis.

9

Workshop

The quiz questions and answers are provided for your further understanding. See Appendix A, "Answers," for the answers.

Quiz

1. What is a software process?

2. What is an iterative process?

3. At the end of OOA, what should you have accomplished?

4. What do the system requirements tell you?

5. What is a use case?

6. What steps must you take to define your use cases?

7. What is an actor?

8. What are some questions that you can ask to discover the actors?

9. How can use cases relate to one another?

10. What is a use case variant?

11. What is a scenario?

12. What are some ways that you can model your use cases?

13. Describe the differences between the various models used to visualize use cases.

14. What good is a domain model?

15. What good are use cases?

Exercises

1. What other use cases might you add to the list of use cases for the online store?

2. Take one of the use cases from Question 1 and develop it.

3. A use case variant is a specific case of a more general use case. What variants can you identify in the guest user and registered user use cases.

4. What other domain objects can you find?

Introduction to Object Oriented Design (OOD)

Yesterday, you saw how Object Oriented Analysis (OOA) helps you to understand a problem and its requirements. Through the analysis of use cases and the construction of a domain model you can capture the "real-world" or domain level details of your problem. However, OOA is only part of the overall development story.

Object Oriented Design (OOD) helps you to take the domain that you found in OOA and design a solution. While the OOA process helped you to discover many of the problem's domain objects, OOD helps you to discover and design the objects that will appear in the problem's specific solution.

Today you will learn

- How to transform your analysis into a solution
- How to identify and design the objects that will appear in your solution
- How Class Responsibility Collaboration (CRC) cards can help you to discover object responsibilities and relationships
- How you can use the UML to capture your design

Object Oriented Design (OOD)

NEW TERM   *OOD* is the process of constructing a solution's object model. Said another way, OOD is the process of breaking down a solution into a number of constituent objects.

NEW TERM   The *object model* is the design of the objects that appear in a problem's solution. The final object model may contain many objects not found in the domain. The object model will describe the various object's responsibilities, relationships, and structure.

The OOD process helps you to figure out how you will implement the analysis that you completed during OOA. Mainly, the object model will contain the main classes in the design, their responsibilities, and a definition of how they will interact and get their information.

Think of OOD in terms of building a single-family home. Before you build the home of your dreams, you decide what kinds of rooms that you want in your house. Through your analysis you might find that you want a home that has a kitchen, two bedrooms, two and a half bathrooms, a living room, and a dining room. You might also need a den, a two-car garage, and a Jacuzzi. All of the rooms and the Jacuzzi comprise the idea and design of your home.

What do you do next? Does a builder just start building? No. First, an architect figures out how the rooms best fit together, how the wiring should be run, and what beams are necessary to hold the house up. Then the architect prepares a set of detailed blueprints that capture the design. The builder then uses those blueprints as a guide while constructing the house.

Using the terms of the construction world, you use OOD to create your program's blueprints.

A formal design process helps you to determine what objects will appear in your program, and how they will interact or fit together. The design will tell you the structure of your objects, and a design process will help you discover many of the design issues that you will encounter while coding.

When working as part of a team, it is important to identify and solve as many design issues as possible before you begin construction. By solving problems up front, everyone will work under the same set of assumptions. A consistent approach to the design will make it easier to put all components together later. Without a clear design, each developer will make his own set of, assumptions, often incompatible with other sets of assumptions. Work will be duplicated, and the proper balance of responsibility between the objects will break down. All in all, the design that emerges could easily become a muddled mess if everyone isn't on the same page.

In addition, mistakes are exponentially more expensive to fix, the later in the development sequence they are discovered. Errors in design are very low cost to fix.

While designing your solution, you will find that there is often more than one solution to the problem. OOD allows you to explore each interesting solution and decide upfront what path to follow. Through design you can make well-informed decisions, and through your documentation you can document why you decided upon the choices that you made.

The object model identifies the significant objects that appear in the solution; however, the object model is a superset of the domain. While many of the objects that appear in the domain model will find their way into the design, many objects not found in the domain will also appear. Likewise, objects not found in the analysis may find their way into the design, just as wiring does not appear in the initial analysis of a new home. Once you have your design, you can begin coding.

With that being said, don't take design to the extreme. Just as OOA can suffer from *analysis paralysis*, OOD can suffer from *design paralysis*.

You should avoid over-designing your solution. It's simply not possible to foresee every design decision you will need to make before you make it, and some design can be left until construction. You don't want to get caught up trying to create the perfect design; you need to start coding at some time. What you need to do is design the architecturally significant aspects of the system.

How do you know what aspects of your system are *architecturally significant*? The significant pieces are those aspects of the system where a different decision would completely alter the structure or behavior of the system.

Think back to the online store and the shopping cart discussed yesterday. Knowing that you have a shopping cart object in your analysis, you need to design what specific abstractions will be used to represent the shopping cart—such as a pricer, a persistent store, and an expiration monitor. But you don't need to design whether a hash table or vector will be used to represent the cart contents—that is an appropriate subject for a detailed (implementation) design phase, but is too detailed for this phase.

How Do You Apply OOD?

OOD is an iterative process that identifies the objects and their responsibilities in your system, and how these objects relate. You continually refine the object model as you iterate through the design process. Each iteration should give you a deeper insight into the design and perhaps even the domain itself.

As you learn more about the problem that you are trying to solve during design, you may need to apply additional analysis. Remember, there's no shame in going back and refining your analysis! The only shame is in creating useless software.

There are a number of loosely defined steps that you can follow to build your object model. Normally you will

1. Generate an initial list of objects.

2. Refine your objects' responsibilities.

3. Develop the points of interaction.

4. Detail the relationships between objects.

5. Build your model.

Your understanding of the design will increase as you complete these steps and repeat the process.

There are many ways to complete OOD. The steps outlined above make up an informal process that combines aspects from many different methodologies.

The actual methodology that you follow will depend on experience, the domain, company edict, and good taste. By the end of OOD, you should have decomposed the solution into a number of objects. How you get to those objects is up to you and your design team.

Step 1: Generate an Initial List of Objects

When you start designing your system, you need to start with the domain that you defined during analysis. Each domain object and each actor should become a class in your fledgling object model. You will find that some of the domain objects will not find their way into your final object model; however, at this point you can't be sure which will go, so you need to include all of them.

Think back to the online store of Day 9, "Introduction to Object Oriented Analysis (OOA)." Figure 10.1 illustrates the core classes that will appear in your early object model.

FIGURE 10.1

The core online store classes.

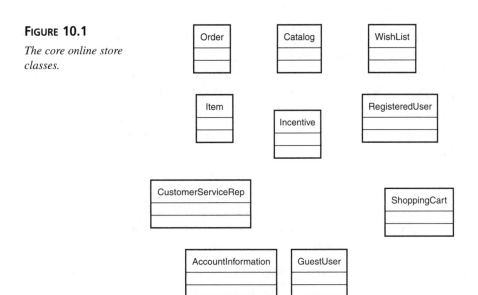

When searching for the initial list of classes, you'll also want to consider any events that may affect your system. Each of these events should appear initially as a class. The same holds true for any reports, displays, and devices. All of these elements should translate into a class.

> **Tip**
>
> Here are a few tips for flushing out that initial list of classes:
> - Turn each actor into a class.
> - Turn each domain object into a class.
> - Turn any event into a class.
> - Consider how the system will display information, and turn each display into an object.
> - Represent any third party systems or devices that the system interacts with as classes.

At this point you cannot say too much about the classes that you've listed. You might have a general idea of the objects' responsibilities and relationships; however, you need to do a little more digging before you can finalize your understanding of the new classes.

Step 2: Refine Your Objects' Responsibilities

A list of objects is a good start, but it's only a small part of your overall design. A complete design will capture each object's responsibilities as well as the object's structure and relationships. A design will show how everything fits together.

To work towards this understanding you need to identify what each object does. There are two aspects that you need to explore so you can answer the question, "What does the object do?"

You first need to explore responsibility. Through encapsulation you know that each object should have a small number of responsibilities. During design you need to identify each object's responsibilities and break the object up when it starts doing too much. You also need to make sure that each responsibility only appears once, and that knowledge is evenly spread among all of the objects.

Next, you need to explore how each object gets its work done. Objects will often delegate work to other objects. Through your design you need to identify these collaborations.

 An *object* delegates work to *collaborators*.

 Collaboration is the relationship where objects interact in order to accomplish some purpose.

A deep understanding of an object's relationships and responsibilities is important. On a practical level, responsibilities will translate into methods. Relationships will translate into structure; however, an overall understanding of responsibility will help you effectively divide responsibility among the objects. You need to avoid having a small set of large objects. Through design you'll be sure to spread out responsibilities.

What Are CRC Cards?

One way to flesh out responsibilities and collaborations is through the use of CRC (Class Responsibility Collaboration) cards. As the name suggests, a CRC card is nothing more than a lined 4×6 index card.

When you first start the design, it is difficult to simply start listing methods and attributes. Instead, you need to start by identifying each object's purpose.

CRC cards help define an object's purpose by drawing attention to the object's responsibilities. When you use CRC cards, you simply create a card for each class. You write the class name at the top of the card and then divide the card into two sections. List responsibilities on the left side, and list any other object that the card needs to perform its responsibility on the right side.

Figure 10.2 illustrates a CRC card template.

Figure 10.2

A CRC card template.

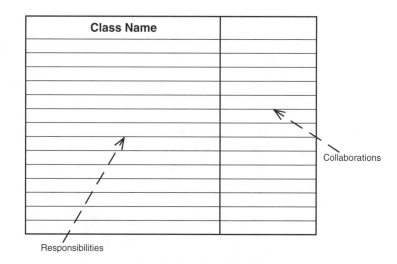

CRC cards are intentionally low tech. You are intentionally limited by the size of the card. If you find that the card is not large enough, chances are good that you need to break up the class. One big advantage of CRC cards is that you are not tied to a computer. Believe it or not, having to design in front of a computer is not always desirable. Design is not a solitary exercise, and can require conversation and discussion among the designers. CRC cards free you and your fellow designers to design whenever and wherever you want. Design over lunch; go to a conference room, or to a park bench. As long as you can bring your cards, you can design.

CRC cards also free you from having to keep an electronic model up to date. Early on, your model will change frequently and having to keep the model up to date can be a major inconvenience. Instead, you simply take your cards and erase, scratch out, bend, write on, and rip them up as necessary. The cost of changing a card is much cheaper (and more immediate) than having to update something on your computer. Having to stop the CRC session and update a computer can bring the flow of the session to a screeching halt.

Finally, CRC cards appeal to our more primitive instincts. It just helps to have something concrete that you can hold. Instead of having to model various design alternatives, you can just move your cards around. To model interactions, you can sit with other designers, divide up cards, and step through the interactions. Such an interactive process encourages discussion.

How Do You Apply CRC Cards?

Creating CRC cards is not a solitary exercise. Instead, you should hold CRC sessions with other designers/developers so that the design process is as interactive as possible.

You begin a session by choosing a number of use cases. The number that you choose depends upon the amount of time that you have and the difficulty of the use cases. If you have a few very large use cases, it might make sense to have one session per use case. If you have many small ones you'll want to tackle multiple use cases during the session. What is important is that you handle related use cases and that you make noticeable progress in your design. Don't let the process get bogged down.

Once you choose the use cases, identify the main classes and create a card for each one. Once you have the cards, divide them among the designers and then begin the session. During the session you will trace through each use case's scenario. As you go through the scenario, each designer should concentrate on the responsibilities and collaborations of his class. When his class is needed in the scenario, he will note its use and tell any other designer if he needs to delegate to another object.

The approach that you take to the design session is one of personal preference. Some methodologies call for role-playing where each designer takes a card and acts out the class's role. Other methodologies are a bit more formal. The approach that you choose is up to you and your design team. What is important is that everyone stays engaged in the process, and that no one hides in the corner or gets shouted down. It is during these sessions that you will discuss design alternatives, discover new objects, and build team camaraderie.

An Example CRC Card

Let's consider the Order use case from Day 9, and see how you might use CRC cards to assign responsibility for it.

- Order
    - Registered user proceeds to the checkout.
    - Registered user provides shipping information.
    - System displays the order total.
    - Registered user provides payment information.
    - System authorizes payment.
    - System confirms the order.
    - System sends a confirmation email.
- Preconditions
    - A non-empty shopping cart.
- Post Conditions
    - An order in the system.

- Alternative: Cancel Order
  - During steps 1-4, the user chooses to cancel the order. The user is returned to the homepage.
- Alternative: Authorization Failed
  - At step 5, the system fails to authorize the payment information. The user can reenter the information or cancel the order.

Start by identifying the classes. Right away you'll see: `RegisteredUser`, `Order`, `Payment`, `OrderConfirmation`, `ShoppingCart`, `ShippingInformation`. You might also want to include `System`; however, there is a problem. In the use cases, anything not done by an actor was done by the "all inclusive" system. The point of analysis was to understand the problem. So instead of trying to break the system into its parts, analysis treated it as a big black box. Through design you will decompose the system into its pieces.

Whether or not to include a system card really depends on the complexity of the system. It may help to list all of the system responsibilities on one card and then break that card into a number of classes at a later time. In this case, however, you can try to deconstruct the system before you begin. If you miss something, you can always add it in later.

Begin by reading the steps in the scenario. Here the system authorizes payment, displays the order, and confirms the order. The system also creates and enters the order. You can start by breaking the system into a `Clerk`, `OrderDisplay`, and `PaymentTerminal`.

Once you feel comfortable with your list of classes you can create the CRC cards, as illustrated in Figure 10.3.

FIGURE 10.3

Some of the CRC cards for Order.

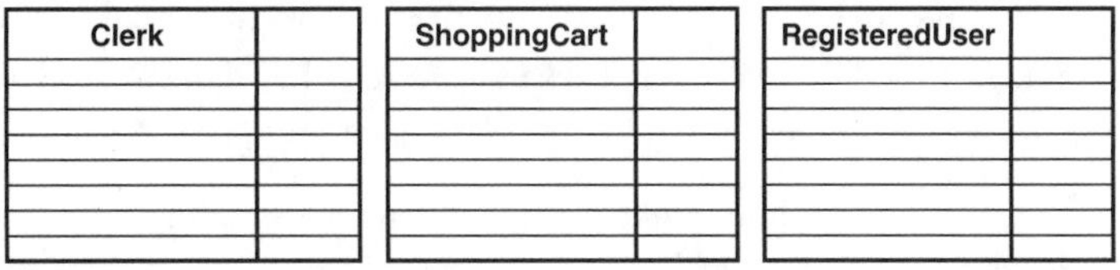

Clerk		ShoppingCart		RegisteredUser	

The next step is to go through each step of the scenario and identify responsibilities. Step 1, "Registered user proceeds to the checkout," is simply a click of a link in the interface. For simplicity we'll ignore the UI. Step 2, "Registered user provides shipping information," is a bit more interesting. Here you see that the `RegisteredUser` is responsible for providing its shipping information to the `Clerk`.

Figure 10.4 illustrates the resulting card.

FIGURE **10.4**

The CRC card for RegisteredUser.

RegisteredUser	
provides shipping information	ShippingInformation

Note

Whenever you see that an object "provides" or "supplies" something, you need to be sure that the object isn't acting as a simple data structure.

If the object does nothing but provide access to information, you'll want to combine that object with the one that manipulates the data.

Step 3, "System displays the order total," is a bit more involved. Before the system can display anything, the Clerk must enter the order, price the order, and total the order.

The Clerk will use the ShoppingCart to retrieve the items and the OrderDisplay to display the resulting order; however, the Clerk probably shouldn't also be responsible for pricing or totaling the order. These tasks are better delegated to another object. Remember, an object should only have a small number of responsibilities.

The Order object should take care of pricing and totaling the order. Figure 10.5 summarizes the Clerk's responsibilities so far.

The Order object should also hold onto the items being purchased. The Item object was overlooked during the creation of the class list, so you should add it now. The Item contains pricing and product information as well as a quantity. The Item will also hold onto any incentives that the user may have applied. Incentive is another class that you should add to the list.

The remaining steps are much like the others. The RegisteredUser provides Payment information, the Clerk authorizes the payment and finalizes the order.

Figures 10.6 and 10.7 summarize the responsibilities for the Clerk and RegisteredUser.

FIGURE 10.5

The CRC card for `Clerk`.

Clerk	
retrieve shipping and payment information	ShippingInformation
enter the order	ShippingCart Order
display the order	OrderDisplay

FIGURE 10.6

The complete CRC card for `Clerk`.

Clerk	
retrieve shipping and payment information	RegisteredUser
enter the order	ShippingCart Order
display the order	OrderDisplay
authorize the order	PaymentTerminal
confirm the order	Order

How Many Responsibilities Per Class?

When developing your CRC cards, you need ensure that each class has only two or three main responsibilities. If you have any more responsibilities, you should break the class into two or more separate classes.

Caution

You should consider breaking up the class, but in real systems this is not necessarily realistic.

10

FIGURE 10.7

The CRC card for RegisteredUser.

RegisteredUser	
provides shipping information	ShippingInformation
provides payment information	Payment

Take the Clerk class, for example. The Clerk is responsible for:

- Retrieving payment and shipping information.
- Entering the order.
- Displaying the order.
- Authorizing payment.
- Confirming the order.

As Figure 10.8 illustrates, however, all of these responsibilities fall under the "Process Order" responsibility.

FIGURE 10.8

Process Order.

Clerk	
retrieve shipping and payment information	RegisteredUser
enter the order	ShippingCart Order
display the order	OrderDisplay
authorize the order	PaymentTerminal
confirm the order	Order

— Process Order

It is important to list sub-tasks; however, you don't want to over do it. What is important is that all of the sub-responsibilities work towards a common goal. Here, all of the tasks work toward processing an order.

While working with CRC cards, you also need to keep in mind that they fulfill a specific purpose: defining responsibilities and simple collaboration relationships. Do not use CRC cards to describe complex relationships.

You should also keep CRC cards low tech—don't try to automate the CRC card process.

CRC Card Limitations

Like any good tool, CRC cards have their uses as well as limitations.

CRC cards were originally developed as a teaching tool. As a result, they are an excellent way to approach the initial design of a system—especially if you are new to OO.

CRC cards, however, are difficult to use as the design becomes more complicated. Complex inter-object interactions can be difficult to track simply through the use of CRC cards. A large number of classes also make the use of cards unwieldy. It can also become difficult to continue to use CRC cards once you begin modeling. Keeping the two in sync can be a challenge.

The best advice is to use what works. Use CRC cards until they no longer add to the design process. At that time, simply stop using them.

10

 Tip

When should you use CRC cards?
- During the initial stages of design.
- When you're still new to OO.
- To flesh out responsibilities and collaborations.
- To walk through a scenario. Not only will the cards find responsibilities and collaboration, they may help you to understand the scenario better.
- On smaller projects or to focus in on a smaller section of a larger project. Don't try to tackle an entire project with CRC cards.

Step 3: Develop the Points of Interaction

Once you have completed your CRC cards for a set of use cases, you need to develop the points of interaction. A point of interaction is any place where one object uses another.

NEW TERM   A *point of interaction* is any place where one object uses another.

There are a number of issues to consider at the point of interaction.

Interfaces

You need a well-defined interface wherever one object uses another. You want to be sure that a change in one implementation will not break the other object.

Agents

You also need to look at the interactions critically. Take a library, for example. A library has shelves and books. When it comes time to remove a book from the shelf, does the book call a `removeBook()` method on the shelf, or does the shelf call a `removeBook()` method on the book? Really, the responsibility doesn't belong to the book or the shelf. Neither choice adequately models the real world. In the real world a librarian or patron will remove the book. Librarians and patron can appear in the OO world as well; however, the OO world calls such actors *agents* or intermediaries.

NEW TERM   An *agent* mediates between two or more objects to accomplish some goal.

When developing points of interaction, you'll want to keep an eye out for places to use agents.

Future Considerations

When considering interactions you'll want to look for places where the object being used may change. If you can pinpoint such places, you'll want to design the interaction in such a way that it won't break if you introduce new objects. Planning for change is what future proof software is all about. In such places you'll want to establish pluggability relationships, and use polymorphism so that you can introduce new objects at any time.

Like anything else, however, don't overdo it. Plan for change only in places where you absolutely know change will occur. There are two general ways to predict the future:

- Change is a requirement. If the requirements call for future changes, design for the change.

- If you're using a third party library, and you want to upgrade to a new version seamlessly in the future, plan for change.

The first case is best solved through establishing some sort of substitutability relationship through inheritance. The second takes a bit more work. You'll want to wrap the library in classes that you've created. You should be careful to design these wrappers to take advantage of pluggability and polymorphism.

Data Transformation

During design you may find places where you need to translate data before you pass it to another object. Normally, you would delegate such data transformation to another object; if you need to alter the transformation, you'll only need to update the transformation class. This practice also helps to spread out responsibilities.

As you consider these points of interaction and add new classes, you may need to revisit and update your CRC cards or object model (if you've begin formal modeling).

Step 4: Detail the Relationships Between Objects

Once you've established responsibility and basic collaboration relationships, you need to detail the complex relationships between the classes. This is where you define the dependencies, associations, and generalizations. Detailing these relationships is an important step because it defines how the objects fit together. It also defines the internal structure of the various objects.

Start with the CRC cards. While these do not capture every relationship, they do capture collaboration. They will also suggest some of the other relationships.

Look for classes that share similar responsibilities. If two or more classes shares the same set of responsibilities, chance are good that you can factor the commonality out into a base class. You'll also want to revisit step 3 and consider any substitutability relationships that you might need.

Step 5: Build Your Model

By the time you reach step 5, you are ready to formally model the system. A complete model will consist of class diagrams and interaction diagrams. These diagrams will describe the structure and relationship of the various classes in the system. The UML also defines models for modeling interactions, state transition, and activities. For the purposes of this book, however, you will concentrate on class and interaction diagrams. You've seen both types in previous days.

Figure 10.9 models the Order structure.

The Order model illustrates all of the important relationships between the Order and the classes that display it. Conceivably, you will also have models that illustrate the relationships between the Clerk, Orders, and the RegisteredUser.

Again, you only want to model what makes sense—the architecturally interesting components. Keep in mind that you are trying to convey specific information through your models, not simply churn out models for the sake of documentation.

Figure 10.10 illustrates the updated sequence diagram for the Order use case.

FIGURE **10.9**

Order model.

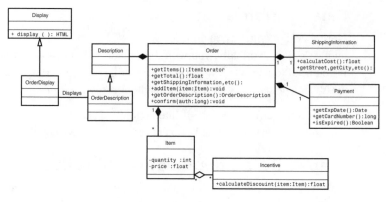

FIGURE **10.10**

Order sequence diagram.

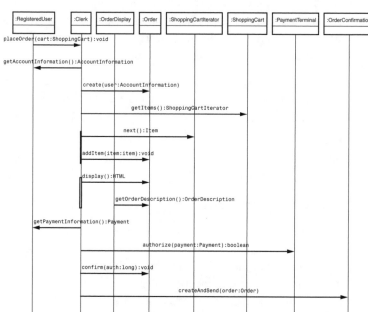

You can also create sequence and collaboration diagrams to model the important interactions in the system.

When you are done creating the models, you should have descriptions of all of the major structures and interactions found in the system. These models tell you how the various objects are structured, how they relate, and how they fit together to model the solution to the problem elaborated during analysis.

Summary

OOD picks up where OOA leaves off by taking the domain and transforming it into a solution to your problem. Through the process of OOD, you take your domain model and construct the object model of your solution. The object model describes the architecturally significant aspects of your system, such as object structure and object relationships—how the objects fit together. By the end of OOD, you should have a good idea of what you will implement in code.

Roughly, there are five iterative steps that you can follow while performing OOD:

Step 1: Generate an initial list of objects.

Step 2: Refine your objects' responsibilities through CRC cards.

Step 3: Develop the points of interaction.

Step 4: Detail the relationships between objects.

Step 5: Build your model.

Each step further refines your object model and brings you closer to the blueprint of your system.

Q&A

Q Why is it important to design the system before you begin coding?

A There are a number of factors that make design important. Design helps you foresee implementation problems before you start to code. It is much easier to fix a problem in a model than to go through all of your code to fix a problem.

Design also ensures that all of the developers on a development team are on the same page. The design will clarify many of the architecturally important assumptions that would have otherwise been decided during development. By leaving architectural decisions until implementation, you risk having each developer make his own, incompatible decisions.

Q Why is it important to model your design before you begin coding?

A Modeling is important for the same reason that most people write out a speech before delivering it. By modeling the design, you can see how the pieces fit together. By having a visual view of the design, you can decide if you're comfortable with it. You can check that everything fits together nicely and sanely.

Sometimes the solution to a problem will seem simple when you think about it. Taking the solution and formally writing it down forces you to be intellectually honest about the solution. Having to formally translate a problem forces you to think critically and exactly about the solution. What seems simple in your head may have you tearing out your hair before you are done!

Q How do you know when your design is finished?

A There are no hard and fast rules that govern when a design is done. If you worry about having a perfect design, you can easily fall into design paralysis.

It all goes back to what you are trying to convey through your models, your experience level, and the experience level of your team. If you have an experienced team, you can probably get away with simply modeling the high level architecture of the system. If you or the members of your team are new to objects, you'll probably want to spend more time designing. Either way, you are done when you feel confident enough that you can take the design and implement the solution.

The OO development process is iterative. You should use that to your advantage and iterate toward your final architecture.

Workshop

The quiz questions and answers are provided for your further understanding. See Appendix A, "Answers," for the answers.

Quiz

1. What are the three benefits of a formal design?
2. What is OOD?
3. What is the object model?
4. What are the downsides to over-design?
5. How do you know what aspects of your system are *architecturally significant*?
6. What are the five basic steps to OOD?
7. How do you generate the initial list of objects?
8. What does a complete design capture?
9. What do CRC cards help you identify?
10. What is a collaboration?
11. Why is a deep understanding of an object's relationships and responsibilities important?
12. What is a CRC card?
13. Describe one reason that CRC cards are intentionally low-tech.
14. When should you use CRC cards?

15. What is a major problem with CRC cards?

16. What is a point of interaction?

17. What four considerations can you make at a point of interaction?

18. What is an agent?

19. What will you do as you detail the complex relationships among the objects, and why is it important?

20. What type of models might you create?

Exercises

1. In Day 9, Exercise 2, you developed the following use case:

- Remove Item

    - Guest user selects an item from the shopping cart.

    - Guest user asks the cart to remove the item.

- Preconditions

    - The cart contains an item to remove.

- Post Conditions

    - The item no longer appears in the cart.

- Alternative: Operation Canceled

    - The user may opt to cancel the transaction after step #1.

To the best of your abilities, use CRC cards to flesh out the responsibilities. What responsibilities will the ShoppingCart have?

10

DAY 11

Reusing Designs Through Design Patterns

In yesterday's chapter, you saw how Object Oriented Design helps you design a solution for a problem. Through OOD you build a blueprint that diagrams the objects that comprise your system. Once you have this design, you can begin to implement your solution.

You probably have a few questions, however.

- How do you know that yours is a good design?
- Will your design have unforeseen consequences in the future?
- How have other designers solved this or a similar problem in the past?
- What about reuse? OOP gives you code reuse, but does OOD allow for reuse?

This chapter will help you answer these questions and more as you explore the topic of design patterns.

Today you will learn

- How to use design patterns
- How to apply four common patterns
- How a design can benefit from the use of patterns
- How to avoid a common pattern pitfall

Design Reuse

An important goal of OOP is code reuse. When you reuse code you gain peace of mind, knowing that your software is built on a foundation of reliable, time-tested code. Furthermore, you know that the code you reuse will solve your problem. Such peace of mind while you program is great, but what about peace of mind while you design? How do you know if your design is any good?

Luckily, design patterns can help put to rest many of the doubts that you will encounter as you design. As time has gone by, many designers and programmers have noticed that the same design elements appear over and over again throughout their designs. The OO community has made it a point to identify, name, and describe these recurring design concepts. The result is an ever-growing list of design patterns.

NEW TERM   A *design pattern* is a reusable design concept.

It turns out that you can reuse design patterns throughout your design just as you would reuse a class within your program. This reuse brings the benefits of OOP reuse to OOD. When you use design patterns, you know that you have based your design on a foundation of reliable, time-proven designs. Such reuse enables you to know that you're on the right track to a reliable solution. When you reuse a design pattern, you're using a design that others have successfully used many times before.

Design Patterns

Design Patterns—Elements of Reusable Object-Oriented Software by Gamma, Helm, Johnson, and Vlissides first introduced the concept of design patterns to many in the OO community. This groundbreaking work not only defined a set of reusable design patterns, but also formally defined design pattern.

According to this work, a design pattern consists of four elements:

- The pattern name
- The problem

- The solution
- The consequences

The Pattern Name

A name uniquely identifies each design pattern. Just as the UML gives you a common design language, pattern names gives you a common vocabulary for describing your design elements to others. Other developers can understand your design quickly and easily when you use a common vocabulary.

A simple name reduces an entire problem, solution, and consequences to a single term. Just as objects help you program at a higher, more abstract level, these terms allow you to design from a higher, more abstract level and not get caught up in details that repeat themselves from design to design.

The Problem

Each design pattern exists to solve some discrete set of design problems, and each design pattern describes the set of problems that it is designed to solve. That way, you can use the problem description to determine whether the pattern applies to the specific problem that you face.

The Solution

The solution describes how the design pattern solves the problem, and identifies the architecturally significant objects in the solution as well as the responsibilities and relationships that those objects share.

Note

It is important to note that you can apply a design pattern to an entire class of problems. The solution is a general solution, and does not present an answer to a specific or concrete problem.

Suppose that you would like to find the best way to scan over the items in the shopping cart from Chapter 10, "Introduction to Object Oriented Design (OOD)." The Iterator design pattern proposes a way to do just that; however, the solution stated by the Iterator pattern is not given in terms of shopping carts and items. Instead, the solution describes the process of scanning over any list of elements.

When you set out to use a design pattern, you must map the general solution to your specific problem. Sometimes it can be difficult to make that mapping; however, the design pattern itself needs to remain generic so that it remains applicable to many different specific problems.

11

The Consequences

There is no such thing as the perfect design. Every good design will have good compromises, and every compromise you make has its own special set of consequences. A design pattern will enumerate the major consequences inherent in the design.

Consequences are nothing new. You make tradeoffs every time you choose between two alternatives when you program. Consider the difference between using an array and using a linked list. An array provides for quick lookup by index, but works very slowly when you need to shrink or expand the array to insert or delete elements. On the other hand, the linked list provides for quick additions and deletions, but has a higher memory overhead and slower index lookups. Here, the consequences of a linked list are memory overhead and slower lookups. The consequence of using an array is the fact that resizing the array is costly, but indexed lookups are very quick. Which you choose depends on the importance of memory and speed in your design, if you'll be doing a lot of addition and deletion of elements, and if you will do many lookups.

It is always important to document your design decisions as well as the resulting consequences. Having these decisions documented helps others to understand the choices that you have made, and determine whether the design can help solve their own problems. Likewise, design pattern consequences will factor heavily into your decision of whether to use the pattern. If a design pattern has consequences that do not match your design goals, you should not use it—even if it might otherwise solve your problem.

Pattern Realities

When you first begin to learn about patterns it is important to know what patters can and cannot do. The following lists can help keep the intentions behind patterns straight.

Patterns are

- Reusable designs that have proven to work in the past
- Abstract solution to a general design problem
- Solutions to recurring problems
- A way to build a design vocabulary
- A public record of design experience
- A solution to one problem

Patterns are not

- A solution to a specific problem
- The magical answer to all of your problems

- A crutch, you still need to do your design work yourself
- Concrete classes, libraries, pre made solutions

Patterns by Example

There are many books that catalog design patterns. There's no reason to formally repeat those catalogs here; however, there is a set of design patterns that you will encounter almost daily. No introductory OO text would be complete without presenting those patterns to you.

Instead of formally presenting these patterns, let's take a more informal approach through example.

Today, this chapter will introduce three important patterns:

- Adapter
- Proxy
- Iterator

The Adapter Pattern

11

Chapter 4, "Inheritance: Getting Something for Nothing," introduced the concept of substitutability relationships. Chapter 6, "Polymorphism: Learning to Predict the Future," showed you how you can use those relationships to add new objects to your system at any time. When you use inheritance to define substitutability, however, your objects can become constrained by the resulting hierarchies. To be able to plug into your program, an object must be part of the substitutability hierarchy.

So what do you do if you would like to plug an object into your program, but it doesn't belong to the proper hierarchy? One solution is to take the class that you would like to use and then edit it so that it inherits from the right class. This solution is not optimal for a couple of reason.

You will not always have the source code to the classes that you want to use. Furthermore, if that class already uses inheritance, you'll be in trouble if your language doesn't support multiple inheritance.

Even if you do have the source code, it's simply not practical or reasonable to rewrite an object each time you would like it to be part of the "proper" hierarchy. The definition of the "proper" hierarchy will change for each program. If you have a reasonably abstracted class, you won't want to keep editing it each time that you want to reuse it. Instead, you should simply use it unaltered. Rewriting it each time defeats the purposes of reuse and abstraction. If you keep creating special editions of a class, you'll be left with a lot of redundant classes to maintain.

The Adapter pattern presents an alternative solution that solves the problem of incompatibility by transforming the incompatible interface into the one that you need. The Adapter pattern works by wrapping the incompatible object inside of a compatible adapter object. The adapter object holds onto an instance of the object, and exposes the object through the interface that fits into your program. Because the adapter class wraps an object, this pattern is sometimes referred to as the Wrapper pattern.

NEW TERM   An *adapter* is an object that transforms the interface of another object.

Implementing an Adapter

Figure 11.1 summarizes the MoodyObject hierarchy presented in Chapter 7, "Polymorphism: Time to Write Code."

FIGURE 11.1

The MoodyObject hierarchy.

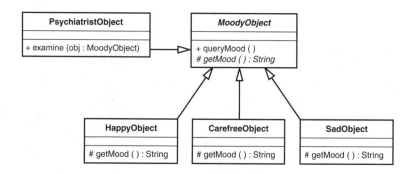

The PsychiatristObject can only examine an object if it is a MoodyObject. The PsychiatristObject's examine() method depends upon MoodyObject's queryMood() method. Any other type of object will need to find a different psychiatrist.

Figure 11.2 presents the new Pet hierarchy.

FIGURE 11.2

The Pet hierarchy.

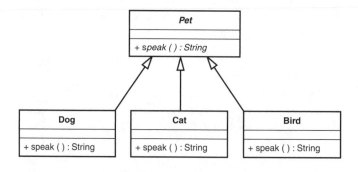

Each Pet speaks in its own specialized way, and provides its own implementation of speak().

So, what's the problem?

Today, even pets go to psychiatrists, but the PsychiatristObject cannot examine a Pet because a Pet is not a MoodyObject. For the PsychiatristObject to be able to examine a Pet, you'll need to create a Pet adapter.

Listing 11.1 presents one possible Pet adapter.

LISTING 11.1 PetAdapter.java

```java
public class PetAdapter extends MoodyObject {

    private Pet pet;

    public PetAdapter( Pet pet ) {
        this.pet = pet;
    }

    protected String getMood() {
        // only implementing because required to by
        // MoodyObject, because also override queryMood
        // we don't really need it
        return pet.speak();
    }

    public void queryMood() {
        System.out.println( getMood() );
    }
}
```

11

The PetAdapter wraps a Pet instance. Instead of exposing the Pet interface, the adapter hides the Pet interface behind the MoodyObject interface, in essence transforming Pet's interface. Whenever a request comes into the PetAdapter, the adapter delegates to the Pet instance as needed.

Listing 11.2 shows the adapter in action.

LISTING 11.2 Using the Adapter

```java
PetAdapter dog  = new PetAdapter( new Dog() );
PetAdapter cat  = new PetAdapter( new Cat() );
PetAdapter bird = new PetAdapter( new Bird() );
```

LISTING 11.2   continued

```
PsychiatristObject psychiatrist = new PsychiatristObject();

psychiatrist.examine( dog );
psychiatrist.examine( cat );
psychiatrist.examine( bird );
```

Once wrapped, the `Pet` instance looks like any other `MoodyObject` to the
`PsychiatristObject`. This solution is more efficient than the alternatives because it
requires you to only write one adapter class. This adapter class can handle any `Pet` that
comes along. The tricky part is to make sure that the `PetAdapter` wraps any `Pet`
instances before you pass the `Pet` to the `PsychiatristObject`.

> The implementation provided above is called an *object adapter* because the adapter uses
> composition to transform the interface of an instance. You can also implement an
> adapter through inheritance. Such an adapter is known as a *class adapter* since it adapts
> the class definition itself.
>
> If your language supports multiple inheritances, you can always inherit from the class you
> want to use as well as from a class in the hierarchy.
>
> If your language lacks multiple inheritance, like Java, your choices may be limited
> depending on how the hierarchy was constructed. In fact, you may have to forego inheri-
> tance entirely and use composition, at which point you might as well create an object
> adapter.
>
> While multiple inheritance works, this solution is limited. Creating a new subclass for
> each class that you want to use can lead to an unacceptable proliferation in wrapper
> classes.
>
> Each approach has its own limitation. A class adapter will only work for the class that it
> inherits. You'll need a separate adapter for each subclass.
>
> Likewise, while an object adapter can work with each subclass, you'll need subclasses of
> the adapter if you want to change the way it wraps various subclasses.

When to Use the Adapter Pattern

The Adapter pattern is useful when you want to use an object that has an incompatible
interface. The Adapter pattern allows you to directly reuse objects that you would have
otherwise needed to alter or throw away.

Adapters are also useful in a proactive sense. From time to time, you will need to employ
third-party libraries in your programs. Unfortunately, the APIs of third-party tools can

vary dramatically between releases, especially for new products or maturing technologies. The APIs can also vary greatly from the libraries of a competing product.

The Adapter pattern can help insolate your program from changing APIs and from vendor lock in. By creating an adapter interface that you control, you can swap in new versions of a library at any time. Simply create a subclass of the adapter for each library that you would like to use.

It's also important to point out that an adapter can be simple or complicated, and the level of complexity depends on the object being wrapped. Some adapters will boil down to simply mapping a request to the proper method. Others will need to do more processing.

Use the Adapter pattern when

- You want to use incompatible objects in your program.
- You want your program to remain independent of third party libraries.

Table 11.1 outlines the user of the Adapter pattern.

TABLE 11.1 The Adapter Pattern

Pattern Name	Adapter, Wrapper
Problem	How to reuse incompatible objects
Solution	Provides an object that converts the incompatible interface into a compatible one
Consequences	Makes incompatible objects compatible; results in extra classes—perhaps many—if you use inheritance or need to handle each subclass differently

The Proxy Pattern

Normally, when an object wants to interact with another object, it does so by acting directly upon the other object. In most cases this direct approach is the best approach, but there are times when you will want to transparently control access between your objects. The Proxy pattern addresses such cases.

Publish/Subscribe and the Proxy Pattern

Consider the problem of a publish/subscribe event service where an object will register its interest in an event. Whenever the event occurs, the publisher will notify the subscribing objects of the event.

Figure 11.3 illustrates one possible publish/subscribe relationship.

FIGURE 11.3

*A publish/subscribe
relationship.*

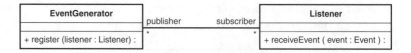

In Figure 11.3, many `Listeners` register their interest in events generated by an
`EventGenerator`. Whenever the `EventGenerator` generates an event, it will push the
event to each of its `Listeners`.

While this solution works, it places a great burden on the `EventGenerator`. Not only
does the `EventGenerator` have the responsibility of generating events, it is also responsible for keeping track of all its listeners and pushing them the events.

The Proxy pattern presents an elegant solution to this problem. Consider Figure 11.4.

FIGURE 11.4

A proxy solution.

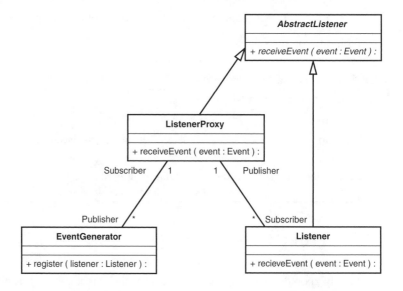

Instead of holding onto its listeners directly, the `EventGenerator` can hold onto one
`ListenerProxy`. Whenever the generator needs to push an event, it pushes it once to the
proxy. It is then up to the proxy to track and update all of the listeners.

The General Proxy Pattern

The publish/subscribe scenario describes one possible use for a proxy; however, you can
use proxies in many places.

First, what is a proxy?

A *proxy* is a surrogate or placeholder that brokers access to the actual object of interest. You can use a proxy anyplace where you need a surrogate or placeholder for another object. Instead of using an object directly, you use the proxy. The proxy takes care of all the details of communicating with the actual object or objects.

New Term   A *proxy* is a surrogate or placeholder that brokers access to the actual object of interest. For all intents and purposes, the *proxy* is indistinguishable from the actual object that it brokers.

A proxy brokers access to an underlying object (or objects) transparently. You can think of a proxy as a way of tricking your objects. For example, while the `EventGenerator` thinks that it is only communicating with one `Listener`, the `ListenerProxy` might actually broadcast the message to many different `Listeners`.

Being able to trick your objects is an important ability because it allows you to perform all kind of magic behind the scenes. A proxy enables you to put responsibilities in the proxy without having to embed those responsibilities in the user of the proxy. More importantly, your proxy can perform all of these responsibilities without the other objects being aware of what you are doing.

The responsibilities that you can put in the proxy are endless; however, common use includes adding optimizations, performing housekeeping tasks, making remote resources appear local, and for deferring expensive operations.

When to Use the Proxy Pattern

Use proxies when

- You want to defer an expensive operation. Consider an object that pulls back information from a database. While your program may need to know about the objects that it can pull back, the program doesn't need to pull all of the information back until it actually access the object. A proxy can stand in for the actual object and load the extra information once it is needed.

  Another example is a file proxy that allows you to write to a file, but only does the actual file IO when you are done. Instead of making a multiple number of slow writes, the proxy will do one large write.

- You want to transparently protect how an object is used. Most objects are mutable, such as Java's collection classes. A protective proxy could make a collection immutable by intercepting requests that would otherwise alter a collection. By filtering all method invocations through a proxy, you can transparently govern the allowable operations on an object.

11

- The actual object exists remotely across a network or process. Proxies are important to distributed computing. A proxy can make a distributed resource appear as if it were a local resource by forwarding requests over a network or across a process space.

- When you want to perform additional actions transparently when using an object. For example, you may want to count the number of times that a method is called without the caller knowing. A counting proxy could track access to an object.

Table 11.2 outlines the user of the Proxy pattern.

TABLE 11.2   The Proxy Pattern

Pattern Name	Proxy, Surrogate
Problem	Need to control access to an object
Solution	Provides an object that transparently brokers access to an object
Consequences	Introduces a level of indirection to object use

The Iterator Pattern

Design patterns often describe solutions to common problems. When you program, chances are good that you will spend a lot of time writing code that loops over objects in a collection. As you learned in Chapter 8, "Introduction to the UML," the relationship between a collection and its elements is an *aggregation*. The collection contains items.

Listing 11.3 presents a familiar method that loops over the contents of a deck of cards (a collection) and constructs a string representation of the deck.

LISTING 11.3   Looping Over the Contents of a Deck of Cards

```
public String deckToString( Deck deck ) {
    String cards = "";
    for( int i = 0; i < deck.size(); i ++ ) {
        Card card = deck.get( i );
        cards = cards + card.display();
    }
    return cards;
}
```

Suppose that you wanted to loop over an array of cards. Listing 11.4 shows the method that can handle just that case.

LISTING 11.4 Looping Over the Contents of an Array

```
public String deckToString( Card [] deck ) {
    String cards = "";
    for( int i = 0; i < deck.length; i ++ ) {
        cards = cards + deck[i].display();
    }
    return cards;
}
```

Finally, what if you want to loop over the deck of cards in reverse order? You'll need to add yet another method. Listing 11.5 shows a method that loops over the deck in reverse.

LISTING 11.5 Looping Over the Contents of a Deck of Cards in Reverse

```
public String reverseDeckToString( Deck deck ) {
    String cards = "";
    for( int i = deck.size() - 1; i > -1; i — ) {
        Card card = deck.get( i );
        cards = cards + card.display();
    }
    return cards;
}
```

11

If you think back to the lessons on coupling and responsibilities, you should hear a voice in your head screaming, "Bad code!" Every time that you would like to loop over a collection of cards, you need to add a method that knows how to loop over that specific type of collection. In fact, the logic isn't really all that different from case to case. The only elements that do change are the methods and attributes you access on the collection. Right away you see a warning: repeated code.

The problem is that each of the methods listed above is dependent on the implementation of the collection, such as a Deck or an Array. When you program, you always want to make sure that you don't get coupled to a specific implementation. Coupling makes your program resistant to change.

Think about it. What happens if you want to change the collection that holds your cards? You'll need to update or add a new method that performs the loop. If you're not lucky, simply changing the collection's implementation could necessitate changes throughout your program.

 Note

While a single object might only contain one loop, your entire program will probably repeat the loops many times in many different places.

Another problem with these examples stems from the fact that the mechanics of the traversal is hard coded into the method. That's why you need one method for forward looping and yet another for reverse looping. If you want to randomly loop over the cards, you'll need a third method (and one for each collection type). Not only will you need multiple methods, you'll need to reimplement the traversal logic each time you define a loop. Unfortunately, such logic replication is a symptom of responsibility muddling. The traversal logic should appear in one place and one place only.

Luckily, the Iterator pattern solves many of the problems of tight coupling and responsibility muddling by placing the loop, or iteration, logic into its own object.

Figure 11.5 illustrates the Iterator interface.

FIGURE 11.5

The Iterator
interface.

Iterator
+ first ( ) : void
+ next ( ) : void
+ isDone ( ) : boolean
+ currentItem ( ) : Object

The Iterator interface provides a generic interface for iterating over a collection. Instead of writing your loops and methods to use a specific collection, you can simply program to the Iterator's generic interface. The Iterator interface completely hides the underlying collection implementation.

 Note

Java defines a slightly different iterator interface: java.util.Iterator. The Java Iterator only defines three methods: public boolean hasNext(), public void remove(), and public Object next().

The Java Iterator interface only allows you to iterate in one direction. Once you reach the end, you cannot go back to the beginning. Other than that shortcoming, the Java Iterator is similar to the one presented earlier.

When writing Java programs you should use java.util.Iterator so that other Java programs can use your iterator implementations. For the purposes of this book, however, this lesson will stay true to the classical iterator definition provided in Figure 11.5.

Listing 11.6 presents an alternative deckToString() that loops over an instance of Iterator.

LISTING 11.6 Looping Over the Contents of an `Iterator` Instance

```
public String deckToString( Iterator i ) {
    String cards = "";
    for ( i.first(); !i.isDone(); i.next() ) {
        Card card = (Card) i.currentItem();
        cards = cards + card.display();
    }
    return cards;
}
```

Just because an object passes back an iterator doesn't mean that the object actually stores its items inside of the iterator. Instead, an iterator will provide access to the object's contents.

There are three benefits to using an iterator to traverse a collection.

First, an iterator will not tie you to a specific collection. The original methods all looped over specific collection implementations. As a result, each method only differed in the methods that it calls on the collection. If those methods had looped over an iterator, such as Listing 11.4, you would only have needed to write one `deckToString()` method.

Second, the iterator can return its elements in any order that it sees fit. This means that one iterator implementation might return the elements in order. Another iterator could return the elements in reverse order. By using an iterator, you can write the traversal logic once and have it appear in only one place: the iterator itself.

Finally, an iterator makes it simple to change the underlying collection whenever you need to. Because you haven't programmed to a specific implementation, you can swap in a new collection at any time, as long as the collection knows how to return an instance of `Iterator`.

Implementing an Iterator

 Note

> Most Java collections already provide access to an iterator. For example the `LinkedList` used internally by the Deck object already has an `iterator()` method that returns a `java.util.Iterator`; however, it helps to see an actual iterator implementation and this pattern is not specific to Java. So please, ignore the Java `LinkedList` `iterator()` method for a moment.

Listing 11.7 lists an implementation of `Iterator` that allows a user to scan over the elements of a `LinkedList` collection.

LISTING 11.7   An Iterator Implementation

```java
public class ForwardIterator implements Iterator {

    private Object [] items;
    private int index;

    public ForwardIterator( java.util.LinkedList items ) {
        this.items = items.toArray();
    }

    public boolean isDone() {
        if( index == items.length ) {
            return true;
        }
        return false;
    }

    public Object currentItem() {
        if( !isDone() ) {
            return items[index];
        }
        return null;
    }

    public void next() {
        if( !isDone() ) {
            index++;
        }
    }

    public void first() {
        index = 0;
    }

}
```

Another implementation might provide a reverse iteration (please see the full source for such an example).

Listing 11.8 illustrates the changes that you will need to make to Deck so that it can return an Iterator.

LISTING 11.8   An Updated Deck

```java
public class Deck {
    private java.util.LinkedList deck;

    public Deck() {
```

LISTING **11.8**   continued

```
        buildCards();
    }

    public Iterator iterator() {
        return new ForwardIterator( deck );
    }
    // snipped for brevity
}
```

Alternatively, it is fully valid from an OO point of view to consider an iterator as an extension of the collection that it provides access to. As a result, you have a few other implementation options.

Java allows for a construct known as the inner class. An inner class is a class that is defined within another class. Because the inner class is defined within another class, it has full access to all of that class' public, as well as protected and private methods and internal variables. The closest analogy in C++ is a `friend` class. `friend` gives special access to other trusted object.

Both the `friend` and inner class are easy to abuse since they can easily destroy encapsulation; however, an iterator is really part of the collection. Listing 11.9 shows an inner class implementation of the `Iterator` for the `Deck` class.

LISTING 11.9   An Inner Class `Iterator` Implementation

```
public class Deck {

    private java.util.LinkedList deck;

    public Deck() {
        buildCards();
    }

    public Iterator iterator() {
        return new ForwardIterator();
    }

    //snipped for brevity

    private class ForwardIterator implements Iterator {

        int index;
```

11

LISTING **11.9**   An Inner Class Iterator Implementation

```
        public boolean isDone() {
            // notice that the inner class has unfettered
            // access to Deck's internal variable deck
            if( index == deck.size() ) {
                return true;
            }
            return false;
        }

        public Object currentItem() {
            if( !isDone() ) {
                return deck.get( index );
            }
            return null;
        }

        public void next() {
            if( !isDone() ) {
                index++;
            }
        }

        public void first() {
            index = 0;
        }
    }

    }
```

When to Use the Iterator Pattern

There are a number of reasons to use the Iterator pattern:

- You can use an iterator when you want to hide the implementation of a collection.
- You can use an iterator when you want to provide different kinds of loops over a collection (such as forward loop, reverse loop, filtered loop, and so on).
- You can use an iterator to keep a collection's interface simple. You will not need to add methods to aid looping over the contents. Just let the object's users use an iterator.

- You can define a base collection class that returns an iterator. If all of your collections inherit from this base the iterator allows you to treat all of your collections generically. In fact, `java.util.Collection` does just that. This usage is also the general form of the Iterator pattern. The `Deck` example is an abridged version of the Iterator pattern. The `Deck` does not inherit from an abstract base collection class, thus you cannot treat it generically.
- Iterators are also useful for providing optimized access to collections. Some data structures, such as the hashtable, do not provide an optimized way of iterating over the elements. An iterator can provide such an ordering at the cost of a little extra memory. However, depending upon your application, the time savings might more than make up for the memory overhead.

Table 11.3 outlines the user of the Iterator pattern.

TABLE 11.3 The Iterator Pattern

Pattern Name	Iterator, Cursor
Problem	Looping over a collection without becoming dependent upon the collection's implementation
Solution	Provides an object that handles the iteration details, thus hiding the details from the user
Consequences	Decoupled traversal, simpler collection interface, encapsulated looping logic

Making a Pattern Yours

Some patterns are harder to understand than others; however, complexity can be deceptive. Before you can apply or even think about altering a pattern, you need to understand the pattern: In other words "make it yours." There are a few steps that you must take to be able to master a pattern:

1. Read the pattern
2. Read the pattern again paying close attention to the main participants and the sample code
3. Practice implementing the pattern
4. Apply the pattern to a real life problem

Once you have completed these four steps, you probably have full understanding of the pattern. At this point you can start to alter the pattern to fit the specific needs of your problem; however, you shouldn't attempt to augment a pattern with which you are still unfamiliar.

Summary

Design patterns are a useful aid while designing your solutions. In their own way, patterns are the collective conscience of the OO community that tap years of design experience. Design patterns can provide valuable guidance while designing.

You need to keep the limits of design patterns in mind when you use them. A design pattern addresses one abstract problem, and one problem only. A design pattern does not provide the solution to a specific problem. Instead, the pattern provides an abstract solution to a general problem. It is up to you to provide the mapping between the abstract problem and your specific problem.

Mapping a design pattern is probably the greatest challenge that you will face while using patterns. It is a skill that only comes through time, study, and practice.

Q&A

Q Does the Java language use patterns?

A Yes, many of the Java APIs employ patterns. In fact, each of the patterns that you read about today are represented in Java. Here is a brief list of the patterns that you have seen:

Iterator:	the Java Collection classes
Proxy:	Java's RMI
Adapter:	used extensively for event listeners

Q Do all patterns translate to all languages?

A No. Every language is different. Some patterns are impossible to implement under certain languages, while other patterns are unnecessary because of built-in language features.

Workshop

The quiz questions and answers are provided for your further understanding. See Appendix A, "Answers," for the answers.

Quiz

1. What is an adapter class?
2. What problem does the Iterator pattern solve?
3. Why would you use the Iterator pattern?
4. What problem does the Adapter pattern solve?
5. Why would you use the Adapter pattern?
6. What problem does the Proxy pattern solve?
7. Why would you use the Proxy pattern?
8. Consider the following situation; what pattern would you use and why?

   Sun Microsystems, IBM, and Apache all provide libraries for parsing XML documents. You have chosen to use the Apache library in your XML application. In the future, though, you might decide to go with a different vendor.
9. Consider the following situation; what pattern would you use and why?

   You must write an application that retrieves data from a file-based datastore. Sometimes your application will run locally and can access the datastore through direct means. Other times, the client will run remotely and will need to talk to a server in order to read the datastore.
10. The Adapter pattern transforms an interface. Does the Proxy pattern change an object's interface?

Exercises

1. Listings 11.10 and 11.11 present a shopping cart class and an item class. Listing 11.12 presents an iterator interface. Use these definitions to create an iterator that will allow you to iterate over the contents of the shopping cart.

LISTING 11.10   Item.java

```
public class Item {

    private int    id;
    private int    quantity;
    private float  unit_price;
    private String description;
    private float  discount;

    /**
     *  Create a new item with the given quantity, price,
     *  description, and unit discount.
```

11

LISTING 11.10   continued

```
 *    @param id the product id
 *    @param quantity the number of items selected
 *    @param unit_price the before discount price
 *    @param description the product description
 *    @param discount the dollar amount to subtract per item
 */
public Item( int id, int quantity, float unit_price, float discount,
String desc) {
    this.id = id;
    this.quantity = quantity;
    this.unit_price = unit_price;
    this.discount = discount;
    this.description = desc;
}

/**
 *    @return int the item quantity
 */
public int getQuantity() {
    return quantity;
}

/**
 *    @param quantity the new quantity
 */
public void setQuantity( int quantity ) {
    this.quantity = quantity;
}

/**
 *    @return the item unit price
 */
public float getUnitPrice() {
    return unit_price;
}

/**
 *    @return float the total price of the item minus any discounts
 */
public float getTotalPrice() {
    return ( unit_price * quantity ) - ( discount * quantity );
}

/**
 *    @return String the product description
 */
public String getDescription() {
    return description;
}
```

LISTING 11.10   continued

```
/**
 *  @return int the product id
 */
public int getID() {
    return id;
}
```

LISTING 11.11   ShoppingCart.java

```java
public class ShoppingCart {

    java.util.LinkedList items = new java.util.LinkedList();

    /**
     * adds an item to the cart
     * @param item the item to add
     */
    public void addItem( Item item ) {
        items.add( item );
    }

    /**
     * removes the given item from the cart
     * @param item the item to remove
     */
    public void removeItem( Item item ) {
        items.remove( item );
    }

    /**
     * @return int the number of items in the cart
     */
    public int getNumberItems() {
        return items.size();
    }

    /**
     * retrieves the indexed item
     * @param index the item's index
     * @retun Item the item at index
     */
    public Item getItem( int index ) {
        return (Item) items.get( index );
    }
}
```

11

LISTING 11.12 Iterator.java

```
public interface Iterator {
    public void first();
    public void next();
    public boolean isDone();
    public Object currentItem();
}
```

2. The PetAdapter presented earlier in the chapter is limited to only wrap one Pet instance. Alter the adapter so that you can change the object that it wraps at any time.

   Why might you want a mutable adapter?

Answers to Quiz

1. An adapter class transforms an object's interface to one expected by your program. An adapter contains an object and delegates messages from the new interface to the contained object's interface.

2. The Iterator pattern describes a mechanism for looping over elements in a collection.

3. You would use the Iterator pattern to contain traversal logic in one place, provide a standard way for traversing collections, and to hide the implementation of the collection from the user.

4. The Adapter pattern describes a mechanism that allows you to transform an objects interface.

5. You would use the Adapter pattern whenever you need to use an object that has an incompatible interface. You can also proactively use wrappers to isolate your code from API changes.

6. The Proxy pattern transparently brokers access to an object. Proxies add indirection to object use.

7. You would use the Proxy pattern any time that you would like to broker access to an object in a way that a simple reference does not allow. Common examples include remote resources, optimizations, and for general object housekeeping such as reference counting or usage statistics collecting.

8. In this situation you can use the Adapter pattern to create an interface that is independent of the one provided by Sun, IBM, or Apache. By creating your own interface, you can remain independent of each vendor's slightly different API. By wrapping the

library you are free to switch the library at any time whether to upgrade to a new version or to switch vendors since you control the adapter's interface.

9. In this situation you can use the Proxy pattern to hide the identity of the datastore object that your objects talk to. Depending upon the client's location, you can instantiate a networked proxy or a local proxy. Either way, the rest of the program will not know the difference, so all your objects can use one proxy interface without having to worry about the underlying implementation.

10. The Proxy pattern does not change an interface in that it doesn't take anything away from it. A proxy is free to add additional methods and attributes to the interface, however.

Answers to Exercises

1.

LISTING 11.13   ShoppingCart.java

```java
public class ShoppingCart {

    java.util.LinkedList items = new java.util.LinkedList();

    /**
     * adds an item to the cart
     * @param item the item to add
     */
    public void addItem( Item item ) {
        items.add( item );
    }

    /**
     * removes the given item from the cart
     * @param item the item to remove
     */
    public void removeItem( Item item ) {
        items.remove( item );
    }

    /**
     * @return int the number of items in the cart
     */
    public int getNumberItems() {
        return items.size();
    }

    /**
```

11

LISTING 11.13   continued

```
         * retrieves the indexed item
         * @param index the item's index
         * @retun Item the item at index
         */
        public Item getItem( int index ) {
            return (Item) items.get( index );
        }

        public Iterator iterator() {
            // ArrayList has an iterator() method that returns an iterator
            // however, for demonstration purposes it helps to see a simple iterator
            return new CartIterator( items );
        }
    }
```

LISTING 11.14   CartIterator.java

```
    public class CartIterator implements Iterator {

        private Object [] items;
        private int index;

        public CartIterator( java.util.LinkedList items ) {
            this.items = items.toArray();
        }

        public boolean isDone() {
            if( index >= items.length ) {
                return true;
            }
            return false;
        }

        public Object currentItem() {
            if( !isDone() ) {
                return items[index];
            }
            return null;
        }

        public void next() {
            index++;
        }

        public void first() {
```

LISTING 11.14   continued

```
        index = 0;
    }

}
```

2. By making the adapter mutable, you can use the same wrapper to wrap many different objects, and you don't need to instantiate a wrapper for each object that
   needs to be wrapped. Wrapper reuse makes better use of memory, and frees your
   program from having to pay the price of instantiating many wrappers.

LISTING 11.15   MutableAdapter.java

```
public class MutableAdapter extends MoodyObject {

    private Pet pet;

    public MutableAdapter( Pet pet ) {
        setPet( pet );
    }

    protected String getMood() {
        // only implementing because required to by
        // MoodyObject, since also override queryMood
        // we don't really need it
        return pet.speak();
    }

    public void queryMood() {
        System.out.println( getMood() );
    }

    public void setPet( Pet pet ) {
        this.pet = pet;
    }
}
```

11

DAY 12

Advanced Design Patterns

In yesterday's chapter, you saw how design patterns allow you to reuse time-tested designs. Today, you will continue your study of design patterns by examining three more patterns.

Today you will learn

- About three important design patterns
- How to make sure that your objects remain single
- How to enhance a previous example
- About some common pattern pitfalls that you should avoid

More Patterns by Example

Let's continue your study of design patterns by considering three important patterns:

- Abstract Factory
- Singleton
- Typesafe Enum

Each of these patterns find their way into almost every design. In fact, you can use the Typesafe Enum pattern to fix up an example from Chapter 3, "Encapsulation: Time to Write Code!"

The Abstract Factory Pattern

Chapter 7, "Polymorphism: Time to Write Code," showed you how you can combine inheritance and polymorphism to write "future-proof" software. Inheritance's pluggability relationships combined with polymorphism allows you to plug new objects into your program at any time; however, there is a downside.

For your program to be able to instantiate these new objects, you must go into the code and alter it so that it instantiates the new objects instead of the old ones. (And you'll need to do this in every place where the old objects are instantiated!) Wouldn't it be nice if there was an easier way to plug in your new objects?

The Abstract Factory pattern solves this problem through delegation. Instead of instantiating objects throughout your program, you can delegate that responsibility to an object called a *factory*. Whenever an object needs to create another object, it will ask the factory to do it. By using a factory, you can isolate all object creation in one place. When you need to introduce new objects into your system, you'll only need to update the factory so that it creates instance of your new classes. The objects that use the factory will never know the difference.

Figure 12.1 illustrates the general design of the Abstract Factory pattern.

The Abstract Factory pattern uses inheritance and pluggability. The base factory class defines all of the object creation methods, and each factory subclass defines which objects it creates by overriding the methods.

Implementing an Abstract Factory

There are times when you will need to use third-party libraries within your program. Unfortunately, when it comes time to upgrade to a new version, you may find that the libraries' public APIs have changed slightly. Luckily, the Abstract Factory pattern offers a solution that makes upgrading the library painless.

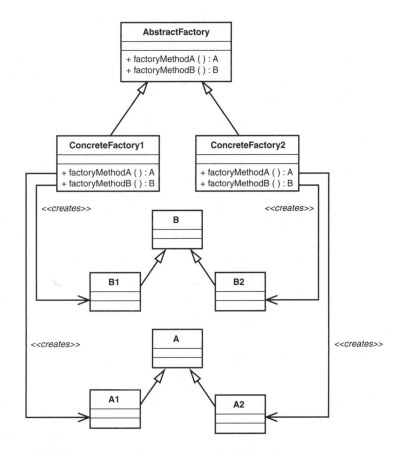

FIGURE 12.1

The Abstract Factory Pattern.

Imagine that you are working on a project that uses an XML parser. An XML parser will take an XML document as a `String` and return an object representation of the document known as `Document`. If you know that you will update the library in the future, and that the API will change, there are a few steps that you can take to protect yourself.

XML

XML, the Extensible Markup Language, is a language for writing tags that describe data. Just as HTML offers you tags for formatting and displaying your data, XML allows you to define your own custom tags to describe the conceptual meaning of your data.

HTML is an excellent way of marking up data for display. However, HTML lacks the ability to convey the meaning of the data. HTML can tell you to make a word bold, but HTML cannot tell you that the word that is bold is the title of the document. Instead, you have to apply that meaning externally to the document.

XML, on the other hand, provides you with a mechanism that lets you say that some word in a document is a title. If you use these tags to markup your data different programs can read your documents and know what each piece of data means. So, for example, you can write a program that knows to format titles as bold. Or you can write another program that reads through a list of documents and formulates a list of titles for your selection. Trying to write the same programs to read an HTML document would be much more difficult.

Over the past few years XML has become an important standard for the interchange of data. Two unrelated entities can communicate as long as they both understand the XML tags. As a result, XML has emerged as the standard for business-to-business communication. In order to buy and sell, two businesses can agree on a set of common tags. Once they have these tags they can exchange XML documents freely.

Consider the following recipe XML document:

```
<Recipe>
    <Name>Chicken Tacos</Name>
    <Ingredients>
        <Ingredient>
            <Name>Chicken</Name>
            <Quantity UOM="lb">1</Quantity>
        </Ingredient>
        <!— cut for brevity —>
    </Ingredients>
</Recipe>
```

This XML document has tags that describe the data in a recipe. If you understand the tag markup you know that the data between the <Name> tags is the name of the recipe. Any data between the <Ingredients> tags contains ingredient information.

You can write programs that recognize the Recipe markup. One program might allow you to select the recipes that you would like to cook over the course of a week. This program could use the Recipe documents that you choose to formulate and print out a shopping list. Another program might print out the week's menu.

In order for a program to read and understand an XML document, it must parse the document. An XML parser will take a document and convert it into a tree of objects. Each object will contain part of the document. Your program can simply traverse these objects to pull out information from the document. So, if you write a program that reads recipes, it can traverse through all of the Ingredient objects in order to construct a list of ingredients.

Currently, many different XML parsers are available to choose from. Each parser has a slightly different API, so once you write a program to use a specific parser, it can be difficult to switch parsers at a later time. The Abstract Factory pattern presents a way for you to protect from becoming locked into using any one particular parser.

NEW TERM An *XML parser* takes an XML document and transforms it into an object representation.

You initially need to wrap the parser in an object that you control.

Note   Remember, a *wrapper* is an adaptor. A *wrapper* converts an object's interface into an alternative interface. Normally, you use a *wrapper* to convert
the interface into one expected by your program.

Because you control the wrapper's API, you guarantee a stable API that your program
can use. Listing 12.1 illustrates a possible parser wrapper.

LISTING 12.1   Parser.java

```java
public interface Parser {
    public org.w3c.dom.Document parse( String document );
}
```

Note   org.w3c.dom.Document is an interface defined by the W3C for representing
an XML document as a structure of objects. You can find more information
about the Document interface at http://www.w3.org/TR/2000/
CR-DOM-Level-2-20000510/java-binding.html.

Listings 12.2 and 12.3 show two possible implementations: VersionOneParser that uses
version 1.0 of the library, and VersionTwoParser that uses version 2.0 of the library.

LISTING 12.2   VersionOneParser.java

```java
public class VersionOneParser implements Parser{

    public org.w3c.dom.Document parse( String document ) {
        // instantiate the version 1 parser
        // XMLParser p = new XMLParser();
        // pass the document to the parser and return the result
        // return p.parseXML( document );
    }

}
```

LISTING 12.3   VersionTwoParser.java

```java
public class VersionTwoParser implements Parser{

    public org.w3c.dom.Document parse( String document ) {
        // instantiate the version 2 parser
```

12

LISTING 12.3   continued

```
        // DOMParser parser = new DOMParser();
        // pass the document to the parser and return the result
        // return parser.parse( document );
    }

}
```

Your program can use the Abstract Factory pattern to create the proper version of the parser each time it needs to parse a document. Listing 12.4 presents the base factory interface.

LISTING 12.4   ParserFactory.java

```
public interface ParserFactory {
    public Parser createParser();
}
```

You will need two concrete factory implementations because there are two parser implementations. Listing 12.5 and 12.6 present those implementations.

LISTING 12.5   VersionOneParserFactory.java

```
public class VersionOneParserFactory implements ParserFactory {
    public Parser createParser() {
        return new VersionOneParser();
    }
}
```

LISTING 12.6   VersionTwoParserFactory.java

```
public class VersionTwoParserFactory implements ParserFactory {
    public Parser createParser() {
        return new VersionTwoParser();
    }
}
```

Now, instead of instantiating parsers directly, your program can use one of the factories to retrieve parser objects whenever it needs to parse a document. You'll simply need to instantiate the proper factory at the beginning of the program, and make it available to the objects in your program.

> The Factory Method pattern is closely related to the Abstract Factory pattern. In fact, an abstract factory can use factory methods to create the objects that it returns.
>
> A factory method is nothing more than a method that creates objects. `createParser()` is an example of a factory method. You can also find examples of factory methods throughout the Java API.
>
> `Class.newInstance()` is an example of a factory method.
>
> As you can see a factory method can appear in an ordinary class or in an abstract factory. In either case, it creates objects, thus hiding the actual class of the created object.

When to Use the Abstract Factory Pattern

Use the Abstract Factory pattern when

- You want to hide how an object is created.

- You want to hide the actual class of the object created.

- You want a set of objects used together. This prevents you from using incompatible objects together.

- You want to be able to use different versions of a class implementation. An abstract factory allows you to swap these different versions in and out of your system.

Table 12.1 outlines the user of the Abstract Factory pattern.

TABLE 12.1 The Abstract Factory Pattern

Pattern Name	Abstract Factory
Problem	Need a way to transparently swap in pluggable objects
Solution	Provides an abstract interface that provides methods for instantiating the objects
Consequences	Allows you to easily swap new class types into your system; however, it is expensive to add unrelated types

12

The Singleton Pattern

As you design your systems, you will find that some classes should logically only have one instance, such as a factory or an object that accesses some unshareable resource (database connection, region of memory, and so on). Nothing, however, will prevent one object from instantiating another object. How do you enforce your design?

The Singleton pattern provides the answer to this question. The Singleton pattern enforces your design by placing the responsibility of creating and brokering access to the instance in the object itself. Doing so guarantees that only one instance will get created, plus it provides a single point of access for that instance. Figure 12.2 illustrates the signature of a singleton class.

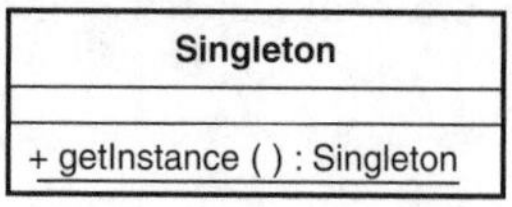

FIGURE **12.2**

The Singleton Pattern

Singleton
+ getInstance ( ) : Singleton

Listing 12.7 illustrates a possible singleton class.

LISTING 12.7   An Implementation of the Singleton pattern

```
public class Singleton {

    // a class reference to the singleton instance
    private static Singleton instance;

    // the constructor must be hidden so that objects cannot instantiate
    // protected allows other classes to inherit from Singleton
    protected Singleton() {}

    // a class method used to retrieve the singleton instance
    public static Singleton getInstance() {
        if( instance == null ) {
            instance = new Singleton();
        }
        return instance;
    }

}
```

The Singleton class holds onto a static Singleton instance and provides access to the Singleton instance through the getInstance() class method.

Implementing a Singleton

Chapter 7, lab 1 introduced a Payroll class. A "real life" payroll class would probably access an employee database. It might be a good idea to only have one Payroll instance to avoid resource conflicts. The Payroll is a good candidate for the Singleton pattern.

Listing 12.8 presents a Payroll singleton.

LISTING 12.8   A Payroll Singleton

```java
public class Payroll {

    // a class reference to the single singleton instance
    private static Payroll instance;

    private int    total_hours;
    private int    total_sales;
    private double total_pay;

    // hide the constructor so that other objects cannot instantiate
    protected Payroll() {}

    // note the use of static, you don't have an instance when you go to
retrieve
    // an instance, so the method must be a class method, thus static
    public static Payroll getInstance() {
        if( instance == null ) {
            instance = new Payroll();
        }
        return instance;
    }

    public void payEmployees( Employee [] emps ) {
        for( int i = 0; i < emps.length; i ++ ) {
            Employee emp = emps[i];
            total_pay += emp.calculatePay();
            emp.printPaycheck();
        }
    }

    public void calculateBonus( Employee [] emps ) {
        for( int i = 0; i < emps.length; i ++ ) {
            Employee emp = emps[i];
            System.out.println("Pay bonus to " + emp.getLastName() + ", " +
emp.getFirstName() + " $" + emp.calculateBonus() );
        }
    }

    public void recordEmployeeInfo( CommissionedEmployee emp ) {
        total_sales += emp.getSales();
    }

    public void recordEmployeeInfo( HourlyEmployee emp ) {
        total_hours += emp.getHours();
    }

    public void printReport() {
        System.out.println( "Payroll Report:" );
```

12

LISTING 12.8   continued

```
            System.out.println( "Total Hours: " + total_hours );
            System.out.println( "Total Sales: " + total_sales );
            System.out.println( "Total Paid: $" + total_pay );
     }


  }
```

The `Payroll` singleton adds a `getInstance()` method. This method is responsible for creating and providing access to the `singleton` instance. Take special note of the constructor; here, the constructor is protected so that other objects cannot inadvertently instantiate additional `Payroll` objects. Because it is protected, other objects may inherit from `Payroll`.

Listing 12.9 provides an example of how you can use the singleton.

LISTING 12.9   Using the `Payroll` Singleton

```
// retrieve the payroll singleton
Payroll payroll = Payroll.getInstance();

// create and update some employees
CommissionedEmployee emp1 = new CommissionedEmployee( "Mr.", "Sales", 25000.00,
1000.00);
CommissionedEmployee emp2 = new CommissionedEmployee( "Ms.", "Sales", 25000.00,
1000.00);
emp1.addSales( 7 );
emp2.addSales( 5 );

HourlyEmployee emp3 = new HourlyEmployee( "Mr.", "Minimum Wage", 6.50 );
HourlyEmployee emp4 = new HourlyEmployee( "Ms.", "Minimum Wage", 6.50 );
emp3.addHours( 40 );
emp4.addHours( 46 );

// use the overloaded methods
payroll.recordEmployeeInfo( emp2 );
payroll.recordEmployeeInfo( emp1 );
payroll.recordEmployeeInfo( emp3 );
payroll.recordEmployeeInfo( emp4 );
```

Once you have a singleton instance, it works just like any other instance. What is interesting about Listing 12.9 is:

```
Payroll payroll = Payroll.getInstance();
```

Note that you no longer say

```
Payroll payroll = new Payroll();
```

Inheritance and the Singleton Pattern

The Singleton pattern introduces some inheritance difficulties. Specifically, who manages the singleton instance, the parent or the child? You have a few choices.

The first choice is to simply create the singleton subclass and update the parent to instantiate the child. Listings 12.10 and 12.11 outline this approach.

LISTING 12.10   The `ChildSingleton`

```
public class ChildSingleton extends Singleton {

    protected ChildSingleton() {}

    public String toString() {
        return "I am the child singleton";
    }

}
```

LISTING 12.11   The Updated `Singleton`

```
public class Singleton {

    // a class reference to the singleton instance
    private static Singleton instance;

    // the constructor must be hidden so that objects cannot instantiate
    // protected allows other classes to inherit from Singleton
    protected ParentSingleton() {}

    // a class method used to retrieve the singleton instance
    public static Singleton getInstance() {
        if( instance == null ) {
            instance = new ChildSingleton();
        }
        return instance;
    }

    public String toString() {
        return "I am the singleton";
    }
}
```

12

This solution has the drawback of requiring changes in the parent class. An alternative solution includes having the singleton read a configuration variable the first time `getInstance()` gets called. The singleton can instantiate whatever object is specified in the configuration value.

You can also let each child provide its own implementation of `getInstance()`. This approach will not require changes to the parent.

This sidebar relies on a Java trick, although there is an analog in C++. It is an interesting solution that takes advantage of the fact that static blocks are executed as a class is loaded in Java.

Through another approach you can add a protected `register( Singleton s)` method to the parent. You can put a static block in the child that instantiates the child. Within the constructor, the child can register itself with the parent singleton.

Here is the code to the updated `Singleton`:

```java
public class Singleton {

    // a class reference to the singleton instance
    private static Singleton instance;

    // the constructor must be hidden so that objects cannot instantiate
    // protected allows other classes to inherit from Singleton
    protected Singleton() {}

    // a class method used to retrieve the singleton instance
    public static Singleton getInstance() {
        if( instance == null ) {
            // default value
            instance = new Singleton();
        }
        return instance;
    }

    protected static void register( Singleton s ) {
        if( instance == null ) {
            instance = s;
        }
    }
}
```

And the updated ChildSingleton:

```java
public class ChildSingleton extends Singleton {

    static {
        new ChildSingleton();
    }

    protected ChildSingleton() {
```

```
          Singleton.register( this );
      }

  }
```

To make all of this work, you will need to call Class.forName("ChildSingleton") before calling the singleton's getInstance() method. Here's an example:

```
Class.forName( "ChildSingleton" );
Singleton s = Singleton.getInstance();
System.out.println( s.toString() );
```

When to Use the Singleton Pattern

Use the Singleton pattern when you want to constrain a class to only having one instance.

Table 12.2 outlines the user of the Singleton pattern.

TABLE 12.2   The Singleton Pattern

Pattern Name	Singleton
Problem	Only one instance of an object should exist in the system at any one time.
Solution	Enables the object to manage its own creation and access through a class method.
Consequences	Controlled access to the object instance. Can provide access to a set number of instances as well (such as only six instances) with a slight change to the pattern. It is a bit more difficult to inherit a singleton.

12

The Typesafe Enum Pattern

Listing 12.12 lists a selection from the Card class, first introduced in Chapter 3, Lab 3.

LISTING 12.12   A Selection from Card.java

```java
public class Card {

    private int rank;
    private int suit;
    private boolean face_up;

    // constants used to instantiate
```

LISTING 12.12   continued

```
// suits
public static final int DIAMONDS = 4;
public static final int HEARTS   = 3;
public static final int SPADES   = 6;
public static final int CLUBS    = 5;
// values
public static final int TWO   = 2;
public static final int THREE = 3;
public static final int FOUR  = 4;
public static final int FIVE  = 5;
public static final int SIX   = 6;
public static final int SEVEN = 7;
public static final int EIGHT = 8;
public static final int NINE  = 9;
public static final int TEN   = 10;
public static final int JACK  = 74;
public static final int QUEEN = 81;
public static final int KING  = 75;
public static final int ACE   = 65;

// creates a new card - only use the constants to initialize
public Card( int suit, int rank ) {
    // In a real program you would need to do validation on the arguments.

    this.suit = suit;
    this.rank  = rank;
}
```

When instantiating Card objects, you have to pass in a valid rank and suit constant. The usage of constants in this way can lead to a host of problems. Nothing prevents you from passing in any int that you wish. And while you should just reference the constant name, this does open up the Card's internal representation. For example, to be able to learn the Card's suit, you must retrieve the int value and then compare it to the constants. While this works, this is not a clean solution.

The problem really stems from the fact that suit and rank are objects in their own right. int doesn't cut it because you need to apply a meaning to the int. Again, this muddles responsibility because you'll need to re-apply that meaning every time that you encounter an int that represents a rank or a suit.

Languages such as C++ have a construct known as an *enumeration*; however, enums simply boil down to shorthand for declaring a list of integer constants. These constants are limited. For example, they cannot provide behavior. It is also difficult to add additional constants.

Instead, the Typesafe Enum pattern provides an OO way to declare your constants. Instead of declaring simple integer constants, you create classes for each type of constant. For the Card example, you would create a Rank class and a Suit class. You then create an instance for each constant value that you would like to represent and make it publicly available from the class (through public final just like other constants).

Implementing the Typesafe Enum Pattern

Let's look at the implementation of the Rank and Suit classes in Listings 12.13 and 12.14.

LISTING 12.13   Suit.java

```java
public final class Suit {

    // statically define all valid values of Suit
    public static final Suit DIAMONDS = new Suit( (char)4 );
    public static final Suit HEARTS   = new Suit( (char)3 );
    public static final Suit SPADES   = new Suit( (char)6 );
    public static final Suit CLUBS    = new Suit( (char)5 );

    // helps to iterate over enum values
    public static final Suit [] SUIT = { DIAMONDS, HEARTS, SPADES, CLUBS };

    // instance variable for holding onto display value
    private final char display;

    // do not allow instantiation by outside objects
    private Suit( char display ) {
        this.display = display;
    }

    // return the Suit's value
    public String toString() {
        return String.valueOf( display );
    }
}
```

Suit is straightforward. The constructor takes a char that represents the Suit. Because Suit is a full-fledged object, it can also have methods. Here, the Suit provides a toString() method. A typesafe enumeration can add any methods that prove useful.

You'll also notice that the constant is private. This prevents objects from instantiating Suit objects directly. Instead, you are restricted to only use the constant instances declared by the class. The class is also declared final so that other classes cannot subclass it. There are times where you would allow inheritance. At those times make the constructor protected and remove the final declaration.

Note

> Because of the way Java works, be sure to provide final versions of `equals()` and `hashCode()` that call super if you open your enum to inheritance. If not, you'll open yourself to weird problems if your subclasses redefine these methods incorrectly.

You'll notice that the `Suit` class defines a number of constant instances, one for each of the valid suits. When you need a constant `Suit` value, you can say `Suit.DIAMONDS`.

The `Rank` class in Listing 12.14 works similar to `Suit`; however, it adds a few more methods. The `getRank()` method returns the value of the `Rank`. This value can be important for calculating the value of a hand. Unlike the original constants, you no longer have to apply meaning to the `Rank` or `Suit` constants. Instead, they hold onto their own meaning because they are objects.

LISTING 12.14   Rank.java

```
public final class Rank {

    public static final Rank TWO   = new Rank( 2, "2" );
    public static final Rank THREE = new Rank( 3, "3" );
    public static final Rank FOUR  = new Rank( 4, "4" );
    public static final Rank FIVE  = new Rank( 5, "5" );
    public static final Rank SIX   = new Rank( 6, "6" );
    public static final Rank SEVEN = new Rank( 7, "7" );
    public static final Rank EIGHT = new Rank( 8, "8" );
    public static final Rank NINE  = new Rank( 9, "9" );
    public static final Rank TEN   = new Rank( 10, "10" );
    public static final Rank JACK  = new Rank( 11, "J" );
    public static final Rank QUEEN = new Rank( 12, "Q" );
    public static final Rank KING  = new Rank( 13, "K" );
    public static final Rank ACE   = new Rank( 14, "A" );

    public static final Rank [] RANK =
            { TWO, THREE, FOUR, FIVE, SIX, SEVEN,
              EIGHT, NINE, TEN, JACK, QUEEN, KING, ACE };

    private final int    rank;
    private final String display;

    private Rank( int rank, String display ) {
        this.rank = rank;
        this.display = display;
    }

    public int getRank() {
```

LISTING 12.14   continued

```
            return rank;
        }

        public String toString() {
            return display;
        }
    }
```

For example, you no longer need to apply meaning to the int 4 and know that 4 stands for DIAMONDS. When you need to determine the constant's value, you can do object comparisons using equals().

Listing 12.15 shows the changes that you would need to make to Card to be able to use the new constants. (Updated Deck and Dealer classes are available from the source to this chapter).

LISTING 12.15   The Updated Card.java

```
public class Card {

    private Rank rank;
    private Suit suit;
    private boolean face_up;

    // creates a new card - only use the constants to initialize
    public Card( Suit suit, Rank rank ) {
        // In a real program you would need to do validation on the arguments.
        this.suit = suit;
        this.rank = rank;
    }

    public Suit getSuit() {
        return suit;
    }

    public Rank getRank() {
        return rank;
    }

    public void faceUp() {
        face_up = true;
    }

    public void faceDown() {
```

12

LISTING 12.15   continued

```
        face_up = false;
    }

    public boolean isFaceUp() {
        return face_up;
    }

    public String display() {
        return rank.toString() + suit.toString();
    }
}
```

You might have also noticed that both `Rank` and `Suit` declare arrays of constants. This makes it easy to loop over the available constant values. Listing 12.16 shows how this fact greatly simplifies the `Deck`'s `buildCards()` method.

LISTING 12.16   The Updated `buildCards()` Method

```
private void buildCards() {

    deck = new java.util.LinkedList();

    for( int i = 0; i < Suit.SUIT.length; i ++ ) {
        for( int j = 0; j < Rank.RANK.length; j ++ ) {
            deck.add( new Card( Suit.SUIT[i], Rank.RANK[j] ) );
        }
    }
}
```

When to Use the Typesafe Enum Pattern

Use the Typesafe Enum pattern when:

- You find yourself writing numerous public primitive or String constants.
- You find yourself enforcing identity on a value instead of deriving the identity from the value itself. Table 12.3 outlines the user of the Typesafe Enum pattern.

TABLE 12.3   The Typesafe Enum Pattern

Pattern Name	Typesafe Enum.
Problem	Integer constants are limited.

TABLE 12.3   continued

Solution	Creates a class for each constant type and then provide constant instances for each constant value.
Consequences	Extendible OO constants. Useful constants that have behavior. You still need to update code to use new constants as they are added. Requires more memory than a simple constant.

Pattern Pitfalls

You can abuse design patterns like you can any other tool by using them incorrectly. Design patterns do not guarantee a good design; in fact, including a pattern in a place where it really doesn't belong will ruin your design. You have to be judicious in your decision to include a pattern in your design.

Design patterns have recently come under an increasing amount of criticism. Unfortunately, there is a tendency, especially among beginners, to get caught up in trying to apply as many patterns to a design as possible. The enthusiasm to use patterns has caused many developers to lose sight of the point of patterns, and even the design process itself. Do not fall into this trap! Do not be blinded by a zest to apply patterns, and let design boil down to a race to cram as many patterns into your design as possible. You won't win points from your peers for using the most patterns, but you **will** win points from your peers for producing a clean, coherent design. Such a design might not even use patterns!

 Tip

There are some guidelines that will help you avoid pattern pitfall:

Tip 1: Placing Round Pegs In Square Holes. If you find yourself thinking, "How can I use <insert your favorite pattern here> in my design?" you're in trouble. Instead, you should be thinking, "I've seen this design before; I think there is a pattern that solves it." Now, go and look through a book of patterns. Always start from the point of view of the problem, not the solution (the pattern).

Tip 2: Fits Of Amnesia. You're in trouble if you can't explain, in two sentences or less, why you've chosen a pattern and what benefits it offers. You should easily be able to explain why you included a pattern, and what it contributes to a design. The situation is hopeless if you can't think of any explanation whatsoever.

12

There is a second, more subtle pitfall to patterns: *pattern babble*. Don't use patterns in an attempt to appear smart, and try not to suggest the use of a pattern that you have not studied. You might mention the pattern, but be clear if you are not familiar with it. You should not only use patterns appropriately in your design, but also in your conversation as well. It's not a good idea to contribute to the factors that harm the practice of using patterns.

Summary

Design patterns are a useful aid while designing your solutions. In their own way, patterns are the collective conscience of the OO community that tap years of design experience.

Keep in mind the limits of design patterns when you use them. A design pattern addresses one abstract problem, and one problem only. A design pattern does not provide the solution to a specific problem. Instead, the pattern provides an abstract solution to a general problem. It is up to you to provide the mapping between the abstract problem and your specific problem.

Mapping a design pattern is probably the greatest challenge that you will face while using patterns. It is a skill that only comes through time, study, and practice.

Q&A

Q How do you pick a design pattern?

A Each design pattern has a problem and related patterns. Study the pattern if the problem description seems to match your problem,. It will also help if you review any related patterns. If, after studying the pattern, it seems to address your problem, try to apply the pattern to your problem. Be sure to review the consequences. If any of the consequences clash with your requirements, you should probably pass on the pattern.

Q How do you know when to use a design pattern?

A There's no easy answer to this question.

You can't use a pattern if you don't know about it, and no one can know about every design pattern available. As you design, try to get as much input as possible. Ask other people if they know of any patterns that might help you make your design decisions.

Study patterns. The more patterns that you know, the more opportunities you will see for using them.

Q Does Java use any of the patterns covered today?

A Yes. Java uses many of the patterns covered today.

Factory Method Pattern: Many Java classes have factory methods (a pattern closely related to the Abstract Factory pattern).

Singleton Pattern: `java.lang.System` is an example of a singleton in Java.

Typesafe Enum Pattern: The Typesafe Enum pattern was not yet defined when many of the Java APIs were created. Future additions to the Java API will use the Typesafe Enum pattern.

Workshop

The quiz questions and answers are provided for your further understanding. See Appendix A, "Answers," for the answers.

Quiz

1. What is a wrapper class?
2. What problem does the Abstract Factory pattern solve?
3. Why would you use the Abstract Factory pattern?
4. What problem does the Singleton pattern solve?
5. Why would you use the Singleton pattern?
6. What problem does the Typesafe Enum pattern solve?
7. Why would you use the Typesafe Enum pattern?
8. Will patterns ensure a perfect design? Why, or why not?

12

Exercises

Listing 12.17 presents the `Bank` from Chapter 7. Turn `Bank` into a singleton.

LISTING 12.17   `Bank.java`

```java
public class Bank {

    private java.util.Hashtable accounts = new java.util.Hashtable();

    public void addAccount( String name, BankAccount account ) {
        accounts.put( name, account );
    }

    public double totalHoldings() {
```

LISTING 12.17   continued

```
        double total = 0.0;

        java.util.Enumeration enum = accounts.elements();
        while( enum.hasMoreElements() ) {
            BankAccount account = (BankAccount) enum.nextElement();
            total += account.getBalance();
        }
        return total;
    }

    public int totalAccounts() {
        return accounts.size();
    }

    public void deposit( String name, double ammount ) {
        BankAccount account = retrieveAccount( name );
        if( account != null ) {
            account.depositFunds( ammount );
        }
    }

    public double balance( String name ) {
        BankAccount account = retrieveAccount( name );
        if( account != null ) {
            return account.getBalance();
        }
        return 0.0;
    }

    private BankAccount retrieveAccount( String name ) {
        return (BankAccount) accounts.get( name );
    }
}
```

2. Consider the Error class presented in Listing 12.18. This class defines a number of level constants. Apply the Typesafe Enum pattern to this class's design.

LISTING 12.18   Error.java

```
public class Error {

    // error levels
    public final static int NOISE   = 0;
    public final static int INFO    = 1;
    public final static int WARNING = 2;
    public final static int ERROR   = 3;
```

LISTING 12.18   continued

```
    private int level;

    public Error( int level ) {
        this.level = level;
    }

    public int getLevel() {
        return level;
    }

    public String toString() {
        switch (level) {
            case 0: return "NOISE";
            case 1: return "INFO";
            case 2: return "WARNING";
            default: return "ERROR";
        }
    }
}
```

3. Design and create an abstract factory for the BankAccount hierarchy presented as a solution to Chapter 7, lab 3.

Answers to Quiz

1. A wrapper class transforms an object's interface to one expected by your program. A wrapper contains an object and delegates messages from the new interface to the contained object's interface.

2. The Abstract Factory pattern provides a mechanism that instantiates specific descendant class instances without revealing which descendant is actually created. This allows you to transparently plug in different descendants into your system.

3. You use the Abstract Factory pattern to hide the details of instantiation, to hide which class of object gets instantiated, and when you want a set of objects used together.

4. The Singleton pattern ensures that an object is instantiated only once.

5. You use the Singleton pattern when you want an object to be instantiated only once.

6. Using primitive constants is not an OO approach to programming, because you have to apply an external meaning to the constant. You saw how much trouble the breakdown of responsibility could cause!

12

The Typesafe Enum pattern solves this problem by turning the constant into a higher-level object. By using a higher-level object, you can better encapsulate responsibility within the constant object.

7. You should use the Typesafe Enum pattern whenever you find yourself declaring public constants that should be objects in their own right.

8. No, patterns do not ensure a perfect design because you could end up using a pattern incorrectly. Also, correctly using a pattern does not mean that the rest of your design is valid. Many valid designs might not even contain a pattern.

Answers to Exercises

1.

LISTING 12.19   Bank.java

```java
public class Bank {

    private java.util.Hashtable accounts = new java.util.Hashtable();

    private static Bank instance;

    protected Bank() {}

    public static Bank getInstance() {
        if( instance == null ) {
            instance = new Bank();
        }
        return instance;
    }

    public void addAccount( String name, BankAccount account ) {
        accounts.put( name, account );
    }

    public double totalHoldings() {
        double total = 0.0;

        java.util.Enumeration enum = accounts.elements();
        while( enum.hasMoreElements() ) {
            BankAccount account = (BankAccount) enum.nextElement();
            total += account.getBalance();
        }
        return total;
    }

    public int totalAccounts() {
        return accounts.size();
    }
```

LISTING 12.19   continued

```
    public void deposit( String name, double ammount ) {
        BankAccount account = retrieveAccount( name );
        if( account != null ) {
            account.depositFunds( ammount );
        }
    }

    public double balance( String name ) {
        BankAccount account = retrieveAccount( name );
        if( account != null ) {
            return account.getBalance();
        }
        return 0.0;
    }

    private BankAccount retrieveAccount( String name ) {
        return (BankAccount) accounts.get( name );
    }
}
```

2.

LISTING 12.20   Level.java

```
public final class Level {

    public final static Level NOISE   = new Level( 0, "NOISE" );
    public final static Level INFO    = new Level( 1, "INFO" );
    public final static Level WARNING = new Level( 2, "WARNING" );
    public final static Level ERROR   = new Level( 3, "ERROR" );

    private int    level;
    private String name;

    private Level( int level, String name ) {
        this.level = level;
        this.name  = name;
    }

    public int getLevel() {
        return level;
    }

    public String getName() {
        return name;
    }
}
```

12

LISTING 12.21   Error.java

```java
public class Error {

    private Level level;

    public Error( Level level ) {
        this.level = level;
    }

    public Level getLevel() {
        return level;
    }

    public String toString() {
        return level.getName();
    }
}
```

3. The solution consists of an abstract bank account factory (written as an interface; however, it can be an abstract class as well) and a concrete bank account factory. The factory has a method for creating each type of bank account.

   This factory hides the details of instantiation, not necessarily the object's subtype.

LISTING 12.22   AbstractAccountFactory.java

```java
public interface AbstractAccountFactory {

    public CheckingAccount createCheckingAccount( double initDeposit, int trans,
    double fee );

    public OverdraftAccount createOverdraftAccount( double initDeposit, double
    rate );

    public RewardsAccount createRewardsAccount( double initDeposit, double
    interest, double min );

    public SavingsAccount createSavingsAccount( double initBalance, double
    interestRate );

    public TimedMaturityAccount createTimedMaturityAccount( double initBalance,
    double interestRate, double feeRate );

}
```

LISTING 12.23   ConcreteAccountFactory.java

```java
public class ConcreteAccountFactory implements AbstractAccountFactory {

    public CheckingAccount createCheckingAccount( double initDeposit, int trans,
    double fee ) {
        return new CheckingAccount( initDeposit, trans, fee );
    }

    public OverdraftAccount createOverdraftAccount( double initDeposit, double
    rate ) {
        return new OverdraftAccount( initDeposit, rate );
    }

    public RewardsAccount createRewardsAccount( double initDeposit, double
    interest, double min ) {
        return new RewardsAccount( initDeposit, interest, min );
    }

    public SavingsAccount createSavingsAccount( double initBalance, double
    interestRate ) {
        return new SavingsAccount( initBalance, interestRate );
    }

    public TimedMaturityAccount createTimedMaturityAccount( double initBalance,
    double interestRate, double feeRate ) {
        return new TimedMaturityAccount( initBalance, interestRate, feeRate );
    }

}
```

12

WEEK 2

DAY 13

OO and User Interface Programming

The user interface (UI) provides the interface between the user and your system. Almost every modern system will have some form of UI, whether graphical, command-line driven, or even phone or speech based. (Some systems may combine all four types!). In any case, you need to take special care in the design and implementation of your user interfaces. Luckily, OOP can bring the same benefits to your UI that it brings to other aspects of the system.

Today you will learn

- How OOP and UI construction interrelate
- About the importance of a decoupled UI
- What patterns help you to decouple the UI

OOP and the User Interface

The process of designing and programming user interfaces is fundamentally no different than the process of designing and programming any other aspect of your system. You may need to learn some new APIs so that you can construct your UIs, but in the end you need to apply the same object-oriented principles to the UI as you would to the other parts of your system.

 Note

You will learn how to approach UI development from the point of view of a developer. As a developer, you will design and implement the classes that make up and support the user interface.

Today's lesson will not cover the general subject of UI design. UI design encompasses all aspects of how the capabilities of a program are made available to a user. The general subject of UI design is one that is completely removed from programming, and more rooted in graphic arts and psychology. The ACM Special Interest Group on Computer-Human Interaction (SIGCHI) is an excellent resource for information on the topic of UI design and usability.

The point deserves emphasis: When designing and programming your user interfaces you *must* apply the same OO principals to your UIs that you would apply to the rest of your system! Too often, user interfaces are simply thrown together and tacked onto the system as an after thought.

Instead, your UI code needs to be just as object-oriented as the code in the rest of the system. The UI implementation has to use encapsulation, inheritance, and polymorphism properly.

You also need to consider the UI while performing OOA and OOD. Without a proper analysis and design, you may miss certain requirements and find that you've written a UI that isn't flexible enough to provide the desired level of functionality, or a UI that can't adapt to future changes.

The Importance of Decoupled UIs

You will find that the same system often requires many different, often unrelated, user interfaces. For example, a provisioning system may allow people to place orders over the Web, by phone, by PDA, or through a custom desktop application. Each of these interfaces will hook into the same system; however, each approach will hook into the system and display the information in its own way.

You will also find that user interface requirements can become a moving target. Systems mature over time as new features are added and as users expose areas of weakness. In response, you will need to continually update the user interface to be able to expose each new feature and correct any shortcomings. This reality calls for a user interface whose design is flexible and can readily accept change.

The best way to achieve flexibility is to design a system that is completely decoupled from its UI. A decoupled design allows you to add any UI to the system, and to make changes to the existing UIs without having to make corresponding changes to the system itself. A decoupled design also allows you to test the capabilities of the system even if you have not finished developing the UI. Furthermore, a decoupled design allows you to pinpoint bugs as either being UI bugs or being system errors.

Luckily, OOP is the perfect solution to these problems. By properly isolating responsibilities, you can lessen the impact of changes on unrelated parts of the system. By isolating functionality, you should be able to add any interface to your system at any time without making changes to the underlying system. The key is to not embed the UI code inside of the system itself. The two *must* be separate.

Let's take a look at an example that improperly decouples the UI. Listing 13.1 shows how *not* to write a UI.

LISTING 13.1   VisualBankAccount.java

```java
import javax.swing.JPanel;
import javax.swing.JLabel;
import java.awt.BorderLayout;
import java.awt.event.ActionListener;
import java.awt.event.ActionEvent;
import javax.swing.JTextField;
import javax.swing.JButton;

public class VisualBankAccount extends JPanel implements ActionListener {

    // private data
    private double balance;

    // UI elements
    private JLabel      balanceLabel   = new JLabel();
    private JTextField  amountField    = new JTextField( 10 );
    private JButton     depositButton  = new JButton( "Deposit" );
    private JButton     withdrawButton = new JButton( "Withdraw" );

    public VisualBankAccount( double initDeposit ) {
        setBalance( initDeposit );
        buildUI();
```

13

LISTING 13.1 Continued

```java
    }

    // handles the events from the buttons
    public void actionPerformed( ActionEvent e ) {
        if( e.getSource() == depositButton ) {
            double amount = Double.parseDouble( amountField.getText() );
            depositFunds( amount );
        } else if( e.getSource() == withdrawButton ) {
            double amount = Double.parseDouble( amountField.getText() );
            if( amount > getBalance() ) {
                amount = getBalance();
            }
            withdrawFunds( amount );
        }
    }

    private void buildUI() {

        setLayout( new BorderLayout() );

        // build the display
        JPanel buttons = new JPanel( new BorderLayout() );
        JPanel balance = new JPanel( new BorderLayout() );
        buttons.add( depositButton, BorderLayout.WEST );
        buttons.add( withdrawButton, BorderLayout.EAST );
        balance.add( balanceLabel, BorderLayout.NORTH );
        balance.add( amountField, BorderLayout.SOUTH );
        add( balance, BorderLayout.NORTH );
        add( buttons, BorderLayout.SOUTH );

        // set up the callbacks so that the buttons do something
        // the deposit button should call depositFunds()
        depositButton.addActionListener( this );
        // the withdraw button should call withdrawFunds
        withdrawButton.addActionListener( this );
    }

    public void depositFunds( double amount ) {
        setBalance( getBalance() + amount );
    }

    public double getBalance() {
        return balance;
    }

    protected void setBalance( double newBalance ) {
        balance = newBalance;
        balanceLabel.setText( "Balance: " + balance);
    }
```

LISTING 13.1   Continued

```
    public double withdrawFunds( double amount ) {
        setBalance( getBalance() - amount );
        return amount;
    }

}
```

The VisualBankAccount uses Java's Swing library to display itself. Every OO language has libraries for creating and displaying graphical user interfaces (GUI). Don't worry if you don't understand everything in this example. It's just important that you understand the general meaning of the example.

A bit of background may help. Swing provides a class for each major GUI element, such as buttons (JButton), labels (JLabel), and entry fields (JTextField). You put those elements together, such as inside of panels (JPanel), to build your UI.

Each GUI element has an addActionListener() method. This method allows you to register an object that implements the ActionListener interface as a callback. Whenever the GUI element generates an event (usually as a result of a mouse click), it will inform each of its action listeners. Here, the VisualBankAccount acts as the listener. When it receives an event from one of the buttons, it takes the proper action and then either deposits or withdraws money.

VisualBankAccount provides all of the functionality of the BankAccount class presented in earlier lessons. The VisualBankAccount also knows how to display itself, as shown in Figure 13.1.

FIGURE 13.1

The VisualBankAccount *embedded within a frame.*

13

Whenever you type in an amount and click the Deposit or Withdraw button, the bank account will extract the amount from the entry field and either call its withdrawFunds() or depositFunds() method with the value.

Because VisualBankAccount is a Jpanel, you can embed it in any Java GUI. Unfortunately, the UI is not decoupled from the bank account class. Such tight coupling makes it impossible to use the bank account in other forms of user interfaces, or to provide a different UI without having to alter the VisualBankAccount class itself. In fact, you'll need to create a separate version of the class for each type of UI that you would like to have it participate within.

How to Decouple the UI Using the Model View Controller Pattern

The Model View Controller (MVC) design pattern provides one approach to the design of user interfaces that completely decouples the underlying system from the user interface.

Note

> MVC is only one approach to designing object-oriented user interfaces. There are other valid approaches to user interface design; however, MVC is a time-tested approach that is popular in the software industry. If you end up doing user interface work, especially in relation to the Web and Sun's J2EE, you will encounter MVC.
>
> Both the Document/View Model popularized by the Microsoft Foundation Classes and the Presentation Abstraction Control (PAC) design pattern provide alternatives to the MVC. See *Pattern–Oriented Software Architecture A System of Patterns* by Frank Buschmann, et al (Wiley, ISBN 0-471-95869-7) for a complete presentation of these alternatives.

The MVC pattern decouples the UI from the system by breaking the UI design into three separate pieces:

- The model, which represents the system
- The view, which displays the model
- The controller, which processes user input

Each piece of the MVC triad has its own set of unique responsibilities.

The Model

The model is responsible for providing

- Access to the system's core functionality
- Access to the system's state information
- A state change notification system

The model is the layer of the MVC triad that manages the core behavior and state of the system. The model responds to queries about its state from the view and controller and to state change requests from the controller.

> **Note**
>
> A system may have many different models. For example a banking system may be made up of an account model and a teller model. A number of smaller models breaks up responsibility better than one large model.
>
> Don't let the term *model* confuse you. A model is just an object that represents the system.

The controller is the layer of the MVC triad that interprets user input. In response to the user input, the controller may command the model or the view to change or perform some action.

The view is the layer of the MVC triad that displays the graphical or textual representation of the model. The view retrieves all state information about the model from the model.

In either case, the model is completely unaware that a view or controller is making a method call. The model is only aware that an object is calling one of its methods. The only connection that a model maintains to the UI is through the state change notification system.

If a view or controller is interested in state change notification, it will register itself with the model. When the model changes its state, it will go through its list of registered objects (often called listeners or observers) and inform each object of the state change. To construct this notification system, models will normally employ the Observer pattern.

The Observer Pattern

The Observer pattern provides a design for a publish/subscribe mechanism among objects. The Observer pattern allows an object (the observer) to register its interest in another object (the observable). Whenever the observable wants to notify its observers of a change, it will call an update() method on each observer.

Listing 13.2 defines the Observer interface. All observers that want to register with the observable object must implement the Observer interface.

LISTING 13.2 *Observer.java*

```
public interface Observer {

    public void update();
}
```

An observable will provide a method through which the observers can register and deregister their interest in updates. Listing 13.3 presents a class that implements the Observer pattern.

13

Implementing The Model

Applying the MVC pattern to the VisualBankAccount can make it much more flexible. Let's start by ripping the core "system" functionality out of the display code to be able to create the model.

Listing 13.3 presents the core bank account functionality—the model.

LISTING 13.3 BankAccountModel.java

```java
import java.util.ArrayList;
import java.util.Iterator;

public class BankAccountModel {

    // private data
    private double    balance;
    private ArrayList listeners = new ArrayList();

    public BankAccountModel( double initDeposit ) {
        setBalance( initDeposit );
    }

    public void depositFunds( double amount ) {
        setBalance( getBalance() + amount );
    }

    public double getBalance() {
        return balance;
    }

    protected void setBalance( double newBalance ) {
        balance = newBalance;
        updateObservers();
    }

    public double withdrawFunds( double amount ) {
        if( amount > getBalance() ) {
            amount = getBalance();
        }
        setBalance( getBalance() - amount );
        return amount;
    }

    public void register( Observer o ) {
        listeners.add( o );
        o.update();
    }
```

LISTING 13.3 Continued

```
    public void deregister( Observer o ) {
        listeners.remove( o );
    }

    private void updateObservers() {
        Iterator i = listeners.iterator();
        while( i.hasNext() ) {
            Observer o = (Observer) i.next();
            o.update();
        }
    }
}
```

The BankAccountModel is similar to the original BankAccount class presented in earlier lessons; however, the model also uses the Observer pattern to add support for registering and updating objects that are interested in state change notification.

You'll also notice that this class contains all of the system logic. withdrawFunds() now checks the withdraw amount ensure that it is not greater than the balance. It's critical to keep such domain rules within the model. If these rules were to leak out into the view or controller, each view and controller for this model would need to maintain the rule. As you've seen, having each view or controller enforce this rule is a muddling of responsibilities, and is error prone. Muddling the responsibility also makes it difficult to change the rule because you must change it in each place.

Substitutability relationships also make placing rules in the view a dangerous practice. Because of substitutability relationships, a view will work for any subclass; however, if you put the withdraw rules into the view, the view will no longer work for an OverdraftAccount. This is because the OverDraftAccounts allow you to withdraw amounts greater than the current balance.

The View

The view is responsible for

- Displaying the model to the user
- Registering with the model for state change notification
- Retrieving state information from the model

The view is the layer of the MVC triad that displays information to the user. The view obtains display information from the model using the model's public interface, and will also register itself with the model so that it can be informed of state change and update itself accordingly.

13

Note

A single model may have many different views.

Implementing the View

Now that there is a model it's time to implement the bank account view. Listing 13.4 presents the BankAccountModel's view.

LISTING 13.4   *BankAccountView.java*

```java
import javax.swing.JPanel;
import javax.swing.JLabel;
import java.awt.BorderLayout;
import javax.swing.JTextField;
import javax.swing.JButton;

public class BankAccountView extends JPanel implements Observer {

    public final static String DEPOSIT  = "Deposit";
    public final static String WITHDRAW = "Withdraw";

    private BankAccountModel model;
    private BankAccountController controller;

    // GUI Elements, pre-allocate all to avoid null values
    private JButton depositButton  = new JButton( DEPOSIT );
    private JButton withdrawButton = new JButton( WITHDRAW );
    private JTextField amountField = new JTextField();
    private JLabel balanceLabel    = new JLabel();

    public BankAccountView( BankAccountModel model ) {
        this.model = model;
        this.model.register( this );
        attachController( makeController() );
        buildUI();
    }

    // called by model when the model changes
    public void update() {
        balanceLabel.setText( "Balance: " + model.getBalance() );
    }

    // provides access to the amount entered into the field
    public double getAmount() {
        // assume that the user entered a valid number
        return Double.parseDouble( amountField.getText() );
    }
```

LISTING 13.4 Continued

```
    // wires the given controller to the view, allows outside object to set con-
troller
    public void attachController( BankAccountController controller ) {
        // each view can only have one controller, so remove the old one first
        if( this.controller != null ) { // remove the old controller
            depositButton.removeActionListener( controller );
            withdrawButton.removeActionListener( controller );
        }

        this.controller = controller;
        depositButton.addActionListener( controller );
        withdrawButton.addActionListener( controller );
    }

    protected BankAccountController makeController() {
        return new BankAccountController( this, model );
    }

    private void buildUI() {

        setLayout( new BorderLayout() );

        // associate each button with a commend string
        // the controller will use this string to interpret events
        depositButton.setActionCommand( DEPOSIT );
        withdrawButton.setActionCommand( WITHDRAW );

        // build the display
        JPanel buttons = new JPanel( new BorderLayout() );
        JPanel balance = new JPanel( new BorderLayout() );
        buttons.add( depositButton, BorderLayout.WEST );
        buttons.add( withdrawButton, BorderLayout.EAST );
        balance.add( balanceLabel, BorderLayout.NORTH );
        balance.add( amountField, BorderLayout.SOUTH );
        add( balance, BorderLayout.NORTH );
        add( buttons, BorderLayout.SOUTH );
    }
}
```

13

The BankAccountView's constructor accepts a reference to a BankAccountModel. Upon creation, the BankAccountView registers itself with the model, creates and attaches itself to its controller, and constructs its UI. The view uses the model to retrieve all of the information that it needs for display. Whenever the balance changes, the model will call the view's update() method. When this method gets called, the view will update its balance display.

Normally a view will create its own controller, as BankAccountView does within the makeController() factory method. Subclasses can override this factory method to create a different controller. Within the `attachController()` method the view registers the controller with the deposit and withdraw buttons so that the controller can receive user event.

You will notice, however, that the view first removes any pre-existing controller. A view will normally have only one controller.

You'll also notice that `attachController()` is a public method. Using this method you can switch the controller without having to subclass the view. This method allows you to create different controllers and pass them to the view. The controller that you see in the next section will interpret the user events just as `VisualBankAccount` interpreted them (with only slight modification). Nothing stops you from writing controllers that lock out the user, or limit what the user can do.

Unlike a view that can only have one controller at a time, a model may have many different views. Listing 13.5 presents a second view for the bank account.

LISTING 13.5   `BankAccountCLV.java`

```java
public class BankAccountCLV implements Observer {

    private BankAccountModel model;

    public BankAccountCLV( BankAccountModel model ) {
        this.model = model;
        this.model.register( this );
    }

    public void update() {
        System.out.println( "Current Balance: $" + model.getBalance() );
    }
}
```

`BankAccountCLV` simply prints the balance to the command line. While this behavior is simple, `BankAccountCLV` is an alternate view into the `BankAccountModel`. You'll notice that this view does not require a controller because it does not accept user events. You do not always need to provide a controller.

Tip

A view may not always display to the screen.

Take a word processor as an example. The model of the word processor will keep track of the entered text, formatting, footnotes, and so on. One view will display the text in the main editor; however, another view may convert the data in the model into PDF, HTML, or Postscript and then write it out to a file. The view that writes to a file doesn't display to the screen; instead, the view displays to a file. Other programs can then open, read, and display the data in the file.

The Controller

The controller is responsible for

- Intercepting user events from the view
- Interpreting the event, and calling the proper methods on the model or the view
- Registering with the model for state change notification, if interested

The controller acts as the glue between the view and the model. The controller intercepts events from the view and then translates them into requests for the model or the view.

> **Note** A view only has one controller, and a controller only has one view. Some views allow you to set their controller directly.

Each view has one controller, and all user interaction goes through that controller. If the controller is dependent upon state information, it will also register with the model for state change notification.

Implementing the Controller

With a model and view already created, all that is left to construct is the BankAccountView's controller. Listing 13.6 presents the view's controller.

LISTING 13.6 BankAccountController.java

```java
import java.awt.event.ActionListener;
import java.awt.event.ActionEvent;

public class BankAccountController implements ActionListener {

    private BankAccountView  view;
    private BankAccountModel model;

    public BankAccountController( BankAccountView view, BankAccountModel model )
    {
        this.view  = view;
        this.model = model;
    }

    public void actionPerformed( ActionEvent e ) {

        String command = e.getActionCommand();
        double amount = view.getAmount();
```

13

LISTING 13.6   Continued

```
        if( command.equals( view.WITHDRAW ) ) {
            model.withdrawFunds( amount );
        } else if( command.equals( view.DEPOSIT ) ) {
            model.depositFunds( amount );
        }

    }

}
```

Upon construction the controller accepts a reference to both the view and model. The controller will use the view to obtain the amounts entered into the entry field. The controller will use the model to actually withdraw and deposit money into the account.

The `BankAccountController` itself is fairly simple. The controller implements the `ActionListener` interface so that it can receive events from the view. The view takes care of registering the controller for events, so the controller doesn't need to do anything other than interpret events as it receives them.

Whenever the controller does receive an event, it checks the event's command to determine whether the event is a withdraw or deposit event. In either case, it makes the corresponding call on the model. Unlike the original `VisualBankAccount`, the controller only needs to call `depositFunds()` or `withdrawFunds()`. It no longer needs to make sure that the withdraw amount is not greater than the balance because the model now takes care of this domain detail.

Putting the Model View and Controller Together

Listing 13.7 presents a small main that glues the model and two views together. The main doesn't need to do anything to the controller because the view takes care of that detail.

LISTING 13.7   Putting the Model, Views, and Controller Together

```
import java.awt.event.WindowListener;
import java.awt.event.WindowAdapter;
import java.awt.event.WindowEvent;
import javax.swing.JFrame;

public class MVCDriver {

    public static void main( String [] args ) {

        BankAccountModel model = new BankAccountModel( 10000.00 );
```

LISTING 13.7 Continued

```
            BankAccountView view   = new BankAccountView( model );
            BankAccountCLV  clv    = new BankAccountCLV( model );

            JFrame frame = new JFrame();

            WindowAdapter wa = new WindowAdapter() {
                public void windowClosing( WindowEvent e ) {
                    System.exit( 0 );
                }
            };

            frame.addWindowListener( wa );

            frame.getContentPane().add( view );
            frame.pack();
            frame.show();
        }

}
```

The main first creates an instance of the model. When the main has the model, the main can then create the various views. In the case of the BankAccountView, the main also needs to imbed the view in a frame so that the view can be displayed. Figure 13.2 illustrates the resulting output.

FIGURE 13.2

A bank account model with multiple views.

If you execute MVCDriver, you will see two separate views into the same model. Using the MVC pattern you can create as many views of your underlying models that you need.

Problems with the Model View Controller

As with any design, the Model View Controller has its shortcomings and its critics alike. The problems include

13

- An emphasis on data
- A tight coupling between the view/controller and the model
- An opportunity for inefficiency

The severity of these shortcomings depends upon the problem that you are solving and its requirements.

An Emphasis on Data

On an OO scale of purity, the MVC pattern does not rate near the top because of its emphasis on data. Instead of asking an object to do something with its data, the view asks the model for data and then displays it.

You can lessen the severity of this problem by displaying only the data that you remove from the model. Do not perform additional processing on the data. If you find yourself doing extra processing on the data after you retrieve it, or before you call a method on the model, chances are good that the model should do that work for you. There is a fine line between doing too much and doing what is necessary to the data. Over time you will learn to differentiate between too much to the data and only doing what is necessary.

| **Tip** | If you find that you repeat the same code in each view, consider moving that logic into the model. |

Avoiding the MVC pattern solely for purity reasons can fly in the face of some programming realities. Take a Web site as an example. Some companies mandate a clear separation between presentation (the view) and business logic (the model). Forcing such a separation has a valid business basis: The programmers can program and the content people can write content. Taking the content out of the programming layer means that non-programmers can create content. Forcing content into the programming layer means that the person writing content must either be a programmer, or that a programmer has to take the content and embed it within the code. It is much harder to update a site if you embed content in the code.

Reality also tells you that requirements are not written in stone, much less known. Again, the Web site provides an excellent example. A Web site has to generate HTML for display in a desktop web browser. What about PDAs, cell phones, and other display devices? None of those displays use basic HTML. How about six months into the future? Chances are good there will be other forms of display. To meet unknown requirements, you need a design that is flexible. If you have a fairly static system with well-defined requirements, you can use an alternative such as PAC. If you aren't lucky enough to have such clear requirements, you'll need to consider MVC.

Tight Coupling

Both the view and controller are tightly coupled to the model's public interface. Changes to the model's interface will require changes in both the view and the controller. When you use the MVC pattern, you implicitly make the assumption that the model is stable, and that the view is likely to change. If this is not the case, you will either need to pick a different design, or be prepared to make changes to the view and controller.

The view and controller are also closely related to one another. A controller is almost always used exclusively with a specific view. You can try to find reuse through careful design; but even if you don't, the MVC pattern still provides a good division of responsibility between the objects. OO is not simply a means for reuse.

Inefficiency

You must be careful to avoid inefficiencies when designing and implementing an MVC-based UI. Inefficiencies can find their way into the system in any piece of the MVC triad.

The model should avoid propagating unnecessary state change notifications to its observers. A model can queue related change notifications so that one notification may signify many state changes. Java's Abstract Window Toolkit (AWT) event model uses this approach for redrawing the screen. Instead of redrawing after each event, the AWT queues up the events and does one redraw.

When designing the controller and view you may want to consider caching the data, if data retrieval from the model is slow. After a state change notification, only retrieve the state that has changed. You can augment the observer pattern so that the model passes an identifier to the update() method. The view can use that identifier to decide whether or not it needs to update itself.

Summary

The user interface is an important part of any system. To some it may be the only part of the system with which they interact; to them, the UI *is* the system. You should always approach the UI's analysis, design, and implementation just as you approach any other part of the system. A UI should never be an afterthought, or something tacked onto the system at the last minute.

While there are many approaches to UI design, the MVC pattern provides a design that offers flexibility by decoupling the UI from the underlying system. But as with any other design decision, you'll still need to weigh the pros and cons of MVC before you decide to use it. The MVC does not decouple you from the realities of your system.

13

Q&A

Q **Your BankAccountModel class contains all of the system logic. Does the model always have to hold the logic or can it act as a gateway into the actual system?**

A It depends. Sometimes the model will act as a gateway into the system; other times, the model will actually be embedded within the real system. It all boils down to a design decision. In either case, the UI has no way of knowing if the model acts as a gateway or not.

Q **In Listing 13.6 you wrote**

```
if( command.equals( view.WITHDRAW ) ) {
        model.withdrawFunds( amount );
    } else if( command.equals( view.DEPOSIT ) ) {
        model.depositFunds( amount );
    }
```

Isn't this case logic? I thought that you said case logic is "bad" OO.

A Yes. That is an example of case logic.

To keep this example simple, I decided to make the controller an ActionListener that would handle both events. In a real implementation, you can avoid the case logic by catching the original event inside of the view itself and having the view generate its own custom events. For example, the view could generate deposit and withdraw events. The controller could listen for each of these events separately. Perhaps the controller would implement a depositPerformed() and withdrawPerformed() methods. The view would call the proper method on the controller depending on the event; thus, no more case statement, but a much harder example to understand.

Q **Okay. Your previous answer makes me feel a little better. But if you implement the controller as explained above, doesn't the view have to do case logic to figure out which button fired the event?**

A No. The view can avoid case logic by providing a separate listener for each button. When there is a one-to-one correspondence between an element and its listener, you do not need to do case logic to figure out where the event originates. (See exercise 2 for the alternative implementation.)

Workshop

The quiz questions and answers are provided for your further understanding. See Appendix A, "Answers," for the answers.

Quiz

1. How are the UI's analysis, design, and implementation different from that of the rest of the system?

2. Why should you decouple the UI from the underlying system?

3. What are the three components of the MVC triad?

4. What are two alternatives to the MVC pattern?

5. Describe the model's responsibilities.

6. Describe the view's responsibilities.

7. Describe the controller's responsibilities.

8. How many models can a system have? How many views can a model have? How many controllers can a view have?

9. What inefficiencies must you avoid while using the MVC pattern?

10. What assumptions does the MVC pattern make?

11. What is the history of the MVC pattern? (Please note that this question requires you to do a quick web search.)

Exercises

1. Listing 13.8 presents an employee class. Alter the employee class so that it can register and unregister listeners, as well as inform them of state changes. Listing 13.2 presents an Observer interface that you can use for this exercise.

LISTING 13.8 EmployeeModel.java

```java
public abstract class Employee {

    private String first_name;
    private String last_name;
    private double wage;

    public Employee(String first_name,String last_name,double wage) {
        this.first_name = first_name;
        this.last_name  = last_name;
        this.wage = wage;
    }

    public double getWage() {
        return wage;
    }

    public void setWage( double wage ) {
```

13

LISTING 13.8   Continued

```
            this.wage = wage;
        }


        public String getFirstName() {
            return first_name;
        }

        public String getLastName() {
            return last_name;
        }

        public abstract double calculatePay();

        public abstract double calculateBonus();

        public void printPaycheck() {
            String full_name = last_name + ", " + first_name;
            System.out.println( "Pay: " + full_name + " $" + calculatePay() );
        }
    }
```

2. Using Listing 13.9 and 13.10 as a starting point, write a new
   `BankAccountController` that implements the new `BankActivityListener` interface and handles the events without case logic.

   Listing 13.9 presents a `BankActivityEvent` and its corresponding
   `BankActivityListener`.

LISTING 13.9   `BankActivityListener.java` and `BankActivityEvent.java`

```
public interface BankActivityListener {

    public void withdrawPerformed( BankActivityEvent e );

    public void depositPerformed( BankActivityEvent e );

}

public class BankActivityEvent {

    private double amount;

    public BankActivityEvent( double amount ) {
        this.amount = amount;
    }
```

LISTING 13.9 Continued

```java
    public double getAmount() {
        return amount;
    }

}
```

Listing 13.10 presents an updated BankAccountView. This BankAccountView intercepts the button's ActionEvents and forwards the new BankActivityEvent to the controller.

LISTING 13.10 BankAccountView.java

```java
import javax.swing.JPanel;
import javax.swing.JLabel;
import java.awt.BorderLayout;
import javax.swing.JTextField;
import javax.swing.JButton;
import java.util.ArrayList;
import java.awt.event.ActionListener;
import java.awt.event.ActionEvent;

public class BankAccountView extends JPanel implements Observer {

    public final static String DEPOSIT  = "Deposit";
    public final static String WITHDRAW = "Withdraw";

    private BankAccountModel model;
    private BankAccountController controller;

    // GUI Elements, pre-allocate all to avoid null values
    private JButton depositButton  = new JButton( DEPOSIT );
    private JButton withdrawButton = new JButton( WITHDRAW );
    private JTextField amountField = new JTextField();
    private JLabel balanceLabel    = new JLabel();

    public BankAccountView( BankAccountModel model ) {
        this.model = model;
        this.model.register( this );
        attachController( makeController() );
        buildUI();
    }

    // called by model when the model changes
    public void update() {
        balanceLabel.setText( "Balance: " + model.getBalance() );
    }
```

13

LISTING 13.10   Continued

```
    // wires the given controller to the view, allows outside object to set
controller
    public void attachController( BankAccountController controller ) {
        this.controller = controller;
    }

    protected BankAccountController makeController() {
        return new BankAccountController( this, model );
    }

    // provides access to the amount entered into the field
    private double getAmount() {
        // assume that the user entered a valid number
        return Double.parseDouble( amountField.getText() );
    }

    private void fireDepositEvent() {
        BankActivityEvent e = new BankActivityEvent( getAmount() );
        controller.depositPerformed( e );
    }

    private void fireWithdrawEvent() {
        BankActivityEvent e = new BankActivityEvent( getAmount() );
        controller.withdrawPerformed( e );
    }

    private void buildUI() {

        setLayout( new BorderLayout() );

        // associate each button with a commend string
        depositButton.setActionCommand( DEPOSIT );
        withdrawButton.setActionCommand( WITHDRAW );

        // build the display
        JPanel buttons = new JPanel( new BorderLayout() );
        JPanel balance = new JPanel( new BorderLayout() );
        buttons.add( depositButton, BorderLayout.WEST );
        buttons.add( withdrawButton, BorderLayout.EAST );
        balance.add( balanceLabel, BorderLayout.NORTH );
        balance.add( amountField, BorderLayout.SOUTH );
        add( balance, BorderLayout.NORTH );
        add( buttons, BorderLayout.SOUTH );

        depositButton.addActionListener(
            new ActionListener() {
                public void actionPerformed( ActionEvent e ) {
                    fireDepositEvent();
                }
```

LISTING 13.10 Continued

```
            }
        );

        withdrawButton.addActionListener(
            new ActionListener() {
                public void actionPerformed( ActionEvent e ) {
                    fireWithdrawEvent();
                }
            }
        );
    }
}
```

13

DAY 14

Building Reliable Software Through Testing

When you use object-oriented programming, you strive to write software that is natural, reliable, reusable, maintainable, extendable, and timely. To be able to meet these goals, you must understand that good OO does not happen by accident. You must attack your problems through careful analysis and design, at the same time never losing sight of the core tenets of OOP. Only then can OO begin to deliver on its promises. Even with careful analysis and design, however, OOP is not a magical formula. It will not protect you from your own mistakes or the mistakes of others. And mistakes will happen! To produce reliable software, you need to test the software.

Today you will learn

- Where testing falls in the iterative process
- About the different types of testing
- How to test your classes
- How to test incomplete software
- What you can do to write more reliable code
- How to make your testing more effective

Testing OO Software

OO won't prevent bugs from finding their way into your software. Even the best programmers make mistakes. Bugs are commonly thought of as a software defect arising from a typo, an error in logic, or just a silly mistake made while coding. While the implementation of an object is a common source of errors, bugs can come in other forms.

Bugs can also result when one object uses another object incorrectly. Bugs may even come about from fundamental flaws in the analysis or design itself. By its very nature, an OO system is full of interacting objects. These interactions can be the source of all kinds of errors.

Luckily, you can protect your software from bugs through software testing where you can validate your software's analysis, design, and implementation.

 Caution

> Like OO, testing is not a magical solution; it is extremely difficult to completely test your software. The total number of possible paths through a non-trivial program makes it difficult and time consuming to achieve total coverage of the code. So even tested code may harbor hidden bugs.
>
> The best that you can do is to perform an amount of testing that ensures the quality of your code while also allowing you to meet your deadlines and stay within budget. The actual "amount" of testing that you perform will depend on the scope of the project and your own comfort levels.

Testing and the Iterative Software Development Process

Figure 14.1 illustrates the iteration first presented in Chapter 9, "Introduction to Object Oriented Analysis." Testing is the last step of an iteration.

Before you leave an iteration, testing is an important step. The testing stage verifies that any changes you made during that iteration do not break any existing functionality. The testing stage also verifies that any new functionality you have added now works correctly. For these reasons, the tests performed before leaving an iteration are often referred to as *functional* or *acceptance* testing.

FIGURE 14.1

An iteration.

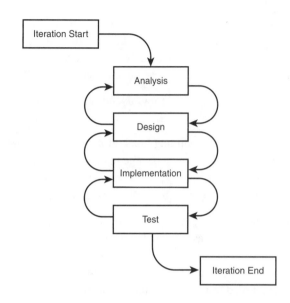

Note

Testing at the end of an iteration is an important milestone. To leave the iteration, your system must pass the tests; however, testing must also occur during other stages of an iteration. Today's lessons will show you how to effectively use testing during the implementation and testing stages of the iteration.

Make testing a goal, and something that you do throughout development. If you give no thought to testing until the end of development, you may find that it is not possible to test your software. Instead, you need to develop with testing in mind. You must make testing an integral part of the development process.

If bugs are found, you must go back and fix them. Normally you will go back to the implementation and try to fix the problem in the code. Sometimes, that is all you will need to do: simply fix the implementation, retest everything, and move on. Bugs, however, may actually stem from a design flaw, or even an overlooked or misunderstood requirement. You may need to go all the way back to design or analysis before you can fix a bug in the implementation.

Caution

After fixing a bug, it is not sufficient to simply test for the fixed bug. Instead, you need to perform all tests. While fixing one bug you can easily introduce one or more new ones!

14

A misunderstanding in the analysis means that the system will not function as the customer expects. A system must work as expected, and the customer that drives the system must agree with what behavior is expected. Not only do you need to test the code for implementation flaws, you also need to test that the code to see if it functions as expected.

To be able to test a system, you need to write and run test cases. Each test case will test a specific aspect of the system.

NEW TERM   A *test case* is the basic building block of the testing process. The testing process runs a number of *test cases* to be able to completely validate a system. Each *test case* consists of a set of inputs and expected outputs. The test will either execute a specific path through the system (white box) or test some defined behavior (black box).

A test case exercises a specific piece of functionality to see if the system behaves as it should. If the system behaves as expected, the test case passes. If the system does not behave as expected, the test case fails. A failed test case indicates that there is a bug in the system. You always want all of your test cases to pass 100% of the time. Don't be tempted to ignore a failed test case if a hundred other cases pass. Every test must pass or you cannot continue your work!

There are two ways to base your test cases: black box and white box testing. An effective test strategy will have a mix of black box- and white box-based test cases.

NEW TERM   *Black box testing* tests that the system functions as expected. Given a specific input *black box testing* tests that the proper externally visible output or behavior results as defined by the class' or system's specification.

NEW TERM   In *white box testing,* the tests are based solely on a method's implementation. White box tests try to achieve 100% code coverage.

When testing individual classes, black box testing is based upon the functional requirements of the class. When testing the entire system, black box testing is based upon the use cases. In either case, black box testing verifies that an object or system behaves as expected. For example, if a method is supposed add two numbers, a black box test will send two numbers to the method and then verify whether or not the output is the correct sum of the two numbers. If a system is supposed to allow you to add and remove items from a shopping cart, a black box test will attempt to add and remove items from the cart.

White box testing, on the other hand, is based upon the implementation of a method. Its purpose is to ensure that every branch of the code is executed. Black box testing is estimated to only cover a third to a half of the actual code. With white box testing, you design your tests so that you exercise each branch of code, and hopefully flush out any latent errors.

> **Tip**
>
> White box testing, except for the simplest programs, can rarely attain even reasonable coverage of the combination of paths through the program. There are two steps that you can take to improve the efficiency of your tests:
>
> Write you programs so that they have a minimal number of paths.
>
> Identify critical paths and be sure to test them.

For example, if a method divides two numbers, and there is an error branch that executes when you try to divide by 0, you'll need to ensure that you have a test case that exercises that error condition. Unless specified in the interface's documentation, you would only know about this branch by looking at the code itself. So white box tests must be based upon the code itself.

In either case, black box and white box testing govern how you create your test cases. Each plays an important part in the form of testing that you can perform.

Forms of Testing

In all, there are four important forms of testing. These tests range from lower-level tests that examine the individual objects, to upper-level tests that examine the entire system. Performing each will help to ensure the overall quality of your software.

Unit Testing

Unit testing is the lowest level unit of testing. A unit test examines only one feature at a time.

NEW TERM A *unit test* is the lowest level testing device. A unit test sends a message to an object and then verifies that it receives the expected result from the object. A unit test only checks one feature at a time.

In OO terms, a unit test examines a single class of object. A unit test checks an object by sending that object a message and verifying that the object returns the expected result. You can base unit tests on both black box and white box testing. In fact, you should do both to ensure that your objects work properly. While each class that you write should have a corresponding unit test, you should probably write the test case before you write the class. You'll read more on that point later.

Today, we will focus on unit testing because it is so central to writing reliable OO software. In fact, you should perform unit testing throughout development.

14

Integration Testing

OO systems are made up of interacting objects. While unit testing examines each class of object in isolation, integration testing checks that the objects that make up your system interact properly. What might work in isolation may blow up when combined with other objects! Common sources of integration errors stem from errors in or misunderstanding about input/output formats, resource conflicts, and the incorrect sequence of method calls.

NEW TERM   An *integration test* checks that two or more objects work together properly.

Like unit tests, the tests that you perform during integration testing can be based on both white box and black box testing concepts. You should have an integration test for each important interaction in the system.

System Testing

System testing verifies that the entire system performs as described by the use cases. While performing system tests, you must also test the system in ways not described by the use cases. By doing so, you can verify that the system handles and recovers from unforeseen conditions gracefully.

Tip

Try throwing these tests at your system when testing:

Random Action Tests

Random access tests consist of trying operations in random order.

Empty Database Tests

Empty database tests ensure that the system can fail gracefully if there is a major problem with the database.

Mutant Use Cases

A mutant use case changes a valid use case into an invalid use case and ensures that the system can properly recover from the interaction.

You would be surprised at what a user might try to do to your system. It may not fall under one of the "normal" use cases, so it is better to be prepared for the worst.

NEW TERM   A *system test* examines the entire system. A system test verifies that the system works as stated in the use cases, and that it can handle unusual and unexpected situations gracefully.

System testing also includes stress and performance tests. These tests ensure that the system satisfies any performance requirements and can function under expected loads. If possible, it is best to run these tests in an environment that matches the production environment as closely as possible.

System tests are an important aspect of acceptance testing. System testing checks entire functional units at once, so a single test may touch many different objects and subsystems. To be able to leave an iteration, the system must pass these tests successfully.

Regression Testing

A test is only valid as long as the tested piece doesn't change. When an aspect of a system does change, that piece—as well as any dependent pieces—must be retested. Regression testing is the process of repeating unit, integration, and system tests after changes are made.

NEW TERM *Regression tests* examine changes to parts of the system that have already been validated. Whenever a change is made, the piece that was changed—as well as any dependent pieces—must be retested.

It is absolutely critical to retest even after a small change. A small change can introduce a bug that could potentially break the entire system. Luckily, regression testing is as easy as rerunning your unit, integration, and system tests.

A Guide to Writing Reliable Code

While each form of testing is important to the overall quality of your software, today you will focus on what you can do best in your day-to-day work to ensure the quality of the systems that you write. To be able to write reliable code, you need to unit test, learn to differentiate between error conditions and bugs, and write useful documentation.

Combining Development and Testing

One fact lost in Figure 14.1 is that testing should be an ongoing process. Testing should not be something avoided, put off until the end, done by someone else, or skipped entirely. In fact, it can be impossible to suddenly begin testing once the system is done. Instead, you need to learn to begin testing while you develop. To test as you develop, you need to write unit tests for each class that you create.

An Example Unit Test

Let's take a look at a unit test for the SavingsAccount class first presented in Chapter 5, "Inheritance: Time to Write Code." Listing 14.1 presents the SavingsAccountTest class.

14

LISTING 14.1   SavingsAccountTest.java

```java
public class SavingsAccountTest {

    public static void main( String [] args ) {
        SavingsAccountTest sat = new SavingsAccountTest();
        sat.test_applyingInterest();
    }

    public void test_applyingInterest() {

        SavingsAccount acct = new SavingsAccount( 10000.00, 0.05 );

        acct.addInterest();

        print_getBalanceResult( acct.getBalance(), 10500.00, 1 );

    }

    private void print_getBalanceResult( double actual, double expected, int
➥test ) {

        if( actual == expected ) {  // passed
            System.out.println( "PASS: test #" + test + " interest applied
➥properly" );
            System.out.println();
        } else { // failed
            System.out.println( "FAIL: test #" + test + " interest applied
➥incorrectly" );
            System.out.println( "Value returned: " + actual );
            System.out.println( "Expected value: " + expected );
            System.out.println();
        }

    }

}
```

The SavingsAccountTest is a unit test that examines the SavingsAccount class. A unit test can be made up of a number of test cases. Here, the SavingsAccountTest class only has one test case: test_applyingInterest. The test_applyingInterest test case checks to be sure that a SavingsAccount instance properly applies interest to its balance. A unit test can have many test cases, but each test case should only check one feature of the object.

SavingsAccountTest is referred to as a unit test because it examines the lowest level building block, or unit, in the OO world: the object. A unit test should only examine one object at a time. This means that each object must be testable as well as a standalone entity. If not, you may not be able to test the object at all. Even if you can, you may end up inadvertently testing many objects at the same time.

When writing unit tests you should avoid manual validation of the output as much as possible. As you can see in `test_applyingInterest`, the test case does all of the necessary validation automatically. Manual validation is often time consuming and error prone. When running test cases, you want accurate results as fast as possible, and with the least amount of effort. Otherwise, you may start to neglect testing.

Why You Should Write Unit Tests

Unit tests help you to detect errors. If you break something in your class, you'll know right away because the unit test will tell you. The unit test is your first line of defense against bugs. Catching a bug at the unit level is much easier to handle than trying to trace a bug during integration or system test.

Unit tests also enable you to know when you are done writing a class: A class is done when your unit tests all pass! As a developer, it can be extremely helpful to have such a clear-cut end point. Otherwise, it can be difficult to know when a class is "done." Knowing that you are done and can move on prevents you from being tempted to add more functionality than you need to a class.

Writing unit tests can help you to think about the design of your classes, especially if you write your test case before you write your class; however, to be able to write the test case, you have to use your imagination and pretend that the class already exists. Doing so gives you great freedom to experiment with your classes interface. Once you finish writing the test you can write the class and then everything will compile.

Unit tests can help you to refactor your code. It is easier to make changes to your code if you have a unit test because you have instant feedback on your changes. You don't have to worry as much about introducing bugs; you can simply rerun your test to see if anything broke. By using unit tests you don't have to be haunted by the nagging question, "Did I break something?" You can make changes with more confidence.

Finally, you might not always be around to test the system. You may move onto other projects, or other members of your team may need to perform testing. Unit tests allow someone other than the author to test an object.

Writing Unit Tests

`SavingsAccountTest` and `test_applyingInterest()` are fairly straightforward examples of a unit test and test case; however, writing unit tests from scratch for each class can become time consuming. Imagine a system where you must write hundreds of test cases. If you write each unit test from scratch, you'll end up doing a lot of redundant work. You need to either create or reuse a testing framework.

14

NEW TERM A *framework* is a reusable domain model. The framework contains all of the classes common to an entire domain of problems, and serves as the basis for a specific application in the domain.

The classes in a framework define the general design of an application. As a developer, you simply extend these classes and then provide your own problem-specific classes to create an application.

In the case of a testing framework, the framework defines a skeleton that you can reuse for writing and executing unit tests. A testing framework allows you to write unit tests quickly and conveniently by eliminating redundant, error-prone work. Remember, anything that you program can contain bugs, even your test code. Having a well-tested testing framework can take care of a lot of testing errors. Without a framework, the extra overhead of testing could be enough to keep you from doing it.

A complete testing framework will contain base classes for writing unit tests, built-in support for test automation, and utilities to help interpret and report output. Today you will learn to use JUnit, a free testing framework released under the "IBM Public License" for testing Java classes. You can download JUnit from `http://www.junit.org/`.

Note
> The JUnit download includes source code. JUnit has an excellent design, and you would be well served by studying the code and included documentation. In particular, the documentation does an excellent job of documenting the design patterns used to write JUnit.

JUnit

JUnit provides classes for writing unit tests, for validating output, and for running the test cases in a GUI or command line environment. `junit.framework.TestCase` is the base class for defining unit tests. To write unit tests, you simply write a class that inherits from `TestCase`, overrides a few methods, and provides its own test case methods.

Note
> When writing JUnit test cases, you should begin the name of any test case method with `test`. JUnit provides a mechanism that will automatically load and run any method that begins with `test`.

Listing 14.2 presents a JUnit version of `SavingsAccountTest`.

LISTING 14.2   SavingsAccountTest.java

```java
import junit.framework.TestCase;
import junit.framework.Assert;

public class SavingsAccountTest extends TestCase {

    public void test_applyingInterest() {

        SavingsAccount acct = new SavingsAccount( 10000.00, 0.05 );

        acct.addInterest();

        Assert.assertTrue( "interest applied incorrectly", acct.getBalance() ==
➥10500.00 );

    }

    public SavingsAccountTest( String name ) {
        super( name );
    }

}
```

The JUnit version of SavingsAccountTest is much simpler than the original. When using JUnit, there is no reason to reproduce display code or logical tests. You can simply use JUnit's supplied Assert class. The Assert class provides a number of methods that take a boolean as argument. If the boolean is false, an error is recorded. So here, the test passes Assert the boolean returned by the comparison acct.getBalance() == 10500.00. If the comparison evaluates to false, JUnit will flag an error.

So, how do you run these tests?

JUnit offers you a number of options for running your test cases. These options fall into two categories: static and dynamic. If you choose to use the static method, you will need to override the runTest() method to call the test that you want to run.

In Java, the most convenient way is to write an anonymous class so that you won't have to create a separate class for each test that you would like to run. Listing 14.3 shows the anonymous declaration:

LISTING 14.3   An Anonymous SavingsAccountTest

```java
SavingsAccountTest test =
    new SavingsAccountTest( "test_applyingInterest" ) {
        public void runTest() {
```

14

LISTING 14.3   Continued

```
            test_applyingInterest();
        }
    };
    test.run();
```

Anonymous classes are convenient because they allow you to override a method as you instantiate an object, all without having to create a named class in a separate file. Here, the main instantiates a `SavingsAccountTest`, but overrides the `runTest()` method to run the `test_applyingInterest()` test case.

 An *anonymous class* is a class that does not have a name. Anonymous classes lack a name because they are simply defined when they are instantiated. They are not declared in a separate file or as an inner class.

Anonymous classes are an excellent choice for one-time use classes (if the class is small). By using an anonymous class, you avoid having to create a separate named class.

As convenient as they are, anonymous classes have shortcomings. You will need to create one for each test case method that you would like to call. If you have a lot of test cases, using anonymous classes can call for a lot of redundant code.

To overcome that shortcoming, JUnit also provides a dynamic mechanism that will search for and run any method that begins with `test`. For the purposes of today's lesson, we will rely on this dynamic mechanism.

> **Note**
>
> JUnit also provides a mechanism known as a *test suite* for running multiple test cases. JUnit provides a mechanism for statically defining the set of tests to run as a suite; however, the dynamic mechanism will search out and find each test method. Today, we will rely on this automatic mechanism to find and run the tests.

JUnit also provides a few other convenient features. Consider the updated version of `SavingsAccountTest` in Listing 14.4 that also tests the `withdrawFunds()` method.

LISTING 14.4   `SavingsAccountTest.java`

```
import junit.framework.TestCase;
import junit.framework.Assert;

public class SavingsAccountTest extends TestCase {
```

LISTING 14.4 Continued

```
    private SavingsAccount acct;

    public void test_applyingInterest() {

        acct.addInterest();

        Assert.assertTrue( "interest applied incorrectly", acct.getBalance() ==
➥10500.00 );

    }

    public void test_withdrawFunds() {

        acct.withdrawFunds( 500.00 );

        Assert.assertTrue( "incorrect amount withdrawn", acct.getBalance() ==
➥9500.00 );

    }

    protected void setUp() {

        acct = new SavingsAccount( 10000.00, 0.05 );

    }

    public SavingsAccountTest(String name) {
        super( name );
    }

}
```

In this version, you will notice that the test contains two new methods:
test_withdrawFunds() and setUp(). setUp() overrides a method in the TestCase
base class. Each time that JUnit calls a test method, it will first make a call to setUp()
to establish the testing fixture.

A testing *fixture* defines the set of objects on which a test will operate. Establishing a
testing fixture can consume most of the time it takes to write test cases.

NEW TERM The testing fixture prepares the set of objects upon which a test case will act.
Fixtures are also convenient because they allow you to share the same fixture
among an entire set of test cases without having to duplicate code.

JUnit guarantees that the fixture objects will be in a known state by calling setUp()
before running each test. JUnit also supplies a corresponding tearDown() method for
performing any cleaning up of the fixture after the test runs.

14

To be able to run your test cases, JUnit provides test runners for exercising and collecting the results from a test. JUnit provides both a graphical and command-line based version of this utility.

To run `SavingsAccountTest` graphically, simply type

```
java junit.swingui.TestRunner
```

Figure 14.2 illustrates the JUnit main window.

FIGURE 14.2

The main JUnit UI.

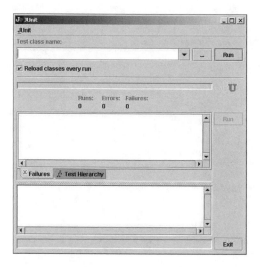

Using the UI, you can browse for the `SavingsAccountTest` class. Once loaded, you can simply run the test by hitting the run button.

As Figure 14.3 shows, the JUnit UI displays the number of tests run as well as the number of failed tests. The UI also provides a graphical bar that display whether or not any tests failed.

JUnit is a great tool because it allows you to receive clear, instant feedback from your test cases. So if that little voice in your head ever nags you with, "What if I broke something?" you can find out quickly by rerunning your unit tests.

Writing Advanced Unit Tests

Let's consider a slightly more complicated example. Exercise 1 from Chapter 11, "Reusing Design through Design Patterns," presented one possible implementation of an `Item`. Currently, to be able to display an `Item`, you must call a number of getter methods and process the data for display. Unfortunately, asking an object for its data is not the best OO approach. You should ask the object to do something with its data.

FIGURE 14.3

The main JUnit UI after successfully running the test cases.

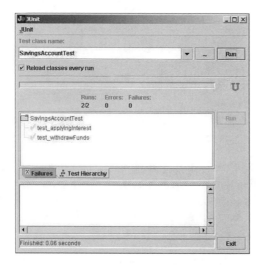

Consider Listing 14.5, which presents an alternative implementation of Item.

LISTING 14.5 Item.java

```java
public class Item {

    private int    id;
    private int    quantity;
    private float  unitPrice;
    private String description;
    private float  discount;

    public Item( int id, int quantity, float unitPrice, float discount, String
➥desc) {
        this.id = id;
        this.quantity = quantity;
        this.unitPrice = unitPrice;
        this.discount = discount;
        this.description = desc;
    }

    public void display( ItemDisplayFormatter format ) {

        format.quantity( quantity );
        format.id( id );
        format.unitPrice( unitPrice );
        format.discount( discount );
        format.description( description );
        format.adjustedPrice( getTotalPrice() );
```

14

LISTING 14.5 Continued

```
    }

    public float getTotalPrice() {
        return ( unitPrice * quantity ) - ( discount * quantity );
    }

}
```

Here, you can ask the Item to display itself using a display formatter. The formatter will take care of formatting the data for display. Having a separate formatting object is a better approach than having another object call getters, or embedding the display logic in the Item object itself. When display requirements change, you can simply create new implementations of ItemDisplayFormatter.

Listing 14.6 defines the ItemDisplayFormatter interface, and Listing 14.7 presents one possible implementation of the interface.

LISTING 14.6 ItemDisplayFormatter.java

```
public interface ItemDisplayFormatter {
    public void quantity( int quantity );
    public void id( int id );
    public void unitPrice( float unitPrice );
    public void discount( float discount );
    public void description( String description );
    public void adjustedPrice( float total );
    public String format();
}
```

LISTING 14.7 ItemTableRow.java

```
public class ItemTableRow implements ItemDisplayFormatter {

    private int    quantity;
    private int    id;
    private float  unitPrice;
    private float  discount;
    private String description;
    private float  adjPrice;

    public void quantity( int quantity ) {
        this.quantity = quantity;
    }
```

Listing 14.7 Continued

```
public void id( int id ) {
    this.id = id;
}

public void unitPrice( float unitPrice ) {
    this.unitPrice = unitPrice;
}

public void discount( float discount ) {
    this.discount = discount;
}

public void description( String description ) {
    this.description = description;
}

public void adjustedPrice( float total ) {
    this.adjPrice = total;
}

public String format() {
    String row = "<tr>";
    row = row + "<td>"  + id          + "</td>";
    row = row + "<td>"  + quantity    + "</td>";
    row = row + "<td>"  + description + "</td>";
    row = row + "<td>$" + unitPrice   + "</td>";
    row = row + "<td>$" + adjPrice    + "</td>";
    row = row + "</tr>";
    return row;
}
}
```

The `ItemTableRow` formatter creates an HTML table row representation for the `Item` using US currency symbols. Other formatters could format the data in other ways.

This example presents some interesting testing challenges as well as some opportunities. For these classes, simply calling a method and checking an output won't do the job.

Testing `Item`'s `display()` method is of special interest because a unit test should only check one class in isolation; however, to be able to test `display()`, you must also pass an `ItemDisplayFormatter` to it.

Luckily, mock objects offer an alternative that will still allow you to test `Item` in isolation.

NEW TERM   A *mock object* is a simplistic substitute for a real object. It's called a mock object because the object has been mocked-up for testing purposes. While the mock object may have a simplistic implementation, it can hold extra functionality to aid in testing.

14

Mock objects are closely related to stubs. However, mock objects differ in that they actually perform some function instead of simply accepting a call and returning some canned value.

Mock objects are sometimes called *simulators*.

A mock object provides a simplistic substitute for a real object. This substitute will not appear in the actual system, just in the test code.

The point of a mock object isn't to provide the actual functionality of the object that it mimics. Instead, the mock object should provide a simplistic implementation that may have added support for testing.

 Caution

Keep mock objects as simple as possible. A mock object should normally be a standalone object that does not rely on any other mock objects. If your mock object has too many dependencies, it is probably too complicated.

For example, consider a database accessor that returns Item objects. You would hardcode the mock accessor to return the same Item over and over; however, if you're unit testing an object that retrieves Items using the accessor, it will not know the difference. Such an approach isolates the object being tested from defects in the objects that it uses.

You can use a mock object to test whether the Item's display() method properly uses ItemDisplayFormatter objects. Listing 14.8 presents a mock ItemDisplayFormatter.

LISTING 14.8   MockDisplayFormatter.java

```java
import junit.framework.Assert;

public class MockDisplayFormatter implements ItemDisplayFormatter {

    private int    test_quantity;
    private int    test_id;
    private float  test_unitPrice;
    private float  test_discount;
    private String test_description;
    private float  test_adjPrice;

    private int    quantity;
    private int    id;
    private float  unitPrice;
    private float  discount;
    private String description;
    private float  adjPrice;
```

LISTING **14.8**   Continued

```
    public void verify() {
        Assert.assertTrue( "quantity set incorrectly", test_quantity == quantity
);
        Assert.assertTrue( "id set incorrectly", test_id == id );
        Assert.assertTrue( "unitPrice set incorrectly", test_unitPrice ==
➥unitPrice );
        Assert.assertTrue( "discount set incorrectly", test_discount == discount
);
        Assert.assertTrue( "description set incorrectly", test_description ==
➥description );
        Assert.assertTrue( "adjPrice set incorrectly", test_adjPrice == adjPrice
);
    }

    public void test_quantity( int quantity ) {
        test_quantity = quantity;
    }

    public void test_id( int id ) {
        test_id = id;
    }

    public void test_unitPrice( float unitPrice ) {
        test_unitPrice = unitPrice;
    }

    public void test_discount( float discount ) {
        test_discount = discount;
    }

    public void test_description( String description ) {
        test_description = description;
    }

    public void test_adjustedPrice( float total ) {
        test_adjPrice = total;
    }

    public void quantity( int quantity ) {
        this.quantity = quantity;
    }

    public void id( int id ) {
        this.id = id;
    }

    public void unitPrice( float unitPrice ) {
        this.unitPrice = unitPrice;
```

14

LISTING 14.8   Continued

```
        }

        public void discount( float discount ) {
            this.discount = discount;
        }

        public void description( String description ) {
            this.description = description;
        }

        public void adjustedPrice( float total ) {
            this.adjPrice = total;
        }

        public String format() { // we're not testing formatter functionality
            return "NOT IMPLEMENTED";
        }
    }
```

MockDisplayFormatter is similar in some ways to the actual implementation; however, you'll notice that it does not implement a true format() method. You will also notice that it adds a number of methods for setting the expected values as well as a method for checking the inputs from Item against those values.

Listing 14.9 illustrates how you might use the mock display to unit test the Item class.

LISTING 14.9   ItemTest.java

```
import junit.framework.TestCase;
import junit.framework.Assert;

public class ItemTest extends TestCase {

    private Item item;

    // constants for constructor values
    private final static int ID            = 1;
    private final static int QUANTITY      = 10;
    private final static float UNIT_PRICE  = 100.00f;
    private final static float DISCOUNT    = 5.00f;
    private final static String DESCRIPTION = "ITEM_TEST";

    protected void setUp() {
        item = new Item( ID, QUANTITY, UNIT_PRICE, DISCOUNT, DESCRIPTION );
    }
```

LISTING 14.9 Continued

```
    public void test_displayValues() {
        MockDisplayFormatter formatter = new MockDisplayFormatter();
        formatter.test_id( ID );
        formatter.test_quantity( QUANTITY );
        formatter.test_unitPrice( UNIT_PRICE );
        formatter.test_discount( DISCOUNT );
        formatter.test_description( DESCRIPTION );

        float adj_total = ( UNIT_PRICE * QUANTITY ) - ( DISCOUNT * QUANTITY );
        formatter.test_adjustedPrice( adj_total );

        item.display( formatter );

        formatter.verify();
    }

    public ItemTest( String name ) {
        super( name );
    }
}
```

ItemTest's test_displayValues() method creates a MockDisplayFormatter, sets the expected inputs, passes it to the Item, and uses the formatter to validate the input. Internally, the formatter's verify() method uses JUnit's Assert class to validate the input.

Mock objects are a powerful concept because you can program them to do anything. You may have mock objects that count the number of times a method is called, or one that keeps track of the amount of data an object sends over a network. It all depends upon your application and what you need to monitor. Mock objects allow you to perform all kinds of monitoring and testing that isn't possible if an object simply creates all of the objects that it needs itself.

This raises the question, "What if my objects create the objects that they themselves need?" Most of the examples in this book actually fall into that category (hopefully that kept the examples more understandable, though!). One solution is to edit the classes so that the objects instantiate a mock object instead of the real object. Such an approach, however, isn't clean because it forces you to alter code that you're testing. If you change the implementation of the code before you test, you're not really testing the class that will find its way into your system. The best solution is to write code that is easy to test.

Such advice may seem backwards. Conventional wisdom dictates that you normally write tests to test code that you have already written. You don't write code so that you can test! The Item example illustrates an important lesson. Designing your classes so that they are easy to test can actually result in code that is more OO! In this case, passing in the dependent objects actually made the object less dependent on a specific class, thus more pluggable.

14

> Design your classes so that you can test them easily. Design with mock objects in mind. Your code may actually become more object-oriented!

> Write your classes so that dependent objects are passed in, not instantiated within the object itself. This practice leads to stand alone objects.

While it is true that Item's display() method is dependent upon the ItemDisplayFormatter interface, it is not dependent upon a specific implementation of the interface, such as TableRowFormatter or even MockDisplayFormatter. Instead, Item is free to use any ItemDisplayFormatter implementation because it doesn't force itself to use any specific one by creating the instance itself.

> Tips to effective testing:
> - You should optimize your tests for speed. Quick tests provide instant feedback, so you might be more apt to use them.
> - Compile your test cases along with your normal classes. This practice will force you to keep your test cases up to date with the code.
> - Avoid visual/manual validation of test output because it is error prone. Use some automatic mechanism instead.
> - If you have to maintain a codebase that lacks unit tests, write the tests as you need them.

Writing Exceptional Code

Testing is an important way to ensure the quality of the code that your write; however, it is not the only step that you can take. You also need to learn to tell the difference between an error condition and a bug. An error condition and a bug are not the same!

You know what a bug is; a bug is a defect. An error condition is slightly different. An error condition, or exception, is a predictable failure that happens under certain circumstances in the domain. Take the online store, for example. Network outages happen all of the time. A network outage is not a bug (unless your code causes it!). Instead of treating error conditions as bugs, you need to code around them.

For example, if your database connection fails, you need to try reconnecting. If it is still down, you need to handle the condition gracefully, and inform the user of the error.

Every language has its own way of reporting error conditions. Java and C++ employ a mechanism known as exceptions to signal error conditions. Languages such a C rely on return codes. Whatever language you use, you must write your code to detect and recover gracefully from error conditions.

Java and C++ exceptions work similarly. Exceptions are just another type of object; however, the Java compiler forces you to handle them if it determines that an exception may occur and you do not handle it.

Here is one of the methods from Java's URL class:

```
public URLConnection openConnection() throws IOException
```

You see that the method has some extra information. The method indicates that it may throw IOException, meaning that under normal conditions the method will return a URLConnection. If there is an error opening the connection, however, the method will throw an IOException instead.

In Java, you handle exceptions in try/catch blocks. Listing 14.10 shows how you could handle a call to openConnection.

LISTING 14.10   Handling an Exception

```
java.net.URL url = new java.net.URL("http://www.samspublishing.com/");
java.net.URLConnection conn;
try {
    conn = url.openConnection();
} catch ( java.io.IOException e ) { // an error has occurred
    // log an error, write something out to the screen
    // do something to handle the error
}
```

When you make a call to openConnection, you do so normally; however, you must make the call within try/catch blocks or explicitly state that the method the call is made in also throws an IOException.

If the call to openConnection() results in an exception being thrown, conn will not be set. Instead, execution will continue within the catch block where you can try to recover, log an error, print a message to the screen, or throw another exception.

If you do not explicitly catch the exception or throw a new exception, the exception will bubble up the call stack until it reaches the top or someone finally catches it.

14

What is important is that you program for error conditions by using whatever mechanism is built into your language. This means that when you design your classes, you should also give consideration to the various error conditions, model them through exception objects, and have your methods throw them.

Writing Effective Documentation

There is one more step that you can take to improve the quality of your work: document it. There are many forms of documentation, each with its own level of effectiveness.

Source Code as Documentation

The source code, even your unit tests, is a form of documentation. When others have to take and maintain your code, it is important that it is readable and well laid out. Otherwise, no one will be able to make any sense out of it.

Source code is the most important form of documentation, because it is the only documentation that you *must* maintain.

Coding Conventions

The first step that you can take to turning your code into good documentation is to pick a coding convention and stick to it. Coding conventions can cover everything from how you indent your braces to how you name your variables. The specific convention is not all that important. What is important is that your project team, and preferably your company, pick a convention and stick with it. That way, anyone can pick up a piece of code and follow it—well, at least not be distracted by the formatting.

Listing 14.11 presents one way of declaring Java classes.

LISTING **14.11**   An Example Class

```
public class <ClassName>
    extends <ParentClassName>
    implements <LIST OF INTERFACES>
{
    // public variables
    // protected variables
    // private variables
    // constants

    // public methods
    // protected methods
    // private methods
}
```

Tip

Class names should always begin with an uppercase letter. Method names should always begin with a lowercase letter. Variable names should always begin with a lowercase letter.

Any name containing multiple words should begin nested words with caps. For example: someMethod() and HappyObject.

Constants should always be in CAPS. Normal variables should be in lower-case.

(Please note that these conventions are Java centric. Smalltalk and C++ conventions may differ.)

Here's one way to declare methods and nest if/else statements:

```
public void method() {
    if( conditional ) {

    } else {

    }
}
```

Constants

Constants can also serve as a form of documentation. Use constants wherever you find yourself using a hard coded value. A well-named constant can provide insight into the purpose of your code.

Comments

Like a well-placed constant, nothing helps make code more understandable than a well-placed comment; however, you need to find a balance in your commenting. Comment too much, and your comments will lose meaning.

Here's a useless, but common, commenting mistake:

```
public void id( int id ) {
    this.id = id;  // set id
}
```

Useless comments tell you what code is doing. If you need to explain code, the code may be too complicated. Comments should tell you what the code is for. Comments should describe non-intuitive implementations.

14

Note

Please note that a comment under a method signature is no substitute for a good, clear method name.

Names

Variable, method, and class names should be meaningful. Spell them out and be consistent in your spelling. For example, always capitalize the second word in a multi-word name such as testCase. As an alternative, you can split the words with a hyphen (-),as in test-case. Again, the most important aspect is consistency. Make your naming rule part of your convention and then use it consistently.

Method and Class Headers

When you write a class or method, always be sure to include a header. A method header will include a description, a list of arguments, a description of the return, as well as an exception conditions and side effects. A header may even include pre-conditions. A class header will normally include a description, version number, author list, and revision history.

When you program in Java, be sure to take advantage of Javadoc. (See Appendix B for more information.) Javadoc provides a number of tags for writing headers. If you use Javadoc, you can simply run your classes through a processor that will automatically generate convenient Web-based API documentation for your classes.

Tip

When you have documented something you have committed yourself to keeping that documentation up to date, whether it is Javadoc, a design document, or a comment. Out-of-date documentation is worthless. Keep it up to date!

Summary

Today you learned about testing and what you can do as a developer to ensure the quality of your work. In all, there are four overall forms of testing:

- Unit Testing
- Integration Testing
- System Testing
- Regression Testing

In your day-to-day work, the unit test is your first line of defense against bugs. Unit testing also has the benefits of forcing you to consider your design from the point of view of testing, and provides you with a mechanism that makes refactoring easier.

You also saw the importance of handling error conditions properly and keeping documentation. All of these practices add up to higher quality code.

Q&A

Q Why do developers hate to test?

A There does seem to be a culture of "test avoidance" among programmers. I feel that this is a cultural problem. In most companies the Quality Assurance (QA) group is a group separate from the developers. They come in, test the system, and write up bug reports. This approach puts the programmer on the defensive, especially if the project manager puts an undo amount of pressure on the developer. In a way, testing becomes punishment, and a source of extra work.

Viewing testing as extra work is also part of the problem. Many project teams put off testing until the end of development thus it becomes something that you do when you're done with the "real" work. Unfortunately, the more that you delay testing, the harder it will be to do. When you do start testing, you will likely encounter a large number of bugs because you hadn't tested up to that point. This puts you back in the punishment phase, especially because you're probably close to your deadline. And if you're close to your deadline, the pressure from the project manager will increase.

Test avoidance is a problem that feeds itself.

Q Why is testing often done by a separate Quality Assurance group?

A Independent testing helps to ensure that the testers don't subconsciously avoid areas where problems may exist—a failing to which developers can be prone.

Q Throughout today's lessons you used JUnit. Why did you choose JUnit?

A JUnit is a free testing tool that does its job well. JUnit is designed well and is small enough that you can get your hands around the design easily. It also lacks the bells and whistles that many other products have.

In my opinion, avoiding the bells and whistles during unit testing is a benefit. JUnit puts you closer to the code because you have to write your own tests, set up the data, and validate the output. It forces you to consider your design, and even augment it so that it is easy to test.

With some of the more automated testing tools, you can lose these benefits; however, JUnit is a unit-testing framework. You will need to find other tools for some of the integration and system testing.

Q Unit testing seems like a burden. I don't have time to unit test. What should I do?

A Unit testing may seem like a burden the first time that you write a unit test. In all honesty, at times, unit tests are expensive to write. Unit tests pay off over time. When you write a test, you can reuse it over and over again. Each time that you change the implementation of your class, you simply rerun your unit test. Unit tests make it much easier to make changes to your code.

14

Not having time is a weak argument. Imagine how much more time it will take to find, trace, and fix bugs if you put off testing until the end—a time when you are usually under even more pressure.

Q How do you know if you've tested enough?

A You've tested at a minimal level when you have a unit test for each class, an integration test for each major interaction in the system, and a system test for each use case. Whether or not you do additional testing depends on your deadline as well as your comfort level.

Workshop

The quiz questions and answers are provided for your further understanding. See Appendix A, "Answers," for the answers.

Quiz

1. How can bugs find their way into your software? (Or maybe the question should be, "How do you cause bugs in your software?")
2. What is a test case?
3. What are the two ways upon which you can base your tests?
4. Define white box and black box testing.
5. What are the four forms of testing?
6. Define *unit test*.
7. What is the point behind integration testing and system testing?
8. Why should you avoid delaying testing until the end of a project?
9. Why should you avoid manual or visual validation while testing? What is the alternative?
10. What is a framework?
11. What is a mock object?
12. Why should you use mock objects?
13. What is the difference between a bug and an error condition?
14. When writing your code, how can you ensure its quality?

Exercises

1. Download JUnit and read `cookstour`, which is found in the doc directory.
2. Write a unit test for the HourlyEmployee from Chapter 7, "Polymorphism: Time to Write Code," that tests the `calculatePay()` method.

WEEK 2

In Review

This week, you learned about the iterative approach to the software development process. The software development process includes analysis, design, implementation, and testing stages. You learned that the iterative approach to the software development allows you to go back and refine any stage in the process. This continual refinement leads to a more complete, correct solution to your problem.

Day 8 introduced you to the Unified Modeling Language. In Day 9 you learned about OOA, the first step in the development process. OOA allows you to understand the problem you are trying to solve. One method of OOA is through the use of use cases to describe how the users will use the system. Once you have your use cases mapped out, you can use modeling languages such as the UML to graphically visualize your problem domain.

Day 10 describes OOD, the process of taking the domain model and creating the objects model you will use during implementation. The following list presents the basic steps necessary to complete OOD.

1. Generate an initial list of objects
2. Refine your objects' responsibilities
3. Develop the points of interaction
4. Detail the relationships between objects
5. Build your model

CRC cards aid you in mapping out the responsibilities of and interactions between each object. The next two days covered design patterns, reusable design concepts that provide shortcuts to OOD. You learned about patterns, such as the Adapter,

Proxy, Iterator, Abstract Factory, Singleton, and Typesafe Enum, and when it is appropriate to use them.

Day 13 explains UI design with the MVC pattern. The MVC pattern provides flexibility be decoupling the UI from the underlying system. It also stresses the need to carry out the software design process for the UI as for any other part of the system.

Finally, Day 14 introduced you to testing in the implementation and testing stages of each iteration. You learned about the two way of testing your code: white box and black box testing. You also learned the four forms of testing: unit, integration, system, and regression testing. Testing is the final way to ensure the quality of your code. If it is not taken into consideration throughout the development process, you could face serious consequences.

Now that you have finished this week's lessons, you should understand the software development process.

WEEK 3

Putting It All Together: A Complete OO Project

15 Learning to Combine Theory and Process

16 Blackjack Iteration 2: Adding Rules

17 Blackjack Iteration 3: Adding Betting

18 Blackjack Iteration 4: Adding a GUI

19 Applying an Alternative to MVC

20 Having Some Fun with Blackjack

21 The Final Mile

15

16

17

18

19

20

21

WEEK 3

At a Glance

In the first week, you learned the theory behind OOP. The second week gave you a process to follow while applying that theory. This week, you will put the lessons of the first two weeks together in a complete OOP project. This project will step you through all phases of development—from project inception to completion.

Your final project is the development of a Blackjack card game. Day 15, the first day this week, will step you through the first iteration of the game and add basic functionality from OOA through implementation and testing. In Days 16 and 17, you will add more functionality to the game through two more iterations. Day 18 shows you how to add a GUI to the system.

Day 19 provides an alternate way to implement a GUI through the PAC design pattern. In Day 20 you will learn how to add multiple non-human players and see how to turn your game into a simulator. Finally, Day 21 pulls everything together and ties up any loose ends.

DAY 15

Learning to Combine Theory and Process

Week 1 helped you understand the theory behind OOP. Week 2 gave you a process to follow while applying that theory. Week 3 will show you how to put the lessons of Week 1 and Week 2 together by presenting a complete OOP project. This project will step you through all phases of development, all the way from project inception to completion.

Today's lesson introduces you to Blackjack, a popular card game. By the end of today's lesson, you will complete an initial analysis, design, and working implementation of the game. You will not create an entire Blackjack game in one large step. Instead, you will apply the iterative process over the course of the week as you work towards a complete Blackjack game.

Today you will learn how to:

- Apply OO analysis and design to a real life card game
- Use the iterative process to achieve and see quick results
- Avoid many common development temptations
- Prevent procedural characteristics that can sneak into your program

Blackjack

Blackjack is a popular card game where the goal is to get a higher count of cards than the dealer without going over 21. This week's goal is to create a fairly complete Blackjack game written in Java using the OOP concepts that you have learned throughout the book. While some features will be left out for the sake of clarity and brevity, you should be left with a game as addictive and time-consuming as the Solitaire or FreeCell games that are shipped with many popular operating systems.

 Caution   The author does not assume any liability for the time lost while playing this game!

Why Blackjack?

The question may come to mind, "Why Blackjack?"

The goal of programming Blackjack is not to turn you into a professional gambler. There are two reasons for using Blackjack as an introductory OOP project:

- Almost everyone is familiar with at least one card game.
- It just so happens that the game of Blackjack fits well into the OOP paradigm.

In general, most people are familiar with the card game domain. An important part of OOA and OOD is to have a domain expert present while fleshing out the use cases and domain model. It is simply not possible for you to obtain a domain expert as part of completing these lessons.

A card game does not require a domain expert. Instead, your own experience and a good rules book or web site provides everything you need to complete the analysis and design on your own. If you get confused, you can even take out a pack of cards and work through a scenario.

As a result, a card game is much more accessible than trying to learn a completely unfamiliar domain. A familiar domain will not distract you from the true point of these lessons—learning to apply OO principles.

Blackjack—in fact, most card games in general—also tend to fit well into the OOP paradigm. The interactions between dealers, players, their hands, and the cards can help you to see that an OO system is made up by the interactions between the various objects.

Card games also tend to retain enough procedural characteristics that it is easy to see how an OOP approach can differ vastly from a procedural one, especially when applying game rules.

Vision Statement

When beginning a project it often helps to start out with a statement of vision or objective. The point of the statement is to frame the overall purpose of the system that you will create. The point of the statement is not to capture every aspect of the problem that you're trying to solve. Instead, the statement simply states the intent and gives you a starting point for analysis.

 The *vision statement* frames the overall purpose of the system that you will create and the problem that you are trying to solve.

Here is the statement of vision for the Blackjack system:

> The Blackjack game allows a player to play a game of Blackjack according to common casino rules.

While seemingly obvious, this statement serves as an excellent catalyst to analysis.

Overriding Requirements

Before beginning analysis it helps to enumerate any overriding requirements. There are just a handful of constrains to the game of Blackjack. The only constraint that is important now is how the user will interact with the system.

The Blackjack game will allow the user to interact with the system through either a command line or graphical UI. Of course, the initial iterations will only allow interaction through a command line interface.

The Blackjack game must also be implemented in the Java programming language.

It is important to list such constraints up front so that you do not come up with a design that makes adhering to these constraints impossible.

Initial Blackjack Analysis

Chapter 9, "Introduction to Object Oriented Analysis," introduced you to OOA as well as the iterative development process. Staying true to the information in Chapter 9, this project will follow an iterative development process and will begin each iteration of that process with analysis.

When beginning analysis it is often helpful to start with the vision statement stated earlier:

> The Blackjack game allows a player to play a game of Blackjack according to common casino rules.

You can use the statement to generate an initial list of questions. It is these questions that will drive your analysis.

The Blackjack Rules

From the Blackjack vision statement, you can naturally ask, "What are the common casino rules of Blackjack?" You will use these rules to model the game of Blackjack.

The main goal of Blackjack is to collect a hand of cards whose value is greater than that of the dealer's hand without exceeding 21. Each card is assigned a numeric value from 1 to 11, where the ace is worth 1 or 11 (depending on which gives you a better hand), number cards are worth their respective number value, and all picture cards are worth 10. Suit has no bearing on card value.

Figure 15.1 shows some example hands.

Of course the actual game is a bit more involved. Let's look at each major component of the game.

Betting

Before the dealer deals any cards, each player must place a bet. Normally betting is capped off by some limit such as $25 or $50 per game.

Dealing

After each player has placed a bet, the dealer may deal the cards. Beginning with the first player the dealer deals one card face up to each player, finishing with himself.

The dealer then repeats this process, but deals his own card face down. The dealer's down card is known as the hole card.

Dealing ends once the dealer deals each player, including himself, two cards. Play commences once the deal is through.

Playing

Play may differ depending upon the dealer's up card. If the dealer's up card is worth 10 (called a 10-count) or it is an ace (worth 11), the dealer must check his hole card. If the hole card gives him a total of 21 (called a natural 21 or Blackjack) play automatically ends and the game moves to settlement. If the hole card does not give him 21, play commences normally.

If the dealer's up card is not a 10-count or an ace, play automatically moves to the first player. If the player has a natural 21, the player has Blackjack and play skips to the next player. If the player does not have 21, the player has two choices: to hit or to stand:

FIGURE 15.1

Example Blackjack hands.

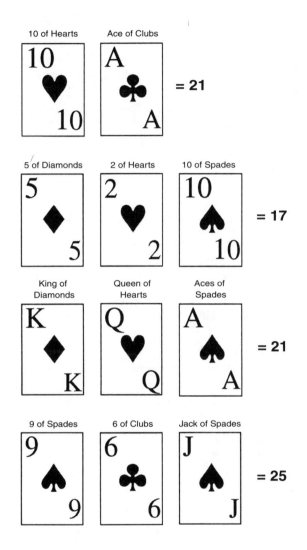

hit—If the player is not satisfied with his hand, he may choose to draw another card, which is called a hit. The player may hit until he goes over 21 (busts) or stands (stops needing cards).

stand—If the player is satisfied with his hand, he may choose to stand and receive no further cards.

After the player busts or stands, play moves on to the next player. This process repeats itself until each player has played. After each player plays, the dealer then plays his hand. When the dealer completes his turn, the game moves into settlement where scoring and payout occur.

Settlement

After the dealer finishes his turn (or learns that he has Blackjack), play moves into settlement. During settlement each busted player loses his bet; each player with a hand less than the dealer's loses his bet; each player with a hand better than the dealer wins his bet; and each player with a count equal to the dealer's is said to standoff and no payout is made. Bets are paid off evenly.

If a player has a Blackjack and the dealer does not, the player is paid off at three to two odds. For example, if the player had bet $100 he is paid $150 ([100 * 3]/2).

Miscellaneous

I need to mention a few more important details about the game of Blackjack:

The Deck—Blackjack is played with four standard 52-card decks. These four decks are combined into one large pile of cards.

Number of players—One to seven players may play Blackjack.

Doubling Down—After being dealt his two cards, the player may choose to double down. When the player double downs, he doubles his bet, receives one more card, and ends his turn.

Insurance—When the dealer's face up card is an ace the player may elect to place an insurance bet. The insurance bet is equal to half of the original bet. If the dealer's hole card gives the dealer a natural 21, the player breaks even. If the dealer's hole card does not give the dealer 21, the player loses his insurance bet.

Splitting pairs—A player is said to have a pair if the initial two cards dealt have the same value. If the player is dealt a pair, he may choose to split the hand into two new hands. If the player splits the pair, the dealer deals each new hand one additional card and then the player must place an equal bet on the new hand. A player can split any pair that results from a subsequent split (except for a pair of aces). Also of note is the fact that any 21-count resulting from a split is not treated as a natural 21. Once split, the player goes on normally to hit or to stand for each hand in turn.

Identifying the Actors

There are two reasons for performing analysis. Through analysis, you create the use case model: the description of how the user will use the system. Through analysis, you also create the domain model: a description of the main vocabulary of the system.

The first step in defining your use cases is to define the actors that will use the system. Going by the description in the last section, it is easy to see that there are two main actors in the game of Blackjack—the player(s) and the dealer.

These two actors answer the question, "Who will primarily use the system." Through use cases, you can define how these actors will use the system.

Creating a Preliminary List of Use Cases

An effective way of generating the initial use cases is to ask what each of these actors can do.

Players can do the following:

1. Place bets
2. Hit
3. Stand
4. Bust
5. Get Blackjack
6. Place insurance
7. Split pairs
8. Double down
9. Decide to play again
10. Quit

The dealer can do the following:

1. Deal cards
2. Fulfill the game
3. Hit
4. Stand
5. Bust
6. Get Blackjack

There may be more use cases but this list provides you with plenty of starting material.

Planning the Iterations

Chapter 9 introduced you to the iterative development process. Following an iterative development process will allow you to quickly build a bare bones Blackjack implementation. Each iteration will continue to add additional functionality to the game.

Such an approach allows for quick, quantifiable results. Following such an approach allows you to deal with issues as they come up—not all at once at the end of development. An iterative approach prevents you from being overwhelmed by an avalanche of problems at the end of development.

Key to an iterative development is planning the iterations as best you can from the beginning. As additional facts present themselves it is fully acceptable to revisit the plan; however, a rough sketch of the iterations from the start gives a project direction, goals—and more importantly, it gives you a feeling of achievement as the goals are met.

Normally you plan your iterations by rating the use cases by importance. When working with a customer it is best to let the customer rank the importance of each use case. In the case of Blackjack, you should rank the use cases based on its importance to game play. Pick the use cases absolutely necessary for game play, and do those use cases first. Other use cases can wait for later iterations. Such an approach allows you to create a working game as soon as possible.

For the purposes of the Blackjack project there will be four main iterations.

Iteration 1: Basic Game Play

Iteration 1 will create the basic game play. Iteration 1 will refine and implement the following preliminary use cases.

Player use cases:

1. Hit
2. Stand
3. Bust

Dealer use cases:

1. Deal cards
2. Hit
3. Stand
4. Bust

At the end of Iteration 1, you should have a game that plays on the command line. The game will have two participants: the dealer and one player. The dealer will deal the cards and allow each player to hit until the player decides to stand or busts. After each player plays, the game will terminate.

Iteration 2: Rules

Iteration 2 will add rules to the game. Iteration 2 will refine and implement the following preliminary use cases:

Player use cases:

1. Get Blackjack

The dealer can

1. Fulfill the game (detect winners, losers, and standoff)
2. Get Blackjack

At the end of Iteration 2, everything from Iteration 1 will still work. In addition the game will detect and indicate when a player has blackjack, busts, stands, wins, loses, and standoffs.

Iteration 3: Betting

Iteration 3 will add basic betting and doubling down to the game. Iteration 3 will refine and implement the following preliminary use cases:

Player use cases:

1. Place bets
2. Double down

Dealer use cases:

1. Fulfill the game (for betting)

At the end of Iteration 3, everything from Iterations 2 and 1 will still work. In addition the game will allow basic betting and doubling down.

Iteration 4: User Interface

Iteration 4 will put some final touches on the command line UI and build a graphical UI. Iteration 4 will refine and implement the following preliminary use cases:

Player use cases:

1. Decide to play again
2. Quit

Note

For the purposes of this project, insurance betting and split pairs are omitted. These features are left wholly as an exercise to the reader. Blackjack is a game with many variants. Often, insurance is not allowed and splitting overly complicates the system. Think of this variant as the *Teach Yourself Object Oriented Programming in 21 Days* Blackjack variant!

Just remember that you heard it here first.

Iteration 1: Basic Game Play

Today's lesson will step you through the first iteration of the Blackjack card game. By the end of today's lesson you will have the basic skeleton of a Blackjack game.

 Note

> Before each section you may want to put the book down and try your hand at the analysis, design, or implementation.
>
> If you experiment on your own be sure to come back, read each section, and compare your work with the presented materials before continuing. Try to judge any discrepancies between your solution and the book's solution judiciously. While you may have a superior solution (there are many ways to approach this game), be sure that you are correct and that your solution follows the tenets of OOP.

Blackjack Analysis

Today's iteration will refine and implement the following use cases:

Player use cases:

1. Hit
2. Stand
3. Bust

Dealer use cases:

1. Deal cards
2. Hit
3. Stand
4. Bust

After you have a set of refined use cases, you can create an initial model of the domain and begin design.

Refining the Use Cases

Let's begin with the dealer's deal use case as this action starts the game.

You first need to describe the use case in a paragraph:

> Beginning with the first player, the dealer deals one card face up to each player, finishing with himself. The dealer then repeats this process, but deals his own card face

down. Dealing ends and then play commences once the dealer has dealt each player, including himself, two cards.

- Deal cards:
    1. Dealer deals one card face up to every player including himself.
    2. Dealer deals a second card face up to all non-dealer players.
    3. Dealer deals a card face down to himself.

- Preconditions:
    - New game
- Post conditions:
    - All players and the dealer have a hand with two cards

The Player Hits and Player Stands use cases naturally follow. Let's start with the Player Hits use case:

The player decides he is not satisfied with his hand. The player has not yet busted, so the player decides to hit. If the player does not bust, he can choose to either hit again or stand. If the player does bust, play transfers to the next player.

- Player hits:
    1. Player decides he is not satisfied with his hand.
    2. The player requests another card from the dealer.
    3. The player can decide to hit again, or stand if his hand totals less than or equal to 21.

- Preconditions:
    - Player has a hand whose total value is less than or equal to 21
- Post conditions:
    - A new card is added to the player's hand
- Alternative: Player busts:

    New card causes player's hand to exceed 21. Player busts (loses). Next player's/dealer's turn begins.

Player Stands is a simple use case:

The player decides he is satisfied with his hand and stands.

- Player stands:
    1. Player decides he is happy with his hand and stands

- Preconditions:
  - Player has a hand whose value is less than or equal to 21
- Post conditions:
  - Player's turn ends

At this point it is becoming apparent that Player/Dealer Busts is not a use case because it is a byproduct of other actions. The dealer and player will never take a bust action; however, the players will choose to take a hit or stand.

With the bust use cases removed only the Dealer Hits and Dealer Stands use cases remain. Let's start with the Dealer Hits use case:

The dealer must hit if his hand's total is less than 17. If the dealer does not bust after the hit and his hand's total is still less than 17, he must hit again. The dealer must stand on any total greater than or equal to 17. When the dealer busts or stands, play terminates.

- Dealer hits:
  1. The dealer hits if his hand is less than 17
  2. New card added to dealer's hand
  3. If the total is less than 17, dealer must hit again
- Preconditions:
  - Dealer has a hand whose total is less than 17
- Post conditions:
  - New card in dealer's hand
  - Play ends
- Alternative: Dealer busts:
  New card causes dealer's hand to be greater than 21. Dealer busts.
- Alternative: Dealer stands:
  New card causes dealer's hand to be greater than or equal to 17. Dealer stands.

Like Player Stands, Dealer Stands is relatively simple:

The dealer has a hand total greater than or equal to 17 and stands.

- Dealer stands:
  4. Dealer's hand has a total greater than or equal to 17 and stands.

- Preconditions:
  - Dealer's hand greater than or equal to 17
- Post conditions:
  - Play ends

Modeling the Use Cases

For Iteration 1, the use cases are fairly simple. Use case models would be more overhead then they are worth, so they will be omitted.

The interactions between the dealer and players are a bit more interesting. Figure 15.2 shows the sequence of events followed within the Deal Cards use case. Figure 15.3 shows the sequence of event followed within the Player Hits use case.

FIGURE 15.2

The sequence diagram for Deal Cards use case.

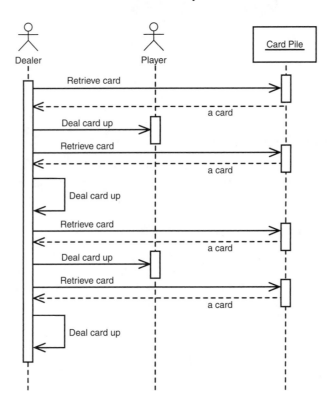

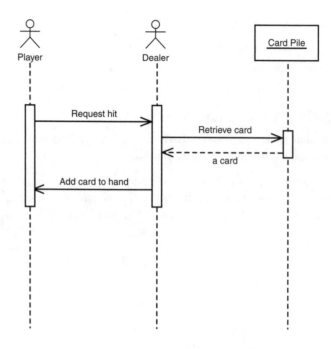

Figure 15.3

The sequence diagram for Player Hits use case.

Modeling The Domain

Using the use cases as a basis for the domain model, you can isolate seven distinct domain objects: `BlackjackGame`, `Dealer`, `Player`, `Card`, `Deck`, `DeckPile`, and `Hand`. Figure 15.4 diagrams the resulting domain model.

Blackjack Design

By applying object-oriented design to the previous analysis, you will arrive at a model of the main classes in the design, their responsibilities, and a definition of how they will interact and get their information. You can then take the design and work on the implementation.

CRC Cards

The domain model gives you a good starting point for an initial list of objects. With this list of objects you can use CRC cards to flesh out the object's various responsibilities and collaborations.

Note

Before continuing it may be a good exercise to try and generate a list of CRC cards on your own.

FIGURE 15.4

The Blackjack domain model.

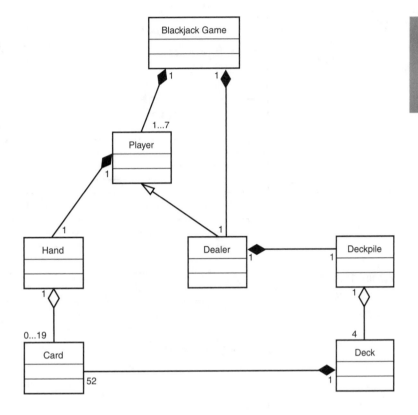

Figures 15.5 through 15.11 illustrates the possible output from a CRC card session.

FIGURE 15.5

The Blackjack game CRC card.

Blackjack	
create players	Player
create hands	Hand
create dealer	Dealer
create Deckpile	Deck, Deckpile
connect all of the players, dealer, and console together	Console, Dealer, Player, Deckpile
start game	Dealer

15

FIGURE **15.6**

The Deck CRC card.

Deck	
add itself to the Deckpile	Deckpile
construct 52 cards	Card

FIGURE **15.7**

The Card CRC card.

Card	
hold a suit	Suit
hold a rank	Rank
display itself	Rank, Suit, Console
hold and toggle a face state: up or down	

FIGURE 15.8

The Player CRC card.

Player	
hold a hand	Hand
add cards to hand	Hand, Card
decide whether to hit or stand	Hand
inform dealer when done playing	Dealer
update observers	Player Listener
display itself	Hand, Console
detect busted hand	Hand

FIGURE 15.9

The Dealer CRC card.

Dealer inherits from Player	
hit a player	Player
pass the turn to the next player/self	Players/self
track players in game	Player
start a new game	
deal cards	Deckpile, Card, Player, self
decide whether to hit or stand	
tell players when they can play	Player/self

15

FIGURE **15.10**

The Hand CRC card.

Hand	
hold onto cards	Card
add cards to itself	Card
reset itself	
turn all cards over	Card
display itself	Card, Console
calculate its total	Card, Rank
detect bust	Card

FIGURE **15.11**

The Deckpile card.

Deckpile	
accept cards to hold onto	Card
shuffle the cards	Card
deal cards up	Card
deal cards down	Card
reset itself	

The Command Line UI

Chapter 13, "OO and User Interface Programming," presented the MVC design pattern. The Blackjack game's UI will utilize the MVC design pattern. As a result of this design decision, you need to add an observer mechanism to the `Player` as well as a `Console` object for displaying the players and retrieving user input.

Because there is only one `Console`, the `Console` object is a candidate for the Singleton pattern.

The Blackjack Model

In all, nine classes and two interfaces make up the complete Blackjack class model. Figure 15.12 illustrates the model.

FIGURE 15.12

The Blackjack *class model.*

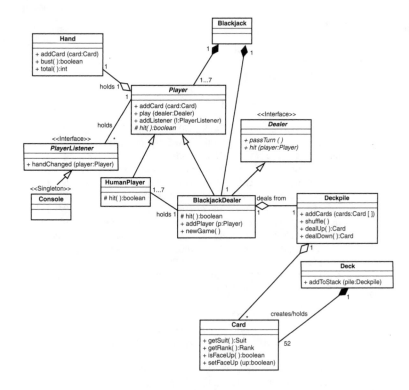

The next section details the implementation of this model.

The Implementation

The following sections provide the implementation for the major parts of the model illustrated in Figure 15.12.

Note All source code is available for download from this book's Web page. Visit www.samspublishing.com, and search for ISBN number 0672321092; then, click the Source Code link on the book's page.

The Card

The Card is implemented much as the Card class presented in Chapter 12, "Advanced Design Patterns". Rank has changed a bit. Listing 15.1 presents the new implementation of Rank.

LISTING 15.1   Rank.java

```
import java.util.Collections;
import java.util.List;
import java.util.Arrays;

public final class Rank {

    public static final Rank TWO   = new Rank( 2, "2" );
    public static final Rank THREE = new Rank( 3, "3" );
    public static final Rank FOUR  = new Rank( 4, "4" );
    public static final Rank FIVE  = new Rank( 5, "5" );
    public static final Rank SIX   = new Rank( 6, "6" );
    public static final Rank SEVEN = new Rank( 7, "7" );
    public static final Rank EIGHT = new Rank( 8, "8" );
    public static final Rank NINE  = new Rank( 9, "9" );
    public static final Rank TEN   = new Rank( 10, "10" );
    public static final Rank JACK  = new Rank( 10, "J" );
    public static final Rank QUEEN = new Rank( 10, "Q" );
    public static final Rank KING  = new Rank( 10, "K" );
    public static final Rank ACE   = new Rank( 11, "A" );

    private static final Rank [] VALUES =
            { TWO, THREE, FOUR, FIVE, SIX, SEVEN,
              EIGHT, NINE, TEN, JACK, QUEEN, KING, ACE };

    // provide an unmodifiable list to loop over
    public static final List RANKS =
        Collections.unmodifiableList( Arrays.asList( VALUES ) );

    private final int    rank;
    private final String display;

    private Rank( int rank, String display ) {
        this.rank = rank;
        this.display = display;
    }

    public int getRank() {
        return rank;
    }

    public String toString() {
        return display;
    }
}
```

You will notice that the Rank constants have been updated to reflect the numeric values of Blackjack. The class has also been changed to hold onto a public unmodifiable List instead of the modifiable array presented in Chapter 12. Using an unmodifiable List prevents inadvertent modifications of the enumeration List.

The Deck and Deckpile

Deck has changed considerably from the one presented in Chapter 12. Listing 15.2 presents the new implementation.

LISTING 15.2   Deck.java

```java
import java.util.Iterator;
import java.util.Random;

public class Deck {

    private Card [] deck;
    private int index;

    public Deck() {
        buildCards();
    }

    public void addToStack( Deckpile stack ) {
        stack.addCards( deck );
    }

    private void buildCards() {

        deck = new Card[52];

        Iterator suits = Suit.SUITS.iterator();

        int counter = 0;
        while( suits.hasNext() ) {
            Suit suit = (Suit) suits.next();
            Iterator ranks = Rank.RANKS.iterator();
            while( ranks.hasNext() ) {
                Rank rank = (Rank) ranks.next();
                deck[counter] = new Card( suit, rank );
                counter++;
            }
        }

    }

}
```

The Deck simply knows how to construct its Cards and then add itself to a Deckpile.
Listing 15.3 presents the Deckpile.

LISTING 15.3 Deckpile.java

```java
import java.util.ArrayList;
import java.util.Iterator;
import java.util.Random;

public class Deckpile {

    private ArrayList stack = new ArrayList();
    private int index;
    private Random rand = new Random();

    public void addCards( Card [] cards ) {
        for( int i = 0; i < cards.length; i ++ ) {
            stack.add( cards[i] );
        }
    }

    public void shuffle() {
        reset();
        randomize();
        randomize();
        randomize();
        randomize();
    }

    public Card dealUp() {
        Card card = deal();
        if( card != null ) {
            card.setFaceUp( true );
        }
        return card;
    }

    public Card dealDown() {
        Card card = deal();
        if( card != null ) {
            card.setFaceUp( false );
        }
        return card;
    }

    public void reset() {
        index = 0;
        Iterator i = stack.iterator();
        while( i.hasNext() ) {
            Card card = (Card) i.next();
            card.setFaceUp(false);
```

LISTING 15.3 continued

```
        }
    }

    private Card deal() {
        if( index != stack.size() ) {
            Card card = (Card) stack.get( index );
            index++;
            return card;
        }
        return null;
    }

    private void randomize() {
        int num_cards = stack.size();
        for( int i = 0; i < num_cards; i ++ ) {
            int index = rand.nextInt( num_cards );
            Card card_i = (Card) stack.get( i );
            Card card_index = (Card) stack.get( index );
            stack.set( i, card_index );
            stack.set( index, card_i );
        }
    }
}
```

The Deckpile knows how to shuffle its Cards, deal its Cards, and add Cards to itself. Unlike the original Deck the Deckpile maintains a reference to all of the Cards that it returns. That way it can easily retrieve all Cards and reset itself. While this does not completely model the real world, it simplifies card management greatly.

Understanding the rationale behind these changes is important. Both the Deck and Deckpile only implement the behaviors that the game needs. These classes do not provide additional functionality "just in case we need it someday." It's impossible to tell the future and you don't have any requirements for extra functionality, so you should not add it until you know that you need it.

If you try to implement every "what if" possibility or perform premature abstraction you'll never finish implementing your classes. If you do manage to finish them, chances are good that the added functionality or abstraction is not correct. Plus you'll only make more work for yourself because you'll have to maintain functionality that no one else needs or uses.

Trying to program for every "what if" is a common problem encountered by programmers new to OO. You must avoid the temptation to add more functionality that absolutely required to your objects! However, you should insulate those parts of the system that you know will change.

The `Player` and `HumanPlayer`

The `Player` class holds onto a `Hand`. Listing 15.4 presents the `Hand` class.

LISTING 15.4   `Hand.java`

```
import java.util.ArrayList;
import java.util.Iterator;

public class Hand {

    private ArrayList cards = new ArrayList();
    private static final int BLACKJACK = 21;

    public void addCard( Card card ) {
        cards.add( card );
    }

    public boolean bust() {
        if( total() > BLACKJACK ) {
            return true;
        }
        return false;
    }

    public void reset() {
        cards.clear();
    }

    public void turnOver() {
        Iterator i = cards.iterator();
        while( i.hasNext() ) {
            Card card = (Card)i.next();
            card.setFaceUp( true );
        }
    }

    public String toString() {
        Iterator i = cards.iterator();
        String string = "";
        while( i.hasNext() ) {
            Card card = (Card)i.next();
            string = string + " " + card.toString();
        }
        return string;
    }

    public int total() {
        int total = 0;
        Iterator i = cards.iterator();
```

LISTING 15.4   continued

```
        while( i.hasNext() ) {
            Card card = (Card) i.next();
            total += card.getRank().getRank();
        }
        return total;
    }


}
```

The Hand knows how to add Cards to itself, reset itself, turn its cards over, calculate its total, and represent itself as a String. You might notice that the Hand only counts aces as 11. The next iteration will add support for counting aces as 1 or 11.

Listing 15.5 and 15.6 present the Player and HumanPlayer respectively.

LISTING 15.5   Player.java

```
import java.util.ArrayList;
import java.util.Iterator;

public abstract class Player {

    private Hand hand;
    private String name;
    private ArrayList listeners = new ArrayList();

    public Player( String name, Hand hand ) {
        this.name = name;
        this.hand = hand;
    }

    public void addCard( Card card ) {
        hand.addCard( card );
        notifyListeners();
    }

    public void play( Dealer dealer ) {
        // as before, play until the player either busts or stays
        while( !isBusted() && hit() ) {
            dealer.hit( this );
        }
        // but now, tell the dealer that the player is done, otherwise nothing
        // will happen when the player returns
        stopPlay( dealer );
    }

    public void reset() {
```

LISTING 15.5   continued

```java
            hand.reset();
        }

        public boolean isBusted() {
            return hand.bust();
        }

        public void addListener( PlayerListener l ) {
            listeners.add( l );
        }

        public String toString() {
            return ( name + ": " + hand.toString() );
        }

        protected Hand getHand() {
            return hand;
        }

        protected void notifyListeners() {
            Iterator i = listeners.iterator();
            while( i.hasNext() ) {
                PlayerListener pl = (PlayerListener) i.next();
                pl.handChanged( this );
            }
        }

        /**
         * The call to passTurn MUST be inside of a protected method. The Dealer
         * needs to override this behavior! Otherwise it will loop forever.
         */
        protected void stopPlay( Dealer dealer ) {
            dealer.passTurn();
        }

        protected abstract boolean hit();


    }
```

LISTING 15.6   HumanPlayer.java

```java
    public class HumanPlayer extends Player {

        private final static String HIT   = "H";
        private final static String STAND = "S";
        private final static String MSG   = "[H]it or [S]tay";
        private final static String DEFAULT = "invalid";
```

LISTING 15.6   continued

```
    public HumanPlayer( String name, Hand hand ) {
        super( name, hand );
    }

    protected boolean hit() {
        while( true ) {
            Console.INSTANCE.printMessage( MSG );
            String response = Console.INSTANCE.readInput( DEFAULT );
            if( response.equalsIgnoreCase( HIT ) ) {
                return true;
            } else if( response.equalsIgnoreCase( STAND ) ) {
                return false;
            }
            // if we get here loop until we get meaningful input
        }
    }

}
```

The Player abstract class defines all of those behaviors and attributes common to both Players and Dealers. These behaviors include manipulating the Hand, tracking PlayerListeners, and playing a turn.

Player defines one abstract method: public boolean hit(). While playing, the Player base class will make a call to this method to determine whether to hit or to stand. Subclasses can implement this method to provide their own specific behaviors. For example, the HumanPlayer asks the user whether or not to hit or stand. When the Player is done playing it informs the Dealer by calling the Dealer's passTurn() method. When the Player calls this method, the Dealer tells the next Player to play.

The Dealer

Dealer is an interface that specifies the extra methods that a Dealer will expose. Listing 15.7 presents the Dealer interface.

LISTING 15.7   Dealer.java

```
public interface Dealer {

    public void hit( Player player );

    public void passTurn();
}
```

Listing 15.8 presents the BlackjackDealer.

LISTING 15.8   BlackjackDealer.java

```java
import java.util.ArrayList;
import java.util.Iterator;

public class BlackjackDealer extends Player implements Dealer {

    private Deckpile cards;
    private ArrayList players = new ArrayList();
    private int player_index;

    public BlackjackDealer( String name, Hand hand, Deckpile cards ) {
        super( name, hand );
        this.cards = cards;
    }

    public void passTurn() {
        if( player_index != players.size() ) {
            Player player = (Player) players.get( player_index );
            player_index++;
            player.play( this );
        } else {
            this.play( this );
        }
    }

    public void addPlayer( Player player ) {
        players.add( player );
    }

    public void hit( Player player ) {
        player.addCard( cards.dealUp() );
    }

    // override so that the dealer shows his cards before he starts play
    public void play( Dealer dealer ) {
        exposeCards();
        super.play( dealer );
    }

    public void newGame() {
        // deal the cards and tell the first player to go
        deal();
        passTurn();
    }

    public void deal() {

        cards.shuffle();
```

LISTING 15.8   continued

```
        // reset each player and deal 1 card up to each and self
        Player [] player = new Player[players.size()];
        players.toArray( player );
        for( int i = 0; i < player.length; i ++ ) {
            player[i].reset();
            player[i].addCard( cards.dealUp() );
        }
        this.addCard( cards.dealUp() );

        // deal 1 more up card to each player and one down to self
        for( int i = 0; i < player.length; i ++ ) {
            player[i].addCard( cards.dealUp() );
        }
        this.addCard( cards.dealDown() );

    }

    protected void stopPlay( Dealer dealer ) {
        // do nothing here in the dealer, simply let the game stop
        // if this were not overridden it would call passTurn() and
        // loop forever
    }

    protected boolean hit() {
        if( getHand().total() <= 16 ) {
            return true;
        }
        return false;
    }

    private void exposeCards() {
        getHand().turnOver();
        notifyListeners();
    }

}
```

BlackjackDealer inherits from Player because a Dealer is also a Player. In addition to
the behaviors provided by a Player, the dealer also holds onto the Player, deals cards
to those Players, and tells each Player to play when its turn starts. When a Player calls
the Dealer's passTurn() method, it knows to let the next Player play.

Figure 15.13 illustrates the interaction between the dealer and the players.

FIGURE **15.13**

*The interaction
between players and
the dealer.*

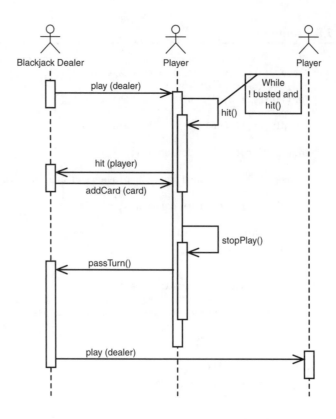

The BlackjackDealer overrides its stopPlay() method so that it terminates play. The dealer also implements the hit() method so that it returns true when the hand is less than 17, and true when the hand is equal to or greater than 17.

The BlackjackGame

Listing 15.9 and 15.10 presents the Blackjack game and Console classes respectively.

LISTING 15.9   Blackjack.java

```
public class Blackjack {

    public static void main( String [] args ) {

        Deckpile cards = new Deckpile();
        for( int i = 0; i < 4; i ++ ) {
            cards.shuffle();
            Deck deck = new Deck();
            deck.addToStack( cards );
```

LISTING 15.9   continued

```
            cards.shuffle();
        }

        Hand dealer_hand = new Hand();
        BlackjackDealer dealer = new BlackjackDealer( "Dealer", dealer_hand,
cards );
        Hand human_hand = new Hand();
        Player player = new HumanPlayer( "Human", human_hand );
        dealer.addListener( Console.INSTANCE );
        player.addListener( Console.INSTANCE );
        dealer.addPlayer( player );

        dealer.newGame();
    }

}
```

LISTING 15.10   Console.java

```
import java.io.BufferedReader;
import java.io.InputStreamReader;
import java.io.IOException;

public class Console implements PlayerListener {

    // console singleton
    public final static Console INSTANCE = new Console();

    private BufferedReader in =
        new BufferedReader( new InputStreamReader( System.in ) );

    public void printMessage( String message ) {
        System.out.println( message );
    }

    public String readInput( String default_input ) {
        String response;
        try {
            return in.readLine();
        } catch (IOException ioe) {
            return default_input;
        }
    }

    public void handChanged( Player player ) {
        printMessage( player.toString() );
    }
```

LISTING 15.10 continued

```
// private to prevent instantiation
private Console() {}

}
```

The Blackjack game constructs the Dealer, Hands, Deckpile, Decks, and connects them all together. Once connected, it starts the game by telling the Dealer to start a new game.

The Console is a singleton that provides access to the command line. It also listens to the Players and then prints them to the screen each time they are updated.

A Procedural Pitfall

If you come from a procedural background it could be tempting to implement the BlackjackDealer's newGame() method as illustrated in Listing 15.11.

LISTING 15.11 A Procedural Implementation of BlackjackDealer

```
public void newGame() {

    cards.shuffle();

    // reset each player and deal 1 card up to each and self
    Player [] player = new Player[players.size()];
    players.toArray( player );
    for( int i = 0; i < player.length; i ++ ) {
        player[i].reset();
        player[i].addCard( cards.dealUp() );
    }
    this.addCard( cards.dealUp() );

    // deal 1 more up card to each player and one down to self
    for( int i = 0; i < player.length; i ++ ) {
        player[i].addCard( cards.dealUp() );
    }
    this.addCard( cards.dealDown() );

    // have each player play and then dealer
    for( int i = 0; i < player.length; i ++ ) {
        player[i].play(this);
    }
    exposeCards();
    this.play( this );

}
```

This implementation removes the need for the passTurn() method; however, this is a procedural approach to the game loop. Instead of Player objects communicating to the Dealer that they are done playing, the Dealer simply loops sequentially through the Players.

Figure 15.14 illustrates the interaction between the Dealer and its Players.

FIGURE 15.14

The procedural inter-action between players and the dealer.

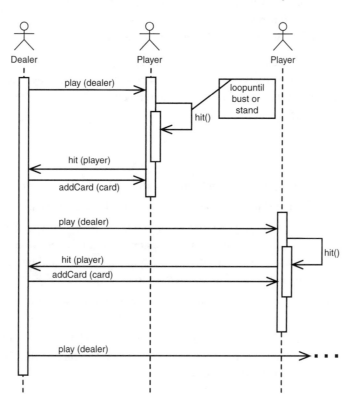

You will notice that the interactions in Figure 15.13 are much more dynamic than the interactions taking place in Figure 15.14. Figure 15.13 is truly a system of interacting objects. In 15.14 the Dealer simply waits for the Player to return and then sequentially calls the next Player. There is no interaction beyond the Dealer statically telling each Player to play in turn. While this approach does work, it is not very flexible and it is certainly not as object-oriented as the approach presented in 15.13.

Testing

As Chapter 14, "Building Reliable Software Through Testing," showed testing should be an ongoing process. A complete set of tests is available along with the source code for download. These tests consist of a set of unit tests and mock objects that thoroughly test the Blackjack system. Studying the tests is left as an important exercise to the reader.

Summary

Today you analyzed, designed, and implemented a basic game of Blackjack. By using an iterative approach you were able to gain results that you could see quickly. Over the course of the week, you will continue to add functionality to this Blackjack game.

You also learned a few new lessons today. When programming, you need to avoid falling into procedural traps even though a procedural approach may seem like the natural solution. You must also learn to avoid the temptation of adding more to a class definition than you need.

Q&A

Q If testing is so important, why did you skip it?

A I did not skip testing at all. All downloadable sources are packed full of test cases.

The text did skip the discussion of testing for space and efficiency constraints. I don't think that you would have appreciated it if you were forced to read through countless pages of test code. Studying and understanding the test code (and all code really) is left as an exercise to the reader.

Q There seems to be a lot more code than the code published in the chapter— what's up with that?

A There is a lot more code. It's simply not possible to cover all of the code effectively within the text. Think of the text as the "highlights film" of the code. You will need to expend a considerable amount of personal study to fully understand the code.

The purpose of these final chapters is to present an overall project of which code is only one component. Analysis and design are equally as important. You will need to spend extra time within that framework studying the code, if you want to fully understand it.

Workshop

The quiz questions and answers are provided for your further understanding. See Appendix A, "Answers," for the answers.

Quiz

1. List two of the design patterns that you saw today. Where were the patterns used?

2. Find one example of polymorphism from the source.

3. Find one example of inheritance from the source.

4. How does the `Deck` encapsulate its cards?

5. How do both the `BlackjackDealer` and `HumanPlayer` act polymorphically?

Exercises

1. Download the source code for today's iteration. After you have the code, compile it, run it by executing Blackjack, and then try to understand how it works. Gaining a full understanding of the code will take some time and patience.

2. Today lesson was rather long. There are no other exercises. Be sure to review the source and lesson.

DAY **16**

Blackjack Iteration 2: Adding Rules

Yesterday you performed the initial analysis and design of a Blackjack game. Today you will continue that process and add additional rules to the Blackjack game.

Today you will learn how to

- Model the Blackjack game states
- Use states to remove conditional logic

Blackjack Rules

Yesterday you built a simple Blackjack game. The game that you designed and built dealt cards and allowed a player to play until he either stood or busted. A real Blackjack game will do a bit more. In a real Blackjack game, aces are worth 1 or 11 points. Players can get blackjack, bust, standoff, lose, or win. A dealer won't even play if all of the players bust or he is dealt a blackjack hand.

Today you will add the necessary logic to support these and other additional game features. As always, you will begin by analyzing the use cases.

Rules Analysis

To fully understand all of the rules of Blackjack, you'll need to revisit each of yesterday's use cases and add any required new use cases. Once the use cases are fleshed out, you'll need to update the domain model.

Blackjack Rules Use Case Analysis

The addition of rules affects many of the use cases fleshed out yesterday. There is also one new use case: Dealer Fulfills Game. Let's begin with the Deal Cards use case that you discovered yesterday:

> Beginning with the first player, the dealer deals one card face up to each player, finishing with himself. The dealer then repeats this process but deals his own card face down. Dealing ends and then play commences once the dealer has dealt each player, including himself, two cards.

- Deal cards
    1. Dealer deals one card face up to every player including himself
    2. Dealer deals a second card face up to all non-dealer players
    3. Dealer deals a card face down to himself
- Preconditions
    - New game
- Post conditions
    - All players and the dealer have a hand with two cards
    - The turn of the first player who does not have blackjack (two cards totaling 21) begins
    - Play continues for each player who does not have blackjack
- Alternative: Dealer has blackjack

    If the dealer has a natural 21 or blackjack, the game moves to fulfillment. The players do not get to take a turn.

The Deal Cards use case now adds a number of new post conditions as well as an alternative. What is important to note is that if the dealer has blackjack the game automatically ends. Likewise, any player with blackjack does not play.

Next, revisit Player Hits:

The player decides he is not satisfied with his hand. The player has not yet busted so the player decides to hit. If the player does not bust he can choose to either hit again or stand. If the player does bust, play transfers to the next player.

- Player hits
    1. Player decides he is not satisfied with his hand
    2. The player requests another card from the dealer
    3. The player can decide to hit again or stand if his hand totals less than or equal to 21
- Preconditions
    - Player has a hand whose total value is less than or equal to 21
    - Player does not have blackjack
    - Dealer does not have blackjack
- Post conditions
    - A new card is added to the player's hand
- Alternative: Player busts

    New card causes player's hand to be greater than 21. Player busts (loses); next player's/dealer's turn begins
- Alternative: Player's hand > 21, but player has an ace

    New card causes player's hand to be greater than 21. Player has an ace. Value of the ace changes from 11 to one, bringing the player's hand to less than or equal to 21. The player can decide to hit again or stand.

Of note is the fact that a player can only play if he or the dealer does not have blackjack. This use case also introduces the fact that an ace can have a value of 1 or 11, depending on which makes the hand better.

Player stands also gets some additional preconditions.

The player decides he is satisfied with his hand and stands.

- Player stands
    1. Player decides he is happy with his hand and stands
- Preconditions
    - Player has a hand whose value is less than or equal to 21
    - Player does not have blackjack
    - Dealer does not have blackjack

16

- Post conditions
  - Player's turn ends

Like Player Hits, you'll need to update Dealer Hits:

- The dealer must hit if his hand's total is < less than 17. If the dealer does not bust after the hit and his hand's total is still less than< 17 he must hit again. The dealer must stand on any total >= greater than or equal to 17. When the dealer busts or stands, play terminates.

- Dealer hits
  1. The dealer hits if his hand less than 17
  2. New card added to dealer's hand
  3. Total is less than 17, dealer must hit again

- Preconditions
  - Dealer has a hand whose total is less than 17
  - Must be a player in the standing state

- Post conditions
  - New card in dealer's hand
  - Play ends

- Alternative: Dealer busts

  New card causes dealer's hand greater than 21; dealer busts

- Alternative: Dealer stands

  New card causes dealer's hand to be greater than or equal to 17; dealer stands

- Alternative: Dealer has ace, stands

  New card causes dealer's hand to be greater than or equal to 21, but includes an ace. The value of the ace changes from 11 to 1 bringing the dealer's total to 17; dealer stands.

- Alternative: Dealer has ace, hits

  New card causes dealer's hand to be greater than or equal to 21, but includes an ace. The value of the ace changes from 11 to 1 bringing the dealer's total to less than 17; dealer hits.

This use case adds a number of preconditions and variants. The precondition, "Must be a player in the standing state," signifies that a dealer will only hit if there is a player to beat. If no player is standing, that means that all of the players are either busted or have blackjack. In addition, the new alternatives take the fact that an ace can be counted as a 1 or an 11.

Likewise, a dealer will automatically stand if there are no other standing players.

> The dealer has a hand total greater than or equal to >= 17 and stands.

- Dealer stands
    1. Dealer's hand has a total greater than or equal to 17 and stands
- Preconditions
    - Dealer's hand greater than or equal to 17
    - Must be a player in the standing state
- Post conditions
    - Play ends
- Alternative: No standing players

    If there are no standing players the dealer will automatically stand regardless of hand count

When the game is done the dealer needs to figure out who has won, lost, and standoffs. The Dealer Fulfills Game use case handles that use:

> After all playing in done, the dealer checks each hand and determines for each player if they win or lose or if the game is a standoff.

- Dealer fulfills game
    1. Dealer checks the first player's hand and compares it with his own
    2. The player's hand is greater than the dealer, but not busted; the player wins
    3. The dealer repeats this comparison for all players
- Preconditions
    - Each player has passed their turns
    - The dealer has passed his turn
- Post conditions
    - Player's final results determined
- Alternative: Player loses
    - Dealer checks the player's hand and compares it with his own. The player's hand is less than the dealer's. The player loses.

16

- Alternative: Standoff
  - Dealer checks the player's hand and compares it with his own. The player's hand is equal to the dealer's. The game is a standoff.
- Alternative: Dealer busts
  - If the dealer is busted, every standing and blackjack player wins. All others lose.

Modeling the Use Cases

Most of the changes to the use cases are straightforward. It may be helpful to draw the sequence of events for the Dealer Fulfills Game, however. Figure 16.1 illustrates the sequence of events found in the Dealer Fulfills Game use case.

FIGURE 16.1

The sequence diagram for Dealer Fulfills Game use case.

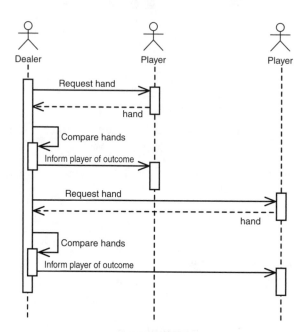

Updating the Blackjack Domain Model

From a domain perspective these new and updated use cases do not change the domain.

Rules Design

At this point it can be extremely tempting to go directly into implementation. On the surface, it seems as if you can implement the rules through conditionals. In fact, you can implement the rules through conditionals. Listing 16.1 presents what one of those conditionals might look like.

LISTING 16.1 Conditional Rules Inside the `BlackjackDealer`

```
protected void stopPlay( Dealer dealer ) {
    // the game is over, pick the winners and point out the losers
    if( isBusted() ) {
        Iterator i = players.iterator();
        while( i.hasNext() ) {
            Player player = (Player) i.next();
            if( !player.isBusted() ) {
                Console.INSTANCE.printMessage( player.toString() + " WINNER!" );
            }
        }
    } else {
        if( hasBlackjack() ) {
            Iterator i = players.iterator();
            while( i.hasNext() ) {
                Player player = (Player) i.next();
                if( player.hasBlackjack() ) {
                    Console.INSTANCE.printMessage( player.toString() +
" STANDOFF!" );
                } else {
                    Console.INSTANCE.printMessage( player.toString() +
" LOSER!" );
                }
            }
        } else { // deal is not busted and does not have blackjack
            Iterator i = players.iterator();
            while( i.hasNext() ) {
                Player player = (Player) i.next();
                if( player.hasBlackjack() ) {
                    Console.INSTANCE.printMessage( player.toString() +
" WINNER WITH BLACKJACK!" );
                } else if( player.isBusted() ) {
                    Console.INSTANCE.printMessage( player.toString() +
" BUSTED!" );
                } else if( player.getHand().greaterThan( getHand() ) ){
                    Console.INSTANCE.printMessage( player.toString() +
" WINNER!" );
                } else if( player.getHand().equalTo( getHand() ) ) {
                    Console.INSTANCE.printMessage( player.toString() +
" STANDOFF!" );
                } else {
                    Console.INSTANCE.printMessage( player.toString() +
" LOSER!" );
                }
            }
        }
    }
}
```

16

Of course, this conditional only deals with fulfilling the game. The dealer will need many more conditionals to know whether or not to start play after the deal, and whether or not to let a player play. For example, if a dealer has blackjack hand, play should automatically end. You will need a conditional for that and all other branches of play.

Such an approach is fragile, difficult to maintain, error prone, and simply ugly. When dealing with conditionals you will often find that the addition of a new conditional causes an old behavior to fail. It is also extremely difficult to understand code that is packed with conditionals. Good luck to anyone who has to maintain such a conditional mess.

Conditionals are not particularly object-oriented. The improper use of conditionals breaks down the proper divisions of responsibility that are so key to OOP. When using conditionals the dealer devolves into a procedural function that checks a flag on the player, makes a decision, and then tells the player what to do. OO does not work that way! Conditionals do have their uses; however, they should never extract responsibilities from an object.

Instead, the knowledge of whether a player busted or was dealt blackjack should be contained within the `Player` object itself; then, when one of those events does occur, the `Player` object can take the proper action and inform the `BlackjackDealer`, if appropriate. Instead of the dealer instructing the players in what to do, the players should use their own internal states to make those decisions. Such an approach more closely models the real-world Blackjack game anyway.

The first step to getting rid of conditionals is the realization that events and states drive the game of Blackjack. Throughout a game of Blackjack, the various players move through states. At one point the player is waiting; then he is playing. After playing the player either moves into a standing or busted state. Likewise, the dealer moves from dealing, to waiting for his turn, to playing, and finally to standing or busted.

There are also alternative state transitions. After being dealt his cards, the dealer or player may automatically transition to the blackjack state if he is dealt a blackjack hand.

To gain a full understanding of the various states as well as the events that move the player from state to state, it helps to model the various states through a state diagram.

State Diagrams

The UML defines a rich set of notations for modeling state diagrams. Instead of getting lost in the details, we'll only use those aspects necessary for modeling the Blackjack game.

For the purposes of Blackjack modeling, there are states, transitions, events, activities, and conditions.

In Blackjack a state is the current playing condition for a player. Such conditions include waiting, playing, busted, standing, and blackjack, among others.

Transitions occur when a player moves among its states. For example a player transitions from the playing state to the busted state when he busts.

Events are one type of stimulus that can cause a player to transition among its states. For example, when the player's hand busts, the player will move from the playing to busted state.

Activities are those actions taken when in a state. For example, when playing in the playing state a player will choose to hit until he either decides to stand or busts.

Guard Conditions are a boolean expression that place some kind of constraint on a transition. For example, a player will move to standing if he decides not to hit.

Figure 16.2 presents the notation that you will use to model the Blackjack states.

FIGURE 16.2

The state diagram notation.

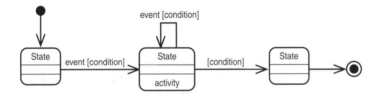

In the model, transitions are symbolized through arrows. Transitions can occur as a result of an event or a condition (or a combination of the two). The event and condition should appear on the transition arrow so that it is obvious why the transition occurs.

You'll also notice that a transition can transition right back to the current state. Such a transition is known as a *self transition*.

Finally, if the object takes a certain action when in the state, the action is recorded as an activity inside of the state symbol. It is completely valid for a state to lack an activity.

Modeling the Player States

Figure 16.3 presents the player state diagram.

The player has five main states: Waiting, Blackjack, Playing, Standing, and Busted. The player begins in the Waiting state. After the deal the player either moves into the Blackjack or Playing state, depending upon the hand he is dealt.

FIGURE 16.3

The player state diagram.

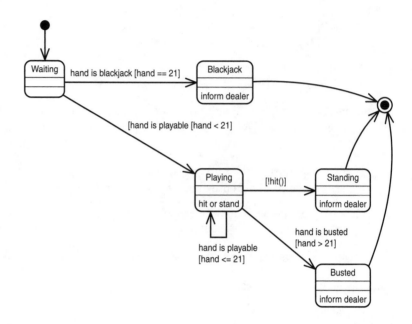

When it is his turn to play, the player plays (the activity of the Playing state). While playing the player decides to either hit or stay. If the player decides to stay, he transitions into the Standing state. If the player hits, he transitions to the Busted state if his hand busts, or goes back to the Playing state if the hand remains playable. This continues until the player either busts or stands.

Modeling the Dealer States

Figure 16.4 presents the dealer state diagram.

The dealer has six main states: Dealing, Waiting, Blackjack, Playing, Standing, and Busted. The dealer begins in the Dealing state and deals cards to each player and himself. After the deal the dealer either moves into the Blackjack or Waiting state, depending upon the hand he is dealt.

While in the Waiting state the dealer waits for all players to finish their turns. When all players have finished, the dealer transitions to the Playing state and begins his turn.

Like the player the dealer decides whether to hit or to stay in the Playing state. Unlike the players, however, the dealer is constrained to hit when his hand is less than 17 and stand when his hand is greater than or equal to 17.

Like the player if the dealer hits and busts, he automatically transitions into the Busted state. If the dealer decides to stand, he moves into the Standing state.

FIGURE 16.4

The dealer state diagram.

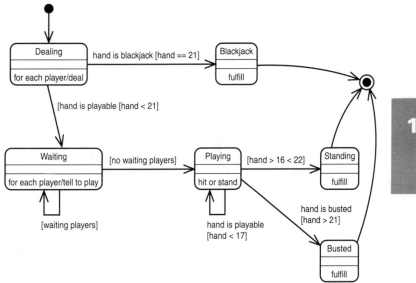

Of note are the activities in the Blackjack, Busted, and Standing states. While in these states, the dealer fulfills the game and ends play.

The Updated Blackjack Model

When the game states are modeled and fully understood, you need to decide how to fit them into the design. Start by turning each game state into its own class. Next, you'll need to figure out what generates the events.

This use of the term *state* fits with the original definition presented earlier. Here you just base an object around each state that the Player may have at a given time. This frees you from having to have many different internal variables. Instead, the state object nicely encapsulates all of those different values inside one object that has both state and behavior.

You'll quickly realize that all events revolve around the hand's state. So you should probably let the Hand generate and send these events as Cards are added to the Hand. You'll also need to establish a mechanism for the states to receive events from the Hand.

States themselves are fairly simple and have three responsibilities. States are responsible for

- Performing any activities
- Listening for and responding to events
- Knowing what state to transition to in response to an event or condition

Figure 16.5 illustrates the class diagram for the State interface.

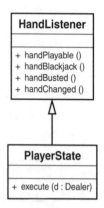

FIGURE 16.5

The State *class diagram.*

You'll note that each event has a corresponding method on the state. The Hand will call one of these methods depending on what state the Hand would like to report. The State also adds an execute() method. This method is called when the State should perform its actions.

Figure 16.6 models the relationships between the Player, Hand, and States.

FIGURE 16.6

The State *framework class diagram.*

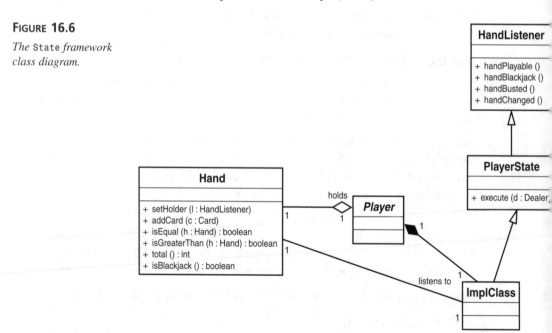

The Player holds onto a State object. When it is the Player's turn to do something, the Player simply execute the State's execute() method. The State will then perform any activities, listen

Hand, and transition to the next State as appropriate. Once transitioned, the next State will perform any activities, listen to the Hand, and transition as appropriate. This pattern will repeat itself until the game is over.

Figure 16.7 illustrates the complete class diagram for the Blackjack card game.

FIGURE 16.7

The complete Blackjack *class diagram.*

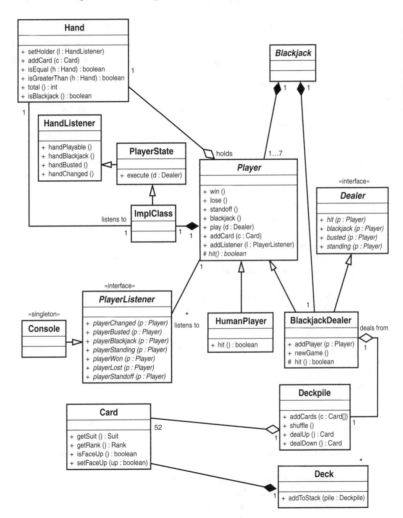

While the addition of a State framework is the major change taken during this iteration, other interfaces and classes have been updated to be able to support the reporting and display of the new game conditions.

Rules Implementation

To support the new game features, changes are required in the Player, Dealer, BlackjackDealer, and Hand classes. A number of new classes and interfaces need to be added, as well. The following sections will review every major change.

Changes to Hand

To support the new game features, a Hand must report its state to a listener. Listing 16.2 presents the new HandListener interface.

LISTING 16.2   HandListener.java

```java
public interface HandListener {

    public void handPlayable();

    public void handBlackjack();

    public void handBusted();

    public void handChanged();

}
```

Listing 16.3 presents the updated Hand class.

LISTING 16.3   Hand.java

```java
import java.util.ArrayList;
import java.util.Iterator;

public class Hand {

    private ArrayList cards = new ArrayList();
    private static final int BLACKJACK = 21;
    private HandListener holder;
    private int number_aces;

    public Hand() {
        // set the holder to a blank listener so it will not be null if not
        // externally set
        setHolder(
            new HandListener() {
```

LISTING 16.3   continued

16

```
                public void handPlayable() {}
                public void handBlackjack() {}
                public void handBusted() {}
                public void handChanged() {}
            }
        );
    }

    public void setHolder( HandListener holder ) {
        this.holder = holder;
    }

    public Iterator getCards() {
        return cards.iterator();
    }

    public void addCard( Card card ) {
        cards.add( card );

        holder.handChanged();

        if( card.getRank() == Rank.ACE ) {
            number_aces++;
        }

        if( bust() ) {
            holder.handBusted();
            return;
        }
        if( blackjack() ) {
            holder.handBlackjack();
            return;
        }
        if ( cards.size() >= 2 ){
            holder.handPlayable();
            return;
        }
    }

    public boolean isEqual( Hand hand ) {
        if( hand.total() == this.total() ) {
            return true;
        }
        return false;
    }

    public boolean isGreaterThan( Hand hand ) {
        return this.total() > hand.total();
```

LISTING 16.3 continued

```
        }

    public boolean blackjack() {
        if( cards.size() == 2 && total() == BLACKJACK ) {
            return true;
        }
        return false;
    }

    public void reset() {
        cards.clear();
        number_aces = 0;
    }

    public void turnOver() {
        Iterator i = cards.iterator();
        while( i.hasNext() ) {
            Card card = (Card)i.next();
            card.setFaceUp( true );
        }
    }

    public String toString() {
        Iterator i = cards.iterator();
        String string = "";
        while( i.hasNext() ) {
            Card card = (Card)i.next();
            string = string + " " + card.toString();
        }
        return string;
    }

    public int total() {
        int total = 0;
        Iterator i = cards.iterator();
        while( i.hasNext() ) {
            Card card = (Card) i.next();
            total += card.getRank().getRank();
        }
        int temp_aces = number_aces;
        while( total > BLACKJACK && temp_aces > 0 ) {
            total = total - 10;
            temp_aces--;
        }
        return total;
    }

    private boolean bust() {
```

LISTING 16.3   continued

```
            if( total() > BLACKJACK ) {
                return true;
            }
            return false;
        }

    }
```

16

Changes to the Hand's total() method now makes it possible for an ace to have either a value of 1 or 11. Likewise, changes to the addCard() method now allow the Hand to inform its listener of changes to the Hand contents as they happen.

Finally, the addition of isEqual() and isGreaterThan() methods allow for the easy, encapsulated comparison of Hands.

Changes to Player

The biggest change to the Player hierarchy revolves around the addition of States. Listing 16.4 presents the new PlayerState interface.

LISTING 16.4   PlayerState.java

```
public interface PlayerState extends HandListener {
    public void execute( Dealer dealer );
}
```

PlayerState inherits from HandListener and adds an execute() method. A PlayerState implementation will implement PlayerState, respond appropriately to any of the HandListener events, and execute its activities within execute().

The Player maintains a reference to its current state through the variable current_state. The play() method has been changed to simply execute the current state:

```
public void play( Dealer dealer ) {
    current_state.execute( dealer );
}
```

Instead of defining some behavior inside of the play() method, the Player simply delegates to its state. That way you can provide new behavior by simply swapping in different state objects. Swapping in different states is a much more elegant solution than switching through a list of conditional logic.

Listings 16.5 through 16.9 present the default `Player` `PlayerState` implementations. These states directly implement the state models from the previous section.

LISTING 16.5 The Default Waiting State

```
private class Waiting implements PlayerState {
    public void handChanged() {
        notifyChanged();
    }
    public void handPlayable() {
        setCurrentState( getPlayingState() );
        // transition
    }
    public void handBlackjack() {
        setCurrentState( getBlackjackState() );
        notifyBlackjack();
        // transition
    }
    public void handBusted() {
        // not possible in waiting state
    }
    public void execute( Dealer dealer ) {
        // do nothing while waiting
    }
}
```

LISTING 16.6 The Default Busted State

```
private class Busted implements PlayerState {
    public void handChanged() {
        // not possible in busted state
    }
    public void handPlayable() {
        // not possible in busted state
    }
    public void handBlackjack() {
        // not possible in busted state
    }
    public void handBusted() {
        // not possible in busted state
    }
    public void execute( Dealer dealer ) {
        dealer.busted( Player.this );
        // terminate
    }
}
```

LISTING 16.7   The Default Blackjack State

```
private class Blackjack implements PlayerState {
    public void handChanged() {
        // not possible in blackjack state
    }
    public void handPlayable() {
        // not possible in blackjack state
    }
    public void handBlackjack() {
        // not possible in blackjack state
    }
    public void handBusted() {
        // not possible in blackjack state
    }
    public void execute( Dealer dealer ) {
        dealer.blackjack( Player.this );
        // terminate
    }
}
```

16

LISTING 16.8   The Default Standing State

```
private class Standing implements PlayerState {
    public void handChanged() {
        // not possible in standing state
    }
    public void handPlayable() {
        // not possible in standing state
    }
    public void handBlackjack() {
        // not possible in standing state
    }
    public void handBusted() {
        // not possible in standing state
    }
    public void execute( Dealer dealer ) {
        dealer.standing( Player.this );
        // terminate
    }
}
```

LISTING 16.9   The Default Playing State

```
private class Playing implements PlayerState {
    public void handChanged() {
        notifyChanged();
    }
```

LISTING 16.9 continued

```
        public void handPlayable() {
            // can ignore in playing state
        }
        public void handBlackjack() {
            // not possible in playing state
        }
        public void handBusted() {
            setCurrentState( getBustedState() );
            notifyBusted();
        }
        public void execute( Dealer dealer ) {
            if( hit() ) {
                dealer.hit( Player.this );
            } else {
                setCurrentState( getStandingState() );
                notifyStanding();
            }
            current_state.execute( dealer );
            // transition
        }
    }
}
```

All of these states are implemented as Player inner classes because they are, in essence, extensions of the Player class. As inner classes, these states have full access to all methods and variables of the Player class. Inner classes allow you to efficiently encapsulate state logic within its own class without having to break the encapsulation of the Player class.

Subclasses can provide their own state implementation by overriding the following methods in Player:

```
protected PlayerState getBustedState() {
    return new Busted();
}
protected PlayerState getStandingState() {
    return new Standing();
}
protected PlayerState getPlayingState() {
    return new Playing();
}
protected PlayerState getWaitingState() {
    return new Waiting();
}
protected PlayerState getBlackjackState() {
```

```
      return new Blackjack();
}
protected PlayerState getInitialState() {
      return new WaitingState();
}
```

As long as the states use these methods to retrieve the other states, subclasses can intro-duce their own custom states. getInitialState() is used by the Player base class to set the Player's initial state. If a subclass starts in another state, it will need to override this method as well.

Finally, a number of notify methods have been added to the Player class. The states use these methods to inform any listener of changes. These methods correspond to the new methods found in the PlayerListener interface. New methods were added to the listener in order to support the new game functionality. Listing 16.10 presents the update PlayerListener interface.

LISTING 16.10   PlayerListener.java

```
public interface PlayerListener {

    public void playerChanged( Player player );

    public void playerBusted( Player player );

    public void playerBlackjack( Player player );

    public void playerStanding( Player player );

    public void playerWon( Player player );

    public void playerLost( Player player );

    public void playerStandoff( Player player );

}
```

Because the Console is a PlayerListener, the following methods are added to the Console:

```
public void playerChanged( Player player ) {
    printMessage( player.toString() );
}

public void playerBusted( Player player ) {
    printMessage( player.toString() + " BUSTED!" );
}
```

```
public void playerBlackjack( Player player ) {
    printMessage( player.toString() + " BLACKJACK!" );
}

public void playerStanding( Player player ) {
    printMessage( player.toString() + " STANDING" );
}

public void playerWon( Player player ) {
    printMessage( player.toString() + " WINNER!" );
}

public void playerLost( Player player ) {
    printMessage( player.toString() + " LOSER!" );
}

public void playerStandoff( Player player ) {
    printMessage( player.toString() + " STANDOFF" );
}
```

These changes allow the Console to display all of the major game events.

A few new methods have been added to the Player as well:

```
public void win() {
    notifyWin();
}

public void lose() {
    notifyLose();
}

public void standoff() {
    notifyStandoff();
}

public void blackjack() {
    notifyBlackjack();
}
```

These methods allow the Dealer to tell the Player if he won, lost, tied, or had blackjack.

Changes to Dealer and BlackjackDealer

Both the Dealer and BlackjackDealer need to be updated to fit into the new state framework. Listing 16.11 presents the updated Dealer interface.

LISTING 16.11   Dealer.java

```
public interface Dealer {
    // used by the player to interact with the dealer
    public void hit( Player player );

    // used by the player to communicate state to dealer
    public void blackjack( Player player );
    public void busted( Player player );
    public void standing( Player player );
}
```

The Player uses these new methods to report state to the Dealer. So, for example, when the Player has blackjack, the Player will call the Dealer's blackjack() method. The Dealer can then pass the turn to the next player. These methods are akin to the previous passTurn() method. They are just more specific.

The Dealer uses calls to these methods to filter the Players into buckets based on their state. This makes fulfilling the game much easier for the Dealer.

For example, here is an implementation of busted() from the BlackjackDealer:

```
public void busted( Player player ) {
    busted_players.add( player );
    play( this );
}
```

The other methods work similarly.

The BlackjackDealer adds a DealerDealing state. It also customizes many of the default Player states. Listings 16.12 through 16.16 present these modified states.

LISTING 16.12   The Customized Dealer Busted State

```
private class DealerBusted implements PlayerState {
    public void handChanged() {
        // not possible in busted state
    }
    public void handPlayable() {
        // not possible in busted state
    }
    public void handBlackjack() {
        // not possible in busted state
    }
    public void handBusted() {
        // not possible in busted state
    }
```

LISTING 16.12   continued

```
public void execute( Dealer dealer ) {
    Iterator i = standing_players.iterator();
    while( i.hasNext() ) {
        Player player = (Player) i.next();
        player.win();
    }
    i = blackjack_players.iterator();
    while( i.hasNext() ) {
        Player player = (Player) i.next();
        player.win();
    }
    i = busted_players.iterator();
    while( i.hasNext() ) {
        Player player = (Player) i.next();
        player.lose();
    }
}
}
```

LISTING 16.13   The Customized Dealer Blackjack State

```
private class DealerBlackjack implements PlayerState {
    public void handChanged() {
        notifyChanged();
    }
    public void handPlayable() {
        // not possible in blackjack state
    }
    public void handBlackjack() {
        // not possible in blackjack state
    }
    public void handBusted() {
        // not possible in blackjack state
    }
    public void execute( Dealer dealer ) {
        exposeHand();
        Iterator i = players.iterator();
        while( i.hasNext() ) {
            Player player = (Player) i.next();
            if( player.getHand().blackjack() ) {
                player.standoff();
            } else {
                player.lose();
            }
        }
    }
}
```

LISTING 16.14 The Customized Dealer Standing State

```
private class DealerStanding implements PlayerState {
    public void handChanged() {
        // not possible in standing state
    }
    public void handPlayable() {
        // not possible in standing state
    }
    public void handBlackjack() {
        // not possible in standing state
    }
    public void handBusted() {
        // not possible in standing state
    }
    public void execute( Dealer dealer ) {
        Iterator i = standing_players.iterator();
        while( i.hasNext() ) {
            Player player = (Player) i.next();
            if( player.getHand().isEqual( getHand() ) ) {
                player.standoff();
            } else if( player.getHand().isGreaterThan( getHand() ) ) {
                player.win();
            } else {
                player.lose();
            }
        }
        i = blackjack_players.iterator();
        while( i.hasNext() ) {
            Player player = (Player) i.next();
            player.win();
        }
        i = busted_players.iterator();
        while( i.hasNext() ) {
            Player player = (Player) i.next();
            player.lose();
        }
    }
}
```

LISTING 16.15 The Customized Dealer Waiting State

```
private class DealerWaiting implements PlayerState {
    public void handChanged() {
        // not possible in waiting state
    }
    public void handPlayable() {
        // not possible in waiting state
```

LISTING 16.15 continued

```
    }
    public void handBlackjack() {
        // not possible in waiting state
    }
    public void handBusted() {
        // not possible in waiting state
    }
    public void execute( Dealer dealer ) {
        if( !waiting_players.isEmpty() ) {
            Player player = (Player) waiting_players.get( 0 );
            waiting_players.remove( player );
            player.play( dealer );
        } else {
            setCurrentState( getPlayingState() );
            exposeHand();
            getCurrentState().execute( dealer );
            // transition and execute
        }
    }
}
```

LISTING 16.16 The customized Dealer Dealing state

```
private class DealerDealing implements PlayerState {
    public void handChanged() {
        notifyChanged();
    }
    public void handPlayable() {
        setCurrentState( getWaitingState() );
        // transition
    }
    public void handBlackjack() {
        setCurrentState( getBlackjackState() );
        notifyBlackjack();
        // transition
    }
    public void handBusted() {
        // not possible in dealing state
    }
    public void execute( Dealer dealer ) {
        deal();
        getCurrentState().execute( dealer );
        // transition and execute
    }
}
```

You might notice that the `BlackjackDealer` does not define its own playing state. Instead, it uses the `Player`'s default playing state; however, to use its custom states, the `BlackjackDealer` must override the state getters found in the `Player` base class:

```
protected PlayerState getBlackjackState() {
    return new DealerBlackjack();
}
protected PlayerState getBustedState() {
    return new DealerBusted();
}
protected PlayerState getStandingState() {
    return new DealerStanding();
}
protected PlayerState getWaitingState() {
    return new DealerWaiting();
}
```

Testing

As with the code for Chapter 15, "Learning to Combine Theory and Process" a complete set of tests is available for download from www.samspublishing.com along with the source code for this chapter. These tests consist of a set of unit tests and mock objects that thoroughly test the Blackjack system.

Testing is an important part of the development process; however, study of the test code is left as an exercise for the reader.

Summary

Today you completed the second iteration of the Blackjack game. By stepping through this exercise you got to see first hand how you could use the iterative process to incrementally work towards a complete solution.

Each prior iteration acts as the basis or foundation for the next. Instead of beginning analysis or design anew today, you started by building on the use cases and design discovered yesterday.

Tomorrow you will further build on top of this foundation as you add betting features to the Blackjack program.

16

Q&A

Q **If states are so important, why did you want until this iteration to include them?**

A The initial iteration was simple. The initial iteration played a basic game of Blackjack that did not detect natural blackjack hands, winners, or losers (though it did detect busts). There was no reason to attack the problem with a complex solution. The requirements of this iteration justify a more complicated solution, because it adds blackjack detection as well as game fulfillment.

Q **Could you have implemented the states outside of the `Player` and `BlackjackDealer` or must they be inner classes?**

A You can implement the states outside of the class. But if you do define them outside of the `Player` you may need to add some new methods so that the states can retrieve all of the data that they need.

I would warn against such an approach for three reasons:

First, moving the state definition outside of the class doesn't really buy you all that much. In fact, it causes extra work because of the methods that you will need to add.

Second, adding extra methods so that the states can retrieve data breaks encapsulation.

Finally, moving the states out of the `Player` class does not model the state/player relationship very well. States are in essence an extension of `Player`. As such, the states act as the `Player`'s brains. Brains are best left within the body.

It is important to note that the implementation of states as inner classes works nicely in Java. Other languages may require a slightly different approach.

Workshop

The quiz questions and answers are provided for your further understanding. See Appendix A, "Answers," for the answers.

Quiz

1. When are conditionals dangerous?
2. List two ways to remove conditionals.
3. The version of Hand presented today is better encapsulated than yesterday's. How does the new version of Hand encapsulate itself?

4. What pattern does the `Hand` and `HandListener` implement?

5. Search the web for more information on the State pattern.

Exercises

1. Download the source code for today's iteration. When you have the code, compile it, run it by executing Blackjack, and then try to understand how it works. Gaining a full understanding of the code will take some time and patience.

2. The following code appears in the `Player` class definition:

```
protected void notifyChanged() {
    Iterator i = listeners.iterator();
    while( i.hasNext() ) {
        PlayerListener pl = (PlayerListener) i.next();
        pl.playerChanged( this );
    }
}

protected void notifyBusted() {
    Iterator i = listeners.iterator();
    while( i.hasNext() ) {
        PlayerListener pl = (PlayerListener) i.next();
        pl.playerBusted( this );
    }
}

protected void notifyBlackjack() {
    Iterator i = listeners.iterator();
    while( i.hasNext() ) {
        PlayerListener pl = (PlayerListener) i.next();
        pl.playerBlackjack( this );
    }
}

protected void notifyStanding() {
    Iterator i = listeners.iterator();
    while( i.hasNext() ) {
        PlayerListener pl = (PlayerListener) i.next();
        pl.playerStanding( this );
    }
}

protected void notifyStandoff() {
    Iterator i = listeners.iterator();
    while( i.hasNext() ) {
        PlayerListener pl = (PlayerListener) i.next();
        pl.playerStandoff( this );
    }
}
```

16

```
protected void notifyWin() {
    Iterator i = listeners.iterator();
    while( i.hasNext() ) {
        PlayerListener pl = (PlayerListener) i.next();
        pl.playerWon( this );
    }
}

protected void notifyLose() {
    Iterator i = listeners.iterator();
    while( i.hasNext() ) {
        PlayerListener pl = (PlayerListener) i.next();
        pl.playerLost( this );
    }
}
```

The methods work. Functionally there is nothing wrong with them; however, each method performs the exact same action up until the point a call is made on the PlayerListener.

How might you use objects so that you only have to write one notify method? Design and implement a solution.

DAY **17**

Blackjack Iteration 3: Adding Betting

In yesterday's chapter you saw how to take a fairly primitive Blackjack implementation and iterate it towards a more mature game. Today you will build upon the same Blackjack game by adding simple betting support.

Today's lesson will give you further experience with the iterative process as well as with OOA and OOD. By the end of today's lesson, you should also begin to feel more comfortable with the state-based architecture presented yesterday. In fact, one of today's exercises will ask you to add a new state to the system.

Today you will learn

- How to extend the Blackjack game's state architecture in order to add functionality
- About the benefits that a true OO approach can bring to a system by working on an OO based system

Blackjack Betting

Yesterday's iteration produced a fairly full-featured game of Blackjack. Almost every nonbetting-related feature is now part of the game. Today you will add some of those missing betting features.

As with the other lessons this week we will follow the process outlined in Chapter 9, "Introduction to Object Oriented Analysis (OOA)." Let's start by exploring the betting use cases.

Betting Analysis

To fully understand betting you'll need to finalize the Place Bets and Double Down use cases identified during the initial analysis of Blackjack. You'll also need to revisit the other use cases to make sure that they do not require updating. Once you have finished the use cases you'll need to update the domain model.

Blackjack Betting Use Case Analysis

Let's begin with the new Player Places Bet use case:

Players begin the game with $1000 in their pot. Before any cards are dealt, each player must place a bet. Beginning with the first player, each player bets an amount of $10, $50, or $100.

- Player places bet
    1. Player places a bet of $10, $50, or $100
    2. Moves to the next player and repeats until all players have placed a bet
- Preconditions
    - New game
- Post conditions
    - Player has placed bet

In the real game of Blackjack, every game has its own rules about betting. These rules will include a minimum bet, a maximum bet, and the bet increment. In this game of Blackjack a player can bet $10, $50, or $100. For the sake of simplicity this game will offer the player an unlimited line of credit. Each player will start out with $1000. When the player exhausts his pot, his balance will become negative; however, the player is allowed to play as long as he wishes.

The other new betting use case is Player Doubles Down:

The player decides he is not satisfied with his initial hand. Instead of simply hitting, the player decides to double down. This doubles the player's bet and adds one card to the hand. The player's turn ends and play moves to the next player/dealer.

- Player doubles down
  1. Player decides he is not satisfied with his initial hand
  2. The player wants to double down
  3. The player's bet is doubled
  4. The dealer adds another card to his hand
- Preconditions
  - This is the player's initial hand and has not yet taken a hit or stand
  - Player does not have blackjack
  - Dealer does not have blackjack
- Post conditions
  - Player's hand has three cards
  - Player's turn ends
- Alternative: Player busts

  New card causes player's hand to bust (loses)
- Alternative: Player's hand is greater than 21, but player has an ace

  New card causes player's hand to be greater than 21. Player has an ace. Value of the ace changes from 11 to 1, bringing the player's hand to less than or equal to 21.

The only pre-existing use cases affected by the addition of betting are the Deal Cards use case and the Dealer Fulfills Game use case. The other use cases remain unchanged:

Beginning with the first player the dealer deals one card face up to each player, finishing with himself. The dealer then repeats this process but deals his own card face down. Dealing ends and play commences once the dealer has dealt each player, including himself, two cards.

- Deal cards
  1. Dealer deals one card face up to every player including himself
  2. Dealer deals a second card face up to all non-dealer players
  3. Dealer deals a card face down to himself
- Preconditions
  - All players have placed their bets

17

- Post conditions
    - All players and the dealer have a hand with two cards
- Alternative: Dealer has blackjack

    If the dealer has a natural 21 or blackjack, the game moves to fulfillment. The players do not get to take a turn.

Dealing will now not begin until every player has placed a bet. Let's see how betting changes game fulfillment:

After all playing in done, the dealer checks each hand and determines for each player if they win or lose or if the game is a standoff.

- Dealer fulfills game
    1. Dealer checks the first player's hand and compares it with his own
    2. The player's hand is greater than the dealer, but not busted; the player wins
    3. The amount of the bet is added to the player's pot
    4. The dealer repeats this comparison for all players

- Preconditions
    - Each player has passed their turns
    - The dealer has passed his turn
- Post conditions
    - Player's final results determined
- Alternative: Player loses

    Dealer checks the player's hand and compares it with his own. The player's hand is less than the dealer's. The player loses. The bet is removed from the player's pot.
- Alternative: Standoff

    Dealer checks the player's hand and compares it with his own. The player's hand is equal to the dealer's. The game is a standoff. Nothing is added or subtracted from the player's pot.
- Alternative: Dealer busts

    If the dealer is busted every standing and blackjack player wins. All else lose. Winners receive the amount the bet.
- Alternative: Player wins with blackjack

    If the player has blackjack and the dealer does not, the player wins and gets paid 3:2 (for example, if the player bet $100, the player would win $150).

That concludes the changes to the use cases. All of these use cases are relatively straight-forward. Interaction diagrams would probably be overkill. Let's see how these updated use cases have changed the domain model.

Updating the Blackjack Domain Model

The betting analysis does require you to update the domain model, but only slightly. You'll need to add one additional domain object: the Bank. Every Player in the game has his own personal Bank. Figure 17.1 illustrates the updated domain model.

FIGURE 17.1

The Blackjack domain model.

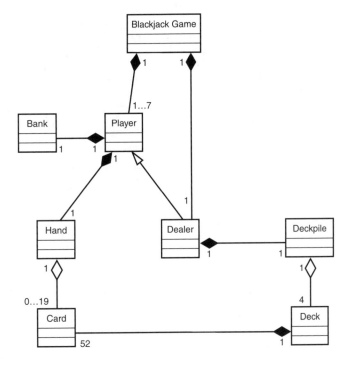

17

Betting Design

You should begin design by designing the new Bank class. When the Bank is done you'll need to figure out how to work betting into the game. For the purposes of today's lesson, the use case Player Doubles Down is left as an exercise at the end of the lesson.

Designing the Bank

When setting out to design the Bank, you must first identify the Bank's responsibilities. Figure 17.2 illustrates the resulting CRC card for the Bank class.

FIGURE **17.2**

The Bank CRC card.

Bank	
hold total $ for player	
place $100 bet	
place $50 bet	
place $10 bet	
payoff win	
payoff blackjack	
settle loss	
settle standoff	
represent itself as a string	String

Good OO calls for the proper division of responsibility. As such, the Bank is responsible for keeping track of all betting activities. The Bank keeps all betting details internal and provides access to the bet and balance through a well-defined interface. Figure 17.3 illustrates the class diagram for the Bank as well as the Bank's relationship with the Player.

FIGURE **17.3**

The Bank *class diagram.*

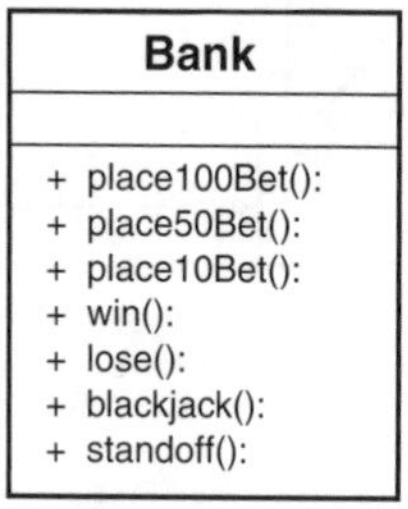

Bank
+ place100Bet():
+ place50Bet():
+ place10Bet():
+ win():
+ lose():
+ blackjack():
+ standoff():

The Betting Design

As it turns out, betting should fit well into the state architecture that you saw yesterday. Both the player and dealer will need one additional state to support basic betting. The dealer will need a CollectingBets state, and the player will need a Betting state. Figures 17.4 and 17.5 illustrate the new state diagrams for the dealer and player respectively.

As you can see, the player now starts off in the Betting state while the dealer begins in the CollectingBets state. When all bets are collected, the dealer moves into the Dealing state as before. When done betting, the players move into the Waiting state.

FIGURE 17.4

The state diagram for the dealer.

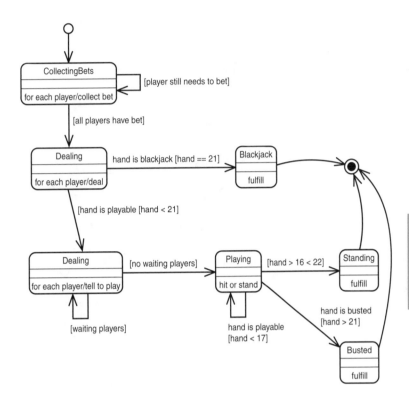

Refactoring the Player Hierarchy

At this point of the design it seems that the Player and BlackjackDealer are diverging. While the BlackjackDealer extends Player, it does not need a Bank. This is unlike a HumanPlayer because the dealer does not bet. If you add betting support directly to the Player, BlackjackDealer will inherit all kinds of useless behavior that it will need to override (plus Player will get awfully cluttered).

This is a good time to refactor the Player inheritance hierarchy by breaking common elements out into subclasses. In the new hierarchy, no betting support should be added to the base Player class. Instead, a new class, BettingPlayer, should inherit from Player and then add the necessary states and methods for betting support.

BlackjackDealer can continue to inherit from Player; however, HumanPlayer should now inherit from BettingPlayer. Figure 17.6 illustrates the resulting hierarchy.

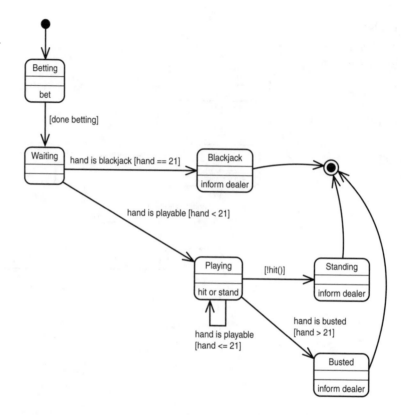

FIGURE 17.5

The state diagram for the players.

The Updated Blackjack Model

Now that you are finished with design, it's a good idea to update the Blackjack class diagram. Figure 17.7 illustrates the class diagram.

You are now ready to move on to the implementation.

Betting Implementation

Implementing betting will require the creation of the Bank and BettingPlayer classes as well as changes to the BlackjackDealer, Dealer, and HumanPlayer. Let's begin with the Bank class.

FIGURE **17.6**

The Player hierarchy.

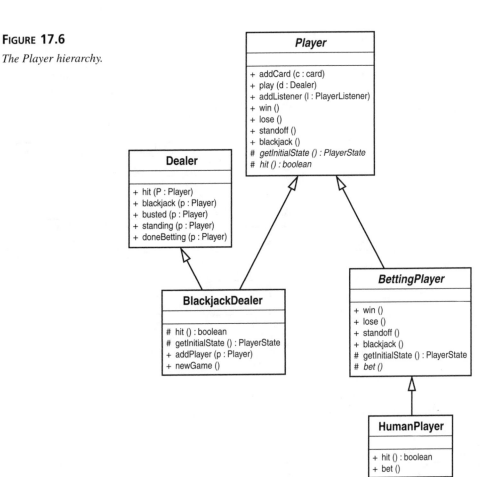

The Bank Implementation

As you discovered the Bank is responsible for holding onto a total as well as managing bets. Listing 17.1 presents one possible Bank implementation.

FIGURE 17.7

The Blackjack *class diagram.*

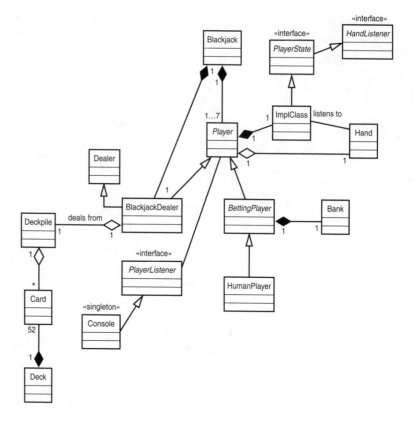

LISTING 17.1   Bank.java

```
public class Bank {

    private int total;
    private int bet;

    public Bank( int amount ) {
        total = amount;
    }

    public void place100Bet() {
        placeBet( 100 );
    }

    public void place50Bet() {
```

LISTING 17.1 continued

```
        placeBet( 50 );
    }

    public void place10Bet() {
        placeBet( 10 );
    }

    public void win() {
        total += ( 2 * bet );
        bet = 0;
    }

    public void lose() {
        // already taken out of total
        bet = 0;
    }

    public void blackjack() {
        total += ( ( ( 3 * bet ) / 2 ) + bet );
        bet = 0;
    }

    public void standoff() {
        total += bet;
        bet = 0;
    }

    public String toString() {
        return ( "$" + total + ".00" );
    }

    private void placeBet( int amount ) {
        bet = amount;
        total -= amount;
    }

}
```

17

When the player needs to place a bet, it does so through the Bank interface. Of note is how the Bank completely hides the details of the bet. When the player wins, loses, hits blackjack, or standoffs he simply informs the Bank. The Bank does the rest.

The `BettingPlayer` Implementation

The BettingPlayer needs to inherit from Player, define a Betting state, make sure that it's initial state gets set to the Betting state, and add support for a Bank (as well as updating it properly). Listing 17.2 presents the new BettingPlayer.

LISTING 17.2   BettingPlayer.java

```java
public abstract class BettingPlayer extends Player {

    private Bank bank;

    public BettingPlayer( String name, Hand hand, Bank bank ) {
        super( name, hand );
        this.bank = bank;
    }

    //******************************************************************
    // overridden behavior
    public String toString() {
        return ( getName() + ": " + getHand().toString() + "\n" +
bank.toString() );
    }

    public void win() {
        bank.win();
        super.win();
    }

    public void lose() {
        bank.lose();
        super.lose();
    }

    public void standoff() {
        bank.standoff();
        super.standoff();
    }

    public void blackjack() {
        bank.blackjack();
        super.blackjack();
    }

    protected PlayerState getInitialState() {
        return getBettingState();
    }

    //******************************************************************
    // newly added for BettingPlayer
    protected final Bank getBank() {
        return bank;
    }

    protected PlayerState getBettingState() {
        return new Betting();
```

LISTING 17.2   continued

```
    }

    protected abstract void bet();

    private class Betting implements PlayerState {
        public void handChanged() {
            // not possible in busted state
        }
        public void handPlayable() {
            // not possible in busted state
        }
        public void handBlackjack() {
            // not possible in busted state
        }
        public void handBusted() {
            // not possible in busted state
        }
        public void execute( Dealer dealer ) {
            bet();
            setCurrentState( getWaitingState() );
            dealer.doneBetting( BettingPlayer.this );
            // terminate
        }
    }
}
```

17

You'll also note that the BettingPlayer adds a new abstract method: protected
abstract void bet(). The bet() method is called within the Betting state's activity.
Each subclass must override this method as it sees fit.

Changes to Dealer and HumanPlayer

From reviewing the code for the BettingPlayer, you probably noticed that a new
method has been added to the Dealer: public void doneBetting(Player p).

The BettingPlayer calls this method to inform the Dealer that it is done betting. That
way the Dealer can know that the player is done, and the next player can begin betting.

The changes to HumanPlayer are rather tame. Listing 17.3 lists the new HumanPlayer.

LISTING 17.3   HumanPlayer.java

```
public class HumanPlayer extends BettingPlayer {

    private final static String HIT  = "H";
    private final static String STAND = "S";
```

LISTING 17.3   continued

```java
private final static String PLAY_MSG = "[H]it or [S]tay";
private final static String BET_MSG = "Place Bet: [10] [50] or [100]";
private final static String BET_10  = "10";
private final static String BET_50  = "50";
private final static String BET_100 = "100";
private final static String DEFAULT = "invalid";

public HumanPlayer( String name, Hand hand, Bank bank ) {
    super( name, hand, bank );
}

protected boolean hit() {
    while( true ) {
        Console.INSTANCE.printMessage( PLAY_MSG );
        String response = Console.INSTANCE.readInput( DEFAULT );
        if( response.equalsIgnoreCase( HIT ) ) {
            return true;
        } else if( response.equalsIgnoreCase( STAND ) ) {
            return false;
        }
        // if we get here loop until we get meaningful input
    }
}

protected void bet() {
    while( true ) {
        Console.INSTANCE.printMessage( BET_MSG );
        String response = Console.INSTANCE.readInput( DEFAULT );
        if( response.equals( BET_10 ) ) {
            getBank().place10Bet();
            return;
        }
        if( response.equals( BET_50 ) ) {
            getBank().place50Bet();
            return;

        }
        if( response.equals( BET_100 ) ) {
            getBank().place100Bet();
            return;
        }
        // if we get here loop until we get meaningful input
    }
}

}
```

HumanPlayer now inherits from BettingPlayer rather than directly from Player. HumanPlayer also provides an implementation of bet(). Whenever bet() gets called, it queries the command line for feedback from the user.

Changes to BlackjackDealer

BlackjackDealer implements the new doneBetting() method defined in Dealer. When this method is called, the BlackjackDealer takes the player and inserts him into a waiting players bucket.

The BlackjackDealer also defines a new state: DealerCollectingBets. Too, DealerCollectingBets acts as the BlackjackDealer's new initial state. Listing 17.4 presents the new state.

17

LISTING 17.4   The New DealerCollectingBets State

```
private class DealerCollectingBets implements PlayerState {
    public void handChanged() {
        // not possible in betting state
    }
    public void handPlayable() {
        // not possible in betting state
    }
    public void handBlackjack() {
        // not possible in betting state
    }
    public void handBusted() {
        // not possible in betting state
    }
    public void execute( Dealer dealer ) {
        if( !betting_players.isEmpty() ) {
            Player player = (Player) betting_players.get( 0 );
            betting_players.remove( player );
            player.play( dealer );
        } else {
            setCurrentState( getDealingState() );
            getCurrentState().execute( dealer );
            // transition and execute
        }
    }
}
```

The new state goes through and tells each player to bet. Of note is that this state does not loop. Instead, the activity gets executed each time a player indicates that he is done betting. This behavior is defined within the doneBetting() method:

```
public void doneBetting( Player player ) {
    waiting_players.add( player );
```

```
        play( this );
    }
```

Remember that a call to play() executes the current state.

Miscellaneous Changes

The only other change of note is the fact that the Player method getInitialState() is now declared abstract in the Player base class. Making the method abstract works as a form of documentation that enables anyone who subclasses the class to know that they should provide their own initial state definition.

The practice of making a method abstract so that it works as a form of documentation is an effective way to establish an inheritance protocol.

A Little Testing: A Mock Object

As usual, test cases are available along with the source; however, it is valuable to take a look at one clever use of mock objects. Listing 17.5 presents a Deckpile mock object that ensures that the dealer is dealt a blackjack.

LISTING 17.5   DealerBlackjackPile.java

```java
public class DealerBlackjackPile extends Deckpile {

    private Card [] cards;
    private int index = -1;

    public DealerBlackjackPile() {
        cards = new Card[4];
        cards[0] = new Card( Suit.HEARTS, Rank.TWO );
        cards[1] = new Card( Suit.HEARTS, Rank.ACE );
        cards[2] = new Card( Suit.HEARTS, Rank.THREE );
        cards[3] = new Card( Suit.HEARTS, Rank.KING );
    }

    public void shuffle() {
        // do nothing
    }

    public Card dealUp() {
        index++;
        cards[index].setFaceUp( true );
        return cards[index];
    }

    public Card dealDown() {
        index++;
```

LISTING 17.5 continued

```
        return cards[index];
    }

    public void reset() {
        // do nothing
    }

}
```

You can use this mock object to test that the game responds correctly when the dealer receives a blackjack hand. This mock object truly stacks the deck.

Summary

17

Today you completed the third iteration of the Blackjack game project—only one more to go!

In this chapter, you saw how you could extend the state architecture to support simple gambling in the game. You also saw that it is sometime necessary to revisit and refactor a hierarchy as new requirements present themselves. Though refactoring presents a little extra work upfront, refactoring when appropriate tends to pay for itself as you move forward.

Because you did refactor the hierarchies now, the code base will be much easier to understand, extend, and maintain later.

Tomorrow, you will put a graphical UI on top of the game.

Q&A

Q Why didn't you model fulfillment as a state?

A You could have modeled fulfillment as a state; however, a fulfillment state would have amounted to design noise. Activities within the Busted, Blackjack, and Standing states can fulfill the game adequately. Furthermore, these states can fulfill the game very specifically.

If the dealer were to transition into a fulfillment state, it would lose its previous state information. If you fulfill within a specific state, however, the dealer can score the game easily because the dealer will know what state he ended in.

Workshop

The quiz questions and answers are provided for your further understanding. See Appendix A, "Answers," for the answers.

Quiz

1. How can you effectively establish inheritance protocols?

2. The lesson on inheritance during week 1 pointed out that inheritance hierarchies are often discovered, not planned out from the beginning. What hierarchy did you discover today?

3. Given quiz question #2, why should you wait to perform abstraction until you've done something a few times?

4. Today you refactored the Player hierarchy. List two of the benefits that you gained by making the changes.

Exercises

1. Download the source code for today's iteration. When you have the code, compile it, run it by executing Blackjack, and then try to understand how it works. Gaining a full understanding of the code will take some time and patience.

2. Design and implement the Player Doubles Down use case. Base your solution on the source for today's lesson.

DAY 18

Blackjack Iteration 4: Adding a GUI

So far this week you've analyzed, designed, and built a Blackjack card game. By working from a simple implementation and iterating towards a more complex application, you've been able to add rules and betting capabilities to the game. Today you will continue the iterative process and make improvements to the game's presentation layer.

Today you will learn how to

- Apply analysis, design, and implementation when writing user interfaces
- Apply the MVC pattern to the Blackjack game

Blackjack Presentation

So far the only interface into the Blackjack card game has been a rudimentary command-line-based user interface (UI). Not much has been said about this UI. In fact, very little, if any, analysis or design has been applied to the UI beyond stating that you will use the MVC pattern. Instead of going through a round of analysis and design for the command line UI, the simplest possible UI was created to allow you to interact with the Blackjack system.

During development you will often find that you need to develop supporting materials, such as stubs, or system harnesses, such as the UI. Often these materials will not be driven by the analysis. Instead, these items are driven by necessities that present themselves during implementation. In the case of Blackjack you absolutely needed a way to interact with the system; however, writing a graphical UI from the beginning was just not practical. Because the command line UI wasn't meant to be part of the final system, there was no need to perform additional analysis for it.

Today you will make one final tweak to the original command line UI and then go into the analysis, design, and implementation of a full fledged graphical UI (GUI) for the Blackjack game.

Command Line Tweaks

Before moving on to working on the actual GUI for the Blackjack game, it is valuable to make one final tweak to the command line UI.

It's an inconvenience, having to restart the game each time you would like to play. Listing 18.1 presents a new main that allows you to play as many Blackjack games as you like without having to restart.

LISTING 18.1   Blackjack.java

```
public class Blackjack {

    public static void main( String [] args ) {
        Deckpile cards = new Deckpile();
        for( int i = 0; i < 4; i ++ ) {
            cards.shuffle();
            Deck deck = new Deck();
            deck.addToStack( cards );
            cards.shuffle();
        }

        Hand dealer_hand = new Hand();
        BlackjackDealer dealer = new BlackjackDealer( "Dealer", dealer_hand,
cards );
        Bank human_bank = new Bank( 1000 );
        Hand human_hand = new Hand();
        Player player = new CommandLinePlayer( "Human", human_hand, human_bank
);
```

LISTING 18.1   continued

```
        dealer.addListener( Console.INSTANCE );
        player.addListener( Console.INSTANCE );
        dealer.addPlayer( player );

        do {
            dealer.newGame();
        } while( playAgain() );

        Console.INSTANCE.printMessage( "Thank you for playing!" );

    }

    private static boolean playAgain() {
        Console.INSTANCE.printMessage( "Would you like to play again? [Y]es
[N]o" );
        String response = Console.INSTANCE.readInput( "invalid" );
        if( response.equalsIgnoreCase( "y" ) ) {
            return true;
        }
        return false;
    }

}
```

18

Adding this functionality to the Blackjack main has a practical value because it helps us to detect any errors that might be hidden in the program when you play multiple games. For example, each hand needs to be properly reset before the next game. By flushing out any errors now, you won't be caught by the bug later and think that the new GUI is to blame.

Blackjack GUI Analysis

To be able to complete the analysis of the GUI, you must perform use case analysis just as you did during the past iterations. When performing GUI analysis it is also imperative that you sit down with your customers, users, and usability experts to design the layout of the GUI. In reality, the less say that you have as a developer in the actual layout of the GUI the better. Everyone has his or her own specialty. As a developer your specialty is normally to analyze problems, design solutions, and implement those solutions. When you sit down with your customer, you will discover how he wants his GUI set out.

Unfortunately, usability experts, customers, and users do not come in a convenient book form, so you'll need to make do without them today. Instead we'll work out a rough sketch of the screen before moving on to design.

GUI Use Cases

Unlike the Blackjack use cases that you analyzed during the previous iterations the GUI use cases do not affect the Blackjack domain per se. Instead, the GUI use cases help establish how the user will manipulate the ongoing Blackjack game through the UI.

As such, the first use case that you need to investigate is the use case that begins a new game:

When the program is first starting or the player has just finished a game, he may elect to play a new game

- GUI new game
    1. Player clicks the New Game button and a new game starts
- Preconditions
    - Player must have either just started the program or just finished a game
- Post conditions
    - New game started

As you can see this use case does not alter the Blackjack domain. It simply sets the ground rules for the UI. The next UI use case analyzes betting:

Players begin the game with $1000 in their pot. Before any cards are dealt, each player must place a bet. Beginning with the first player, each player bets an amount of $10, $50, or $100. If a player goes below $0, he is still allowed to play. The amount in his pot is reflected as a negative number.

- GUI player places bet
    1. Player selects one of the following bet levels: 10, 50, or 100, which immediately places the bet.
    2. Bet moves to the next player and repeats until all players have placed a bet
- Preconditions
    - New game started
- Post conditions
    - Player has placed bet
    - Dealer may begin to deal

You still need support for hitting and standing. The next use case fleshes out hitting:

The player decides he is not satisfied with his hand. The player has not yet busted so the player decides to hit. If the player does not bust, he can choose to either hit again or stand. If the player does bust, play transfers to the next player.

- GUI player hits
    1. Player decides he is not satisfied with his hand
    2. The player clicks the Hit button, which requests another card from the dealer
    3. The player can decide to hit again or stand if his hand totals less than or equal to 21

- Preconditions
    - Player has a hand whose total value is less than 21
    - Player does not have blackjack
    - Dealer does not have blackjack

- Post conditions
    - A new card is added to the player's hand

- Alternative: Player busts

    New card causes player's hand to be greater than 21. Player busts (loses). Next player's/dealer's turn begins.

- Alternative: Player's hand greater than 21, but player has an ace

    New card causes player's hand to be greater than 21. Player has an ace. Value of the ace changes from 11 to one, bringing the player's hand to be less than or equal to 21. The player can decide to hit again or stand.

If a payer does not hit, he must stand. The next use case analyzes using the GUI to stand:

The player decides he is satisfied with his hand and stands.

- Player stands
    1. Player decides he is happy with his hand and clicks the Stand button.

- Preconditions
    - Player has a hand whose value is less than or equal to 21
    - Player does not have blackjack
    - Dealer does not have blackjack

- Post conditions
    - Player's turn ends

18

And last but not least, you need to consider quitting the game:

The player decides that he doesn't want to play anymore and quits.

- GUI player quits
    1. Player clicks the Quit button
    2. Game closes
- Preconditions
    - Game must not be in progress (either no games have been played or a game has been finished)
- Post conditions
    - Game shutdown

GUI Visual Mock Ups

Based on the use cases enumerated in the previous section, you'll need to design the GUI's layout. Figure 18.1 presents one possible GUI that fulfills all of the requirements discovered during analysis.

FIGURE 18.1

The Blackjack GUI.

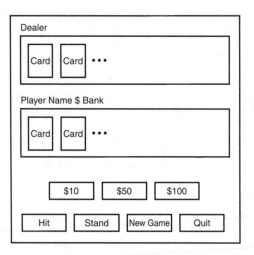

There are some additional GUI behaviors that you can work out now. Figure 18.2 illustrates the status of the buttons when the user first starts the game.

FIGURE 18.2

The initial button status.

All buttons are visible when the game first starts up; however, only New Game and Quit are active. Figure 18.3 illustrates the status of the buttons after clicking New Game.

FIGURE 18.3

The button status after clicking New Game.

The player must place a bet after clicking New Game. As a result only the betting buttons are active. Figure 18.4 illustrates the status of the buttons after playing a game.

FIGURE 18.4

The button status after placing a bet.

After placing a bet a user may hit or stand. Thus, only the Hit and Stand buttons are active after placing a bet. All of the other buttons are disabled. The buttons remain in such a state until the player stands or busts, at which point the game ends and the buttons return to the status illustrated in 18.2.

After the completion of a game, the cards remain on the screen until the user clicks New Game. The cards are then removed from the screen. During play, the player's graphical hand is updated whenever a card is dealt to the player.

This GUI layout will factor heavily into the views that you design in the next section.

Blackjack GUI Design

Designing the classes that make up a GUI is no different from designing any other type of class. You must identify the individual classes and their responsibilities.

Using Figure 18.1 as a starting point, you can generate an initial list of classes. You will need a class for the main display, a class to view a player, and a class to visualize the player's options.

18

GUI CRC Cards

A CRC card session may or may not be warranted here. It really depends on your own comfort level. For a larger GUI you'll definitely want to go through a number of sessions to ensure that you've done a good job splitting up responsibilities.

For our purposes the Blackjack GUI is simple enough that it is okay to skip a full-fledged CRC session. Instead, we will list the responsibilities here.

PlayerView

The PlayerView is responsible for visualizing a Player in the Blackjack game. The view must display the Player's hand, name, and pot balance (if applicable). The PlayerView is simply a visualization vehicle. As such, it does not require a controller. It simply needs to listen to and display its Player.

OptionView and OptionViewController

The OptionView is responsible for visualizing the human player's options. The OptionView also needs to respond to user interaction so it requires a controller: OptionViewController.

CardView

The CardView is responsible for visualizing the individual Card objects. The CardView is not interactive, thus it does not require a controller. The PlayerView will use CardView to visualize the Hand.

BlackjackGUI

The BlackjackGUI is responsible for aggregating and displaying all of the various views. Because the BlackjackGUI acts as a simple shell, it does not require a controller.

Miscellaneous

The CardView will need a way to map a Card to an image for display. You can implement a lengthy if/else if switch to map the Card inside of CardView; however, such an approach is fairly ugly (not to mention slow).

Instead of creating a conditional solution you should subclass Deck and Card. You can call the two resulting classes VDeck and VCard, respectively. VCard will take an extra constructor argument, the name of a bitmap file. VDeck will construct VCards.

Because you pass the Deckpile to the BlackjackDealer instead of letting the BlackjackDealer create its own pile, you can transparently pass the visual cards to the dealer instead.

You will also need to create a new human player for the GUI. This new `GUIPlayer` can inherit directly from `BettingPlayer`; however, it will need to provide its own custom Betting and Playing states.

Instead of basing a decision on the `hit()` or `bet()` method the `GUIPlayer` will need to get this information from the GUI. As a result you'll need methods that the GUI can call for betting, hitting, and standing. When these methods get called, they'll put the player into the proper states and communicate any information to the dealer.

In all, you'll need to add or override the following methods to the `GUIPlayer`: `place10Bet()`, `place50Bet()`, `place100Bet()`, `takeCard()`, `stand()`, `getBettingState()`, and `getPlayingState()`.

GUI Structure

Sometimes when working with a GUI it helps to sketch out how the pieces will fit together. Because the GUI is itself visual, sketching the GUI out can actually be a bit more powerful than standard class diagrams. Figure 18.5 visualizes the `PlayerView`.

FIGURE 18.5

Visualizing the `PlayerView`.

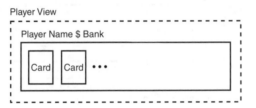

You see that the `PlayerView` in Figure 18.5 is made up of a number of `CardViews`. The `PlayerView` also draws a border around itself with the `Player`'s name and pot balance (if applicable) in the upper-left corner.

Luckily, Java's `javax.swing.JPanel` provides all of the functionality that you need to lay out other components as well as draw a labeled border.

Continuing, Figure 18.6 visualizes the `OptionView`.

FIGURE 18.6

Visualizing the `OptionView`.

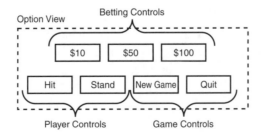

18

The `OptionView` is simply a collection of buttons. A combination of `javax.swing.JPanel` (for nesting the buttons) and `javax.swing.JButton` should provide everything that you need to implement this view.

Figure 18.7 puts all of the pieces together visually.

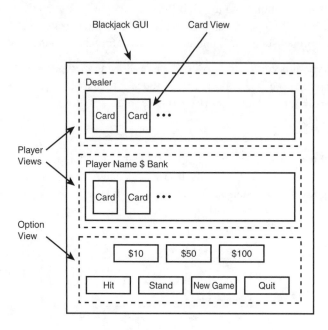

The preceding pictures should help visualize how all of the views fit together. Understanding how the pieces fit together can help while implementing a GUI.

Refactoring

Now that there are two types of human players—GUI and CLUI—it probably makes sense to rename `HumanPlayer` to `CommandLinePlayer`. You should make that change today.

GUI Class Diagram

Now that all of the new classes are identified you can model the resulting class structure. Like the class diagram in Chapter 17, "Blackjack Iteration 3: Adding Betting," the model presented in Figure 18.8 focuses in on structure.

FIGURE 18.8

The GUI class structure.

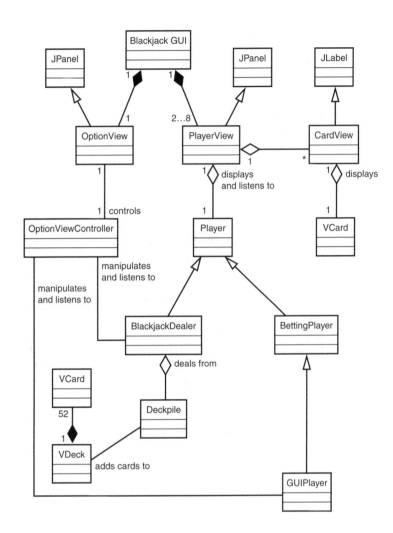

18

Blackjack GUI Implementation

When implementing a GUI, in general, it is often easiest to work from the bottom up. In that vein you should implement in the following order: VCard, VDeck, CardView, PlayerView, OptionView, OptionViewController, GUIPlayer, and BlackjackGUI. Let's review the highlights of each class.

Implementing the VCard, VDeck, and CardView

VCard has a relatively simple implementation because it only adds one additional attribute to the Card class. Listing 18.2 presents the new VCard class definition.

LISTING 18.2   VCard.java

```java
public class VCard extends Card {

    String image;

    public VCard( Suit suit, Rank rank, String image ) {
        super( suit, rank );
        this.image = image;
    }

    public String getImage() {
        if( isFaceUp() ) {
            return image;
        } else {
            return "/bitmaps/empty_pile.xbm";
        }
    }

}
```

VDeck's implementation is almost as simple. To be able to create VCards instead of Card, you will need to override Deck's buildCards() method. To override the method you will first need to change the method to protected in Deck. Originally the method was private. Listing 18.3 shows a partial listing of the VDeck implementation.

LISTING 18.3   VDeck.java

```java
public class VDeck extends Deck {

    protected void buildCards() {

        // This is ugly, but it is better than the alternative loops/if/elseif
        Card [] deck = new Card[52];
        setDeck( deck );

        deck[0] = new VCard( Suit.HEARTS, Rank.TWO, "/bitmaps/h2" );
        deck[1] = new VCard( Suit.HEARTS, Rank.THREE, "/bitmaps/h3" );
        deck[2] = new VCard( Suit.HEARTS, Rank.FOUR, "/bitmaps/h4" );
        deck[3] = new VCard( Suit.HEARTS, Rank.FIVE, "/bitmaps/h5" );
        deck[4] = new VCard( Suit.HEARTS, Rank.SIX, "/bitmaps/h6" );
        deck[5] = new VCard( Suit.HEARTS, Rank.SEVEN, "/bitmaps/h7" );
        deck[6] = new VCard( Suit.HEARTS, Rank.EIGHT, "/bitmaps/h8" );
        // rest cut for brevity
```

For the GUI we'll use a set of bitmaps that are contained in the bitmaps directory along with the source download. The names of the bitmaps follow a specific naming convention, so you can also implement buildCards() as a loop. While ugly, simply hardcoding the values is a bit easier to understand (and maintain).

Caution	Hard coding the card creation may not be the most maintainable solution either. The problem is that each approach that you might take has a short-coming. VDeck is an example of one of those times where you must make a choice between two evils, and just live with it.
	The solution outlined above is flawed because of the errors inherent in key-ing in all of the calls. Plus, if the constructor ever changes, you'll need to update each call.
	Alternatively you could loop over the List representation of the Ranks. Such a solution forces you to assume a specific order of elements in the list (so that you can properly generate the image filename). If the ordering ever changes, the loop will mysteriously break. Anyone maintaining the code will have a difficult time tracking down the source of the error. I avoided the loop approach because changes to an unrelated class could break the VDeck.

The CardView will display the VCard bitmap. javax.swing.JLabel provides the neces-sary functionality to display a bitmap. Listing 18.4 presents the implementation of CardView.

18

LISTING 18.4   CardView.java

```java
import javax.swing.*;
import java.awt.*;

public class CardView extends JLabel {

    private ImageIcon icon;

    public CardView( VCard card ) {
        getImage( card.getImage() );
        setIcon( icon );
        setBackground( Color.white );
        setOpaque( true );
    }

    private void getImage( String name ) {
        java.net.URL url = this.getClass().getResource( name );
        icon = new ImageIcon( url );
    }

}
```

The CardView takes a VCard, extracts the bitmap path, converts the path to a url, creates an ImageIcon, and adds the icon to itself. That's all you need to do to be able to load and display a bitmap!

Implementing the PlayerView

The PlayerView will display any subclass of Player. Unlike OptionView, which you will see in the next section, PlayerView only needs to present the Player; it does not accept user interaction. As a result the implementation is rather straightforward. Listing 18.5 presents the method that gets called when the Player changes.

LISTING **18.5** The PlayerView Update Code

```
public void playerChanged( Player player ) {
    border.setTitle( player.getName() );
    cards.removeAll();
    Hand hand = player.getHand();
    Iterator i = hand.getCards();
    while( i.hasNext() ) {
        VCard vcard = (VCard) i.next();
        JLabel card = new CardView( vcard );
        cards.add( card );
    }
    revalidate();
    repaint();
}
```

As you can see the playerChanged() method extracts the Player's VCards and creates a CardView for each. Finally, it adds the view to itself so that the VCard get displayed.

The implementation presented here is not the most efficient because it creates a new CardView for each VCard each time the Player changes. A more efficient implementation could perform some caching of the view. Because you're using objects, you can change the implementation to a more efficient one at any time. Performance seems okay so the overhead of adding caching just isn't worth the effort at this point.

PlayerView must also display the outcome of the Player's game. Listing 18.6 presents two methods that get called at the end of the Player's game.

LISTING **18.6** A Sample of PlayerView's PlayerListener Methods

```
public void playerBusted( Player player ) {
    border.setTitle( player.getName() + " BUSTED!" );
    cards.repaint();
```

LISTING 18.6   continued

```
}

public void playerBlackjack( Player player ) {
    border.setTitle( player.getName() + " BLACKJACK!" );
    cards.repaint();
}
```

These methods set the border of the view with the outcome of the game.
PlayerListener defines more than two methods, but like the two listed here,
PlayerView's implementation of the methods all follow a similar pattern. Please review
the source if you are interested in seeing the entire list of update methods.

Implementing the OptionView and the OptionViewController

The OptionView inherits from JPanel and adds a number of buttons to itself.
OptionView does not listen to the model. Instead, the OptionViewController listens to
the model and enables or disables the buttons in the OptionView as appropriate.

Neither class is very interesting from an implementation standpoint. If you're interested
in the specifics, be sure to download and read over the code.

Implementing the GUIPlayer

GUIPlayer is probably the most interesting class in this iteration. When implementing a
GUI, you should keep in mind that all user interaction is asynchronous—it can come in
at any time.

Writing a command line player was rather easy. You only had to override hit() or bet()
so that it would read from the command line. Because the command line blocks until it
receives user input, the player was very easy to implement. A GUI player is a bit harder
to write.

Instead of being able to call a method and block until we get input, the GUIPlayer just
has to wait until the user decides to click a button. As a result, all stimuli comes from
outside of the player.

In response to this reality you need to add a number of methods that the GUI can call to
the GUIPlayer. Listing 18.7 lists the betting methods that you must add.

18

LISTING 18.7   GUIPlayer's Betting Methods

```
// these bet methods will get called by the GUI controller
// for each: place the proper bet, change the state, let the
// dealer know that the player is done betting
public void place10Bet() {
    getBank().place10Bet();
    setCurrentState( getWaitingState() );
    dealer.doneBetting( this );
}

public void place50Bet() {
    getBank().place50Bet();
    setCurrentState( getWaitingState() );
    dealer.doneBetting( this );
}

public void place100Bet() {
    getBank().place100Bet();
    setCurrentState( getWaitingState() );
    dealer.doneBetting( this );
}
```

You'll notice that these methods have to place bets and set the user to the proper state. Listing 18.8 lists the hit and stand methods.

LISTING 18.8   GUIPlayer's Hit and Stand Methods

```
// takeCard will get called by the GUI controller when the player
// decides to hit
public void takeCard() {
    dealer.hit( this );
}
// stand will get called by the GUI controller when the player chooses
// to stand, when standing change state, let the world know, and then
// tell the dealer
public void stand() {
    setCurrentState( getStandingState() );
    notifyStanding();
    getCurrentState().execute( dealer );
}
```

Like the betting methods, the methods in Listing 18.8 must perform their action and update the state. Because the state can not simply call hit() or bet() to be able to play or bet, you'll need to provide some customized Playing and Betting states. Listing 18.9 presents the overridden getPlayingState() and getBettingState() methods.

LISTING 18.9   GUIPlayer's Overridden State Getter Methods

```
protected PlayerState getPlayingState() {
    return new Playing();
}

protected PlayerState getBettingState() {
    return new Betting();
}
```

By overriding these methods, the GUIPlayer can provide its own customized states. Listing 18.10 presents the GUIPlayer's customized Playing state.

Note   Methods such as getPlayingState() and getBettingState() are factory methods.

LISTING 18.10   GUIPlayer's Custom Playing State

```
private class Playing implements PlayerState {

    public void handPlayable() {
        // do nothing
    }

    public void handBlackjack() {
        setCurrentState( getBlackjackState() );
        notifyBlackjack();
        getCurrentState().execute( dealer );
    }

    public void handBusted() {
        setCurrentState( getBustedState() );
        notifyBusted();
        getCurrentState().execute( dealer );
    }

    public void handChanged() {
        notifyChanged();
    }

    public void execute( Dealer d ) {
        // do nothing here, actions will come from the GUI which is
        // external to the state, but when events do come in be sure to
        // force state transition right away
    }
}
```

18

When executed the customized Playing state does not do anything. Instead, the
GUIPlayer needs to wait for asynchronous interaction from the GUI. You'll notice that
the Playing state still transitions in response to events from the Hand.

Listing 18.11 presents the customized Betting state. You'll notice that this state doesn't
do anything at all. Instead, the GUIPlayer must wait for the player to hit some button on
the GUI. Once that happens the button will call the proper betting method on the
GUIPlayer.

LISTING 18.11   GUIPlayer's Custom Betting State

```
private class Betting implements PlayerState {
    public void handChanged() {
        // not possible in busted state
    }
    public void handPlayable() {
        // not possible in busted state
    }
    public void handBlackjack() {
        // not possible in busted state
    }
    public void handBusted() {
        // not possible in busted state
    }
    public void execute( Dealer d ) {
        // do nothing here, actions will come from the GUI which is
        // external to the state, since no events come in as part of
        // betting the state will need to be changed externally to this state
    }
}
```

Putting It All Together with the BlackjackGUI

The BlackjackGUI creates and displays the Blackjack system. Listing 18.12 highlights
the BlackjackGUI's setUp() method.

LISTING 18.12   BlackjackGUI's setUp() Method

```
private void setUp() {
    BlackjackDealer dealer = getDealer();
    PlayerView v1 = getPlayerView( dealer );

    GUIPlayer human = getHuman();
    PlayerView v2 = getPlayerView( human );

    PlayerView [] views = { v1, v2 };
```

LISTING 18.12   continued

```
        addPlayers( views );

        dealer.addPlayer( human );

        addOptionView( human, dealer );
    }
```

The `setUp()` method creates each player, the views, and puts everything together. The other methods mainly construct the various objects. If you're interested in the full source, be sure to review the code. Figure 18.9 illustrates the final game screen.

FIGURE 18.9

The Blackjack GUI.

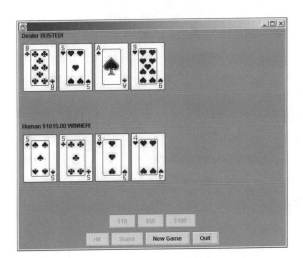

Summary

Today you saw the MVC pattern as applied to a real program. Sometimes it helps to see an extended example to be able to fully understand a pattern. Today's lesson also drives home the point that a GUI is not an afterthought. The GUI deserves the same level of analysis and design as any other part of a system.

Today's lesson actually completes the Blackjack game. Tomorrow you will see an alternative design and implementation of the Blackjack GUI.

18

Q&A

Q **You mentioned earlier that you shouldn't just tack the GUI on at the end. Well, this is the last iteration and we are adding a GUI. Doesn't it go against what you said earlier?**

A No, absolutely not!

When I say "tack on," I mean to add a GUI without doing any design at all. We've planned a GUI from the start. In the beginning we stated that we would use MVC. That was all the design that we needed to do until we were finally ready to add the GUI. Once we were ready to add the GUI, we did additional design in an iteration totally dedicated to the GUI.

Early on saying that we would use MVC and adding an observer mechanism was all that we needed to do to know that we could support a GUI.

Q **Where/what are the different pieces of MVC (I found mention of various Views and a controller)? Elaborate on what the model and the controller are.**

A The model is the system. In this case the `BlackjackDealer`, `BettingPlayers`, and so on make up the model layer.

The design only called for one controller—the `OptionViewController`—thus there wasn't much to say about controllers.

Workshop

The quiz questions and answers are provided for your further understanding. See Appendix A, "Answers," for the answers.

Quiz

1. How did you use inheritance and polymorphism to introduce a "visual" card?

2. In the lesson on inheritance it was pointed out that if a method is not needed by an outside classes and there is no requirements for a subclass to use the method then you should define the method as private. If a subclass ever does need it, you can make it protected at that time, but no earlier. Find an example of this advice in the Blackjack project.

Exercises

1. Download the source code for today's iteration. The code is broken into two separate directories: `mvc_gui` and `exercise_2`.

   `mvc_gui` contains the GUI code that was created during today's iteration.

exercise_2 contains the files that you will need for Exercise 2 as well
as the solutions.

Study the code in mvc_gui. Try to understand how it all works and then complete
Exercise 2.

2. Exercise 2 from Chapter 17 asked you to add doubling down to the Blackjack
   game. You need to add doubling down to the game again. This time, add it to the
   graphical version of the game that you downloaded for exercise 1. The download
   includes all of the files that you will need to start this exercise.

18

DAY 19

Applying an Alternative to MVC

Yesterday you analyzed, designed, and implemented a GUI for the Blackjack game. Today you will use an alternative approach to the design and implementation of the Blackjack GUI.

Today you will learn

- About an alternative to the MVC design pattern
- How to apply the alternative to the Blackjack GUI
- When to base your GUIs on MVC and when not to do so

An Alternative Blackjack GUI

Yesterday you created an MVC based GUI for the Blackjack game. MVC is just one approach to GUI design. Today you will redesign and reimplement the GUI using a different approach.

The approach that you employ today is a specialization of the Presentation Abstraction Control (PAC) design pattern. Like the MVC design pattern, the PAC design pattern breaks the GUI's design into three separate layers:

- The presentation layer, which displays the system
- The abstraction layer, which represents the system
- The control layer, which assembles all of the presentation layer components

PAC's similarities with the MVC design pattern are deceiving. In fact, PAC follows an entirely different philosophy than the one followed by the MVC pattern.

The PAC Layers

PAC's abstraction layer is akin to the model layer in the MVC pattern. The abstraction layer houses the core functionality of the system. It is this core that the presentation layer displays and manipulates. The abstraction layer is also responsible for providing access to presentation level objects.

In the PAC the functionality in view and controller layers from MVC are not split; instead, these two entities are combined within the presentation. The presentation layer is responsible for displaying and manipulating the abstraction layer as well as for responding to user interaction.

Because the MVC controller and view are combined into the presentation layer, the control serves an entirely different purpose in PAC. In PAC, the control assembles all of the different presentations. It does not listen for and respond to user interaction like the MVC controller.

The PAC Philosophy

MVC goes to great lengths to completely decouple each part of its design. When you use the MVC pattern, it is easy to swap in new views to your system at any time, thus using the MVC pattern gives you great freedoms in how you display your system. Chapter 13, "OO and User Interface Programming," points out, however, that greater freedoms come with the price of encapsulation.

PAC's approach is different. The PAC does not decouple the presentation and abstraction layers. Instead, the two layers are tightly coupled. This isn't to say that, for example, Player will extend JComponent directly. What it does say is that the abstraction layer will create and return its presentation. So the Player and its presentation are still two separate objects.

To get a different presentation of a part of the abstraction, you'll have to alter the abstraction's definition so that it returns a different presentation object. It is a bit more difficult to change the presentation, or to provide two or more different views of the same system.

Construction of the GUI is easier, however. When the control goes out to assemble the screen, it will ask each member of the abstraction layer for its presentation. All the control needs to do is add that presentation to the main screen. There's no view and controller to wire together.

When to Use the PAC Design Pattern

The underlying assumption of PAC is that you will not need to provide multiple views into the system. Instead, when you use PAC, you need to be sure that the system has only one well-defined interface. If your system will have only one interface, PAC can provide a very elegant alternative to MVC.

PAC does have a number of benefits. Because the abstraction layer can create its presentation, you do not need to destroy the encapsulation of your system. Instead, you can define the presentation classes as inner classes. As an inner class the presentation can have complete access to its parent abstraction class. When it needs to visualize the abstraction, it can directly access and display the abstraction's state.

Using PAC simplifies the communication between the presentation and its abstraction. When the abstraction changes, the abstraction can simply call an update method on the presentation that it has created.

When you use the PAC pattern, you can think of the presentation as a direct extension of the abstraction. By acting on the presentation, you act directly upon the underlying system. In a way, the presentation acts much as a proxy to the system. Such direct manipulation greatly simplifies the overall design.

19

Analyzing the PAC Blackjack GUI

To apply the PAC design pattern to the Blackjack GUI, you can simply reuse the analysis that you did yesterday. Nothing about the analysis changes because you decide to use the PAC pattern instead of MVC.

Designing the PAC Blackjack GUI

For the Blackjack game there is only one main interface: a GUI. You won't be deploying this game as a HTML web application (though you could easily turn it into an applet) or to a PDA, thus it is safe to use the PAC design pattern.

It's important to note that nothing forces you to remove the listener mechanisms that you've already built into the system. It is still possible to have a command-line-based and PAC-based GUI at the same time. In fact, through careful subclassing, you can leave all of the original class definitions intact. When you want a GUI, you can simply instantiate

the classes that support a GUI. When you want a command-line game, you can instantiate the older classes. Choosing MVC or PAC does not necessarily exclude you from
using the other.

Just as in Chapter 18, "Blackjack Iteration 4: Adding a GUI," you can take the completed
design and implementation from Chapter 17, "Blackjack Iteration 3: Adding Betting," as
the basis for the new GUI. What you do need to do is figure out which of those classes
need their own presentation object. When you have those classes identified, you need to
design the abstraction layer. When that is done you can design the control.

Identifying the Presentation Layer Components

To identify the presentation layer components it helps to draw some sketches of the GUI
screen. This time you should associate parts of the screen with the underlying class
instead of associating them with a separate view.

Figure 19.1 isolates one part of the GUI. By carefully dissecting this screen segment, you
can identify some of the presentation components.

FIGURE 19.1

A screen segment.

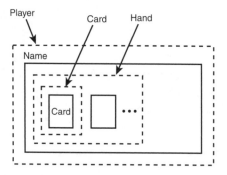

By slicing up the screen segment, you can see that the Card, Hand, and Player will need
to provide presentation objects. Figure 19.2 dissects the remaining part of the screen.

FIGURE 19.2

The GUI buttons.

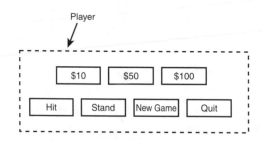

All of the buttons belong to the human `Player`, so the class that represents the human player will need to extend the `Player`'s presentation and add buttons. The `GUIPlayer` should have the same design as the one created for Chapter 18. Instead of repeating that design here, go back and read the section "Implementing the `GUIPlayer`" in Chapter 18 if you need a refresher. The only difference between Chapter 18's `GUIPlayer` and this one is that this one will also provide a presentation of itself.

Designing the Abstraction Layer Components

From the last section you've identified that `Card`, `Hand`, and the various `Player` subclasses need to provide a presentation of themselves.

For each of these classes you need to create an abstraction subclass. In particular you need to subclass `BlackjackDealer`, `BettingPlayer`, `Hand`, and `Card`. In addition you need to create a `GUIPlayer` as in Chapter 18. However, this `GUIPlayer` also needs to provide a presentation as well.

Figure 19.3 illustrates the resulting `Player` inheritance hierarchy.

FIGURE 19.3

The `Player` *abstraction hierarchy.*

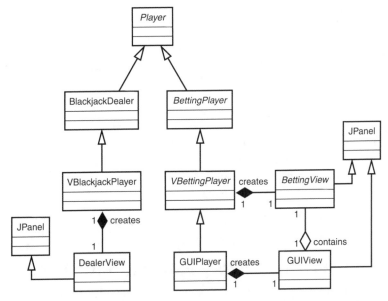

You need to create a `VBlackjackDealer BlackjackDealer` subclass. You also need to create a `VBettingPlayer BettingPlayer` subclass. These subclasses will add support for creating and returning presentation objects.

Figure 19.4 illustrates the resulting `Hand` and `Card` hierarchies.

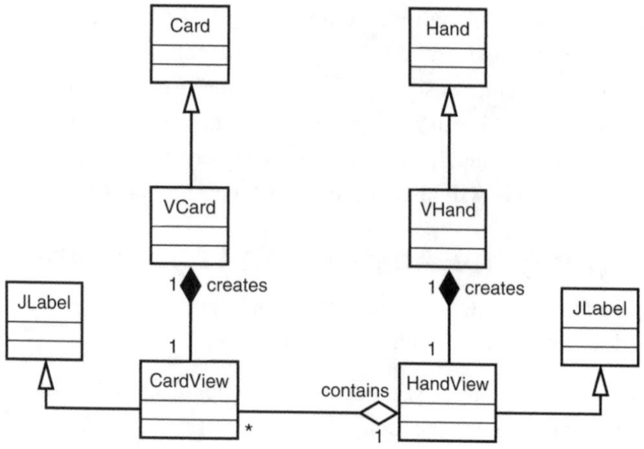

FIGURE 19.4

The Hand and Card abstraction hierarchy.

You'll need to create a VCard Card subclass as well as a VHand Hand subclass. These subclasses will visualize the Card and Hand respectively. As in yesterday's design, you also need a VDeck. The VDeck will create a deck of VCards.

Designing the Control

The control is a relatively simple class. An instance of control will retrieve a VBlackjackDealer as well as the various players. From each of these objects the control will request a presentation object. The control will take that presentation object, and add it to the display.

You'll need to design a mechanism that the console can use to ask the abstraction layer for its presentation objects. The easiest approach is to define an interface—let's call it Displayable. Displayable has one method: public JComponent view() which retrieves a presentation object. Each abstraction class that provides a presentation will need to implement this method.

Figures 19.5 and 19.6 show the updated hierarchies. The abstraction classes now realize the Displayable interface.

Using the Factory Pattern to Avoid Common Errors

There is one small problem with the resulting hierarchy: nothing stops you from creating a Deckpile of plain old un-displayable Cards and passing those to the dealer. Substitutability relationships allow such a substitution. Unfortunately, you will experience run time errors if you mix and match the GUI and non-GUI classes incorrectly.

Chapter 12, "Advanced Design Patterns," introduced the Abstract Factory design pattern. One reason to use that pattern was to ensure that a set of objects get used together. This prevents you from using incompatible objects together.

FIGURE 19.5

The updated Player *abstraction hierarchy.*

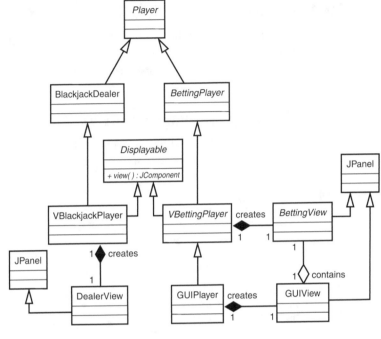

FIGURE 19.6

The updated Hand *and* Card *abstraction hierarchy.*

19

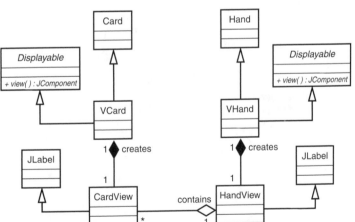

You can use a factory to ensure that the correct objects are used together. You'll need to create a factory that returns a VBlackjackDealer and a GUIPlayer that have been instantiated with the correct types of arguments. When the control goes out to retrieve the players and the dealer, it should only do so through the factory. This extra layer will ensure that all of the objects get instantiated properly.

Implementing the PAC Blackjack GUI

Yesterday's lesson pointed out that while implementing a GUI, it is often easiest to work from the bottom up. Following that advice you should implement in the following order: VCard, VHand, VBettingPlayer, VBlackjackGUI, and the GUIPlayer. Let's review each implementation.

Implementing the VCard and VHand

The VCard inherits from Card and represents itself through the internal class: CardView. Listing 19.1 presents the implementation of VCard.

LISTING 19.1   VCard.java

```java
public class VCard extends Card implements Displayable {

    private String image;
    private CardView view;

    public VCard( Suit suit, Rank rank, String image ) {
        super( suit, rank );
        this.image = image;
        view = new CardView( getImage() );
    }

    public void setFaceUp( boolean up ) {
        super.setFaceUp( up );
        view.changed();
    }

    public JComponent view() {
        return view;
    }

    private String getImage() {
        if( isFaceUp() ) {
            return image;
        } else {
            return "/bitmaps/empty_pile.xbm";
        }
    }

    private class CardView extends JLabel {

        public CardView( String image ) {
            setImage( image );
            setBackground( Color.white );
            setOpaque( true );
```

LISTING 19.1 continued

```
        }

        public void changed() {
            setImage( getImage() );
        }

        private void setImage( String image ) {
            java.net.URL url = this.getClass().getResource( image );
            ImageIcon icon = new ImageIcon( url );
            setIcon( icon );
        }

    }

}
```

This implementation of VCard is much like the one presented earlier with the exception of the inner presentation class. Upon creation, the VCard creates and holds onto a presentation view of itself.

You'll also notice that the new image attribute is now completely encapsulated within the VCard. For an outside entity to display the image, it must ask the VCard for a view. Furthermore, whenever the card is turned over, the VCard automatically tells its presentation view to update itself by calling changed() on the view. Unlike the MVC pattern, all of the control is held within the abstraction itself.

VHand is similar to VCard. Upon creation the VHand creates a presentation of itself. Listing 19.2 presents VHand's implementation.

19

LISTING 19.2 VHand.java

```
public class VHand extends Hand implements Displayable {

    private HandView view = new HandView();

    public JComponent view() {
        return view;
    }

    // you need to override addCard and reset so that when the hand changes, the
    // change propagates to the view
    public void addCard( Card card ) {
        super.addCard( card );
        view.changed();
    }
```

LISTING 19.2   continued

```java
public void reset() {
    super.reset();
    view.changed();
}

private class HandView extends JPanel {
    public HandView() {
        super( new FlowLayout( FlowLayout.LEFT ) );
        setBackground( new Color( 35, 142, 35 ) );
    }
    public void changed() {
        removeAll();
        Iterator i = getCards();
        while( i.hasNext() ) {
            VCard card = (VCard) i.next();
            add( card.view() );
        }
        revalidate();
    }
}
}
```

Like VCard, VHand tells its view to update itself whenever the VHand changes.

Implementing the VBettingPlayer

The idea behind the VBettingPlayer is much the same as that behind VHand and VCard. Listing 19.3 presents the VBettingPlayer implementation.

LISTING 19.3   VBettingPlayer.java

```java
public abstract class VBettingPlayer extends BettingPlayer implements
Displayable {

    private BettingView view;

    public VBettingPlayer( String name, VHand hand, Bank bank ) {
        super( name, hand, bank );
    }

    public JComponent view() {
        if( view == null ) {
            view = new BettingView( (VHand) getHand() );
            addListener( view );
        }
```

LISTING 19.3 continued

```
        return view;
    }

    private class BettingView extends JPanel implements PlayerListener {

        private TitledBorder border;

        public BettingView( VHand hand ) {
            super( new FlowLayout( FlowLayout.LEFT ) );
            buildGUI( hand.view() );
        }

        public void playerChanged( Player p ) {
            String name = VBettingPlayer.this.getName();
            border.setTitle( name );
            repaint();
        }

        public void playerBusted( Player p ) {
            String name = VBettingPlayer.this.getName();
            border.setTitle( name + " BUSTED!" );
            repaint();
        }

        // the rest of the PlayerListener methods have been snipped for brevity
        // they all follow the same pattern, please see source for full listing

        private void buildGUI( JComponent hand ) {
            border = new TitledBorder( VBettingPlayer.this.getName() );
            setBorder( border );
            setBackground( new Color( 35, 142, 35 ) );
            border.setTitleColor( Color.black );
            add( hand );
        }
    }
}
```

19

VBettingPlayer creates its view and sets it as a listener. Whenever the player changes, the view automatically knows to update itself. Of interest is the buildGUI() method. The buildGUI() method sets up the view.

You'll notice that instead of grabbing each card in the hand and constructing a view, BettingView simply takes the VHand's view and inserts it into itself. The VHand will manage the display of the cards. All that BettingView has to do is insert the view into itself and keep the title status up to date.

Implementing the `VBlackjackDealer`

`VBlackjackDealer` works exactly the same as `VBettingPlayer`. Listing 19.4 presents the implementation of `VBlackjackDealer`.

LISTING 19.4 `VBlackjackDealer.java`

```java
public class VBlackjackDealer extends BlackjackDealer implements Displayable {

    private DealerView view;

    public VBlackjackDealer( String name, VHand hand, Deckpile cards ) {
        super( name, hand, cards );
    }

    public JComponent view() {
        if( view == null ) {
            view = new DealerView( (VHand) getHand() );
            addListener( view );
        }
        return view;
    }


    private TitledBorder border;

    public DealerView( VHand hand ) {
        super( new FlowLayout( FlowLayout.LEFT ) );
        String name = VBlackjackDealer.this.getName();
        border = new TitledBorder( name );
        setBorder( border );
        setBackground( new Color( 35, 142, 35 ) );
        border.setTitleColor( Color.black );

        add( hand.view() );
        repaint();
    }

    public void playerChanged( Player p ) {
        String name = VBlackjackDealer.this.getName();
        border.setTitle( name );
        repaint();
    }

    public void playerBusted( Player p ) {
        String name = VBlackjackDealer.this.getName();
        border.setTitle( name + " BUSTED!" );
        repaint();
    }
```

LISTING 19.4 continued

```
        // the rest of the PlayerListener methods have been snipped for brevity
        // they all follow the same pattern, please see source for full listing

    }

}
```

DealerView listens for changes to the VBlackjackDealer. As these changes occur the view updates its title. The VHand takes care of keeping the card view up to date.

Implementing the GUIPlayer

Every non-GUI aspect of the GUIPlayer class is the same as the one presented yesterday. Like the other abstraction layer classes, GUIPlayer defines an inner presentation class.

This class combines Chapter 18's OptionView and OptionViewController classes. The presentation code isn't all that different than the original view and controller classes. For a full listing please be sure to download today's source code from www.samspublishing.com.

Putting It All Together with the Control

Before creating the control, you need to create the player factory. Listing 19.5 presents the implementation of VPlayerFactory.

LISTING 19.5 VPlayerFactory.java

```
public class VPlayerFactory {

    private VBlackjackDealer dealer;
    private GUIPlayer human;
    private Deckpile pile;

    public VBlackjackDealer getDealer() {
        // only create and return one
        if( dealer == null ) {
            VHand dealer_hand = getHand();
            Deckpile cards = getCards();
            dealer = new VBlackjackDealer( "Dealer", dealer_hand, cards );
        }
        return dealer;
    }

    public GUIPlayer getHuman() {
```

19

LISTING **19.5**   continued

```
            // only create and return one
            if( human == null ) {
                VHand human_hand = getHand();
                Bank bank = new Bank( 1000 );
                human = new GUIPlayer( "Human", human_hand, bank, getDealer() );
            }
            return human;
        }

        public Deckpile getCards() {
            // only create and return one
            if( pile == null ) {
                pile = new Deckpile();
                for( int i = 0; i < 4; i ++ ) {
                    pile.shuffle();
                    Deck deck = new VDeck();
                    deck.addToStack( pile );
                    pile.shuffle();
                }
            }
            return pile;
        }

        private VHand getHand() {
            return new VHand();
        }
    }
```

VPlayerFactory ensures that VBlackjackDealer and GUIPlayer are instantiated properly. Listing 19.6 presents the setup() method from BlackjackGUI: the control.

LISTING **19.6**   The setUp() Method from the BlackjackGUI Control

```
public class BlackjackGUI extends JFrame {

    // SNIP!! some code omitted for brevity

    private JPanel players = new JPanel( new GridLayout( 0, 1 ) );

    private void setUp() {
        VBlackjackDealer dealer = factory.getDealer();

        GUIPlayer human = factory.getHuman();
```

LISTING 19.6   continued

```
        dealer.addPlayer( human );

        players.add( dealer.view() );
        players.add( human.view() );
        getContentPane().add( players, BorderLayout.CENTER );
    }
}
```

`setUp()` simply retrieves each player, adds their views to itself, and connects the dealer to the players. Contrast that with Listing 19.7, yesterday's `setUp()` method.

LISTING 19.7   The `setUp()` Method from the MVC `BlackjackGUI`

```
private void setUp() {
    BlackjackDealer dealer = getDealer();
    PlayerView v1 = getPlayerView( dealer );

    GUIPlayer human = getHuman();
    PlayerView v2 = getPlayerView( human );

    PlayerView [] views = { v1, v2 };
    addPlayers( views );

    dealer.addPlayer( human );

    addOptionView( human, dealer );
}
```

19

It seems that simply asking the abstraction for a view is much simpler than creating and hooking together the various views from the MVC version.

Summary

Today you saw an alternative to the MVC. If your system is relatively stable and has one well defined UI, the PAC approach may offer a more elegant solution than MVC.

Even if you do need to support multiple interfaces, today's lesson shows how you can use inheritance to separate the abstraction layer from the core of the system. Thus, to support multiple interfaces, you need only to create a subclass for each presentation type.

Q&A

Q If PAC provides a better choice, why did we bother doing the MVC implementation?

A PAC simply provides an alternative. One is not necessarily better than the other. It's just a design decision.

The fact is you'll run into MVC a lot in the industry. You may run into PAC but it's much less likely. So covering MVC first is more pragmatic. Personally, I tend to favor PAC.

Keep both options in mind. What you never want to do is code your business logic (classes such as BettingPlayer) directly as a GUI component. For example, the BettingPlayer should *never* extend JComponent (or some other GUI component) directly. Both the MVC and PAC provide you with a mechanism that avoids muddling your model and the GUI together. The patterns just take different approaches. Which you choose depends on your design and your design team.

Workshop

The quiz questions and answers are provided for your further understanding. See Appendix A, "Answers," for the answers.

Quiz

1. What are the three layers of the PAC design pattern?

2. Give a brief description of each of the PAC layers.

3. How can you use inheritance to decouple the GUI from the underlying system classes?

4. Before using the PAC, what characteristics should your project exhibit?

5. Even though you used PAC throughout this lesson, how were you still able to provide a command line UI for the system?

6. How was the factory pattern used in this chapter?

Exercises

1. Download the source code for today's iteration. When you have the code, compile it, run it by executing BlackjackGUI, and then try to understand how it works. Gaining a full understanding of the code will take some time and patience.

2. Exercise 2 from Chapter 17 asked you to add doubling down to the Blackjack game. You need to add doubling down to the game again. This time, add it to the graphical version of the game that you downloaded for Exercise 1.

DAY 20

Having Some Fun with Blackjack

Over the past few days, you've worked on a fairly intense OOP project. Today you get to kick back and have a little fun with the Blackjack game by using polymorphism to add a number of non-human players to the game. You'll also get to see how OO lends itself to simulators.

Today you will learn how you can

- Use polymorphism to add players to the Blackjack game
- Use OO to create simulators

Having Fun with Polymorphism

The game of Blackjack allows for up to seven players to play at any given time. Up until now the game that you've created has only included a human player and the dealer. Luckily, polymorphism allows you to add non-human players to the game.

Creating a Player

To create a new non-human player, simply create a new class that inherits from `BettingPlayer`. All that your new class needs to do is implement the following two abstract methods:

- `public boolean hit()`
- `public void bet()`

The behavior that you provide for these two methods will determine how the player plays its turn. You won't need to alter any states or override any other methods. The default states know how to use the methods that you implement.

When you've finished defining the new player class, you can alter `BlackjackGUI` to create the player and add it to the game.

The Safe Player

Let's create a new player: `SafePlayer`. `SafePlayer` never hits and always bets the smallest allowed bet. Listing 20.1 presents the `SafePlayer` definition.

LISTING 20.1   `SafePlayer.java`

```
public class SafePlayer extends BettingPlayer {

    public SafePlayer( String name, Hand hand, Bank bank ) {
        super( name, hand, bank );
    }

    public boolean hit() {
        return false;
    }

    public void bet() {
        getBank().place10Bet();
    }
}
```

You'll note that `hit()` always returns false; the `SafePlayer` will never hit. Likewise, the `SafePlayer` always calls `place10Bet()`.

Adding the `SafePlayer` to the GUI

Adding the `SafePlayer` to the game is relatively straightforward. First, add the following method to `BlackjackGUI`:

LISTING 20.2   The getSafePlayer() Method

```
private Player getSafePlayer() {
    // return as many as called for
    Hand safe_hand = new Hand();
    Bank safe_bank = new Bank( 1000 );
    return new SafePlayer( "Safe", safe_hand, safe_bank );
}
```

getSafePlayer() is a factory method that instantiates SafePlayers. When you have the method, you can update setUp() so that it adds the new player to the game. Listing 20.3 presents the updated setUp() method.

LISTING 20.3   The Updated setUp() Method

```
private void setUp() {
    BlackjackDealer dealer = getDealer();
    PlayerView v1 = getPlayerView( dealer );

    GUIPlayer human = getHuman();
    PlayerView v2 = getPlayerView( human );

    Player safe = getSafePlayer();
    PlayerView v3 = getPlayerView( safe );

    PlayerView [] views = { v1, v2, v3 };
    addPlayers( views );

    dealer.addPlayer( human );
    dealer.addPlayer( safe );

    addOptionView( human, dealer );
}
```

You'll also want to alter the GUI's main method so that it makes the window a bit bigger so that the new player can fit. Figure 20.1 illustrates the new player as it appears in the GUI.

Here the player is added as a second player who plays after the human. Nothing stops you from letting the non-human play first.

Polish

You can add any number and type of BettingPlayer to the game that you like. As the number of player options gets larger, you may want to provide the user with a dialog box that allows him to set the player mix. At very least, you'll want to make the setUp() method protected so that subclasses can overwrite the method. When protected, you can write subclasses that create games with different player mixes.

20

*The GUI containing
three players.*

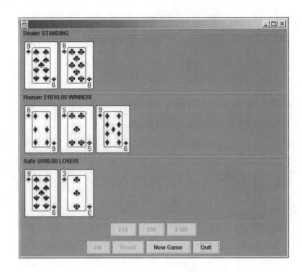

OOP and Simulations

As pointed out in an earlier lesson, when you write an OOP system you are actually writing a living simulator a some real life problem. This week you've written a system that simulates the game of Blackjack.

So far, the game has been human-player centric. You want a person with which to play the game, yet the system does not care if there is a human playing or not. To the system, all players are Player objects. The system just cares that there are Players.

By creating different types of players and adding them to the system, you can have a game of Blackjack that plays by itself without human interaction: a Blackjack simulator.

A Blackjack simulator can be useful for a number of reasons. Maybe you would like to create players that utilize different strategies so you can see which strategies work best.

Perhaps you are doing AI research and would like to write a neural network that learns how to play an optimal game of Blackjack. You can use a Blackjack simulator to accomplish all of these goals.

In today's chapter and exercises you will create a number of players to be able to find out if you can beat the blackjack dealer over time.

The Blackjack Players

You've already seen a SafePlayer. It'll be interesting to see how the SafePlayer performs over time. In addition to the SafePlayer let's define

- FlipPlayer: a player who alternates between hitting and staying
- OneHitPlayer: a player who always hits once per turn
- SmartPlayer: a player who stands on any hand greater than 11

Note

> You may notice the lack of use cases for these players. As an exercise, you might want to work through use cases for the players. However, a tenet of this book has been to perform only the amount of analysis that makes sense and adds value to your understanding of the problem. In my opinion, use cases wouldn't help your understanding in this case, and seem more like creating documentation simply for the sake of documentation.

Implementing the `FlipPlayer`

The implementation of FlipPlayer is a little more complicated than that of SafePlayer. Listing 20.4 presents the FlipPlayer implementation.

LISTING 20.4   FlipPlayer.java

```java
public class FlipPlayer extends BettingPlayer {

    private boolean hit = false;
    private boolean should_hit_once = false;

    public FlipPlayer( String name, Hand hand, Bank bank ) {
        super( name, hand, bank );
    }

    public boolean hit() {
        if( should_hit_once && !hit ) {
            hit = true;
            return true;
        }
        return false;
    }

    public void reset() {
        super.reset();
        hit = false;
        should_hit_once = !should_hit_once;
    }

    public void bet() {
        getBank().place10Bet();
    }
}
```

20

The FlipPlayer needs to keep two boolean flags. One flag tells the player whether it should hit at all that turn, and the other flag tracks whether the player has taken a hit during that round. The flags ensure that the player only hits once every other game.

To enable all of the boolean logic to work out, you'll need to override the reset() method to flip the boolean state of should_hit_once. Overriding reset() in this way ensures that the player will hit every other game, and only once per game when it does hit.

Implementing the OneHitPlayer

OneHitPlayer is similar in implementation to FlipPlayer. Unlike FlipPlayer, OneHitPlayer will hit every game, but only once. Listing 20.5 presents the implementation of OneHitPlayer.

LISTING 20.5 OneHitPlayer.java

```java
public class OneHitPlayer extends BettingPlayer {

    private boolean has_hit = false;

    public OneHitPlayer( String name, Hand hand, Bank bank ) {
        super( name, hand, bank );
    }

    public boolean hit() {
        if( !has_hit ) {
            has_hit = true;
            return true;
        }
        return false;
    }

    public void reset() {
        super.reset();
        has_hit = false;
    }

    public void bet() {
        getBank().place10Bet();
    }
}
```

Again, you need to override reset() so that it clears the has_hit flag. This flag ensures that the player only hits once per turn.

Implementing the `SmartPlayer`

`SmartPlayer` has a very simple implementation. Listing 20.6 presents the implementation.

LISTING 20.6 SmartPlayer.java

```java
public class SmartPlayer extends BettingPlayer {

    public SmartPlayer( String name, Hand hand, Bank bank ) {
        super( name, hand, bank );
    }

    public boolean hit() {
        if( getHand().total() > 11 ) {
            return false;
        }
        return true;
    }

    public void bet() {
        getBank().place10Bet();
    }
}
```

The `SmartPlayer` checks its `Hand`'s total. If the total is greater than eleven, the player stands. If it is lower, the player hits.

Setting Up the Simulator

To turn the game into a simulator, you can simply alter the `main` found in the `Blackjack` class. Here we'll copy and rename the class to `BlackjackSim`. Listing 20.7 presents the new simulator.

LISTING 20.7 BlackjackSim.java

```java
public class BlackjackSim {

    public static void main( String [] args ) {

        Console.INSTANCE.printMessage( "How many times should the simulator
play?" );
        String response = Console.INSTANCE.readInput( "invalid" );
        int loops = Integer.parseInt( response );

        Deckpile cards = new Deckpile();
        for( int i = 0; i < 4; i ++ ) {
            cards.shuffle();
```

20

LISTING 20.7 continued

```
            Deck deck = new Deck();
            deck.addToStack( cards );
            cards.shuffle();
        }

        // create a dealer
        Hand dealer_hand = new Hand();
        BlackjackDealer dealer = new BlackjackDealer( "Dealer", dealer_hand,
    cards );

        // create a OneHitPlayer
        Bank one_bank = new Bank( 1000 );
        Hand one_hand = new Hand();
        Player oplayer = new OneHitPlayer( "OneHit", one_hand, one_bank );

        // create a SmartPlayer
        Bank smart_bank = new Bank( 1000 );
        Hand smart_hand = new Hand();
        Player smplayer = new SmartPlayer( "Smart", smart_hand, smart_bank );

        // create a SafePlayer
        Bank safe_bank = new Bank( 1000 );
        Hand safe_hand = new Hand();
        Player splayer = new SafePlayer( "Safe", safe_hand, safe_bank );

        // create a FlipPlayer
        Bank flip_bank = new Bank( 1000 );
        Hand flip_hand = new Hand();
        Player fplayer = new FlipPlayer( "Flip", flip_hand, flip_bank );

        // hook all of the players together
        dealer.addListener( Console.INSTANCE );
        oplayer.addListener( Console.INSTANCE );
        dealer.addPlayer( oplayer );
        splayer.addListener( Console.INSTANCE );
        dealer.addPlayer( splayer );

        smplayer.addListener( Console.INSTANCE );
        dealer.addPlayer( smplayer );
        fplayer.addListener( Console.INSTANCE );
        dealer.addPlayer( fplayer );

        int counter = 0;
        while( counter < loops ) {
            dealer.newGame();
            counter ++;
        }
    }

  }
```

The simulator will first query you for a number of times to play. When it has that information it will create a `BlackjackDealer`, a `OneHitPlayer`, a `SmartPlayer`, and a `FlipPlayer`. It will then connect these players to the `Console` and add them to the dealer.

When it is done with the setup, it will play the game for the number of times that you specified.

The Results

After running the simulator a few times at 1000 games per run, it becomes easy to see how the players stack up. Here are the results from greatest to smallest holdings:

- `SmartPlayer`
- `SafePlayer`
- `FlipPlayer`
- `OneHitPlayer`

It appears that of these four players staying on a hand that is greater that 11 is the best approach. In fact, the `SmartPlayer` was the only player left with any money at all after 1000 games.

`SafePlayer` comes a close second, but it actually ended up losing money. And whatever you do don't flip or take one hit. These players lost more money than their initial pot.

Note

> None of these players ended up with more money than they started. The players only differed in the rate at which they lost their money.

Summary

You learned an important lesson today: Don't follow any of today's strategies while playing blackjack. You'll lose all of your money!

You also got to see first hand how polymorphism allows you to write future proof software. You were able to introduce player types to the system without having to alter the core system. These player types were not even considered when you built the initial system.

20

Q&A

Q Is there a reason that you didn't use the GUI as a basis for your simulator?

A I could have used the GUI instead of the console. It could have been entertaining to see the games flash by. Usually a simulator has no UI. Instead, the simulator will spit out some statistics at the end.

There are also practical limits to a GUI. GUIs do take some time to refresh. Playing 1000 visual games could take a bit longer than playing them on the command line.

Various versions of Swing also suffer from slow memory leaks. These leaks might come and bite you if you run through 10,000 visual games.

For testing purposes however, you might consider using the GUI as a basis for the simulator.

Workshop

The quiz questions and answers are provided for your further understanding. See Appendix A, "Answers," for the answers.

Quiz

1. How did polymorphism allow the game to play without a human player?
2. Which betting strategy will you never emulate?

Exercises

1. Download the source code for today's iteration from www.samspublishing.com. The code is broken into four separate directories: gui, simulation, exercise_2, and exercise_3.

   gui contains a GUI that has a human player and a SafePlayerU.

   simulation contains the simulation code. simulation has the following players: OneHitPlayer, FlipPlayer, SafePlayer, and SmartPlayer.

   exercise_2 and exercise_3 contain the files that you will need for Exercises 2 and 3 as well as the solutions.

   Study the code in gui and simulator. Try to understand how it all works. When you have done that, complete Exercises 2 and 3.

2. The download contains all of the starting files that you will need to complete this exercise. The starting files make changes to the hit method first declared in Player.

   The changes add Dealer as a parameter. The method getUpCard has been added to Dealer so that you can obtain the Dealer's up card. In a real game of Blackjack, the players can see the dealer's up card. You can use that information to make some smarter moves.

For this exercise, write one or two new players that base their hit decision on their own total as well as the dealer's up card. Here are two suggestions, but feel free to implement your own players and add them to the simulator and see how they do:

KnowledgeablePlayer

KnowledgeablePlayer should base the decision whether or not to hit on the following rules:

No matter what, if the hand total is greater than 15, stand.

If the hand total is 11 or less, hit.

If the hand is 15 or less and greater than 11, base the decision to hit on the dealer's card. If the dealer's card is greater than 7, hit; otherwise, you should stand.

OptimalPlayer

OptimalPlayer is as close to optimal that you can get without differentiating between soft and hard hands. (Differentiating is left as an exercise to the reader.)

OptimalPlayer should base the decision whether or not to hit on the following rules:

If the hand total is greater than or equal to 17, stand.

If the hand total is 11 or less, hit.

If the hand total is 16, base the decision to hit or stand on the dealer's up card. If the up card is seven, eight, or nine, hit; otherwise, stand.

If the hand total is 13, 14, or 15, base the decision to hit or stand on the dealer's up card. If the up card is 2, 3, 4, 5, or 6, stand; otherwise, hit.

If the hand total is 12, base the decision to hit or stand on the dealer's up card. If the up card is 4, 5, or 6, stand; otherwise, hit.

3. The download contains all of the starting files that you need to complete this exercise. The starting files add doubling down support to the classes. Additionally the new doubleDown method now accepts a Dealer as argument.

The changes add Dealer as a parameter to doubleDown. The method getUpCard has been added to Dealer so that you can obtain the Dealer's up card. In a real game of Blackjack the player's can see the dealer's up card. You can use that information to make some smarter moves.

For this exercise, write one or two new players that base their hit and double-down decision on their own total as well as the dealer's up card. Here are two suggestions, but feel free to implement your own players and add them to the simulator and see how they do:

20

KnowledgeablePlayer

For hitting, follow the rules laid out in Exercise 2.

For the doubling down, follow these rules:

If the hand total is 10 or 11, double down. In all other cases, do not double down.

OptimalPlayer

For hitting, follow the rules laid out in Exercise 2.

For the doubling down, follow these rules:

If the hand total is 11, always double down.

If the hand total is 10, base the decision to double down on the dealer's up card. If the up card is worth 10 or is an ace, double down; otherwise, do not double down.

If the hand total is 9, base the decision to double down on the dealer's up card. If the up card is 2, 3, 4, 5, or 6, double down; otherwise, do not double down.

In all other cases, do not double down.

DAY 21

The Final Mile

Congratulations! You've made it to the final lesson in this book. You've come a long way. You should now have the foundation that you need to be successful as you continue your studies of OOP.

Today we will clean up some loose ends and then send you on your way!

Today you will learn about

- Refactoring the Blackjack design for reuse in other systems
- The benefits that OOP brought to the Blackjack game
- Realities in the industry that may prevent total OO solutions

Tying Up the Loose Ends

You've covered a lot of ground during the past three weeks. You started by considering basic OO theory and worked your way through an entirely OOP based project. You should now have a good idea what OOP truly means.

Before completing the book, however, there are three issues left to cover:

- Refactoring the Blackjack design for reuse in other systems
- A survey of the benefits that OOP brought to the Blackjack system
- A word about industry realities and OOP

Refactoring the Blackjack Design for Reuse in Other Systems

There is a small issue related to the Blackjack game design that we need to examine. This issue does not impact the Blackjack game, but it could negatively impact another OO system if it reuses the design incorrectly.

On Day 15 you saw two alternative solutions. In one solution the dealer loops over its players telling each to play after the previous player completes. You then saw a more object based approach to the game loop.

Instead of the dealer going through the players one by one and telling them what to do, the OO dealer started each player and waited for the player to tell him when it was done playing.

This offered a cleaner solution because you left it up to the player to tell the dealer when it was done—only then did the dealer continue. It also turns out that this design was absolutely required for the GUI to work; otherwise, a human player would instantly return, and if the dealer were looping, the dealer would tell the next player to go. The human player would never get a turn in the procedural approach!

The Design Problem

There is a small problem with the approach as outlined in the lessons. Let's trace through the method calls in a game where there is one player and a dealer. Both players stand during their turn.

Listing 21.1 represents a trace of all method calls in the game. The stack terminates when a method returns.

LISTING 21.1   A Method Stack Track

```
BlackjackSim.main
 BlackjackDealer.newGame
  Player.play
   BlackjackDealer$DealerCollectingBets.execute
    Player.play
     BettingPlayer$Betting.execute
```

LISTING 21.1   continued

```
BlackjackDealer.doneBetting
 Player.play
  BlackjackDealer$DealerCollectingBets.execute
   BlackjackDealer$DealerDealing.execute
    BlackjackDealer$DealerWaiting.execute
     Player.play
      Player$Playing.execute
       Player$Standing.execute
        BlackjackDealer.standing
         Player.play
          BlackjackDealer$DealerWaiting.execute
           Player$Playing.execute
            BlackjackDealer$DealerStanding
```

The problem is subtle. None of the methods return until the dealer finishes his turn! The methods recursively call one another. So for example, the `notifyChanged` method in Listing 21.2 will not execute until the current game ends.

LISTING 21.2   A Method That Will Not Get Called Until After the Current Game Ends

```
public void execute( Dealer dealer ) {
    if( hit( dealer ) ) {
        dealer.hit( Player.this );
    } else {
        setCurrentState( getStandingState() );
        notifyStanding();
    }
    current_state.execute( dealer );
    // transition

    // will not get called until stack unwinds!!!!
    notifyChanged();
}
```

In the Blackjack game, this is not really a problem because there is a limit of seven players and the method call stack unwinds after every game. You can also code carefully around problems like the one demonstrated in Listing 21.2.

However, imagine a simulator with hundreds or thousands of objects that follow the Blackjack game design. If these objects call one another recursively, even if the stack does eventually unwind, you could end up running out of memory. Either way, each method call will allocate more memory. If you follow this design unaltered, your system either will not run or will require a whole lot more memory than absolutely necessary.

21

Sewing a Solution with Threads

Luckily there is a solution: threads. While a full discussion of threading is well beyond the scope of this book, you'll see how you can use threading to solve the method call problem quickly.

> **Note**
>
> Almost every non-trivial system will share two characteristics:
> - They will be threaded
> - They will have state logic
>
> The Blackjack system shares both of these characteristics.

A thread is simply a path of execution through your program. So far, the Blackjack system has one thread of execution. Figure 21.1 helps visualize that single thread.

FIGURE 21.1

The single threaded Blackjack system.

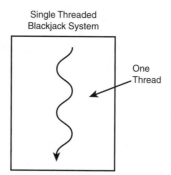

Because the Blackjack game is single threaded (it only has one thread), that single thread does everything.

Threading allows you to create multiple threads of execution through your program. By creating multiple threads, your program can do many different things at the same time. Figure 21.2 helps visualize two threads running through the Blackjack system.

Threading the Blackjack system can allow a method to return right away. Let's look at a simple thread example from Java. Listing 21.3 presents a simple thread that prints out `"Hello World!"`.

Figure 21.2

The multithreaded *Blackjack system.*

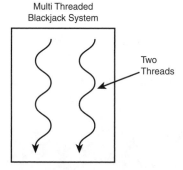

Multi Threaded
Blackjack System

Two
Threads

Listing 21.3   A Threaded `"Hello World!"`

```java
public class HelloWorld {

    public void sayHello() {
        System.out.println( "Hello World!" );
    }

    public static void main( String [] args ) {
        final HelloWorld hw = new HelloWorld();

        Runnable runnable = new Runnable() {
            public void run() {
                hw.sayHello();
            }
        };

        Thread thread = new Thread( runnable );
        thread.start();

        System.out.println( "All Done!" );

    }

}
```

HelloWorld itself is a simple class that has one method: sayHello. sayHello prints out a message to the command line.

The main is where it gets interesting. First, the main instantiates HelloWorld. It then creates an anonymous Runnable class. Runnables have one method: run. run tells the thread what to do when it is started. In this case it will tell the HelloWorld instance to print its message.

21

After creating the `Runnable`, the main instantiates a Java `Thread`. When you create a `Thread` you need to pass it a `Runnable`. The `Runnable`'s run method tells the `Thread` what to do when you tell the `Thread` to `start`. After starting the `Thread` the `main` prints out a message of its own.

You may be surprised when you see the main run. Figure 21.3 presents the output of `HelloWorld`.

FIGURE 21.3

The output of
HelloWorld.

When running `HelloWorld`, you'll find that "All Done" gets printed before "Hello World!" The call to `Thread.start` does not block like other method calls. Because `start` starts a new thread of execution it automatically returns. After you call `start` you have two threads of execution in the `HelloWorld` program. It just so happens that the `main` prints its message before the new thread gets a chance to call `sayHello`.

You can use the fact that `start` does not block to fix the design shortcoming in the Blackjack game. Listing 21.4 presents a new `Waiting` state for the `BlackjackDealer` that starts each player on its own thread.

LISTING 21.4   A Threaded `DealerWaiting`

```
private class DealerWaiting implements PlayerState {
    public void handChanged() {
        // not possible in waiting state
    }
    public void handPlayable() {
        // not possible in waiting state
    }
    public void handBlackjack() {
        // not possible in waiting state
    }
    public void handBusted() {
        // not possible in waiting state
    }
```

LISTING 21.4   continued

```java
public void execute( final Dealer dealer ) {
    if( !waiting_players.isEmpty() ) {
        final Player player = (Player) waiting_players.get( 0 );
        waiting_players.remove( player );
        Runnable runnable = new Runnable() {
            public void run() {
                player.play( dealer );
            }
        };
        Thread thread = new Thread( runnable );
        thread.start();
    } else {
        setCurrentState( getPlayingState() );
        exposeHand();
        getCurrentState().execute( dealer );
        // transition and execute
    }
}
}
```

By starting each player on its own thread, the `BlackjackDealer`'s state `execute` method can return right away, thus unrolling the stack. This does interject some difficulties if you loop calls to `newGame` because `newGame` will now return before the game is actually finished. If you loop, you'll start another game before the last has finished and then you'll run into all kinds of nasty problems. You can solve this problem by telling the `BlackjackDealer` how many times to loop. At the end of each game, it can check to see if it needs to play again.

Note

> Threading is just one way to solve the problem with recursion. I presented a threaded solution here to give you some exposure to threads.
>
> The loop/thread problem raises some concerns. You could also create a `GameTable` object that would start and stop the threads. The `Dealer` could then listen to the table's state and deal, hit, fulfill, and so on based on the state. However, such an approach is a bit more involved than simply threading the players as they start.
>
> You could also get rid of the recursion through iteration over the players.

The good news is that if you don't loop, such as in the GUI, you can easily thread by simply changing the `BlackjackDealer`'s `DealerWaiting` state! The downloadable source contains threaded versions of the GUI.

21

Caution   It is easy to thread the Blackjack game because only one player thread runs
at any given time. You don't have many different player threads running
concurrently.

Threading becomes tricky when many threads run concurrently and share
the same data!

Identifying the Benefits the OOP Brought to the Blackjack System

The first week pointed out some of the goals and benefits of OOP. To recap, OOP
attempts to produce software that is

1. Natural

2. Reliable

3. Reusable

4. Maintainable

5. Extendable

6. Timely

OOP brought each of these benefits to the Blackjack system. The Blackjack system fulfills each of the goals of OOP:

- Natural: The Blackjack system naturally models a game of Blackjack.

  The Blackjack system exists in the terms of an actual Blackjack game. The
  Blackjack system is made up of `Players`, a `BlackjackDealer`, `Cards`, `Decks`, and a
  `DeckPile`. As you see, the Blackjack game is a living simulation of the Blackjack
  domain.

- Reliable: The Blackjack system is reliable.

  Through a combination of careful testing and encapsulation you've created a reliable Blackjack system. Because you have isolated knowledge and responsibility
  and placed them where they belong, you can make enhancements to the system
  without worrying about negatively impacting unrelated parts of the system.

- Reusable: The Blackjack system is reusable.

  Because this was the first card game that you have written, there wasn't a lot of
  emphasis placed on writing an abstract card game framework. Instead, you wrote a
  Blackjack game. As a result the game is not completely reusable; however, classes
  such as `Card`, `Deck`, and `Deckpile` can be reused across almost any card game.

Furthermore, many of the design ideas are reusable across many problems. As you write more card games, you will be able to abstract further and create a fully reusable framework.

- Maintainable: The Blackjack system is maintainable.

  By encapsulating knowledge and responsibility where they belong, it is simple to make changes to one part of the system without negatively impacting other unrelated parts of the system.

  Such divisions make it possible to make improvements to the system at any time. You've also seen first hand how inheritance and polymorphism make it possible to add new players to the system at any time.

- Extendable: The Blackjack system is extendable.

  You saw firsthand how you can add new players to the system. Furthermore, through careful inheritance you can introduce new types of cards (such as visual cards) and hands. The iterative process proved just how extendable an OOP system can be.

- Timely: The Blackjack system is timely.

  You were able to produce a full Blackjack game in four iterations—a week's worth of time. Now that's timely!

Industry Realities and OOP

The lessons of this book have assumed that you're starting your OOP projects from scratch. When you start from scratch you don't have to integrate into legacy, non-OO, backend systems. You don't have to reuse procedural libraries. You can start fresh and everything that you use can be OO.

You'll find that a standalone OOP project is rare. Most times you will need to interact with non-OO components. Take the case of relational databases. Relational databases are not particularly object-oriented, and object-oriented databases are still rarely used outside of some niche industries.

Java itself is not even fully object oriented. The reliance on non-OO primitives make you perform some non-OO coding from time to time.

When faced with these realities, it is best to bite the bullet and wrap these non-OO aspects in an object-oriented wrapper. For example, when dealing with relational databases, it helps to write an object persistence layer. Instead of going directly to a database and reconstituting your objects through a number of SQL queries, the persistence layer can do that work for you.

21

It's really not possible to cover every type of non-OO system that you will encounter here. But it would have been negligent not to point out these realities before sending you out to apply OOP.

It will be a long time before every legacy system is converted to an object-based architecture (if it ever happens). You must be prepared for this eventuality and ready to deal with it as elegantly as possible.

Summary

You're done! In three short weeks, this book has given you a solid foundation in OOP. The rest is up to you. You now have enough knowledge to begin applying OOP to your daily projects. Good luck!

Q&A

Q Why did you wait until now to tell us about threading?

A The design issue does not really affect the Blackjack game. Bringing up the possible issues sooner would have confused the issue.

It is important that you do realize the shortcomings of the design as well as a possible solution.

Threading is also an advanced topic. Threading the Blackjack game was rather easy. But threading other applications may not prove so simple.

Q What can make threading difficult?

A If you have multiple threads sharing data, one thread could change the data and break another thread. Such concurrency issues are extremely difficult to design, implement, and debug.

Workshop

The quiz questions and answers are provided for your further understanding. See Appendix A, "Answers," for the answers.

Quiz

1. How does threading take care of the recursive method call problem?

Exercises

1. Download the source code for today's iteration. The code is broken into four separate directories: `threaded_hello_world`, `threaded_mvc_gui`, `threaded_pac_gui`, and `threaded_simulator`. Study the code and be sure to understand how it works.

2. Your study of OOP should not end with this book. Generate a list of topics that you would like to learn more about. Rank those topics by importance search the web for materials, and start studying!

21

WEEK 3

In Review

You have now finished the third and final week of this book, and in the past seven days you learned how to develop your own OO Blackjack game.

Day 15 presented the basic rules for Blackjack. You developed a list of potential use cases and selected a few of those to develop in the first iteration of the game. You followed the design process from analysis to implementation and testing and at the end of the day, you had a working version of Blackjack that dealt cards and let you play.

In Day 16, you completed a second iteration of the game. You added more functionality, such as the capability to determine the results of the game. In doing so, you learned about states and how to use them to improve your design.

Day 17 showed you how to complete yet another iteration of the Blackjack game—betting. By doing this, you saw how you could extend the state architecture to support simple gambling in the game. You also saw that it is sometime necessary to revisit and refactor a hierarchy as new requirements present themselves. Though refactoring presents a little extra work upfront, refactoring when appropriate tends to pay for itself as you move forward.

In Day 18, you completed the Blackjack game by adding a GUI. To do so, you revisited the MVC pattern discussed in an earlier chapter.

Day 19 provided an alternate GUI, using the PAC pattern, to the one developed in Day 18. This helped to refine your understanding of which patterns are appropriate for specific scenarios.

During Day 20, you revisited the concepts of polymorphism that allow you to write future proof software. You had some fun as you added multiple non-human players to the system and turned the Blackjack game into a simulator. By playing around with various player strategies, you learned what not to do when playing a game. You also learned that you were able to introduce player types to the system without having to alter the core system. These player types were not even considered when you built the initial system.

Finally, in Day 21, you learned about threading. The chapter also covered any loose ends with the project and presented a discussion about pure OO as opposed to what you are likely to see in the real world.

The lessons this week nailed down your understanding of OO, plus you ended up with a fun, time-wasting OO Blackjack game to prove it.

After completing this book, you have the necessary foundation in OO to begin developing OO software. All you need now is practice and experience. Good luck.

For further resources, Appendix D, "Selected Bibliography," provides a starting point for more OO information.

Appendices

A Answers

B Java Primer

C UML Reference

D Selected Bibliography

E Blackjack Code Listings

A

B

C

D

E

APPENDIX A

Answers

Day 1 Quiz Answers

Answers to Quiz

1. As a software discipline, procedural programming decomposes a program into data and procedures for manipulating that data. Procedural programming has a sequential nature. Lists of procedural calls that execute sequentially drive a procedural program's flow. A procedural program terminates after it calls its last procedure.

2. Procedural programming gives a program an overall structure: data and procedures. Procedures also help you to see how to program a task. Instead of writing one large processing block, you keep breaking up the procedures into subprocedures. Procedures do give you a level of reuse. You can create libraries of reusable procedures.

3. Modular programming tightly couples data and procedures for manipulating that data into units known as modules. Modules hide a program's inner workings and data representation. However, most modular languages still allow you to use those modules in a procedural environment.

4. Modular programming hides implementation and thereby protects data from inconsistent or improper manipulation. Modules also give a higher-level structure to a program. Instead of thinking in terms of data and procedures, modules allow you to think at a conceptual, behavioral level.

5. Both procedural and modular programming have limited support for reuse. Although you can reuse procedures they are highly dependent upon their data. The global nature of data in the procedural world makes reuse difficult. Procedures may have dependencies that are hard to quantify.

   Modules themselves are readily reusable. It is possible to take a module and use it in any of your programs. However, modules limit reuse. Your program can only use the modules directly. You cannot use an existing module as the basis for a new module.

6. OOP is a software discipline that models the program in terms of real-world objects. OOP breaks the program into a number of interrelating objects. It builds upon modular programming by supporting encapsulation as well as cleaning up reuse deficiencies through inheritance and typing shortcomings through polymorphism.

7. The six benefits of OOP are programs that are

   Natural

   Reliable

   Reusable

   Maintainable

   Extendable

   Timely

8. OOP is natural. Instead of modeling problems in terms of data or procedures, OOP allows you to model your programs in the terms of the problem. Such an approach frees you to think in the terms of the problem and focus on what you are trying to accomplish. It takes the focus away from implementation details.

9. Class defines all of the attributes and behaviors common to a group of objects. You use this class definition to create instances of those objects.

   An object is an instance of a class. Your programs manipulate these objects.

   An object performs behaviors. You can also call an object's behaviors its public interface. Other objects may exercise any behavior in an object's interface.

10. Objects communicate by sending each other messages. Calling a message is synonymous with making a method or procedure call.

11. A constructor is a method that defines how to create an object instance. Using the constructor will instantiate an object and make it available to your program.

12. An accessor is a behavior that gives you access to an object's internal data.

13. A mutator is a behavior that can alter an object's internal state.

14. `this` is a reference that each instance has to itself. The `this` reference gives the instance access to its internal variables and behaviors.

Day 2 Quiz and Exercise Answers

Answers to Quiz

1. Encapsulation is natural. Encapsulation allows you to model the software in terms of the problem, not in the terms of the implementation.

   Encapsulation leads to reliable software. Encapsulation hides the inner workings of a software component and guarantees that it is accessed properly. Encapsulation allows you to isolate and validate responsibility. Once a component is shown to act correctly, you can reuse it with confidence.

   Encapsulation gives you reusable software. Since each software component is independent, you can reuse the component in many different situations.

   Encapsulation leads to maintainable code because each component is independent. A change to one component will not break another component. Thus, maintenance and enhancement are simplified.

   Encapsulation makes your software modular. Changes to one part of a program will not break code in another part. Modularity allows you to make bug fixes of functionality enhancements without breaking the rest of your code.

   Encapsulation leads to timely code development because it removes unnecessary code coupling. Too often, hidden dependencies lead to bugs that are difficult to find and fix.

2. Abstraction is the process of simplifying a difficult problem. When you set out to solve a problem, you don't overwhelm yourself with every detail surrounding the domain. Instead, you simplify it by only addressing those details germane to actually formulating a solution.

   Your computer's graphical desktop is an example of abstraction. The desktop completely hides the details of the file system from you.

3. An implementation defines how a component actually provides a service. The implementation defines the internal details of the component.

A

4. An interface defines what you can do to a component. The interface completely hides the underlying implementation.

5. An interface describes what a software component does; the implementation tells you how the component does it.

6. Without clear division, responsibilities become muddled. Muddled responsibilities lead to two related problems.

   First, code that could be centralized becomes decentralized. Decentralized responsibility must be repeated, or reimplemented, in each place where it is needed. Think back to the BadItem example presented earlier.

   It is easy to see that each user would need to re-implement the code for calculating the adjusted total for an item. Each time you rewrite the logic you open yourself up to bugs. You also open up your code to improper use because the responsibility of keeping internal state no longer lies within the component. Instead, you place that responsibility in the hands of others.

7. A type is a language element that represents some unit of computation or behavior. If lines of code are sentences, types are the words. Types are normally treated as independent, self-contained, atomic units.

8. An ADT is a set of data and a set of operations on that data. ADTs enable us to define new language types by hiding internal data and state behind a well-defined interface. This interface presents the ADT as a single atomic unit.

9. There are a number of ways to achieve implementation hiding and loosely coupled code. The easy answer is to use encapsulation. However, effective encapsulation is no accident. Here are a few tips to effective encapsulation:

   • Access your ADT only through an interface of methods; never allow internal structures to become part of the public interface.

   • Do not provide access to inner data structures; abstract all access.

   • Do not give inadvertent access to inner data structures by accidentally returning pointers or references.

   • Never make assumptions about the other types that you use. Unless a behavior appears in the interface or in the documentation, do not rely on it.

   • Be careful while writing two closely related types. Do not let yourself accidentally program in assumptions and dependencies.

10. You need to beware of a few abstraction pitfalls.

    Do not fall into abstraction paralysis. Solve the problems that you face first. Solving problems is your primary job. Look at abstraction as a bonus, not the end goal. Otherwise, you face the possibility of missed deadlines and incorrect abstraction. There are times to abstract and times when abstraction is not appropriate.

Abstraction can be dangerous. Even if you have abstracted some element, it may not work in every case. It is very difficult to write a class that will satisfy every user's need.

Don't put more into a class than is necessary to solve the problem.

Don't set out to solve all problems. Solve the problem at hand, and then look for ways to abstract what you have done.

Answers to Exercises

1. One possible stack ADT:

```
public interface Stack {
    public void push( Object obj );
    public Object pop();
    public boolean isEmpty();
    public Object peek();
}
```

2. The stack is best implemented as a singly linked list with a front pointer. When you push or pop an element, you use the front pointer to find the first element.

3. Looking back at the answer to Exercise 1 and the implementation in Exercise 2, you see that the interface was adequate. The interface gives us the benefits that any well-defined interface provides. Here is a short list of benefits:

   - The interface defines the stack as a type. By studying the interface, you know exactly what the stack will do.

   - The interface completely hides the internal representation of the stack.

   - The interface clearly defines the stack's responsibilities.

Day 3 Quiz and Exercise Answers

Answers to Quiz

1. Account has two mutators: depositFunds() and withdrawFunds().

   Account has one accessor: getBalance().

2. There are two types of constructors: those that have arguments and those that do not (noargs).

   Account from Lab 2 has both types of constructors.

3. (Optional) Public is acceptable in the case of Boolean since the variables are constants. Having public access to constants does not break encapsulation since it is not exposing the implementation to outside use.

A

Furthermore, the use of constant `Booleans` for true and false saves memory. There is no need to ever instantiate your own copies of `Boolean`. You can simply share these global instance constants.

4. The `Card` instances are immutable. It would be more efficient to define 52 `Card` constants—one for each card. There is no need to instantiate multiple representations of the same card, even when there are multiple `Deck` instances. It is perfectly safe to share the same `Card` instances among the decks.

5. When designing your classes you must ask yourself what makes this "thing" a class? Specifically, think back to the discussion of how classes classify related objects. How are cards related? Cards all hold onto a value, a suit, and know how to display themselves.

The value or a suit doesn't make one card a different kind of card. It is still a poker card. The poker cards just might have different values. Just as a brown mammal is still a mammal, a 10 of hearts is still just a card.

Sometimes it can be extremely difficult to decide what should and should not be a class of its own. There is a rule of thumb that you can follow though.

If you see that an object's behavior changes fundamentally when the value of an attribute changes, chances are you should create separate classes: one for each possible value of that attribute. Clearly, the value of the card does not change the card's behavior in any fundamental way.

6. The proper division of responsibility made the `Deck`, `Dealer`, and `Card` design more modular. Instead of one large class, poker cards nicely break up into three classes. Each class is responsible for doing its job and hiding that implementation from the other classes. As a result, these classes can easily change their implementation at any time without harming any of their users.

With separate classes you also get the benefit that you can reuse the `Card` class separate from the `Deck` and `Dealer` class.

Answers to Exercises

1. Here is one possible solution to Exercise 1:

```
public class DoubleKey {

    private Object key1, key2;

    // a no args constructor
    public DoubleKey() {
        key1 = "key1";
        key2 = "key2";
    }
```

```
    // a constructor with arguments
    // should check for and handle null case
    public DoubleKey( Object key1, Object key2 ) {
        this.key1 = key1;
        this.key2 = key2;
    }

    // accessor
    public Object getKey1() {
        return key1;
    }

    // mutator
    // should check for and handle null case
    public void setKey1( Object key1 ) {
        this.key1 = key1;
    }

    // accessor
    public Object getKey2() {
        return key2;
    }

    // mutator
    // should check for and handle null case
    public void setKey2( Object key2 ) {
        this.key2 = key2;
    }

    // the following two methods are required in order to
....// properly work as a keyif passed to a HashMap or Hashtable
    public boolean equals( Object obj ) {

        if( this == obj ) {
            return true;
        }

        if( this.getClass() == obj.getClass() ) {
            DoubleKey dk = ( DoubleKey ) obj;
            if( dk.getKey1().equals( getKey1() ) &&
                dk.getKey2().equals( getKey2() ) ) {
                return true;
            }
        }
        return false;
    }

    public int hashCode() {
        return key1.hashCode() + key2.hashCode();
    }

}
```

A

2. Here is one possible solution to Exercise 2:

```java
public class Deck {

    private java.util.LinkedList deck;

    public Deck() {
        buildCards();
    }

    public String display() {
        int num_cards = deck.size();
        String display = "";
        int counter = 0;
        for( int i = 0; i < num_cards; i ++ ) {
            Card card = ( Card ) deck.get( i );
            display = display + card.display() + " ";
            counter++;
            if( counter == 13 ) {
                counter = 0;
                display = display + "\n";
            }
        }
        return display;
    }

    public Card get( int index ) {
        if( index < deck.size() ) {
            return (Card) deck.get( index );
        }
        return null;
    }

    public void replace( int index, Card card ) {
        deck.set( index, card );
    }

    public int size() {
        return deck.size();
    }

    public Card removeFromFront() {
        if( deck.size() > 0 ) {
            Card card = (Card) deck.removeFirst();
            return card;
        }
        return null;
    }

    public void returnToBack( Card card ) {
        deck.add( card );
```

```
    }

    private void buildCards() {

        deck = new java.util.LinkedList();

        deck.add( new Card( Card.CLUBS, Card.TWO   ) );
        deck.add( new Card( Card.CLUBS, Card.THREE ) );
        deck.add( new Card( Card.CLUBS, Card.FOUR  ) );
        deck.add( new Card( Card.CLUBS, Card.FIVE  ) );
        // full definition clipped for brevity
        // see source for full listing
    }


}
```

Day 4 Quiz and Exercise Answers

Answers to Quiz

1. Simple reuse provides no mechanism for reuse beyond instantiation. To directly reuse code, you need to cut and paste the code you wish to reuse. Such a practice results in multiple code bases that differ in only a small number of ways. Code that lacks inheritance is static. It cannot be extended. Furthermore, static code is type limited. Static code cannot share type. Thus you lose the benefits of type pluggability.

2. Inheritance is a built-in mechanism for the safe reuse and extension of pre-existing class definitions. Inheritance allows you to establish "Is-a" relationships between classes.

3. The three forms of inheritance are

   Inheritance for implementation reuse

   Inheritance for difference

   Inheritance for type substitution

4. Implementation inheritance can blind a developer. Implementation reuse should never be the only goal of inheritance. Type substitution should always be your first priority. Blind reuse inheritance leads to class hierarchies that simply do not make sense.

5. Programming by difference is one of the forms of inheritance. It means that when you inherit, you only program those features that differentiate the new class from the old. Such a practice leads to smaller, incremental classes. Smaller classes are easier to manage.

A

6. The three types of methods and attributes are

   Overridden

   New

   Recursive

   An overridden attribute or method is an attribute or method declared in the parent (or ancestor) and re-implemented in the child. The child alters the behavior of the method or the definition of the attribute.

   A new method or attribute is a method or attribute that appears in the child but not in the parent or ancestors.

   A recursive attribute or method is defined in the parent or the ancestor but is not redefined by the child. The child simply inherits the method or attribute. When a call to this method or attribute is made on the child, the call passes up the hierarchy until someone is found who knows how to handle it.

7. Programming by difference gives you smaller classes that define a smaller number of behaviors. Smaller classes should contain fewer bugs, be easier to debug, easier to maintain, and easier to understand.

   Programming by difference allows you to program incrementally. As a result, a design can evolve over time.

8. `AllPermission`, `BasicPermission`, and `UnresolvedPermission` are all children of `Permission`. `SecurityPermission` is a descendant of `Permission`.

   `Permission` is the root class. `AllPermission`, `UnresolvedPermission`, and `SecurityPermission` are all leaf classes since they lack children.

   Yes, `Permission` is an ancestor of `SecurityPermission`.

9. Inheritance for type substitution is the process of defining substitutability relationships. Substitutability allows you to substitute a descendant for an ancestor so long as you don't need to use any new methods defined by the descendant.

10. Inheritance can destroy encapsulation by giving a subclass inadvertent access to the internal representation of a superclass.

    Inadvertent destruction of encapsulation is a pitfall that can sneak up on you. Inheritance quietly gives a child class more liberal access to the parent. As a result, if the proper steps are not taken, a child could gain direct access to the parent's implementation. Direct implementation access is just as dangerous between parent and child as it is between two objects. Many of the same pitfalls still apply.

    Avoid encapsulation destruction by making internal implementation private. Only make those methods absolutely needed by a subclass protected.

    Most of the time children should only exercise the parent's public interface.

Answers to Exercises

1. Any subclass will have direct access to the `Point`'s internal representation. Such unrestricted access destroys encapsulation and opens the class up to the problems addressed in Question 10.

   Remedying the situation is as easy as making x and y private. Please note that this `Point` class is modeled after `java.awt.Point`.

Day 5 Quiz Answers

Answers to Quiz

1. In `CheckingAccount, public double withdrawFunds( double amount )` is an example of a redefined method. `CheckingAccount` overrides `withdrawFunds()` so that it can keep track of the number of transactions.

   In `BankAccount, public double getBalance()` is an example of a recursive method. The method appears in the parent, but none of the subclasses redefine it. However, the subclasses do call it.

   Finally, `SavingsAccount`'s `public double getInterestRate()` method is an example of a new method. The method only appears in the `SavingsAccount` class, not in the parent.

2. You would use an abstract class for planned inheritance. An abstract class gives its subclasses a clue as to what it will need to redefine. Abstract classes guarantee that your subclasses use the base class properly.

3. Lab 3 shows "Has-a." The `Deck` has `Cards`. `DoubleKey` from Lab 2 also has two `Strings`.

4. The labs preserved encapsulation by hiding all data members. If you look back through the solutions, you will see that all data is private. For example, the `BankAccount` class declares the balance as private. Instead, each class provides access to the data representation through a well-defined interface.

5. The `SavingsAccount` is an example of specialization. It specializes upon its parent, `BankAccount`, by adding methods to set, query, and apply interest to the account.

6. Lab 3 uses inheritance to reuse the basic behavior defined by the `BankAccount` class. The `BankAccount` defines a common implementation for withdrawing funds, depositing funds, and querying the balance. Through inheritance, account subclasses get this implementation.

   Lab 4 starts off by presenting a case of inheritance for implementation, but ends by using composition to achieve a cleaner form of reuse.

A

Day 6 Quiz and Exercise Answers

Answers to Quiz

1. Inclusion

   Parametric

   Overridding

   Overloading

2. Inclusion polymorphism enables you to treat one object as if it were a different type of object. As a result, an object may demonstrate many different kinds of behavior.

3. Overloading and parametric polymorphism allow you to model something at the conceptual level. Instead of worrying about the types of parameters something processes, you can write your code more generically. Instead, you model your methods and types at the conceptual level of what they do, not what they do things to.

4. An interface may have any number of implementations. By programming to an interface, you do not get tied to any specific implementation. As a result, your program can automatically use any implementation that comes along. This freedom from implementation allows you to swap-in different implementations to change your program's behavior.

5. When you override a method polymorphism ensures that the proper version of the method is called.

6. Ad-hoc polymorphism is another name for overloading.

7. Overloading allows you to define a method name multiple times. Each definition simply differs in the number and types of arguments. Overloading expresses different behavior because you simply call the method. You don't have to do anything to be sure that the correct version of the method gets called.

   Overloading allows you to model a method at the conceptual level of what it does. Overloading's polymorphic nature takes care of the specific arguments.

8. Parametric polymorphism enables you to write truly generic types and methods by deferring type definitions until runtime. This type of polymorphism enables you to write truly natural code because you can program very generic, conceptual types and methods. You write these types and methods from the conceptual view of what they do not what they specifically do it to. For example, if you program a `compare( [T] a, [T] b)` method you think in terms of the higher concept of comparing two objects of type [T] together. Arguments of type [T] would simply need to share a common structure such as < or a `compare()` method. The important point

is that you simply write one method and it can compare many different kinds of objects.

9. Polymorphism will normally incur a cost in efficiency. Some forms and implementations of polymorphism requires checks and lookups at runtime. These checks are costly when compared to statically typed languages.

   Polymorphism tempts the developer to break the inheritance hierarchy. You must never move functionality up a hierarchy to simply increase the opportunities for polymorphic behavior.

   When you treat a subtype as if it were the base type you lose access to any behaviors added by the subtype. So when you create a new subtype, you'll need to make sure that the base type interface is adequate for interacting with your new subtype in methods that work with the base type.

10. Effective inheritance directly impacts inclusion polymorphism. In order to enjoy the pluggability offered by subtype polymorphism, you must have a proper object hierarchy.

    Encapsulation protects an object from getting tied to a specific implementation. Without encapsulation, one object could easily become dependent on the internal implementation of another object. Such a tight coupling makes substitution difficult if not impossible.

Answers to Exercises

1. Imagine a program that writes its status out to the command line while executing. In Java, you could simply use `System.write.println()` to write these messages to the screen. However, what if you wanted these messages to write to a file? What if you wanted these messages sent to an alarm GUI on another computer? Obviously, you would need to alter your code as the requirements change.

   However, what if your requirements call you to support both at the same time? Instead of one or the other, you want to let the user choose which to write to through a command line argument. Without polymorphism, you would need to program cases for each write out type. With polymorphism, however, you can simply declare a class named log that has a write method. Subclasses can specify where the messages are logged. You can add new subtypes to your program at any time. The program will automatically know how to use the new subtypes as long as you program to the log interface. So you can swap in new log behavior at any time.

2. `int i = 2 + 3.0`

   Depending on the definition of +, this statement may be coercive. Here, the statement attempts to add an integer and a real number. It takes the result and places it into an `int` variable. Depending upon the language the compiler may coerce the integer 2 into a real number, perform the arithmetic, and then coerce the result back to an integer.

This statement is interesting because it may also demonstrate an instance of overloading. + may overload to the following operations:

```
+(real,real)
```

```
+(integer,integer)
```

```
+(integer,real)
```

In either case you have ad-hoc polymorphism because instead of one polymorphic method, you either have a number of monomorphic methods or coercion.

3. Overloading:

   Consider `java.util.SimpleTimeZone`. `SimpleTimeZone` defines the following two overloaded methods: `setEndRule` and `setStartRule`. As a result, these methods respond differently depending on the number and types of input.

   Inclusion Polymorphism:

   Consider `java.io.Writer`. The abstract writer class defines a number of methods for writing data. Currently, Java defines a number of `Writer` subclasses: `BufferedWriter`, `CharArrayWriter`, `FilterWriter`, `OutputStreamWriter`, `PipedWriter`, `PrintWriter`, and `StringWriter`. Each subclass defines the behavior for the close, flush, and write (an overloaded method by the way) methods.

   When programming, you should write your objects and methods to act on instances of `Write`. That way, you can swap in the different subclasses depending upon how you want the data to be written out. If you program that way, `Writer` will express a number of different behaviors depending on the underlying implementation that you are really using.

Day 7 Quiz Answers

Answers to Quiz

1. The `PsychiatristObject`'s `observe()` method is an example of method overloading.

2. The `observe()` method nicely illustrates the problem with overloading. Each time that you add a new subtype, you will need to add another overloaded method. As the number of methods increases, you will want to find a way to add a common function to your objects so that you can treat them generically and remove the overridden methods.

3. There are two steps to adding new behavior to a polymorphic hierarchy. First, create the new type. Second, alter your program so that it can create instances of the new type. You shouldn't have to change anything else unless you need to take advantage of some special feature of the new class.

4. The `PsychiatristObject`'s `examine()` method is an example of inclusion polyorphism. It can work on any `MoodyObject` subtype.

5. You can eliminate conditionals by attacking the data that you switch over. If the data is not an object, turn it into an object. If the data is an object, add a method that provides the necessary behavior. Once you do that, ask the object to do something, don't do something to data.

6. Inclusion polymorphism will allow a method to work for the argument type and any subtype. You do not need a different method for each subtype. Only having one method cuts down on the number of methods that you would need otherwise. It also simplifies the addition of new features.

7. In OO you should not ask an object for its data. Instead, you should ask an object to do something to its data.

8. Conditionals force you to break the relationship outlined in #7. Breaking the relationship forces you to muddle responsibility because every user will need to know what the data represents and how to manipulate it.

9. If you find yourself updating a number of conditionals each time you add a new type, the conditional is a problem. If you find yourself writing the same conditional in multiple places (or calling a method that has the conditional), the conditional is a problem.

10. Polymorphism allows you to treat a subtype as if it were the supertype. However, polymorphism allows you to use the behavior of the actual underlying type. Polymorphism makes it seem that the supertype manifests many different behaviors.

Day 8 Quiz and Exercise Answers

Answers to Quiz

1. The UML is the Unified Modeling Language. The UML is an industry standard modeling language.

2. A methodology describes how to design software. A modeling language helps capture that design graphically. A methodology will often contain its own modeling language.

A

3. The lab demonstrates a dependency relationship.

4. You can make two statements about `MoodyObject`. `MoodyObject` has a method named `queryMood()`. `MoodyObject` is also an abstract class. The italicized name indicates that the class is abstract.

5. The `Employee`/`Payroll` relationship from lab 1 is an example of a dependency. `Payroll`'s `payEmployees()` method depends upon the `Employee`'s public interface.

6. Each of these symbols conveys visibility information. + is public, # is protected, and - is private.

7. A `Queue` and its elements is an example of aggregation.

8. The `Deck` has many cards. However, if you destroy the deck you should destroy the cards. The `Deck` is an example of a composition relationship.

9. Simply italicize a class or method name to show that it is abstract.

10. The end goal of modeling is to convey your design. Consequently, you shouldn't concern yourself with using every modeling notation available. Instead, you should use the bare minimum notation that still successfully conveys your message.

11. An association models structural relationships among objects. Aggregation and composition are subtypes of association that model "whole/part" relationships. An aggregation is a structural relationship among peers. Composition is a structural relationship where the part is not independent of the whole. The part cannot exist separately from the whole.

12. Model association when the point of your model is to model the roles between the objects. Use aggregation or composition when you are trying to convey structural design.

Answers to Exercises

1.

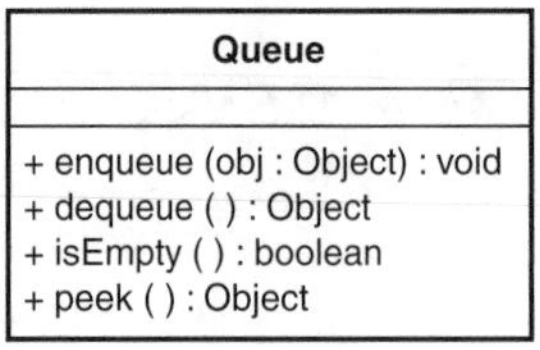

FIGURE A.1

A Queue.

Queue
+ enqueue (obj : Object) : void
+ dequeue ( ) : Object
+ isEmpty ( ) : boolean
+ peek ( ) : Object

2.

FIGURE A.2

A Honeybee/Hive Composition Relationship.

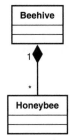

3.

FIGURE A.3

A Bank/BankAccount Aggregation Relationship.

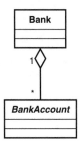

4.

FIGURE A.4

The Shopper/Merchant Association.

A

5.

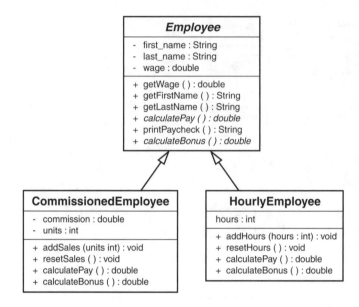

6.

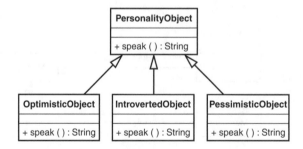

Day 9 Quiz and Exercise Answers

Answers to Quiz

1. A software process lays out the various stages of software development.

2. An iterative process is a process that allows you to continually go back and redo or enhance the product of previous iterations. An iterative process takes an iterative and incremental approach to software development.

   Incremental means that each iteration adds a small increase in functionality. Not so small as to be unnoticeable, but not so large as to be too costly to throw away.

3. At the end of OOA you should have a good understanding of the system's requirements as well as the system's domain vocabulary.

4. The requirements tell you what the users want to do to the system and what kind of responses they expect back.

   The requirements are those features that the system must have to solve a given problem.

5. A use case describes the interaction between the user of the system and the system. The use case describes how the user will use the system from the user's point of view.

6. You must take the following steps to define your use cases:

   1. Identify the actors

   2. Create a preliminary list of use cases

   3. Refine and name the use cases

   4. Define each use case's sequence of events

   5. Model your use cases

7. An actor is anything that interacts with the system.

8. You can ask the following questions to help find actors:

   • Who will primarily use the system?

   • Are there any other systems that will use the system? For example, are there any nonhuman users?

   • Will the system communicate with any other system? For example, is there an existing database that you need to integrate?

   • Does the system respond to nonuser-generated stimulus? For example, does the system need to do something on a certain calendar day each month? A stimulus can come from sources not normally considered when thinking from a purely user point of view.

9. A use case can contain and use another use case or extend another use case. One use case may also be a variant of another use case.

10. A use case variant is a special case of a more general use case.

11. A scenario is a sequence or flow of events between the user and system.

12. You can model your use cases through interaction diagrams and activity diagrams. There are two kinds of interaction diagrams: sequence and collaboration diagrams.

13. Sequence diagrams model the sequence of events over time. A collaboration diagram models the interactions between the actors of a use case. Both types of diagrams are interaction diagrams. However, each takes a different point of view

A

towards the system. Use sequence diagrams when you want to trace events and collaboration diagrams when you want to highlight relationships.

Activity diagrams help you model parallel processes. Use activity diagrams when you want to convey that a process may run in parallel with other processes during a use case scenario.

14. A domain model presents a number of benefits. The domain model can serve as the foundation or skeleton of your object model. You can use this base as a start and build off it.

    Domain models also give you a common vocabulary and understanding of the problem.

15. Use cases help you to understand the system, its requirements, and its uses.

    Use cases can help you plan the iterations of your project.

    Finally, use cases help you to define your domain model.

Answers to Exercises

1. Some other use cases:

    - Remove Item: A user can remove an item from the cart

    - Delete User: An administrator can remove inactive accounts

    - Reward User: The system can reward frequent customers by offering on-the-fly discounts

2. The user selects an item from the shopping cart. The user removes the selected item from the shopping cart.

    - Remove Item

        1. Guest user selects an item from the shopping cart

        2. Guest user asks the cart to remove the item

    - Preconditions

        - The cart contains an item to remove

    - Post Conditions

        - The item no longer appears in the cart

    - Alternative: Operation Canceled

    The user may opt to cancel the transaction after Step 1

3. The following two use cases are variants of the Search Product Catalog use case:

    - Guest users can search the product catalog.

    - Guest users can search for a specific item.

The following two use cases are variants of the Sign Up For Correspondence use case:

- Registered users can sign up for notifications.
- Registered users can sign up for various mailing lists.

4. There are many other domain objects. Here are a few: Administrator, Highlighted Product List, and Wish List.

Day 10 Quiz and Exercise Answers

Answers to Quiz

1. There are three benefits to a formal design. A formal design helps you figure out what objects will appear in your program, and how they will interact or fit together.

   A design helps you foresee many of the design issues that would have come up during implementation. It is much easier to fix a design before there is code.

   Finally, a design helps ensure that all of the developers are on the same page; otherwise, you run the risk of each developer developing incompatible pieces.

2. OOD is the process of constructing a solution's object model. Said another way, OOD is the process of decomposing a solution into a number of constituent objects.

3. The *object model* is the design of the objects that appear in a problem's solution. The final *object model* may contain many objects not found in the domain. The *object model* will describe the various object's responsibilities, relationships, and structure.

4. It's simply not possible to foresee every design decision before you make it, and it's not always worth the time. Some design can be left until construction. Also, you don't want to get caught up trying to create the perfect design. You need to start coding some day.

5. The significant pieces are those aspects of the system that completely alter the structure or behavior of the system. These are the pieces that really matter when you code the solution. A change to an architectural important piece will change the structure of the solution.

6. The five basic steps to OOD are

   1. Generate an initial list of objects.

   2. Refine your objects' responsibilities through CRC cards.

   3. Develop the points of interaction.

A

    4. Detail the relationships between objects.

    5. Build your model.

7. Start with the domain to generate your initial list of objects. Each domain object and actor should become a class in your object model.

Third-party systems, hardware interfaces, reports, displays, and devices should also become classes.

8. A complete design will capture each object's responsibilities as well as the object's structure and relationships. A design will show how everything fits together.

9. CRC cards help you to identify class responsibilities and collaborations.

10. *Collaboration* is the relationship of delegation between two objects. You can think of a collaboration as a client/server relationship between two objects.

11. Practically, responsibilities will translate into methods. Relationships will translate into structure; however, an overall understanding of responsibility will help you effectively divide responsibility among the objects. You need to avoid having a small set of very large objects. Through design you'll be sure to spread responsibilities out.

12. A CRC cards is a 4x6 index card that helps you to discover an object's responsibilities and collaborations by exploring use cases.

13. You are intentionally limited by the size of a CRC card. If you find that you are running out of room, chances are good that your class is doing too much.

14. You should use CRC cards during the initial stages of development, especially when you are still new to OO development. CRC cards lend themselves to small projects, or a small section of a larger project.

You should only use CRC cards to flesh out responsibilities and collaborations. Don't try to describe complex relationships through CRC cards.

15. CRC cards do not work well for large projects or development groups. A large number of classes can overwhelm a CRC session. To many developers can also fracture a CRC session.

16. A *point of interaction* is any place where one object uses another.

17. At a point of interaction, you should consider data transformation, future change, interfaces, and the use of agents.

18. An *agent* is an object that mediates between two or more objects to accomplish some goal.

19. You will define the dependencies, associations, and generalizations. Detailing these relationships is an important step because it defines how the objects fit together. It also defines the internal structure of the various objects.

20. You might create class diagrams, activity diagrams, and interaction diagrams to model you design. The UML also defines object diagrams and state diagrams.

Answers to Exercises

1. The ShoppingCart instances will have the overall responsibility of holding onto items. Specifically, a ShoppingCart can add an item to itself, remove an item from itself, and allow an outside object to select an item without removing it.

Day 11 Quiz and Exercise Answers

Answers to Quiz

1. An adapter class transforms an object's interface to one expected by your program. An adapter contains an object and delegates messages from the new interface to the contained object's interface.

2. The Iterator pattern describes a mechanism for looping over elements in a collection.

3. You would use the Iterator pattern to contain traversal logic in one place, provide a standard way for traversing collections, and to hide the implementation of the collection from the user.

4. The Adapter pattern describes a mechanism that allows you to transform an objects interface.

5. You would use the Adapter pattern whenever you need to use an object that has an incompatible interface. You can also proactively use wrappers to isolate your code from API changes.

6. The Proxy pattern transparently brokers access to an object. Proxies add indirection to object use.

7. You would use the Proxy pattern any time that you would like to broker access to an object in a way that a simple reference does not allow. Common examples include remote resources, optimizations, and for general object housekeeping such as reference counting or usage statistics collecting.

8. In this situation you can use the Adapter pattern to create an interface that is independent of the one provided by Sun, IBM, or Apache. By creating your own interface, you can remain independent of each vendor's slightly different API. By wrapping the library you are free to switch the library at any time whether to upgrade to a new version or to switch vendors since you control the adapter's interface.

9. In this situation you can use the Proxy pattern to hide the identity of the datastore object that your objects talk to. Depending upon the client's location, you can

A

instantiate a networked proxy or a local proxy. Either way, the rest of the program will not know the difference, so all your objects can use one proxy interface without having to worry about the underlying implementation.

10. The Proxy pattern does not change an interface in that it doesn't take anything away from it. A proxy is free to add additional methods and attributes to the interface, however.

Answers to Exercises

1.

LISTING 11.13   ShoppingCart.java

```java
public class ShoppingCart {

    java.util.LinkedList items = new java.util.LinkedList();

    /**
     * adds an item to the cart
     * @param item the item to add
     */
    public void addItem( Item item ) {
        items.add( item );
    }

    /**
     * removes the given item from the cart
     * @param item the item to remove
     */
    public void removeItem( Item item ) {
        items.remove( item );
    }

    /**
     * @return int the number of items in the cart
     */
    public int getNumberItems() {
        return items.size();
    }

    /**
     * retrieves the indexed item
     * @param index the item's index
     * @return Item the item at index
     */
    public Item getItem( int index ) {
        return (Item) items.get( index );
    }
```

LISTING 11.13   continued

```
        public Iterator iterator() {
            // ArrayList has an iterator() method that returns an iterator
            // however, for demonstration purposes it helps to see a simple iterator
            return new CartIterator( items );
        }
    }
```

LISTING 11.14   CartIterator.java.

```
    public class CartIterator implements Iterator {

        private Object [] items;
        private int index;

        public CartIterator( java.util.LinkedList items ) {
            this.items = items.toArray();
        }

        public boolean isDone() {
            if( index >= items.length ) {
                return true;
            }
            return false;
        }

        public Object currentItem() {
            if( !isDone() ) {
                return items[index];
            }
            return null;
        }

        public void next() {
            index++;
        }

        public void first() {
            index = 0;
        }

    }
```

A

2. By making the adapter mutable, you can use the same wrapper to wrap many different objects, and you don't need to instantiate a wrapper for each object that
   needs to be wrapped. Wrapper reuse makes better use of memory, and frees your
   program from having to pay the price of instantiating many wrappers.

LISTING 11.15 MutableAdapter.java

```
public class MutableAdapter extends MoodyObject {

    private Pet pet;

    public MutableAdapter( Pet pet ) {
        setPet( pet );
    }

    protected String getMood() {
        // only implementing because required to by
        // MoodyObject, since also override queryMood
        // we don't really need it
        return pet.speak();
    }

    public void queryMood() {
        System.out.println( getMood() );
    }

    public void setPet( Pet pet ) {
        this.pet = pet;
    }
}
```

Day 12 Quiz and Exercise Answers

Answers to Quiz

1. A wrapper class transforms an object's interface to one expected by your program. A wrapper contains an object and delegates messages from the new interface to the contained object's interface.

2. The Abstract Factory pattern provides a mechanism that instantiates specific descendant class instances without revealing which descendant is actually created. This allows you to transparently plug in different descendants into your system.

3. You use the Abstract Factory pattern to hide the details of instantiation, to hide which class of object gets instantiated, and when you want a set of objects used together.

4. The Singleton pattern ensures that an object is instantiated only once.

5. You use the Singleton pattern when you want an object to be instantiated only once.

6. Using primitive constants is not an OO approach to programming, because you have to apply an external meaning to the constant. You saw how much trouble the breakdown of responsibility could cause!

The Typesafe Enum pattern solves this problem by turning the constant into a higher-level object. By using a higher-level object, you can better encapsulate responsibility within the constant object.

7. You should use the Typesafe Enum pattern whenever you find yourself declaring public constants that should be objects in their own right.

8. No, patterns do not ensure a perfect design because you could end up using a pattern incorrectly. Also, correctly using a pattern does not mean that the rest of your design is valid. Many valid designs might not even contain a pattern.

Answers to Exercises

1.

LISTING 12.19   Bank.java

```java
public class Bank {

    private java.util.Hashtable accounts = new java.util.Hashtable();

    private static Bank instance;

    protected Bank() {}

    public static Bank getInstance() {
        if( instance == null ) {
            instance = new Bank();
        }
        return instance;
    }

    public void addAccount( String name, BankAccount account ) {
        accounts.put( name, account );
    }

    public double totalHoldings() {
        double total = 0.0;

        java.util.Enumeration enum = accounts.elements();
        while( enum.hasMoreElements() ) {
            BankAccount account = (BankAccount) enum.nextElement();
            total += account.getBalance();
        }
        return total;
    }

    public int totalAccounts() {
        return accounts.size();
    }
```

A

LISTING 12.19   continued

```java
public void deposit( String name, double ammount ) {
    BankAccount account = retrieveAccount( name );
    if( account != null ) {
        account.depositFunds( ammount );
    }
}

public double balance( String name ) {
    BankAccount account = retrieveAccount( name );
    if( account != null ) {
        return account.getBalance();
    }
    return 0.0;
}

private BankAccount retrieveAccount( String name ) {
    return (BankAccount) accounts.get( name );
}
```

2.

LISTING 12.20   Level.java

```java
public final class Level {

    public final static Level NOISE   = new Level( 0, "NOISE" );
    public final static Level INFO    = new Level( 1, "INFO" );
    public final static Level WARNING = new Level( 2, "WARNING" );
    public final static Level ERROR   = new Level( 3, "ERROR" );

    private int    level;
    private String name;

    private Level( int level, String name ) {
        this.level = level;
        this.name  = name;
    }

    public int getLevel() {
        return level;
    }

    public String getName() {
        return name;
    }
}
```

LISTING 12.21 Error.java

```
public class Error {

    private Level level;

    public Error( Level level ) {
        this.level = level;
    }

    public Level getLevel() {
        return level;
    }

    public String toString() {
        return level.getName();
    }
}
```

3. The solution consists of an abstract bank account factory (written as an interface; however, it can be an abstract class as well) and a concrete bank account factory. The factory has a method for creating each type of bank account.

This factory hides the details of instantiation, not necessarily the object's subtype.

LISTING 12.22 AbstractAccountFactory.java

```
public interface AbstractAccountFactory {

    public CheckingAccount createCheckingAccount( double initDeposit, int trans,
double fee );

    public OverdraftAccount createOverdraftAccount( double initDeposit, double
rate );

    public RewardsAccount createRewardsAccount( double initDeposit, double
interest, double min );

    public SavingsAccount createSavingsAccount( double initBalance, double
interestRate );

    public TimedMaturityAccount createTimedMaturityAccount( double initBalance,
double interestRate, double feeRate );

}
```

A

LISTING 12.23   ConcreteAccountFactory.java

```java
public class ConcreteAccountFactory implements AbstractAccountFactory {

    public CheckingAccount createCheckingAccount( double initDeposit, int trans,
double fee ) {
        return new CheckingAccount( initDeposit, trans, fee );
    }

    public OverdraftAccount createOverdraftAccount( double initDeposit, double
rate ) {
        return new OverdraftAccount( initDeposit, rate );
    }

    public RewardsAccount createRewardsAccount( double initDeposit, double
interest, double min ) {
        return new RewardsAccount( initDeposit, interest, min );
    }

    public SavingsAccount createSavingsAccount( double initBalance, double
interestRate ) {
        return new SavingsAccount( initBalance, interestRate );
    }

    public TimedMaturityAccount createTimedMaturityAccount( double initBalance,
double interestRate, double feeRate ) {
        return new TimedMaturityAccount( initBalance, interestRate, feeRate );
    }

}
```

Day 13 Quiz and Exercise Answers

Answers to Quiz

1. The analysis, design, and implementation of a UI are not any different from the rest of the system. The UI must have equal consideration during all phases of development. If anything else, you must be sure to not neglect UI considerations.

2. You should decouple UIs so that the system and the UI do not become intertwined. It is difficult to make changes to the UI when intertwined with the core functionality of the system.

   It is also impossible to share the system with other UIs or UI types when the UI and system are intertwined.

3. The three components are the model, the view, and the controller.

4. The PAC pattern and the Document/View Model are two alternatives to the MVC pattern.

5. The model is the layer of the MVC triad that manages the core behavior and state of the system.. The controller uses the model to instigate system behavior. The view uses the model to retrieve state information for display.

   The model also provides a change notification mechanism. The view and controller can use this mechanism to stay abreast of state changes in the model.

6. The view is the MVC triad member responsible for displaying the model to the user.

7. The controller is responsible for interpreting events generated by the user. The controller instigates behavior in the model or in the view in response to these events.

8. A system may have many models. A model may have many different views. A view may have one controller, and a controller may control only one view.

9. Inefficiencies may be found in the model of in the view and controller. A model must avoid unnecessary state change notifications. Views and controllers should cache data whenever possible.

10. The MVC pattern assumes a stable model and a changing presentation.

11. A very detailed summary of the history and motivation behind the MVC pattern is "Applications Programming in Smalltalk-80(TM): How to use Model-View-Controller (MVC)" by Steve Burbeck, Ph.D. You can find a copy at

    `http://st-www.cs.uiuc.edu/users/smarch/st-docs/mvc.html`

    So, what's the point of this question? Well, the answer gives you an important perspective into the motivation behind the MVC pattern. By reading the history, you will also note that the MVC pattern was developed initially as part of Smalltalk. Its use is now found in almost any language. This drives an important point home: Patterns are not language usages—they are patterns that work in any language with the requisite features.

    MVC is not about Java or Smalltalk. It's about a design that transcends the implementation language.

Answers to Exercises

1. Listing 13.11 presents the new `Employee` class.

LISTING 13.11 `Employee.java`

```
import java.util.ArrayList;
import java.util.Iterator;
```

LISTING 13.11   continued

```java
public abstract class Employee {

    private String first_name;
    private String last_name;
    private double wage;
    private ArrayList listeners = new ArrayList();

    public Employee(String first_name,String last_name,double wage) {
        this.first_name = first_name;
        this.last_name  = last_name;
        this.wage = wage;
    }

    public double getWage() {
        return wage;
    }

    public void setWage( double wage ) {
        this.wage = wage;
        updateObservers();
    }

    public String getFirstName() {
        return first_name;
    }

    public String getLastName() {
        return last_name;
    }

    public abstract double calculatePay();

    public abstract double calculateBonus();

    public void printPaycheck() {
        String full_name = last_name + ", " + first_name;
        System.out.println( "Pay: " + full_name + " $" + calculatePay() );
    }

    public void register( Observer o ) {
        listeners.add( o );
        o.update();
    }

    public void deregister( Observer o ) {
        listeners.remove( o );
    }

    private void updateObservers() {
        Iterator i = listeners.iterator();
```

LISTING 13.11 continued

```
        while( i.hasNext() ) {
            Observer o = (Observer) i.next();
            o.update();
        }
    }

}
```

2. Listing 13.12 presents the new implementation of `BankAccountController`.

LISTING 13.12 `BankAccountController.java`

```
public class BankAccountController implements BankActivityListener {

    private BankAccountView  view;
    private BankAccountModel model;

    public BankAccountController( BankAccountView view, BankAccountModel model )
    {
        this.view  = view;
        this.model = model;
    }

    public void withdrawPerformed( BankActivityEvent e ) {
        double amount = e.getAmount();
        model.withdrawFunds( amount );
    }

    public void depositPerformed( BankActivityEvent e ) {
        double amount = e.getAmount();
        model.depositFunds( amount );
    }

}
```

This version of `BankAccountController` is much easier to read than the original; however, the view is now much more complex.

Day 14 Quiz and Exercise Answers

Answers to Quiz

1. Bugs can arise from typos, errors in logic, or silly mistakes made while coding. Bugs can also result from incorrect interaction among objects or from flaws in the design or analysis.

A

2. A test case is the building block of testing. Each form of testing is made up of test cases, and each test case tests an aspect of the system.

3. You can base your test cases on black box or white box testing.

4. White box tests are based on the structure of the underlying source code. White box tests are designed to achieve 100% coverage of the tested code.

    Black box tests are based on the specification. Black box tests check to make sure that the system behaves as expected.

5. The four forms of testing are unit test, integration test, system test, and regression test.

6. A unit test is the lowest level testing device. A unit test sends an object a message and verifies that it receives the expected result. A unit test should only check one feature at a time.

7. Integration testing confirms that the objects interact properly. System testing verifies that the system behaves as defined in the use cases, and that it can handle unforeseen use gracefully.

8. You should not put off testing until the end. Testing as you develop helps you find bugs right away. If you put off testing until the end, there will be more bugs and they will be harder to trace and fix.

    Testing as you develop also makes it easier to change your code and may actually improve its design.

9. Manual or visual validation is error prone. You should avoid it as much as possible. Instead, you should rely on an automatic mechanism for validating the unit tests.

10. A framework defines a reusable domain model. You can use the classes in this model as the basis for your specific application.

11. A mock object is a simplistic substitute for a real object that helps you unit test your objects.

12. Mock objects allow you to unit test your classes in isolation. They also open up testing possibilities that would otherwise be difficult or impossible to do.

13. A bug arises from a flaw or defect in the system. An error condition, on the other hand, is not a bug but rather a condition for which your system should be prepared and should handle gracefully.

14. When writing your code, you can ensure quality through unit tests, the proper handling of exceptions, and through proper documentation.

Answers to Exercises

1. `Cookstour` will give you insight into the design and the ideas behind JUnit.

2. Listing 14.12 presents one possible unit test.

LISTING 14.12 `HourlyEmployeeTest.java`

```java
import junit.framework.TestCase;
import junit.framework.Assert;

public class HourlyEmployeeTest extends TestCase {

    private HourlyEmployee emp;

    private static final String FIRST_NAME = "FNAME";
    private static final String LAST_NAME  = "LNAME";
    private static final double WAGE        = 500.00;

    protected void setUp() {
        emp = new HourlyEmployee( FIRST_NAME, LAST_NAME, WAGE );
    }

    public void test_calculatePay() {
        emp.addHours( 10 );

        double expected = WAGE * 10;
        assertTrue( "incorrect pay calculation", emp.calculatePay() == expected
);
    }

    public HourlyEmployeeTest( String name ) {
        super( name );
    }
}
```

Day 15 Quiz and Exercise Answers

Answers to Quiz

1. The `PlayerListener` is an example of the observable pattern.

   The `Console` is a singleton. It implements the singleton pattern.

   `Rank` and `Suit` implement the type safe enumeration pattern.

A

2. The BlackjackDealer treats the HumanPlayer polymorphically as a Player. You could create non-human players and the BlackjackDealer would know how to play Blackjack with them.

3. The Player/BlackjackDealer/HumanPlayer is an example of an inheritance hierarchy.

4. The Deck completely encapsulates the Cards that it holds. It does not provide any getters or setters. Instead, the Deck adds its Cards to Deckpiles.

5. The BlackjackDealer and HumanPlayer act polymorphically by providing their own customized versions of the hit() method. When the play() method calls hit() the play() method's behavior will vary based on the underlying implementation of hit().

Answers to Exercises

1. N/A

2. N/A

Day 16 Quiz and Exercise Answers

Answers to Quiz

1. Conditionals are dangerous when they remove responsibility from an object and put it somewhere else. Behavior belongs in the object, not distributed throughout the program. Distributed logic forces you to repeat logic throughout your program instead of having it in just one place.

   Conditionals are also dangerous because they make it harder to test an object and cover all combinations of paths through the object.

2. Earlier you saw that you could use polymorphism to remove conditionals.

   Today, you saw that you could use a combination of polymorphism and state to be able to remove conditionals. State is an excellent way to implement rules.

3. The previous version of Hand required you to compare the Hand's Cards yourself to be able to check if two Hands are equal or whether one Hand is greater than another. Hand now does this check for you without compromising its internal state.

   The Hand does one other thing to encapsulate itself. The Hand now informs listeners of state changes. Because the Hand readily pushes its state information with listeners, there is no reason for an interested object to query the Hand's state to learn the state of the Hand.

4. The `Hand` and `HandListener` implement the observer pattern.

5. N/A

Answers to Exercises

1. N/A

2. Key to this problem is realizing that the methods all take the same actions up until the point where a call is made on the `PlayerListener`. The solution is to wrap that call in an object.

   Consider the following `notifyListener()` method:

   ```
   protected void notifyListeners( NotifyHelper helper ) {
       Iterator i = listeners.iterator();
       while( i.hasNext() ) {
           PlayerListener pl = (PlayerListener) i.next();
           helper.notifyListener( pl );
       }
   }
   ```

   Note that this method is exactly the same as the old `notifyChanged()` or `notifyBusted()` except for one difference. Instead of calling a method on the `PlayerListener` directly, the `notifyListeners()` method delegates the call to a `NotifyHelper` object.

   Listing 16.17 presents the `NotifyHelper`.

LISTING 16.17   The Customized Dealer Waiting State

```
protected interface NotifyHelper {
    public void notifyListener( PlayerListener pl );
}
```

   The `NotifyHelper` interface defines one method: `notifyListener()`. Implementers will decide which method to call on `PlayerListener`.

   In all, you will need to define seven `NotifyHelper` implementers, one implementation for each method in the `PlayerListener` interface. Listing 16.18 presents those seven implementations.

LISTING 16.18   The `NotifyHelper` Implementations.

```
protected class NotifyBusted implements NotifyHelper {
    public void notifyListener( PlayerListener pl ) { pl.playerBusted(
Player.this ); }
```

A

LISTING 16.18   continued

```
}
protected class NotifyBlackjack implements NotifyHelper {
    public void notifyListener( PlayerListener pl ) { pl.playerBlackjack(
Player.this ); }
}
protected class NotifyWon implements NotifyHelper {
    public void notifyListener( PlayerListener pl ) { pl.playerWon( Player.this
); }
}
protected class NotifyLost implements NotifyHelper {
    public void notifyListener( PlayerListener pl ) { pl.playerLost( Player.this
); }
}
protected class NotifyChanged implements NotifyHelper {
    public void notifyListener( PlayerListener pl ) { pl.playerChanged(
Player.this ); }
}
protected class NotifyStanding implements NotifyHelper {
    public void notifyListener( PlayerListener pl ) { pl.playerStanding(
Player.this ); }
}
protected class NotifyStandoff implements NotifyHelper {
    public void notifyListener( PlayerListener pl ) { pl.playerStandoff(
Player.this ); }
}
```

Now, instead of calling `notifyChanged()` or `notifyBlackjack()` you would call `notifyListeners( new NotifyChanged() )` or `notifyListeners( new NotifyBlackjack() )`.

Whether or not you think that this is a good solution is a matter of personal taste. It does remove the redundant `notifyXXX` methods, however.

Day 17 Quiz and Exercise Answers

Answers to Quiz

1. Making a protected method abstract is a good way to establish an inheritance protocol.

2. After today's analysis and design, a new `Player` hierarchy was discovered. As requirements presented themselves through the use cases, the need for a new inheritance hierarchy presented itself.

3. Programming by speculation rarely works. The hierarchies that you'll need to properly model an abstract domain will present themselves after you've worked

with a domain for a while. If you try to abstract a domain without ever working with that domain, you're mainly guessing at a solution.

4. By refactoring the hierarchy you were left with a model that more closely models the Blackjack game. The code is also easier to understand. Cramming extra responsibility into the base `Player` class would have resulted in code that is difficult to understand.

Answers to Exercises

1. N/A

2. Doubling Down is simply another `BettingPlayer` state. You know that it needs to be a separate state because the `Player` must react differently to the `handPlayable` event. Instead of staying in the Playing state, the `Player` must transition to the Standing state.

Figure A.7 illustrates the new state diagram for a `BettingPlayer` that can double down.

FIGURE A.7

The updated `BettingPlayer` *state diagram.*

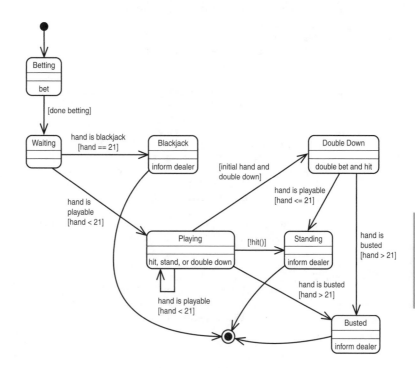

You also need to alter the Playing state so that it can transition into the DoublingDown state. Listing 17.6 presents the new BettingPlayer states.

LISTING 17.6   DoublingDown and Playing

```
private class DoublingDown implements PlayerState {
    public void handChanged() {
        notifyChanged();
    }
    public void handPlayable() {
        setCurrentState( getStandingState() );
        notifyStanding();
    }
    public void handBlackjack() {
        // not possible in doubling down state
    }
    public void handBusted() {
        setCurrentState( getBustedState() );
        notifyBusted();
    }
    public void execute( Dealer dealer ) {
        bank.doubleDown();
        dealer.hit( BettingPlayer.this );
        getCurrentState().execute( dealer );
    }
}
private class BetterPlaying implements PlayerState {
    public void handChanged() {
        notifyChanged();
    }
    public void handPlayable() {
        // can ignore in playing state
    }
    public void handBlackjack() {
        // not possible in playing state
    }
    public void handBusted() {
        setCurrentState( getBustedState() );
        notifyBusted();
    }
    public void execute( Dealer dealer ) {
        if( getHand().canDoubleDown() && doubleDown() ) {
            setCurrentState( getDoublingDownState() );
            getCurrentState().execute( dealer );
            return;
        }
        if( hit() ) {
            dealer.hit( BettingPlayer.this );
        } else {
            setCurrentState( getStandingState() );
```

LISTING 17.6 continued

```
            notifyStanding();
        }
        getCurrentState().execute( dealer );
        // transition
    }
}
```

You'll also need to update HumanPlayer so that it offers a doubling down option.
Listing 17.7 presents the updated HumanPlayer.

LISTING 17.7 HumanPlayer.java

```java
public class HumanPlayer extends BettingPlayer {

    private final static String HIT   = "H";
    private final static String STAND = "S";
    private final static String PLAY_MSG = "[H]it or [S]tay";
    private final static String BET_MSG = "Place Bet: [10] [50] or [100]";
    private final static String DD_MSG  = "Double Down? [Y]es [N]o";
    private final static String BET_10  = "10";
    private final static String BET_50  = "50";
    private final static String BET_100 = "100";
    private final static String NO  = "N";
    private final static String YES = "Y";
    private final static String DEFAULT = "invalid";

    public HumanPlayer( String name, Hand hand, Bank bank ) {
        super( name, hand, bank );
    }

    protected boolean hit() {
        while( true ) {
            Console.INSTANCE.printMessage( PLAY_MSG );
            String response = Console.INSTANCE.readInput( DEFAULT );
            if( response.equalsIgnoreCase( HIT ) ) {
                return true;
            } else if( response.equalsIgnoreCase( STAND ) ) {
                return false;
            }
            // if we get here loop until we get meaningful input
        }
    }

    protected boolean doubleDown() {
        while( true ) {
            Console.INSTANCE.printMessage( DD_MSG );
            String response = Console.INSTANCE.readInput( DEFAULT );
            if( response.equalsIgnoreCase( NO ) ) {
```

A

LISTING 17.7   continued

```
                return false;
            } else if( response.equalsIgnoreCase( YES ) ) {
                return true;
            }
            // if we get here loop until we get meaningful input
        }
    }

    protected void bet() {
        while( true ) {
            Console.INSTANCE.printMessage( BET_MSG );
            String response = Console.INSTANCE.readInput( DEFAULT );
            if( response.equals( BET_10 ) ) {
                getBank().place10Bet();
                return;
            }
            if( response.equals( BET_50 ) ) {
                getBank().place50Bet();
                return;

            }
            if( response.equals( BET_100 ) ) {
                getBank().place100Bet();
                return;
            }
            // if we get here loop until we get meaningful input
        }
    }

}
```

Day 18 Quiz and Exercise Answers

Answers to Quiz

1. To introduce a Vcard, you can simply subclass Card. To get it into the game, you can subclass Deck and then override buildCards so that the subclass will create VCards instead of Cards.

2. Originally the Deck's buildCards method was private. When we found that a subclass needed to override the behavior of buildCards we made it protected.

Answers to Exercises

1. N/A

2. The initial design and implementation that you did for exercise 2 from Chapter 17 is still valid. Doubling down is just another state in BettingPlayer. You should begin writing the code for this exercise by adding the new DoublingDown state to BettingPlayer. You will also need to make the same changes that you made in Chapter 17 to the Bank and Hand classes. When you make those changes you'll need to update the GUIPlayer as well as the OptionView and OptionViewController.

Before going into the changes required to the view and controller classes, we'll review the changes required to BettingPlayer, Hand, and Bank.

Listing 18.13 highlights the changes that were made to the Hand class.

LISTING 18.13   Highlights of the Changes Made to Hand

```
public boolean canDoubleDown() {
    return ( cards.size() == 2 );
}
```

The new canDoubleDown method allows the BettingPlayer to check the Hand to see if the player is allowed to double down.

You also need to add a new doubleDown method to the Bank class. Listing 18.14 presents that new method.

LISTING 18.14   The New doubleDown Method

```
public void doubleDown() {
    placeBet( bet );
    bet = bet * 2;
}
```

The doubleDown method doubles the current bet.

To be able to add doubling down, you need to add a new state to the BettingPlayer. You know that you need a new state because the BettingPlayer has to treat the handPlayable event specially when doubling down. Normally a handPlayable event means that the player can hit again if he so chooses. When doubling down, the player must stand immediately after the double down (if the player does not bust). Listing 18.15 presents the new DoubleDown state.

A

LISTING 18.15   The New `DoubleDown` State

```
private class DoublingDown implements PlayerState {
    public void handChanged() {
        notifyChanged();
    }
    public void handPlayable() {
        setCurrentState( getStandingState() );
        notifyStanding();
    }
    public void handBlackjack() {
        // not possible in doubling down state
    }
    public void handBusted() {
        setCurrentState( getBustedState() );
        notifyBusted();
    }
    public void execute( Dealer dealer ) {
        bank.doubleDown();
        dealer.hit( BettingPlayer.this );
        getCurrentState().execute( dealer );
    }
}
```

When executed this new state tells the `Bank` to double the bet, asks the dealer to hit the player, and then transitions to the next state. The next state will either be standing or busted, depending on which event gets sent to the state by the `Hand`.

To get to the DoublingDown state, you'll need to make some changes to the Playing state. Listing 18.16 presents the new `BetterPlaying` state.

LISTING 18.16   The New `BetterPlaying` State

```
private class BetterPlaying implements PlayerState {
    public void handChanged() {
        notifyChanged();
    }
    public void handPlayable() {
        // can ignore in playing state
    }
    public void handBlackjack() {
        // not possible in playing state
    }
    public void handBusted() {
        setCurrentState( getBustedState() );
        notifyBusted();
    }
    public void execute( Dealer dealer ) {
        if( getHand().canDoubleDown() && doubleDown() ) {
```

LISTING 18.16   continued

```
                setCurrentState( getDoublingDownState() );
                getCurrentState().execute( dealer );
                return;
        }
        if( hit() ) {
            dealer.hit( BettingPlayer.this );
        } else {
            setCurrentState( getStandingState() );
            notifyStanding();
        }
        getCurrentState().execute( dealer );
        // transition
    }
}
```

When executed the BetterPlaying state first checks to see if the player can double down. If so, the state calls the BettingPlayer's doubleDown method (you'll need to add an abstract doubleDown method to the BettingPlayer). If the method indicates that the player would like to double down, the BetterPlaying state sets the current state to DoublingDown and transitions to it.

If the player does not want to double down, the state continues and plays normally. Please see the source for all changes. There were a few other minor changes, such as the addition of a getDoubleDownState method to the BettingPlayer. That effectively adds doubling down to the system.

You now need to update the GUIPlayer and the OptionView and OptionViewController.

The good news is that you do not need to make any changes to the GUIPlayer's states. These states shouldn't do anything because they have to wait until the human player clicks a button. You do need to implement the doubleDown method. Listing 18.17 presents the method.

A

LISTING 18.17   The doubleDown Method

```
protected boolean doubleDown() {
    setCurrentState( getDoublingDownState() );
    getCurrentState().execute( dealer );
    return true;
}
```

The GUI button can call this method if the user decides to double down. The method sets the current state to double down and then transitions to it. The state handles the rest.

The remaining changes all need to go into the `OptionView` and `OptionViewController`. Mainly you need to add a doubling down button to the view and make sure that it is enabled, by the controller, right after the bet and disabled as soon as the player hits it, the stand, or the hit button.

Don't worry too much if you do not fully understand the GUI code. What is important is that you understand how doubling down is added to the system and the basic ideas behind the view and controller.

Day 19 Quiz and Exercise Answers

Answers to Quiz

1. The three layers are the presentation, abstraction, and control.

2. The presentation is responsible for displaying the abstraction as well as for responding to user interaction.

   The abstraction is akin to the model in the MVC. The abstraction represents the core system.

   The control is responsible for taking the various presentations and combining them into a view.

3. You can use inheritance to subclass each of the system classes that will require a presentation. That way, you do not graft a presentation class directly onto the system class. Instead, you can add the presentation class to the subclass.

   By using inheritance in this way, you can provide multiple views of the same system. Each time you need a different view you simply subclass the classes that you need to display and have them create a new presentation. When you need to put all of the classes together as an app, just be sure to instantiate the correct subclasses.

4. It is best to use the PAC on a stable system with well-defined interface requirements. Sometimes the inheritance approach can fail for more complicated designs. When inheritance fails you'll have to graft the presentation directly into the system class. Such an eventuality makes servicing many different views difficult.

5. You were able to maintain two UIs because you left the observer framework intact. Nothing forces you to remove the framework just because you use PAC. In fact, both the `BettingView` and `DealerView` use the `PlayerListener` mechanism to stay abreast of changes to the player and dealer.

6. The factory pattern was used to make sure that the proper class instances were used together. In particular, you must be careful to use a `VDeck` whenever you use the classes that create a presentation.

Answers to Exercises

1. N/A

2. The initial design and implementation that you did for exercise 2 from Chapter 17 is still valid. Doubling down is just another state in BettingPlayer. You should begin writing the code for this exercise by adding the new DoublingDown state to BettingPlayer. You will also need to make the same changes that you made in Chapter 17 to the Bank and Hand classes. When you make those changes you'll need to update the GUIPlayer and its presentation class.

   Before going into the changes required to the GUI classes, we'll review the changes required to BettingPlayer, Hand, and Bank.

   Listing 19.8 highlights the changes that were made to the Hand class.

LISTING 19.8   Highlights of the Changes Made to the Hand

```
public boolean canDoubleDown() {
    return ( cards.size() == 2 );
}
```

The new canDoubleDown method allows the BettingPlayer to check the Hand to see if the player is allowed to double down.

You also need to add a new doubleDown method to the Bank class. Listing 19.9 presents that new method.

LISTING 19.9   The new doubleDown method

```
public void doubleDown() {
    placeBet( bet );
    bet = bet * 2;
}
```

The doubleDown method doubles the current bet.

To add doubling down, you need to add a new state to the BettingPlayer. You know that you need a new state because the BettingPlayer has to treat the handPlayable event in a special manner when doubling down. Normally a handPlayable event means that the player can hit again if he so chooses. When doubling down, the player must stand immediately after the double down (if the player does not bust). Listing 19.10 presents the new DoubleDown state.

A

LISTING **19.10**   The New DoubleDown State

```
private class DoublingDown implements PlayerState {
    public void handChanged() {
        notifyChanged();
    }
    public void handPlayable() {
        setCurrentState( getStandingState() );
        notifyStanding();
    }
    public void handBlackjack() {
        // not possible in doubling down state
    }
    public void handBusted() {
        setCurrentState( getBustedState() );
        notifyBusted();
    }
    public void execute( Dealer dealer ) {
        bank.doubleDown();
        dealer.hit( BettingPlayer.this );
        getCurrentState().execute( dealer );
    }
}
```

When executed, this new state tells the Bank to double the bet, asks the dealer to hit the player, and then transitions to the next state. The next state will either be standing or busted, depending on which event gets sent to the state by the Hand.

To get to the DoublingDown state, you'll need to make some changes to the Playing state. Listing 19.11 presents the new BetterPlaying state.

LISTING **19.11**   The new Playing state

```
private class BetterPlaying implements PlayerState {
    public void handChanged() {
        notifyChanged();
    }
    public void handPlayable() {
        // can ignore in playing state
    }
    public void handBlackjack() {
        // not possible in playing state
    }
    public void handBusted() {
        setCurrentState( getBustedState() );
        notifyBusted();
    }
    public void execute( Dealer dealer ) {
```

LISTING 19.11 continued

```
            if( getHand().canDoubleDown() && doubleDown() ) {
                setCurrentState( getDoublingDownState() );
                getCurrentState().execute( dealer );
                return;
            }
            if( hit() ) {
                dealer.hit( BettingPlayer.this );
            } else {
                setCurrentState( getStandingState() );
                notifyStanding();
            }
            getCurrentState().execute( dealer );
            // transition
        }
    }
```

When executed, the BetterPlaying state first checks to see if the player can double down. If so, the state calls the BettingPlayer's doubleDown method (you'll need to add an abstract doubleDown method to the BettingPlayer). If the method indicates that the player would like to double down, the BetterPlaying state sets the current state to DoublingDown and then transitions to it.

If the player does not want to double down, the state continues and plays normally. See the source for all changes; there were a few other minor changes, such as the addition of a getDoubleDownState method to the BettingPlayer.

You have effectively added doubling down to the system. Now you need to update the GUIPlayer and its presentation class so that it can support doubling down.

The good news is that you do not need to make any changes to the GUIPlayer's states. These states shouldn't do anything because they have to wait until the human player clicks a button. You do need to implement the doubleDown method. Listing 19.12 presents the method.

LISTING 19.12 The doubleDown Method

```
protected boolean doubleDown() {
    setCurrentState( getDoublingDownState() );
    getCurrentState().execute( dealer );
    return true;
}
```

The GUI button can call this method if the user decides to double down. The method sets the current state to double down and then transitions to it. The state handles the rest.

The remaining changes all need to go into the presentation class: GUIView. You need to add a doubling down button, make sure that it is enabled right after the bet, and disabled as soon as the player presses it, the stand, or the hit button.

Don't worry too much if you do not fully understand the GUI code. What is important is that you understand how doubling down is added to the system.

Day 20 Quiz and Exercise Answers

Answers to Quiz

1. Through substitutability relationships and polymorphism you can create any subclass of BettingPlayer that you want and add it to the game.

   The game doesn't know the difference between a human-based player and an automatic non-human player. As a result you can set up the game with no human players. By implementing the hit method in the player subclasses, they will be able to play without human intervention.

2. You should never follow OneHitPlayer's strategy.

Answers to Exercises

1. N/A

2. Your solutions may vary. Listings 20.8 and 20.9 present the implementation of KnowledgeablePlayer and OptimalPlayer respectively.

LISTING 20.8   KnowledgeablePlayer.java

```java
public class KnowledgeablePlayer extends BettingPlayer {

    public KnowledgeablePlayer(String name,Hand hand,Bank bank) {
        super( name, hand, bank );
    }

    public boolean hit( Dealer dealer ) {

        int total = getHand().total();
        Card card = dealer.getUpCard();

        // never hit, no matter what, if total > 15
        if( total > 15 ) {
            return false;
        }

        // always hit for 11 and less
        if( total <= 11 ) {
```

LISTING 20.8   continued

```
            return true;
        }

        // this leaves 11, 12, 13, 14
        // base decision on dealer

        if( card.getRank().getRank() > 7 ) {
            return true;
        }

        return false;

    }

    public void bet() {
        getBank().place10Bet();
    }

}
```

LISTING 20.9   OptimalPlayer.java

```
public class OptimalPlayer extends BettingPlayer {

    public OptimalPlayer( String name, Hand hand, Bank bank ) {
        super( name, hand, bank );
    }

    public boolean hit( Dealer dealer ) {

        int total = getHand().total();
        Card card = dealer.getUpCard();

        if( total >= 17 ) {
            return false;
        }

        if( total == 16 ) {
            if( card.getRank() == Rank.SEVEN ||
                card.getRank() == Rank.EIGHT ||
                card.getRank() == Rank.NINE ) {
                return true;
            } else {
                return false;
            }
        }
```

A

LISTING 20.9   continued

```
            if( total == 13 || total == 14 || total == 15 ) {
                if( card.getRank() == Rank.TWO   ||
                    card.getRank() == Rank.THREE ||
                    card.getRank() == Rank.FOUR  ||
                    card.getRank() == Rank.FIVE  ||
                    card.getRank() == Rank.SIX ) {
                    return false;
                } else {
                    return true;
                }
            }
            if( total == 12 ) {
                if( card.getRank() == Rank.FOUR ||
                    card.getRank() == Rank.FIVE ||
                    card.getRank() == Rank.SIX ) {
                    return false;
                } else {
                    return true;
                }
            }
            return true;
        }

        public void bet() {
            getBank().place10Bet();
        }

    }
```

So, how do these players stack up?

In my testing, both the KnowledgeablePlayer and OptimalPlayer perform better than the SmartPlayer presented in the chapter. In comparison to one another, OptimalPlayer performs the best.

Over time though, both still lose money, just very slowly.

3. Your solutions may vary. Listings 20.10 and 20.11 present the implementation of KnowledgeablePlayer and OptimalPlayer respectively.

LISTING 20.10   KnowledgeablePlayer.java

```
public class KnowledgeablePlayer extends BettingPlayer {

    public KnowledgeablePlayer(String name,Hand hand,Bank bank) {
        super( name, hand, bank );
    }
```

LISTING 20.10 continued

```java
    public boolean doubleDown( Dealer d ) {
        int total = getHand().total();
        if( total == 10 || total == 11 ) {
            return true;
        }
        return false;
    }

    public boolean hit( Dealer d ) {

        int total = getHand().total();
        Card c = d.getUpCard();

        // never hit, no matter what, if total > 15
        if( total > 15 ) {
            return false;
        }

        // always hit for 11 and less
        if( total <= 11 ) {
            return true;
        }

        // this leaves 11, 12, 13, 14
        // base decision on dealer

        if( c.getRank().getRank() > 7 ) {
            return true;
        }

        return false;

    }

    public void bet() {
        getBank().place10Bet();
    }

}
```

LISTING 20.11 OptimalPlayer.java

```java
public class OptimalPlayer extends BettingPlayer {

    public OptimalPlayer( String name, Hand hand, Bank bank ) {
        super( name, hand, bank );
```

LISTING 20.11   continued

```java
        }

    public boolean doubleDown( Dealer d ) {
        int total = getHand().total();
        Card c = d.getUpCard();
        if( total == 11) {
            return true;
        }
        if( total == 10 ) {
            if( c.getRank().getRank() != Rank.TEN.getRank() &&
                c.getRank() != Rank.ACE ) {
                return true;
            }
            return false;
        }
        if( total == 9 ) {
            if( c.getRank() == Rank.TWO   ||
                c.getRank() == Rank.THREE ||
                c.getRank() == Rank.FOUR  ||
                c.getRank() == Rank.FIVE  ||
                c.getRank() == Rank.SIX ) {
                return true;
            }
            return false;
        }
        return false;
    }

    public boolean hit( Dealer d ) {

        int total = getHand().total();
        Card c = d.getUpCard();

        if( total >= 17 ) {
            return false;
        }

        if( total == 16 ) {
            if( c.getRank() == Rank.SEVEN ||
                c.getRank() == Rank.EIGHT ||
                c.getRank() == Rank.NINE ) {
                return true;
            } else {
                return false;
            }
        }
        if( total == 13 || total == 14 || total == 15 ) {
            if( c.getRank() == Rank.TWO   ||
                c.getRank() == Rank.THREE ||
                c.getRank() == Rank.FOUR  ||
```

LISTING 20.11 continued

```
                c.getRank() == Rank.FIVE  ||
                c.getRank() == Rank.SIX ) {
                return false;
            } else {
                return true;
            }
        }
        if( total == 12 ) {
            if( c.getRank() == Rank.FOUR ||
                c.getRank() == Rank.FIVE ||
                c.getRank() == Rank.SIX ) {
                return false;
            } else {
                return true;
            }
        }
        return true;
    }

    public void bet() {
        getBank().place10Bet();
    }
}
```

In my testing, both the KnowledgeablePlayer and OptimalPlayer perform better than the versions in Exercise 2.

Over time though, both still lose money—just very slowly.

Day 21 Quiz and Exercise Answers

Answers to Quiz

1. You can take care of the recursive method call problem by threading each player. When you call Thread.start the call returns right away, unlike a normal method. Because the method returns right away, the method call stack can unwind and return.

Answers to Exercises

1. N/A.

2. Answers will depend upon personal interests. Appendix D, "Selected Bibliography," presents an excellent list of resources upon which you can base your continued study.

A

APPENDIX **B**

Java Primer

Java Developer's Kit: J2SE 1.3 SDK

The Java Developer's Kit (JDK) from Sun Microsystems provides the environment for all Java development. Over the years, Sun has renamed the development kit from the JDK to the Java 2 Standard Edition (J2SE) Software Development Kit (SDK; however, the purpose of the tools and libraries remain the same—to assist developers in their efforts to write quality, platform independent, object oriented software.

Many popular integrated development environments (IDEs) incorporate the SDK in addition to a powerful editor and debugger. Sun's Forte and Borland's JBuilder provide stripped down versions of the IDE for free; however, for the purpose of this discussion, the scope will be limited to using the SDK with a text editor like TextPad, Notepad, or vi.

Sun provides the J2SE SDK for several platforms:

- Windows NT, 2000, 95, 98, ME
- Sun Solaris
- Linux

You can obtain the SDK for other platforms, such as HP or AIX, from the appropriate platform vendor. The J2SE SDK for Windows will be utilized as the default example. Installation and configuration on other platforms will vary little from the procedures discussed below.

Developers can download J2SE SDK from JavaSoft's J2SE website, `java.sun.com/j2se/1.3`. Follow the appropriate links to download the J2SE 1.3 SDK. In addition to the J2SE SDK, you should download the J2SE API documentation. Although not required, the API documentation is tremendously helpful. The J2SE API documentation provides detailed attribute, method, and class level documentation that even highly experienced Java developers will find useful.

Development Environment Configuration

JavaSoft packages the Windows J2SE 1.3 SDK in an InstallShield package. When you download the file, run it and proceed through the dialog boxes to install the SDK in the appropriate target directory. (The default target directory is `C:\jdk1.3`.) Install all components when prompted. This will require around 54MB of hard disk space. When complete, you should see the following directory structure in your installation target directory:

```
C:\jdk1.3
    \bin
    \demo
    \include
    \include-old
    \jre
    \lib
```

The installation package only deploys the SDK to the appropriate directories. To begin development, you should configure the following environment variables.

- JAVA_HOME
- PATH
- CLASSPATH

First, set JAVA_HOME to the appropriate installed directory. For example, you would execute the following at the command line:

```
set JAVA_HOME=c:\jdk1.3
```

Next, configure the PATH environment variable:

```
set PATH=%PATH%;%JAVA_HOME%\bin
```

Finally, configure the CLASSPATH environment variable. The CLASSPATH variable will inform the compiler and the virtual machine where to search for the compiled class files.

In general, this path is the same as the root of the source tree. Choose `c:\projects\src\java\classes`. Thus, you set the `CLASSPATH` variable:

```
set CLASSPATH=c:\projects\src\java\classes
```

Figure B.1 demonstrates the environment settings just described.

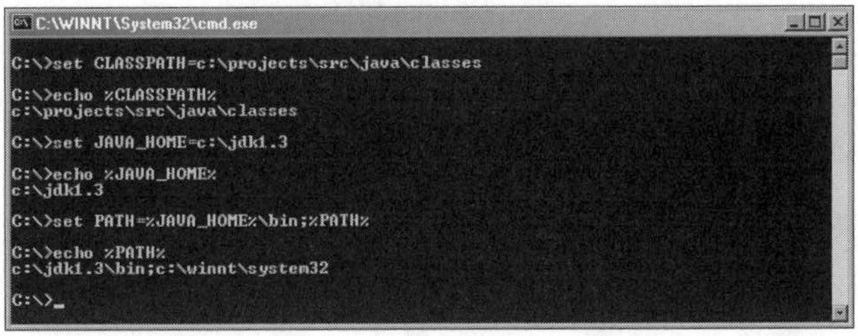

FIGURE B.1

Setting environment variables.

Most third parties will package their libraries in the form of jar or zip files. To use these libraries, you must append the location of the jar file to the `CLASSPATH`. For example, to use `c:\projects\lib\myclasses.jar`, you must perform the following:

```
set CLASSPATH=%CLASSPATH%;c:\projects\lib\myclasses.jar
```

You must append each jar file to the `CLASSPATH` prior to use.

SDK Tools Overview

In addition to providing the Java libraries, the Java SDK provides several tools necessary for development. The most commonly used tools are

- `javac`
- `java`
- `jar`
- `javadoc`

You will need the other tools for additional features, such as remote method invocations and Java native interface.

Java Compiler: `javac`

`javac`, the Java compiler, compiles Java source code to byte code. When you type `javac FirstProgram.java`, the compiler will generate a `FirstProgram.class` file in the current directory—assuming the compiler detects no errors within your Java code.

B

If a Java program utilizes third party libraries, the compiler will attempt to locate these libraries from the specified CLASSPATH; however, you can choose to modify the CLASS-PATH while compiling. The -classpath *<path>* option allows developers to replace the CLASSPATH environment variable.

You can also specify different source and target directories via -sourcepath *<path>* and -d *<path>*, respectively. The -sourcepath option specifies a new location for input source files. Thus, you can choose to compile source files located somewhere other than the current directory. The -d option informs the compiler to deposit the .class files into the specified path rather than in the current directory.

You will not need the -classpath, -sourcepath, or -d options for the exercises in this book.

Java Interpreter: `java`

java, the Java interpreter, provides the runtime environment. It will interpret and execute the compiled class files. To execute a Java program, enter

```
java FirstProgram
```

Note that the command omits the .class extension. The interpreter automatically appends .class to the class name.

As with the compiler, you can specify command line options to the interpreter. Some of the more frequently used options are

- -classpath to specify a classpath other than that defined by the environment variable CLASSPATH
- -DpropName=propValue to specify system properties

These and other interpreter options, however, fall beyond the scope of this discussion.

Java Archive Utility: `jar`

The jar utility generates java archive (jar) files. jar files are equivalent to zip files, compressing files to a smaller size and providing a convenient way to distribute compiled java classes.

To create an archive, simply invoke

```
jar cvf <jarfilename> <files_to_package>
```

You can also specify to jar all files and subdirectories of a given directory via

```
jar cvf <jarfilename> <directory>
```

Note all jar files must have a .jar suffix.

If you want to view the contents of a jar file, invoke

```
jar tvf <jarfile>
```

The `jar tvf` command will display the size, date inserted, and file name of the archive contents.

Additional options are described in the Java SDK documentation.

Java Documentation and the Documentation Generator: `javadoc`

All developers have heard the mantra of code documentation. JavaSoft facilitates the documentation process by providing a tool to generate user-friendly HTML documentation. The developer needs to utilize only standard tags when writing attribute, method, and class level comments and then invoke the `javadoc` tool with the appropriate options to generate API documentation. The Java SDK documentation provides elaborate information about the `javadoc` tool and process; however, let's cover some basic features to get started.

Developers must first document their code with the appropriate comments and tags. It would be great if the documentation tool could introspect our code and decipher exactly what we were thinking when we wrote that particular method; however, the `javadoc` tool is not advanced enough to read minds.

In Java, there are three primary documentation levels: class, method, and attribute. `javadoc` will recognize comments commencing with `/**` as a `javadoc` comment. The comments are terminated with `*/`.

For class-level comments, you will commonly see

- `@author <author_name>` specifies the author of this class. You may have more than one author; however, each author entry should commence with the `@author` tag.
- `@version <version_number>` specifies the version of this class. Some version control software provides tags that will automatically generate the number.
- `@see <classname>` provides links to other classes for further information. You may have more than one reference; however, each reference must commence with a `@see` tag.

A class level documentation would look something similar to

```
/**
 * <Class comments and description>
 *
 * @author Michael C. Han
```

B

```
 * @author Tony Sintes
 * @version 1.0
 * @see SecondJavaClass
 */
```

Method level comments use the previous tags in addition to

- @param *<param_name>* *<comments>* describes method parameters
- @return *<comments>* describes the method return value
- @exception *<ExceptionName>* *<comments>* describes any exceptions thrown by the current method

A method level documentation would look something similar to

```
/**
 * <method description and comments>
 *
 * @param value1 parameter taken by test method
 * @param value2 second parameter taken by test method
 * @return true if value1 == value2
 * @exception NumberFormatException thrown if value1 or value2 are not integers
 */
```

Attribute level javadoc comments tend not to have special tags. Instead, you must denote the comment block as a javadoc comment. The following is a sample attribute javadoc comment:

```
/**
 * Class level attribute to hold state of previous comparison operation
 */
```

Java Playpen: Your First Java Program

To help confirm your SDK installation and practice the tools described so far, you will write the infamous HelloWorld example. First, create a file called HelloWorld.java under the source root. If using the suggested source root (c:\projects\src\java\classes), create the file under c:\projects\src\java\classes.

After creating the file, you can commence writing your first Java program. Listing B.1 contains the HelloWorld example in Java.

LISTING B.1   HelloWorld.java

```
/**
 * A hello world program to confirm the SDK has been configured properly.
 * Also utilized to help demonstrate core SDK tools.
 *
```

LISTING B.1 continued

```java
 * @author Michael C. Han
 * @version 1.0
 */
public class HelloWorld {
    /**
     * Main method for program. All executable Java classes must
 * contain this method.
     *
     * @param args passed in from commandline
     */
    public static void main(String[] args) {
        HelloWorld helloTest = new HelloWorld();
        System.out.println(helloTest.sayHello());
        System.out.println("");
        System.out.println(helloTest.sayHi());
    }

    /**
     * Default Class constructor
     *
     */
    public HelloWorld() {
    }

    /**
     * Method to say hello to the invoker
     * @return String saying "Hello"
     */
    public String sayHello() {
        return "Hello";
    }

    /**
     * Method to say hi to the invoker
     * @return String saying "Hi!"
     */
    public String sayHi() {
        return "Hi!";
    }
}
```

Compiling and Running

To compile the class, run

`javac HelloWorld`

in the source root directory. If successful, you will see a `HelloWorld.class` file generated in the same directory.

B

Next, execute the program by entering

```
java HelloWorld
```

If the HelloWorld program runs successfully and prints out "Hello" and "Hi!" as shown in Figure B.2, you have configured your SDK properly; however, if you see the following when running `java HelloWorld`,

```
Exception in thread "main" java.lang.NoClassDefFoundError: HelloWorld
```

you either did not configure your CLASSPATH properly, or you placed the HelloWorld.java file somewhere other than the source root. In either case, first confirm CLASSPATH contains the source root (c:\projects\src\java\classes) and then confirm the HelloWorld.java file is in the source root.

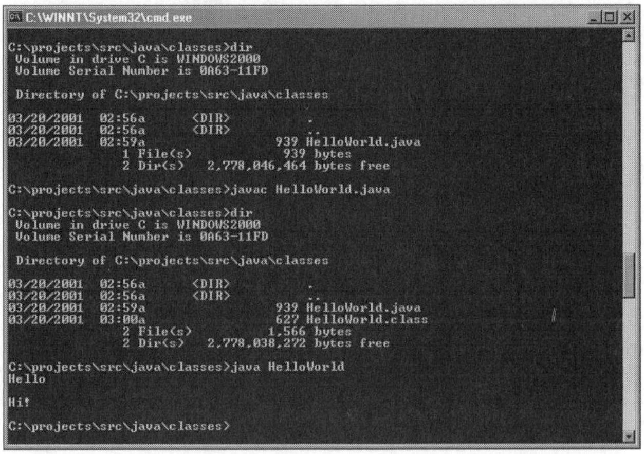

FIGURE B.2

Compiling and executing HelloWorld.

Creating a .jar File

Next try to run the jar utility on the files in the directory. At the source root, execute

```
jar cvf hello.jar *.java *.class
```

You will see a hello.jar file generated.

To confirm the contents of hello.jar, execute

```
jar tvf hello.jar
```

You will see two files—HelloWorld.java and HelloWorld.class—in the listing, as seen in Figure B.3.

FIGURE B.3

Creating, listing, and extracting hello.jar.

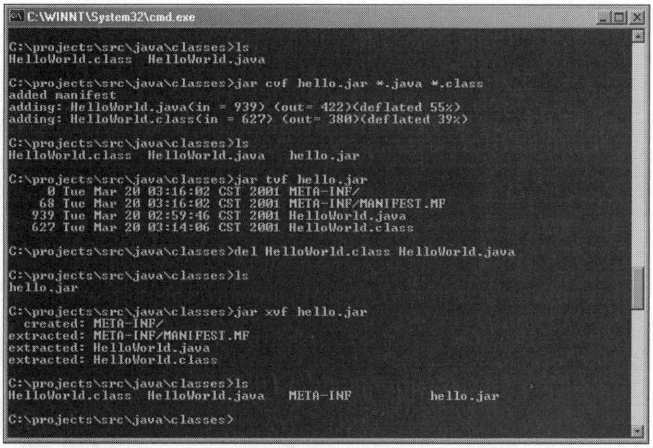

Next, delete HelloWorld.java and HelloWorld.class from the source root (c:\projects\src\java\classes). Finally, you need to execute

```
jar xvf hello.jar
```

This will extract the HelloWorld.java and HelloWorld.class files into the source root (see Figure B.3).

Generating `javadoc`

If you examine the source code for HelloWorld, you will notice javadoc style comments for both the class and the methods of the class.

To generate the documentation, create the documentation directory. Under c:\projects, create a docs directory and then execute:

```
javadoc -public -d c:\projects\docs HelloWorld
```

The command will deposit HTML documentation into the c:\projects\docs directory for all public methods of the HelloWorld class, as shown in Figure B.4. To view the documentation, open c:\projects\docs\index.html in a web browser. Notice the similarity in styles between the generated documentation and the J2SE API documentation from Sun.

B

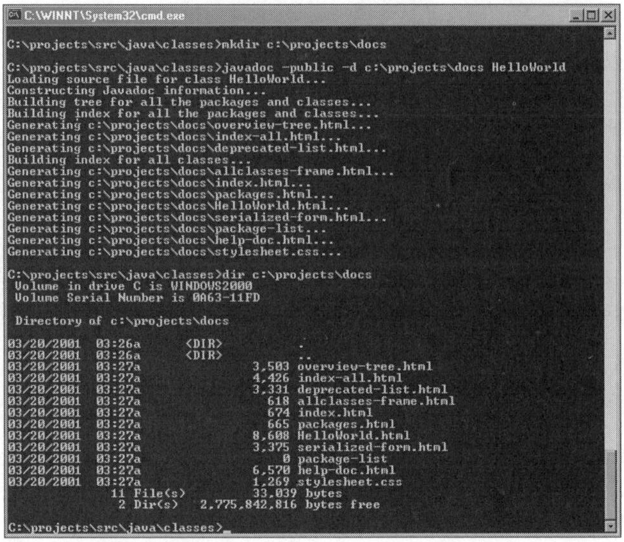

FIGURE B.4

Screen shot of javadoc
generation for
HelloWorld.

FIGURE B.4

Screen shot of javadoc
generation for
HelloWorld.

Java Language Mechanics

After following the steps above, you should have a fully configured Java development environment as well as an understanding of the basic SDK tools. Armed with the development environment, it is now time to write some Java classes.

Simple Java Class

Following is the simplified version of a HelloWorld program introduced in the previous section. Now that you understand how to compile and execute Java programs, you can examine the source in more detail:

```java
public class SimpleHelloWorld {
        public static void main(String args[]) {
                String hi = new String("Hello All");
                System.out.println(hi);
        }
}
```

The first keyword utilized is the keyword public. The word public is termed an access modifier. Similar to C++ or SmallTalk, Java provides access modifiers to specify who can access a particular method, attribute, or class. Public access grants access to all who want to use a particular class, method, or attribute. The other access modifiers are protected, private, and *package level*. Package level is something special in Java. Essentially, a package level modifier grants access to all classes within the same package or directory.

The next keyword in the sample class is class. In Java, a class is the basic foundation and building blocks for programs. It is the encapsulation of data variables or attributes and operations, functions, or methods. Everything in Java must reside within a class.

The name of the sample class is SimpleHelloWorld. In Java, the source code for this class must reside in a file called SimpleHelloWorld.java. If the class resides in any other file, the compiler will complain that "class SimpleHelloWorld is public, should be declared in a file named SimpleHelloWorld.java." The compiled class file resides in SimpleHelloWorld.class.

The SimpleHelloWorld class also contains public static void main(String args[]). Ignore the static and void modifiers. Java requires a main method if you want to execute a Java class via the java command. You can choose to add additional methods and operations to the class; however, without a method of this signature, you cannot execute the class.

Notice the braces ({}) and semicolons (;) in the source code. In Java, braces designate program blocks. A method and class must start with a brace and terminate with a brace. Thus, you must take special care to terminate open braces with close braces. Semicolons designated the end of a statement. If you are a C/C++ programmer, you are already familiar with these and know that you must close all statements with semicolons.

The static and void keywords describe a method. The void keyword is the return value. Similar to other languages, Java methods have a return value. In this case, the main method does not return any value. The static keyword designates the method as accessible via the class. In other words, you can invoke a static method of a class without creating an instance of the class.

The following two lines of code encapsulated by the main method's braces represent the body of the program.

```
String hi = new String("Hello All");
System.out.println(hi);
```

Here, a reference named hi points to a constructed instance of the String class. As in SmallTalk or C++, the new operator performs instance creation. The String instance contains the value "Hello All". It receives the value as parameters of the constructor. In the next line, the System object prints the value of hi to the system console.

Notice also the semicolons at the end of each line of code. Failure to terminate programmatic statements or variable declarations with a semicolon will result in compilation errors.

B

Data Types

Java, like C++ and Smalltalk, is strongly typed. Thus, when declaring variables and return values, you must specify the variable or return type. Java contains eight primitive types. Table B.1 lists the valid primitive types in a Java program and the number of bits associated with a type:

TABLE B.1 Primitive Java Types and Storage Sizes

Type	Number of Bits
byte	8 bits
short	16 bits
char	16 bits
int	32 bits
float	32 bits
double	64 bits
long	64 bits
boolean	1 bit

In most scenarios, you can use int to represent integers and float to represent floating point values; however, certain data types may require larger storage space. For instance, you might want to express the number of milliseconds since 1970. This number is sufficiently large to require a long rather than an integer.

You may represent a long as 1000000000L. The L postfix denotes the number as a long. Similarly, you can represent floats as 4.3405F.

If you are a C++ programmer, you know that characters in C++ are ASCII characters. Java, however, uses Unicode to represent characters. Unicode uses 2 bytes to represent characters as opposed to the 1 byte used by ASCII. This permits representation of a larger character set for purposes of internationalization. For example, most Asian languages require larger storage than standard ASCII. Java does not completely disallow use of ASCII. Instead, you are given a choice to use either. For instance, you can use common ASCII escape sequences, such as \n for new line or \t for tab.

At certain times, you might want to convert one numeric type to another, such as from an int to a long. Java provides automatic convert between numeric types if the conversion leads to no loss of precision. It will convert a 32-bit int automatically to a 64-bit long; however, you must explicitly specify type conversion to convert from a long to an int or from a double to an int. Java terms this operation *casting*. If you do not cast when performing a precision reducing conversion, the compiler will balk.

The following lines demonstrate an explicit cast:

```
long value1 = 40000L;
int value = (int)value1;
float value2 = 4.003F;
double value3 = value2;
```

Notice the `float` to `double` conversion requires no explicit casting because a `float` is 32 bits and a `double` is 64 bits. Thus, the operation increases precision.

Variables

In addition to being strongly typed, Java is also case sensitive. Consequently, Java considers two variables with different capitalization two separate variables. For example, `variableOne` and `variableone` are two different variable declarations. A Java variable name must commence with a letter and contain any alphanumeric characters. The alphanumeric characters can be any Unicode character that denotes a letter in any language; however, the name cannot contain any symbols such as $, %, &, and so on.

The following reserved words cannot be utilized:

abstract	boolean	break	byte
case	catch	char	class
const	continue	default	do
double	Else	extends	final
finally	Float	for	future
generic	Goto	if	implements
import	inner	instanceof	int
interface	Long	native	new
null	operator	outer	package
private	protected	public	rest
return	Short	static	super
switch	synchronized	this	throw
throws	transient	try	var
void	volatile	while	

Following are some sample variable declarations:

```
int value1;
double Value2;
float _value3;
char VALUE4,Value5;
```

Notice the final variable declaration. Java permits multiple variable type declarations per line. In this scenario, both `VALUE4` and `Value5` are `char` values. To declare multiple variables, use a comma to separate each variable name and terminate with a semicolon.

B

There are also attribute modifiers you can add to a variable declaration. For example, variables can be declared `public`, `private`, or `protected` for access control. A variable can also be declared `static` or `final` or both. A `static` variable is one accessible via the class while a `final` variable is unmodifiable.

Although you have little restrictions on variable names, it is highly advisable to follow some form of naming convention or coding standards. Coding standards lead to uniform code, and thus improving code readability. A common variable naming convention is to capitalize the first letter of every word except the first word. Names would look like

```
int anIntegerValue;
char aCharValue;
```

Another convention is to prefix all private and protected variables with an underscore. Thus, variables would look like

```
private int _value;
private char _aCharValue;
```

You should follow your organization's coding standards or follow a common coding standard.

Constants

Constants can be considered a special type of variable. Like in other languages, Java constants are variables with unchanging values. You can declare a constant by prepending the `static final` keywords to the variable declaration.

Sample constant declarations include

```
private static final String _NAME_VALUE = "MyName";
private static final int _AN_INTEGER_CONSTANT = 1;
public static final String PARAMETER_NAME = "MyParam";
protected static final char _TYPE_CHAR_VALUE = 'c';
```

Notice the constant names are in capital letters. Although not a requirement, a commonly followed practice among Java developers is to name constants with all capital letters.

You may access these constants via `<classname>.<constant_name>`. For example, if the previous constants are declared in `MyClass`, you can access the `PARAMETER_NAME` constant via `MyClass.PARAMETER_NAME`. This is the only public constant declared and, thus, this is the only constant available outside of `MyClass`; however, you can use any of the other constants within `MyClass`. You can also use the `_TYPE_CHAR_VALUE` constant in any subclasses of `MyClass`. When using constants within the same class, you can omit the `<classname>.` prefix. For example, to access `_NAME_VALUE` within `MyClass`, you can refer to the constant as either `MyClass._NAME_VALUE` or simply `_NAME_VALUE`.

Operators

Java provides a multitude of operators for arithmetic and boolean operations. For those familiar with C/C++ syntax, you should be familiar with the syntax for these operators. As we mentioned previously, all Java statements must terminate with a semicolon.

Java has the usual +, /, -, * for arithmetic operations. The = operator is used for assignment. In addition, Java supports the mod or remainder operator, %. For instance, 15 / 3 equals 5 while 15 % 3 equals 0. You can also use arithmetic operators when initializing variables. For example, initializing x to n + 2 looks something similar to

```
int x = n + 2;
```

You can also choose to use a shortened syntax when performing operations on the same variable. For example, to increment x by n, you can choose to write

```
x = n + x;
```

You can also take a shortened approach and write

```
x += n;
```

Java also provides support for exponentiation. Java doesn't provide an operator. Instead, you use the pow method provided in the `java.lang.Math` class. So to raise x to power of n, the expression would look similar to

```
int y = Math.pow(x, n);
```

Java also provides increment and decrement operators as in C/C++. To increment x by 1, you can write either of the following:

```
x = x + 1;
x += 1;
```

The best way, however, is to write

```
x++;
```

The same applies for the decrement operator:

```
x--;
```

With both operators, there are two forms. You can place the operator before or after the variable. For example, to decrement x, you can express either of the following:

```
x--;
--x;
```

The location of the operator dictates when the operator is performed. In an arithmetic expression, placing the operator prior to the variable will increment (or decrement) the

B

variable first, before evaluating the expression. If you place the operator after the variable, the expression is evaluated first. Take the following snippet, for example:

```
int x = 5;
int y = 6;
int k =++x;  //after this expression,  k = 6 and x = 6
int j = y++;  //after this expression, j = 6 and y = 7
```

As you can see, the placement of increment or decrement operator is key. Take special care to use the operators appropriately.

Java's boolean operators looks very much like boolean operators in other programming languages. When comparing greater than or less than, Java provides > and < respectively. Also, <= and >= denote less than or equal to and greater than or equal to, respectively. These apply for comparing primitives like integers, longs, doubles, characters, and so on:

```
int x = 5;
int y = 6;
boolean z = x < y;  // z = true
```

When comparing equality, Java provides two different operators. You can use the == operator to compare primitives; however, when comparing two objects (such as String, MyObject), you must use the equals() method defined for the object. If you mistakenly use == to compare two objects, this actually compares the *reference* of the two objects, not the actual objects. Unless you are comparing the same object references, this operation will return false:

```
String x = new String("My String");
String y = new String("My String");
boolean z  = (x == y); // z = false
boolean w = (x.equals(y));  // w = true
```

To compare inequality, Java uses the ! operator. Inequality between primitives will use != and between two objects will be !obj1.equals(obj2).

You can also choose to use && and || to check conditionals (ands and ors, respectively).

Conditional Statements

Conditional statements are a key part to any programming language. Like C/C++, Java provides the if-else operator. The syntax, like in C/C++ looks similar to

```
if (condition) {
        ...  //behavior for when condition is true
}
else {
        ...  //behavior statements
}
```

You can choose to have a single `if`, `if-else`, or `if` with multiple `else` statements.

The following is a sample `if-else` statement with multiple `else`s:

```
if (x == y) {
        x --;
}
else if (x > y) {
        x * 2;
}
else {
        x / 2;
}
```

Notice the braces that denote the beginning and end of an `if` block. Although braces are not required if you only have one statement in the `if` block, using braces in this situation is recommended. By doing so, you can avoid potential headaches later when you decide to add additional statements to the `if` block. Should you forget to add braces at that time, you will have to debug for missing braces.

Java, like C/C++, provides a ternary operator to shorten `if-then` expression. A ternary expression looks something like

```
z = (x > y) ? 3 : 1;
```

The `(x > y)` is the conditional test. The first value following the `?`, represents the value of z if the conditional proves true. The second value represents the value of z if the conditional proves false.

Following the above example, if x = 5 and y = 7, then z = 1. The conditional proves false (5 > 7) and thus z is assigned the second value in the expression, 1.

Loops

Loops are an important component to any programming language. Java, like many other languages, provides a variety of looping mechanisms.

A commonly used loop, the `for` loop, has the following syntax:

```
for (int x = 0; x < 8; x++) {
        //…some operation in loop
}
```

The loop constraint, x, is defined within the parenthesis and initialized to zero. The next statement tests the constraint to ensure it is within the necessary bounds. In this case, x must be less than 8. The final statement increments the loop constraint.

B

Another commonly used loop, the while loop has the following syntax:

```
while (condition is true) {
        //…do some operation
}
```

The loop will continue to execute as long as the conditional statement within the paren-thesis tests true.

Classes and Interfaces—Building Blocks of Java

In Java, you cannot do anything without classes and to a lesser extent, interfaces. Classes comprise the basic building blocks of the language. Thus, when writing your own pro-gram, you will have to create classes and also use classes from existing libraries. You can also need to construct interfaces to better programmatically express your design.

Using Existing Classes

To use existing classes in the Java SDK, you will need to create an instance of the class, initialize it, and then work with the instances. To utilize the existing `java.util.StringBuffer` class, you would create an instance or object of this class:

```
StringBuffer sbTest = new StringBuffer();
```

Now that you have created a new `StringBuffer` to use, you can operate upon the object. For instance, you might want to append another `String` to the buffer.

```
sbTest.append("This is a test String");
```

You might need to create multiple instances of the same class to perform the necessary operations. Thus you can create as many `StringBuffers` as necessary:

```
StringBuffer sbTest2 = new StringBuffer();
```

Now you have created a new instance of a `StringBuffer` identified by the `sbTest2` refer-ence. You may also assign one variable to another via the = sign. This will set both vari-ables to point to the same object. Thus, operations performed on both variables will affect the same object. Take the following statements for instance:

```
StringBuffer sbTest1 = new StringBuffer();
StringBuffer sbTest2 = new StringBuffer();
sbTest = sbTest2;
sbTest.append("Test String 1.");
sbTest2.append("Test String 2.");
System.out.println("Output for sbTest = " + sbTest.toString());
System.out.println("Output for sbTest2 = " + sbTest2.toString());
```

Because you set `sbTest` = `sbTest2`, the append operations on `sbTest` and `sbTest2` will modify the same underlying object. The output from the previous snippet will read

```
Output for sbTest = Test String 1.Test String 2.
Output for sbTest2 = Test String 1.Test String 2.
```

Creating Your Own Classes

The Java syntax for a class is

```
public class ClassName {
    //methods and attributes of the class
}
```

All methods and attributes for the class will reside within the braces. All classes must also reside in a file named `ClassName.java`.

Examine the code snippet from the `Product.java` file shown in Listing B.2.

LISTING B.2   Snippet from `Product.java`

```
/**
 *
 * @author Michael C. Han
 * @version 1.0
 */
public class Product {
      /**
       *
       * @param args passed in from commandline
       */
      public static void main(String[] args) {
            Product prod =
                new Product("widget1", "Acme Inc", "Master Widget",
                    "This is the master widget product to solve all
problems!",
                        90.10f);
            System.out.println(prod.getProductId());
            System.out.println(prod. getManufacturer());
            System.out.println(prod. getProductDesc());
      }

      private String prodName, productId, manufacturer, desc;
      float price;

      /**
       *
       * @param args passed in from commandline
```

B

LISTING B.2   continued

```java
    */
   public Product(String productId, String manufacturer,
                String prodName, String desc, float price) {
        this.prodName = prodName;
        this.productId = productId;
        this.manufacturer = manufacturer;
        this.desc = desc;
     this.price = price;
   }

   /**
    *
    * @return product id
    */
   public String getProductId() {
        return productId;
   }

   /**
    *
    * @return product name
    */
   public String getProductName() {
        return prodName;
   }
   /**
    *
    * @return manufacturer name
    */
   public String getManufacturer() {
        return manufacturer;
   }

   /**
    *
    * @return product description
    */
   public String getProductDesc() {
        return desc;
   }

   /**
    *
    * @return product price
    */
   public float getPrice() {
        return price;
   }
```

LISTING B.2   continued

```
/**
 *
 * @param price - new price for this product
 */
public void setPrice(float price) {
        this.price = price;
}

}
```

The `Product` class has a *constructor method* with five parameters: product name, manu-facturer, product id, description, and price. The constructor performs necessary opera-tions to initialize the object. In this case, you initialize the designated product informa-tion. A constructor must follow the following rules:

- The constructor must have the same name as the class.
- A constructor may take any number of parameters. A constructor with no parame-ter is called a *default constructor*.
- A constructor returns no values.
- A constructor may only be called via the new key word (e.g. `Product prod = new Product(...)`).
- A class may have more than one constructor (or more commonly known as *over-loaded constructors*).

Note the use of the `this` keyword within the constructor. The `this` keyword operates on the current instance of the class. In the constructor, you use the `this` keyword to prevent confusing the private attributes with the constructor parameters.

In addition to constructors, the `Product` class also has four *accessors* or *getters*. The accessors provide read access to the attributes for the `Product` class. To modify attributes of the class, you should use methods called *modifiers* or *setters*. The `Product` class has one modifier, `setPrice`, for modifying the price of a product.

Notice all attributes of the `Product` class are private and only one, `price`, is modifiable after a `Product` is created. It is important to remember that classes should not exposes their internal attributes unless the user of the class has legitimate reasons in reading and/or modifying the attribute. Consequently, you provide access to the attributes via modifiers and accessors.

The `Product` class has only public access methods. You can choose to implement meth-ods with other access levels; you can choose to implement private or protected methods

B

in addition to public methods. It is important to keep in mind that private methods are only accessible within the implementing class and protected methods are accessible within the implementing class and all its subclasses. When deciding on the access levels for a method, keep the following guidelines in mind for private methods:

- A private method has no concern for users of class.
- The method will change should implementation of class change.

Also keep the following in mind about protected methods:

- A protected method has no concern for users of this class; however, classes that extend functionality of the implementing class will require access to the method.
- The method fulfills functional requirements for all subclasses.

Interfaces

Interfaces, like classes, are core features of Java. Unlike classes, however, interfaces do not define attributes and methods for a class. Instead, interfaces provide method definitions that may be implemented by classes. For those familiar with C++, interfaces will look similar to class definitions inside header files.

Take a look at an interface for sortable or comparable objects:

```
/**
 * Interface to compare the equality of two objects
 *
 */
public interface Comparable {

        /**
         * Compare this object to a desired object. If current
         * is larger, then return 1, the toCompare object is larger,
         * then return -1. If the two objects are equal, return 0
         * @param toCompare - object for comparison
         * @return -1 if toCompare > this, 0 if toCompare == this,
         * 1 if this > toCompare
         */
        public int compare(Object toCompare);
}
```

This interface resides within the Java SDK. It defines the methods that all objects of type Comparable must implement. In this case, all Comparable objects must implement the compare method. Simply put, an interface is a contract an implementing class must fulfill. If a class implements a particular interface, it promises to implement all methods designated by the interface.

Currently, Java only provides support for single inheritance. In other words, a Java class may only extend one Java class. Consequently, if you choose to classify an object of ClassA and ClassB (multiple inheritance), you can only do so via interfaces. By using interfaces to simulate multiple inheritance, Java recovers most of the functionality provided by multiple inheritance. Some of the other functionality lost might be partially recovered via design methods like object composition.

Interfaces also have several other properties. You may not instantiate an interface via new. Your class may implement multiple interfaces. For example, the Product class can implement both Sortable and Clonable interfaces:

```
public class Product implements Sortable, Clonable
```

Interfaces can also extend other interfaces. The Sortable interface can also extend a Collectible interface. A class implementing the Sortable interface must also fulfill the contract of the Collectible interface:

```
public interface Sortable extends Clonable
```

Inner Classes and Anonymous Inner Classes

The architects of Java added the concept of inner classes with Java 1.1. An inner class is a class declared within the scope of a public class. Why should you use one? Inner classes have the following distinct advantages:

- An object of an inner class can access any attributes, private or otherwise, of the encapsulating class.

- Anonymous inner classes simplify tasks, such as call-backs and event-handling.

- Inner classes extremely handy for creating data bag objects that really have no meaning outside the context of the wrapping class, such as a specialized hash key for a cache. Outside the cache, the hash key has no meaning. Thus you create a HashKey innerclass within the scope of the ObjectCache class.

Here's what the ObjectCache class with the HashKey inner class would look like

```java
import java.util.Map;
import java.util.HashMap;

public class ObjectCache {
        private Map cache;

        public ObjectCache() {
                cache = new HashMap();
        }

        public void add(String oid, String objName, Object obj) {
```

B

```
            HashKey key = new HashKey(oid, objName);
            cache.put(key, obj);
    }

    public Object get(String oid, String objName) {
            HashKey key = new HashKey(oid, objName);
            Object obj = cache.get(key);
            return obj;
    }

    //.. . . More methods . . .

    private class HashKey {
            private String oid, objName;

       public HashKey(String oid, String objName) {
                    this.oid = oid;
                    this.objName = objName;
            }

            public String getOid() {
                    return oid;
            }

            public String getObjName() {
                    return objName;
            }

            public boolean equals(Object obj) {
                    if (obj instanceof HashKey) {
                            HashKey key = (HashKey)obj;
                            return (key.getOid().equals(getOid()) &&
                                    key.getObjName().equals(getObjName())));
                    }
                    return false;
            }

            public int hashCode() {
                    return 17;
            }
    }
}
```

In the inner classes, just as with normal classes, you can access the attributes of the inner class with the `this` keyword; however, you can also access the attributes of the encapsulating class. You will need to use the `outer` keyword to access those attributes.

Anonymous classes are a special form of inner classes. Anonymous classes are most prevalent in writing event-handling code. Take the following code snippet, for example, for handling action events on an OK button:

```
public class FooFrame {
        //...

        JButton ok = new Jbutton("ok");
        ok.addActionListener(new ActionListener() {
                public void actionPerformed(ActionEvent evt) {
                        // perform some event-handling for the ok button
                }
        });

        //...

}
```

Although the syntax is a little cryptic, anonymous inner classes enables you to reduce the number of classes in your project. Instead of a class or inner class for every event handler, you would inline the class declarations. This is a great time saver; however, due to the cryptic nature of the code, too many anonymous inner classes will reduce code readability. Consequently, if you have to perform a lot of event handling, you might want to use some design patterns (such as the Command pattern) to enhance your design and, thus, clarify your implementation.

Summary

This primer is by no means a complete introduction to Java. It will, however, provide enough information within the context of this text. If you want to obtain additional information, there are several web sites that will provide in depth tutorials on the basics of the Java language. A great resource for beginners and advanced developers is the Java Developer's Connection (JDC) located at developer.java.sun.com. This site provides many tutorials and early access software for Java developers.

B

APPENDIX C

UML Reference

UML Reference

This appendix provides a quick reference to the UML notation used throughout the book.

Classes

The UML represents a class through a box divided into three sections. The top section contains the name, the middle section contains the attributes, and the bottom section contains the methods.

Figure C.1 illustrates how the UML represents a class.

FIGURE C.1

A UML class.

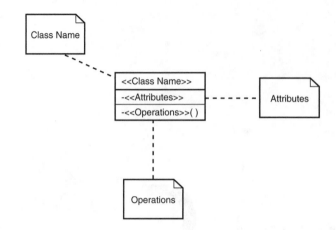

Object

The UML represents objects the same as a class. The only difference is that the object's name is underlined and the methods are omitted. The attributes may also show value.

Visibility

Figure C.2 illustrates how the UML represents attribute and method visibility:

- + represents public visibility
- # represents protected visibility
- - represents private visibility

FIGURE C.2

Method and attribute visibility.

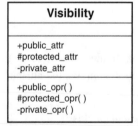

Abstract Classes and Methods

Abstract classes and methods are symbolized by italicizing the abstract name. Figure C.3 provides an example of an abstract class.

FIGURE C.3

An abstract class.

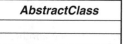

You can also add the {abstract} constraint after the name. Using the constraint label helps when drawing a diagram by hand.

Notes

Sometimes a note will make a model more understandable. In the UML, a note resembles a sticky note and is attached to the element being noted with a dashed line.

Figure C.4 illustrates the UML note. You can attach a note to any part of your UML model.

FIGURE C.4

The UML note.

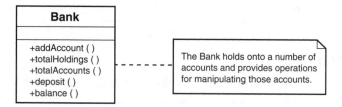

Stereotypes

A *stereotype* is a UML element that allows you to extend the vocabulary of the UML language itself or to classify a marking. A stereotype consists of a word or phrase enclosed in guillemets (<< >>). You place a stereotype above or to the side of an existing element.

Figure C.5 illustrates a stereotype that defines a type of method.

FIGURE C.5

The UML stereotype.

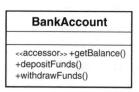

Relationships

A *relationship* describes how classes interact with one another. In the UML, a relationship is a connection between two or more notational elements. In the UML, a relationship is normally illustrated through a line or an arrow between classes.

Dependency

In a *dependency* relationship, one object is dependent on another object's specification. If the specification changes you will need to update the dependent object.

In the UML you represent a dependency as a dashed arrow between the dependent classes. Figure C.6 illustrates the UML dependency notation. The relationship tells you that `ClassA` depends upon `ClassB`.

FIGURE C.6

A simple dependency relationship.

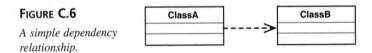

Association

An *association* indicates that one object contains another object. In the UML terms, when in an association relationship one object is connected to another.

In the UML you represent an association as a line that connects the two classes. An association that has no arrow is said to be bidirectional. An arrow signifies that the relationship works only in one way.

Figure C.7 illustrates the UML association notation. The relationship tells you that `ClassA` is associated with `ClassB`.

FIGURE C.7

An association relationship.

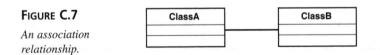

Roles

The UML allows you to denote each class's role in the association. The association *role* is the part that an object plays in a relationship.

Figure C.8 illustrates the UML notation for the role.

FIGURE C.8

The UML role.

Multiplicity

The UML allows you to denote the multiplicity of the association. The *multiplicity* indicates how many objects may take part in the instance of an association.

The range of multiplicity values is listed in Table C.1.

TABLE C.1 Multiplicity Values

Notation	Value
1	One
*	Any number
1..*	At least one
x..y	Any number of values in the range x to y

Figure C.9 illustrates the UML notation for multiplicity.

FIGURE C.9

Multiplicity.

Aggregation

The UML provides notation for aggregation. An *aggregation* is a special type of association that models has-a of whole/part relationships among peers.

You model an aggregation as a line with a hollow diamond on the "whole/part" end. Figure C.10 illustrates the UML notation for aggregation.

FIGURE C.10

Aggregation.

Composition

The UML provides notation for composition. A *composition* is a special type of association that models has-a of whole/part relationships among classes that are not peers. The part is not independent of the whole in a composition relationship.

You model composition as a line with a blackened diamond on the "whole/part" end. Figure C.11 illustrates the UML notation for composition.

FIGURE C.11

Composition.

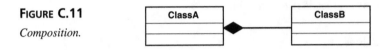

Generalization

A *generalization* relationship exists between the general and the specific. It is inheritance.

Generalization is symbolized through a solid line with a closed hollow arrow head. Figure C.12 illustrates the UML notation for generalization.

FIGURE C.12

Generalization.

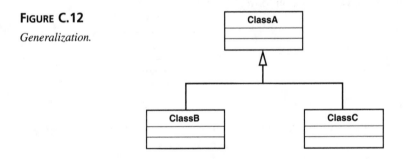

Interaction Diagrams

Interaction diagrams model the interactions between objects.

Collaboration Diagrams

Collaboration diagrams represent the messages that the objects send one another.

Each object in the diagram is symbolized as a box. A line connects each object that interacts. On top of that line, you write the messages that the objects send and the direction of those messages.

Collaboration diagrams highlight the relationships between the actors. Figure C.13 illustrates the UML collaboration diagram.

FIGURE C.13

A collaboration diagram.

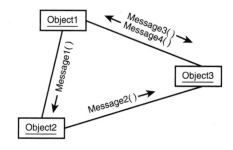

Sequence Diagrams

Sequence diagrams model the sequence of events in a scenario over time.

Each object in the diagram is symbolized at the top of the diagram as a box. The lines descending from the boxes represent the object's lifeline. Messages are passed back and forth between the objects and within the objects. Figure C.14 illustrates the UML sequence diagram.

FIGURE C.14

A sequence diagram.

APPENDIX D

Selected Bibliography

Object mastery can only come with time, practice, and study. No single book can teach you everything there is to learn about object-oriented programming.

This appendix presents a list of categorized OO resources. Use this list as a guide for your next steps in studying and applying OOP. While it is not important that you investigate each resource, this list can guide you to more information on the subjects that you find interesting.

Analysis, Design, and Methodologies

Beck, Kent. *Extreme Programming Explained: Embrace Change*. Boston: Addison-Wesley, 2000.

Booch, Grady. *Object Oriented Analysis And Design: With Applications*. Reading: Addison-Wesley, 1994.

Booch, Grady, James Rumbaugh, and Ivar Jacobson. *The Unified Modeling Language User Guide*. Reading: Addison-Wesley, 1999.

Fowler, Martin, and Kendall Scott. *UML Distilled: A Brief Guide to the Standard Object Modeling Language*. 2nd ed. Reading: Addison-Wesley, 2000.

Johnson, Ralph E., and Brian Foote. "Designing Reusable Classes." *Journal of Object Oriented Programming* 1.2 (June/July 1988): 22-35.

Liberty, Jesse. *Beginning Object Oriented Analysis and Design*. Olton, UK: Wrox, 1998.

C++ Programming

Stroustrup, Bjarne. *The C++ Programming Language*. Special ed. Reading: Addison-Wesley, 2000.

Design Patterns

Buschman, Frank, Regine Meunier, Hans Rohnert, Peter Sommerlad, and Michael Stal. *Pattern-Oriented Software Architecture: A System of Patterns*. Chichester: Wiley, 1996.

Gamma, Erich, Richard Helm, Ralph Johnson, and John Vlissides. *Design Patterns: Elements of Reusable Object-Oriented Software*. Reading: Addison-Wesley, 1995.

General OO Principals and Theory

Booch, Grady. *Object Oriented Analysis And Design: With Applications*. Reading: Addison-Wesley, 1994.

Bud, Timothy. *An Introduction to Object Oriented Programming*. 2nd ed. Reading: Addison-Wesley, 1997.

Fowler, Martin. *Refactoring: Improving the Design of Existing Code*. Boston: Addison-Wesley, 2000.

Rumbaugh, James. "Disinherited! Examples of Misuse of Inheritance." *Journal of Object Oriented Programming* 5.9 (February 1993): 22-24.

Seidewitz, Ed. "Controlling Inheritance." *Journal of Object Oriented Programming* 8.8 (January 1996): 36-42.

Taenzer, David, Murthy Ganti, and Sunil Podar. "Object-Oriented Software Reuse: The Yoyo Problem." *Journal of Object Oriented Programming* 2.3 (September/October 1989): 30-35.

"Hard Core" Theory (But Don't Let That Scare You!)

Cardelli, Luca, and Peter Wegner. "On Understanding Types, Data Abstractions, and Polymorphism." *Computing Surveys* 17.4 (1985): 471-523.

Danforth, Scott, and Chris Tomlinson. "Type Theories and Object Oriented Programming." *ACM Computing Surveys* 20.1 (1988): 29-72.

Snyder, Alan. "Encapsulation and Inheritance in Object Oriented Programming Languages." Proceedings of the 1986 OOPSLA Conference on Object Oriented Programming Systems, Languages and Applications. *Sigplan Notices* 21.11 (1986): 38-45.

Wegner, Peter, and Stanley B. Zdonik. "Inheritance as an Incremental Modification Mechanism or What Like is and isn't Like." *ECOOP* 1988: 55-77.

D

Java Programming

Bloch, Joshua. *Effective Java Programming Language Guide*. Boston: Addison-Wesley, 2001.

Eckel, Bruce. *Thinking in Java*. 2nd ed. Upper Saddle River: Prentice Hall, 2000.

Warren, Nigel, and Philip Bishop. *Java in Practice: Design Styles and Idioms for Effective Java*. Harlow, UK: Addison-Wesley, 1999.

Miscellaneous

Brooks, Frederick P., Jr. *The Mythical Man-Month*. Anniversary ed. Reading: Addison-Wesley, 1995.

Scarne, John. Scarne's Encyclopedia of Card Games: All the Rules for All the Games You'll Want to Play. New York: Harper, 1983.

Smalltalk

Budd, Timothy. *A Little Smalltalk*. Reading: Addison-Wesley, 1987.

Goldberg, Adele, and David Robson. *Smalltalk-80: The Language*. Reading: Addison-Wesley, 1989.

Testing

Beck, Kent. *Extreme Programming Explained: Embrace Change*. Boston: Addison-Wesley, 2000.

Mackinnon, Tim, Steve Freeman, and Philip Craig. "Endo-Testing: Unit Testing with Mock Objects." Paper presented at the eXtreme Programming and Flexible Processes in Software Engineering—XP2000 conference, Cagliari, Sardinia, Italy, June 2000.

APPENDIX E

Blackjack Code Listings

Days 15 through 21 had you build a complete Blackjack game. Many of the exercises also asked you to add additional functionality to the system. This source listing presents the final Blackjack version. The final version combines each feature that was added throughout days 15 through 21.

This appendix contains the complete listing of all code. The code has been packaged to avoid duplicate source files. What can be shared is shared. What cannot be shared is not shared.

The source contains an MVC GUI, a PAC GUI, a CLI UI, and a simulator. The source has been divided into the following packages:

- `blackjack.core`
- `blackjack.core.threaded`
- `blackjack.exe`
- `blackjack.players`
- `blackjack.ui`
- `blackjack.ui.mvc`
- `blackjack.ui.pac`

blackjack.core

blackjack.core contains all of the common classes found in Listings E.1 through E.14. These classes build the core of the blackjack system.

LISTING E.1   Bank.java

```java
package blackjack.core;

public class Bank {

    private int total;
    private int bet;

    public Bank( int amount ) {
        total = amount;
    }

    public void doubleDown() {
        placeBet( bet );
        bet = bet * 2;
    }

    public void place100Bet() {
        placeBet( 100 );
    }

    public void place50Bet() {
        placeBet( 50 );
    }

    public void place10Bet() {
        placeBet( 10 );
    }

    public void win() {
        total += ( 2 * bet );
        bet = 0;
    }

    public void lose() {
        // already taken out of total
        bet = 0;
    }

    public void blackjack() {
        total += ( ( ( 3 * bet ) / 2 ) + bet );
        bet = 0;
    }
```

Listing E.1 continued

```java
    public void standoff() {
        total += bet;
        bet = 0;
    }

    public String toString() {
        return ( "$" + total + ".00" );
    }

    private void placeBet( int amount ) {
        bet = amount;
        total -= amount;
    }

}
```

Listing E.2 BettingPlayer.java

```java
package blackjack.core;

public abstract class BettingPlayer extends Player {

    private Bank bank;

    public BettingPlayer( String name, Hand hand, Bank bank ) {
        super( name, hand );
        this.bank = bank;
    }

    //****************************************************************************
    // overridden behavior
    public String toString() {
        return ( super.getName() + ": " + getHand().toString() + "\n" +
bank.toString() );
    }

    public String getName() {
        return ( super.getName() + " " + bank.toString() );
    }

    public void win() {
        bank.win();
        super.win();
    }

    public void lose() {
        bank.lose();
```

LISTING E.2   continued

```java
            super.lose();
        }

        public void standoff() {
            bank.standoff();
            super.standoff();
        }

        public void blackjack() {
            bank.blackjack();
            super.blackjack();
        }

        protected PlayerState getInitialState() {
            return getBettingState();
        }

        protected PlayerState getPlayingState() {
            return new BetterPlaying();
        }

        //******************************************************************************
        // newly added for BettingPlayer
        protected final Bank getBank() {
            return bank;
        }

        protected PlayerState getBettingState() {
            return new Betting();
        }

        protected PlayerState getDoublingDownState() {
            return new DoublingDown();
        }

        protected abstract void bet();
        protected abstract boolean doubleDown( Dealer dealer );

        private class Betting implements PlayerState {
            public void handChanged() {
                // not possible in busted state
            }
            public void handPlayable() {
                // not possible in busted state
            }
            public void handBlackjack() {
                // not possible in busted state
            }
```

```
            public void handBusted() {
                // not possible in busted state
            }
            public void execute( Dealer dealer ) {
                bet();
                setCurrentState( getWaitingState() );
                dealer.doneBetting( BettingPlayer.this );
                // terminate
            }
        }
        private class DoublingDown implements PlayerState {
            public void handChanged() {
                notifyChanged();
            }
            public void handPlayable() {
                setCurrentState( getStandingState() );
                notifyStanding();
            }
            public void handBlackjack() {
                // not possible in doubling down state
            }
            public void handBusted() {
                setCurrentState( getBustedState() );
                notifyBusted();
            }
            public void execute( Dealer dealer ) {
                bank.doubleDown();
                dealer.hit( BettingPlayer.this );
                getCurrentState().execute( dealer );
            }
        }
        private class BetterPlaying implements PlayerState {
            public void handChanged() {
                notifyChanged();
            }
            public void handPlayable() {
                // can ignore in playing state
            }
            public void handBlackjack() {
                // not possible in playing state
            }
            public void handBusted() {
                setCurrentState( getBustedState() );
                notifyBusted();
            }
            public void execute( Dealer dealer ) {
                if( getHand().canDoubleDown() && doubleDown( dealer ) ) {
                    setCurrentState( getDoublingDownState() );
```

LISTING E.2 continued

```
                getCurrentState().execute( dealer );
                return;
            }
            if( hit( dealer ) ) {
                dealer.hit( BettingPlayer.this );
            } else {
                setCurrentState( getStandingState() );
                notifyStanding();
            }
            getCurrentState().execute( dealer );
            // transition
        }
    }

}
```

LISTING E.3 BlackjackDealer.java

```
package blackjack.core;

import java.util.ArrayList;
import java.util.Iterator;

public class BlackjackDealer extends Player implements Dealer {

    private Deckpile cards;

    private ArrayList players = new ArrayList();

    protected ArrayList waiting_players;
    protected ArrayList betting_players;
    private ArrayList standing_players;
    private ArrayList busted_players;
    private ArrayList blackjack_players;

    public BlackjackDealer( String name, Hand hand, Deckpile cards ) {
        super( name, hand );
        this.cards = cards;
    }

    //*************************************************************************
    // Methods that players can call
    public void blackjack( Player player ) {
        blackjack_players.add( player );
        play( this );
    }
```

LISTING E.3 continued

```java
public void busted( Player player ) {
    busted_players.add( player );
    play( this );
}

public void standing( Player player ) {
    standing_players.add( player );
    play( this );
}

public void doneBetting( Player player ) {
    waiting_players.add( player );
    play( this );
}

public void hit( Player player ) {
    player.addCard( cards.dealUp() );
}

public Card getUpCard() {
    Iterator i = getHand().getCards();
    while( i.hasNext() ) {
        Card card = (Card) i.next();
        if( card.isFaceUp() ) {
            return card;
        }
    }
    // should not get here
    return null;
}

//****************************************************************************
// Game setup methods
public void addPlayer( Player player ) {
    players.add( player );
}
public void reset() {
    super.reset();

    // set up the player buckets
    waiting_players = new ArrayList();
    standing_players = new ArrayList();
    busted_players = new ArrayList();
    blackjack_players = new ArrayList();
    betting_players = new ArrayList();
    betting_players.addAll( players );

    cards.reset();
```

E

LISTING E.3   continued

```
        Iterator i = players.iterator();
        while( i.hasNext() ) {
            Player player = (Player) i.next();
            player.reset();
        }
    }
    public void newGame() {
        reset();
        // go!
        play( this );
    }
    //**************************************************************************

    public void deal() {

        cards.shuffle();

        // reset each player and deal 1 card up to each and self
        Player [] player = new Player[waiting_players.size()];
        waiting_players.toArray( player );
        for( int i = 0; i < player.length; i ++ ) {
            player[i].addCard( cards.dealUp() );
        }
        this.addCard( cards.dealUp() );

        // deal 1 more up card to each player and one down to self
        for( int i = 0; i < player.length; i ++ ) {
            player[i].addCard( cards.dealUp() );
        }
        this.addCard( cards.dealDown() );
    }

    protected boolean hit( Dealer dealer ) {
        if( standing_players.size() > 0 && getHand().total() < 17 ) {
            return true;
        }
        return false;
    }

    protected void exposeHand() {
        getHand().turnOver();
        notifyChanged();
    }

    protected PlayerState getBlackjackState() {
        return new DealerBlackjack();
    }
    protected PlayerState getDealingState() {
```

LISTING E.3   continued

```java
            return new DealerDealing();
        }
        protected PlayerState getCollectingBetsState() {
            return new DealerCollectingBets();
        }
        protected PlayerState getBustedState() {
            return new DealerBusted();
        }
        protected PlayerState getStandingState() {
            return new DealerStanding();
        }
        protected PlayerState getWaitingState() {
            return new DealerWaiting();
        }
        protected PlayerState getInitialState() {
            return new DealerCollectingBets();
        }

        private class DealerCollectingBets implements PlayerState {
            public void handChanged() {
                // not possible in betting state
            }
            public void handPlayable() {
                // not possible in betting state
            }
            public void handBlackjack() {
                // not possible in betting state
            }
            public void handBusted() {
                // not possible in betting state
            }
            public void execute( Dealer dealer ) {
                if( !betting_players.isEmpty() ) {
                    Player player = (Player) betting_players.get( 0 );
                    betting_players.remove( player );
                    player.play( dealer );
                } else {
                    setCurrentState( getDealingState() );
                    getCurrentState().execute( dealer );
                    // transition and execute
                }
            }
        }

        private class DealerBusted implements PlayerState {
            public void handChanged() {
                // not possible in busted state
            }
```

E

LISTING E.3   continued

```java
        public void handPlayable() {
            // not possible in busted state
        }
        public void handBlackjack() {
            // not possible in busted state
        }
        public void handBusted() {
            // not possible in busted state
        }
        public void execute( Dealer dealer ) {
            Iterator i = standing_players.iterator();
            while( i.hasNext() ) {
                Player player = (Player) i.next();
                player.win();
            }
            i = blackjack_players.iterator();
            while( i.hasNext() ) {
                Player player = (Player) i.next();
                player.blackjack();
            }
            i = busted_players.iterator();
            while( i.hasNext() ) {
                Player player = (Player) i.next();
                player.lose();
            }
        }
    }
    private class DealerBlackjack implements PlayerState {
        public void handChanged() {
            notifyChanged();
        }
        public void handPlayable() {
            // not possible in blackjack state
        }
        public void handBlackjack() {
            // not possible in blackjack state
        }
        public void handBusted() {
            // not possible in blackjack state
        }
        public void execute( Dealer dealer ) {
            exposeHand();
            Iterator i = players.iterator();
            while( i.hasNext() ) {
                Player player = (Player) i.next();
                if( player.getHand().blackjack() ) {
                    player.standoff();
                } else {
```

```java
                    player.lose();
                }
            }
        }
    }
    private class DealerStanding implements PlayerState {
        public void handChanged() {
            // not possible in standing state
        }
        public void handPlayable() {
            // not possible in standing state
        }
        public void handBlackjack() {
            // not possible in standing state
        }
        public void handBusted() {
            // not possible in standing state
        }
        public void execute( Dealer dealer ) {
            Iterator i = standing_players.iterator();
            while( i.hasNext() ) {
                Player player = (Player) i.next();
                if( player.getHand().isEqual( getHand() ) ) {
                    player.standoff();
                } else if( player.getHand().isGreaterThan( getHand() ) ) {
                    player.win();
                } else {
                    player.lose();
                }
            }
            i = blackjack_players.iterator();
            while( i.hasNext() ) {
                Player player = (Player) i.next();
                player.blackjack();
            }
            i = busted_players.iterator();
            while( i.hasNext() ) {
                Player player = (Player) i.next();
                player.lose();
            }
        }
    }
    private class DealerWaiting implements PlayerState {
        public void handChanged() {
            // not possible in waiting state
        }
        public void handPlayable() {
            // not possible in waiting state
```

LISTING E.3 continued

```
        }
        public void handBlackjack() {
            // not possible in waiting state
        }
        public void handBusted() {
            // not possible in waiting state
        }
        public void execute( Dealer dealer ) {
            if( !waiting_players.isEmpty() ) {
                Player player = (Player) waiting_players.get( 0 );
                waiting_players.remove( player );
                player.play( dealer );
            } else {
                setCurrentState( getPlayingState() );
                exposeHand();
                getCurrentState().execute( dealer );
                // transition and execute
            }
        }
    }
    private class DealerDealing implements PlayerState {
        public void handChanged() {
            notifyChanged();
        }
        public void handPlayable() {
            setCurrentState( getWaitingState() );
            // transition
        }
        public void handBlackjack() {
            setCurrentState( getBlackjackState() );
            notifyBlackjack();
            // transition
        }
        public void handBusted() {
            // not possible in dealing state
        }
        public void execute( Dealer dealer ) {
            deal();
            getCurrentState().execute( dealer );
            // transition and execute
        }
    }
}
```

LISTING E.4   `Card.java`

```java
package blackjack.core;

public class Card {

    private Rank rank;
    private Suit suit;
    private boolean face_up;

    public Card( Suit suit, Rank rank ) {
        this.suit = suit;
        this.rank = rank;
    }

    public Suit getSuit() {
        return suit;
    }

    public Rank getRank() {
        return rank;
    }

    public void setFaceUp( boolean up ) {
        face_up = up;
    }

    public boolean isFaceUp() {
        return face_up;
    }

    public String toString() {
        if( !isFaceUp() ) {
            return "Hidden";
        }
        return rank.toString() + suit.toString();
    }
}
```

LISTING E.5   `Dealer.java`

```java
package blackjack.core;

public interface Dealer {
    // used by the player to interact with the dealer
    public void hit( Player player );

    // used by the player to communicate state to dealer
```

E

LISTING E.5 continued

```
    public void blackjack( Player player );
    public void busted( Player player );
    public void standing( Player player );
    public void doneBetting( Player player );

    public Card getUpCard();
}
```

LISTING E.6 Deck.java

```
package blackjack.core;

import java.util.Iterator;
import java.util.Random;

public class Deck {

    private Card [] deck;
    private int index;

    public Deck() {
        buildCards();
    }

    public void addToStack( Deckpile stack ) {
        stack.addCards( deck );
    }

    protected void setDeck( Card [] deck ) {
        this.deck = deck;
    }

    protected void buildCards() {

        deck = new Card[52];

        Iterator suits = Suit.SUITS.iterator();

        int counter = 0;
        while( suits.hasNext() ) {
            Suit suit = (Suit) suits.next();
            Iterator ranks = Rank.RANKS.iterator();
            while( ranks.hasNext() ) {
                Rank rank = (Rank) ranks.next();
                deck[counter] = new Card( suit, rank );
                counter++;
```

LISTING E.6 continued

```
            }
        }

    }

}
```

LISTING E.7 Deckpile.java

```java
package blackjack.core;

import java.util.ArrayList;
import java.util.Iterator;
import java.util.Random;

public class Deckpile {

    private ArrayList stack = new ArrayList();
    private int index;
    private Random rand = new Random();

    public void addCards( Card [] cards ) {
        for( int i = 0; i < cards.length; i ++ ) {
            stack.add( cards[i] );
        }
    }

    public void shuffle() {
        reset();
        randomize();
        randomize();
        randomize();
        randomize();
    }

    public Card dealUp() {
        Card card = deal();
        if( card != null ) {
            card.setFaceUp( true );
        }
        return card;
    }

    public Card dealDown() {
        Card card = deal();
        if( card != null ) {
            card.setFaceUp( false );
        }
```

E

LISTING E.7   continued

```
            return card;
        }

        public void reset() {
            index = 0;
            Iterator i = stack.iterator();
            while( i.hasNext() ) {
                Card card = (Card) i.next();
                card.setFaceUp(false);
            }
        }

        private Card deal() {
            if( index != stack.size() ) {
                Card card = (Card) stack.get( index );
                index++;
                return card;
            }
            return null;
        }

        private void randomize() {
            int num_cards = stack.size();
            for( int i = 0; i < num_cards; i ++ ) {
                int index = rand.nextInt( num_cards );
                Card card_i = (Card) stack.get( i );
                Card card_index = (Card) stack.get( index );
                stack.set( i, card_index );
                stack.set( index, card_i );
            }
        }

}
```

LISTING E.8   Hand.java

```
package blackjack.core;

import java.util.ArrayList;
import java.util.Iterator;

public class Hand {

    private ArrayList cards = new ArrayList();
    private static final int BLACKJACK = 21;
    private HandListener holder;
```

LISTING E.8   continued

```
private int number_aces;

public Hand() {
    // set the holder to a blank listener so it will not be null if not
    // externally set
    setHolder(
        new HandListener() {
            public void handPlayable() {}
            public void handBlackjack() {}
            public void handBusted() {}
            public void handChanged() {}
        }
    );
}

public void setHolder( HandListener holder ) {
    this.holder = holder;
}

public Iterator getCards() {
    return cards.iterator();
}

public void addCard( Card card ) {
    cards.add( card );

    holder.handChanged();

    if( card.getRank() == Rank.ACE ) {
        number_aces++;
    }

    if( bust() ) {
        holder.handBusted();
        return;
    }
    if( blackjack() ) {
        holder.handBlackjack();
        return;
    }
    if ( cards.size() >= 2 ){
        holder.handPlayable();
        return;
    }
}

public boolean canDoubleDown() {
    return ( cards.size() == 2 );
```

```java
        }

        public boolean isEqual( Hand hand ) {
            if( hand.total() == this.total() ) {
                return true;
            }
            return false;
        }

        public boolean isGreaterThan( Hand hand ) {
            return this.total() > hand.total();
        }

        public boolean blackjack() {
            if( cards.size() == 2 && total() == BLACKJACK ) {
                return true;
            }
            return false;
        }

        public void reset() {
            cards.clear();
            number_aces = 0;
        }

        public void turnOver() {
            Iterator i = cards.iterator();
            while( i.hasNext() ) {
                Card card = (Card) i.next();
                card.setFaceUp( true );
            }
        }

        public String toString() {
            Iterator i = cards.iterator();
            String string = "";
            while( i.hasNext() ) {
                Card card = (Card)i.next();
                string = string + " " + card.toString();
            }
            return string;
        }

        public int total() {
            int total = 0;
            Iterator i = cards.iterator();
            while( i.hasNext() ) {
                Card card = (Card) i.next();
```

LISTING E.8 continued

```java
                total += card.getRank().getRank();
        }
        int temp_aces = number_aces;
        while( total > BLACKJACK && temp_aces > 0 ) {
            total = total - 10;
            temp_aces--;
        }
        return total;
    }

    private boolean bust() {
        if( total() > BLACKJACK ) {
            return true;
        }
        return false;
    }

}
```

E

LISTING E.9 HandListener.java

```java
package blackjack.core;

public interface HandListener {

    public void handPlayable();

    public void handBlackjack();

    public void handBusted();

    public void handChanged();

}
```

LISTING E.10 Player.java

```java
package blackjack.core;

import java.util.ArrayList;
import java.util.Iterator;

public abstract class Player {

    private Hand hand;
```

LISTING E.10   continued

```java
private String name;
private ArrayList listeners = new ArrayList();
private PlayerState current_state;

public Player( String name, Hand hand ) {
    this.name = name;
    this.hand = hand;
    setCurrentState( getInitialState() );
}

public void addCard( Card card ) {
    hand.addCard( card );
}

public void play( Dealer dealer ) {
    current_state.execute( dealer );
}

public void reset() {
    hand.reset();
    setCurrentState( getInitialState() );
    notifyChanged();
}

public void addListener( PlayerListener l ) {
    listeners.add( l );
}

public String getName() {
    return name;
}

public String toString() {
    return ( name + ": " + hand.toString() );
}

public void win() {
    notifyWin();
}

public void lose() {
    notifyLose();
}

public void standoff() {
    notifyStandoff();
}

public void blackjack() {
```

LISTING E.10 continued

```
        notifyBlackjack();
    }

    public Hand getHand() {
        return hand;
    }

    protected void notifyChanged() {
        Iterator i = listeners.iterator();
        while( i.hasNext() ) {
            PlayerListener pl = (PlayerListener) i.next();
            pl.playerChanged( this );
        }
    }

    protected void notifyBusted() {
        Iterator i = listeners.iterator();
        while( i.hasNext() ) {
            PlayerListener pl = (PlayerListener) i.next();
            pl.playerBusted( this );
        }
    }

    protected void notifyBlackjack() {
        Iterator i = listeners.iterator();
        while( i.hasNext() ) {
            PlayerListener pl = (PlayerListener) i.next();
            pl.playerBlackjack( this );
        }
    }

    protected void notifyStanding() {
        Iterator i = listeners.iterator();
        while( i.hasNext() ) {
            PlayerListener pl = (PlayerListener) i.next();
            pl.playerStanding( this );
        }
    }

    protected void notifyStandoff() {
        Iterator i = listeners.iterator();
        while( i.hasNext() ) {
            PlayerListener pl = (PlayerListener) i.next();
            pl.playerStandoff( this );
        }
    }

    protected void notifyWin() {
```

LISTING E.10   continued

```
            Iterator i = listeners.iterator();
            while( i.hasNext() ) {
                PlayerListener pl = (PlayerListener) i.next();
                pl.playerWon( this );
            }
        }

        protected void notifyLose() {
            Iterator i = listeners.iterator();
            while( i.hasNext() ) {
                PlayerListener pl = (PlayerListener) i.next();
                pl.playerLost( this );
            }
        }

        protected final void setCurrentState( PlayerState state ) {
            current_state = state;
            hand.setHolder( state );
        }

        protected final PlayerState getCurrentState() {
            return current_state;
        }

        protected PlayerState getBustedState() {
            return new Busted();
        }
        protected PlayerState getStandingState() {
            return new Standing();
        }
        protected PlayerState getPlayingState() {
            return new Playing();
        }
        protected PlayerState getWaitingState() {
            return new Waiting();
        }
        protected PlayerState getBlackjackState() {
            return new Blackjack();
        }

        protected abstract PlayerState getInitialState();

        protected abstract boolean hit( Dealer dealer );

        private class Waiting implements PlayerState {
            public void handChanged() {
                notifyChanged();
            }
```

LISTING E.10 continued

```
        public void handPlayable() {
            setCurrentState( getPlayingState() );
            // transition
        }
        public void handBlackjack() {
            setCurrentState( getBlackjackState() );
            notifyBlackjack();
            // transition
        }
        public void handBusted() {
            // not possible in waiting state
        }
        public void execute( Dealer dealer ) {
            // do nothing while waiting
        }
    }

    private class Busted implements PlayerState {
        public void handChanged() {
            // not possible in busted state
        }
        public void handPlayable() {
            // not possible in busted state
        }
        public void handBlackjack() {
            // not possible in busted state
        }
        public void handBusted() {
            // not possible in busted state
        }
        public void execute( Dealer dealer ) {
            dealer.busted( Player.this );
            // terminate
        }
    }
    private class Blackjack implements PlayerState {
        public void handChanged() {
            // not possible in blackjack state
        }
        public void handPlayable() {
            // not possible in blackjack state
        }
        public void handBlackjack() {
            // not possible in blackjack state
        }
        public void handBusted() {
            // not possible in blackjack state
        }
```

E

```
            public void execute( Dealer dealer ) {
                dealer.blackjack( Player.this );
                // terminate
            }
        }
        private class Standing implements PlayerState {
            public void handChanged() {
                // not possible in standing state
            }
            public void handPlayable() {
                // not possible in standing state
            }
            public void handBlackjack() {
                // not possible in standing state
            }
            public void handBusted() {
                // not possible in standing state
            }
            public void execute( Dealer dealer ) {
                dealer.standing( Player.this );
                // terminate
            }
        }
        private class Playing implements PlayerState {
            public void handChanged() {
                notifyChanged();
            }
            public void handPlayable() {
                // can ignore in playing state
            }
            public void handBlackjack() {
                // not possible in playing state
            }
            public void handBusted() {
                setCurrentState( getBustedState() );
                notifyBusted();
            }
            public void execute( Dealer dealer ) {
                if( hit( dealer ) ) {
                    dealer.hit( Player.this );
                } else {
                    setCurrentState( getStandingState() );
                    notifyStanding();
                }
                current_state.execute( dealer );
                // transition
            }
        }
    }

    }
```

LISTING E.11 PlayerListener.java

```java
package blackjack.core;

public interface PlayerListener {

    public void playerChanged( Player player );

    public void playerBusted( Player player );

    public void playerBlackjack( Player player );

    public void playerStanding( Player player );

    public void playerWon( Player player );

    public void playerLost( Player player );

    public void playerStandoff( Player player );

}
```

E

LISTING E.12 PlayerState.java

```java
package blackjack.core;

public interface PlayerState extends HandListener {

    public void execute( Dealer dealer );

}
```

LISTING E.13 Rank.java

```java
package blackjack.core;

import java.util.Collections;
import java.util.List;
import java.util.Arrays;

public final class Rank {

    public static final Rank TWO   = new Rank( 2, "2" );
    public static final Rank THREE = new Rank( 3, "3" );
    public static final Rank FOUR  = new Rank( 4, "4" );
    public static final Rank FIVE  = new Rank( 5, "5" );
```

LISTING E.13 continued

```
        public static final Rank SIX   = new Rank( 6, "6" );
        public static final Rank SEVEN = new Rank( 7, "7" );
        public static final Rank EIGHT = new Rank( 8, "8" );
        public static final Rank NINE  = new Rank( 9, "9" );
        public static final Rank TEN   = new Rank( 10, "10" );
        public static final Rank JACK  = new Rank( 10, "J" );
        public static final Rank QUEEN = new Rank( 10, "Q" );
        public static final Rank KING  = new Rank( 10, "K" );
        public static final Rank ACE   = new Rank( 11, "A" );

        private static final Rank [] VALUES =
                { TWO, THREE, FOUR, FIVE, SIX, SEVEN,
                  EIGHT, NINE, TEN, JACK, QUEEN, KING, ACE };

        // provide an unmodifiable list to loop over
        public static final List RANKS =
            Collections.unmodifiableList( Arrays.asList( VALUES ) );

        private final int    rank;
        private final String display;

        private Rank( int rank, String display ) {
            this.rank = rank;
            this.display = display;
        }

        public int getRank() {
            return rank;
        }

        public String toString() {
            return display;
        }
    }
```

LISTING E.14 Suit.java

```
    package blackjack.core;

    import java.util.Collections;
    import java.util.List;
    import java.util.Arrays;

    public final class Suit {

        // statically define all valid values of Suit
```

LISTING E.14   continued

```
public static final Suit DIAMONDS = new Suit( (char)4 );
public static final Suit HEARTS   = new Suit( (char)3 );
public static final Suit SPADES   = new Suit( (char)6 );
public static final Suit CLUBS    = new Suit( (char)5 );

private static final Suit [] VALUES = { DIAMONDS, HEARTS, SPADES, CLUBS };

// provide an unmodifiable list to loop over
public static final List SUITS =
    Collections.unmodifiableList( Arrays.asList( VALUES ) );

// instance variable for holding onto display value
private final char display;

// do not allow instantiation by outside objects
private Suit( char display ) {
    this.display = display;
}

// return the Suit's value
public String toString() {
    return String.valueOf( display );
}
}
```

blackjack.core.threaded

`blackjack.core.threaded` contains a `BlackjackDealer` that places the players into their own threads (Listing E.15).

LISTING E.15   ThreadedBlackjackDealer.java

```
package blackjack.core.threaded;

import blackjack.core.*;
import java.util.ArrayList;
import java.util.Iterator;

public class ThreadedBlackjackDealer extends BlackjackDealer {

    public ThreadedBlackjackDealer( String name, Hand hand, Deckpile cards ) {
        super( name, hand, cards );
    }

    protected PlayerState getWaitingState() {
```

```java
            return new DealerWaiting();
        }

        protected PlayerState getCollectingBetsState() {
            return new DealerCollectingBets();
        }

        private class DealerCollectingBets implements PlayerState {
            public void handChanged() {
                // not possible in betting state
            }
            public void handPlayable() {
                // not possible in betting state
            }
            public void handBlackjack() {
                // not possible in betting state
            }
            public void handBusted() {
                // not possible in betting state
            }
            public void execute( final Dealer dealer ) {
                if( !betting_players.isEmpty() ) {
                    final Player player = (Player) betting_players.get( 0 );
                    betting_players.remove( player );
                        Runnable runnable = new Runnable() {
                        public void run() {
                            player.play( dealer );
                        }
                    };
                    Thread threaded = new Thread( runnable );
                    threaded.start();
                } else {
                    setCurrentState( getDealingState() );
                    getCurrentState().execute( dealer );
                    // transition and execute
                }
            }
        }

        private class DealerWaiting implements PlayerState {
            public void handChanged() {
                // not possible in waiting state
            }
            public void handPlayable() {
                // not possible in waiting state
            }
            public void handBlackjack() {
                // not possible in waiting state
```

LISTING E.15 continued

```
        }
        public void handBusted() {
            // not possible in waiting state
        }
        public void execute( final Dealer d ) {
            if( !waiting_players.isEmpty() ) {
                final Player p = (Player) waiting_players.get( 0 );
                waiting_players.remove( p );
                    Runnable r = new Runnable() {
                    public void run() {
                        p.play( d );
                    }
                };
                Thread t = new Thread( r );
                t.start();
            } else {
                setCurrentState( getPlayingState() );
                exposeHand();
                getCurrentState().execute( d );
                // transition and execute
            }
        }
    }
}
```

blackjack.exe

blackjack.exe contains the executables for the MVC GUI, PAC GUI, CLI UI, and simulator (Listings E.16 through E.19).

LISTING E.16 BlackjackCLI.java

```
package blackjack.exe;

import blackjack.core.*;
import blackjack.players.*;
import blackjack.ui.*;

public class BlackjackCLI {

    public static void main( String [] args ) {
        Deckpile cards = new Deckpile();
        for( int i = 0; i < 4; i ++ ) {
            cards.shuffle();
            Deck deck = new Deck();
```

LISTING E.16   continued

```
            deck.addToStack( cards );
            cards.shuffle();
        }

        Hand dealer_hand = new Hand();
        BlackjackDealer dealer = new BlackjackDealer( "Dealer", dealer_hand,
➥cards );
        Bank human_bank = new Bank( 1000 );
        Hand human_hand = new Hand();
        Player player = new CommandLinePlayer( "Human", human_hand, human_bank
➥);
        dealer.addListener( Console.INSTANCE );
        player.addListener( Console.INSTANCE );
        dealer.addPlayer( player );

        do {
            dealer.newGame();
        } while( playAgain() );

        Console.INSTANCE.printMessage( "Thank you for playing!" );

    }

    private static boolean playAgain() {
        Console.INSTANCE.printMessage( "Would you like to play again? [Y]es
➥[N]o" );
        String response = Console.INSTANCE.readInput( "invalid" );
        if( response.equalsIgnoreCase( "y" ) ) {
            return true;
        }
        return false;
    }

}
```

LISTING E.17   BlackjackMVC.java

```
package blackjack.exe;

import blackjack.core.*;
import blackjack.core.threaded.*;
import blackjack.ui.mvc.*;
import javax.swing.*;
import java.awt.*;
import java.awt.event.*;

public class BlackjackMVC extends JFrame {
```

LISTING E.17 continued

```java
public static void main( String [] args ) {
    JFrame frame = new BlackjackMVC();
    frame.getContentPane().setBackground( FOREST_GREEN );
    frame.setSize( 580, 480 );
    frame.show();
}

private BlackjackDealer dealer;
private GUIPlayer      human;
private JPanel players = new JPanel( new GridLayout( 0, 1 ) );

private static final Color FOREST_GREEN = new Color( 35, 142, 35 );

public BlackjackMVC() {
    setUp();
    WindowAdapter wa = new WindowAdapter() {
        public void windowClosing( WindowEvent e ) {
            System.exit( 0 );
        }
    };
    addWindowListener( wa );
}

// needs to be protected if subclassed
private PlayerView getPlayerView( Player player ) {
    PlayerView view = new PlayerView( player );
    view.setBackground( FOREST_GREEN );
    return view;
}

// needs to be protected if subclassed
private void setUp() {
    BlackjackDealer dealer = getDealer();
    PlayerView v1 = getPlayerView( dealer );

    GUIPlayer human = getHuman();
    PlayerView v2 = getPlayerView( human );

    PlayerView [] views = { v1, v2 };
    addPlayers( views );

    dealer.addPlayer( human );

    addOptionView( human, dealer );
}

// needs to be protected if subclassed
private void addPlayers( PlayerView [] pview ) {
```

LISTING E.17   continued

```
            players.setBackground( FOREST_GREEN );
            for( int i = 0; i < pview.length; i ++ ) {
                players.add( pview[i] );
            }
            getContentPane().add( players, BorderLayout.CENTER );
        }

        private void addOptionView( GUIPlayer human, BlackjackDealer dealer ) {
            OptionView ov = new OptionView( human, dealer );
            ov.setBackground( FOREST_GREEN );
            getContentPane().add( ov, BorderLayout.SOUTH );
        }

        private BlackjackDealer getDealer() {
            if( dealer == null ) {
                Hand dealer_hand = new Hand();
                Deckpile cards = getCards();
                dealer = new ThreadedBlackjackDealer( "Dealer", dealer_hand, cards
➥);
            }
            return dealer;
        }

        private GUIPlayer getHuman() {
            if( human == null ) {
                Hand human_hand = new Hand();
                Bank bank = new Bank( 1000 );
                human = new GUIPlayer( "Human", human_hand, bank );
            }
            return human;
        }

        private Deckpile getCards() {
            Deckpile cards = new Deckpile();
            for( int i = 0; i < 4; i ++ ) {
                cards.shuffle();
                Deck deck = new VDeck();
                deck.addToStack( cards );
                cards.shuffle();
            }
            return cards;
        }

    }
```

LISTING E.18 BlackjackPAC.java

```java
package blackjack.exe;

import blackjack.core.*;
import blackjack.ui.pac.*;
import javax.swing.*;
import java.awt.*;
import java.awt.event.*;

public class BlackjackPAC extends JFrame {

    public static void main( String [] args ) {
        JFrame frame = new BlackjackPAC();
        frame.getContentPane().setBackground( FOREST_GREEN );
        frame.setSize( 580, 480 );
        frame.show();
    }

    private VPlayerFactory factory = new VPlayerFactory();
    private JPanel players = new JPanel( new GridLayout( 0, 1 ) );

    private static final Color FOREST_GREEN = new Color( 35, 142, 35 );

    public BlackjackPAC() {
        setUp();
        WindowAdapter wa = new WindowAdapter() {
            public void windowClosing( WindowEvent e ) {
                System.exit( 0 );
            }
        };
        addWindowListener( wa );
    }

    // needs to be protected if subclassed
    private void setUp() {
        VBlackjackDealer dealer = factory.getDealer();

        GUIPlayer human = factory.getHuman();

        dealer.addPlayer( human );

        players.add( dealer.view() );
        players.add( human.view() );
        getContentPane().add( players, BorderLayout.CENTER );
    }

}
```

E

LISTING E.19   BlackjackSim.java

```java
package blackjack.exe;

import blackjack.core.*;
import blackjack.ui.*;
import blackjack.players.*;

public class BlackjackSim {

    public static void main( String [] args ) {

        Console.INSTANCE.printMessage( "How many times should the simulator
play?" );
        String response = Console.INSTANCE.readInput( "invalid" );
        int loops = Integer.parseInt( response );

        Deckpile cards = new Deckpile();
        for( int i = 0; i < 4; i ++ ) {
            cards.shuffle();
            Deck deck = new Deck();
            deck.addToStack( cards );
            cards.shuffle();
        }

        // create a dealer
        Hand dealer_hand = new Hand();
        BlackjackDealer dealer = new BlackjackDealer( "Dealer", dealer_hand,
cards );

        // create a OneHitPlayer
        Bank one_bank = new Bank( 1000 );
        Hand one_hand = new Hand();
        Player oplayer = new OneHitPlayer( "OneHit", one_hand, one_bank );

        // create a SmartPlayer
        Bank smart_bank = new Bank( 1000 );
        Hand smart_hand = new Hand();
        Player smplayer = new SmartPlayer( "Smart", smart_hand, smart_bank );

        // create a SafePlayer
        Bank safe_bank = new Bank( 1000 );
        Hand safe_hand = new Hand();
        Player splayer = new SafePlayer( "Safe", safe_hand, safe_bank );

        // create a FlipPlayer
        Bank flip_bank = new Bank( 1000 );
        Hand flip_hand = new Hand();
        Player fplayer = new FlipPlayer( "Flip", flip_hand, flip_bank );
```

```
            // create a knowledgeable player
            Bank kn_bank = new Bank( 1000 );
            Hand kn_hand = new Hand();
            Player knplayer = new KnowledgeablePlayer( "Knowledgeable", kn_hand,
    kn_bank );

            // create an "optimal" player
            Bank opt_bank = new Bank( 1000 );
            Hand opt_hand = new Hand();
            Player optplayer = new OptimalPlayer( "Optimal", opt_hand, opt_bank );

            // hook all of the players together
            dealer.addListener( Console.INSTANCE );
            oplayer.addListener( Console.INSTANCE );
            dealer.addPlayer( oplayer );
            splayer.addListener( Console.INSTANCE );
            dealer.addPlayer( splayer );
            smplayer.addListener( Console.INSTANCE );
            dealer.addPlayer( smplayer );
            fplayer.addListener( Console.INSTANCE );
            dealer.addPlayer( fplayer );
            knplayer.addListener( Console.INSTANCE );
            dealer.addPlayer( knplayer );
            optplayer.addListener( Console.INSTANCE );
            dealer.addPlayer( optplayer );

            int counter = 0;
            while( counter < loops ) {
                dealer.newGame();
                counter ++;
            }
        }
    }
}
```

blackjack.players

blackjack.players contains the various players that were created in the text and for some of the exercises (Listings E.20 through E.26).

LISTING E.20   `CommandLinePlayer.java`

```java
package blackjack.players;

import blackjack.core.*;
import blackjack.ui.*;

public class CommandLinePlayer extends BettingPlayer {

    private final static String HIT   = "H";
    private final static String STAND = "S";
    private final static String PLAY_MSG = "[H]it or [S]tay";
    private final static String BET_MSG = "Place Bet: [10] [50] or [100]";
    private final static String DD_MSG  = "Double Down? [Y]es [N]o";
    private final static String BET_10  = "10";
    private final static String BET_50  = "50";
    private final static String BET_100 = "100";
    private final static String NO  = "N";
    private final static String YES = "Y";
    private final static String DEFAULT = "invalid";

    public CommandLinePlayer( String name, Hand hand, Bank bank ) {
        super( name, hand, bank );
    }

    protected boolean hit( Dealer dealer ) {
        while( true ) {
            Console.INSTANCE.printMessage( PLAY_MSG );
            String response = Console.INSTANCE.readInput( DEFAULT );
            if( response.equalsIgnoreCase( HIT ) ) {
                return true;
            } else if( response.equalsIgnoreCase( STAND ) ) {
                return false;
            }
            // if we get here loop until we get meaningful input
        }
    }

    protected boolean doubleDown( Dealer dealer ) {
        while( true ) {
            Console.INSTANCE.printMessage( DD_MSG );
            String response = Console.INSTANCE.readInput( DEFAULT );
            if( response.equalsIgnoreCase( NO ) ) {
                return false;
            } else if( response.equalsIgnoreCase( YES ) ) {
                return true;
            }
            // if we get here loop until we get meaningful input
        }
    }
```

LISTING E.20 continued

```java
    protected void bet() {
        while( true ) {
            Console.INSTANCE.printMessage( BET_MSG );
            String response = Console.INSTANCE.readInput( DEFAULT );
            if( response.equals( BET_10 ) ) {
                getBank().place10Bet();
                return;
            }
            if( response.equals( BET_50 ) ) {
                getBank().place50Bet();
                return;

            }
            if( response.equals( BET_100 ) ) {
                getBank().place100Bet();
                return;
            }
            // if we get here loop until we get meaningful input
        }
    }

}
```

LISTING E.21 FlipPlayer.java

```java
package blackjack.players;

import blackjack.core.*;

public class FlipPlayer extends BettingPlayer {

    private boolean hit = false;
    private boolean should_hit_once = false;

    public FlipPlayer( String name, Hand hand, Bank bank ) {
        super( name, hand, bank );
    }

    public boolean hit( Dealer dealer ) {
        if( should_hit_once && !hit ) {
            hit = true;
            return true;
        }
        return false;
    }
```

LISTING E.21   continued

```java
        public void reset() {
            super.reset();
            hit = false;
            should_hit_once = !should_hit_once;
        }

        public void bet() {
            getBank().place10Bet();
        }

        public boolean doubleDown( Dealer dealer ) {
            return false;
        }
    }
```

LISTING E.22   KnowledgeablePlayer.java

```java
    package blackjack.players;

    import blackjack.core.*;

    public class KnowledgeablePlayer extends BettingPlayer {

        public KnowledgeablePlayer(String name,Hand hand,Bank bank) {
            super( name, hand, bank );
        }

        public boolean doubleDown( Dealer dealer ) {
            int total = getHand().total();
            if( total == 10 || total == 11 ) {
                return true;
            }
            return false;
        }

        public boolean hit( Dealer dealer ) {

            int total = getHand().total();
            Card card = dealer.getUpCard();

            // never hit, no matter what, if total > 15
            if( total > 15 ) {
                return false;
            }

            // always hit for 11 and less
```

LISTING E.22   continued

```
            if( total <= 11 ) {
                return true;
            }

            // this leaves 11, 12, 13, 14
            // base decision on dealer

            if( card.getRank().getRank() > 7 ) {
                return true;
            }

            return false;

        }

        public void bet() {
            getBank().place10Bet();
        }

    }
```

LISTING E.23   OneHitPlayer.java

```
    package blackjack.players;

    import blackjack.core.*;

    public class OneHitPlayer extends BettingPlayer {

        private boolean has_hit = false;

        public OneHitPlayer( String name, Hand hand, Bank bank ) {
            super( name, hand, bank );
        }

        public boolean hit( Dealer dealer ) {
            if( !has_hit ) {
                has_hit = true;
                return true;
            }
            return false;
        }

        public void reset() {
            super.reset();
            has_hit = false;
```

LISTING E.23   continued

```
    }

    public void bet() {
        getBank().place10Bet();
    }

    public boolean doubleDown( Dealer dealer ) {
        return false;
    }

}
```

LISTING E.24   OptimalPlayer.java

```
package blackjack.players;

import blackjack.core.*;

public class OptimalPlayer extends BettingPlayer {

    public OptimalPlayer( String name, Hand hand, Bank bank ) {
        super( name, hand, bank );
    }

    public boolean doubleDown( Dealer dealer ) {
        int total = getHand().total();
        Card card = dealer.getUpCard();
        if( total == 11) {
            return true;
        }
        if( total == 10 ) {
            if( card.getRank().getRank() != Rank.TEN.getRank() &&
                card.getRank() != Rank.ACE ) {
                return true;
            }
            return false;
        }
        if( total == 9 ) {
            if( card.getRank() == Rank.TWO   ||
                card.getRank() == Rank.THREE ||
                card.getRank() == Rank.FOUR  ||
                card.getRank() == Rank.FIVE  ||
                card.getRank() == Rank.SIX ) {
                return true;
            }
            return false;
        }
```

LISTING E.24 continued

```
            return false;
        }

    public boolean hit( Dealer dealer ) {

        int total = getHand().total();
        Card card = dealer.getUpCard();

        if( total >= 17 ) {
            return false;
        }

        if( total == 16 ) {
            if( card.getRank() == Rank.SEVEN ||
                card.getRank() == Rank.EIGHT ||
                card.getRank() == Rank.NINE ) {
                return true;
            } else {
                return false;
            }
        }
        if( total == 13 || total == 14 || total == 15 ) {
            if( card.getRank() == Rank.TWO   ||
                card.getRank() == Rank.THREE ||
                card.getRank() == Rank.FOUR  ||
                card.getRank() == Rank.FIVE  ||
                card.getRank() == Rank.SIX ) {
                return false;
            } else {
                return true;
            }
        }
        if( total == 12 ) {
            if( card.getRank() == Rank.FOUR ||
                card.getRank() == Rank.FIVE ||
                card.getRank() == Rank.SIX ) {
                return false;
            } else {
                return true;
            }
        }
        return true;
    }

    public void bet() {
        getBank().place10Bet();
    }

}
```

E

LISTING E.25   SafePlayer.java

```java
package blackjack.players;

import blackjack.core.*;

public class SafePlayer extends BettingPlayer {

    public SafePlayer( String name, Hand hand, Bank bank ) {
        super( name, hand, bank );
    }

    public boolean hit( Dealer dealer ) {
        return false;
    }

    public boolean doubleDown( Dealer dealer ) {
        return false;
    }

    public void bet() {
        getBank().place10Bet();
    }
}
```

LISTING E.26   SmartPlayer.java

```java
package blackjack.players;

import blackjack.core.*;

public class SmartPlayer extends BettingPlayer {

    public SmartPlayer( String name, Hand hand, Bank bank ) {
        super( name, hand, bank );
    }

    public boolean hit( Dealer dealer ) {
        if( getHand().total() > 11 ) {
            return false;
        }
        return true;
    }

    public void bet() {
        getBank().place10Bet();
    }
```

LISTING E.26   continued

```
public boolean doubleDown( Dealer dealer ) {
    return false;
}

}
```

blackjack.ui

blackjack.ui contains common UI code (Listing E.27).

LISTING E.27   Console.java

```
package blackjack.ui;

import blackjack.core.*;
import java.io.BufferedReader;
import java.io.InputStreamReader;
import java.io.IOException;

public class Console implements PlayerListener {

    // console singleton
    public final static Console INSTANCE = new Console();

    private BufferedReader in =
        new BufferedReader( new InputStreamReader( System.in ) );

    public void printMessage( String message ) {
        System.out.println( message );
    }

    public String readInput( String default_input ) {
        String response;
        try {
            return in.readLine();
        } catch (IOException ioe) {
            return default_input;
        }
    }

    public void playerChanged( Player player ) {
        printMessage( player.toString() );
    }

    public void playerBusted( Player player ) {
        printMessage( player.toString() + " BUSTED!" );
```

E

LISTING E.27   continued

```
    }

    public void playerBlackjack( Player player ) {
        printMessage( player.toString() + " BLACKJACK!" );
    }

    public void playerStanding( Player player ) {
        printMessage( player.toString() + " STANDING" );
    }

    public void playerWon( Player player ) {
        printMessage( player.toString() + " WINNER!" );
    }

    public void playerLost( Player player ) {
        printMessage( player.toString() + " LOSER!" );
    }

    public void playerStandoff( Player player ) {
        printMessage( player.toString() + " STANDOFF" );
    }

    // private to prevent instantiation
    private Console() {}

}
```

blackjack.ui.mvc

blackjack.ui.mvc contains the mvc code (Listings E.28 through E.34).

LISTING E.28   CardView.java

```
package blackjack.ui.mvc;

import blackjack.core.*;
import javax.swing.*;
import java.awt.*;

public class CardView extends JLabel {

    private ImageIcon icon;

    public CardView( VCard card ) {
        getImage( card.getImage() );
```

LISTING E.28 continued

```
            setIcon( icon );
            setBackground( Color.white );
            setOpaque( true );
        }

        private void getImage( String name ) {
            java.net.URL url = this.getClass().getResource( name );
            icon = new ImageIcon( url );
        }

    }
```

LISTING E.29 GUIPlayer.java

```java
package blackjack.ui.mvc;

import blackjack.core.*;

public class GUIPlayer extends BettingPlayer {

    private Dealer dealer;

    public GUIPlayer( String name, Hand hand, Bank bank) {
        super( name, hand, bank );
    }

    public boolean hit( Dealer dealer ) {
        return true;
    }

    public void bet() {
        // do nothing, this won't get called
        // instead, the human player presses a GUI button
    }

    // these bet methods will get called by the GUI controller
    // for each: place the proper bet, change the state, let the
    // dealer know that the player is done betting
    public void place10Bet() {
        getBank().place10Bet();
        setCurrentState( getWaitingState() );
        dealer.doneBetting( this );
    }

    public void place50Bet() {
        getBank().place50Bet();
```

```
        setCurrentState( getWaitingState() );
        dealer.doneBetting( this );
    }

    public void place100Bet() {
        getBank().place100Bet();
        setCurrentState( getWaitingState() );
        dealer.doneBetting( this );
    }

    // doubling down is a bit different since the player needs to
    // respond to Hand events as a card gets added to the hand
    // so set the state to DoublingDown and then execute it
    protected boolean doubleDown( Dealer d ) {
        setCurrentState( getDoublingDownState() );
        getCurrentState().execute( dealer );
        return true;
    }

    // takeCard will get called by the GUI controller when the player
    // decides to hit
    public void takeCard() {
        dealer.hit( this );
    }

    // stand will get called by the GUI controller when the player chooses
    // to stand, when standing change state, let the world know, and then
    // tell the dealer
    public void stand() {
        setCurrentState( getStandingState() );
        notifyStanding();
        getCurrentState().execute( dealer );
    }

    // you need to override play so that it stores the dealer away for
    // later use
    public void play( Dealer dealer ) {
        this.dealer = dealer;
        super.play( dealer );
    }

    // the following deal w/ states
    protected PlayerState getPlayingState() {
        return new Playing();
    }

    protected PlayerState getBettingState() {
        return new Betting();
    }
```

```
    private class Playing implements PlayerState {

        public void handPlayable() {
            // do nothing
        }

        public void handBlackjack() {
            setCurrentState( getBlackjackState() );
            notifyBlackjack();
            getCurrentState().execute( dealer );
        }

        public void handBusted() {
            setCurrentState( getBustedState() );
            notifyBusted();
            getCurrentState().execute( dealer );
        }

        public void handChanged() {
            notifyChanged();
        }

        public void execute( Dealer dealer ) {
            // do nothing here, actions will come from the GUI which is
            // external to the state, but when events do come in be sure to
            // force state transition right away
        }
    }
    private class Betting implements PlayerState {
        public void handChanged() {
            // not possible in busted state
        }
        public void handPlayable() {
            // not possible in busted state
        }
        public void handBlackjack() {
            // not possible in busted state
        }
        public void handBusted() {
            // not possible in busted state
        }
        public void execute( Dealer dealer ) {
            // do nothing here, actions will come from the GUI which is
            // external to the state, since no events come in as part of
            // betting the state will need to be changed externally to this
state
        }
    }
}
```

E

LISTING E.30 OptionView.java

```java
package blackjack.ui.mvc;

import blackjack.core.*;
import javax.swing.*;
import java.awt.*;

public class OptionView extends JPanel {

    public static final String NEW_GAME = "new";
    public static final String QUIT     = "quit";
    public static final String HIT      = "hit";
    public static final String STAND    = "stand";
    public static final String BET_10   = "BET10";
    public static final String BET_50   = "BET50";
    public static final String BET_100  = "BET100";
    public static final String DOUBLE_DOWN = "dd";

    private JButton bet_10  = new JButton( "$10" );
    private JButton bet_50  = new JButton( "$50" );
    private JButton bet_100 = new JButton( "$100" );
    private JButton deal  = new JButton( "New Game" );
    private JButton quit  = new JButton( "Quit" );
    private JButton hit   = new JButton( "Hit" );
    private JButton stand = new JButton( "Stand" );
    private JButton ddown = new JButton( "Double Down" );
    private BlackjackDealer dealer;
    private GUIPlayer player;

    private static final Color FOREST_GREEN = new Color( 35, 142, 35 );

    public OptionView( GUIPlayer player, BlackjackDealer dealer ) {
        super( new BorderLayout() );
        this.player = player;
        this.dealer = dealer;
        attachController( makeController() );
        buildGUI();
    }

    public void attachController( OptionViewController controller ) {
        deal.addActionListener( controller );
        quit.addActionListener( controller );
        hit.addActionListener( controller );
        stand.addActionListener( controller );
        bet_10.addActionListener( controller );
        bet_50.addActionListener( controller );
        bet_100.addActionListener( controller );
        ddown.addActionListener( controller );
    }
```

```
public void enableDoubleDown( boolean enable ) {
    ddown.setEnabled( enable );
}

public void enableBettingControls( boolean enable ) {
    bet_10.setEnabled( enable );
    bet_50.setEnabled( enable );
    bet_100.setEnabled( enable );
}

public void enablePlayerControls( boolean enable ) {
    hit.setEnabled( enable );
    stand.setEnabled( enable );
}

public void enableGameControls( boolean enable ) {
    deal.setEnabled( enable );
    quit.setEnabled( enable );
}

protected OptionViewController makeController() {
    return new OptionViewController( player, dealer, this );
}

private void buildGUI() {
    JPanel betting_controls = new JPanel();
    JPanel game_controls = new JPanel();
    add( betting_controls, BorderLayout.NORTH );
    add( game_controls, BorderLayout.SOUTH );
    betting_controls.setBackground( FOREST_GREEN );
    game_controls.setBackground( FOREST_GREEN );
    ddown.setActionCommand( DOUBLE_DOWN );
    deal.setActionCommand( NEW_GAME );
    quit.setActionCommand( QUIT );
    hit.setActionCommand( HIT );
    stand.setActionCommand( STAND );
    bet_10.setActionCommand( BET_10 );
    bet_50.setActionCommand( BET_50 );
    bet_100.setActionCommand( BET_100 );
    betting_controls.add( bet_10 );
    betting_controls.add( bet_50 );
    betting_controls.add( bet_100 );
    game_controls.add( ddown );
    game_controls.add( hit );
    game_controls.add( stand );
    game_controls.add( deal );
    game_controls.add( quit );
    enableBettingControls( false );
```

E

LISTING E.30   continued

```
        enablePlayerControls( false );
        enableDoubleDown( false );
    }
}
```

LISTING E.31   OptionViewController.java

```java
package blackjack.ui.mvc;

import blackjack.core.*;
import java.awt.event.*;

public class OptionViewController implements ActionListener, PlayerListener {

    private GUIPlayer model;
    private OptionView view;
    private BlackjackDealer dealer;

    public OptionViewController( GUIPlayer model, BlackjackDealer dealer,
OptionView view ) {
        this.model = model;
        model.addListener( this );
        this.dealer = dealer;
        this.view = view;
        view.enablePlayerControls( false );
    }

    public void actionPerformed( ActionEvent event ) {
        if( event.getActionCommand().equals( OptionView.QUIT ) ) {
            System.exit( 0 );
        } else if( event.getActionCommand().equals( OptionView.HIT ) ) {
            view.enableDoubleDown( false );
            model.takeCard();
        } else if( event.getActionCommand().equals( OptionView.STAND ) ) {
            view.enableDoubleDown( false );
            model.stand();
        } else if ( event.getActionCommand().equals( OptionView.NEW_GAME ) ) {
            view.enableDoubleDown( false );
            view.enableGameControls( false );
            view.enablePlayerControls( false );
            view.enableBettingControls( true );
            dealer.newGame();
        } else if( event.getActionCommand().equals( OptionView.BET_10 ) ) {
            view.enableBettingControls( false );
            view.enablePlayerControls( true );
            view.enableDoubleDown( true );
```

LISTING E.31   continued

```
                model.place10Bet();
            } else if( event.getActionCommand().equals( OptionView.BET_50 ) ) {
                view.enableBettingControls( false );
                view.enablePlayerControls( true );
                view.enableDoubleDown( true );
                model.place50Bet();
            } else if( event.getActionCommand().equals( OptionView.BET_100 ) ) {
                view.enableBettingControls( false );
                view.enablePlayerControls( true );
                view.enableDoubleDown( true );
                model.place100Bet();
            } else if( event.getActionCommand().equals( OptionView.DOUBLE_DOWN ) ) {
                view.enableBettingControls( false );
                view.enablePlayerControls( false );
                view.enableDoubleDown( false );
                view.enableGameControls( true );
                model.doubleDown( dealer );
            }
    }

    public void playerChanged( Player player ) {}

    public void playerBusted( Player player ) {
        view.enablePlayerControls( false );
        view.enableDoubleDown( false );
        view.enableGameControls( true );
    }

    public void playerBlackjack( Player player ) {
        view.enablePlayerControls( false );
        view.enableDoubleDown( false );
        view.enableGameControls( true );
    }

    public void playerStanding( Player player ) {
        view.enablePlayerControls( false );
        view.enableGameControls( true );
    }

    public void playerWon( Player player ) {
        view.enablePlayerControls( false );
        view.enableGameControls( true );
    }

    public void playerLost( Player player ) {
        view.enablePlayerControls( false );
        view.enableDoubleDown( false );
        view.enableGameControls( true );
```

E

LISTING E.31   continued

```
    }

    public void playerStandoff( Player player ) {
        view.enablePlayerControls( false );
        view.enableGameControls( true );
    }

}
```

LISTING E.32   PlayerView.java

```
package blackjack.ui.mvc;

import blackjack.core.*;
import javax.swing.*;
import javax.swing.border.*;
import java.awt.*;
import java.util.Iterator;

public class PlayerView extends JPanel implements PlayerListener {

    private JPanel cards = new JPanel( new FlowLayout( FlowLayout.LEFT ) );
    private TitledBorder border;

    public PlayerView( Player player ) {
        super( new BorderLayout() );
        buildUI( player );
        player.addListener( this );
    }

    public void playerChanged( Player player ) {
        border.setTitle( player.getName() );
        cards.removeAll();
        Hand hand = player.getHand();
        Iterator i = hand.getCards();
        while( i.hasNext() ) {
            VCard vcard = (VCard) i.next();
            JLabel card = new CardView( vcard );
            cards.add( card );
        }
        revalidate();
        repaint();
    }

    public void playerBusted( Player player ) {
        border.setTitle( player.getName() + " BUSTED!" );
```

LISTING E.32 continued

```java
            cards.repaint();
    }

    public void playerBlackjack( Player player ) {
        border.setTitle( player.getName() + " BLACKJACK!" );
        cards.repaint();
    }

    public void playerStanding( Player player ) {
        border.setTitle( player.getName() + " STANDING" );
        cards.repaint();
    }

    public void playerWon( Player player ) {
        border.setTitle( player.getName() + " WINNER!" );
        cards.repaint();
    }

    public void playerLost( Player player ) {
        border.setTitle( player.getName() + " LOSER!" );
        cards.repaint();
    }

    public void playerStandoff( Player player ) {
        border.setTitle( player.getName() + " STANDOFF!" );
        cards.repaint();
    }

    private void buildUI( Player player ) {
        add( cards, BorderLayout.NORTH );
        border = new TitledBorder( player.getName() );
        cards.setBorder( border );
        cards.setBackground( new Color( 35, 142, 35 ) );
        border.setTitleColor( Color.black );
    }

}
```

LISTING E.33 VCard.java

```java
package blackjack.ui.mvc;

import blackjack.core.*;

public class VCard extends Card {
```

LISTING E.33 continued

```
    private String image;

    public VCard( Suit suit, Rank rank, String image ) {
        super( suit, rank );
        this.image = image;
    }

    public String getImage() {
        if( isFaceUp() ) {
            return image;
        } else {
            return "/blackjack/ui/bitmaps/empty_pile.xbm";
        }
    }

}
```

LISTING E.34 VDeck.java

```
package blackjack.ui.mvc;

import blackjack.core.*;
import java.util.Iterator;

public class VDeck extends Deck {

    protected void buildCards() {

        // This is ugly, but it is better than the alternative loops/if/elseif
        Card [] deck = new Card[52];
        setDeck( deck );

        deck[0] = new VCard( Suit.HEARTS, Rank.TWO,
"/blackjack/ui/bitmaps/h2" );
        deck[1] = new VCard( Suit.HEARTS, Rank.THREE,
"/blackjack/ui/bitmaps/h3" );
        deck[2] = new VCard( Suit.HEARTS, Rank.FOUR,
"/blackjack/ui/bitmaps/h4" );
        deck[3] = new VCard( Suit.HEARTS, Rank.FIVE,
"/blackjack/ui/bitmaps/h5" );
        deck[4] = new VCard( Suit.HEARTS, Rank.SIX,
"/blackjack/ui/bitmaps/h6" );
        deck[5] = new VCard( Suit.HEARTS, Rank.SEVEN,
"/blackjack/ui/bitmaps/h7" );
        deck[6] = new VCard( Suit.HEARTS, Rank.EIGHT,
"/blackjack/ui/bitmaps/h8" );
```

LISTING E.34 continued

```
        deck[7] = new VCard( Suit.HEARTS, Rank.NINE,
"/blackjack/ui/bitmaps/h9" );
        deck[8] = new VCard( Suit.HEARTS, Rank.TEN,
"/blackjack/ui/bitmaps/h10" );
        deck[9] = new VCard( Suit.HEARTS, Rank.JACK,
"/blackjack/ui/bitmaps/h11" );
        deck[10] = new VCard( Suit.HEARTS, Rank.QUEEN,
"/blackjack/ui/bitmaps/h12" );
        deck[11] = new VCard( Suit.HEARTS, Rank.KING,
"/blackjack/ui/bitmaps/h13" );
        deck[12] = new VCard( Suit.HEARTS, Rank.ACE,
"/blackjack/ui/bitmaps/h1" );
        deck[13] = new VCard( Suit.DIAMONDS, Rank.TWO,
"/blackjack/ui/bitmaps/d2" );
        deck[14] = new VCard( Suit.DIAMONDS, Rank.THREE,
"/blackjack/ui/bitmaps/d3" );
        deck[15] = new VCard( Suit.DIAMONDS, Rank.FOUR,
"/blackjack/ui/bitmaps/d4" );
        deck[16] = new VCard( Suit.DIAMONDS, Rank.FIVE,
"/blackjack/ui/bitmaps/d5" );
        deck[17] = new VCard( Suit.DIAMONDS, Rank.SIX,
"/blackjack/ui/bitmaps/d6" );
        deck[18] = new VCard( Suit.DIAMONDS, Rank.SEVEN,
"/blackjack/ui/bitmaps/d7" );
        deck[19] = new VCard( Suit.DIAMONDS, Rank.EIGHT,
"/blackjack/ui/bitmaps/d8" );
        deck[20] = new VCard( Suit.DIAMONDS, Rank.NINE,
"/blackjack/ui/bitmaps/d9" );
        deck[21] = new VCard( Suit.DIAMONDS, Rank.TEN,
"/blackjack/ui/bitmaps/d10" );
        deck[22] = new VCard( Suit.DIAMONDS, Rank.JACK,
"/blackjack/ui/bitmaps/d11" );
        deck[23] = new VCard( Suit.DIAMONDS, Rank.QUEEN,
"/blackjack/ui/bitmaps/d12" );
        deck[24] = new VCard( Suit.DIAMONDS, Rank.KING,
"/blackjack/ui/bitmaps/d13" );
        deck[25] = new VCard( Suit.DIAMONDS, Rank.ACE,
"/blackjack/ui/bitmaps/d1" );
        deck[26] = new VCard( Suit.SPADES, Rank.TWO,
"/blackjack/ui/bitmaps/s2" );
        deck[27] = new VCard( Suit.SPADES, Rank.THREE,
"/blackjack/ui/bitmaps/s3" );
        deck[28] = new VCard( Suit.SPADES, Rank.FOUR,
"/blackjack/ui/bitmaps/s4" );
        deck[29] = new VCard( Suit.SPADES, Rank.FIVE,
"/blackjack/ui/bitmaps/s5" );
        deck[30] = new VCard( Suit.SPADES, Rank.SIX,
"/blackjack/ui/bitmaps/s6" );
```

E

LISTING E.34   continued

```
        deck[31] = new VCard( Suit.SPADES, Rank.SEVEN,
"/blackjack/ui/bitmaps/s7" );
        deck[32] = new VCard( Suit.SPADES, Rank.EIGHT,
"/blackjack/ui/bitmaps/s8" );
        deck[33] = new VCard( Suit.SPADES, Rank.NINE,
"/blackjack/ui/bitmaps/s9" );
        deck[34] = new VCard( Suit.SPADES, Rank.TEN,
"/blackjack/ui/bitmaps/s10" );
        deck[35] = new VCard( Suit.SPADES, Rank.JACK,
"/blackjack/ui/bitmaps/s11" );
        deck[36] = new VCard( Suit.SPADES, Rank.QUEEN,
"/blackjack/ui/bitmaps/s12" );
        deck[37] = new VCard( Suit.SPADES, Rank.KING,
"/blackjack/ui/bitmaps/s13" );
        deck[38] = new VCard( Suit.SPADES, Rank.ACE,
"/blackjack/ui/bitmaps/s1" );
        deck[39] = new VCard( Suit.CLUBS, Rank.TWO,
"/blackjack/ui/bitmaps/c2" );
        deck[40] = new VCard( Suit.CLUBS, Rank.THREE,
"/blackjack/ui/bitmaps/c3" );
        deck[41] = new VCard( Suit.CLUBS, Rank.FOUR,
"/blackjack/ui/bitmaps/c4" );
        deck[42] = new VCard( Suit.CLUBS, Rank.FIVE,
"/blackjack/ui/bitmaps/c5" );
        deck[43] = new VCard( Suit.CLUBS, Rank.SIX,
"/blackjack/ui/bitmaps/c6" );
        deck[44] = new VCard( Suit.CLUBS, Rank.SEVEN,
"/blackjack/ui/bitmaps/c7" );
        deck[45] = new VCard( Suit.CLUBS, Rank.EIGHT,
"/blackjack/ui/bitmaps/c8" );
        deck[46] = new VCard( Suit.CLUBS, Rank.NINE,
"/blackjack/ui/bitmaps/c9" );
        deck[47] = new VCard( Suit.CLUBS, Rank.TEN,
"/blackjack/ui/bitmaps/c10" );
        deck[48] = new VCard( Suit.CLUBS, Rank.JACK,
"/blackjack/ui/bitmaps/c11" );
        deck[49] = new VCard( Suit.CLUBS, Rank.QUEEN,
"/blackjack/ui/bitmaps/c12" );
        deck[50] = new VCard( Suit.CLUBS, Rank.KING,
"/blackjack/ui/bitmaps/c13" );
        deck[51] = new VCard( Suit.CLUBS, Rank.ACE,
"/blackjack/ui/bitmaps/c1" );

    }

  }
```

blackjack.ui.pac

blackjack.ui.pac contains the pac code (Listings E.35 through E.42).

LISTING E.35   Displayable.java

```java
package blackjack.ui.pac;

import javax.swing.JComponent;

public interface Displayable {
    public JComponent view();
}
```

E

LISTING E.36   GUIPlayer.java

```java
package blackjack.ui.pac;

import blackjack.core.*;
import javax.swing.*;
import java.awt.*;
import java.awt.event.*;

public class GUIPlayer extends VBettingPlayer implements Displayable {

    private BlackjackDealer dealer;
    private JPanel view;

    public GUIPlayer( String name, VHand hand, Bank bank, VBlackjackDealer
➥dealer ) {
        super( name, hand, bank );
        this.dealer = dealer;
    }

    public boolean hit( Dealer dealer ) {
        return true;
    }

    public void bet() {
        // do nothing, this won't get called
        // instead, the human player presses a GUI button
    }

    // these bet methods will get called by the GUI controller
    // for each: place the proper bet, change the state, let the
    // dealer know that the player is done betting
    public void place10Bet() {
```

LISTING E.36 continued

```
        getBank().place10Bet();
        setCurrentState( getWaitingState() );
        dealer.doneBetting( this );
    }

    public void place50Bet() {
        getBank().place50Bet();
        setCurrentState( getWaitingState() );
        dealer.doneBetting( this );
    }

    public void place100Bet() {
        getBank().place100Bet();
        setCurrentState( getWaitingState() );
        dealer.doneBetting( this );
    }

    // doubling down is a bit different since the player needs to
    // respond to Hand events as a card gets added to the hand
    // so set the state to DoublingDown and then execute it
    protected boolean doubleDown( Dealer d ) {
        setCurrentState( getDoublingDownState() );
        getCurrentState().execute( dealer );
        return true;
    }

    // takeCard will get called by the GUI controller when the player
    // decides to hit
    public void takeCard() {
        dealer.hit( this );
    }

    // stand will get called by the GUI controller when the player chooses
    // to stand, when standing change state, let the world know, and then
    // tell the dealer
    public void stand() {
        setCurrentState( getStandingState() );
        notifyStanding();
        getCurrentState().execute( dealer );
    }

    public JComponent view() {
        if( view == null ) {
            view = new JPanel( new BorderLayout() );
            JComponent pv = super.view();
            GUIView cv = new GUIView();
            addListener( cv );
            view.add( pv, BorderLayout.CENTER );
```

```
            view.add( cv, BorderLayout.SOUTH );
        }
        return view;
    }

    // the following deal w/ states
    protected PlayerState getPlayingState() {
        return new Playing();
    }

    protected PlayerState getBettingState() {
        return new Betting();
    }

    private class Playing implements PlayerState {

        public void handPlayable() {
            // do nothing
        }

        public void handBlackjack() {
            setCurrentState( getBlackjackState() );
            notifyBlackjack();
            getCurrentState().execute( dealer );
        }

        public void handBusted() {
            setCurrentState( getBustedState() );
            notifyBusted();
            getCurrentState().execute( dealer );
        }

        public void handChanged() {
            notifyChanged();
        }

        public void execute( Dealer dealer ) {
            // do nothing here, actions will come from the GUI which is
            // external to the state, but when events do come in be sure to
            // force state transition right away
        }
    }
    private class Betting implements PlayerState {
        public void handChanged() {
            // not possible in busted state
        }
        public void handPlayable() {
            // not possible in busted state
```

E

LISTING E.36 continued

```
        }
        public void handBlackjack() {
            // not possible in busted state
        }
        public void handBusted() {
            // not possible in busted state
        }
        public void execute( Dealer dealer ) {
            // do nothing here, actions will come from the GUI which is
            // external to the state, since no events come in as part of
            // betting the state will need to be changed externally to this
state
        }
    }

    private class GUIView extends JPanel implements PlayerListener,
ActionListener {

        private JButton bet_10  = new JButton( "$10" );
        private JButton bet_50  = new JButton( "$50" );
        private JButton bet_100 = new JButton( "$100" );
        private JButton deal   = new JButton( "New Game" );
        private JButton quit   = new JButton( "Quit" );
        private JButton hit    = new JButton( "Hit" );
        private JButton stand = new JButton( "Stand" );
        private JButton ddown = new JButton( "Double Down" );

        private final String NEW_GAME = "new";
        private final String QUIT     = "quit";
        private final String HIT      = "hit";
        private final String STAND    = "stand";
        private final String BET_10   = "BET10";
        private final String BET_50   = "BET50";
        private final String BET_100  = "BET100";
        private final String D_DOWN   = "DDown";

        private final Color FOREST_GREEN = new Color( 35, 142, 35 );

        public GUIView() {
            super( new BorderLayout() );
            GUIPlayer.this.addListener( this );
            buildGUI();
        }
        private void buildGUI() {
            JPanel betting_controls = new JPanel();
            JPanel game_controls    = new JPanel();

            add( betting_controls, BorderLayout.NORTH );
```

```
        add( game_controls, BorderLayout.SOUTH );

        betting_controls.setBackground( FOREST_GREEN );
        game_controls.setBackground( FOREST_GREEN );
        deal.setActionCommand( NEW_GAME );
        deal.addActionListener( this );
        quit.setActionCommand( QUIT );
        quit.addActionListener( this );
        hit.setActionCommand( HIT );
        hit.addActionListener( this );
        stand.setActionCommand( STAND );
        stand.addActionListener( this );
        bet_10.setActionCommand( BET_10 );
        bet_10.addActionListener( this );
        bet_50.setActionCommand( BET_50 );
        bet_50.addActionListener( this );
        bet_100.setActionCommand( BET_100 );
        bet_100.addActionListener( this );
        ddown.setActionCommand( D_DOWN );
        ddown.addActionListener( this );
        betting_controls.add( bet_10 );
        betting_controls.add( bet_50 );
        betting_controls.add( bet_100 );
        game_controls.add( ddown );
        game_controls.add( hit );
        game_controls.add( stand );
        game_controls.add( deal );
        game_controls.add( quit );
        enableBettingControls( false );
        enablePlayerControls( false );
        enableDoubleDown( false );
    }

    private void enableBettingControls( boolean enable ) {
        bet_10.setEnabled( enable );
        bet_50.setEnabled( enable );
        bet_100.setEnabled( enable );
    }

    private void enablePlayerControls( boolean enable ) {
        hit.setEnabled( enable );
        stand.setEnabled( enable );
    }

    private void enableGameControls( boolean enable ) {
        deal.setEnabled( enable );
        quit.setEnabled( enable );
    }
```

LISTING E.36 continued

```java
private void enableDoubleDown( boolean enable ) {
    ddown.setEnabled( enable );
}

public void actionPerformed( ActionEvent event ) {
    if( event.getActionCommand().equals( QUIT ) ) {
        System.exit( 0 );
    } else if( event.getActionCommand().equals( HIT ) ) {
        enableDoubleDown( false );
        takeCard();
    } else if( event.getActionCommand().equals( STAND ) ) {
        enableDoubleDown( false );
        stand();
    } else if ( event.getActionCommand().equals( NEW_GAME ) ) {
        enableDoubleDown( false );
        enableGameControls( false );
        enablePlayerControls( false );
        enableBettingControls( true );
        dealer.newGame();
    } else if( event.getActionCommand().equals( BET_10 ) ) {
        enableDoubleDown( true );
        enableBettingControls( false );
        enablePlayerControls( true );
        place10Bet();
    } else if( event.getActionCommand().equals( BET_50 ) ) {
        enableDoubleDown( true );
        enableBettingControls( false );
        enablePlayerControls( true );
        place50Bet();
    } else if( event.getActionCommand().equals( BET_100 ) ) {
        enableDoubleDown( true );
        enableBettingControls( false );
        enablePlayerControls( true );
        place100Bet();
    } else if( event.getActionCommand().equals( D_DOWN ) ) {
        enablePlayerControls( false );
        enableDoubleDown( false );
        doubleDown( dealer );
    }
}

public void playerChanged( Player player ) {}

public void playerBusted( Player player ) {
    enablePlayerControls( false );
    enableGameControls( true );
}
```

LISTING E.36 continued

```java
        public void playerBlackjack( Player player ) {
            enableDoubleDown( false );
            enablePlayerControls( false );
            enableGameControls( true );
        }

        public void playerStanding( Player player ) {
            enablePlayerControls( false );
            enableGameControls( true );
        }

        public void playerWon( Player player ) {
            enablePlayerControls( false );
            enableGameControls( true );
        }

        public void playerLost( Player player ) {
            enableDoubleDown( false );
            enablePlayerControls( false );
            enableGameControls( true );
        }

        public void playerStandoff( Player player ) {
            enablePlayerControls( false );
            enableGameControls( true );
        }

    }
}
```

LISTING E.37 VBettingPlayer.java

```java
package blackjack.ui.pac;

import blackjack.core.*;
import java.awt.*;
import javax.swing.*;
import javax.swing.border.*;

public abstract class VBettingPlayer extends BettingPlayer implements
➥Displayable {

    private BettingView view;

    public VBettingPlayer( String name, VHand hand, Bank bank ) {
        super( name, hand, bank );
```

LISTING E.37   continued

```
        }

    public JComponent view() {
        if( view == null ) {
            view = new BettingView( (VHand) getHand() );
            addListener( view );
        }
        return view;
    }

    // Note that all this class does is retrieve the Hand's view, add that view
    // to itself, and update the border as needed. Note what this class does not
do:
    // update the cards as they change. From the point of view of this view the
card
    // update happens automatically because the VHand update's its displayable
behind
    // the scenes
    private class BettingView extends JPanel implements PlayerListener {

        private TitledBorder border;

        public BettingView( VHand hand ) {
            super( new FlowLayout( FlowLayout.LEFT ) );
            buildGUI( hand.view() );
        }

        public void playerChanged( Player player ) {
            String name = VBettingPlayer.this.getName();
            border.setTitle( name );
            repaint();
        }

        public void playerBusted( Player player ) {
            String name = VBettingPlayer.this.getName();
            border.setTitle( name + " BUSTED!" );
            repaint();
        }

        public void playerBlackjack( Player player ) {
            String name = VBettingPlayer.this.getName();
            border.setTitle( name + " BLACKJACK!" );
            repaint();
        }

        public void playerStanding( Player player ) {
            String name = VBettingPlayer.this.getName();
            border.setTitle( name + " STANDING" );
```

LISTING E.37   continued

```
        repaint();
    }

    public void playerWon( Player player ) {
        String name = VBettingPlayer.this.getName();
        border.setTitle( name + " WINNER!" );
        repaint();
    }

    public void playerLost( Player player ) {
        String name = VBettingPlayer.this.getName();
        border.setTitle( name + " LOSER!" );
        repaint();
    }

    public void playerStandoff( Player player ) {
        String name = VBettingPlayer.this.getName();
        border.setTitle( name + " STANDOFF!" );
        repaint();
    }

    private void buildGUI( JComponent hand ) {
        border = new TitledBorder( VBettingPlayer.this.getName() );
        setBorder( border );
        setBackground( new Color( 35, 142, 35 ) );
        border.setTitleColor( Color.black );
        add( hand );
    }

    }

}
```

LISTING E.38   VBlackjackDealer.java

```
package blackjack.ui.pac;

import blackjack.core.*;
import blackjack.core.threaded.*;
import javax.swing.*;
import javax.swing.border.*;
import java.awt.*;

public class VBlackjackDealer extends ThreadedBlackjackDealer implements
Displayable {
```

```
private DealerView view;

public VBlackjackDealer( String name, VHand hand, Deckpile cards ) {
    super( name, hand, cards );
}

public JComponent view() {
    if( view == null ) {
        view = new DealerView( (VHand) getHand() );
        addListener( view );
    }
    return view;
}

// Note that all this class does is retrieve the Hand's view, add that view
// to itself, and update the border as needed. Note what this class does not
do:
// update the cards as they change. From the point of view of this view the
card
// update happens automatically because the VHand update's its displayable
behind
// the scenes
private class DealerView extends JPanel implements PlayerListener {

    private TitledBorder border;

    public DealerView( VHand hand ) {
        super( new FlowLayout( FlowLayout.LEFT ) );
        String name = VBlackjackDealer.this.getName();
        border = new TitledBorder( name );
        setBorder( border );
        setBackground( new Color( 35, 142, 35 ) );
        border.setTitleColor( Color.black );
        add( hand.view() );
        repaint();
    }

    public void playerChanged( Player player ) {
        String name = VBlackjackDealer.this.getName();
        border.setTitle( name );
        repaint();
    }

    public void playerBusted( Player player ) {
        String name = VBlackjackDealer.this.getName();
        border.setTitle( name + " BUSTED!" );
        repaint();
    }
```

LISTING E.38 continued

```java
        public void playerBlackjack( Player player ) {
            String name = VBlackjackDealer.this.getName();
            border.setTitle( name + " BLACKJACK!" );
            repaint();
        }

        public void playerStanding( Player player ) {
            String name = VBlackjackDealer.this.getName();
            border.setTitle( name + " STANDING" );
            repaint();
        }

        public void playerWon( Player player ) {
            String name = VBlackjackDealer.this.getName();
            border.setTitle( name + " WINNER!" );
            repaint();
        }

        public void playerLost( Player player ) {
            String name = VBlackjackDealer.this.getName();
            border.setTitle( name + " LOSER!" );
            repaint();
        }

        public void playerStandoff( Player player ) {
            String name = VBlackjackDealer.this.getName();
            border.setTitle( name + " STANDOFF!" );
            repaint();
        }

    }

}
```

LISTING E.39 VCard.java

```java
package blackjack.ui.pac;

import blackjack.core.*;
import javax.swing.*;
import java.awt.*;

public class VCard extends Card implements Displayable {

    private String image;
    private CardView view;
```

LISTING E.39   continued

```java
public VCard( Suit suit, Rank rank, String image ) {
    super( suit, rank );
    this.image = image;
    view = new CardView( getImage() );
}

public void setFaceUp( boolean up ) {
    super.setFaceUp( up );
    view.changed();
}

public JComponent view() {
    return view;
}

private String getImage() {
    if( isFaceUp() ) {
        return image;
    } else {
        return "/blackjack/ui/bitmaps/empty_pile.xbm";
    }
}

private class CardView extends JLabel {

    public CardView( String image ) {
        setImage( image );
        setBackground( Color.white );
        setOpaque( true );
    }

    public void changed() {
        setImage( getImage() );
    }

    private void setImage( String image ) {
        java.net.URL url = this.getClass().getResource( image );
        ImageIcon icon = new ImageIcon( url );
        setIcon( icon );
    }
}

}
```

LISTING E.40   VDeck.java

```java
package blackjack.ui.pac;

import blackjack.core.*;
import java.util.Iterator;

public class VDeck extends Deck {

    protected void buildCards() {

        // This is ugly, but it is better than the alternative loops/if/elseif
        Card [] deck = new Card[52];
        setDeck( deck );

        deck[0] = new VCard( Suit.HEARTS, Rank.TWO,
"/blackjack/ui/bitmaps/h2" );
        deck[1] = new VCard( Suit.HEARTS, Rank.THREE,
"/blackjack/ui/bitmaps/h3" );
        deck[2] = new VCard( Suit.HEARTS, Rank.FOUR,
"/blackjack/ui/bitmaps/h4" );
        deck[3] = new VCard( Suit.HEARTS, Rank.FIVE,
"/blackjack/ui/bitmaps/h5" );
        deck[4] = new VCard( Suit.HEARTS, Rank.SIX,
"/blackjack/ui/bitmaps/h6" );
        deck[5] = new VCard( Suit.HEARTS, Rank.SEVEN,
"/blackjack/ui/bitmaps/h7" );
        deck[6] = new VCard( Suit.HEARTS, Rank.EIGHT,
"/blackjack/ui/bitmaps/h8" );
        deck[7] = new VCard( Suit.HEARTS, Rank.NINE,
"/blackjack/ui/bitmaps/h9" );
        deck[8] = new VCard( Suit.HEARTS, Rank.TEN,
"/blackjack/ui/bitmaps/h10" );
        deck[9] = new VCard( Suit.HEARTS, Rank.JACK,
"/blackjack/ui/bitmaps/h11" );
        deck[10] = new VCard( Suit.HEARTS, Rank.QUEEN,
"/blackjack/ui/bitmaps/h12" );
        deck[11] = new VCard( Suit.HEARTS, Rank.KING,
"/blackjack/ui/bitmaps/h13" );
        deck[12] = new VCard( Suit.HEARTS, Rank.ACE,
"/blackjack/ui/bitmaps/h1" );
        deck[13] = new VCard( Suit.DIAMONDS, Rank.TWO,
"/blackjack/ui/bitmaps/d2" );
        deck[14] = new VCard( Suit.DIAMONDS, Rank.THREE,
"/blackjack/ui/bitmaps/d3" );
        deck[15] = new VCard( Suit.DIAMONDS, Rank.FOUR,
"/blackjack/ui/bitmaps/d4" );
        deck[16] = new VCard( Suit.DIAMONDS, Rank.FIVE,
"/blackjack/ui/bitmaps/d5" );
        deck[17] = new VCard( Suit.DIAMONDS, Rank.SIX,
"/blackjack/ui/bitmaps/d6" );
```

E

LISTING E.40 continued

```
        deck[18] = new VCard( Suit.DIAMONDS, Rank.SEVEN,
"/blackjack/ui/bitmaps/d7" );
        deck[19] = new VCard( Suit.DIAMONDS, Rank.EIGHT,
"/blackjack/ui/bitmaps/d8" );
        deck[20] = new VCard( Suit.DIAMONDS, Rank.NINE,
"/blackjack/ui/bitmaps/d9" );
        deck[21] = new VCard( Suit.DIAMONDS, Rank.TEN,
"/blackjack/ui/bitmaps/d10" );
        deck[22] = new VCard( Suit.DIAMONDS, Rank.JACK,
"/blackjack/ui/bitmaps/d11" );
        deck[23] = new VCard( Suit.DIAMONDS, Rank.QUEEN,
"/blackjack/ui/bitmaps/d12" );
        deck[24] = new VCard( Suit.DIAMONDS, Rank.KING,
"/blackjack/ui/bitmaps/d13" );
        deck[25] = new VCard( Suit.DIAMONDS, Rank.ACE,
"/blackjack/ui/bitmaps/d1" );
        deck[26] = new VCard( Suit.SPADES, Rank.TWO,
"/blackjack/ui/bitmaps/s2" );
        deck[27] = new VCard( Suit.SPADES, Rank.THREE,
"/blackjack/ui/bitmaps/s3" );
        deck[28] = new VCard( Suit.SPADES, Rank.FOUR,
"/blackjack/ui/bitmaps/s4" );
        deck[29] = new VCard( Suit.SPADES, Rank.FIVE,
"/blackjack/ui/bitmaps/s5" );
        deck[30] = new VCard( Suit.SPADES, Rank.SIX,
"/blackjack/ui/bitmaps/s6" );
        deck[31] = new VCard( Suit.SPADES, Rank.SEVEN,
"/blackjack/ui/bitmaps/s7" );
        deck[32] = new VCard( Suit.SPADES, Rank.EIGHT,
"/blackjack/ui/bitmaps/s8" );
        deck[33] = new VCard( Suit.SPADES, Rank.NINE,
"/blackjack/ui/bitmaps/s9" );
        deck[34] = new VCard( Suit.SPADES, Rank.TEN,
"/blackjack/ui/bitmaps/s10" );
        deck[35] = new VCard( Suit.SPADES, Rank.JACK,
"/blackjack/ui/bitmaps/s11" );
        deck[36] = new VCard( Suit.SPADES, Rank.QUEEN,
"/blackjack/ui/bitmaps/s12" );
        deck[37] = new VCard( Suit.SPADES, Rank.KING,
"/blackjack/ui/bitmaps/s13" );
        deck[38] = new VCard( Suit.SPADES, Rank.ACE,
"/blackjack/ui/bitmaps/s1" );
        deck[39] = new VCard( Suit.CLUBS, Rank.TWO,
"/blackjack/ui/bitmaps/c2" );
        deck[40] = new VCard( Suit.CLUBS, Rank.THREE,
"/blackjack/ui/bitmaps/c3" );
        deck[41] = new VCard( Suit.CLUBS, Rank.FOUR,
"/blackjack/ui/bitmaps/c4" );
```

LISTING E.40 continued

```
        deck[42] = new VCard( Suit.CLUBS, Rank.FIVE,
"/blackjack/ui/bitmaps/c5" );
        deck[43] = new VCard( Suit.CLUBS, Rank.SIX,
"/blackjack/ui/bitmaps/c6" );
        deck[44] = new VCard( Suit.CLUBS, Rank.SEVEN,
"/blackjack/ui/bitmaps/c7" );
        deck[45] = new VCard( Suit.CLUBS, Rank.EIGHT,
"/blackjack/ui/bitmaps/c8" );
        deck[46] = new VCard( Suit.CLUBS, Rank.NINE,
"/blackjack/ui/bitmaps/c9" );
        deck[47] = new VCard( Suit.CLUBS, Rank.TEN,
"/blackjack/ui/bitmaps/c10" );
        deck[48] = new VCard( Suit.CLUBS, Rank.JACK,
"/blackjack/ui/bitmaps/c11" );
        deck[49] = new VCard( Suit.CLUBS, Rank.QUEEN,
"/blackjack/ui/bitmaps/c12" );
        deck[50] = new VCard( Suit.CLUBS, Rank.KING,
"/blackjack/ui/bitmaps/c13" );
        deck[51] = new VCard( Suit.CLUBS, Rank.ACE,
"/blackjack/ui/bitmaps/c1" );

    }

}
```

LISTING E.41 VHand.java

```
package blackjack.ui.pac;

import blackjack.core.*;
import java.awt.*;
import javax.swing.*;
import java.util.Iterator;

public class VHand extends Hand implements Displayable {

    private HandView view = new HandView();

    public JComponent view() {
        return view;
    }

    // you need to override addCard and reset so that when the hand changes, the
    // change propigates to the view
    public void addCard( Card card ) {
        super.addCard( card );
```

LISTING E.41   continued

```
            view.changed();
        }

        public void reset() {
            super.reset();
            view.changed();
        }

        private class HandView extends JPanel {
            public HandView() {
                super( new FlowLayout( FlowLayout.LEFT ) );
                setBackground( new Color( 35, 142, 35 ) );
            }
            public void changed() {
                removeAll();
                Iterator i = getCards();
                while( i.hasNext() ) {
                    VCard card = (VCard) i.next();
                    add( card.view() );
                }
                revalidate();
            }
        }
    }

}
```

LISTING E.42   VPlayerFactory.java

```
package blackjack.ui.pac;

import blackjack.core.*;

public class VPlayerFactory {

    private VBlackjackDealer dealer;
    private GUIPlayer human;
    private Deckpile pile;

    public VBlackjackDealer getDealer() {
        // only create and return one
        if( dealer == null ) {
            VHand dealer_hand = getHand();
            Deckpile cards = getCards();
            dealer = new VBlackjackDealer( "Dealer", dealer_hand, cards );
        }
        return dealer;
```

LISTING E.41 continued

```
    }

    public GUIPlayer getHuman() {
        // only create and return one
        if( human == null ) {
            VHand human_hand = getHand();
            Bank bank = new Bank( 1000 );
            human = new GUIPlayer( "Human", human_hand, bank, getDealer() );
        }
        return human;
    }

    public Deckpile getCards() {
        // only create and return one
        if( pile == null ) {
            pile = new Deckpile();
            for( int i = 0; i < 4; i ++ ) {
                pile.shuffle();
                Deck deck = new VDeck();
                deck.addToStack( pile );
                pile.shuffle();
            }
        }
        return pile;
    }

    private VHand getHand() {
        return new VHand();
    }

}
```

E

INDEX

Symbols

* (asterisk), object associations, 194

A

abstract classes
    code example, 106-107, 131-132
    example requirements, 109
    methods, defining, 108
    UML, 596-597
        notation, 190
Abstract Data Type. *See* ADT
Abstract Factory design pattern, 278
    implementing, 278-282
    when to use, 283
abstract methods, 108
    code example, 139, 151-152
    declaring, 108-109
        code example, 109-110
abstracting, alternatives, 97

abstraction, 30-31
    appropriate situations for, 33
    card game example, 60
    effective implementation of, 46-47
    example of, 31-33
    rules for, 33-34
acceptance testing, 330
access, levels of, 29
access control, overriding methods, 87
accessor methods, setters and getters, 56-57
accessors, 15
    classes, 589
Account class example
    code for, 59
    requirements, 57-58
ACM Special Interest Group on Computer-Human Interaction (SIGCHI), 306
activities, state diagrams, 407
activity diagrams (use case analysis), 222-223
actors, 210-211
    use case analysis, 368
        blackjack card game, 369
        modeling, 218

ad-hoc polymorphism, 139
Adapter design pattern, 253-254
    implementing, 254-256
    when to use, 256-257
adapter objects, 254
adapters, 254, 281
addActionListener( ) method, 309
ADT (Abstract Data Type)
    defining, 38
    effective implementation of, 47
    encapsulation and, 34, 37
    example, 37-39
agents, objects, 242
aggregation relationships, modeling, 194-195
aggregations, UML, 599
analysis
    See also OOA
    resources, 603
ancestors, 92-93
anonymous classes, creating, 339-340
anonymous inner classes, 591-593

APIs (application programming interfaces), 28
   third-party tools, adapters, 256-257
archives, jar utility, 572-573
arguments
   See also parameters, 137
   coercion, 141
association names, 193
association relationships, modeling, 193-194
association role, 193
associations (objects), UML, 598-599
asterisks (*), object associations, 194
attributes, 12
   inheritance, 82-85
   overriding, 83-88
      access control, 87
   recursive, 88-89
   specialization, 91
   visibility, UML, 596

B

Bank class (blackjack card game)
   creating, 433-434
   example code, 163-164
   implementation, 437-439
BankAccount class code example, 115-116
BankAccountCLV code example, 316
BankAccountController code example, 317-318
BankAccountModel code example, 312-313
BankAccountView code example, 314-315, 325-327
BankActivityEvent code example, 324-325
BankActivityListener code example, 324-325
BankDriver class code example, 167-168

banking example
   Bank class code, 163-164
   future-proof code
      example code, 167
      requirements, 166
   inheritance, 110
      checking accounts, 111
      class methods, 114-115
      generic accounts, 111
      overdraft accounts, 112
      requirements, 112
      savings accounts, 111
      timed maturity accounts, 111
   polymorphism
      overview, 160
      requirements, 160-162
base classes. *See* parent classes
BaseLog class example code, 131-132
behavior, 12
   inheritance and, 82
BettingPlayer class, implementation, 439-441
black box testing, 332
blackjack card game
   as simulation, 488
      implementing, 491-493
   Bank class, 433-434
   betting functionality
      Bank class, 437-439
      BettingPlayer class, 439-441
      BlackjackDealer class, 443-444
      Dealer class, 441
      HumanPlayer class, 441-443
      implementing, 436
   collecting bets, 434
   Dealer interface, 420-425
   development
      actors (use case), 369
      analysis, purpose for, 368
      class model, 381
      classes, 376, 380
      command line UI, 380
      implementation, 381-395
      initial questions, 366-368
      iterations, adding betting capability, 371

      iterations, adding rules, 370-371
      iterations, basic game play, 370, 372-376
      iterations, planning, 369-370
      iterations, user interface, 371
      modeling domain, 376
      modeling use cases, 375
      use cases, 372-375
   domain model, updating for betting, 433
   game states, creating classes from, 409-410, 412
   GUI (graphical user interface)
      analysis, 449
      BlackjackGUI, 454
      CardView, 454-455
      class diagram, 456
      CRC card session, 454-455
      design issues, 453-456
      diagrams, 455
      implementing, 457-465
      mock ups, 452-453
      OptionView, 454
      OptionView diagram, 455-456
      overview
         PlayerView, 454
         PlayerView diagram, 455
         use cases, 450-452
   overview (PAC design pattern), 470
      abstraction layer, 473-474
      approach, 470-471
      control design, 474
      design overview, 471-472
      factory patterns, 474-475
      implementing, 476-483
      layers, 470
      presentation layer, 472-473
      when to use, 471
   Hand class, listener for, 412-415
   iterative process and, 365-366
   non-human players
      creating, 486
      FlipPlayer class, 489-490
      OneHitPlayer class, 490

options for, 487
  SafePlayer, 486-487
  SmartPlayer class, 491
OOP benefits, 504-505
Player class
  modifying inheritance
    hierarchy, 435
  PlayerListener interface,
    419-420
  PlayerState interface,
    415-419
purpose for programming,
  364
refactoring for reuse, 498-504
requirements, 365
rules
  analysis, 400
  dealer state diagram,
    408-409
  implementing, 412-425
  implementing through
    conditionals, 404-406
  overview, 399
  player state diagram,
    407-408
  state diagrams, 406-407
  use cases, 400-404
source code packages, 607
testing, 395, 425
  mock objects and,
    444-445
use cases, betting, 430-433
user interface
  command line improve-
    ments, 448-449
  overview, 447-448
vision statement, 365
**Blackjack class diagram,
  updating, 436**
**blackjack.core package (com-
  mon classes), 608-633**
**blackjack.core.threaded pack-
  age, 633-635**
**blackjack.exe, user interfaces,
  635-641**
Blackjack.java, 392
**blackjack.players package,
  641-649**
blackjack.ui package, 649-650
**blackjack.ui.mvc package,
  650-662**

**blackjack.ui.pac package,
  663-679**
**BlackjackDealer class, imple-
  mentation, 443-444**
**BlackjackDealer interface,
  420-425**
BlackjackDealer.java, 390
**BlackjackGUI class, setUp( )
  method, 464-465**
Boolean primitive wrapper
  code example, 67-68, 70-71
  creating, 70
braces ({ }) in source code, 579
bugs, 330
  compared to exceptions, 350
  sources of, 331

C

C++, resources, 604
**Card class code example,
  Typesafe Enum design pattern, 289-294**
**Card class example, code for,
  61-63**
card game example
  abstraction, 60
  division of responsibility, 61
  implementation hiding, 60
  requirements, 61
**CardView class, implementing,
  459**
**CarefreeObject example code,
  164**
**casting, Hashtable class and,
  161-162**
**CheckingAccount class code
  example, 118-119**
child classes, 81-82
  example requirements,
    104-105
  inheritance code example,
    105-106
  new methods, 88
  polymorphism, example code,
    152-154
  specialization, 91
  super keyword, 88

class adapters, 256
class code example, 352
class keyword, 579
class level documentation, 573
class methods, 68-69
class variables, 68-69
classes, 12
  See also user interfaces
  abstract
    code example, 106-107
    example requirements,
      109
    UML notation, 190
  abstract UML, 596-597
  accessors, 589
  account example
    code for, 59
    requirements, 57-58
  ADT (Abstract Data Type),
    effective implementation of,
    47
  aggregations, UML, 599
  anonymous, creating, 339-340
  attributes, 12
  Bank, 433-434
    implementation, 437-439
  Bank example code, 163-164
  BankAccount code example,
    115-116
  BaseLog, example code,
    131-132
  BettingPlayer, implementa-
    tion, 439-441
  black box testing, 332
  Blackjack
    setUp( ) method, 464-465
    updating diagram, 436
  blackjack card game, 376,
    380
    creating non-human play-
      ers, 486
    implementation, 381-395
    model, 381
  BlackjackDealer, implementa-
    tion, 443-444
  card game example, code for,
    61-65
  CardView, implementing, 459
  CheckingAccount code exam-
    ple, 118-119

child, 81-82
    example requirements,
      104-105
    inheritance code example,
      105-106
    new methods, 88
    polymorphism (example
      code), 152, 154
    specialization, 91
    super keyword, 88
code examples,
    DoubleKey.java, 55
collaboration diagrams, UML,
    600
common
    blackjack.core package,
      623-633
    blackjack.core package
      package, 608-623
compiling, 575-576
composition, 80-81
    UML, 600
constructor methods, 589
CountedObject, code exam-
    ple, 69
CRC (Class Responsibility
    Collaboration) cards,
    234-235
    applying, 235-236
    example, 236-238
    limitations, 241
creating, game state and,
    409-410, 412
Dealer, implementation, 441
dependency relationships,
    UML, 598
design considerations, unit
    tests and, 337
DoubleKey, constructors, 56
example code, 13-14
FlipPlayer, implementing,
    489-490
generalization relationships,
    UML, 600
getters, 589
GUIPlayer, implementing,
    461-464, 481
Hand, listener for, 412-415
Hashtable, casting and,
    161-162
headers, documentation and,
    354

HumanPlayer, implementa-
    tion, 441-443
inheritance, basic principles,
    81-83
inheritance hierarchy, 81
inner, 591-593
    anonymous, 591-593
instantiation, preventing mul-
    tiple, 283-284
interaction diagrams, UML,
    600
Java, 578-579, 586-587
    creating, 587-590
leaf, 93
modeling, 198-199
    aggregation relationships,
      194-195
    association relationships,
      193-194
    composition relationships,
      196
    dependency relationships,
      191-193
    documenting code, 187
    generalization relation-
      ships, 197-198
    relationships, 191
    UML advanced notation,
      189-190
    UML notation, 188-189
    UML selecting notation,
      190-191
modifiers, 589
multiplicity, UML, 599
naming conventions, 353
number of responsibilities
    (design issues), 239, 241
object associations, UML,
    598
objects, 11-12
OneHitPlayer, implementing,
    490
OptionView, implementing,
    461
OptionViewController, imple-
    menting, 461
OverdraftAccount code exam-
    ple, 119-120
parent, 81-82
    inheritance code example,
      103-104
    super keyword, 88

Player
    PlayerListener interface,
      419-420
    PlayerState interface,
      415-419
    PlayerView, implementing,
      460-461
    polymorphism and, 130
    relationships, UML, 598
    roles, UML, 598
    root, 93
    SafePlayer
      adding to GUI, 486-487
      creating, 486
    SavingsAccount code exam-
      ple, 116-117
    sequence diagrams, UML,
      601
    setters, 589
    SmartPlayer, implementing,
      491
    Stack
      inheritance problem
        example, 120-121
      inheritance problem
        example requirements,
        121
      inheritance solution code
        example, 121-122
    substitutability relationships,
      Adapter design pattern,
      253-254
    testing, JUnit, 338-342
    TimeMaturityAccount code
      example, 117-118
    UML, 595
    unit testing, 333
    VBettingPlayer, implement-
      ing, 478-479
    VBlackjackDealer, imple-
      menting, 480-481
    VCard, implementing, 457,
      476-477
    VDeck, implementing, 458
    Vhand, implementing, 477
CLASSPATH environment
variable, 570
CLI interface, blackjack.exe
package, 635-641

code

See also design issues; programming
BaseLog class, 131-132
blackjack card game, packages, 607
Card class example, Typesafe
Enum design pattern,
289-290, 293-294
documentation, 352
coding conventions,
352-353
comments, 353
constants, 353
headers (methods and
classes), 354
names, 354
updating, 354
documenting, 187
modeling class aggrega-
tion relationships,
194-195
modeling class association
relationships, 193-194
modeling class composi-
tion relationships, 196
modeling class dependen-
cy relationships,
191-193
modeling class generalization relationships,
197-198
modeling class relation-
ships, 191
modeling classes,
188-191, 198-199
UML (Unified Modeling
Language), 187
Employee class (polymor-
phism), 151-152
examples
A procedural implementa-
tion of BlackjackDealer,
394
abstract classes, 106-107,
131-132
abstract methods, 139,
151-152
Account class, 59
Bank class (polymor-
phism), 163-164

Bank.java, 438-439,
608-609
BankAccount class,
115-116
BankAccountCLV, 316
BankAccountController,
317-318
BankAccountModel,
312-313
BankAccountView,
314-315, 325-327
BankActivityEvent,
324-325
BankActivityListener,
324-325
BankDriver class, 167-168
BettingPlayer.java,
440-441, 609-612
Blackjack.java, 392,
448-449
BlackjackCLI.java,
635-636
BlackjackDealer.java, 390,
612, 618
BlackjackGUI, setUp( )
method, 464
BlackjackMVC.java,
636-638
BlackjackPAC.java, 639
BlackjackSim.java,
491-492, 640-641
Boolean primitive wrap-
per, 67-71
Card class, 61-63
Card.java, 619
CardView.java, 459,
650-651
CheckingAccount class,
118-119
child class (inheritance),
105-106
child classes (polymor-
phism), 152-154
classes, 352
CommandLinePlayer.java,
642-643
Conditional rules inside
the BlackjackDealer,
405
Console.java, 393,
649-650

CountedObject class, 69
customized Dealer
Blackjack state, 422
customized Dealer Busted
state, 421-422
customized Dealer
Dealing state, 424
customized Dealer
Standing state, 423
customized Dealer
Waiting state, 423-424
Dealer class, 65
Dealer.java, 389, 421,
619-620
DealerBlackjackPile.java,
444-445
DealerCollectingBets
state, 443
Deck class, 63-65
Deck.java, 383, 620-621
Deckpile.java, 384,
621-622
declaring abstract meth-
ods, 109-110
default Blackjack state,
417
default Busted state, 416
default Player state,
417-418
default Standing state, 417
default Waiting state, 416
Displayable.java, 663
division of responsibility,
43-45
DoubleKey class, 55
EmployeeModel, 323-324
exception handling, 351
fixing conditionals,
171-176
FlipPlayer.java, 489,
643-644
future-proof code, 167
getSafePlayer( ) method,
487
GUIPlayer's betting meth-
ods, 462
GUIPlayer's custom
Betting state, 464
GUIPlayer's custom
Playing state, 463
GUIPlayer's hit and stand
methods, 462

GUIPlayer's overridden state getter methods, 463

GUIPlayer.java, 651-653, 663-669

Hand.java, 386, 412-415, 622-625

HandListener.java, 412, 625

Hello World, first program, 574-577

Hello World, threaded, 501

HumanPlayer.java, 388, 441-442

implementation, 28-29

implementation hiding, 40-41

inclusion polymorphism, 131-135

inheritance, 77-78

inheritance (new Stack class), 121-122

inheritance adapters, 255-256

instantiating objects, 16

interfaces, 28-29

Item class, 343-344

ItemDisplayFormatter, 344

ItemTableRow, 344-345

ItemTest, 348-349

Iterator design pattern, 262-266

KnowledgeablePlayer.java, 644-645

method inheritance, 83, 85

method stack track, 498-499

methods called after game over, 499

MockDisplayFormatter, 346-348

Observer interface, 311

OneHitPlayer.java, 490, 645-646

OptimalPlayer.java, 646-647

OptionView.java, 654-656

OptionViewController.java, 656-658

OverdraftAccount class, 119-120

overloading methods, 156

overriding (polymorphism), 138-139

parent class (inheritance), 103-104

Player.java, 387, 625, 630

PlayerListener.java, 419

PlayerListerner.java, 631

PlayerState.java, 415, 631

PlayerView update code, 460

PlayerView.java, 658-659

polymorphism, 159-160

future-proof code, 164-165

Product.java file, 587-588

Putting Model, Views, and Controller Together (MVC), 318

Rank.java, 382, 631-632

SafePlayer.java, 486, 648

sample of PlayerView's PlayerListener methods, 460-461

SavingsAccount class, 116-117

SavingsAccountTest class, 336

SavingsAccountTest class (anonymous), 339

SavingsAccountTest class (JUnit), 339

setUp( ) method from BlackjackGUI control, 482-483

setUp( ) method from MVC BlackjackGUI, 483

Singleton design pattern, 284-286

singleton inheritance, 287

SmartPlayer.java, 491, 648-649

substitutability relationships, 154-155

Suit.java, 632-633

threaded DealerWaiting state, 502-503

ThreadedBlackjackDealer.java, 633, 635

TimeMaturityAccount class, 117-118

updated setUp( ) method, 487

VBettingPlayer.java, 478-479, 669-671

VBlackjackDealer.java, 480-481, 671-673

VCard.java, 458, 476-483, 659-660, 673-674

VDeck.java, 458, 660-677

VHand.java, 477-478, 677-678

VisualBankAccount, 307-309

VPlayerFactory.java, 481-482, 678

withdrawFunds( ) method test, 340-341

XML parser, 281-282

PayrollDriver, 156-157

Rank class example, Typesafe Enum design pattern, 292-293

revising, division of responsibility and, 43

samples, classes, 13-14

Suit class example, Typesafe Enum design pattern, 291

coercion methods, polymorphism, 141

collaboration, 234

collaboration diagrams
UML, 600
use case analysis, 221

CollectingBets state, 434

collections, looping over items, Iterator design pattern and, 260-262

command line UI
blackjack card game, 380
improvements to, 448-449

comments, documentation, 353

compatibility, third-party tools, adapters, 256-257

compiling classes, 575-576

composition, 80-81
adapters, 256
UML, 600
when to use, 97

composition relationships, modeling, 196
conditional statements, Java, 584-585
conditionals, 170
   blackjack card game, implementing rules, 404-406
   eliminating, 406
   fixing, 171-173
      code example, 174-176
      example requirements, 173-174
      limitations of, 406
configuration, environment, SDK, 570-571
Console.java, 393
constants
   as documentation, 353
   Java, 582
   naming conventions, 353
constructor methods, 14, 589
   overloaded constructors, 589
constructors
   Account class example, 57
   default, 56
   DoubleKey.java, 56
   noarg, 56
   Singleton design pattern, 286
   super keyword, 113
controller layer (MVC), 317
   combining with model layer, 318-319
   implementing, 317-318
CountedObject class, code example, 69
CRC (Class Responsibility Collaboration) cards, 234-235
   applying, 235-236
   example, 236-238
   GUIs, blackjack card game, 454-455
   limitations, 241

D

data types, 10, 35-37
   See also ADT
   composed of multiple types, 39

encapsulation, 36
first-class objects, 37
generic interfaces, dangers of, 39
implementation inheritance, 90
inheritance, 82
   Has-a test, 80
   Is-a test, 79-80
   type substitution, 94-96
inheritance specialization and, 92
Java, 580-581
parametric, 137-138
second-class objects, 37
subtypes, 96
Deal Cards use case, 400-403
Dealer class
   implementation, 441
   example code, 65
Dealer Fulfills Game use case, 403-404
Dealer interface, 420-425
dealer state diagram (blackjack card game), 408-409
Dealer.java, 389
DealerWaiting state, threads, 502-503
debugging, 330
Deck class example, code for, 63-65
Deck.java, 383
Deckpile.java, 384
declaring
   abstract methods, 108-109
      code example, 109-110
   methods, 353
   parameter types, parametric polymorphism, 135
default constructors, 56
deferred methods, 139
defining
   data types, 35
   methods, abstract classes, 108
definition, ADT (Abstract Data Type), 38
delegation, 77
   compared to inheritance, 81
dependency relationships
   modeling, 191-193
   UML, 598

dependent code, implementation hiding, 40
descendants, 92-93
design issues, 187
   classes, unit tests and, 337
   design patterns, 250
      Abstract Factory, 278
      Adapter, 253-254
      capabilities of, 252-253
      common types, 253
      elements of, 250
      enumerating consequences, 252
      Factory Method, 283
      guidelines, 295
      implementing Abstract Factory, 278-280, 282
      implementing Adapter, 254-256
      implementing Iterator, 263-266
      implementing Singleton, 284-286
      implementing Typesafe Enum, 291, 293-294
      implementing when to use Typesafe Enum, 294-295
      Iterator, 251, 260, 262-263
      Java Iterator interface, 262
      mastering, 267-268
      pattern names, 251
      problem description, 251
      problems with, 295-296
      Proxy, 257-259
      publish/subscribe event services, 257-258
      Singleton, 283-284
      Singleton and inheritance, 287-288
      solution description, 251
      types, 278
      Typesafe Enum, 289-291
      when to use Abstract Factory, 283
      when to use Adapter, 256-257
      when to use Iterator, 266-267

when to use Proxy,
259-260
when to use Singleton,
289
documentation and, 252
exception handling, 351-352
get and set methods, 155
goals, 329
GUIs, blackjack card game,
453-456
inheritance, 97-98
OOD (Object Oriented
Design)
agents (objects), 242
applying CRC cards,
235-236
class responsibilities, 239,
241
CRC cards, 234-235
creating class models,
243-244
data transformation, 243
detailing relationships
(objects), 243
example CRC cards,
236-238
future-proofing, 242
generating list of objects,
232-233
interfaces (objects), 242
limitations of CRC cards,
241
overview, 230-231
points of interaction
(objects), 241-242
refining responsibilities of
objects, 234
steps, 231-232
polymorphism, 141-143
switch logic and, 169-171
testing considerations, 349
user interfaces, 306
decoupling from system,
306-310
Model View Controller
(MVC) design pattern,
310-321
design patterns, resources, 604
Design Patterns: Elements of
Reusable Object Oriented
Software, 250

diagrams (use case analysis),
217-219
difference, programming by,
90-91
displaying
object display formatters, 344
user interface elements,
Swing library, 309
division of responsibility
card game example, 61
implementation hiding, 42-46
Document interface, 281
documentation
comments, 353
constants, 353
design patterns, 252
getInitialState( ) method and,
444
headers (methods and classes), 354
importance of, 187
Java APIs, 61
javadoc, 573-574, 577
names, 354
source code, 352
coding conventions,
352-353
UML (Unified Modeling
Language), 187
modeling class aggrega-
tion relationships,
194-195
modeling class association
relationships, 193-194
modeling class composi-
tion relationships, 196
modeling class dependen-
cy relationships,
191-193
modeling class generalization relationships,
197-198
modeling class relation-
ships, 191
modeling classes,
188-191, 198-199
updating, 354
documents, XML parsers, 280
domain, 11

domain model (use case analysis), 223-225
blackjack card game, 404
updating for betting, 433
prototyping, 225-226
doneBetting( ) method, 443
DoubleKey class
constructors, 56
example code, 55
downloading SDK, 570
dynamically typed languages,
polymorphism and, 143

E

EmployeeModel code example,
323-324
empty database tests, 334
encapsulation, 18, 26-27
abstraction, 30-31
appropriate situations for,
33
card game example, 60
effective implementation
of, 46-47
example of, 31-33
rules for, 33-34
Account class example, 59
ADT (Abstract Data Type),
34, 37
effective implementation
of, 47
basic principles, 30
components of effective, 46
data types and, 36
division of responsibility,
42-46
card game example, 61
enforcing, 34
implementation hiding, 34-42
card game example, 60
effective implementation
of, 48
inheritance and, 98
limitations, 77
non-OOP languages and,
49-50
OOP goals and, 48-49
polymorphism and, 141

enumeration, 290
environment
    configuration, SDK, 570-571
    variables, PATH, 570
errors, 350
events, state diagrams, 407
exception handling, 351-352
exception handling code example, 351
exceptions, compared to bugs, 350
Extensible Markup Language. *See* XML

F

factories, 278
Factory Method design pattern, 283
files, creating .jar files, 576-577
final variables, 582
first-class objects, 37
FlipPlayer class, implementing, 489-490
for loops, 585
formatting, displaying objects, 344
frameworks (testing), 337-338
function polymorphism, 136
functional testing, 330

G

games (blackjack)
    actors (use case), 369
    analysis, purpose for, 368
    class model, 381
    classes, 376, 380
    command line UI, 380
    implementation, 381-395
    initial questions, 366-368
    iterations, adding betting
        capability, 371
    iterations, adding rules,
        370-371

iterations, basic game play,
    370, 372-376
iterations, planning, 369-370
iterations, user interface, 371
iterative process and, 365-366
modeling domain, 376
modeling use cases, 375
purpose for programming,
    364
requirements, 365
testing, 395
use cases, 372-375
vision statement, 365
generalization relationships
    modeling, 197-198
    UML, 600
generating documentation,
    javadoc, 573-574
generic interfaces, dangers of,
    39
get method, design issues, 155
getInitialState( ) method, documenting code with, 444
getter accessor methods, 56-57
getters, classes, 589
graphical user interfaces
    (GUIs). *See* user interfaces
guard conditions, state diagrams, 407
GUIPlayer class, implementing,
    461-464, 481
GUIs (graphical user interfaces). *See* user interfaces

H

Hand class, listener for, 412-415
Hand.java, 386
Has-a test (inheritance), 80
Hashtable class, casting and,
    161-162
headers (methods and classes),
    documentation, 354
Hello World
    first program, 574-577
    SimpleHelloWorld.java file,
        579
hiding implementation, 11

hierarchies. *See* inheritance
    hierarchies
HumanPlayer class, implementation, 441-443
HumanPlayer.java, 388

I

IBM, Java development kit
    Web site, 54
if-else operator, 584-585
if/else statements, nesting, 353
immutable objects, 63
implementation, 11, 28
    blackjack card game
        as simulation, 491-493
        Bank class, 437-439
        betting functionality, 436
        BettingPlayer class,
            439-441
        BlackjackDealer class,
            443-444
        Dealer class, 441
        HumanPlayer class,
            441-443
        GUI, 457-465
        PAC GUI, 476-483
        rules, 404-406, 412-425
    code example, 28-29
    controller layer (MVC),
        317-318
    hiding, 11, 34-42
    model layer (MVC), 312-313
    view layer (MVC), 314-316
implementation hiding
    card game example, 60
    dependent code, 40
    disadvantages, 41
    effective implementation of,
        48
    example code, 40-41
    limitations, 66
    loosely coupled code, 39-40
        creating, 42
        division of responsibility,
            42-46
    tightly coupled code, 40

implementation inheritance, 79
inclusion polymorphism,
   131-135
   advantages, 155
   code examples, 131-135
   methods, 130-131
   overview, 130
inheritance, 76
   access levels, changing, 87-88
   ancestors, 92-93
   attributes, 83, 85
      code example, 83-85
   basic principles, 81-83
   child classes, new methods,
      88
   code example
      child class, 105-106
      parent class, 103-104
   compared to delegation, 81
   data types and implementa-
      tion, 90
   descendants, 92-93
   design issues, 97-98
   encapsulation and, 98
   example code, 77-78
   functionality of, 78-79
   Has-a test, 80
   implementation, 79, 89
      limitations, 89-90
   Is-a test, 79-80
   Java, singletons and, 288-289
   java.util.Stack class
      problem example,
        120-121
      problem example require-
        ments, 121
      solution code example,
        121-122
   leaf classes, 93
   methods, 83, 85
      code example, 83-85
   multiple, 83, 94
   new methods and classes, 88
   overriding methods and class-
      es, 85-87
   passing messages, 78
   pluggability, 96
   polymorphism, 127
   polymorphism and, 142
   programming by difference,
      90-91

   protocols, 88
   recursive methods and attrib-
      utes, 88-89
   root classes, 93
   Singleton design pattern,
      287-288
   specialization, 91-93
   super keyword, 113
   type substitution, 94-96
   usefulness of, 131
inheritance hierarchies
   BankAccount class code
      example, 115-116
   banking example, 110
      checking accounts, 111
      class methods, 114-115
      generic accounts, 111
      overdraft accounts, 112
      requirements, 112
      savings accounts, 111
      timed maturity accounts,
        111
   CheckingAccount class code
      example, 118-119
   design issues, 97
   modifying, Adapter design
      pattern, 253-254
   OverdraftAccount class code
      example, 119-120
   Player class, modifying, 435
   polymorphism, limitations,
      144
   SavingsAccount class code
      example, 116-117
   TimeMaturityAccount class
      code example, 117-118
inheritance hierarchy, 81
inheritance implementation, 89
   limitations, 89-90
inner classes, 591-593
   anonymous, 591-593
InstallShield SDK, 570
instance methods, 68
instance variables, 68
instantiation
   abstract classes, 108
   Abstract Factory design pat-
      tern, 278
   preventing multiple, 283-284
integration testing, 334

interaction diagrams
   UML, 600
   use case analysis, 219-220
interfaces, 27-28, 590-591
   See also classes; user inter-
      faces
   adapter object, 254
   ADT (Abstract Data Type)
      and, 34
   blackjack card game
      Dealer, 420-425
      PlayerListener, 419-420
      PlayerState, 415-419
   code example, 28-29
   generic, dangers of, 39
   objects, 242
   polymorphism, 142
   public, 29
      implementation hiding, 48
      keywords, 29-30
   updating, 40
internal variables, 10
   composition, 80-81
   implementation hiding, 48
   object state, 15
Is-a test (inheritance), 79-80
Item class code example, testing
   and, 343-344
ItemDisplayFormatter interface
   code example, 344
ItemTableRow class code exam-
   ple, 344-345
ItemTest class code example,
   348-349
iterative process, 205
   blackjack card game, 365-366
      actors (use case), 369
      adding betting capability,
        371
      adding rules, 370-371
      analysis, purpose for, 368
      basic game play, 370,
        372-376
      class model, 381
      classes, 376, 380
      command line UI, 380
      implementation, 381-395
      initial questions, 366-368
      modeling domain, 376
      modeling use cases, 375
      planning, 369-370

use cases, 372-375
user interface, 371
incremental approach,
205-207
iteration, 205
limitations of, 207
methodology, 208
OOA (Object Oriented
Analysis), 208-209
activity diagrams,
222-223
collaboration diagrams,
221
combining use cases, 214
defining sequence of
events, 215-217
domain model, 223, 225
identifying actors,
210-211
interaction diagrams,
219-220
listing use cases, 212-213
prototyping, 225-226
refined use cases, 214-215
sequence diagrams,
220-221
splitting use cases,
213-214
use case diagrams,
217-219
use case model, 209
software testing and, 330-333
**Iterator design pattern, 251,
260-263**
benefits, 263
implementing, 263-266
Java implementation, 262
when to use, 266-267

J

**jar (Java archive) utility,
572-573**
jar file creation, 576-577
Java, 572
advantages of, 23
classes, 578-579, 586-587
creating, 587-590

conditional statements,
584-585
constants, 582
data types, 580-581
documentation, APIs, 61
inheritance, singletons and,
288-289
Iterator interface, 262
loops, 585-586
messages, interfaces and, 142
objects in, 39
obtaining, 54
operators, 583-584
platforms supported, 54
primitive wrappers, 67-68, 70
primitives, 66
resources, 605
variables, 581-582
Java SDK. *See* **SDK**
JavaBeans, 56
javac, 571-572
javadoc, 573-574, 577
JAVA_HOME variable, 570
**JDK (Java Developer's Kit),
569**
JUnit, 338-342
Web site, 338

K-L

keys, specifying, 55
keywords
class, 579
public, 578
public interfaces, 29-30
static, 579
super, 88, 113
void, 579

**languages, support for poly-
morphism, 146**
leaf classes, 93
libraries
Swing, 309
third-party tools
adapters, 256-257
upgrading, 278, 280-282
**life lines (use case sequence dia-
grams), 221**

listeners
blackjack card game, Hand
class, 412-415
PlayerListener, 419-420
Proxy design pattern and, 258
listings. *See* **code, examples**
logging code example, 29
**looping, Iterator design pattern
and, 260-262**
loops, Java, 585-586
loosely coupled code
creating, 42
division of responsibility,
42-46
implementation hiding, 39-40

M

machine language, 9
**main( ) method, example code,
16**
message passing, 13
messages, 17
inheritance and, 78
interfaces and, 142
method calls, 13
**method level documentation,
574**
methodologies, 186
methods
abstract, 108
code example, 109-110,
139
declaring, 108-109
example code, 151-152
accessor, 15
setters and getters, 56-57
Account class example, 57
addActionListener( ), 309
banking example, polymor-
phism example require-
ments, 160-162
BlackjackGUI class, setUp( ),
464-465
calling after current game
ends, 499
class, 68-69
coercion, polymorphism, 141

conditionals
    example requirements,
        173-174
    fixing, 171, 173
    fixing (code example),
        174, 176
constructors, 14, 589
declaring, 353
deferred, 139
defining, abstract classes, 108
doneBetting( ), 443
Factory Method design pat-
    tern, 283
get, design issues, 155
getInitialState( ), document-
    ing code and, 444
headers, documentation and,
    354
implementation hiding, 48
inclusion polymorphism,
    130-131
inheritance, 83, 85
    code example, 83-85
instance, 68
main( ), example code, 16
mutators, 15, 57
naming conventions, 353
new, child classes, 88
overloading
    code examples, 156
    polymorphism, 139-140
overriding, 85-86, 88
    Abstract Factory design
        pattern, 278
    access control, 87
    code example, 105-106
    code example (polymor-
        phism), 138-139
    super keyword, 113
parametric polymorphism,
    135-137
Player class, 420
polymorphism, limitations,
    145
private, 590
recursive, 88-89
redefining, 86
set, design issues, 155
specialization, 91

stack termination and,
    498-499
visibility, UML, 596
mock objects, 345-346, 348-349
    testing and, 444-445
MockDisplayFormatter inter-
    face code example, 346-348
model layer (MVC), 310-311
    combining with control layer,
        318-319
    implementing, 312-313
Model View Controller. *See*
    MVC
modeling
    See also UML
    blackjack card game
        domain, 376
        use cases, 375
    languages, 186
modifiers, classes, 589
modular programming, 9-10
    modules compared to objects,
        18
monomorphic languages, 126
multiple inheritance, 83, 94
    adapters, 256
multiplicity, 194
    characters for specifying, 194
    UML, 599
mutant use case tests, 334
mutator methods, 15, 57
MVC (Model View Controller)
    design pattern, 310
    alternatives to, 310
    blackjack.ui.mvc package,
        650-662
    combining model layer and
        control layer, 318-319
    controller layer, 317-318
    coupling, 321
    data handling, 320
    efficiency considerations, 321
    interface, blackjack.exe pack-
        age, 635-641
    model layer, 310-313
    shortcomings, 319
    view layer, 313-316

N

names, documentation, 354
naming
    actors (use case analysis), 211
    association relationships, 193
    test cases, 338
naming conventions
    classes, 353
    constants, 353
    JavaBeans, 56
    methods, 353
    variables, 353
nesting if/else statements, 353
noarg constructors, 56
notes, UML, 597

O

object adapters, 256
object models, 230
object-enabled languages, 67
object-oriented (OO), 8
objective statements, 365
objects, 8, 11
    agents (design issues), 242
    aggregation and, 17
    associations, UML, 598-599
    classes, 12
    collaboration, 234
    collaboration diagrams, 600
    compared to modules, 18
    compared to primitives, 67
    conditionals, fixing, 171-176
    delegation, 77
    detailing relationships (design
        issues), 243
    display formatters, 344
    division of responsibility,
        42-46
    factories, 278
    first-class, 37
    generating list of (design
        issues), 232-233
    immutable, 63
    inheritance, 76
        example code, 77-78
        functionality of, 78-79

instantiating, example code,
16
interaction diagrams, 600
interface, 27-28
interfaces (design issues), 242
internal variables, 10
Java, 39, 66
keys, specifying, 55
messages, 17
mock, testing code and,
444-445
objects, 66
points of interaction (design
issues), 241-242
programming and, 11
proxies, 259
pure object-oriented lan-
guages, 66
references, 15
refining responsibilities
(design issues), 234
relationships, 17
second-class, 37
sequence diagrams, 601
state, 9
substitutability relationships,
Adapter design pattern,
253-254
testing, mock objects and,
345-346, 348-349
testing fixtures, 341
thread-safe, 70
UML, 596
UML definition, 18
variables and state, 15
Observer design pattern, 311
**Observer interface code exam-
ple, 311**
**OneHitPlayer class, implement-
ing, 490**
OO (object-oriented), 8
resources, 604-605
**OOA (Object Oriented
Analysis)**
domain model, activity diagrams, 223-225
overview, 208-209
prototyping, 225-226
purpose, 368
system, 208

use case model, 209
activity diagrams,
222-223
collaboration diagrams,
221
combining cases, 214
defining sequence of
events, 215-217
generating preliminary
list, 212-213
identifying actors,
210-211
interaction diagrams,
219-220
refined use cases, 214-215
sequence diagrams,
220-221
splitting case list, 214
splitting cases, 213
use case diagrams,
217-219
OOD (Object Oriented Design)
class models, creating,
243-244
class responsibilities, 239,
241
CRC cards, 234-235
applying, 235-236
example, 236-238
limitations, 241
data transformation, 243
generating list of objects,
232-233
objects
agents, 242
detailing relationships,
243
future-proofing, 242
interfaces, 242
points of interaction,
241-242
overview, 230-231
refining responsibilities of
objects, 234
steps, 231-232
**OOP (Object Oriented
Programming)**
basic principles, 26
benefits, blackjack card game
and, 504-505
development cycle and, 21

encapsulation, non-OOP languages and, 49-50
extensibility, 20
goals, 19
encapsulation and, 48-49
polymorphism and,
146-147
industry realities and,
505-506
learning curve, 21-22
maintenance and, 20
natural software, 19
objects, 66
overview, 10-17
relationship to past programming paradigms, 18-19
reliability, 19
reusability, 20
**Operation class example code
(switch logic), 171-172**
operators
if-else, 584-585
Java, 583-584
overloading, 140
overriding, 140
**OptionView class, implement-
ing, 461**
**OptionViewController class,
implementing, 461**
org.w3c.dom.document, 281
**OverdraftAccount class code
example, 119-120**
overloaded constructors, 589
overloading
methods
code examples, 156
polymorphism, 139-140
operators, 140
overriding
attributes, 83, 85-86, 88
access control, 87
methods, 85-86, 88
Abstract Factory design
pattern, 278
access control, 87
code example, 105-106
super keyword, 113
operators, 140
polymorphism, 138-139

P-Q

PAC
blackjack.ui.pac package, 663-675, 677-679
interface, blackjack.exe package, 635-641

PAC (Presentation Abstraction Control) design pattern, GUI
abstraction layer, 473-474
control design, 474
design approach, 470-471
design overview, 471-472
factory patterns, 474-475
implementing, 476-483
layers, 470
overview, 470
presentation layer, 472-473
when to use, 471

package level modifiers, 578
packages
blackjack.core, 608-633
blackjack.core.threaded, 633-635
blackjack.exe (user interfaces), 635-641
blackjack.players, 641-649
blackjack.ui, 649-650
blackjack.ui.mvc, 650-660, 662
blackjack.ui.pac, 663-675, 677-679
common classes, blackjack card game, 607

parameters
See also arguments
declaring, parametric polymorphism, 135
methods, overloading, 140

parametric polymorphism
methods, 135-137
overview, 135
support limitations, 138

parametric types, 137-138
parent classes, 81-82
inheritance code example, 103-104
super keyword, 88

parsers
example code, 281-282
XML documents, Abstract Factory design pattern and, 280

passing messages, 17
inheritance and, 78

PATH environment variable, 570

Pattern-Oriented Software Architecture A System of Patterns, 310

PayrollDriver class code example, 156-157

performance tests, 335

Player class
inheritance, modifying hierarchy, 435
PlayerListener interface, 419-420
PlayerState interface, 415-419

Player Places Bet use case, 430-433

player state diagram (blackjack card game), 407-408

Player.java, 387

PlayerListener interface, 419-420

PlayerState interface, 415-419

PlayerView class, implementing, 460-461

pluggability, 96
polymorphic languages, 126
polymorphic variables, 129
polymorphism, 18, 126
Bank class example code, 163-164
banking example
overview, 160
requirements, 160-162
child classes, example code, 152-154
conditionals
example requirements, 173-174
fixing, 171, 173
fixing (code example), 174-176
effective implementation, 141-143

Employee class code example, 151-152
example code, 159-160
example requirements, 158-159
forms of, 130
function, 136
future-proof code example
example code, 167
overview, 164-166
requirements, 166
Hashtable class, casting and, 161-162
inclusion, 131-135
methods, 130-131
overview, 130
interfaces, 142
limitations
adding methods, 145
hierarchy issues, 144
performance issues, 144-145
methods
coercion, 141
overloading, 139-140
OOP goals and, 146-147
overriding, 138-139
overview, 126-130
parametric
methods, 135-137
overview, 135
support limitations, 138
programming language support for, 146
substitutability relationships, example code, 154-155
switch logic and, 169-171
typed languages and, 143

post conditions (use case analysis), 216
preconditions (use case analysis), 216
primitive wrappers, 67-70
code example, 70-71
creating, 70

primitives, 66
limitations, 67

private access, 29
private methods, 590
procedural languages, 9
procedural programming, 18

Product.java file, 587-588
programming
  See also code; design issues;
    software development
    processes
  abstraction, 31
  behavior, 12
  blackjack card game
    actors (use case), 369
    analysis, purpose for, 368
    class model, 381
    classes, 376, 380
    command line UI, 380
    implementation, 381-395
    initial questions, 366-368
    iterations, adding betting
      capability, 371
    iterations, adding rules,
      370-371
    iterations, basic game
      play, 370-376
    iterations, planning,
      369-370
    iterations, user interface,
      371
    iterative process and,
      365-366
    modeling domain, 376
    modeling use cases, 375
    purpose, 364
    requirements, 365
    testing, 395
    use cases, 372-375
    vision statement, 365
  C++, resources, 604
  classes, 12
  constructor methods, 14
  data types, 10
  domain, 11
  encapsulation, 18
  history, 8-10
  implementation, 11
    hiding, 11
  interface, 27-28
  Java
    advantages of, 23
    resources, 605
  machine language, 9
  message passing, 13
  method calls, 13
  methodologies, 186

modeling languages, 186
modular, 9-10
  modules compared to
    objects, 18
monomorphic languages, 126
object references, 15
object-enabled languages, 67
object-oriented, 8
  objects and, 11
OOP, overview, 10-17
polymorphic languages, 126
polymorphism, 18
procedural, 18
procedural languages, 9
typed languages, polymor-
  phism and, 143
vision/objective statements,
  365
programming by difference,
  90-91
programs, running, 575-576
protected access, 29
protocols, inheritance, 88
prototyping, OOA (Object
  Oriented Analysis), 225-226
proxies, 259
Proxy design pattern, 257-259
  publish/subscribe event ser-
    vices, 257-258
  when to use, 259-260
PsychiatristDriver example
  code, 165
public access, 29
public interfaces, 29
  implementation hiding, 48
  keywords, 29-30
public keyword, 578

R

random action tests, 334
random numbers, generating,
  61
Rank class code example
  Typesafe Enum design pat-
    tern, 292-293
Rank.java, 382
recursion, threading and, 503

recursive attributes, 88-89
recursive methods, 88-89
refactoring, 97
refactoring blackjack card
  game for reuse, 498-504
references, 15
regression testing, 335
relationships
  objects, 17
  UML, 598
relationships (classes), 191
resources, 603, 606
RewardsAccount class example
  code, 167
roles, UML, 598
root classes, 93
running programs, 575-576

S

SafePlayer class
  adding to GUI, 486-487
  creating, 486
SavingsAccount class code
  example, 116-117
SavingsAccountTest class code
  example, 336
SavingsAccountTest class code
  example (anonymous), 339
SavingsAccountTest class code
  example (JUnit), 339
  withdrawFunds ( ) method
    test, 340-341
scenarios (use case analysis),
  215
SDK, 569
  downloading, 570
  environment configuration,
    570-571
  InstallShield and, 570
  platforms supported, 569
  tools, 571
    javac, 571-572
SDK tools, Java, 572
second-class objects, 37
self transitions, state diagrams,
  407
semicolons (;) in source code,
  579

sequence diagrams
  UML, 601
  use case analysis, 220-221
set method, design issues, 155
setter accessor methods, 56-57
setters, classes, 589
setUp( ) method, adding non-
human players, 487
SimpleHelloWorld.java file, 579
simulations, uses for, 488
simulators, 346
  blackjack.exe package,
    635-641
Singleton design pattern,
283-284
  constructors, 286
  implementing, 284, 286
  inheritance and, 287-288
  when to use, 289
Smalltalk, resources, 605
SmartPlayer class, implement-
ing, 491
software
  See also design issues
  bugs, 330
  designing, goals of, 329
  exception handling, 351-352
  testing
    advanced, 342-350
    creating unit tests,
     337-338
    during development,
     335-350
    importance of unit tests,
     337
    integration, 334
    iterative design process
     and, 330-333
    JUnit, 338-342
    limitations of, 330
    regression, 335
    system, 334-335
    types of, 333
    unit, 333-337
software development process-
es, 204
  cost of fixing mistakes, 231
  iterative process, 205
    incremental approach,
     205-207
    iteration, 205
    limitations of, 207

methodology, stages, 208
OOA (Object Oriented
Analysis), 208-209
  activity diagrams,
    222-223
  collaboration diagrams,
    221
  combining use cases, 214
  defining sequence of
    events, 215-217
  domain model, 223-225
  identifying actors,
    210-211
  interaction diagrams,
    219-220
  listing use cases, 212-213
  prototyping, 225-226
  refined use cases, 214-215
  sequence diagrams,
    220-221
  splitting use cases,
    213-214
  use case diagrams,
    217-219
  use case model, 209
  system requirements, 208
  waterfall process, 204-205
source code
  See also code
  braces ({ }), 579
  semicolons (;), 579
specialization, 91-93
Stack class, inheritance
  problem example, 120-121
  problem example require-
    ments, 121
  solution code example,
    121-122
state, 9
  blackjack card game, creating
    classes from, 409-410, 412
  diagrams
    blackjack card game,
     406-407
    dealer, 408-409
    player, 407-408
  variables and, 15
State class, blackjack card
game, 409-410, 412
statements, conditional, Java,
584-585

static keyword, 579
static variables, 582
stereotypes, 189
  UML, 597
stress tests, 335
subclasses. *See* **child classes**
substitutability relationships,
94-95
  Adapter design pattern,
    253-254
  design issues, 242
  example code, 154-155
  inclusion polymorphism, 131
  polymorphic variables, 129
  polymorphism, 127-128, 130,
    142
subtypes, 96
Suit class code example,
Typesafe Enum design pat-
tern, 291
super keyword, 88, 113
support, Java, platforms and,
54
Swing library, 309
switch logic
  conditionals, fixing, 171-176
  polymorphism and, 169-171
system, OOA (Object Oriented
Analysis), 208
system requirements
  activity diagrams, 222-223
  analyzing, 209
  collaboration diagrams, 221
  combining use cases, 214
  defining sequence of events,
    215-217
  domain model, 223-225
  identifying actors, 210-211
  interaction diagrams, 219-220
  Java platform support, 54
  listing use cases, 212-213
  prototyping, 225-226
  refined use cases, 214-215
  sequence diagrams, 220-221
  software development
    processes, 209
  splitting use cases, 213-214
  use case diagrams, 217-219
system testing, 334-335

T

test cases, 332
 black box testing, 332
 naming, 338
 white box testing, 332-333
testing
 blackjack card game, 395,
  425
   command line UI,
    448-449
 bugs, sources of, 331
 classes, creating anonymous
  classes, 339-340
 design considerations, 349
 during development, 335-350
 fixtures, 341
 frameworks, 337-338
 importance of, 331
 integration, 334
 iterative software development and, 330-333
 limitations of, 330
 manual validation and, 337
 mock objects and, 345-346,
  348-349, 444-445
 reasons for, 330
 regression, 335
 resources, 606
 system, 334-335
 test cases, 332
   black box, 332
   white box, 332-333
 types of, 333
 unit, 333-337
   advanced, 342-350
   importance of, 337
   JUnit, 338-342
   writing, 337-338
third-party tools
 compatibility, adapter objects,
  256-257
 libraries, upgrading, 278,
  280-282
thread-safe objects, 70
threads, 500-504
**tightly coupled code, implemen-
 tation hiding, 40**
**TimeMaturityAccount class
 code example, 117-118**

transitions, state diagrams, 407
type. *See* **data types**
type substitution, 94-96
typed languages
 polymorphic variables, 129
 polymorphism and, 143
**Typesafe Enum design pattern,
 289-291**
 implementing, 291, 293-294
 when to use, 294-295

U

**UML (Unified Modeling
 Language)**
 abstract classes, 596-597
 aggregations, 599
 attribute and method visibility, 596
 class modeling, 198-199
   advanced notation,
    189-190
   aggregation relationships,
    194-195
   association relationships,
    193-194
   composition relationships,
    196
   dependency relationships,
    191-193
   generalization relation-
    ships, 197-198
   notation, 188-189
   relationships, 191
   selecting notation,
    190-191
 classes, 595
 collaboration diagrams, 600
 composition, 600
 dependency relationships, 598
 documenting code, 187
 generalization relationships,
  600
 interaction diagrams, 600
 notes, 597
 object associations, 598-599
 object definition, 18
 objects, 596
 overview, 186-187

 relationships, 598
 sequence diagrams, 601
 state diagrams, blackjack card
  game, 406-407
 stereotypes, 189, 597
**underscores preceding vari-
 ables, 582**
Unified Modeling Language.
 See **UML**
unit testing, 333-337
 advanced, 342-350
 importance, 337
 JUnit, 338-342
 writing, 337-338
updating
 documentation, 354
 interfaces, 40
   decoupled UI design and,
    307
**upgrading third-party libraries,
 Abstract Factory design pattern, 278, 280-282**
use case analysis, 209
 activity diagrams, 222-223
 blackjack card game
   betting, 430-433
   GUI, 450-452
   rules, 400-404
 collaboration diagrams, 221
 combining use cases, 214
 defining sequence of events,
  215-217
 diagrams, 217-219
 identifying actors, 210-211
 interaction diagrams, 219-220
 listing use cases, 212-213
 rationale for, 489
 refined use cases, 214-215
 sequence diagrams, 220-221
 splitting use cases, 213-214
 tips for writing, 217
 user input and, 210
use cases
 actors, 368
   blackjack card game, 369
   blackjack card game, 372-375
user interfaces, 305
 blackjack card game
   command line improve-
    ments, 448-449
   overview, 447-448

blackjack.exe package, 635-641

blackjack.ui package, 649-650

design issues, 306
    decoupling from system, 306-310
    Model View Controller (MVC) design pattern, 310-321

GUI
    analysis, 449
    BlackjackGUI, 454
    CardView, 454-455
    class diagram, 456
    CRC card session, 454-455
    design issues, 453-456
    diagrams, 455
    implementing, 457-465
    mock ups, 452-453
    OptionView, 454
    OptionView diagram, 455-456
    PlayerView, 454
    PlayerView diagram, 455
    use cases, 450-452

PAC design pattern
    abstraction layer, 473-474
    control design, 474
    design approach, 470-471
    design overview, 471-472
    factory patterns, 474-475
    implementing, 476-483
    layers, 470
    overview, 470
    presentation layer, 472-473
    when to use, 471

PAC design pattern overview, 470

SafePlayer class, adding, 486-487

Swing library, 309

users, roles of (use case analysis), 211

utilities, creating .jar (Java archive) files, 572-573, 576-577

V

variables
    class, 68-69
    CLASSPATH, 570
    data types, 35-37
    final, 582
    instance, 68
    internal, 10
        composition, 80-81
        implementation hiding, 48
    Java, 581-582
    JAVA_HOME, 570
    naming conventions, 353
    object state, 15
    PATH, 570
    polymorphic, 129
    static, 582
    underscores preceding, 582

VBettingPlayer class, implementing, 478-479

VBlackjackDealer class, implementing, 480-481

VCard class, implementing, 457, 476-477

VDeck class, implementing, 458

VHand class, implementing, 477

view layer (MVC), 313
    implementing, 314-316

visability, 188

vision statements, 365

VisualBankAccount code example, 307-309

void keyword, 579

W-Z

waterfall process, 204-205

Web sites
    IBM Java development kit, 54
    Java API documentation, 61
    Java SDK, 54
    JUnit, 338

white box testing, 332-333

whole/part relationships, 194

wrappers, 281
    adapter object, 254
        implementing, 254-256
        when to use, 256-257
    code example, 70-71
    creating, 70
    Java primitives, 67-68, 70

XML (Extensible Markup Language), 279-280
    document parsers, 280-282
        Abstract Factory design pattern and, 280